Digital Advertising Theory

Now in its fourth edition, *Digital Advertising Theory* examines how technological and media transformations are reshaping the foundations of advertising theory and practice. As digital advertising becomes increasingly data-driven, interactive, and complex, this volume revisits core advertising theories and evaluates their relevance within today's evolving media environment.

Building on earlier editions, this book is grounded in a contemporary definition of digital advertising that provides a conceptual foundation for understanding digital advertising as a dynamic, multifaceted system. Across this volume, contributors explore how advertising operates across platforms including social media, mobile environments, video, gaming, and AI-driven systems. This book examines developments, such as artificial intelligence, computational advertising, personalization, immersive media, and algorithmic processes, and considers how these forces are transforming how advertising messages are created, delivered, and evaluated. This volume brings together diverse theoretical perspectives to reassess foundational models of persuasion and audience response in light of contemporary digital conditions. Contributors examine how evolving forms of interactivity, data use, and platform dynamics shape consumer cognition, engagement, and behavior.

Providing both a rigorous theoretical foundation and a forward-looking research agenda, *Digital Advertising Theory* is an essential resource for scholars, students, and professionals in advertising, marketing, communication, media studies, and psychology.

Shelly Rodgers is a Distinguished Curators' Professor and Maxine Wilson Gregory Endowed Chair at the University of Missouri, USA.

Esther Thorson teaches at Colorado State University, USA. She is an Emeritus from the University of Missouri, USA, and Michigan State University, USA.

"This volume takes on the challenging task of theorizing about rapidly changing technologies. It provides many a theoretical lens with which to view the evolving landscape of AI-powered digital advertising. By focusing on core concepts such as interactivity, immersion, and personalization, it helps us to think theoretically about current and future developments in creation, dissemination, reception, and persuasion of advertising appeals."

S. Shyam Sundar, *The Pennsylvania State University, USA*

"While many fundamentals of communication remain, the rapidly changing media context necessities constant reevaluation of applications. As now people live in media, *Digital Advertising Theory*, 4th Edition, is an essential update to spur our thinking about how advertising works in the digital ecosystem. This new edition continues the excellent work of the prior versions, bringing together academicians and practitioners to discuss important theoretical perspectives through which to see and applications of those ideas to advertising practice. It's a valuable resource for the classroom and the workplace."

Eric Haley, *University of Tennessee, USA*

"The radical transformation of the advertising industry requires fresh insights and new perspectives on how to reach audiences. *Digital Advertising Theory* provides actionable and integrated theories and practices to create engagement and impact in this new ecosystem. Marketers have much to gain by understanding the use of AI, augmented reality, trans-media branding, social media, search engine advertising and more by reading this influential book."

Debbie MacInnis, *University of Southern California, USA*

"*Digital Advertising Theory*, 4th Edition, explores how AI, augmented reality, and real-time analytics are redefining advertising's core principles and practices. This thoroughly updated volume offers fresh perspectives into personalization, immersive technologies, and transmedia branding, while critically revisiting foundational theories in today's dynamic digital environment. Offering research-driven insights and practical guidance, it equips scholars, students, and professionals to navigate the complexities of an interactive, data-driven advertising ecosystem."

Hong Cheng, *Southern Illinois University Carbondale, USA*

"Bringing together the classic pillars of advertising theory with timely developments such as artificial intelligence, augmented and extended reality, and real-time social media analytics, this book offers a comprehensive, rigorous, and theoretically rich reflection on advertising in the digital world. It compellingly demonstrates how theory provides the conceptual tools needed to explain, predict, and critically evaluate digital advertising's evolving forms and effects. Readers will encounter a captivating dose of top-tier research spanning diverse topics, offering a stellar illustration of how advertising scholarship maps, explains, and deepens our understanding of digital communication effects. Highly recommended for both scholarly inquiry and professional practice."

Jörg Matthes, *University of Vienna, Austria*

Digital Advertising Theory

Fourth Edition

Edited by
Shelly Rodgers and Esther Thorson

Routledge
Taylor & Francis Group
NEW YORK AND LONDON

Designed cover image: Artificial Intelligence Content Generator © Boy Wirat / Getty Images

Fourth edition published 2027
by Routledge
605 Third Avenue, New York, NY 10158

and by Routledge
4 Park Square, Milton Park, Abingdon, Oxon, OX14 4RN

Routledge is an imprint of the Taylor & Francis Group, an informa business

First edition published by Lawrence Erlbaum Associates, Inc. 1999
Third edition published by Routledge 2017

Library of Congress Cataloging-in-Publication Data
Names: Rodgers, Shelly (Shelly Lannette), 1965– editor |
Thorson, Esther editor
Title: Digital advertising theory / edited by Shelly Rodgers and
Esther Thorson.
Description: Fourth edition. | New York, NY : Routledge, 2027. |
First edition published by Lawrence Erlbaum Associates, Inc. 1999.
Third edition published by Routledge 2017. | Includes bibliographical
references and index.
Identifiers: LCCN 2026024107 (print) | LCCN 2026024108 (ebook) |
ISBN 9781032937625 hardback | ISBN 9781032937618 paperback |
ISBN 9781003567523 ebook
Subjects: LCSH: Internet advertising
Classification: LCC HF6146.I58 A38 2027 (print) | LCC HF6146.I58
(ebook)
LC record available at https://lccn.loc.gov/2026024107
LC ebook record available at https://lccn.loc.gov/2026024108

ISBN: 9781032937625 (hbk)
ISBN: 9781032937618 (pbk)
ISBN: 9781003567523 (ebk)

DOI: 10.4324/9781003567523

Typeset in Times New Roman
by codeMantra

To Jon, for so many reasons. To Brianna and Brandon, who remain my greatest inspiration.

—Shelly

To my grandchildren, Madeline, Dominic, Will, Liliana Lynn, Valentina, and Savannah

—Esther

Contents

About the Co-Editors

Shelly Rodgers is a Distinguished Curators' Professor and Maxine Wilson Gregory Endowed Chair at the University of Missouri.

Esther Thorson is teaching at Colorado State University. She is an Emeritus from the University of Missouri and Michigan State University.

About the Contributors

Sun Joo (Grace) Ahn is a Professor of Advertising in the Grady College of Journalism and Mass Communication at the University of Georgia. She is the Director of the Center for Advanced Computer-Human Ecosystems (CACHE).

Saleem Alhabash is a Professor of Advertising and Public Relations and the Co-Director of the Media and Advertising Psychology Lab, Michigan State University.

Fernando Angulo-Ruiz is a Professor in the Department of International Business, Marketing, Strategy, and Law at MacEwan University, Canada.

Ilse Bruwiere is the Sr. Client Service Director at Ipsos Belgium.

Cristian Buzeta is an Assistant Professor of Digital Marketing at the Universidad de Chile (Chile).

Colin Campbell is an Associate Professor of Marketing at the University of San Diego's Knauss School of Business.

Diotima Chattoraj, PhD, is a Research Manager in the Wee Kim Wee School of Communication and Information, Nanyang Technological University.

Qimei Chen is a Professor of Marketing and the Harold and Sandy Noborikawa Chair of Entrepreneurship, Marketing, and Information Technology, University of Hawaiʻi at Mānoa.

Shu-Chuan Chu is a Professor of Advertising in the College of Communication at DePaul University.

Laurien Desimpelaere is affiliated with the Department of Communication Sciences at Ghent University, Belgium.

Serena D'Hooge is an Assistant Professor of Marketing at EDHEC Business School, France.

Louisa Ha is a University Distinguished Research Professor in the School of Media and Communication at Bowling Green State University.

Seo-Jeong Heo is a PhD student at the Institute of Communications Research, University of Illinois Urbana-Champaign.

Chang-Dae Ham is a Professor of Advertising at the University of Illinois Urbana-Champaign.

Haley R. Hatfield is an Assistant Professor in the School of Journalism and Mass Communications, University of South Carolina.

Jisu Huh is a Professor and Raymond O. Mithun Endowed Chair in Advertising in the Hubbard School of Journalism and Mass Communication, University of Minnesota.

Syed Ali Hussain, PhD, is an External Investigator at the University of Design, Innovation, and Technology, Madrid, Spain.

WooJin Kim is an Assistant Professor in the Department of Advertising, Public Relations, and Design at the University of Colorado Boulder.

Amy Rebecca Jones is an alumnus of the doctoral program of the Department of Marketing and Supply Chain Management at the University of Memphis.

Jae Min Jung is a Professor of Marketing in the College of Business Administration at California State Polytechnic University, Pomona.

Eunjin (Anna) Kim is an Associate Professor in the Annenberg School for Communication and Journalism, University of Southern California.

Hyejin Kim is an Assistant Professor of Marketing at the Dixie L. Leavitt School of Business at Southern Utah University.

Jooyoung Kim is a Professor of Advertising and the Executive Director of the Cox International Center, University of Georgia.

Bingxin Leng is a PhD student in Marketing at the University of Hawaiʻi at Mānoa, studying sustainable marketing through brand communities and digital consumption.

Marian Levy is a Professor and the Associate Dean in the School of Public Health at the University of Memphis.

Zhuoman Li is a doctoral candidate in the Wee Kim Wee School of Communication and Information at Nanyang Technological University, Singapore. Her research focuses on generative AI.

Anthony M. Limperos is a Professor and the Chair in the Department of Communication, University of Kentucky.

Matthew Lombard is an Associate Professor in the Department of Media Studies and Production at Temple University.

Chen Lou is an Associate Professor in the Wee Kim Wee School of Communication and Information at Nanyang Technological University, Singapore.

Man Luo is a doctoral candidate at Bowling Green State University.

Drew Martin is a Professor of Tourism Marketing at the University of South Carolina.

Kyeong Sam Min is the Sidney Baron Professor of Marketing, Louisiana State University (LSU) New Orleans.

Eveline Mollaert is a senior researcher and a lecturer at the Artevelde University of Applied Sciences, Belgium.

Juan Mundel is an Associate Professor of Advertising and Public Relations at Michigan State University.

Patrick De Pelsmacker is a Professor of Marketing at the University of Antwerp, Belgium.

Albena Pergelova is a Professor in the School of Business, MacEwan University, Canada.

Attila Pohlmann is a Professor of Marketing in the College of Business Administration at Universidad San Francisco de Quito, Ecuador.

Kathrynn Pounders is an Associate Professor at the Stan Richards School of Advertising and Public Relations, University of Texas at Austin.

Gudrun Roose is an Assistant Professor of Marketing at Ghent University, Belgium.

Marla Royne Stafford is a Professor in the Department of Marketing and International Business at the University of Nevada, Las Vegas.

Mike Schmierbach is a Professor in the Department of Film-Video and Media Studies, Pennsylvania State University.

Claire M. Segijn is an Associate Professor at the University of Minnesota and a Mithun Program Fellow in Advertising.

Heather Shoenberger is an Associate Professor of Advertising at Pennsylvania State University.

Will R. Silberman, PhD, is a social listening researcher specializing in new media and gaming, and an adjunct instructor in the College of Communication and Information at the University of Kentucky.

Jennifer Snyder-Duch Assistant Provost for Faculty Affairs and Labor Relations at Frostburg State University

Joanna Strycharz is an Assistant Professor of Persuasive Communication at the Amsterdam School of Communication Research, University of Amsterdam, Netherlands.

Jiayue Sun, MS, is with Science Technopreneurship and Innovation Programme, Nanyang Technological University.

Mingxi Sun is a doctoral student in the Wee Kim Wee School of Communication and Information at Nanyang Technological University, Singapore.

Charles R. Taylor is the John A. Murphy Professor of Marketing at the Villanova University School of Business and Faculty Initiatives Senior Research Fellow.

Ting-Hao Tsou is an Assistant Professor of Digital Advertising in the Manship School of Mass Communication, Louisiana State University.

Marijke De Veirman is a senior researcher and a lecturer at the Artevelde University of Applied Sciences, Belgium.

Sukki Yoon is a Professor of Marketing at Bryant University.

Weilu Zhang is an Assistant Professor in the Department of Integrated Strategic Communication, University of Kentucky.

How This Book Is Organized

The organization of this fourth edition reflects both a definition of digital advertising and the *Digital Advertising as a System of Mediated Connection (DASC)* framework introduced in Chapters 1 and 2. Each subsequent part engages one or more of these dimensions—message, experience, data, and ethics—demonstrating how theories, methods, and innovations interact to sustain and reshape connection in digital advertising.

Part I: Defining the System

Chapter 1 – Defining Digital Advertising in a Fragmented, Evolving Landscape

Reviews definitions of digital advertising, introduces an original typology based on academic literature, and lays the conceptual foundation for this volume's theoretical and empirical contributions.

Chapter 2 – From Definition to System: Building a Theory of Connected Advertising

Integrates insights from editors of five leading advertising journals to examine how digital advertising is defined and theorized across the field. Building on Chapter 1's definitional foundation, this chapter identifies converging and diverging perspectives and introduces the *Digital Advertising as a System of Mediated Connection (DASC)* framework, which serves as the conceptual spine for this volume.

Part II: Message: Persuasion and Communication in a Connected System

Chapter 3 – Simulated Persuasion: Theoretical Directions for Virtual Influencers in Interactive Advertising

Reimagines Stern's (1994) Revised Communication Model to theorize how virtual influencers—spanning corporeal, hybrid, and simulated forms—reshape authorship, authenticity, and persuasion in the age of synthetic communicators.

Chapter 4 – Digital Advertising Efficiency: Taking Stock and Looking Forward

Synthesizes literature on digital advertising effectiveness, proposes a comprehensive model including consumer well-being, and outlines methods to measure both consumer- and advertiser-controlled outcomes in participatory, dialogue-based campaigns.

Chapter 5 – Hybrid Pathways to Persuasion: Integrating Online and Offline Advertising and Consumer Behavior

Reviews a decade of research on integrating online and offline advertising, outlining seven key challenges and proposing a future research agenda.

Chapter 6 – Rethinking the Role of Reversal Theory in Digital Advertising

Uses reversal theory to explain shifting consumer motivations in digital environments and their impact on advertising responses, offering a literature review and future research directions.

Part III: Experience: Interactivity, Immersion, and Engagement

Chapter 7 – Theoretical Landscapes in Influencer Advertising: A Framework-Based Review and Future Directions

Identifies key theories in influencer advertising from 2003 to 2025, categorizes them into five focus areas, and highlights gaps in theoretical development despite growing empirical research.

Chapter 8 – What's in a Name? Exploring Consumer Perceptions of Social Media Personalities: Influencers, Content Creators, and Celebrities

Explores how consumers perceive influencers, content creators, and celebrities as brand endorsers, revealing distinct trait attributions through mixed-methods research and offering strategic insights for marketers.

Chapter 9 – Digital Advertising Clutter in an Age of Mobile Media and Artificial Intelligence

Examines the evolution of advertising clutter across traditional, online, and mobile media, defining its causes and effects, and exploring how user and advertiser control—as well as AI—shape the digital clutter landscape.

Chapter 10 – Immersion in Games Exemplifies Why Digital Media Create Complex Responses to Ads

Examines how immersion in video games influences advertising effectiveness, highlighting theoretical gaps and the need to better define immersion and account for game–brand interactions.

Chapter 11 – Advertising in Video Games: An Overview and Future Research Considerations

Reviews advertising in video games, covering current trends, common ad formats, and research on ad effectiveness, with concluding insights and directions for future study.

Chapter 12 – Using Digital Media to Improve Public Health Communication for Both Physical and Emotional Health
Explores how digital media can effectively inform consumers about pressing healthcare issues. It reviews key health topics, examines various digital platforms for health communication, and discusses message strategies for delivering impactful health information.

Part IV: Data: Computational, AI, and Programmatic Systems

Chapter 13 – Past, Present, and Future of Computational Advertising and Research Directions
Examines the evolution of computational advertising (CA), synthesizes key theories and models, and outlines directions for future research.

Chapter 14 – Personalization in the Age of Artificial Intelligence-Powered Digital Advertising
Presents a framework for AI-powered personalization in digital advertising, distinguishing it from related concepts and outlining a typology, recent research, and future directions.

Chapter 15 – Defining Ads in Metaverse: Concept Explication of Augmented and Virtual Reality Advertising
Defines augmented and virtual reality advertising, highlights key properties, and presents a framework to evaluate how A/VR technologies transform advertising formats.

Chapter 16 – The Advertising Experience and the Power of (Tele)Presence
Examines presence theory in digital advertising, highlighting how emerging technologies enhance immersive, interactive ad experiences.

Chapter 17 – Exploring the Roles and Impacts of Artificial Intelligence in Advertising
Synthesizes published research on AI-powered advertising by identifying key topics and theories within the ACET framework and outlining directions for future study.

Part V: Ethics and Responsibility in Digital Systems

Chapter 18 – Targeted Digital Advertising and Privacy
Assesses digital privacy in advertising, exploring the privacy paradox, consumer behavior, and implications for future research in a data-driven landscape.

Chapter 19 – The Role of Culture in Electronic Word-of-Mouth Communication
Explores the role of culture in electronic word-of-mouth (eWOM), reviewing existing research and calling for more cross-cultural studies beyond Western contexts.

Chapter 20 – Algorithmic Absorption: Affective Alignment and Perceived Intrusiveness in ELM Persuasion Routes on Social Media

Explores how algorithmic advertising leverages passive user cues to create ambient persuasion, introducing the Affective Alignment ELM and examining its impact on engagement, emotion, and user agency.

Part VI: The Evolution and Future of Digital Advertising

Chapter 21 – Social Media Advertising

Examines social media use in advertising, marketing, and PR, and reimagines classical persuasion models to better understand its evolving role in influencing consumer behavior.

Chapter 22 – International Digital Advertising: Lessons from around the World

Reviews the rise of international digital advertising, recent trends, and key research across consumer, executional, and strategic brand-building factors. It evaluates these through the lens of the Taylor (2009) framework and identifies future research directions.

Preface

Digital Advertising Theory, 4th Edition

Co-Editors: Shelly Rodgers and Esther Thorson

As the digital landscape continues to evolve, so too must our understanding of advertising. This premise guides the fourth edition of *Digital Advertising Theory*, shaping how we revisit foundational ideas and explore emerging developments.

This edition reflects a field that is both grounded in enduring theoretical traditions and undergoing profound transformation. Core topics—such as theories of persuasion, effects models, and fundamental questions about how advertising works—remain central. Yet, they must now be reconsidered within a media environment defined by fragmentation, interactivity, and rapid technological change.

Digital advertising has expanded into a multifaceted ecosystem, with emerging modes of delivery, evolving platforms for engagement, and increasingly sophisticated targeting capabilities. It is no longer confined to traditional or social media but extends across nearly every digital device, including smartphones, tablets, laptops, and voice-activated technologies. Ads are now woven seamlessly into platform environments—appearing within search, social, streaming, and mobile contexts—where they are delivered algorithmically and personalized in real time. Increasingly interactive and data-driven, digital advertising operates at scale while often targeting individuals rather than broad audiences, fundamentally transforming how brands communicate with consumers.

Earlier editions of this book laid the groundwork for understanding these foundational concepts. In this edition, however, they are revisited in light of a dramatically evolved landscape that includes artificial intelligence (AI), augmented and virtual reality, computational analytics, and evolving content strategies—each reshaping how advertisers engage with audiences.

AI's impact, in particular, has been transformative, enabling real-time data analytics and personalized advertising experiences. From AI-powered chatbots to algorithmically driven content delivery, technology now allows brands to create more relevant and responsive interactions with consumers. At the same time, augmented and virtual reality are pushing the boundaries of traditional advertising formats, creating immersive environments that challenge existing theoretical assumptions. These developments call for renewed attention to the role and effectiveness of digital advertising and to whether models developed in earlier eras remain applicable in today's dynamic context.

The expanding range of media and the growing agency of audiences have fundamentally altered the relationship between advertisers and consumers. Advertisers no longer maintain the same level of control over message delivery, as individuals increasingly determine when, where, and how they engage with advertising. This shift has prompted the development of novel approaches centered on personalization, participation, and social influence.

In this edition, we explore how these changes challenge and reshape our understanding of digital advertising. We argue that it is time for advertising research to revisit established effects models within the context of new technological environments, and for scholars to further investigate the psychological and behavioral implications of this rapidly transforming advertising landscape.

To organize these developments, this edition offers a definition of digital advertising and advances the *Digital Advertising as a System of Mediated Connection (DASC)* framework, as presented in Chapters 1 and 2. The definition is grounded in an extensive review of the scholarly literature and was shared with contributing authors, who were invited to engage with it directly or indirectly in their chapters. Chapter 2 extends this effort through a structured dialogue with editors of leading advertising journals, offering a field-level perspective on how digital advertising is currently defined and theorized. Together, this definition and framework serve as the conceptual foundation for this volume, positioning digital advertising as an interconnected system shaped by four key dimensions: message, experience, data, and ethics. Each part of this book reflects one or more of these dimensions, illustrating how theories, methods, and innovations interact to sustain and reshape connection in digital advertising.

This volume is organized as follows:

Part I (Defining the System) establishes an organizing lens of this volume, revisiting definitions of digital advertising and introducing the DASC framework as a unifying lens for theory and research.

Part II (Message: Persuasion and Communication in a Connected System) focuses on persuasion and communication in a connected environment, extending core theories to contexts such as virtual influencers, hybrid online–offline behavior, and evolving measures of advertising effectiveness.

Part III (Experience: Interactivity, Immersion, and Engagement) explores interactivity, immersion, and engagement, including influencer ecosystems, digital clutter, advertising in games, and applications in public health communication.

Part IV (Data: Computational, AI, and Programmatic Systems) examines the growing centrality of computational systems, including AI-driven personalization, computational advertising, augmented and virtual realities, and the role of presence in shaping consumer responses.

Part V (Ethics and Responsibility in Digital Systems) addresses critical issues such as privacy, algorithmic influence, and cultural dynamics in electronic word-of-mouth, emphasizing the importance of responsible and transparent practices.

Part VI (The Evolution and Future of Digital Advertising) looks ahead to developments in social media and global advertising, identifying key directions for future research and practice.

Across these dimensions, this volume reflects both continuity and innovation, revisiting established theories while extending them to new technological and cultural contexts. Together, the chapters underscore the need to reconsider long-standing models of persuasion and audience effects in a digital environment defined by personalization, interactivity, and rapid change.

Building upon the foundation of earlier editions, this fourth edition of *Digital Advertising Theory* updates and advances prior work:

- Rodgers, S., & Thorson, E. (2017). *Digital Advertising: Theory and Research* (3rd Ed.). Taylor & Francis Group.
- Schumann, D., & Thorson, E. (2007). *Internet Advertising: Theory and Research* (2nd Ed.). Lawrence Erlbaum Associates.
- Schumann, D., & Thorson, E. (1999). *Advertising and the World Wide Web*. Lawrence Erlbaum Associates.

The evolution of this book's title reflects the broader trajectory of the field itself—from *Advertising and the World Wide Web*, to *Internet Advertising*, to *Digital Advertising*. In this fourth edition, we adopt the title *Digital Advertising Theory*, signaling both the maturation of the field and a more focused emphasis on theory as a foundation for understanding ongoing change.

This fourth edition not only updates and expands existing chapters but also introduces new perspectives and contributions from leading scholars across the field. It addresses key developments in digital advertising, including AI, augmented and virtual realities, data-driven systems, and ethical considerations, while also examining emerging areas such as influencer cultures, immersive media, and evolving forms of audience engagement.

Moreover, this edition features contributions from leading scholars across the field who examine digital advertising in the context of human behavior and cognition. This collection provides insights for both researchers and practitioners, offering tools to better understand and navigate the complexities of contemporary digital advertising.

Our aim is not simply to document change, but to provide a coherent framework for understanding it—equipping scholars, students, and practitioners to critically engage with and shape the evolving landscape of digital advertising.

Acknowledgments

We are profoundly grateful to all of our contributors, past and present, whose innovative, insightful, and thought-provoking chapters have been the bedrock of this book. To those who contributed to earlier editions, your lasting influence continues to resonate throughout this work.

Your creativity, expertise, and forward-thinking perspectives have helped ensure that this book remains a vital and evolving resource in the field of digital advertising theory. It has been a privilege to collaborate with each of you, and we are deeply appreciative of your continued inspiration. Quite simply, this book would not be possible without our contributors.

We extend our heartfelt thanks to Emma Ries and Evgeniia Belobrovkina for their meticulous and exceptionally organized assistance.

We also extend our sincere thanks to our publisher partners, Hannah Rich and Zoe Thomson-Kemp. Zoe and Hannah pitched the new edition, offered tremendous input and guidance, and placed their trust in us—we are deeply grateful for their partnership and support. Your professionalism, careful coordination, and steadfast support have made this journey both smooth and enjoyable.

We are especially grateful to the many colleagues who generously shared their insights, helped refine our proposal, suggested contributors, and provided thoughtful feedback on the chapters. Your contributions have helped shape this work, and we deeply value your support.

We also extend our sincere thanks to the anonymous reviewers whose thoughtful feedback helped strengthen this volume. We are equally grateful to the educators who have adopted this book and to the scholars who have engaged with and cited this work and its contributors. Your engagement not only advances ongoing scholarly dialogue but also helps sustain the visibility and impact of research in digital advertising.

A special thank you goes to the many scholars, practitioners, and students who have read this book, engaged with its ideas, and shared their thoughts and feedback. Your curiosity and enthusiasm continue to inspire us and reinforce the importance of this ongoing dialogue.

On a more personal note, Shelly is deeply grateful for the opportunity to collaborate with her dear friend and colleague, Esther—a partnership that now spans 29 years. This journey has been both rewarding and uplifting, and Esther's dedication, insight, and generous spirit have enriched every step along the way.

Esther values Shelly's intellectual and creative vision and is likewise deeply grateful for their ongoing collaboration. She values the opportunity to learn and grow through their work together and looks forward to many more shared endeavors.

Part I

Defining the System

1 Defining Digital Advertising in a Fragmented, Evolving Landscape

Shelly Rodgers and Esther Thorson

In the decade since the last edition of *Digital Advertising Theory*, the digital ecosystem has not only expanded—but it has also fractured, hybridized, and converged. What we once called "web" (Schumann & Thorson, 1999), "online advertising," or "internet advertising" (Schumann & Thorson, 2007) now encompasses a far wider range of environments, from programmatic display ads appearing on mobile news apps to immersive brand experiences emerging in virtual worlds and metaverse platforms. Amid this proliferation of formats, platforms, and technologies, a deceptively simple question continues to challenge scholars, practitioners, and policymakers alike: *What is digital advertising?*

Although definitions of digital advertising vary across the literature, several recurring perspectives appear: persuasive intent, drawing on broader definitions of advertising as brand-initiated communication intended to influence audiences (Dahlen & Rosengren, 2016; Hudders et al., 2019); digital platform infrastructure, focusing on internet-based platforms and digital ecosystems through which advertising is delivered (Ma & Du, 2018; Tauro et al., 2021); interactive communication, emphasizing the participatory nature of digital media where audiences engage with and sometimes co-create advertising content (Rodgers & Thorson, 2018; Lee & Cho, 2020); and data-driven targeting and personalization, highlighting algorithmic targeting, programmatic buying, and automated optimization (McStay, 2017; Huh & Malthouse, 2020).

Even among scholars who agree that digital advertising aims to influence consumer attitudes, behaviors, or actions, there is little agreement about what should count as digital advertising. Some definitions blur the line between advertising and branded content (Rodgers & Thorson, 2019), while others focus more narrowly on persuasion and message intent (Lee & Cho, 2020). As new delivery environments emerge—such as retail media networks, AI-generated influencers, and other hybrid formats—the term *digital advertising* is increasingly used to describe a wide range of overlapping practices rather than a single, clearly defined concept.

This definitional fluidity is not a weakness—it reflects the field's dynamism. Digital advertising today is not a single, fixed concept. Instead, it is a shifting constellation of practices, technologies, and meanings shaped by consumers,

DOI: 10.4324/9781003567523-2

platforms, marketers, and regulators in real time. No single definition can fully capture the institutional, technological, and cultural complexity of digital advertising. In this fourth edition, we treat this definitional fluidity not as a problem to resolve but as an opportunity to clarify how different definitions reflect distinct research traditions, assumptions, and priorities—and how those choices shape the questions scholars ask and the theories they build.

Definitional Synthesis: Focus and Method

The literature informing this chapter focuses on scholarly discussions of digital advertising published primarily from 2016 forward, extending the discussion developed in the third edition of *Digital Advertising Theory* (Rodgers & Thorson, 2017). Anchoring the review in the post-2016 period allows us to trace how conceptualizations of digital advertising have evolved alongside the expansion of algorithmic systems, retail media networks, AI-driven optimization, and platform consolidation.

To revisit this question, we conducted targeted searches of recent scholarship in leading advertising and related journals. Rather than compiling an exhaustive list of definitions, we identified recurring themes in how digital advertising is conceptualized across advertising, marketing, media studies, and related fields. Table 1.1 synthesizes these perspectives into several recurring dimensions

Table 1.1 Key Conceptual Dimensions in Scholarly Definitions (2016–2025)

Conceptual Dimension	*What This Perspective Emphasizes*	*Representative Scholarship*
Persuasive intent	Brand-initiated communication designed to influence audiences.	Dahlen and Rosengren (2016); Hudders et al. (2019)
Digital platform infrastructure	Advertising enabled and distributed through internet-based platforms and technological ecosystems.	Tauro et al. (2021)
Interactive communication	Two-way communication, user participation, sharing, and engagement between brands and audiences in digital environments.	Kumar and Gupta (2016); Lee and Cho (2020); Rodgers and Thorson (2018); Taylor and Kim (2025)
Data-driven targeting and personalization	Advertising delivery informed by behavioral data, audience analytics, and algorithmic personalization systems.	Huh and Malthouse (2020); Koslow and Stewart (2022); Ma and Du (2018); McStay (2017); Pearson (2024)
Algorithmic mediation and optimization	Automated computational systems shaping the delivery and performance of advertising.	Huh and Malthouse (2020); McStay (2017); Pearson (2024)

Note: The categories are heuristic rather than mutually exclusive; some definitions emphasize multiple dimensions of digital advertising.

identified in contemporary scholarship. The table is illustrative rather than exhaustive and provides the foundation for the working definition and typology developed later in this chapter. The following section briefly traces how definitions of digital advertising have evolved alongside changes in digital media technologies and advertising practice.

From Online to Omnichannel: The Evolution of Digital Advertising Definitions

Early definitions of digital advertising—then often labeled "web," "online," or "internet advertising"—focused primarily on the delivery medium: a paid promotional message appearing on the web (Barnes, 2002) or across electronic platforms such as websites, email, and search engines (Strauss & Frost, 2001). These medium-based definitions reflected the initial migration of traditional advertising into emerging digital spaces.

As platforms proliferated, definitions expanded to emphasize interactivity, ubiquity, and targeting sophistication. Yoo et al. (2010) highlighted the interactive and boundary-transcending nature of digital advertising, while Kannan and Li (2017) underscored data-enabled, algorithmically mediated interactions across mobile and social platforms. Koslow and Stewart (2022) emphasize the fluidity of formats and devices, noting that digital advertising may appear in forms ranging from a simple logo to embedded video across televisions, computers, and phones. More recently, Taylor and Kim (2025) conceptualize digital advertising as an "always-on," AI-enabled, and data-driven environment structured by six core principles: privacy, trust, relevance, interactivity, entertainment, and brand building.

Parallel developments place digital advertising within increasingly data-rich and computational infrastructures. Contemporary formulations emphasize algorithmic mediation (McStay, 2017), precision targeting (Mills et al., 2019), and the construction of audiences through predictive modeling and automated optimization (Huh & Malthouse, 2020). In this view, digital advertising is not simply a message placed within media; it is an ongoing, systemically mediated process shaped by data flows, platform governance, and computational decision-making.

These developments reflect a broader conceptual shift. Earlier definitions emphasized what and where—the message and the medium—whereas contemporary formulations increasingly foreground who, when, and how: audience construction, behavioral segmentation, and predictive delivery systems. This shift from static message placement to dynamic, algorithmically optimized interaction reflects broader transformations in media infrastructures and market logics. Foundational work in advertising theory provides a useful anchor for this discussion. Dahlen and Rosengren (2016) define advertising as "brand-initiated communication intent on impacting people" (p. 334), shifting the emphasis from specific media formats to the persuasive purpose of advertising.

This formulation accommodates interactive, digital, and multi-platform channels while emphasizing the continuing role of persuasion in contemporary marketing communication. Thus, while the technological environments of advertising have become increasingly interactive and data-driven, its foundational role as persuasive brand communication remains unchanged (Hudders et al., 2019).

These evolving formulations also reveal tensions. Some retain a narrow focus on paid persuasion, while others incorporate branded content, gamified experiences, and dialogic engagement. Rodgers and Thorson (2018), for example, conceptualize digital engagement with advertising as consumers' interactions with brands that strengthen emotional, psychological, or behavioral investment, highlighting the interactive nature of contemporary advertising environments. Scholarship on brand communication in social media further complicates definitional boundaries. Platform characteristics, influencer practices, and personalized content reshape how promotional communication becomes embedded in everyday digital interactions (e.g., Voorveld, 2019). Work examining specific dimensions of digital advertising—such as consumer empowerment (Hudders et al., 2019)—illustrates how definitional boundaries expand when users act as distributors, commentators, and co-creators of branded content.

Consequently, advertising may be difficult to distinguish from content, community, or conversation. Some scholars treat digital advertising as a subset of marketing communication, while others situate it within broader socio-technical systems. The variety of definitions reflects how the field has grown and diversified over time, including conceptualizations of digital advertising alongside related constructs and approaches.

Taken together, these perspectives reveal five recurring conceptual dimensions used to define and analyze digital advertising: persuasive intent, digital platform infrastructure, interactive communication, data-driven targeting and personalization, and algorithmic mediation and optimization. Table 1.1 illustrates how these dimensions appear in recent scholarship. The categories are not mutually exclusive, and many formulations incorporate multiple perspectives simultaneously. For example, Pearson's (2024) definition of computational advertising emphasizes the data-driven and algorithmic foundations of digital advertising systems, highlighting the role of behavioral data, mathematical models, and computational infrastructures in delivering and optimizing advertising messages. Even when definitions fall within the same conceptual dimensions, they may emphasize different components of digital advertising; for example, Huh and Malthouse (2020) foreground the automated advertising process, whereas Pearson (2024) emphasizes the computational infrastructure enabling it, a distinction that the dimensional framework in Table 1.1 helps clarify.

Importantly, not all definitions of digital environments constitute definitions of digital advertising. For example, Kim (2021) defines the metaverse as "an interoperated persistent network of shared virtual environments where people can interact synchronously through their avatars with other agents and objects" (p. 142). While such definitions describe emerging digital infrastructures within which advertising may occur, they do not themselves define advertising as persuasive, data-driven, or algorithmically mediated communication.

This dimensional framework also helps situate emerging forms of digital advertising without treating each technological development as a wholly new category. Innovations such as artificial intelligence (AI)–enabled advertising, computational advertising systems, and immersive brand experiences within virtual or metaverse environments are often described as distinct forms of advertising. AI advertising refers to the use of machine-learning systems capable of performing tasks that typically require human intelligence, including learning from data and improving performance over time (Rodgers, 2021). Rather than representing entirely separate forms of advertising, these developments can be understood as emphasizing different combinations of the conceptual dimensions identified here. AI-enabled advertising intensifies algorithmic mediation and data-driven targeting and personalization. Computational advertising foregrounds the infrastructural and optimization systems through which ads are generated and delivered, while immersive or metaverse advertising emphasizes digital platform infrastructure and interactive audience engagement. From this perspective, such developments do not fall outside the domain of digital advertising but instead represent evolving configurations of the technological, data-driven, and experiential dimensions that structure the field.

Ultimately, how digital advertising is defined has implications for the questions researchers ask, the units of analysis they prioritize, and the theories they apply.

Definitions Have Consequences: Theoretical Implications of a Shifting Field

How we define digital advertising shapes what we study, how we measure it, and which theories we use to explain it. A narrow, medium-based definition often focuses attention on questions of media effectiveness or pricing strategies. A broader, experience-oriented definition shifts attention to engagement, co-creation, and identity, reflecting the growing importance of digital engagement within advertising scholarship (Rodgers & Thorson, 2018). A data-driven definition directs attention to algorithmic governance, predictive modeling, and the ways audiences are constructed through data (Huh & Malthouse, 2020; McStay, 2017).

Definitions also shape the unit of analysis and the outcomes measured by researchers. Is the focus the advertisement itself, the consumer, the platform, the algorithmic system, or the interaction among them? As definitions expand, the theories used to study digital advertising expand as well. When digital advertising is viewed primarily as persuasive messaging, researchers often draw on frameworks such as the Elaboration Likelihood Model or the Theory of Planned Behavior. When it is understood as interaction between brands and audiences, theories of networks or engagement may be more useful. When it is viewed as part of a data-driven system, perspectives from algorithm studies, surveillance capitalism, or socio-technical systems research become more relevant.

Likewise, the outcomes examined depend on how advertising is conceptualized. If advertising is treated mainly as a message, researchers may focus on awareness or attitude change. If it is treated as a digital experience, outcomes might include engagement, sharing, or co-creation. If it is understood as part of a data exchange, outcomes may involve behavioral tracking, conversion events, or audience profiling.

These choices are not neutral. They reflect assumptions about the role of advertising in society, the agency of consumers, and the goals of advertisers. They also shape how ethical questions are framed, including concerns about transparency, manipulation, privacy, and consent.

As Rodgers and Thorson (2019) illustrated in their "theory of theories" framework (see Figure 1.1), advertising research draws on a wide range of intellectual traditions. In this edition, we build on that perspective by examining how changing definitions of digital advertising reshape those traditions, particularly in areas such as algorithmic mediation, predictive modeling, and data-driven optimization.

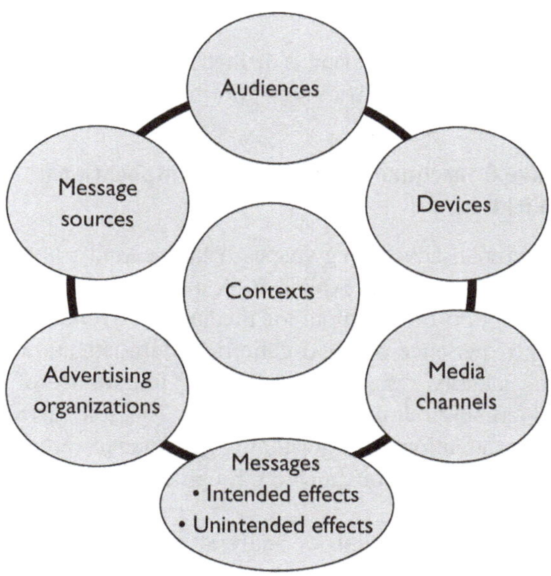

Figure 1.1 Components of the Advertising Process Circle.

Source: Reproduced from Rodgers and Thorson (2019), with permission.

Toward a Working Definition and Typology

Earlier in this chapter, we described how definitions of digital advertising have shifted alongside changes in technology, platforms, and industry practice. No single definition can fully capture the field's complexity. At the same time, an edited volume requires some shared point of reference in order to create coherence across chapters. For that reason, we offer the following working definition—not as a final answer, but as a practical guide for this chapters that follow. Table 1.1 summarizes several recurring ways scholars define and analyze digital advertising. Building on those perspectives, we define digital advertising as follows:

> *Digital advertising refers to brand communication delivered through networked digital technologies that enable interactive, data-driven, and algorithmically mediated promotion across platforms, devices, and media environments.*

Our definition builds on prior work that emphasizes technology-driven and interactive advertising environments (e.g., Lee & Cho, 2020), while more explicitly foregrounding the role of algorithmic mediation and cross-platform digital ecosystems. This definition reflects the multidimensional nature of digital advertising. It recognizes the continuing importance of persuasion while acknowledging that modern advertising operates within complex digital systems shaped by platforms, data, and algorithms. In this sense, digital advertising encompasses a range of practices that operate within networked digital environments, including programmatic advertising, computational advertising, AI-driven advertising, and immersive advertising in virtual or augmented settings. Together these elements reflect a broader shift in digital advertising from static message placement toward relational, behavioral, and computational systems in which advertising operates as an ongoing, data-informed process.

Earlier editions of this book highlighted interactivity, targeting capabilities, and cross-platform integration as defining features of digital advertising. Today's ecosystem introduces an additional structural layer: algorithmic mediation. Advertising processes are now shaped not only by persuasive strategies but also by computational systems that automate targeting, generate creative variations, predict behavioral responses, and determine how advertising appears across platforms.

With this working definition in place, we now turn to a framework that helps organize these ideas. The typology presented in Table 1.2 builds on the conceptual dimensions identified in Table 1.1 by translating them into analytic continua that capture how digital advertising varies across experience design, communication dynamics, platform ecosystems, data infrastructures, and algorithmic control. Although these dimensions are analytically distinct, they operate together in practice.

Table 1.2 A Typology of Digital Advertising in an Algorithmically Mediated Ecosystem

Dimension	*Continuum*	*Illustrative Examples*
Communication Initiation & Amplification	Brand-initiated → Consumer-amplified → Algorithmically amplified	Sponsored brand post → Influencer or user-generated sharing and remixing → Platform-curated or algorithmically prioritized content within feeds or recommendation systems
Experience Design	Passive → Interactive → Immersive	Static display banner → Instagram Story poll or playable ad → Branded virtual world in Roblox or AR-enabled live commerce event
Ecosystem Structure	Single-platform → Cross-platform → Platform ecosystem integration	Search ads within Google → Coordinated campaign across YouTube and Instagram → Integrated advertising across interconnected retail media, streaming, and platform ecosystems
Data & Audience Construction	Contextual → Behavioral → Predictive/AI-driven	Ad placed next to relevant article content → Retargeting based on prior website visits → Machine-learning audience modeling and automated segmentation systems
Algorithmic Mediation & Control	Human-planned → Platform-optimized → Autonomous AI optimization	Manual media buying and creative selection → Automated bidding and dynamic creative optimization → Generative AI systems producing, testing, and deploying creative variants with minimal human intervention

This typology complements earlier frameworks, including the "theory of theories" model presented in Rodgers and Thorson (2019). Whereas Figure 1.1 maps the broader theoretical traditions that inform advertising research, Table 1.2 focuses more specifically on the structural features of contemporary digital advertising environments. Together, Table 1.1, Figure 1.1, and Table 1.2 provide three complementary perspectives on digital advertising: conceptual orientations in the literature, theoretical traditions shaping advertising research, and analytic dimensions for studying contemporary digital advertising environments.

As digital advertising continues to evolve, the frameworks used to study it must evolve as well. The typology proposed here offers an organizing structure for the theoretical and methodological approaches represented throughout this volume. Some chapters extend these dimensions, while others question or refine them. Taken together, the contributions in this fourth edition both reflect and advance the definition and analytic dimensions outlined here, offering new perspectives alongside a shared vocabulary for studying an increasingly automated and data-driven advertising environment.

Chapter 2 continues this definitional discussion through a dialogue with editors of leading advertising journals, who respond to a set of questions about the field, including the one that anchors this chapter: *What is digital advertising?* Their reflections reveal both areas of convergence and productive disagreement, illustrating how definitional choices shape research agendas, theoretical commitments, and ethical concerns.

Acknowledgment

We thank Emma Ries for her assistance with the literature search for this chapter.

References

Barnes, S. J. (2002). Wireless digital advertising: Nature and implications. *International Journal of Advertising, 21*(3), 399–420.

Dahlen, M., & Rosengren, S. (2016). If advertising won't die, what will it be? Toward a working definition of advertising. *Journal of Advertising, 45*(3), 334–345.

Hudders, L., Van Reijmersdal, E.A., & Poels, K. (2019). Digital advertising and consumer empowerment. *Cyberpsychology: Journal of Psychosocial Research on Cyberspace, 13*(2), Article 1.

Huh, J., & Malthouse, E. C. (2020). Advancing computational advertising: Conceptualization of the field and future directions. *Journal of Advertising, 49*(4), 367–376.

Kannan, P. K., & Li, H. A. (2017). Digital marketing: A framework, review, and research agenda. *International Journal of Research in Marketing, 34*(1), 22–45.

Kim, J. (2021). Advertising in the metaverse: Research agenda. *Journal of Interactive Advertising, 21*(3), 141–144.

Koslow, S., & Stewart, D. W. (2022). Message and media: The future of advertising research. *International Journal of Advertising, 41*(5), 827–849.

Kumar, V., & Gupta, S. (2016). Conceptualizing the evolution and future of advertising. *Journal of Advertising, 45*(3), 302–317.

Lee, H., & Cho, C. H. (2020). Digital advertising: present and future prospects. *International Journal of Advertising, 39*(3), 332–341.

Ma, J., & Du, B. (2018). Digital advertising and company value: Implications of reallocating advertising expenditures. *Journal of Advertising Research, 58*(3), 326–337.

McStay, A. (2017). *Digital Advertising*. Bloomsbury Publishing.

Mills, A. J., Pitt, C., & Ferguson, S. L. (2019). The relationship between fake news and advertising: Brand management in the era of programmatic advertising and prolific falsehood. *Journal of Advertising Research, 59*(1), 3–8.

Pearson, S. (2024). Computational advertising for meaningful brands, the public purpose, and a sustainable ecology: A call for research into a systems approach and modeling applications of LLMs in marketing and advertising. *Journal of Current Issues & Research in Advertising, 45*(3), 357–367.

Rodgers, S. (2021). Themed issue introduction: Promises and perils of artificial intelligence and advertising. *Journal of Advertising, 50*(1), 1–10.

Rodgers, S., & Thorson, E. (2017). *Digital Advertising Theory and Research*, 3rd ed. New York and London: Routledge.
Rodgers, S., & Thorson, E. (2018). Special issue introduction: Digital engagement. *Journal of Advertising, 47*(1), 1–3.
Rodgers, S., & Thorson, E. (2019). *Advertising Theory*, 2nd ed. New York and London: Routledge.
Schumann, D., & Thorson, E. (Eds.) (1999). *Advertising and the Worldwide Web.* Hillsdale, NJ: Lawrence Erlbaum Associates, Inc.
Schumann, D., & Thorson, E. (Eds.) (2007). *Internet Advertising: Theory and Research.* Hillsdale, NJ: Lawrence Erlbaum Association, Inc.
Strauss, J., & Frost, R. (2001). *E-marketing*, 2nd ed. Upper Saddle River, NJ: Prentice Hall.
Tauro, D., Panniello, U., & Pellegrino, R. (2021). Risk management in digital advertising. *The International Journal on Media Management, 23*(1/2), 29–57.
Taylor, C. R., & Kim, E. (2025). What are the unique features of digital advertising? The six principles of digital advertising in the 21st century. *Journal of Interactive Advertising, 25*(4), 328–346.
Voorveld, H. A. M. (2019). Brand communication in social media: A research agenda. *Journal of Advertising, 48*(1), 14–26.
Yoo, C. Y., Kim, K., & Stout, P. A. (2010). Assessing the effects of animation in online banner advertising: Hierarchy of effects model. *Journal of Interactive Advertising, 10*(2), 49–60.

2 From Definition to System

Toward a Theory of Digital Advertising as Connection

Shelly Rodgers and Esther Thorson, with contributions from Charles R. Taylor, Jisu Huh, Colin Campbell, Sukki Yoon, and Jooyoung Kim

Context and Approach

This chapter, curated and synthesized by Shelly Rodgers and Esther Thorson, draws on original written responses from the editors-in-chief of five leading U.S. advertising journals—an approach that brings leading editorial perspectives directly into the process of theory development. Listed alphabetically by journal title, these contributors include Charles R. Taylor (*International Journal of Advertising*), Jisu Huh (*Journal of Advertising*), Colin Campbell (*Journal of Advertising Research),* Sukki Yoon (*Journal of Current Issues & Research in Advertising* [*JCIRA*]), and Jooyoung Kim (*Journal of Interactive Advertising*). Their reflections form the foundation for the integrated analysis presented here and inform the Digital Advertising as a System of Mediated Connection (DASC) framework we develop in this chapter.

The synthesis that follows integrates the editors' perspectives based on written responses to a structured set of questions (see Table 2.1), distributed via email in 2025. These responses, paraphrased and selectively quoted with permission, are organized thematically to foreground areas of convergence and productive tension rather than to reproduce each exchange verbatim.

Collectively, these editors lead five of the field's most influential journals, each advancing distinct yet overlapping perspectives on how advertising research evolves within an increasingly digital, data-driven, and algorithmically mediated environment.

From Editorial Perspectives to Definitional Debates

In Chapter 1, we began with what has long been the field's most deceptively simple question: What is digital advertising? We found that, far from having a settled answer, this question continues to fuel debate across research traditions, technologies, and disciplinary boundaries. The definitions identified in our Chapter 1 review reflected both convergence and contradiction—some grounded in persuasion and message effects, others in interaction and experience design,

DOI: 10.4324/9781003567523-3

Table 2.1 Core Questions Posed to Editors of Leading Advertising Journals

Question	*Purpose*	*Representative Topics in Editors' Responses*
1. How does your journal define digital advertising?	Establish the scope and conceptual foundations of each journal.	Definitions emphasizing persuasion, mediation, interactivity, or systems.
2. What developments most shape the field today?	Identify emerging technological and theoretical influences.	AI, influencer marketing, personalization, immersive media, ethics.
3. Which topics dominate recent submissions?	Track trends and possible saturation points.	Generative AI and social media influencers remain prevalent.
4. What gaps or underexplored areas exist?	Encourage future-oriented theorizing.	Data access, ethics, interdisciplinary bridges.
5. What types of studies would you like to see more of?	Link editorial direction to methodological innovation.	Mixed methods, qualitative insights, conceptual reviews.
6–11. Additional questions on theory, application, accessibility, and author guidance.	Explore the balance between theoretical rigor and applied relevance.	Accessibility, industry engagement, storytelling in research.

Note. This table summarizes the structured questions distributed to participating advertising journal editors in 2025. Editors were encouraged to respond to as many—or as few—questions as they wished and were invited to add their own questions and answers if desired. Their responses informed both the qualitative synthesis presented in this chapter and the development of the DASC framework.

still others in data infrastructures, platform ecosystems, and the algorithmic mediation of visibility and control. That definitional multiplicity, we argued, is not a sign of conceptual weakness but of disciplinary vitality.

To deepen that definitional inquiry, we reached beyond the published literature and asked those who sit at the nexus of research and practice—the editors-in-chief of five leading U.S. advertising journals—to reflect on how they and their publications now define, frame, and advance the study of digital advertising. Their written responses, summarized from a series of structured questions detailed in Table 2.1 (Editors' written response, 2025), represent a panoramic snapshot of how the field currently understands itself: its boundaries, its challenges, and its theoretical directions.

Because each editor's perspective is shaped by the mission and scope of their respective journal, understanding these outlets helps contextualize their reflections. The *Journal of Advertising Research* bridges theory and managerial practice; the *Journal of Advertising* emphasizes theoretical and interdisciplinary inquiry; the *Journal of Interactive Advertising* advances interactive and experiential perspectives; the *International Journal of Advertising* emphasizes global scope and theoretical rigor; and the *JCIRA* embraces experimentation and emerging issues. Together, these journals form the intellectual core of advertising research, reflecting both the breadth and coherence of the field.

The working definition developed in Chapter 1 was intentionally broad and adaptive, recognizing advertising's evolution into a system of technologies, data infrastructures, and mediated relationships rather than a fixed set of media forms. Yet, as the editors' reflections reveal, this evolution brings renewed pressure to clarify what, precisely, counts as "digital advertising" in an environment where persuasion, participation, platform ecosystems, audience data, and algorithmic mediation are tightly interwoven.

Across their responses, one message emerged clearly: digital advertising has become too expansive and dynamic to be confined by medium-based definitions (Editors' written response, 2025). At the same time, definitional clarity remains essential. A field without boundaries risks diffusion; a field with boundaries that are too rigid risks irrelevance. What follows is an effort to navigate that balance—integrating the editors' perspectives to extend the definitional foundation established in Chapter 1.

Why Definitions Still Matter

In the decade since the previous edition of *Digital Advertising Theory*, the digital ecosystem has fractured and recombined in ways few could have anticipated. Advertising has shifted from discrete placements to ambient experiences, and from isolated campaigns to ongoing systems of connection. In this context, definitions are not mere formalities. They function as epistemological boundaries—shaping what counts as advertising, what counts as data, and how human agency is understood.

The editors we consulted collectively emphasized that definitional work remains essential because it structures the field's questions, methods, and ethical commitments. As Jisu Huh's perspective suggests, definitions shape what scholars study and how they conceptualize the field. Definitions also serve a strategic function: they signal to practitioners, policymakers, and the public what advertising scholars believe they are studying—and why that work matters.

Our Chapter 1 working definition framed digital advertising as follows:

> Digital advertising refers to brand communication delivered through networked digital technologies that enable interactive, data-driven, and algorithmically mediated promotion across platforms, devices, and media environments.

Designed to be both integrative and adaptive, this definition recognizes advertising's expansion into a system of technologies, infrastructures, and mediated relationships rather than a fixed set of media forms. When presented to the editors, it was not only largely affirmed for its breadth but also used as a point of departure for more specific interpretations. Their responses ranged from managerial pragmatism to theoretical rearticulation, and from ethical caution to creative speculation. In the sections that follow, these perspectives are organized thematically rather than alphabetically, beginning with Colin Campbell, whose reflections can be understood as pointing toward a view of digital advertising as increasingly shaped by algorithmic and adaptive forms of persuasion, providing a useful bridge from definitional debate to the systemic model developed in this chapter.

Colin Campbell: Digital Advertising as Algorithmic Persuasion

For Colin Campbell, Editor-in-Chief of the *Journal of Advertising Research*, digital advertising can be understood as increasingly shaped by algorithmic and adaptive processes (Editors' written response, 2025). In his response, he emphasizes the growing role of generative AI in creative development, the expansion of personalized and scalable content through technologies such as digital twins, and the shift toward AI-driven search environments, all of which point to the central role of computational systems in designing, delivering, and refining advertising.

Campbell's response highlights how digital advertising is increasingly shaped by adaptive processes in which human creativity and machine learning intersect. He points to the role of generative AI in enabling rapid experimentation and personalization, as well as emerging formats such as digital twins and AI-driven search, which together reflect a system in which advertising content is continually refined through data-driven processes.

These developments also carry important implications for theory and research. Campbell highlights the need for studies grounded in real-world data, including field experiments and longitudinal approaches, suggesting that evolving digital environments require methods capable of capturing dynamic consumer responses over time. Campbell also emphasizes the importance of maintaining strong connections between research and practice. He encourages collaboration with industry partners and highlights the value of research that is both theoretically grounded and practically impactful, particularly in understanding how emerging technologies reshape advertising strategy and execution. Taken together, Campbell's perspective suggests that digital advertising extends beyond traditional notions of brand-initiated communication, reflecting a system in which data, technology, and creative processes are increasingly intertwined.

This perspective not only aligns with our Chapter 1 emphasis on brand intent but also points toward its transformation within increasingly data-driven and computational environments. Persuasion remains central, but it is now shaped through systems that integrate human input with algorithmic processes. In this way, Campbell's response highlights the need to understand advertising not only as communication but also as part of a broader technological and managerial system—an idea that connects directly to the systemic framework developed in this chapter and sets up the transition to Huh's emphasis on networked communication.

Jisu Huh: Digital Advertising as Networked Communication

If Campbell's orientation is algorithmic, Jisu Huh, Editor-in-Chief of the *Journal of Advertising*, can be understood as approaching digital advertising as networked communication. Her perspective is shaped by the journal's growing interdisciplinary focus on computational advertising, artificial intelligence, and data ethics (Editors' written response, 2025). From this vantage point, digital advertising can be understood as a social and informational system in which meaning and influence circulate across interconnected networks of consumers, technologies, and platforms.

This systems perspective reframes advertising as part of a broader communication ecology rather than a one-to-one persuasion exchange, emphasizing how advertising operates within complex environments of content, data, and interaction. These dynamics extend beyond commercial messaging to include broader informational and societal contexts in which digital communication unfolds.

Huh's editorial perspective also provides insight into how the field's topics have diversified. Analysis of recent *Journal of Advertising* submissions reveals strong and growing interest in areas such as social media, artificial intelligence, influencer marketing, and computational advertising. Her discussion further highlights the importance of examining the societal and ethical dimensions of these developments—including algorithmic bias, transparency, accountability, and policy implications—areas that suggest a need for continued attention alongside ongoing technical advances.

Her perspective suggests an expansion of brand-initiated intent to include broader societal impact. In contemporary data ecosystems, advertising does not operate in isolation but circulates through networks of sharing, interaction, and algorithmic amplification, extending its influence beyond immediate target audiences. She also emphasizes the importance of theorizing responsibility as an integral component of digital advertising systems. At the same time, Huh highlights structural challenges facing researchers, particularly the limited access to proprietary platform data and the resulting concerns around transparency, reproducibility, and data governance. These constraints underscore the need for methodological innovation, data-sharing partnerships, and interdisciplinary collaboration in advancing the field.

If Campbell's framing highlights the technological engine of persuasion, Huh's perspective stresses its social and infrastructural dimensions. Both recognize advertising's dependence on data, but Huh's discussion draws particular attention to the broader systems through which data circulate and shape both market behavior and societal outcomes. This progression sets the stage for Jooyoung Kim's focus on the experiential dimension of connection, where advertising becomes less a discrete message and more a mode of participation in everyday digital life.

Jooyoung Kim: Digital Advertising as Connected Experience

Where Colin Campbell views digital advertising through the logic of algorithms and Jisu Huh situates it within social systems, Jooyoung Kim, Editor-in-Chief of the *Journal of Interactive Advertising*, offers a more philosophical reorientation. For Kim, digital advertising is not primarily a message, nor even a technology, but a connected experience—a continuous process of human–machine interaction through which persuasion becomes lived rather than delivered (Editors' written response, 2025).

In his 2025 editorial essay, "Rethinking Digital Advertising in a Connected Age," Kim argues that every digital encounter—whether a programmatic banner, a TikTok branded filter, or a conversational AI assistant—functions simultaneously as communication and as experience. Advertising, he writes, "does more than interrupt experience—it frequently facilitates and frames it" (Kim, 2025). In this view, interactivity is both the precondition and the consequence of connection: users engage not only with content but also with the connective infrastructures—networks, interfaces, and algorithmic systems—that make engagement possible.

Kim's connection-centered perspective has recently been formalized as Connectism, which treats connection as a fundamental unit of analysis. Digital advertising is thus defined less by platform or format than by the relational systems through which persuasion emerges among humans, algorithms, and environments. These systems vary in potential (connectibility), fit (connexity), quality (connectedness), density (connectance), and performance (connexus).

This perspective expands our Chapter 1 definition in two key respects. First, it emphasizes that connection is not simply a channel outcome but a defining condition of digital life: people increasingly experience brands as ambient presences woven into everyday interactions. Second, it introduces what Kim describes as artificial influence—AI agents that simulate social presence through voice, gesture, or personality cues. Such agents blur the boundaries between human and algorithmic interaction, raising new questions about authenticity and engagement.

Kim's framework thus points toward a broader reconceptualization of communication as emerging from interactions among human and technological actors. In this view, the ad is less a discrete text and more a node within an adaptive, affective system. Persuasion becomes continuous—an evolving process shaped by the alignment between human attention and machine mediation. If Kim's vision highlights transformation and fluidity, Taylor offers a counterbalance, restoring a sense of continuity and grounding. He reminds us that even in algorithmic environments, persuasion still depends on enduring human principles.

Charles R. Taylor: Digital Advertising as Principled Evolution

Charles R. Taylor, Editor-in-Chief of the *International Journal of Advertising*, offers a complementary yet cautionary perspective. Where Kim emphasizes transformation, Taylor stresses continuity. His decades of editorial leadership suggest that, although technology reshapes delivery, the principles of effective advertising remain remarkably stable (Editors' written response, 2025).

Taylor's historical lens traces digital advertising's evolution from early banner placements to today's AI-driven ecosystems. Despite technological change, he argues that successful advertising continues to depend on enduring human factors: privacy, relevance, trust, interactivity, entertainment, and brand building (Taylor, 2009; Taylor & Kim, 2025). These six principles, first articulated more than a decade ago, continue to serve as touchstones for evaluating digital effectiveness.

While new platforms—such as the metaverse, augmented reality, or programmatic audio—deserve study, he emphasizes that they should be understood as means rather than ends, with advertising effectiveness still grounded in enduring principles such as attention, trust, and meaningful engagement.

In this view, digital advertising is best understood as an evolutionary rather than revolutionary phenomenon. This perspective does not diminish innovation but situates it within a lineage of persuasion grounded in psychology, creativity, and consumer insight. For Taylor, the field's challenge lies in adapting classical principles to digital architectures without losing theoretical depth or managerial relevance.

Taylor's approach complements the DASC framework articulated in this chapter: enduring principles act as the ethical and cognitive scaffolding of connection. Where Kim maps advertising's experiential expansion, Taylor anchors it in the constants of human judgment and affect.

Sukki Yoon: Digital Advertising as Shape-Shifting Persuasion

Sukki Yoon, Editor-in-Chief of the *JCIRA*, embraces the field's experimental frontier. He defines digital advertising as "any form of persuasive communication mediated by digital technology"—a deliberately open and evolving conception of "a living, shape-shifting phenomenon." For Yoon, this indeterminacy is not a weakness but a source of theoretical vitality (Editors' written response, 2025).

Under his editorial direction, *JCIRA* has become a venue for research that captures emerging and unconventional phenomena at early stages of development. Yoon emphasizes that "quirkiness is not a liability but a signal of innovation," encouraging work that explores new forms of digital persuasion before they become fully established theoretical domains.

Yet Yoon's optimism is tempered by concern. He notes that AI is "infiltrating nearly every facet of the advertising process," raising new questions about authorship, authenticity, and audience response. Earlier scholarship suggested that "AI can think but it cannot feel" (Bakpayev et al., 2022), but more recent research points to increasingly complex consumer reactions. Yoon cites emerging work (e.g., Ryoo et al., 2025) indicating that audiences may respond uneasily to AI–human creative hybrids, sometimes perceiving them as inauthentic or unsettling.

This ambivalence reflects a broader tension in contemporary advertising, as human and machine-generated creativity become increasingly intertwined. It suggests that future advertising may depend less on replicating human emotion than on reimagining how emotion is represented and experienced in machine-mediated contexts.

In this sense, Yoon's position converges with Kim's notion of artificial influence while retaining a distinctly creative orientation. Both view advertising as a site of negotiation between human and algorithmic agency. Yoon's open-ended definition thus complements Taylor's emphasis on enduring principles, Campbell's focus on adaptive systems, and Huh's concern with social and ethical dimensions—together forming a constellation of perspectives that chart the field's evolving intellectual landscape.

Together, these perspectives form a dialogue that mirrors the complexity of the field itself—sometimes divergent, often overlapping, and always evolving. Their collective insights set the stage for understanding where points of convergence emerge and why these differences matter.

Threads of Convergence: A Field in Constructive Tension

Across their varied emphases—managerial, ethical, experiential, historical, and creative—the written responses of the five editors (2025) reveal a discipline held together by constructive tension. Beneath these differences lie several profound points of consensus that both validate and extend the definitional framework introduced in Chapter 1.

A central point of agreement is the shift from message to system. All five editors recognize that digital advertising can no longer be defined solely as a message; it has become an interconnected ensemble of technological, social, and affective processes. Whether reflected in Campbell's emphasis on algorithmic and adaptive processes, Huh's focus on networked and computational advertising systems, Kim's conception of connected experience, or in Taylor's emphasis on enduring principles and Yoon's focus on emergent and experimental forms, each perspective situates advertising within infrastructures of computation and interaction. This shared orientation affirms the move we outlined in Chapter 1—from delivery mode to data strategy—as a defining dimension of the field.

A second convergence centers on connection as both infrastructure and outcome. Kim's theory of Connectism and Yoon's exploration of AI-mediated creativity converge on the insight that connection functions simultaneously as precondition and product. Advertising not only travels through networks—but it also helps build them. Taylor's emphasis on trust and interactivity reinforces this view, reminding us that connection must be meaningful to be persuasive.

Another area of agreement concerns the human–machine continuum. Each editor acknowledges that agency in digital advertising is increasingly distributed across human and algorithmic actors. Algorithms curate exposure, AI systems generate and test content, and consumers co-produce meaning through engagement and data. Campbell emphasizes managerial adaptation to this evolving landscape; Kim and Yoon examine how authenticity and emotion are reshaped in human–machine interaction; Huh foregrounds the ethical implications of computational persuasion; and Taylor underscores the continued importance of human-centered principles such as trust, relevance, and meaning in guiding how these technologies are used. Together, these perspectives point toward an emerging understanding of advertising as a system in which human and technological actors operate in tandem.

There is also consensus around theoretical and methodological pluralism. Taylor advocates for mixed methods that balance rigor and relevance; Huh emphasizes interdisciplinary integration across communication, psychology, and data science; and Yoon encourages exploratory and innovative approaches that capture emerging phenomena. Campbell highlights the importance of testing theory in applied, real-world contexts, while Kim's framework points toward the need for conceptual innovation grounded in evolving technological realities. From this perspective, definitional debates are not obstacles but engines of theoretical development.

Finally, the editors converge in emphasizing ethical reflexivity and access as defining challenges for the discipline. Yoon highlights the limited availability of proprietary data, describing scholars as "standing outside a well-stocked kitchen watching others cook with the finest ingredients." Huh connects these constraints to broader concerns about transparency, reproducibility, and public trust, while Taylor emphasizes privacy as a foundational principle of effective advertising. Both Kim and Campbell further underscore that ethical considerations are integral to sustaining meaningful and responsible forms of connection. Together, these perspectives suggest that defining digital advertising also entails defining its boundaries—who controls data, who bears responsibility, and who benefits from connectivity.

Taken together, these convergences suggest that digital advertising is not a static category but a living system of mediation. Its coherence arises not from uniformity but from the dynamic equilibrium among persuasion, participation, computation, and ethics—a balance that continues to evolve as technologies and values change.

Having traced the points of convergence among leading editors' perspectives, we now turn to how these insights refine and extend the definitional foundation established in Chapter 1.

Bridging Typology and System

In Chapter 1, Table 1.1 mapped the structural dimensions of digital advertising—delivery modes, initiation sources, platform dependencies, and data strategies. That typology provided a descriptive snapshot of how digital advertising manifests across contexts. Building on that foundation, the DASC framework extends the analysis from structure to system, revealing the relational forces that animate and connect those elements. Put another way, if Table 1.1 charted the terrain of digital advertising, Table 2.2 explores its geology—the deeper strata of message, experience, data, and ethics that make that terrain coherent and dynamic.

The Four Dimensions of the DASC Framework

At its core, the DASC model positions connection as both the organizing principle and the outcome of digital advertising. This connection is shaped by four interdependent dimensions—message, experience, data, and ethics—each corresponding to a particular kind of mediated relationship that sustains the system.

The first of these, message, centers on intent and meaning. Advertising still begins with purpose—the deliberate creation of messages designed to inform, persuade, or engage. Campbell's emphasis on generative AI, personalization, and adaptive digital systems, together with Taylor's emphasis on enduring principles of effectiveness, suggests that message design remains central even as its forms evolve. Yet in contemporary systems, the message is increasingly fluid, reshaped through feedback, targeting, and computational optimization. Prior to the digital revolution, advertising messages were often designed for broad audiences with the expectation of repeated exposure. In contrast, contemporary digital advertising increasingly involves the development of multiple related message variants, calibrated for individuals operating in changing contexts.

This shift toward developing multiple related message variants aligns with this chapter's broader view of advertising as adaptive and data-responsive, even as the precise mechanisms vary across platforms and contexts. Taylor's six enduring principles—privacy, relevance, trust, interactivity, entertainment, and brand building—anchor this evolution in human-centered values. Within the DASC model, the message dimension represents dynamic intent: the ongoing negotiation between brand meaning and algorithmic adaptation. It calls for renewed theoretical attention to how intent is preserved, reshaped, or distributed when AI systems participate in the creative process.

While message highlights persuasion, experience foregrounds participation. For Kim and Yoon, digital advertising is increasingly co-constructed through interaction—an experience that is lived rather than merely received. Kim's concept of connected experience reframes engagement as relational and embedded across time, platforms, and systems, while Yoon's emphasis on digital advertising as a "living, shape-shifting phenomenon" highlights the fluidity of emerging forms of persuasion and creative practice. In the DASC model, experience denotes the relational depth of these encounters—the quality of connection rather than the quantity of clicks. It shifts the unit of analysis from discrete exposure to sustained, co-created experience.

Again, the idea of message families rather than a single, unchanging entity is relevant. Algorithmic control means these families of messages can be flexibly presented to maximize persuasion. Messages may affect individuals differently depending on the experiential context in which they are encountered. In principle, this flexibility may reduce repetitive wear-out and increase the overall relevance and impact of advertising encounters.

If experience represents the phenomenological layer of connection, data provide its infrastructural core. Data form the connective tissue of digital advertising: they make personalization possible while simultaneously defining the boundaries of visibility, agency, and fairness. Huh's discussion of computational advertising, AI, algorithmic bias, transparency, and accountability highlights the extent to which data operate not merely as technical inputs but as structural conditions of contemporary advertising systems. Campbell's emphasis on AI-driven optimization and personalization complements this view by showing how computational processes increasingly shape advertising strategy and execution. Together, their perspectives suggest that data are not neutral material but active mediators of what can be known, targeted, and measured. Within the DASC framework, the data dimension captures this infrastructural logic—the systems that enable connection while simultaneously shaping its contours.

Finally, ethics operates as the system's internal regulator. Huh and Taylor emphasize transparency, accountability, privacy, and broader societal implications, while Yoon extends ethical concern to include data access, reproducibility, and equity in research conditions. This dimension transforms ethics from a peripheral consideration into a structural principle. The feedback loops of digital advertising—between message, data, and experience—must be governed by reflexive awareness of consequence. Ethical design, in this sense, is not an afterthought but an integral element of system stability.

The DASC framework therefore positions ethics as a recursive loop: every connection produced by advertising must be mirrored by mechanisms of accountability. As illustrated in Table 2.2, the model visualizes these interdependencies as a dynamic system of mediated connection, in which message, experience, data, and ethics continually shape and reshape one another through feedback and adaptation.

Of course, algorithmically controlled feedback loops—continually adjusting messages in response to user behavior—are largely invisible to consumers. Huh's discussion of transparency, accountability, and the limits of access to digital systems suggests that such invisibility may itself pose an ethical challenge. From the perspective of this chapter, that challenge also implies a growing need for digital advertising literacy among both professionals and the publics they seek to persuade.

Table 2.2 Relationship between Typology (Table 1.1 in Chapter 1) and the DASC Framework

Aspect	*Table 1.1 – Typology*	*DASC – Framework*	*Relationship*
Level of analysis	Descriptive, structural	Explanatory, systemic	DASC provides theoretical scaffolding for typological categories.
Orientation	Horizontal (variation across formats)	Vertical (function across mediation levels)	Each DASC dimension cuts through all four typological dimensions.
Temporal logic	Snapshot of formats	Continuous, adaptive process	DASC captures feedback and evolution.
Goal	Define *what*	Explain *how* and *why*	Together they form a more complete field model.

Note. This table aligns conceptually with the typology introduced in Chapter 1 and illustrates how the DASC framework advances the analysis from surface description to systemic explanation.

Digital Advertising as a System of Mediated Connection

At the center of the model lies connection, surrounded by four interacting dimensions—message (intent), experience (relation), data (infrastructure), and ethics (accountability). Arrows among these dimensions indicate continuous feedback: messages are shaped by data; data are interpreted through experience; and ethics govern and reflect all three. The model depicts an evolving, mediated system operating across platforms and through time, in which connection functions as both the precondition for and the result of interaction.

Synthesizing across the editors' perspectives reveals an ecosystem balanced by opposing forces—productive contradictions that sustain theoretical growth. One enduring tension lies between persuasion and participation. While Taylor and Campbell emphasize persuasion as the core intent of advertising, Kim and Yoon highlight participation as co-creation, seeing advertising as a shared experiential process. Huh bridges the two, framing digital advertising as simultaneously persuasive and participatory—an evolving dialogue between influence and engagement. However, it is important to point out that unless the consumer can successfully opt out of participation, the imbalance of persuasive power will be problematic. This leads directly to the question of human versus algorithmic agency.

The tension between the two is recognized by all of the editors. They acknowledge that agency in digital advertising has become a hybrid, distributed across humans, machines, and data systems. The next frontier for research lies in understanding how meaning, trust, and accountability operate when creative and analytical authority is shared with algorithms.

Another point of contrast concerns continuity and disruption. Taylor's continuity thesis underscores the endurance of advertising's core principles—trust, relevance, and meaning—while Kim's systemic reframing views digital advertising as a radical restructuring of communication itself. Yet both perspectives converge on the recognition that advertising's success depends on adapting human values to new technological architectures.

Finally, the dialogue between access and control reflects one of the most pressing issues facing the field. Huh and Yoon underscore barriers to data access and the power asymmetries they create, whereas Campbell views responsible analytics as a space for innovation. The challenge ahead lies in reconciling the open-science ideals of transparency and reproducibility with the proprietary constraints of commercial platforms. Again, the field must focus on the issue of consumer versus advertising power.

These tensions do not divide the discipline; they energize it. The DASC model visualizes this equilibrium: each dimension exerts pressure on the others, keeping the system responsive rather than rigid and ensuring that digital advertising remains a dynamic, adaptive field of inquiry.

From Definition to Diagnosis: Implications for Theory and Research

What emerges from this dialogue is not a single, final definition but a shared commitment to definitional openness. Campbell's pragmatic systems, Huh's networked ethics, Kim's connected experiences, Taylor's enduring principles, and Yoon's creative pluralism together reveal a field defined more by conversation than by closure. This implies that creative thinking by advertising researchers will be welcomed across the five gatekeepers of the main U.S. advertising journals.

Our working definition from Chapter 1 remains robust precisely because it is adaptable. Yet, as this chapter demonstrates, definitions must evolve alongside their media. Digital advertising today exists simultaneously as message, experience, dataset, and moral practice—at once designed and emergent, persuasive and participatory, human and algorithmic.

The field, like its medium, is perpetually in beta.

While the synthesis presented here draws on insights from editors of five leading U.S. advertising journals, it represents only a beginning in a broader scholarly conversation. The DASC framework will continue to grow stronger through dialogue with global researchers and editors across advertising, marketing, communication, media studies, and information systems. The chapters that follow in this fourth edition stand as a testament to that ongoing exchange—each extending, testing, and refining elements of the DASC framework through new theory, data, and application. In this sense, the framework introduced here is not a conclusion but an invitation: a living model designed to evolve alongside the field it seeks to describe.

By engaging diverse perspectives, advertising scholars enhance the field's ability to theorize complexity, anticipate change, and bridge the distance between theory and practice. Moving forward, our task is not to narrow definition but to refine connection—to examine how definitions shape methods, how methods shape ethics, and how these, together, structure the evolving ecology of digital advertising persuasion.

About the Contributing Editors

The authors gratefully acknowledge the following editors for their generosity and insight. Listed alphabetically by journal title to underscore parity among publications, these scholars—and the research areas they represent—collectively reflect the field's most influential U.S. editorial voices. Information about these journals is available through their respective publisher websites.

Charles R. Taylor, Editor-in-Chief, *International Journal of Advertising* (Taylor & Francis)

Taylor's research bridges theory and practice in global advertising strategy, creativity, regulation, and public policy.

Jisu Huh, Editor-in-Chief, *Journal of Advertising* (Taylor & Francis)

A leading scholar in computational and AI-driven advertising research, Huh's work explores data ethics, algorithmic communication, and the transformation of advertising systems in the age of automation.

Colin Campbell, Editor-in-Chief, *Journal of Advertising Research* (Taylor & Francis)

Campbell's research examines digital marketing strategy, social media engagement, and the intersection of academic theory and managerial practice in evolving media environments.

Sukki Yoon, Editor-in-Chief, *Journal of Current Issues & Research in Advertising* (Taylor & Francis)

Yoon investigates consumer psychology, cross-cultural advertising, and the cognitive and ethical implications of AI-mediated media forms.

Jooyoung Kim, Editor-in-Chief, *Journal of Interactive Advertising* (Taylor & Francis)

Kim's scholarship focuses on consumer engagement, interactive media, and the psychology of persuasion in digital and hybrid environments.

Acknowledgments

The authors acknowledge that the perspectives represented in this chapter reflect the personal views of participating journal editors. Their written responses (2025), as summarized and synthesized here, informed the development of the DASC framework; all interpretations and conclusions are those of the authors.

References

Ahn, S. J. G., Kim, J., & Kim, J. (2022). The bifold triadic relationships framework: A theoretical primer for advertising research in the metaverse. *Journal of Advertising, 51*(5), 592–607.

Bakpayev, M., Baek, T., van Esch, P., & Yoon, S. (2022). Programmatic creative: AI can think but it cannot feel. *Australasian Marketing Journal, 30*(1), 90–95.

Cho, C.-H., & Cheon, H. J. (2004). Why do people avoid advertising on the internet? *Journal of Advertising, 33*(4), 89–97.

Editors' written response (2025). *Unpublished correspondence collected by authors via email, (used with permission.)*

Kim, J. (2025). Rethinking digital advertising in a connected age. *Journal of Interactive Advertising, 24*(4), 382–400.

Kim, J. (2026). Advertising's movement to the connection era: A new paradigm for understanding connections among brands, people, content, and technology. *International Journal of Advertising*. https://doi.org/10.1080/02650487.2025.2611696

Kim, J., Lee, K. H., & Kim, J. (2023). Linking blockchain technology and digital advertising: How blockchain technology can enhance digital advertising to be more effective, efficient, and trustworthy. *Journal of Business Research, 160*, 113778.

Kerr, G., & Richards, J. (2020). Redefining advertising in research and practice. *International Journal of Advertising, 40*(2), 175–198.

Leckenby, J. D., & Li, H. (2000). From the editors: Why we need the journal of interactive advertising. *Journal of Interactive Advertising, 1*(1), 1–3.

Redden, J. P. (2025). Test for the best: Using ChatGPT to create effective ad taglines. *Journal of Current Issues & Research in Advertising, 47*(1), 1–27.

Rodgers, S., & Thorson, E. (2019). *Advertising theory* (2nd ed.). Routledge.

Ryoo, Y., Bakpayev, M., Jeon, Y., Kim, K., & Yoon, S. (2025). High hopes, hard falls: Consumer expectations and reactions to AI-human collaboration in advertising. *International Journal of Advertising*, *45*(1), 48–80.

Taylor, C. R. (2009). Editorial: The six principles of digital advertising. *International Journal of Advertising, 28*(3), 411–418.

Taylor, C. R., & Kim, E. (2025). What are the unique features of digital advertising? The six principles of digital advertising in the 21st century. *Journal of Interactive Advertising*, *25*(4), 328–346.

Part II

Message

Persuasion and Communication
in a Connected System

3 Simulated Persuasion

Theoretical Directions for Virtual Influencers in Interactive Advertising

Haley R. Hatfield and Sun Joo (Grace) Ahn

The dramatic growth of digital platforms has reshaped how consumers encounter brands and connect with the source delivering persuasive messages. As audiences spend more time in algorithmically curated social media environments, traditional lines between advertising and entertainment and advertisers and audiences have become increasingly blurred (Schultz, 2016), leading to the emergence of new types of hybrid promotional content that seamlessly embed brand messaging within social experiences. Among these changes, influencer marketing has emerged as a powerful persuasive strategy, enabling brands to leverage the perceived authenticity, relatability, and personal connection associated with social media figures in selling their products and services.

While early research on influencers primarily focused on human endorsers, or social media users with real-world identities and offline visibility (Hudders et al., 2021), technological advancements are quickly and dramatically reshaping this field. Artificial intelligence (AI), computer-generated imagery, and automated content production have introduced a new category of synthetic, simulated endorsers known as virtual influencers (VIs; Byun & Ahn, 2023; Ham et al., 2024; Kim et al., 2025; Li & Ma, 2024; Lou et al., 2023). These digitized personas replicate the presence and style of human influencers (HIs), offering unmatched scalability and control over brand messaging and targeting. Their emergence challenges traditional theories of advertising persuasion, which are often based on assumptions about the credibility, agency, and authenticity of human communicators who serve as influencers on social media. As the industry continues to adopt algorithmic identities and synthetic relationships between VIs and audiences, researchers and practitioners must revisit core advertising principles and frameworks to keep pace with the rapidly shifting realities of modern digital communication.

We address this need by applying the Revised Communication Model for Advertising to VIs, which views the communication process as a dynamic interaction among the *source*, the *message*, and the *recipient* (Stern, 1994). In doing so, we explore how VIs expand and complicate traditional advertising theories. Although this model has been used to analyze the commercialization of social

DOI: 10.4324/9781003567523-5

media stars (i.e., HIs; Hudders et al., 2021), more recent work by Byun and Ahn (2023) systematically applied it to examining VIs, revealing both conceptual parallels and critical distinctions.

Building on these foundations, this chapter situates VIs within the broader development of digital advertising theory, adapting foundational concepts to reflect new technological realities. We begin by tracing the evolution of influencers from human to virtual and explaining their similarities and differences through the framework of the Revised Communication Model for Advertising (Stern, 1994). We then critically re-examine key advertising concepts—persuasion, interactivity, and authenticity—in light of emerging tools such as AI, transmedia branding, and simulated persuasion. This chapter aims to highlight the psychological, cognitive, and behavioral effects of synthetic endorsers and to suggest directions for updating theories to meet the demands of modern advertising practice.

From Living Bodies to Virtual Beings

The rapidly evolving digital landscape has altered how many people consume, share, and engage with media. Platforms such as Snapchat, Facebook, Instagram, and TikTok have created highly interactive environments where users connect with celebrities, peers, and brands in various ways, from social interaction and information gathering to simply enjoying entertainment (Arsenyan & Mirowska, 2021; Byun & Ahn, 2023). Over time, these interactions have helped establish a new class of media figures called influencers—social media figures recognized for their online presence, rather than celebrity status or offline public roles—who build visibility and trust through specialized personal branding typically used to generate profit (Arsenyan & Mirowska, 2021; Djafarova & Rushworth, 2017; Khamis et al., 2017).

Global influencer marketing, projected to surpass US$30 billion in market value by the end of 2025 (Ross, 2025), relies on these distinctive spokespeople whose reach and status are largely derived from their social media followings (Byun & Ahn, 2023; Hudders et al., 2021). For example, "megainfluencers" have over one million followers, "macroinfluencers" have between 100,000 and one million, "microinfluencers" range from 10,000 to 100,000, and "nanoinfluencers" have between one and 10,000 followers (Block & Lovegrove, 2021). While micro- and nanoinfluencers have smaller audiences, they are often recognized for cultivating more emotionally rich relationships with their followers and can also target smaller, more niche demographics (Block & Lovegrove, 2021).

Influencers strategically utilize their platforms to promote products, brands, and services by leveraging their extensive social networks (Byun & Ahn, 2023; Hudders et al., 2021). Research shows that influencers significantly enhance brand engagement online through their connections with social media users and their creative content, while maintaining qualities of peer relationships, such as approachability and familiarity, unlike celebrities who are relatively psychologically distant from viewers and audiences (Byun & Ahn, 2023; Hudders et al., 2021; Ye et al., 2021). Social media offer media affordances that provide opportunities for bidirectional communication, allowing audiences to engage in activities from the bottom up (e.g., likes, comments, replies, shares), contrasting with the top-down diffusion common in traditional media (Dijkmans et al., 2015; Hanus & Fox, 2015). Influencers utilize the interactive affordances of platforms to appear more relatable and connect with their audiences through direct engagement, influencing purchasing decisions, as well as broader social and political opinions (Block & Lovegrove, 2021; Choudhry et al., 2022; Peter & Muth, 2023).

Historically, influencer roles have been understood as living, breathing, flesh-and-blood humans whose credibility and popularity emerge from their personal experiences, identities, and audience connection (Brooks et al., 2021; Byun & Ahn, 2023; Kim & Kim, 2021; Lou, 2022). However, as technologies such as AI and computer-generated imagery progress, this once-obvious assumption now requires a clearer distinction; in today's advertising, not all influencers are human or even real. VIs are defined as "digitized entities with anthropomorphized appearances that have human bodies, social roles, and their own identity; they can play the role of HIs by interacting with other humans, controlled either by humans or computer algorithms" (Byun & Ahn, 2023, p. 298). Often mimicking the content and visual presentation of HIs, VIs adopt human-like personas and carefully crafted narratives designed to engage audiences and persuade consumers (Haikel-Elsabeh, 2023). Unlike HIs, VIs never age, make a mistake, or take a day off. The AI-based VIs market was valued at around US$4.6 billion in 2018 and is projected to grow at an annual rate of 26% from 2019 to 2025 (The Influencer Marketing Factory, 2023; Jin & Viswanathan, 2025).

At the time of writing, some VIs have been active for nearly a decade, gradually gaining popularity and legitimacy in digital culture and advertising. One of the most widely recognized and studied examples is Lil Miquela (@LilMiquela), launched in 2016 by tech startup Brud Inc. (Block & Lovegrove, 2021; Choudhry et al., 2022; Hofeditz et al., 2022; Neri, 2022). Lil Miquela is depicted as a perpetual 19-year-old Brazilian-American singer and model based in Los Angeles. With over five million followers across platforms and recognized as a megainfluencer, she has collaborated with celebrities such as Bella Hadid and Tracee Ellis Ross and appeared in campaigns for Calvin Klein and Prada (Choudhry et al., 2022; Park et al., 2021; Sands et al., 2022a, 2022b). Despite being virtual, Lil Miquela was named one of *Times*' Most Influential People on the Internet in 2018 (TIME, 2018). More recently, her creators aged her to 22, breaking the "teenager" narrative to likely evolve her character in sync with her maturing audience—just one of many strategies that these technology companies can control, which they could not do with HIs.

However, not all VIs follow the same model. Figures like Lil Miquela and Imma—a hyperreal pink-haired Japanese VI—are developed by creative technology companies that manage their personas independently. These VIs often feature evolving narrative arcs and curated backstories, making them feel more lifelike and relatable. They are then licensed to brands for partnerships and campaigns (Sands et al., 2022b). In contrast, brand-owned VIs such as Lu do Magalu (@magazineluiza) and KFC's Virtual Colonel Sanders function more like digital mascots (see Gambetti & Kozinets, 2024). Lu do Magalu, launched in 2009 by Brazilian retailer Magazine Luiza, is now one of the most-followed VIs globally (Wang et al., 2025) and promotes products and tech reviews with minimal narrative depth. KFC's Colonel Sanders was digitally reimagined as a youthful, sexy influencer to drive cross-brand collaborations with companies like Casper and Old Spice (KFC: Virtual Colonel, 2019; Zhang & Zhu, 2025).

Somewhere between these models are VIs like Shudu (@shudu.gram), with a highly photorealistic appearance and often described as the world's first digital supermodel (Wang et al., 2025), and Noonoouri (@noonoouri), a cartoon-like high-fashion figure with big eyes and a digitally exaggerated appearance (Stein et al., 2022). Both were created by independent digital artists and are not directly tied to a single brand. While they lack the deeply engaging backstories of VIs like Lil Miquela and Imma, they similarly rely on visual storytelling, political signaling, and fashion-forward aesthetics to attract large followings and collaborate with luxury brands (Stein et al., 2022).

As VIs proliferate within media ecosystems and audience expectations evolve, it becomes essential to understand how these synthetic entities both resemble and diverge from their human counterparts in persuasive processes and outcomes. As traditional tenets of advertising, grounded in mass media, increasingly lose relevance, scholars and practitioners must revisit the fundamental ideas of persuasion, interactivity, and authenticity. The next section applies the Revised Communication Model for Advertising (Stern, 1994) to systematically explore how human and VIs function as sources, messages, and recipients in today's advertising environment. By mapping their dynamics within this framework, we can better assess how digital advertising is evolving in the era of algorithmic and simulated persuasion.

Applying the Revised Communication Model for Advertising to Virtual Influencers

Advertising research has traditionally relied on linear communication models to explain how messages move from sender to receiver. Classic frameworks, such as Lasswell's (1948) "who, says what, in which channel, to whom, with what effect" model, conceptualized the process as unidirectional, where a source sends a message to an audience through a specific medium. While useful, this view often misses the complex and interactive nature of real-world advertising. Although such models recognize feedback and noise as inherent to the communication process, audiences are generally portrayed as passive recipients, ignoring how meaning is dynamically co-created through audience interpretation, resistance, remixing, and sharing across various media and contexts (Hudders et al., 2021; Stern, 1994).

To address these limitations, Stern (1994) introduced the Revised Communication Model for Advertising, arguing that traditional models derived from oral speech (see Jakobson, 1960) and word-of-mouth paradigms (see Mullen & Johnson, 1990) do not fully capture how advertising functions in mediated, mass communication contexts. Drawing from literary theory (see Ong, 1982) and discourse analysis (see Martin, 1986), Stern (1994) defines advertising as "mass communication in the media that is paid for by identifiable sponsors" (p. 6) and reframes advertising as a dynamic, interactive exchange (i.e., active discourse). Rather than a one-way flow of information, advertising becomes an act of ongoing interpretation shaped by multilayered communication roles and cultural codes (Stern, 1994).

The revised model retains the core triad of *source* (advertisers), *message* (promotional content), and *recipient* (consumers) but reimagines each as multidimensional and context-dependent (Stern, 1994). The source is comprised of the *sponsor* (e.g., the brand or company funding and controlling the ad), the *author* (e.g., the creative agency responsible for message construction), and the *persona* (e.g., the spokesperson or voice in the ad) (Byun & Ahn, 2023; Hudders et al., 2021; Stern, 1994). Each source role contributes differently to how the ad is constructed, interpreted, and received, especially in the context of VIs. For instance, the *persona* is often the most public-facing and interactive element in VI advertising because, unlike traditional spokespersons, VIs are branded identities performing authenticity, emotion, and social relevance through computer-generated algorithms (Byun & Ahn, 2023). Consequently, the persona's *message* is not a static block of information but a layered text that operates on multiple narrative and performative levels simultaneously (Stern, 1994).

Stern suggests that message strategies can use the persona in unique ways to evoke different responses from the audience. For example, the point of view a persona adopts when communicating with an audience can vary, such as using first-person autobiographical content to share emotional or personal information, allowing audiences to imagine they are sharing personal experiences (Hudders et al., 2021; Stern, 1994). Narrative messages adopt a third-person persona to tell a story about others to an audience who must use additional information and their existing knowledge to make sense of the story (Stern, 1994). Message strategies that use drama or playacting enable personas to perform events directly for an audience, encouraging vicarious experience through performance (Stern, 1994). In other words, advertising messages aim to convey the endorser's persona to build a connection with the audience, stylized and crafted to evoke relatability, authority, and information to influence consumer behavior (Byun & Ahn, 2023; Stern, 1994).

The recipient, or audience, is the third and final element of communication in the revised model. Drawing on reader-response theory (see Staton, 1987), Stern emphasizes that consumers do not passively absorb messages but actively interpret, deconstruct, and make meaning of advertising content based on personal, cultural, and social contexts (Byun & Ahn, 2023; Hudders et al., 2021; Stern, 1994). The model identifies three recipient roles: *implied consumers* (those imagined and idealized by the ad's persona), *sponsorial consumers* (the sponsor's internal gatekeepers who approve or reject ads before public release), and *actual consumers* (those in the real world who see the ad). Consumers act as co-creators of meaning, and no meaning remains fixed because actual consumers may agree or disagree with the sponsor's intended message, which is usually designed for the implied consumer. Importantly, Stern introduces *interactive consumers* as a concept for future research. These consumers go beyond understanding the message; they are expected to act to engage with the message, such as sharing content, making purchases, or interacting with the message on social media. This shifts the ad's impact from mere interpretation to real behavior (Stern, 1994).

Stern (1994) concludes by urging scholars to explore what is called "interactive advertising," defined at the time as "a dialogue between human and machine [interactive], based on integrated digital streams of video, audio text, and graphics [multimedia]" (Salomon Brothers, 1993, p. 30). Though this early vision predates today's algorithmic and immersive technologies, it anticipated many of the concerns that now dominate advertising research, such as source credibility in synthetic environments (Hofeditz et al., 2022; Liu & Lee, 2022; Park & Sun, 2023; Pearson et al., 2019; Sands et al., 2022a), media effects in multimodal platforms (Sands et al., 2022b; Stein et al., 2022; Sundar et al., 2017), and the behaviors of digital consumers navigating real and virtual ecosystems (Ahn et al., 2022a; Arsenyan & Mirowska, 2021; Mrad et al., 2022).

Revised Communication Model in the Age of Influencers

Nearly three decades after Stern introduced the Revised Communication Model for Advertising (1994), Hudders et al. (2021) updated the framework to account for the rise of influencer marketing within participatory digital platforms (e.g., social media). While retaining Stern's multidimensional triadic structure of *source*, *message*, and *recipient*, Hudders et al. (2021) emphasized the co-creative, relational, and interactive dynamics that define contemporary influencer-brand-audience relationships. Their framework captures how communication is no longer linear or top-down, but collaborative and shaped by the influencer's dual role as both content creator and persona (Ahn et al., 2022a; Byun & Ahn, 2023).

Sources in Human Influencer Marketing

One of the most significant shifts in the updated revised model is the way the traditional boundaries between source roles—sponsor, author, and persona—increasingly converge in influencer communication (Byun & Ahn, 2023; Hudders et al., 2021). Influencers blur the boundary of these roles, serving as the face of the brand (persona), the creator of the content (author), and in some cases, a surrogate for the sponsor through brand partnerships. Unlike Stern's original distinctions (e.g., creative agencies as authors, spokespersons as personas), Hudders et al. (2021) argue that influencers collapse these roles into one. Influencers often have creative control of content, share legal and reputational responsibility for sponsored messages, and perform stylized versions of themselves for their audience (Byun & Ahn, 2023; Hudders et al., 2021). Hudders and colleagues thus propose three modified source dimensions that reflect these shifts: the *sponsor*, the *intermediary* (a bridging agent such as an agency partner or digital platform), and the *influencer* (combining author and persona; Hudders et al., 2021). This convergence makes influencer not only marketing highly personalized but also challenging to assess using traditional communication theory, as it disrupts clear role distinctions and complicates questions of authorship and intent.

In their systematic review of 154 studies conducted between 2011 and 2020, Hudders et al. (2021) identified two key characteristics of the influencer-as-source: reach and impact. Reach refers to the size and visibility of an influencer's audience, often measured by follower count (Murray & Jenkins, 1992). This metric plays a critical role in determining the influencer's perceived status (i.e., megainfluencer, nanoinfluencer). Conversely, impact concerns the degree to which an influencer can shape the opinions, decisions, or behaviors of their followers, often through content that spans multiple formats and modalities (i.e., static posts or live videos; Hudders et al., 2021). Together, reach and impact metrics are commonly used by brands and intermediaries to assess partnership potential, although Hudders et al. (2021) note that many companies still lack formalized strategies for selecting influencers that align with their values or goals.

Influencers also tend to specialize in specific and niche domains (e.g., fashion, travel, fitness) and are often regarded as opinion leaders within these focused areas (Hudders et al., 2021). Their effectiveness depends largely on their perceived expertise and ability to cultivate an authentic, engaging online presence (Khamis et al., 2017). This sense of authenticity is typically achieved by sharing aspects of everyday life, personal preferences, and social relationships (Hudders et al., 2021). However, authenticity can be fragile, where excessive overt self-promotion can backfire and lead to perceptions of inauthenticity, diminishing the influencer's credibility and appeal (Marwick & Boyd, 2011). Unlike traditional celebrities, influencers are often seen as more approachable and relatable, in part because they use social media to engage directly with followers, shaping an ongoing sense of connection and community.

The influencer-audience relationship is frequently theorized through the lens of parasocial interaction, where followers form one-sided imaginary bonds with media figures (Horton & Wohl, 1956). These interactions can deepen over time into parasocial relationships, particularly when influencers post regularly, respond to comments, and offer personal glimpses into their lives (Byun & Ahn, 2023; Chung & Cho, 2017). These connections strengthen feelings of similarity, familiarity, and likability, which are essential for building trust and persuasive influence (Stein et al., 2022). Additionally, influencers often act as moderators, balancing the demands of sponsors and agencies for profit with their audience's expectations of authentic content (Enke & Borchers, 2019). In many campaigns, influencers adjust their tone and messaging to ensure the content resonates with their existing community.

Hudders et al. (2021) argued that source characteristics in influencer marketing borrow heavily from earlier celebrity endorsement literature. Traits such as trustworthiness and expertise (dimensions of source credibility), as well as likeability, similarity, and familiarity (dimensions of source attractiveness), remain central to how audiences evaluate influencers. These qualities shape message reception and campaign effectiveness, especially when influencers demonstrate alignment or congruency with the brand's values and product category (Woodcock & Johnson, 2019). The number of followers an influencer has can also influence perceptions of expertise and legitimacy, especially within a given niche (De Veirman et al., 2017). Moreover, when influencers effectively foster parasocial interactions and relationships, they become powerful agents for shaping brand awareness, purchase intentions, and even broader shifts in public opinion (Hudders et al., 2021). Finally, Hudders et al. (2021) found that using influencers with a broad reach can boost brand awareness. However, micro- or nanoinfluencers, who often have close personal connections with their followers, may be more effective at shaping attitudes or behaviors (Gaenssle & Budzinski, 2021; Wellman et al., 2020).

Messages in Human Influencer Marketing

Hudders et al. (2021) simplified Sterns' (1994) advertising message strategies into two key types for influencer marketing: autobiographical sharing and storytelling. While Stern's framework draws from literary theory to characterize advertising messages, influencer marketing blends more flexible and participatory strategies. Hudders et al. (2021) note that autobiographical messages (e.g., personal experiences, preferences, or behind-the-scenes moments) form the foundation of how influencers cultivate emotional closeness and authenticity with their followers. These personalized narratives help shape the influencer's persona and foster parasocial relationships through feelings of intimacy and trust (Enke & Borchers, 2019; Marôpo et al., 2020; Porter, 2020).

In Hudders et al.'s (2021) review, few studies (21 of 154) focused directly on the content of influencers' posts. However, these studies underscore how carefully curated messaging shapes both influencers' identity and audience response. Influencers are often concerned with projecting a desirable yet relatable image while maintaining authenticity, all while managing the commercial goals of their partnerships. To do this, they incorporate personal anecdotes, expressions of endearment, and backstage glimpses into their lives to establish emotional bonds with their audiences (Abidin & Thompson, 2012; Hudders et al., 2021). Importantly, messages that adopt a storytelling format, whether told directly or acted out, garner longer viewer engagement than purely informational posts (Stubb, 2018). Still, autobiographical messages tend to generate stronger perceptions of authenticity, particularly when the product is embedded naturally within the influencer's ongoing personal narrative (Hudders et al., 2021).

Hudders et al. (2021) emphasized that in the influencer context, message credibility is often influenced by the degree to which the endorsement appears seamlessly integrated with the influencer's established persona. When product promotion seems forced or overly commercial, it risks harming the trust between the influencer and their followers. To mitigate this, many influencers employ subtle branding tactics, such as referral links or casual verbal mentions in video content (Hudders et al., 2021; Jorge et al., 2018; Qutteina et al., 2019; Schwemmer & Ziewiecki, 2018). Techniques such as text in captions, hashtags, images, background settings, and facial expressions allow influencers to promote products while maintaining a sense of spontaneous or unscripted interaction (Holiday et al., 2023). Furthermore, varying content formats (e.g., posts, stories, reels) allow influencers to creatively leverage multimodal tools to craft sponsored content without losing their personal touch.

Influencers also navigate multiple messaging roles, from content creators and storytellers to moderators and distributors of brand messaging (Hudders et al., 2021). Their ability to serve as cultural and discursive intermediaries reflects their dual position as both market actors and meaning-makers (Hutchinson, 2020). As cultural intermediaries, influencers help shape and circulate values, beauty ideals, body image, and lifestyle norms that resonate with their audiences, often translating commercial content into aspirational narratives (Hudders et al., 2021). As discursive intermediaries, they engage in ongoing meaning-making processes through language, imagery, and symbolic cues, constantly negotiating their self-brand to remain relevant to both marketers and audiences. Influencers can bridge personal and commercial goals in ways that traditional advertising formats cannot. However, the intertwined impact of sponsored messages and native cultures raises ethical concerns, as many promoted products and particularly those within food and wellness categories are unhealthy or unrealistic and often reinforce unattainable beauty standards (Campbell et al., 2021; Hudders et al., 2021; Pfeuffer et al., 2024; Tiggemann et al., 2017).

Finally, message effectiveness is also shaped by how products are visually framed. Posts that are product-centric (i.e., focus primarily on the item) are often perceived as more trustworthy when coming from brands; however, these posts tend to generate less parasocial interaction compared to influencer-centric posts (i.e., where the influencer is posed with the product; De Veirman et al., 2017; Kim & Kim, 2021; Schouten et al., 2020). Thus, the integration of branded content into autobiographical or narrative messages serves to enhance authenticity and activate stronger bonds between the influencer and the audience. Hudders et al. (2021) argued that in influencer marketing, autobiographical messaging that aligns closely with the influencer's persona remains the most persuasive strategy, particularly when coupled with authentic storytelling and subtle brand integration.

Audiences in Human Influencer Marketing

In Stern's (1994) Revised Communication Model, the audience is repositioned as an active interpreter of meaning through individual cultural and social lenses, rather than a passive receiver. In influencer marketing, Hudders et al. (2021) expanded this view, emphasizing that audiences are not monolithic and should be understood and differentiated by their roles and engagement levels. Specifically, Hudders et al. (2021) distinguish between an influencer's immediate follower base, broader online networks reached through shares and reports, and niche audiences targeted through specific content strategies. Therefore, their updated revised model identified three key influencer-audience dimensions: large reach (i.e., total potential audience), engaged audience (e.g., likes, comments), and specific audience (e.g., tailored content for niche groups). These categories relate to different audience outcomes, including message attention, awareness, knowledge, attitudes, and behavioral responses (Hudders et al., 2021).

Audience-related inquiries dominated Hudders et al.'s (2021) review of influencer research, with 77 of 154 studies focused on how followers perceive influencers and their content. Most examined how source, message, and disclosure cues affect persuasion, while others explored audience trust and perceptions of authenticity. Positive personality traits such as honesty, relatability, and ambition consistently emerged as key to influencer appeal (Balaban & Mustătea, 2019; Coates et al., 2020; Djafarova & Trofimenko, 2019; Freberg et al., 2011; Konstantopoulou et al., 2019). Parasocial interactions were also found to drive engagement (Daniel et al., 2018), particularly when influencers disclosed personal information and maintained a conversational tone, even if one-sided (Hwang & Jeong, 2016).

However, sponsorship often complicates these relationships. Some audiences viewed branded posts as less genuine, which weakened trust and authenticity (Hudders et al., 2021; Marôpo et al., 2020). While younger audiences were more forgiving, seeing sponsorship as a way to support creators (Stubb et al., 2019; Van Dam & Van Reijmersdal, 2019), others found that overt commercialism reduced credibility (Konstantopoulou et al., 2019). Emotional responses were further shaped by the physical appearance of the influencer, with eye-tracking research showing that audiences focused more on an influencer's face and body than on the product (Mañas-Viniegra et al., 2020). However, imperfections such as acne elicited stronger reactions than idealized images (Mañas-Viniegra et al., 2020), and upward social comparisons sometimes led to envy, especially in individuals with low self-esteem (Chae, 2018).

Authenticity remains a paradox in influencer marketing. It is essential for cultivating trust and engagement, yet it does not always translate into persuasive outcomes. Studies show that authenticity is most effective when paired with expertise and product congruence (Carter, 2016; Hudders et al., 2021; Lin et al., 2018; Marwick & Boyd, 2011; Wellman et al., 2020). Storytelling formats and advertising disclosures can increase transparency (Evans et al., 2017); however, if disclosures are overly descriptive, they may undermine perceptions of honesty (Pfeuffer & Huh, 2021; Pfeuffer et al., 2024). Additionally, while some problematic effects, such as promoting unhealthy eating habits (De Jans et al., 2018), emerged in short-term exposure for youth, long-term behavioral changes were less evident (De Jans et al., 2020, 2022).

Hudders et al. (2021) also emphasized the need for clearer ethical standards. Many influencers, particularly minors, may be unaware of their regulatory obligations, raising questions about accountability. Hudders et al. (2021) proposed that advertisers should bear full responsibility for the content influencers post on their behalf, though international regulation remains uneven across countries. Standardized global guidelines, better advertising literacy (i.e., ad recognition), and more transparent collaboration between influencers, brands, and platforms could help improve trust while maintaining the effectiveness of influencer messaging.

As influencer marketing evolves, brands are shifting away from mega-reach and are instead seeking micro- and nanoinfluencers with more targeted, engaged audiences (Hudders et al., 2021). While this shift enables deeper relationships, it also introduces new risks, such as fake followers (e.g., bots), scandals, or damage to the brand or influencer's reputation. These challenges have increased interest in VIs, which are designed to deliver controlled, customizable, and controversy-free messages (Byun & Ahn, 2023). The following sections examine how VIs are transforming audience interactions and propose potential solutions to the limitations of human influence, along with ethical concerns related to emerging technologies.

Revised Communication Model in the Age of Virtual Influencers

The rapid growth of interactive and immersive media technologies has improved the ability to create realistic, human-like VIs, moving beyond static posts to include complex animations like nonverbal cues (i.e., facial expressions or body gestures) and synchronized voice overlays (Byun & Ahn, 2023). As VIs become more popular, many well-known VIs are recognized for mimicking HIs on social media. These VIs, such as Lil Miquela mentioned earlier, resemble and behave like humans, portraying an anthropomorphized representation (Byun & Ahn, 2023).

The programmatic and consistent nature of VIs makes them an attractive marketing tool. Unlike HIs, VIs do not get tired or hungry, are not affected by humane working conditions (such as overtime limits or mandated lunch breaks), and can manage multiple online accounts simultaneously (Byun & Ahn, 2023). VIs can appear in static posts on Instagram or animated videos on TikTok or YouTube and, more recently, in interactive three-dimensional social virtual environments (i.e., metaverse) like Roblox (Joel-Edgar et al., 2025; Koles et al., 2024; McDowell, 2024). VIs' consistency and flexibility allow for high-quality brand communication at scale, with less risk of burnout or scandal (Byun & Ahn, 2023). These efficiencies contribute to their perceived cost-effectiveness, where matching these efforts with consistent quality and audience engagement would be incredibly difficult for HIs to replicate since they often take on the labor of filming, editing, and managing audience engagement (Byun & Ahn, 2023; Sands et al., 2022b).

Conversely, while VIs can be programmed to look and act like humans, they further complicate the influencing process. Social influence—the process of changing others' thoughts, feelings, attitudes, or behaviors through interaction—is often nuanced and context-dependent (Byun & Ahn, 2023; Cialdini & Goldstein, 2004). HIs often succeed because audiences believe they are building a relationship with a real person, which fosters parasocial interactions. In contrast, research shows that audiences tend to prefer and are more influenced by content controlled and delivered by humans over content controlled and delivered by algorithms or machine-controlled entities (Fox et al., 2015). These preferences are partly due to how humans interpret authenticity, or how much a communicative act is seen as real and genuine (Lee, 2020). While HIs are often praised for creating intimate, relatable online personas, VIs may fall short of this due to their constructed and corporate-controlled nature.

Moreover, the uncanny valley hypothesis (Mori et al., 2012) offers additional insight into audience discomfort with VIs. Recent research suggests that the unsettling emotional effects of almost-human VIs may undermine trust and limit their persuasive power (Arsenyan & Mirowska, 2021; Liu & Lee, 2022). Although audiences might still interact with VI content, the perception that they are ultimately engaging with a company rather than an individual shifts the dynamic. Unlike HIs, which are perceived as having autonomy and personality, VIs may be viewed as digital spokespersons representing a carefully crafted brand identity, thereby limiting their ability to form meaningful or believable connections with followers.

Using the Revised Communication Model for Advertising (Stern, 1994) as a guiding framework, Byun and Ahn's (2023) systematic review expanded the model to highlight key differences between VIs and HIs based on earlier work (e.g., Hudders et al., 2021). While most studies (28 of 44) referred to VIs as "virtual influencers," others used terms like virtual stars, AI influencers, social robots, or digital human avatars (Byun & Ahn, 2023). This inconsistency reflects the conceptual ambiguity surrounding VIs and highlights the need for clearer theoretical distinctions. To explore these differences, the following sections apply the source-message-recipient triad of the Revised Communication Model (Stern, 1994) to VIs, examining how these roles are mediated and interpreted within interactive advertising. By drawing from Byun and Ahn's (2023) review and related scholarship, we can better understand how VIs function as communicative agents and how they differ from their human counterparts.

Sources in Virtual Influencer Marketing

In adapting Stern's (1994) Revised Communication Model for Advertising to VIs, the source dimension must consider the layered and computational aspects of VI design and operation. Traditionally, the source includes the sponsor (brand), the author (creative agency), and the persona (spokesperson) (Stern, 1994). In influencer marketing, Hudders et al. (2021) reframed these roles as the sponsor, intermediary (e.g., agency or platform), and the influencer. Regarding VIs, Byun and Ahn (2023) suggest a similar three-way structure—comprising the sponsor, creator (a combined author/intermediary), and the VI as the persona. Although audiences may perceive VIs as autonomous sources, the actual authorship belongs to the teams of developers, strategists, and brands behind them, making it important to distinguish VIs as sources of social influence and to understand VIs' source effects from the perspectives of sponsors or creative agencies (Byun & Ahn, 2023).

VIs demonstrate source-like features through social influence markers like those of HIs, such as reach (e.g., the size of a follower count), impact (e.g., the ability to shape audiences' attitudes and behaviors), and parasocial interaction (Byun & Ahn, 2023). Studies have found that VIs can rival or even surpass the engagement of HIs (HypeAuditor, 2019), often due to their novelty, idealized appearance, and strategic use of anthropomorphism (Breves et al., 2021; Miao et al., 2022). However, VIs' lack of consciousness and physicality means they are ultimately extensions of brand strategy, as programmable and controllable beings, and immune to fatigue or scandal, unlike HIs. This high level of predictability and flexibility makes VIs appealing to advertisers, who can tailor content more precisely to campaign needs (da Silva Oliveira & Chimenti, 2021; Robinson, 2020).

At the same time, because VIs are generated by multiple sources (e.g., designers, coders, brand managers), their perceived authenticity is often lower than HIs. Research applying source orientation theory, or the perceived psychological distance audiences feel in their interactions with VIs (Liu & Lee, 2022), suggests audiences view VIs as psychologically distal compared to HIs, which may reduce their persuasive impact. The layering of authorship and lack of transparency about who is communicating can hinder trust. Moreover, VIs may be more cognitively grouped as an out-group (machines) rather than as distinct individuals like us (humans), meaning a single VI's brand misstep could generalize to the entire group (Tajfel & Turner, 2000; Thomas & Fowler, 2021).

Importantly, the evolving realism of VIs increases their potential and risks. As AI-generated influencers become more human-like, they approach the "uncanny valley," where nearly human-like representations cause discomfort (Mori et al., 2012). However, recent research challenges the idea that hyperrealism is always detrimental; scholars suggest that having a well-defined persona and consistent responsiveness may be more important than physical realism in building audience trust (Stein et al., 2022; Yang et al., 2023). Transparency also plays a key role; research shows that audiences report discomfort when VIs are not clearly labeled virtual but are more accepting when VIs are honest about their virtual nature and when they respond to user interactions to build parasocial relationships (Franke et al., 2023; Liu & Lee, 2022; Lou et al., 2022). While their anthropomorphic features, algorithmic control, and responsiveness provide unique marketing advantages, their effectiveness as sources depends on audience perceptions of authenticity, psychological distance, and transparency. Understanding these factors is crucial for the growing use of VIs in interactive marketing.

Messages in Virtual Influencer Marketing

According to Stern's (1994) Revised Communication Model for Advertising, the message serves as a crucial link between the source and the audience, aiming to persuade and build relational intimacy. In influencer marketing, the message is often used to convey authenticity, which is achieved through autobiographical storytelling (Hudders et al., 2021). Although VIs lack lived experience, their messages can mimic autobiographical depth by using strategic first-person narration and consistent storytelling. For example, in 2025, Lil Miquela posted a selfie outside and looked displeased with this caption: "when you're on your daily hot girl walk and remember who you let disrupt your peace in your last era…never again lol" (Lil Miquela, 2025). Though entirely fabricated by her creators, the post mirrors familiar patterns of self-reflection to portray Lil Miquela as having relatable, human-like experiences to her followers. Like many other VIs, Lil Miquela's posts often imitate human self-disclosure (e.g., "having a hard week"; Byun & Ahn, 2023), creating emotional storylines (e.g., public breakup with her human boyfriend), replying to fan comments, and reflecting on fictional yet human-like milestones (e.g., celebrating a birthday) (da Silva Oliveira & Chimenti, 2021).

VIs can adopt similar narrative strategies as HIs to signal authenticity and intimacy despite their artificiality. Research indicates that when posts are consistent and combine commercial content with emotional or entertaining elements, audiences tend to respond positively to VIs who share "personal" insights, opinions on products, or lifestyle choices (Wang & Huang, 2023). Like HIs, VIs must balance the tension between appearing authentic and promoting products transparently (Hudders et al., 2021). In both instances, the persuasive message is not just informative but also performative, influencing perceptions of trust and credibility.

However, the unique visual presence of VIs introduces new messaging dynamics. For example, in a sentiment analysis, Park et al. (2021) found that mixed visual compositions featuring both VIs and HIs together elicited stronger emotional responses, including anxiety, especially when viewers could not easily distinguish between virtual and human (Byun & Ahn, 2023). These reactions may result from subtle visual cues of unnaturalness or confusion about authenticity, which complicate the processing of VI messages. This unnaturalness may also highlight the importance of message-product congruence with VIs given their digital origin. That is, VIs tend to be more persuasive when endorsing technical or futuristic products (e.g., computer graphics cards) than those requiring physical presence, such as skincare or food (Franke et al., 2023). Message-product congruence for VIs may be especially crucial for effective messaging, considering the psychological distance audiences may feel toward digital entities (Mrad et al., 2022).

Finally, the visual format and platform can influence how VI messages are understood. Unlike static images, videos or interactive content may evoke different emotional and cognitive responses (Sundar et al., 2017). Similarly, revealing the VI's sponsorship or digital nature may affect audience trust (Kim et al., 2024; Pfueffer et al., 2024). However, as with VIs as sources, research shows mixed results on whether transparency enhances or diminishes persuasive impact (Vrontis et al., 2021). Although research is limited, there is evidence that message design in VI campaigns involves complex emotional and perceptual processes not yet fully addressed in traditional influencer studies.

Audiences in Virtual Influencer Marketing

The final component focuses on the audience: how users interpret, respond to, and co-create meaning from advertising content (Hudders et al., 2021; Stern, 1994). In interactive media ecosystems, audiences are seen as active participants in meaning-making (Aho & Mackie, 1993), a role that is even more prominent in influencer marketing (Hudders et al., 2021). Compared to traditional advertising, audiences typically show higher engagement and regard such content as more credible when interacting with HIs, due to perceived authenticity and relational qualities (Casaló et al., 2020; Wang & Huang, 2023). Nonetheless, the advent of VIs introduces new dynamics, often blurring the boundary between human connection and algorithmic simulation.

At first glance, VIs seem to share many of the same appealing qualities that attract audiences to HIs. Like HIs, VIs can be designed to display traits such as attractiveness, expertise, and consistency—qualities that increase parasocial interaction and brand endorsement effectiveness (Mrad et al., 2022; Ye et al., 2021). VIs also generate audience interest through unique features like anthropomorphism and scalability (da Silva Oliveira & Chimenti, 2021). However, audience engagement with VIs is not always simple. Even when virtual characters convincingly mimic human behavior, studies show that audiences often recognize them as nonhuman and may categorize them as out-group members or dehumanized objects (Seymour et al., 2021).

This inconsistency is evident in mixed findings on trust and influence. VIs are sometimes held to higher standards than HIs and are only viewed as credible when they demonstrate exceptional expertise or novel content (Byun & Ahn, 2023; Franke et al., 2023; Hofeditz et al., 2022). While one study found that audiences trust VIs more than HIs when they believe the virtual agents have higher expertise, this trust quickly declined when the illusion of expertise was disrupted (Pearson et al., 2019). Moreover, audiences often assign greater credit for successful product endorsements to HIs due to stronger feelings of psychological closeness and similarity (Liu & Lee, 2022). These perceptions of authenticity and proximity are essential to the influencer-audience relationship and cannot be easily reproduced by algorithmically controlled personas (Byun & Ahn, 2023).

Despite these limitations, VIs can still foster parasocial relationships, especially when audiences are curious about the boundary between real and virtual. As Sands et al. (2022b) pointed out, the novelty of interacting with a computer-generated persona may be a factor in attracting interest. In other words, VI-related advertising can satisfy audience desires for entertainment, aesthetics, and surveillance (Lou et al., 2022), indicating that VIs might address different psychological needs than HIs. One study found that audiences felt comparable levels of parasocial engagement with both HIs and VIs when they viewed the content as authentic and emotionally expressive (Stein et al., 2022). However, when anthropomorphism and perceived similarity were low, these parasocial responses weakened, emphasizing the delicate nature of audience connection to VIs.

Interestingly, concerns about misinformation and manipulation through VIs have not shown strong empirical support. Jayles et al. (2020) found that false information provided by VIs did not significantly impair group decision-making, as human users were often able to identify and correct inaccuracies through social interaction. This suggests that interpersonal audience dynamics, such as collective intelligence, may buffer against the potential harms of VI-driven content (Byun & Ahn, 2023). Though VIs can display many qualities similar to HIs, they are often required to outperform to earn comparable trust.

A Revised Communication Model for Virtual Influencer Advertising

Building from Stern's (1994) Revised Communication Model for Advertising and extending insights from Hudders et al. (2021), we propose an updated framework that reconfigures the traditional source-message-audience triad to better accommodate the layered authorship, algorithmic behavior, and relational interactivity that define VI communication in interactive advertising. Stern's (1994) revised model introduced the distinction between "within-text" and "without-text" communicators, where fictional narrators and implied audiences were situated inside the advertising text (virtual), while the sponsor and actual audience lived outside the text (real). Yet in VI advertising, these boundaries blur. The traditional binary between "real" and "virtual" no longer holds, as simulated agents perform authenticity, emotion, and expertise, while real humans orchestrate, respond to, and engage with personas in ways that mirror human-to-human interactions (Ahn et al., 2022a).

Insights from decades of virtual reality (VR) and avatar-based research help clarify this shift. Studies have shown that people frequently respond to simulated environments as if they are real (Ahn, 2021; Behm-Morawitz et al., 2016; Slater & Wilbur, 1997; Yee & Bailenson, 2007). These effects are also found when interacting with virtual avatars (controlled by another human) or agents (controlled by algorithms; Nowak & Fox, 2018), exhibiting emotional (Sundar et al., 2017), cognitive (Ahn et al., 2022b), and even physiological reactions (Jenkins & Obhi, 2020; Katsumi et al., 2020) that closely mirror those in face-to-face contexts (Blascovich et al., 2002; Blascovich & Bailenson, 2011; Maloney et al., 2020). Through mechanisms such as spatial presence, or feeling "there" in a mediated environment (Lombard & Ditton, 2006), even brief VR experiences can lead to short-term attitudinal and behavioral changes (Ahn et al., 2014, 2016; Lee et al., 2023). In this light, it becomes less surprising that audiences form parasocial bonds with VIs and attribute human qualities (e.g., authenticity, expertise, relatability) to entirely simulated personas.

To account for this blurring of boundaries, we instead lay out the source-message-audience relationship across a spectrum of *corporeal* (flesh and blood), *hybrid/augmented*, and *simulated* (pixels and code) ontologies and compare it against Stern's 1994 model (see Figure 3.1). Our framework captures the distinction between different actors—real and virtual, human and nonhuman—as well as the layered and often entangled ways in which authorship, control, and audience response are co-constructed across media systems. Unlike earlier models that treat communicative roles as discrete and static, our framework visualizes how VI campaigns emerge through the coordinated and dynamic inputs of human agents, algorithmic processes, and audience behaviors. It also clarifies how these roles may also be shaped by platform infrastructures (e.g., engagement metrics, platform algorithms) rather than solely by narrative content.

The top half of the figure emphasizes *authorship and control,* including the source and message, while the bottom half emphasizes *audience experience and response,* covering the message and audience. Regarding source dimensions (sponsor, creator, VI), we position the sponsor (e.g., company or brand) within the corporeal domain. Even when campaigns are supported through

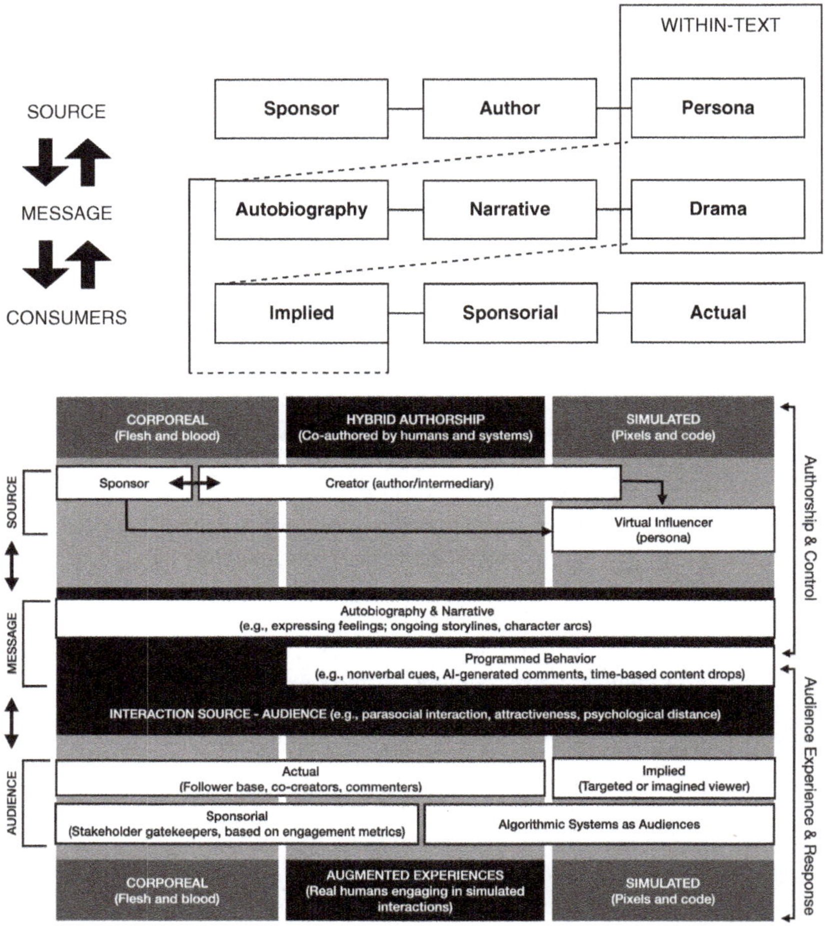

Figure 3.1 Revised Communication Model for Virtual Influencer Advertising.

Source: Adapted from Stern (1994).

digital assets (e.g., NFTs, digital currency), the core funding decisions are typically made by human stakeholders. The creator (e.g., creative agencies or tech developers) extends from corporeal through hybrid to simulated. As authors and intermediaries (Byun & Ahn, 2023), this positioning spanning corporeal to simulated reflects a broad range of creative influence, from fully human authorship to AI-generated content pipelines. The VI persona, situated within the simulated domain, is the output of this collaboration: animated, curated, and controlled by sponsors, creators, and systems. Although VIs are not (yet) sentient, they are presented with coherence and intentionality that enable audiences to perceive them as autonomous figures who may even be emotionally aware. This raises new interpretive challenges for understanding the "source" of a message, since influence is no longer tied to a singular entity but is dispersed across a network of human and algorithmic collaborations.

The message layer in the middle of the framework reflects the spectrum that spans from corporeal and simulated, while serving as a bridge between source and audience. While not always to the extent as Lil Miquela, many VIs communicate through autobiography and narrative, such as drawing from human experiences (e.g., captions written in first-person voice) (corporeal), to confronting their constructed identities (e.g., behind-the-scenes showing creators) (hybrid), or exhibiting character arcs not possible for humans (e.g., changing ages on demand) (simulated). Currently, these message components are designed to mimic the intimacy and relatability of HIs; however, they may become entirely AI-driven based on autonomous experiences (e.g., agentic AI). Messages also reflect a degree of programmed behavior spanning hybrid and simulated control, such as stylized animations, nonverbal cues and gestures, algorithmically scheduled posts, or AI-generated comments that simulate spontaneity. Though highly scripted, these features often mimic the stylistic conventions of human self-presentation and can evoke comparable affective responses (Byun & Ahn, 2023). As with the source, the line between human-created narrative and automated delivery is becoming harder to separate—and often intentionally so.

In the audience section, we clarify several types of engagement. Actual audiences, or users who follow, comment, and engage, occupy both the corporeal and hybrid space, as real people participate in simulated interactions. This is where we shift from the language of "hybrid authorship" to "augmented experiences," highlighting the way human responses are shaped by immersion and interaction within digitally constructed spaces. Implied audiences are situated within the simulated domain, representing idealized or imagined viewers constructed by the campaign logic (Stern, 1994) and often through data proxies like target demographics or algorithmic profiles. Sponsorial audiences (e.g., institutional gatekeepers such as brand managers or content strategists) stretch from corporeal decision-making to augmented inputs, as their assessments are often based on quantified data (e.g., impressions, likes, shares). Finally, we treat algorithmic systems as a kind of audience. These systems are coded to observe, evaluate, and respond in ways that actively shape circulation, prioritizing certain content through ranking, visibility, or recommendation engines. In emerging cases, brands are even developing simulated audiences—algorithms and AI trained on engagement data—to test content before deployment (Ahmadi et al., 2024; Liu et al., 2025). These systems shape both message circulation and the feedback loop that influences how future content is created and distributed.

By positioning source, message, and audience within a shared ontological spectrum of corporeal, hybrid/augmented, and simulated zones, this revised model frames VI campaigns as emergent, co-authored processes. These campaigns unfold through a dynamic interplay of human labor, creative intent, machine behavior, and audience response. As such, they challenge legacy models of persuasion communication and demand frameworks capable of grappling with blurred authorship, flexible identity, and responsive media systems. VIs may be simulated, but their effects, and the experiences they help construct, are very much real.

This revised model offers a clearer framework for navigating the complexity of VI campaigns, anticipating how audiences attribute credibility, authenticity, and engagement across human and algorithmic agents. For advertisers, the framework supports more intentional message design by mapping where human creative input ends and system-driven behaviors begin, creating insights that can guide creative transparency (e.g. disclosures), ethical storytelling, and more meaningful audience connection with VI personas. For platforms, the model underscores their evolving role not just as distributors but also as algorithmic participants in meaning-making, with the power to shape visibility, interaction patterns, and campaign outcomes (Noble, 2018). Finally, for policymakers, the visualization of hybrid authorship and augmented audience engagement reveals new forms of persuasion influence that challenge legacy norms of disclosure, consent, and agency. As audiences increasingly distort the lines between entertainment, interaction, and commerce, regulatory bodies must consider how simulated content mimics interpersonal intimacy and supports simulated relationships while operating outside the expectations of traditional advertising frameworks.

Generated and Agentic: The Role of Artificial Intelligence in Virtual Influencer Advertising

As VIs become more prevalent and technology continues to advance, we will continue to see AI integration in the creation, distribution, and evaluation of VI advertising. Not all VIs and digital characters are created with AI; also, how and during what process AI is integrated shifts the characteristics and features of the VI, ultimately shaping how it generates rapport and parasocial relationships with audiences (Thomas & Fowler, 2021).

The very beginnings of VIs are calculated and strategic, with marketing experts collecting a large amount of existing social media user-generated content to accurately profile their target audience and carefully curate the appearance (Stein et al., 2022), traits, and persona of the VI (Looi & Kahlor, 2024). Once the VI is generated, most of the content creation, user interaction, and assessment on consumer impact can be obtained through unsupervised machine learning algorithms; based on the machine learning's iteratively enhanced simulation, VIs can produce content that aligns with the brand's pre-existing image and incorporate consumer preferences when responding to human followers, effectively managing consumer relationships (Lou et al., 2023).

Despite initial concerns over AI's perceived inauthenticity, studies show that when consumers perceive utility in persuasive attempts, they are satisfied and even entertained by novel advertising efforts (Kim et al., 2025; Sweetser et al., 2016). Research demonstrates that VIs are far more transparent about their sponsored roles as influencers than HIs and readily reveal that they are synthetically created (e.g., "virtual human," "digital art") (Looi & Kahlor, 2024). Despite VI's ability to personalize content by optimizing the integration of user preferences (Lakshika et al., 2025), HIs still elicit more user engagement (Looi & Kahlor, 2024), suggesting that VIs may complement but not necessarily replace HIs by playing distinct roles in interactive advertising.

Despite findings that indicate lower user engagement with VIs relative to HIs, there are abundant reasons for integrating them into a company's advertising portfolio as a potent tool of persuasion. Many of these reasons were made possible through the integration of AI, allowing VIs to develop and distribute content with minimal human supervision. As generative AI continues to advance, advertising researchers as well as industry professionals (including HIs) will have to rapidly understand the strengths and limitations of VIs to maintain a balanced advertising ecosystem between humans and machines.

Scalability

Perhaps the greatest strength of AI-integrated VIs is their ability to process an unprecedented amount of data rapidly and produce evidence-based content, reducing the likelihood of failure. HIs also closely observe their followers to gather anecdotal data that allows them to build intimate bonds with followers, driven by inspiring personas to fulfill followers' emotional needs. Contrary to earlier research on celebrity endorsers (Liu & Brock, 2011), research demonstrates that the development of emotional bonds between HIs and their followers depends far more on the relatability and ideality of HI personas than their physical attractiveness (Ki et al., 2020).

VIs, on the other hand, are limited in their ability to generate original ideas to inspire human followers. Instead, they are equipped with the ability to cater to consumer preferences, serving them the content consumers are most likely to engage with based on their prior social media posts and engagement statistics. Because VIs are not as limited by working hours and the need to rest relative to HIs, they may soon be able to participate in as many advertising campaigns as needed and maintain the same level of productivity across all campaigns. Although the content produced by VIs may not be as inspirational as HI content, VIs are designed to please and elicit positive emotions in followers through AI-driven iterative corrections and enhancements; content (e.g., text, images, video) that activates positive reactions from followers is remembered and used frequently (Looi & Kahlor, 2024). Making a large number of consumers generally happy at scale, even if consumers are not necessarily inspired, is likely to yield profitable outcomes for brands and advertising agencies.

Control

In the early years of VIs, human moderators were actively involved in content curation, ensuring that social media posts that were released under the name of the VI were appropriate and relevant. Therefore, earlier literature argued that VIs can provide stronger control over content creation for advertising agencies than HIs, who can be unpredictable and become involved in scandals (Thomas & Fowler, 2021). With the integration of unsupervised machine learning and more recently generative AI, human moderators are increasingly handing over the reins to algorithms. However, when AI algorithms are trained on large amounts of unsupervised data, they can sometimes generate seemingly realistic but non-sensical (also plausible but incorrect) results, often referred to as "artificial hallucination" (Ji et al., 2022). Scholars have noted that AI-generated VIs are at risk of hallucination and that it can negatively impact consumers' decision-making processes, raising ethical and legal concerns (Yang et al., 2025).

With rigorous application of human monitoring, an appropriate balance between control over content generation and safeguards against hallucination may be struck in VI advertising. Efforts to maintain control may be particularly important when VIs are applied at scale across a number of different campaigns. This challenge echoes that of AI-integrated medical and legal services, where AI agents may be the consumer-facing entity, but the final approval is provided by a human doctor or lawyer. Until artificial hallucinations are effectively eradicated, human gatekeepers will be necessary for most AI-generated services (Frohock, 2025). Eventually, with the development of agentic AI, VIs may become fully autonomous with minimal, if any, human involvement. Even then, scholars urge for safeguard considerations given the risks of unsupervised VI activity related to content creation and consumer relations, and the rise of deepfake technologies (Whittaker et al., 2025).

Relative to HIs, VIs' strategic advantage lies in the control agencies have over data, wherein every interaction between the VI and consumers is tracked, logged, and analyzed. Based on the wide array of consumer engagement data being collected and analyzed as well as rapid changes in regulations and policies, VI behaviors can be updated as often as needed. High control over data allows for rapid evolution of the algorithms that drive the VI's actions which may ultimately allow for precise personalization of interactions that cater to individual follower needs at a granular level that was not possible with HIs. Imagine the same VI who can interact effectively with a wide range of audiences by answering product-related questions, providing honest testimonials, providing personalized recommendations, listening to grievances, and sharing stories about themselves to build an emotional bond with consumers to meet individual needs. AI algorithms would remember past interactions and shape future VI responses to reach optimal levels of data-driven personalization in their interactions with followers.

Multilingual, Multicultural

The wide appeal of VIs may also transcend physical and cultural boundaries, with generative AI's ability to translate language with little latency and integrate culturally appropriate content. VIs would be able to connect with even larger bodies of audiences around the world, with granular localization of sponsored content that aligns with cultural views and appropriate language use—imagine a spokesperson that can speak unlimited numbers of languages, with in-depth understanding of cultural norms and trends encased within each language (Biswas et al., 2024).

Despite the potential of AI as a transformative tool, at the moment, a dearth of culturally diverse training data and the resultant limited capacity for understanding and interpreting the nuanced context of complex situations (e.g., medical consultation, Genovese et al., 2024) remains a roadblock for widespread AI application in multilingual and multicultural situations. There is a large body of literature emphasizing the critical role that culture plays on all elements of the advertising process, including source, message, and audience (Lee & Yoo, 2012). Although AI can provide rapid rote translation of multiple languages at a rate that human translators cannot match, it will still be a while before AI can understand the intricacies of individual vs. collective, horizontal vs. vertical, and high vs. low structures of culture to respond and interact appropriately in the respective cultural context.

Future Research Considerations and Directions

As VIs continue to gain cultural and commercial influence, new questions arise about how their hybridity and fluidity can reshape traditional advertising dynamics. Our revised communication framework for VI advertising offers a conceptual foundation for understanding these shifts, particularly by mapping communicative roles (i.e., source, message, and audience) and functions across corporal, hybrid/augmented, and simulated domains. Future research should empirically test and refine this model to better understand how configurations of authorship and interaction shape advertising outcomes, such as persuasion, trust, authenticity, and relational dynamics.

One key area of research involves reconsidering the idea of "source" in interactive advertising. Traditional advertising models assume a clearly identifiable human sender, whereas VI campaigns add complexity with layered authorship that may include human creators, creative agencies, brands, and, increasingly, AI systems. As authorship and control become more decentralized, new questions emerge: How do audiences react when the "creator" is algorithmic, unknown, or corporate? What impact does trust or perceived authenticity have when audiences discover that a seemingly personal VI message is entirely scripted by AI? These questions are especially important when VIs express personal values or support for social issues (e.g., Black Lives Matter; Hong et al., 2024), raising concerns about sincerity and performative allyship. Research should examine whether transparency about creator identity affects credibility, message interpretation, or ethical judgment.

At the level of the message, VIs blur the boundary between storytelling and automation. While some VIs adopt elaborate narrative arcs that simulate autobiographical self-disclosure, others are more overt brand vehicles or stylized visual entities with minimal narrative substance. These messages are often delivered through hybrid means, relying on different levels of programmed behaviors, such as algorithmic comment replies, scheduled posts, or AI-generated captions. Future work should examine how audiences interpret these hybrid messages: Are first-person narratives perceived as authentic even when delivered by a simulated persona? How does the presence of programmed cues (e.g., automated posting, AI-generated scripts) affect psychological distance or emotional engagement? By investigating narrative depth, authorship style, and how platform aesthetics interact, researchers can clarify the mechanisms that make VI messaging persuasive or uncanny.

Audience dynamics also warrant further investigation. A key concern is how audiences perceive the creator behind the VI, raising several questions: Do audiences feel deceived or manipulated upon learning who or what is "behind" the VI? And does it matter? While some viewers may develop connections with the VI, there is a growing recognition that these figures are extensions of brand strategy, rather than autonomous individuals (Liu & Lee, 2022). Therefore, the revised model expands the audience category by distinguishing between actual users, implied audiences, sponsor gatekeepers, and algorithmic systems as quasi-audiences. These layered audiences influence how content is produced, circulated, and evaluated. For instance, algorithmic audiences, or systems that assess engagement and determine visibility, can significantly shape which VIs succeed and which disappear. Future studies should explore how audience types influence the feedback loop in VI campaigns.

Research should also examine how immersive or augmented experiences, such as engaging with VIs in VR or metaverse settings, change the quality of parasocial interaction, presence, and user behavior. These environments typically intensify the sense of "being there" (i.e., spatial presence) or "being with another" (i.e., social presence) in virtual environments, which is known as a double-edged sword effect in VR literature (Ahn et al., 2022b; Barreda-Ángeles et al., 2021; Li & Chen, 2019). These immersive environments may either accelerate or hinder emotional bonding and brand attachment in ways that differ from traditional social media. Additionally, with the growing popularity of social virtual environments like Roblox, especially among children and teens, examining the impacts of such simulated influence is crucial.

Finally, issues of cultural representation and algorithmic bias must remain central to VI research. As VIs increasingly represent racially ambiguous, feminized, hyper-stylized, or decontextualized identities (i.e., lack grounding in a coherent social, historical, or geographic context), scholars must examine how these representations are read by diverse audiences and what broader implications they carry (Miyake, 2022; Neri, 2022). This includes scrutinizing how race, gender, and identity are encoded, commodified, and how audiences assess authenticity or appropriation in virtual spokes figures. Moreover, as VI creation increasingly draws on generative AI, existing concerns around algorithmic bias and embedded discrimination become more urgent. Scholars like Benjamin (2019) and Noble (2018) remind us that algorithms often replicate the biases of their human authors, whether intentional or not. Similarly, evidence suggests that audiences project real-world biases onto virtual humans (see Hatfield et al., 2022, for a review). Future work should critically evaluate the social costs and benefits of using VIs to advocate for causes that disproportionately affect marginalized communities.

Ultimately, VI campaigns exist at the intersection of human intention, computational logic, and audience perception. By interrogating the fluid relationships among sources, messages, and audiences across corporeal, hybrid, and simulated realms, future research can deepen our understanding of VIs as advertising tools and as emergent forms of mediated identity, social influence, and persuasive communication.

Conclusion

VIs represent a profound shift in the source-message-audience dynamic of advertising communication. Building on Stern's (1994) original framework and earlier revisions of the framework, we propose an updated model that recognizes the complexity of simulated and hybrid entities in interactive media environments. By conceptualizing VI communication across a spectrum of interactive advertising—from corporeal to simulated—this framework accounts for the blurred boundaries between author and algorithm, fiction and reality, and audience and participant.

This chapter has also highlighted the pressing ethical, cultural, and methodological challenges posed by VIs. From the commodification of identity to questions of agency and authenticity, VIs demand new theoretical and empirical tools to understand their role in persuasive messaging. As immersive technologies continue to evolve and VIs become more autonomous, scalable, and interactive, scholars must remain attentive to how these changes affect user experience, power structures, and societal values. The revised model presented here offers a foundation for this kind of inquiry, connecting digital advertising theory with the changing realities of synthetic identities and simulated persuasion.

References

Abidin, C., & Thompson, E. C. (2012). Buymylife.com: Cyber-femininities and commercial intimacy in blogshops. *Women's Studies International Forum*, *35*(6), 467–477. https://doi.org/10.1016/j.wsif.2012.10.005

Ahmadi, I., Abou Nabout, N., Skiera, B., Maleki, E., & Fladenhofer, J. (2024). Overwhelming targeting options: Selecting audience segments for online advertising. *International Journal of Research in Marketing, 41*(1), 24–40. https://doi.org/10.1016/j.ijresmar.2023.08.004

Ahn, S. J. (2021). Designing for persuasion through embodied experiences in virtual reality. In Teresa de La Hera, Jeroen Jansz, Joost Raessens, & Ben Schouten (Eds.), *Persuasive Gaming in Context* (pp. 163–180). Amsterdam University Press. https://doi.org/10.2307/j.ctv1hw3z1d.13

Ahn, S. J. G., Bostick, J., Ogle, E., Nowak, K. L., McGillicuddy, K. T., & Bailenson, J. (2016). Experiencing nature: Embodying animals in immersive virtual environments increases inclusion of nature in self and involvement with nature. *Journal of Computer Mediated Communication, 21*(6), 399–419. https://doi.org/10.1111/jcc4.12173

Ahn, S. J. (grace), Bailenson, J. N., & Park, D. (2014). Short- and long-term effects of embodied experiences in immersive virtual environments on environmental locus of control and behavior. *Computers in Human Behavior, 39*, 235–245. https://doi.org/10.1016/j.chb.2014.07.025

Ahn, S. J. (grace), Kim, J., & Kim, J. (2022a). The bifold triadic relationships framework: A theoretical primer for advertising research in the metaverse. *Journal of Advertising, 51*(5), 592–607. https://doi.org/10.1080/00913367.2022.2111729

Ahn, S. J. (grace), Nowak, K. L., & Bailenson, J. N. (2022b). Unintended consequences of spatial presence on learning in virtual reality. *Computers & Education, 186*, 104532. https://doi.org/10.1016/j.compedu.2022.104532

Aho, D., & Mackie, V. (1993). How to get your company on the interactive highway: Agency experts tell where to look for opportunities now. *Advertising Age: Interactive Media & Marketing, 64*(October 2), 24.

Arsenyan, J., & Mirowska, A. (2021). Almost human? A comparative case study on the social media presence of virtual influencers. *International Journal of Human-Computer Studies, 155*(102694), 102694. https://doi.org/10.1016/j.ijhcs.2021.102694

Balaban, D., & Mustățea, M. (2019). Users' perspective on the credibility of social media influencers in Romania and Germany. *Romanian Journal of Communication and Public Relations, 21*(1), 31.

Barreda-Ángeles, M., Aleix-Guillaume, S., & Pereda-Baños, A. (2021). Virtual reality storytelling as a double-edged sword: Immersive presentation of nonfiction 360°-video is associated with impaired cognitive information processing. *Communication Monographs, 88*(2), 154–173. https://doi.org/10.1080/03637751.2020.1803496

Behm-Morawitz, E., Pennell, H., & Speno, A. G. (2016). The effects of virtual racial embodiment in a gaming app on reducing prejudice. *Communication Monographs, 83*(3), 396–418. https://doi.org/10.1080/03637751.2015.1128556

Benjamin, R. (2019). *Race After Technology: Abolitionist Tools for the New Jim Code*. John Wiley & Sons. https://play.google.com/store/books/details?id=G6-hDwAAQBAJ

Biswas, P., Neogi, S. G., Arockiam, D., & Mitra, A. (2024, March 14). The importance of multi-lingual sentiment analysis in digital marketing. *2024 11th International Conference on Reliability, Infocom Technologies and Optimization (Trends and Future Directions) (ICRITO)*, Noida, India. https://doi.org/10.1109/icrito61523.2024.10522115

Blascovich, J., & Bailenson, J. N. (2011). *Infinite Reality: Avatars, Eternal Life, New Worlds, and the Dawn of the Virtual Revolution*. William Morrow.

Blascovich, J., Loomis, J., Beall, A. C., Swinth, K. R., Hoyt, C. L., & Bailenson, J. N. (2002). Target Article: Immersive virtual environment technology as a methodological tool for social psychology. *Psychological Inquiry*, *13*(2), 103–124. https://doi.org/10.1207/s15327965pli1302_01

Block, E., & Lovegrove, R. (2021). Discordant storytelling, "honest fakery", identity peddling: How uncanny CGI characters are jamming public relations and influencer practices. *Public Relations Inquiry*, *10*(3), 265–293. https://doi.org/10.1177/2046147x211026936

Breves, P., Amrehn, J., Heidenreich, A., Liebers, N., & Schramm, H. (2021). Blind trust? The importance and interplay of parasocial relationships and advertising disclosures in explaining influencers' persuasive effects on their followers. *International Journal of Advertising*, *40*(7), 1209–1229. https://doi.org/10.1080/02650487.2021.1881237

Brooks, G., Drenten, J., & Piskorski, M. J. (2021). Influencer celebrification: How social media influencers acquire celebrity capital. *Journal of Advertising*, *50*(5), 528–547. https://doi.org/10.1080/00913367.2021.1977737

Byun, K. J., & Ahn, S. J. (grace). (2023). A systematic review of virtual influencers: Similarities and differences between human and virtual influencers in interactive advertising. *Journal of Interactive Advertising*, *23*(4), 293–306. https://doi.org/10.1080/15252019.2023.2236102

Campbell, C., Plangger, K., Sands, S., & Kietzmann, J. (2021). Preparing for an era of deepfakes and AI-generated ads: A framework for understanding responses to manipulated advertising. *Journal of Advertising*, 1–17. https://doi.org/10.1080/00913367.2021.1909515

Carter, D. (2016). Hustle and brand: The sociotechnical shaping of influence. *Social Media + Society*, *2*(3), 205630511666630. https://doi.org/10.1177/2056305116666305

Casaló, L. V., Flavián, C., & Ibáñez-Sánchez, S. (2020). Influencers on Instagram: Antecedents and consequences of opinion leadership. *Journal of Business Research*, *117*, 510–519. https://doi.org/10.1016/j.jbusres.2018.07.005

Chae, J. (2018). Explaining females' envy toward social media influencers. *Media Psychology*, *21*(2), 246–262. https://doi.org/10.1080/15213269.2017.1328312

Choudhry, A., Han, J., Xu, X., & Huang, Y. (2022). I felt a little crazy following a "doll": Investigating real influence of virtual influencers on their followers. *Proceedings of the ACM on Human-Computer Interaction*, *6*(GROUP), 1–28. https://doi.org/10.1145/3492862

Chung, S., & Cho, H. (2017). Fostering parasocial relationships with celebrities on social media: Implications for celebrity endorsement. *Psychology & Marketing*, *34*(4), 481–495. https://doi.org/10.1002/mar.21001

Cialdini, R. B., & Goldstein, N. J. (2004). Social influence: Compliance and conformity. *Annual Review of Psychology*, *55*(1), 591–621. https://doi.org/10.1146/annurev.psych.55.090902.142015

Coates, A. E., Hardman, C. A., Halford, J. C. G., Christiansen, P., & Boyland, E. J. (2020). "it's just addictive people that make addictive videos": Children's understanding of and attitudes towards influencer marketing of food and beverages by YouTube video bloggers. *International Journal of Environmental Research and Public Health*, *17*(2), 449. https://doi.org/10.3390/ijerph17020449

Daniel, E. S., Jr, Crawford Jackson, E. C., & Westerman, D. K. (2018). The influence of social media influencers: Understanding online vaping communities and parasocial interaction through the lens of Taylor's six-segment strategy wheel. *Journal of Interactive Advertising, 18*(2), 96–109. https://doi.org/10.1080/15252019.2018.1488637

da Silva Oliveira, A. B., & Chimenti, P. (2021). "Humanized robots": A proposition of categories to understand virtual influencers. *Australian Journal of Information Systems, 25*. https://doi.org/10.3127/ajis.v25i0.3223

De Jans, S., Cauberghe, V., & Hudders, L. (2018). How an advertising disclosure alerts young adolescents to sponsored vlogs: The moderating role of a peer-based advertising literacy intervention through an informational vlog. *Journal of Advertising, 47*(4), 309–325. https://doi.org/10.1080/00913367.2018.1539363

De Jans, S., Hudders, L., Naderer, B., & De Pauw, V. (2022). Impact of thin-ideals in influencer posts promoting healthy vs. Unhealthy foods on tweens' healthy food choice behavior. *Frontiers in Psychology, 13*, 789069. https://doi.org/10.3389/fpsyg.2022.789069

De Jans, S., Van De Sompel, D., De Veirman, M., & Hudders, L. (2020). #Sponsored! How the recognition of sponsoring on Instagram posts affects adolescents' brand evaluations through source evaluations. *Computers in Human Behavior, 109*(106342), 106342. https://doi.org/10.1016/j.chb.2020.106342

De Veirman, M., Cauberghe, V., & Hudders, L. (2017). Marketing through Instagram influencers: The impact of number of followers and product divergence on brand attitude. *International Journal of Advertising, 36*(5), 798–828. https://doi.org/10.1080/02650487.2017.1348035

Dijkmans, C., Kerkhof, P., & Beukeboom, C. J. (2015). A stage to engage: Social media use and corporate reputation. *Tourism Management, 47*, 58–67. https://doi.org/10.1016/j.tourman.2014.09.005

Djafarova, E., & Rushworth, C. (2017). Exploring the credibility of online celebrities' Instagram profiles in influencing the purchase decisions of young female users. *Computers in Human Behavior, 68*, 1–7. https://doi.org/10.1016/j.chb.2016.11.009

Djafarova, E., & Trofimenko, O. (2019). "Instafamous" – credibility and self-presentation of micro-celebrities on social media. *Information, Communication and Society, 22*(10), 1432–1446. https://doi.org/10.1080/1369118x.2018.1438491

Enke, N., & Borchers, N. S. (2019). Social media influencers in strategic communication: A conceptual framework for strategic social media influencer communication. *International Journal of Strategic Communication, 13*(4), 261–277. https://doi.org/10.1080/1553118x.2019.1620234

Evans, N. J., Phua, J., Lim, J., & Jun, H. (2017). Disclosing Instagram influencer advertising: The effects of disclosure language on advertising recognition, attitudes, and behavioral intent. *Journal of Interactive Advertising, 17*(2), 138–149. https://doi.org/10.1080/15252019.2017.1366885

Fox, J., Ahn, S. J. (grace), Janssen, J. H., Yeykelis, L., Segovia, K. Y., & Bailenson, J. N. (2015). Avatars versus agents: A meta-analysis quantifying the effect of agency on social influence. *Human-Computer Interaction, 30*(5), 401–432. https://doi.org/10.1080/07370024.2014.921494

Franke, C., Groeppel-Klein, A., & Müller, K. (2023). Consumers' responses to virtual influencers as advertising endorsers: Novel and effective or uncanny and deceiving? *Journal of Advertising, 52*(4), 523–539. https://doi.org/10.1080/00913367.2022.2154721

Freberg, K., Graham, K., McGaughey, K., & Freberg, L. A. (2011). Who are the social media influencers? A study of public perceptions of personality. *Public Relations Review*, *37*(1), 90–92. https://doi.org/10.1016/j.pubrev.2010.11.001

Frohock, C. (2025). Ghosts at the gate: A call for vigilance against AI-Generated case hallucinations. *Penn State Law Review*. *130*, 1–26.

Gaenssle, S., & Budzinski, O. (2021). Stars in social media: New light through old windows? *Journal of Media Business Studies*, *18*(2), 79–105. https://doi.org/10.1080/16522354.2020.1738694

Gambetti, R. C., & Kozinets, R. V. (2024). From killer bunnies to talking cupcakes: Theorizing the diverse universe of virtual influencers. *European Journal of Marketing*, *58*(13), 205–251. https://doi.org/10.1108/ejm-12-2022-0948

Genovese, A., Borna, S., Gomez-Cabello, C. A., Haider, S. A., Prabha, S., Forte, A. J., & Veenstra, B. R. (2024). Artificial intelligence in clinical settings: A systematic review of its role in language translation and interpretation. *Annals of Translational Medicine*, *12*(6), 117. https://doi.org/10.21037/atm-24-162

Haikel-Elsabeh, M. (2023). Virtual influencers versus real influencers advertising in the metaverse, understanding the perceptions, and interactions with users. *Journal of Current Issues & Research in Advertising*, *44*(3), 252–273. https://doi.org/10.1080/10641734.2023.2218420

Ham, J., Li, S., Shah, P., & Eastin, M. S. (2024). Are virtual influencers more effective in real-world advertisement settings?: The impact of product type and social cues on consumers' perceptions and behaviors. *Journal of Advertising Research*, PAP_015. https://doi.org/10.2501/jar-2024-015

Hanus, M. D., & Fox, J. (2015). Assessing the effects of gamification in the classroom: A longitudinal study on intrinsic motivation, social comparison, satisfaction, effort, and academic performance. *Computers & Education*, *80*, 152–161. https://doi.org/10.1016/j.compedu.2014.08.019

Hatfield, H. R., Ahn, S. J. G., Klein, M., & Nowak, K. L. (2022). Confronting whiteness through virtual humans: A review of 20 years of research in prejudice and racial bias using virtual environments. *Journal of Computer Mediated Communication*, *27*(6), zmac016. https://doi.org/10.1093/jcmc/zmac016

Hofeditz, L., Nissen, A., Schütte, R., & Mirbabaie, M. (2022). *Trust me, I'm an influencer! - A comparison of perceived trust in human and virtual influencers*. AIS Electronic Library (AISeL). https://aisel.aisnet.org/ecis2022_rip/27

Holiday, S., Hayes, J. L., Park, H., Lyu, Y., & Zhou, Y. (2023). A multimodal emotion perspective on social media influencer marketing: The effectiveness of influencer emotions, network size, and branding on consumer brand engagement using facial expression and linguistic analysis. *Journal of Interactive Marketing*, *58*(4), 414–439. https://doi.org/10.1177/10949968231171104

Hong, J.-W., Cruz, I. F., & Kim, D. (2024). Justice behind the virtual mask: The influence of race of the virtual influencer and the creator on promoting the Black Lives Matter movement. *New Media & Society*. https://doi.org/10.1177/14614448241262806

Horton, D., & Wohl, R. R. (1956). Mass communication and para-social interaction; observations on intimacy at a distance. *Psychiatry*, *19*(3), 215–229. https://doi.org/10.1080/00332747.1956.11023049

Hudders, L., De Jans, S., & De Veirman, M. (2021). The commercialization of social media stars: A literature review and conceptual framework on the strategic use of social media influencers. *International Journal of Advertising*, *40*(3), 327–375. https://doi.org/10.1080/02650487.2020.1836925

Hutchinson, J. (2020). Digital first personality: Automation and influence within evolving media ecologies. *Convergence the International Journal of Research into New Media Technologies*, *26*(5–6), 1284–1300. https://doi.org/10.1177/1354856519858921

Hwang, Y., & Jeong, S.-H. (2016). "This is a sponsored blog post, but all opinions are my own": The effects of sponsorship disclosure on responses to sponsored blog posts. *Computers in Human Behavior*, *62*, 528–535. https://doi.org/10.1016/j.chb.2016.04.026

HypeAuditor. (2019). The Top Instagram Virtual Influencers. https://hypeauditor.com/blog/the-top-instagram-virtual-influencers-in-2019/

Jakobson, R. (1960). Closing statement: Linguistics and poetics. In T. Sebeok (Ed.), *Style in Language* (pp. 350–377). MIT Press.

Jayles, B., Escobedo, R., Cezera, S., Blanchet, A., Kameda, T., Sire, C., & Theraulaz, G. (2020). The impact of incorrect social information on collective wisdom in human groups. *Journal of the Royal Society, Interface*, *17*(170), 20200496. https://doi.org/10.1098/rsif.2020.0496

Jenkins, M., & Obhi, S. S. (2020). Neurophysiological and psychological consequences of social exclusion: The effects of cueing in-group and out-group status. *Cerebral Cortex Communications*, *1*(1), tgaa057. https://doi.org/10.1093/texcom/tgaa057

Ji, Z., Lee, N., Frieske, R., Yu, T., Su, D., Xu, Y., Ishii, E., Bang, Y., Madotto, A., & Fung, P. (2022). Survey of hallucination in natural Language Generation. *ACM Computing Surveys*. https://doi.org/10.1145/3571730

Jin, S. V., & Viswanathan, V. (2025). "Threatened and empty selves following AI-based virtual influencers": Comparison between followers and non-followers of virtual influencers in AI-driven digital marketing. *AI & Society*, *40*(1), 117–131. https://doi.org/10.1007/s00146-023-01832-9

Joel-Edgar, S., Chowdhury, S., Nagy, P., & Ren, S. (2025). Virtual influencers in social media versus the metaverse: Mind Perception, blame judgements and brand trust. *Journal of Business Research*, *189*(115139), 115139. https://doi.org/10.1016/j.jbusres.2024.115139

Jorge, A., Marôpo, L., & Nunes, T. (2018). I am not being sponsored to say this: A teen youtuber and her audience negotiate branded content. *Observatorio*, 76–96. https://www.scopus.com/inward/record.uri?eid=2-s2.0-85054557001&partnerID=40&md5=daf2ce9f9d38f111a57772a76b28a0c8

Katsumi, Y., Dolcos, F., Moore, M., Bartholow, B. D., Fabiani, M., & Dolcos, S. (2020). Electrophysiological correlates of racial in-group bias in observing nonverbal social encounters. *Journal of Cognitive Neuroscience*, *32*(1), 167–186. https://doi.org/10.1162/jocn_a_01475

KFC: Virtual Colonel. (2019, April). Wieden Kennedy. https://www.wk.com/work/kfc-virtual-colonel/

Khamis, S., Ang, L., & Welling, R. (2017). Self-branding, "micro-celebrity" and the rise of Social Media Influencers. *Celebrity Studies*, *8*(2), 191–208. https://doi.org/10.1080/19392397.2016.1218292

Ki, C.-W. (chloe), Cuevas, L. M., Chong, S. M., & Lim, H. (2020). Influencer marketing: Social media influencers as human brands attaching to followers and yielding positive marketing results by fulfilling needs. *Journal of Retailing and Consumer Services, 55*(102133), 102133. https://doi.org/10.1016/j.jretconser.2020.102133

Kim, D. Y., & Kim, H.-Y. (2021). Influencer advertising on social media: The multiple inference model on influencer-product congruence and sponsorship disclosure. *Journal of Business Research, 130*, 405–415. https://doi.org/10.1016/j.jbusres.2020.02.020

Kim, E. (anna), Shoenberger, H., Kim, D., Thorson, E., & Zihang, E. (2024). Novelty vs. trust in virtual influencers: Exploring the effectiveness of human-like virtual influencers and anime-like virtual influencers. *International Journal of Advertising*, 1–31. https://doi.org/10.1080/02650487.2024.2386916

Kim, J., Kim, M., & Lee, S.-M. (2025). Unlocking trust dynamics: An exploration of playfulness, expertise, and consumer behavior in virtual influencer marketing. *International Journal of Human-Computer Interaction, 41*(1), 378–390. https://doi.org/10.1080/10447318.2023.2300018

Koles, B., Audrezet, A., Moulard, J. G., Ameen, N., & McKenna, B. (2024). The authentic virtual influencer: Authenticity manifestations in the metaverse. *Journal of Business Research, 170*(114325), 114325. https://doi.org/10.1016/j.jbusres.2023.114325

Konstantopoulou, A., Rizomyliotis, I., Konstantoulaki, K., & Badahdah, R. (2019). Improving SMEs' competitiveness with the use of Instagram influencer advertising and eWOM. *International Journal of Organizational Analysis, 27*(2), 308–321. https://doi.org/10.1108/ijoa-04-2018-1406

Lakshika, V. G. P., Chathuranga, B. T. K., & Jayarathne, P. G. S. A. (2025). The evolving role of AI and ML in digital promotion: A systematic review and research agenda. *Journal of Marketing Analytics, 13*(2), 288–307. https://doi.org/10.1057/s41270-024-00367-2

Lasswell, H. D. (1948). *The structure and function of communication in society.* In L. Bryson (Ed.), *The communication of ideas: A series of addresses* (pp. 37–51). New York, NY: Institute for Religious and Social Studies.

Lee, E.-J. (2020). Authenticity model of (mass-oriented) computer-mediated communication: Conceptual explorations and testable propositions. *Journal of Computer-Mediated Communication: JCMC, 25*(1), 60–73. https://doi.org/10.1093/jcmc/zmz025

Lee, J., Wu, D.-Y., Lin, J., Kim, J., & Ahn, S. J. (2023). Using time travel in virtual reality (VR) to increase efficacy perceptions of influenza vaccination. *Journal of Computer Mediated Communication, 28*(3), zmad010. https://doi.org/10.1093/jcmc/zmad010

Lee, W.-N., & Yoo, J. J. (2012). Understanding the role of culture in advertising. In Shintaro Okazaki (Ed.), *Handbook of Research on International Advertising*. Edward Elgar Publishing. https://doi.org/10.4337/9781781001042.00010

Li, J., & Ma, Y. (2024). Virtual influencers in advertisements: Examining the role of authenticity and identification. *Journal of Interactive Advertising, 24*(1), 1–12. https://doi.org/10.1080/15252019.2023.2270478

Lil Miquela [@lilmiquela]. (2025, April 1). "When you're on your daily hot girl walk and remember who you let disrupt your peace in your last era…never again lol" [Photograph]. Instagram. https://www.instagram.com/p/DH6dKQ7v2Fx

Lin, H.-C., Bruning, P. F., & Swarna, H. (2018). Using online opinion leaders to promote the hedonic and utilitarian value of products and services. *Business Horizons, 61*(3), 431–442. https://doi.org/10.1016/j.bushor.2018.01.010

Li, T., & Chen, Y. (2019). Will virtual reality be a double-edged sword? Exploring the moderation effects of the expected enjoyment of a destination on travel intention.

Journal of Destination Marketing & Management, *12*, 15–26. https://doi.org/10.1016/j.jdmm.2019.02.003

Liu, F., & Lee, Y.-H. (2022, June 21). Unveiling behind-the-scenes human interventions and examining source orientation in virtual influencer endorsements. *ACM International Conference on Interactive Media Experiences. IMX '22: ACM International Conference on Interactive Media Experiences*, Aveiro JB Portugal. https://doi.org/10.1145/3505284.3529962

Liu, R., Yen, H., Marjieh, R., Griffiths, T., & Krishna, R. (2025). Improving interpersonal communication by simulating audiences with large language models. *Proceedings of the Annual Meeting of the Cognitive Science Society*, *47*(0). https://escholarship.org/uc/item/87p4v2h1

Lombard, M., & Ditton, T. (2006). At the heart of it all: The concept of presence. *Journal of Computer-Mediated Communication: JCMC*, *3*(2), 0–0. https://doi.org/10.1111/j.1083-6101.1997.tb00072.x

Looi, J., & Kahlor, L. A. (2024). Artificial intelligence in influencer marketing: A mixed-method comparison of human and virtual influencers on Instagram. *Journal of Interactive Advertising*, *24*(2), 107–126. https://doi.org/10.1080/15252019.2024.2313721

Lou, C. (2022). Social media influencers and followers: Theorization of a trans-parasocial relation and explication of its implications for influencer advertising. *Journal of Advertising*, *51*(1), 4–21. https://doi.org/10.1080/00913367.2021.1880345

Lou, C., Kiew, S. T. J., Chen, T., Lee, T. Y. M., Ong, J. E. C., & Phua, Z. (2023). Authentically fake? How consumers respond to the influence of virtual influencers. *Journal of Advertising*, *52*(4), 540–557. https://doi.org/10.1080/00913367.2022.2149641

Maloney, D., Freeman, G., & Wohn, D. Y. (2020). Talking without a voice: Understanding non-verbal communication in social virtual reality. *Proceedings of the ACM on Human-Computer Interaction*, *4*(CSCW2), 1–25. https://doi.org/10.1145/3415246

Mañas-Viniegra, L., Núñez-Gómez, P., & Tur-Viñes, V. (2020). Neuromarketing as a strategic tool for predicting how Instagramers have an influence on the personal identity of adolescents and young people in Spain. *Heliyon*, *6*(3), e03578. https://doi.org/10.1016/j.heliyon.2020.e03578

Marôpo, L., Jorge, A., & Tomaz, R. (2020). "I felt like I was really talking to you!": Intimacy and trust among teen vloggers and followers in Portugal and Brazil. *Journal of Children and Media*, *14*(1), 22–37. https://doi.org/10.1080/17482798.2019.1699589

Martin, W. (1986). *Recent Theories of Narrative*. Cornell University Press.

Marwick, A. E., & Boyd, D. (2011). I tweet honestly, I tweet passionately: Twitter users, context collapse, and the imagined audience. *New Media & Society*, *13*(1), 114–133. https://doi.org/10.1177/1461444810365313

McDowell, M. (2024, February 27). *Influencer marketing has arrived on Roblox*. Vouge Business. https://www.voguebusiness.com/story/technology/influencer-marketing-has-arrived-on-roblox

Miao, F., Kozlenkova, I. V., Wang, H., Xie, T., & Palmatier, R. W. (2022). An emerging theory of avatar marketing. *Journal of Marketing*, *86*(1), 67–90. https://doi.org/10.1177/0022242921996646

Miyake, E. (2022). I am a virtual girl from Tokyo: Virtual influencers, digital-orientalism and the (Im)materiality of race and gender. *Journal of Consumer Culture*, 14695405221171. https://doi.org/10.1177/14695405221117195

Mori, M., MacDorman, K., & Kageki, N. (2012). The uncanny valley [from the field]. *IEEE Robotics & Automation Magazine*, *19*(2), 98–100. https://doi.org/10.1109/mra.2012.2192811

Mrad, M., Ramadan, Z., & Nasr, L. I. (2022). Computer-generated influencers: The rise of digital personalities. *Marketing Intelligence & Planning*, *40*(5), 589–603. https://doi.org/10.1108/mip-12-2021-0423

Mullen, B., & Johnson, C. (1990). *The Psychology of Consumer Behavior*. Erlbaum Associates.

Murray, G. B., & Jenkins, J. R. G. (1992). The concept of "effective reach" in advertising. *Journal of Advertising Research*, *32*(3), 34–42. https://doi.org/10.1080/00218499.1992.12466831

Neri, F. C. (2022). Artificial intelligence or a neoliberal marketing scheme? *The iJournal: Student Journal of the Faculty of Information*, *7*(2). https://doi.org/10.33137/ijournal.v7i2.38617

Noble, S. U. (2018). *Algorithms of Oppression: How Search Engines Reinforce Racism*. New York University Press. https://play.google.com/store/books/details?id=-ThDDwAAQBAJ

Nowak, K. L., & Fox, J. (2018). Avatars and computer-mediated communication: A review of the definitions, uses, and effects of digital representations. *Review of Communication Research*, *6*, 30–53. https://doi.org/10.12840/ISSN.2255-4165.2018.06.01.015

Ong, W. J. (1982). *Orality and Literacy*. Methuen.

Park, G., Nan, D., Park, E., Kim, K. J., Han, J., & del Pobil, A. P. (2021). Computers as social actors? Examining how users perceive and interact with virtual influencers on social media. *2021 15th International Conference on Ubiquitous Information Management and Communication (IMCOM)*, 1–6. https://doi.org/10.1109/imcom51814.2021.9377397

Park, S., & Sung, Y. (2023). The interplay between human likeness and agency on virtual influencer credibility. *Cyberpsychology, Behavior and Social Networking*, *26*(10), 764–771. https://doi.org/10.1089/cyber.2023.0060

Pearson, C. J., Geden, M., & Mayhorn, C. B. (2019). Who's the real expert here? Pedigree's unique bias on trust between human and automated advisers. *Applied Ergonomics*, *81*(102907), 102907. https://doi.org/10.1016/j.apergo.2019.102907

Peter, C., & Muth, L. (2023). Social media influencers' role in shaping political opinions and actions of young audiences. *Media and Communication*, *11*(3). https://doi.org/10.17645/mac.v11i3.6750

Pfeuffer, A., Hatfield, H. R., Evans, N., & Kim, J. (2024). Illegally beautiful? The role of trust and persuasion knowledge in online image manipulation disclosure effects. *International Journal of Advertising*, *44*(4), 1–22. https://doi.org/10.1080/02650487.2024.2403311

Pfeuffer, A., & Huh, J. (2021). Effects of different sponsorship disclosure message types on consumers' trust and attitudes. *International Journal of Advertising*, *40*(1), 49–80. https://doi.org/10.1080/02650487.2020.1807229

Porter, A. (2020). The influence of intimacy. *Performance Research*, *25*(1), 59–62. https://doi.org/10.1080/13528165.2020.1751536

Qutteina, Y., Hallez, L., Mennes, N., De Backer, C., & Smits, T. (2019). What do adolescents see on social media? A diary study of food marketing images on social media. *Frontiers in Psychology*, *10*, 2637. https://doi.org/10.3389/fpsyg.2019.02637

Robinson, B. (2020). Towards an ontology and ethics of virtual influencers. *Australian Journal of Information Systems*, *24*. https://doi.org/10.3127/ajis.v24i0.2807

Ross, C. (2025, May 16). *Influencer marketing worldwide - statistics & facts*. Statista. https://www.statista.com/topics/2496/influence-marketing/

Salomon Brothers. (1993). Interaction. *Advertising Age: Interactive Media & Marketing, 64*(30).

Sands, S., Campbell, C. L., Plangger, K., & Ferraro, C. (2022a). Unreal influence: Leveraging AI in influencer marketing. *European Journal of Marketing*, *56*(6), 1721–1747. https://doi.org/10.1108/ejm-12-2019-0949

Sands, S., Ferraro, C., Demsar, V., & Chandler, G. (2022b). False idols: Unpacking the opportunities and challenges of falsity in the context of virtual influencers. *Business Horizons*, *65*(6), 777–788. https://doi.org/10.1016/j.bushor.2022.08.002

Schouten, A. P., Janssen, L., & Verspaget, M. (2020). Celebrity vs. Influencer endorsements in advertising: The role of identification, credibility, and Product-Endorser fit. *International Journal of Advertising*, *39*(2), 258–281. https://doi.org/10.1080/02650487.2019.1634898

Schultz, D. (2016). The future of advertising or whatever we're going to call it. *Journal of Advertising*, *45*(3), 276–285. https://doi.org/10.1080/00913367.2016.1185061

Schwemmer, C., & Ziewiecki, S. (2018). Social media sellout: The increasing role of product promotion on YouTube. *Social Media + Society*, *4*(3), 205630511878672. https://doi.org/10.1177/2056305118786720

Seymour, M., University of Sydney, Australia, Yuan, L. (ivy), Iowa State University, USA, Dennis, A. R., Indiana University, USA, Riemer, K., & University of Sydney, Australia. (2021). Have we crossed the uncanny valley? Understanding affinity, trustworthiness, and preference for realistic digital humans in immersive environments. *Journal of the Association for Information Systems*, *22*(3), 591–617. https://doi.org/10.17705/1jais.00674

Slater, M., & Wilbur, S. (1997). A framework for immersive virtual environments (FIVE): Speculations on the role of presence in virtual environments. *Presence, 6*(6), 603–616. https://doi.org/10.1162/pres.1997.6.6.603

Staton, S. F. (1987). *Literary Theories in Praxis*. The University of Pennsylvania Press.

Stein, J.-P., Linda Breves, P., & Anders, N. (2022). Parasocial interactions with real and virtual influencers: The role of perceived similarity and human-likeness. *New Media & Society*, *26*(6), 3433–3453. https://doi.org/10.1177/14614448221102900

Stern, B. B. (1994). A revised communication model for advertising: Multiple dimensions of the source, the message, and the recipient. *Journal of Advertising*, *23*(2), 5–15. https://www.jstor.org/stable/4188924

Stubb, C. (2018). Story versus info: Tracking blog readers' online viewing time of sponsored blog posts based on content-specific elements. *Computers in Human Behavior*, *82*, 54–62. https://doi.org/10.1016/j.chb.2018.01.001

Stubb, C., Nyström, A.-G., & Colliander, J. (2019). Influencer marketing. *Journal of Communication Management*, *23*(2), 109–122. https://doi.org/10.1108/jcom-11-2018-0119

Sundar, S. S., Kang, J., & Oprean, D. (2017). Being there in the midst of the story: How immersive journalism affects our perceptions and cognitions. *Cyberpsychology, Behavior and Social Networking*, *20*(11), 672–682. https://doi.org/10.1089/cyber.2017.0271

Sweetser, K. D., Ahn, S. J. (grace), Golan, G. J., & Hochman, A. (2016). Native advertising as a new public relations tactic. *The American Behavioral Scientist*, *60*(12), 1442–1457. https://doi.org/10.1177/0002764216660138

Tajfel, H., & Turner, J. (2000). An integrative theory of intergroup conflict. In Mary Jo Hatch & Majken Schultz (Eds.), *Organizational Identity* (pp. 56–65). Oxford University PressOxford. https://doi.org/10.1093/oso/9780199269464.003.0005

The Influencer Marketing Factory. (2023). Virtual Influencers Survey + INFOGRAPHIC. https://theinfluencermarketingfactory.com/virtual-influencers-survey-infographic/

Thomas, V. L., & Fowler, K. (2021). Close encounters of the AI kind: Use of AI influencers as brand endorsers. *Journal of Advertising*, *50*(1), 11–25. https://doi.org/10.1080/00913367.2020.1810595

Tiggemann, M., Brown, Z., Zaccardo, M., & Thomas, N. (2017). "Warning: This image has been digitally altered": The effect of disclaimer labels added to fashion magazine shoots on women's body dissatisfaction. *Body Image*, *21*, 107–113. https://doi.org/10.1016/j.bodyim.2017.04.001

TIME. (2018, June 30). *The 25 Most Influential People on the Internet*. TIME. https://time.com/5324130/most-influential-internet/

Tingchi Liu, M., & Brock, J. L. (2011). Selecting a female athlete endorser in China. *European Journal of Marketing*, *45*(7/8), 1214–1235. https://doi.org/10.1108/03090561111137688

Van Dam, S., & Van Reijmersdal, E. (2019). Insights in adolescents' advertising literacy, perceptions and responses regarding sponsored influencer videos and disclosures. *Cyberpsychology*, *13*(2). https://doi.org/10.5817/cp2019-2-2

Vrontis, D., Makrides, A., Christofi, M., & Thrassou, A. (2021). Social media influencer marketing: A systematic review, integrative framework and future research agenda. *International Journal of Consumer Studies*, *45*(4), 617–644. https://doi.org/10.1111/ijcs.12647

Wang, B., Han, Y., Kandampully, J., & Lu, X. (2025). How language arousal affects purchase intentions in online retailing? The role of virtual versus human influencers, language typicality, and trust. *Journal of Retailing and Consumer Services*, *82*(104106), 104106. https://doi.org/10.1016/j.jretconser.2024.104106

Wang, P., & Huang, Q. (2023). Digital influencers, social power and consumer engagement in social commerce. *Internet Research*, *33*(1), 178–207. https://doi.org/10.1108/intr-08-2020-0467

Wellman, M. L., Stoldt, R., Tully, M., & Ekdale, B. (2020). Ethics of authenticity: Social media influencers and the production of sponsored content. *Journal of Media Ethics*, *35*(2), 68–82. https://doi.org/10.1080/23736992.2020.1736078

Whittaker, L., Weismueller, J., & Pallant, J. (2025). Avatars, assemble! Digital human avatars for public figure engagement and marketing. *Business Horizons*. https://doi.org/10.1016/j.bushor.2025.06.004

Woodcock, J., & Johnson, M. R. (2019). Live streamers on twitch. Tv as social media influencers: Chances and challenges for strategic communication. *International Journal of Strategic Communication*, *13*(4), 321–335. https://doi.org/10.1080/1553118x.2019.1630412

Yang, J., Chuenterawong, P., Lee, H., & Chock, T. M. (2023). Anthropomorphism in CSR endorsement: A comparative study on humanlike vs. Cartoonlike virtual influencers' climate change messaging. *Journal of Promotion Management*, *29*(5), 705–734. https://doi.org/10.1080/10496491.2022.2163041

Yang, Y., Li, S., & Qiu, S. (2025). A systematic literature review on the negative impacts of AI-generated virtual digital humans. *IEEE Access: Practical Innovations, Open Solutions*, *13*, 80047–80062. https://doi.org/10.1109/access.2025.3564041

Yee, N., & Bailenson, J. (2007). The Proteus effect: The effect of transformed self-representation on behavior. *Human Communication Research*, *33*(3), 271–290. https://doi.org/10.1111/j.1468-2958.2007.00299.x

Ye, G., Hudders, L., De Jans, S., & De Veirman, M. (2021). The value of influencer marketing for business: A bibliometric analysis and managerial implications. *Journal of Advertising*, *50*(2), 160–178. https://doi.org/10.1080/00913367.2020.1857888

Zhang, W. Q., & Zhu, D. H. (2025). I'm "KFC": How brand-exclusive digital human influences brand intimacy. *Journal of Business Research*, *197*(115451), 115451. https://doi.org/10.1016/j.jbusres.2025.115451

4 Digital Advertising Efficiency

Taking Stock and Looking Forward

Albena Pergelova and Fernando Angulo-Ruiz

Introduction: Digital Advertising, Consumer Well-Being, and the Continuous Impetus for Efficiency

The rise of digital advertising is no surprise since it offers advertisers more precise targeting, and consumers get more personalized messages. For instance, in the context of social media influencer advertising, where individuals with large following on social media are paid to promote products/services to their followers, the promotional message is naturally embedded in the conversation and is delivered in a context where potential consumers are already engaged and interested in the conversation (Pergelova & Hachey, 2023). In an era of constantly increasing clutter and competition for the audience's attention, better targeting is especially important for advertisers because it means increased cost-effectiveness and improved efficiency. Better targeting is also important for consumers and their well-being, as consumers are exposed to messages that are more relevant to them. Indeed, digital technologies, such as artificial intelligence (AI) and digital platforms, have the ability to enhance consumer well-being (e.g., by providing opportunities for increased connectedness with others and more personalized messages); however, they can also detract from consumer well-being via, e.g., rising security and privacy concerns that induce anxiety, overuse of social media, and the negative effects of constant "social comparison" (Boninsegni et al., 2022).

Research has demonstrated that digital advertising can, indeed, help advertisers by increasing the overall advertising efficiency (e.g., Kim, 2020; Pergelova et al., 2010) because of its more dynamic content, more efficient targeting, and higher reach per dollar compared with traditional channels (Ma & Du, 2018). However, there is also research indicating that we should be careful when assessing the effects of digital advertising. Even though personalization decreases ad avoidance (Baek & Morimoto, 2012), online ads could lead to negative brand attitudes if they are perceived as distractors (e.g., Duff & Faber, 2011). Similarly, in the context of AI use in video advertisements, Wang et al. (2024) caution that AI-generated voice-over can increase consumers' cognitive load thus decreasing

DOI: 10.4324/9781003567523-6

purchase intentions. Digital advertising campaigns typically employ multiple sources and can lead to multiple outcomes (both positive and negative, such as negative electronic word-of-mouth [eWOM] and negative brand attitudes); therefore, the methods for assessing the efficiency of digital advertising should ideally be able to reflect this reality and incorporate the multitude of potential results.

Rodgers and Thorson (2000), in their Interactive Advertising Model (IAM), directed the attention of researchers to the consumer-controlled and advertiser-controlled elements of the model. The importance of thinking about both aspects—and carefully considering the new multiplicity of consumer-controlled aspects—has only increased since the publication of the original IAM in 2000. Consumer-controlled aspects are increasingly not only at the level of outcomes (e.g., click on ad, form attitude) but also at the level of input into the communication through, for example, consumer-generated advertising, eWOM, and parasocial relationships (PSRs) between consumers and influencers on social media. Conceptual developments in communications, advertising, and marketing have long suggested that we are moving toward greater appreciation and preference for more participative, dialogue-based communication between companies/brands and consumers that is mutually controllable and responsive (Deighton & Kornfeld, 2009; Jenkins et al., 2013; Yadav & Varadarajan, 2005). While such a view is intuitively appealing given the shift of power to former consumer-audiences (which are now co-creators), the challenges of measuring digital advertising effectiveness and efficiency are only compounded. Against this backdrop, this chapter's objective is to synthesize the digital advertising effectiveness and efficiency literature, propose a digital advertising efficiency model that incorporates a broader set of metrics, including consumer well-being, and outline a methodological measurement approach that can capture the diversity of inputs and outputs (both consumer and advertiser-controlled) generated as a result of digital advertising campaigns. We refer to digital advertising effectiveness as the proper utilization of resources to achieve the organization's objectives with regard to its advertising strategy (thus, the focus is on desired objectives/results), while efficiency is the minimization of resources in implementing the strategy and achieving the objectives; thus, efficiency requires the consideration of both inputs (cost, resources) and outputs (results) with attention to minimizing the inputs for a given set of outputs (Sheth & Sisodia, 2002).

Current Ways to Measure Digital Advertising Effects

In this section, we provide a review of the digital advertising literature organizing it around two themes: advertiser-controlled inputs into the ad campaign and consumer-controlled inputs (Rodgers & Thorson, 2000), with the caveat that the distinction is fluid because of the consumer-advertiser interaction and interdependence in the process (Stewart & Pavlou, 2002). The review is not meant to be exhaustive, but rather to illustrate the types of inputs into and outcomes from digital advertising campaigns.

Digital Advertising Metrics from the Perspective of Advertiser-Controlled Elements

The ad type, ad format, and ad features are all advertiser-controlled elements of digital communication campaigns (Rodgers & Thorson, 2000). Looking at the digital advertising effectiveness and efficiency literature from this perspective generates a picture of the diversity of ad formats/features and their (relative) effectiveness. Studies within this stream of literature have examined display (e.g., banner) ads, paid search, social media advertising, mobile advertising, AI, etc., either in isolation or in combination, including comparing digital and traditional advertising. The variables considered outcomes (i.e., variables measuring how effective ads are) tend to be different depending on whether this study takes a broader marketing perspective or focuses on advertising-specific theoretical approaches. From an advertising point of view, the effectiveness variables used typically fall within the cognition (e.g., recall), affection (e.g., attitude toward the ad or brand), behavior (e.g., purchase intention) model in advertising. Given that marketing's key contribution to the organization is to stimulate demand for organizational products or services (Clark et al., 2014), current literature on digital advertising effectiveness from this perspective studies the impact of firm-controlled digital advertising inputs on consumers' mind-set metrics (e.g., brand awareness, liking) and on firm top-line performance (e.g., sales).

Early Research into the Effectiveness of Digital Advertising

In the topic about the relative effectiveness of digital advertising, literature has studied the impact of digital and traditional advertising on sales, brand recall, and consumer spending and cross-buying behavior. For example, Danaher and Dagger (2013) studied the impact of advertisements in television, newspapers, radio, magazines, catalogs, mail, search, and email on sales, while Dinner et al. (2014) examined the impact of traditional advertisements, online display ads, and paid search ads on sales. Another stream of literature is focused on paid search and assesses digital advertising's impact on click-through rates, brand evaluations, and conversion (e.g., Agarwal et al., 2011; Kumar et al., 2016; Rutz et al., 2012; Yoo, 2014; Jerath et al., 2014). Studies have also looked into online display ads (Hoban & Bucklin, 2015), e-mail ads (Li & Kannan, 2014), banner ads (Chun et al., 2014), and online video ads (Li & Lo, 2015; Baron et al., 2014) to assess their effect on impressions, conversions, brand memory, recognition and attitudes, and purchase behavior.

Social Media and Influencer Advertising

Social media advertising has attracted a lot of research attention because of the high personalization possibilities of advertising on social media sites (De Keyzer et al., 2015). The most significant trend in social media advertising is influencer advertising. Indeed, social media influencers have become a key part of many brands' marketing campaigns, and research has investigated the effectiveness of using influencers as an advertising tool (e.g., Kay et al., 2020; Martínez-López et al., 2020; Reinikainen et al., 2020). The general consensus is that influencer advertising can generate more sales than other forms of paid advertising because they are perceived as more credible and relatable. It is important to note, however, that this effect is contingent on the degree to which influencers are able to project an image of authenticity, as consumers will punish brands (e.g., less purchase intention, more negative brand attitudes) and influencers (e.g., less followers) if they perceive manipulative intent (An et al., 2019).

Recent research has differentiated between (1) traditional (human) influencers (real individual who create content on social media and have amassed a large following); (2) virtual influencers (digital personas who create content and promote products and services and are controlled by institutions or corporate entities); and (3) AI influencers (more advanced enterprise-generated digital personas utilizing algorithms and models to mimic human behavior) (Zhang et al., 2025, p. 868). Guo et al. (2025) discuss how, in contrast to traditional influencers, virtual influencers can be freely modified in various aspects according to the brand needs and consumers preferences, they are completely controlled by companies/brands, and many virtual influencers have become trusted "key opinion leaders." For example, one virtual influencer—Lil Miquela (@ lil-miquela)—has millions of followers and has been engaged in brand collaborations with Prada, Dior, and Calvin Klein. This virtual influencer was created by Trevor McFedries and Sara DeCou, co-founders of the company Brud. Moreover, companies can imbue virtual influencers with the desired characteristics and behaviors that match their brands. The remarkable anthropomorphic characteristics of virtual influencers and the high degree of control over their content and conduct makes them especially appealing to brands (Melnychuk et al., 2024).

According to Zhang et al. (2025), "AI influencers represent a quantum leap in virtual influencer technology" (p. 867) enabling AI influencers to simulate creative human behavior, while offering brands consistency and scalability. However, AI influencers may be at a disadvantage if advertising products are deeply personal; in such cases, human influencers have the upper hand, as they can leverage their experiences, stories, and most importantly emotions to establish deeper connections with consumers (Hu & Ma, 2023).

Influencer advertising's effectiveness is usually measured with metrics such as engagement rates (likes, follows, etc.), brand-related metrics (e.g., brand awareness, brand attitudes), and the ability to influence purchase decisions (e.g., purchase intentions, sales) (e.g., Boerman, 2020; De Jans et al., 2020; Pergelova & Hachey, 2023). Recent developments have critiqued the use of engagement as a metric, as an influencer ad could be engaging for the "wrong" reason, that is, what makes the ad engaging may not be related to the product and may not lead to sales lift (Yang et al., 2025). Thus, those authors propose a product engagement score metric which they demonstrate is a significant predictor of how much sales revenue lift the ad can generate.

Use of AI to Increase Digital Advertising Efficiency and Effectiveness

While AI has been used in the creation of virtual/AI influencers, it is rapidly becoming used to enhance the efficiency of other aspects of advertising as well. Generative AI, in particular, can generate new content (e.g., audio, code, image, text) based on pre-trained data and identified patterns which makes it particularly appealing to advertisers to increase the efficiency of the ad creation process (Yang et al., 2024). Shi and Wang (2023) use AI in the application of the genetic algorithm back propagation neural network to predict the click-through rate of website advertising applications, thus promoting resource efficiency. Another area where AI is favored by advertisers is in the creation of voice-over in video advertisements, because it offers ad creators efficiency and reduces production costs. Wang et al. (2024) investigated the relative effectiveness of AI vs human voice-over in video ads and found that human voice-over not only has the advantage of reducing consumers' cognitive load (thus increasing purchase intentions) but also offers insights on how to use AI in ways that mitigate this effect.

Mobile Advertising

The mobile advertising literature focuses on the impact of mobile advertising on attitude, intention, coupon redemption, and locational targeting. For example, Bart et al. (2014) found that mobile display ads positively affected attitudes and intentions. Danaher et al. (2015) assessed the impact of mobile phone coupon characteristics on redemption and found that location affected coupon redemption of snack foods. Ghose et al. (2019) proposed a "trajectory-based" targeting strategy for mobile ads which is based on consumers' physical-movement trajectories. They demonstrate the advantages of this strategy for increasing the efficiency of customers' shopping processes, thus leading to higher revenues.

Virtual Reality and Metaverse

Virtual reality (VR) technology allows users to experience a situation or place by embodying a virtual avatar. VR has become an important new trend for digital advertising. For example, Li et al. (2024) investigate the effect of VR in the context of prosocial advertising and demonstrate that VR advertising increases both the number of people who decide to donate, and the amount donated. Another setting in which VR has become increasingly used is in the tourism sector, where VR is found to help consumer adoption (Stylos et al., 2024; Rafdinal et al., 2024).

Zaki et al. (2023) conduct a bibliometric review of the VR literature in digital marketing. They propose several avenues for future research on VR, including measuring the impact and engagement of VR, consumers' perceptions and behavior in VR, and how brands can leverage VR to support digital marketing efforts.

From this perspective, studies have investigated metaverse perception of consumers. Metaverse employs immersive technologies, incorporating augmented reality, VR, and mixed reality, and understanding consumer acceptance and behavior of it is important for assessing its potential advertising effectiveness (Sharma et al., 2025). As companies and brands have started to invest in metaverse advertising campaigns, researchers have started to investigate topics such as consumers' adoption of avatars (Kim et al., 2023) and consumers' intentions toward metaverse-based virtual stores (Chakraborty et al., 2024).

Potential Negative Impacts of Digital Advertising

One important emerging stream of literature focuses on the potential negative effects of firm-controlled aspects of digital ad campaigns. For instance, Goldstein et al. (2014) studied the role of annoying ads and found that these ads increased the tendency of consumers to abandon the website. Baek and Morimoto (2012) found that privacy concerns and ad irritation had a direct positive effect on ad avoidance. Goodrich et al. (2015) investigated intrusive online video advertisements and found that they negatively affected attitudes and intentions toward both the advertised brand and the host website.

More recent research has investigated a growing variety of potentially negative effects on consumers. For example, Pergelova and Hachey (2023) in the context of social media influencer advertising identify consumer overconfidence as a result of being constantly exposed to social media advertising, which can be detrimental to making optimal purchase decisions. Another study in the context of AI vs human influencers found that consumers with lower levels of knowledge are more easily influenced by functional product appeals shared by AI influencers (Zhang et al., 2025). This raises concerns about whether consumers with low knowledge are well served by this kind of advertising, and the impact on consumers' well-being. Consumers may suffer from cognitive dissonance after sub-optimal purchases (which was the case in Pergelova and Hachey's 2023 study), and this can affect brand perceptions and potentially reduce future purchase intentions. The study of Guo et al. (2025) provides another interesting effect of the use of virtual influencers by brands. The authors found evidence of the "uncanny valley effect" (the unsettling feeling people may experience when faced with computer-generated characters that resemble humans but are not quite realistic) and suggest that excessive use of virtual influencers can negatively impact the number of brand followers.

Thus, the inclusion of both potentially positive and negative effects in measurement models is important because, as Duff and Faber (2011) postulate, the majority of advertising studies assume that ads that are not fully processed will either result in no impact or may have a positive effect on the consumer due to mere exposure. Yet, this view does not reflect the reality of many consumers that are annoyed by ads online and actively try to avoid them, or consumers whose opinion of the brand has changed after sub-optimal purchases.

Digital Advertising Metrics from the Perspective of Consumer-Controlled Inputs

Consumer engagement has been suggested as an antidote to consumers that are empowered and connected in digital spaces. Early studies in this field suggested that many people reject behavioral targeting based on their prior search and browsing behavior (Turow et al., 2009). Thus, authors have emphasized that to succeed in the new digital world, brands must relinquish control (e.g., Fournier & Avery, 2011). An implicit recognition of the need for more participative, mutually controllable, and responsive view toward digital advertising would inform studies that focus on consumers' inputs into the communication process. Such studies have investigated consumer-generated ads (CGAs) and eWOM/forwarding messages (viral advertising) and more recently a key focus of the literature has been on parasocial interactions (PSIs) and PSRs between social media personalities and consumers/followers.

Consumer-Generated Ads

Motivated by the contention that CGAs may be more effective than traditional company ads, Lawrence et al. (2013) posited that CGAs engaged viewers more on cognitive, personal, emotional, and behavioral grounds because of the presence of credible, authentic, and non-corporate consumer source. Orazi et al. (2016) similarly showed that the disclosure of consumer participation in the ad creation process resulted in positive ad evaluations. More recent research has confirmed those early findings. For instance, in the context of Facebook ads, Mayrhofer et al. (2020) found that user-generated content performed better (higher purchase intention) than brand-generated content. Similarly, Diwanji et al. (2024) in the context of X (formerly Twitter) found that consumer-generated brand-related content was more effective in increasing purchase intention.

Viral Advertising and eWOM

Viral advertising and eWOM have also received a good deal of research attention (e.g., Cho et al., 2014; Hennig-Thurau et al., 2015). Although viral advertising initiates with a marketer-designed ad, it is consumers' decisions to pass along the ad and spread eWOM that is the essence of virality.

Kareklas et al. (2015) investigated the key influence of perceived source credibility on the effectiveness of health-related public service announcements and eWOM communications. Alhabash et al. (2015) reported a mediating effect of viral behavioral intentions (e.g., likes, shares, comments) on the relationship between attitudes toward the message and offline behavioral intentions. Srivastava et al. (2023) have emphasized the need to better understand the link between eWOM and consumer brand engagement, linking the two and proposing theoretical and managerial implications. More recently, Liu et al. (2024) have redirected attention toward what they call eWOM 2.0 and propose that future research should pay attention to how the availability of big data and AI shape consumers' information adoption and eWOM.

Parasocial Interactions and Relationships

PSIs and PSRs have become increasingly important from the perspective of consumer-controlled inputs/behavior into the digital advertising space. PSI refers to the one-sided interaction between a media user and an audience member (e.g., in the case of social media, the one-sided interaction between an influencer and followers), which after experience and numerous online interactions can develop into PSR (Breves et al., 2021; Yuan & Lou, 2020). PSRs are referred to as "illusory bonds" between consumers/followers and the influencers they follow, because they are inherently one-sided. PSRs have been found to play a crucial role in the success of the social media influencers (e.g., influencer's reputation, number of followers) (Boerman & Reijmersdal, 2020).

If influencers are able to build PSRs with their followers, this translates into tangible benefits for the brands they work it, such as purchase intentions and word-of-mouth recommendations, and consumer brand engagement (Gomes et al., 2022; Manchanda et al., 2022). Because PSRs are a manifestation of consumers' trust, brands can reap the benefits from strong PSR between consumers and influencers.

Toward a More Inclusive Model of Digital Advertising Efficiency: Consumer Well-Being, Long-Term Company Performance, and Cost-Effectiveness of Digital Advertising

The common tie among studies cited above is that they look at digital advertising through the "stickiness" lens, i.e., they apply a traditional marketing "funnel" approach in which companies produce marketing communications content, deliver it to consumers, and use the marketing tools with the higher probability of making consumers "stick" with the ad and consequently make a purchase decision. Even when researchers look at consumer-initiated and consumer-controlled aspects of the communication, such as comments, eWOM, and PSRs, the research question is typically concerned with the issue of how to increase such behavior for the benefits of the marketer, instead of how to maximize positive outcomes for both/all parties involved (for an exception, see, e.g., Levesque et al., 2023). This is surprising given the advancement in conceptual developments focused on participative, dialogue-based, co-creation approaches in both communications and marketing (Deighton & Kornfeld, 2009; Jenkins et al., 2013; Stewart & Pavlou, 2002; Yadav & Varadarajan, 2005).

Consumers are motivated to participate in digital advertising interactions by needs for social support, reinforcement of self through social interactions, and psychological well-being, which includes self-esteem and life satisfaction (Kwon et al., 2014). Yet, digital advertising effectiveness and efficiency studies only approach these issues as motivations and do not take into consideration those measures as outputs for the consumer (i.e., does a participant's self-esteem increase as a result of the interaction online?). Newer studies have looked at consumer well-being outcomes such as consumers' advertising literacy in the context of digital advertising (Pergelova & Hachey, 2023). Digital advertising literacy is important because it allows consumers to discern when they are being exposed to advertising and to make more beneficial purchasing decisions for themselves (Hudders et al., 2017).

Consumers' appreciation for companies that engage in digital advertising from the stance of openness and transparency will likely result in better and longer term relationships and support (e.g., loyalty) to the organization. Thus, we advocate the use of metrics that reflect not only effectiveness and efficiency for the advertiser but also desirable effects for consumers (Kwon et al., 2014) and measures that empower consumers to make decisions and participate on their own terms, thus increasing their well-being.

We suggest that if organizations are effective in generating outputs that empower consumers, this will lead to increased efficiency of advertising campaigns because of earned (not paid) media and increased willingness of consumers to engage with and respond favorably to companies that provide avenues for openness and dialogue. In Figure 4.1, we present a model which incorporates both advertiser-controlled inputs (e.g., social media ads, influencers ads, AI, and VR) and consumer-controlled inputs into the process. We suggest two types of intermediate outputs: one focused on traditional metrics used to evaluate advertising based on, e.g., brand recall and brand attitude, while the other introduces consumer well-being metrics such as perceived control, self-efficacy, and digital advertising literacy. Lastly, the final outputs in the model include both the traditional economic outputs (e.g., sales, financial performance) and non-economic outputs (e.g., social performance). This expanded view of the inputs and outputs of efficiency measurement of digital advertising is forward-looking and reflective of the dialogical nature of interactions in the digital space, and the multitude of outcomes available.

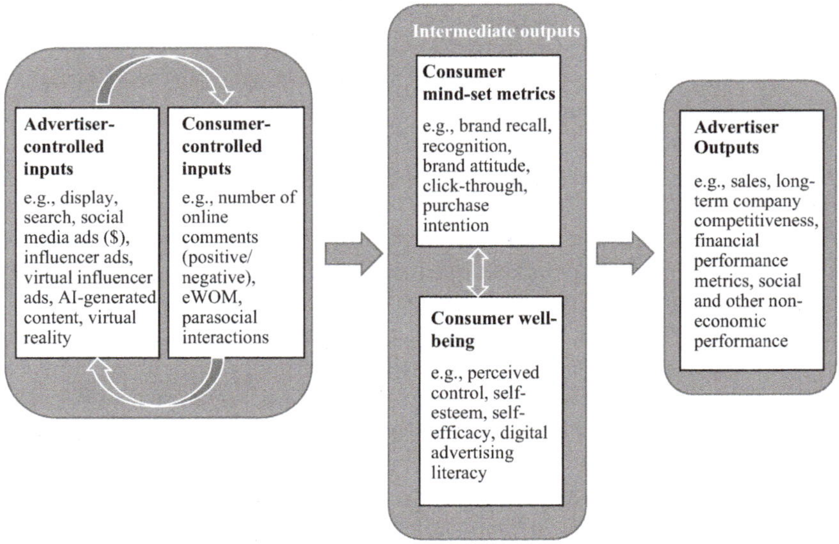

Figure 4.1 Integrative Model of Digital Advertising Efficiency.

Proposed Measurement Approaches: Network Data Envelopment Analysis (DEA) and Other Developments

Network DEA

The new reality (message movement across platforms, content creation, and well-being of consumers) necessitates a new way of measuring the effect of digital advertising that can capture the diversity of inputs and outputs generated as a result of digital advertising campaigns, as presented in Figure 4.1. While one can envision different methodological approaches for empirically testing this model (e.g., structural equation modeling), we present network Data Envelopment Analysis (DEA) as a method that easily incorporates multiple inputs and outputs and offers efficiency estimation. Network DEA matches the IAM (Rodgers & Thorson, 2000) and the integrative model in Figure 4.1 to assess digital advertising efficiency.

The challenge of assessing the effects of diverse digital advertising measures comes from the fact that such measures usually have multiple objectives, related not only to build awareness, consideration, and preference but also to enhance performance. We argue that this chain of effects should be addressed as a whole: digital advertising (advertiser-controlled and consumer-controlled elements)—mind-set metrics, and consumer well-being—performance. Indeed, as a relationship between the inputs, intermediate outputs and final outputs has to be established, network DEA is necessary (Angulo-Ruiz et al., 2014, 2022).

In our model for capturing digital advertising efficiency presented in Figure 4.1, the generation of performance is the result of two consecutive and interdependent stages. During stage one of network DEAs, digital advertising efforts (expended in *t or t−1*) are oriented toward the fulfillment of customer mind-set metrics or consumer well-being maximization (in t or t+1). In stage two, the optimal level of customer mind-set metrics or consumer well-being is added to the previous resources (advertising resources, expended in *t or t−1*) to optimize the level of long-term performance (in *t or t+1*). A firm oriented toward the optimization of long-term performance should manage efficiently all stages in order to guarantee the achievement of the final goal. More details on network DEA can be found in Angulo-Ruiz et al. (2014, 2022), Choi (2020), Sexton and Lewis (2003), Lewis and Sexton (2004), and Yeh and Chang (2023).

Another aspect that needs consideration is the role of undesirable outputs. Examples of such outputs can be negative reviews, negative word-of-mouth, and others. Directional distance function (DDF) based on DEA can help in measuring efficiency of digital advertising taking into consideration desirable and undesirable outputs. DDF aims to increase the desirable outputs while simultaneously decreasing the undesirable outputs (Chung et al., 1997).

To summarize, advancements in the DEA method make it especially suitable for assessing digital advertising efficiency: the method can accommodate multiple inputs and outputs, including undesirable ones; it can provide a measure of efficiency and is able to work with complex multi-stage models.

Developments from Computer Science and Information Technology

Computer science and information technology fields are pushing the boundaries for measuring digital advertising efficiency. For instance, Musku and Yadav (2021) recommend integrating DEA with a statistical and machine-learning hybrid scoring method based on classification modeling to help us decide the best video ad. This model reduced cost-per-thousand impressions by 6%–12% and increased video completion rate by 1%–4%. Han et al. (2022) propose a cost-effective item-influencer selection algorithm with acceleration techniques (such as adopter caching, lazy utility estimation), Monte Carlo simulation, and network-based adoption modeling. In their model, they maximize marketers' utility by selecting appropriate pairwise combinations of influencers and items (e.g., articles or videos about products) based on realistic conditions (e.g., marketers' budget, influencers' payments, item-user fitness, social propagation, and influencers' marketing slots). The proposed algorithm improved company returns by 21%–117%.

Following on measuring digital advertising efficiency of influencers, Yang et al. (2025) propose an algorithm to measure the concept of the product engagement score to capture how engaging the product itself is as presented in a video. They proposed a pixel-level engagement by training a deep three-dimensional convolutional neural network on video-level engagement data from video ads on TikTok and product sales data on Taobao. Influencers advertising showed 35% higher product engagement scores, and these scores are a significant predictor of sales lift. To note, in this modeling, influencer popularity and ads pricing do not impact sales lift.

Assessing digital advertising efficiency using textual data is an area that has garnered attention for many years now. Su et al. (2024), for example, propose a semi-supervised machine-learning approach, guided latent Dirichlet allocation, which incorporates human insights into the discovery and classification of topics. Because their model integrates human insights, the model performs better than traditional latent Dirichlet allocation. On a similar note, the efficiency of digital advertising content has become more tractable with the emergence of generative AI. However, when creating personalized advertising content, AI collects user's behavior data without the user's knowledge, and this brings security risks to digital advertising. Jing et al. (2024) propose a security-enhanced digital platform in the context of digital outdoor advertising. They combine blockchain and edge computing technology to provide a decentralized platform which contains non-tamperable and traceable features. Results show that the platform not only can effectively manage user identities and advertising plans but also improves data security, credibility, and performance.

Qualitative Research to Understand Digital Advertising Efficiency

Network DEA, AI, computer science, information technology, and other quantitative methodologies can help us understand the chain of effects of inputs, intermediary outputs, and final outputs proposed in Figure 4.1. However, qualitative methodologies can help us understand the dynamics and theoretical mechanisms of the influence of a digital advertising input on certain intermediary or final outputs (explain the arrows in Figure 4.1). Qualitative methodologies will help us interpret and develop dynamic process models to understand in-depth the whys and how of the relationships among digital advertising inputs and outputs. Readers can refer to Gehman et al. (2018) and Gioia et al. (2013) to have a better understanding of qualitative methodologies, and Levesque et al. (2023) and Pergelova and Hachey (2023) for a creative application of qualitative and mixed methodologies in digital advertising.

Implications

Theoretical Implications

We offer several key takeaways based on the literature and the proposed model. First, the proliferation of digital advertising formats and the advancement of digital technologies bring both opportunities (e.g., increased efficiency of digital ads on social media and via AI) and concerns (e.g., effects on consumer well-being, negative eWOM) that need to be considered in measurement models. The integration of multiple inputs and (intermediate) outputs from the process is more complex to model, but it is also closer to reality. Second, the rise of importance of PSRs in influencer advertising speaks to the continuous need to attend to the dialogical, interactive nature of digital advertising, and the impetus of integrating consumer-controlled inputs and outputs. Third, while most of the literature examines effectiveness measures based on desired results of advertising campaigns (e.g., attitude and purchase intentions), digital advertising offers the potential of increased efficiency which requires inclusion in theoretical models. Empirical advancements in network DEA and in computational approaches have brought new possibilities for precise efficiency measurements. Fourth, the existing literature on digital advertising efficiency and effectiveness predominantly focuses on economic outcomes within for-profit contexts. However, organizations are increasingly attentive to the social and other non-economic implications of their (marketing) activities. Future research should put greater emphasis on exploring the trade-offs that arise when companies pursue both economic and non-economic objectives, which may at times appear to be in tension. In this regard, organizations such as social enterprises or certified benefit corporations (or others operating in marginalized communities) offer valuable contexts for investigation. These organizations serve as compelling laboratories for examining the efficiency and effectiveness of digital advertising, particularly in relation to their dual missions. Studying these novel organizational forms can yield deeper insights into the complex trade-offs involved in digital advertising strategies that aim to balance financial performance with broader societal impact.

Practical Implications: Applications of the Model in Industry Contexts

Our chapter also offers important implications for practitioners. Our conceptual model presented in Figure 4.1 provides a practical framework for marketers and other professionals seeking to assess the efficiency and effectiveness of their digital marketing strategies. Our model is structured around three core components—inputs, intermediate outputs, and final outputs—each of which can serve as a distinct starting point for analysis.

To evaluate advertiser-controlled and consumer-controlled inputs, practitioners should gather archival data from the organization's accounting/financial records (e.g., expenditures on display ads, search advertising, social media ads, influencer ads) as well as data from social media platforms (e.g., volume and sentiment of online comments). These data can be collected at regular intervals—weekly, monthly, quarterly, or annually—and used to conduct analyses to explore directional relationships between advertiser and consumer-controlled inputs.

For intermediate outputs related to consumer mind-set and consumer well-being, marketers can collect survey data (e.g., brand recall, recognition, attitude, purchase intention, self-esteem, self-efficacy) alongside archival metrics such as click-through rates. These data enable analyses that reveal how digital advertising influences both consumer mind-set and well-being responses.

To assess final outputs, practitioners should compile financial performance indicators (e.g., sales, earnings before taxes, depreciation and amortization, and cash flow) and supplement this with archival or primary data capturing social and other non-economic outcomes. With longitudinal data across these three core components, practitioners can apply network DEA to identify periods of optimal efficiency in their digital marketing efforts.

Finally, qualitative methodologies can complement quantitative approaches by offering deeper insights into the mechanisms through which specific digital advertising inputs influence intermediate and final outputs. This mixed-method perspective enhances practitioners' ability to make informed, context-sensitive decisions in complex marketing environments.

Conclusion

The quest to find the next best digital advertising tool and the newest metric to measure advertising's short-term impact (e.g., did yesterday's social media campaign bring enough participants to our online contest?) could leave advertisers with little time to stop and think about the big picture and consider the strategic considerations and the broader implications of their work. Yet, such implications are crucial for the long-term sustainability of any organization. The model presented here takes as a conceptual basis the idea of interactivity as a mutually controllable, responsive, and open-to-dialogue environment, in which consumers will reward openness and transparency on behalf of organizations. From a strategic, long-term perspective, we suggest that such a stance toward digital advertising will bring competitive advantage and enhanced performance outcomes for for-profit, not-for-profit, certified benefit corporations, social enterprises, and other organizations, as it brings about greater levels of consumer well-being. We, therefore, propose that a digital advertising measurement approach from this perspective should incorporate both consumers' and advertisers' efforts (inputs) and consequences (outputs). It is our hope that the model and the measurement approach presented here will stimulate debate and advance research in digital advertising.

Acknowledgments

We gratefully acknowledge the financial support provided by the Social Sciences and Humanities Research Council of Canada through Insight Grant 435-2022-0515. We also extend our sincere thanks to Logan Hoover, Kwizera Bara, and Elise Frederickson for their valuable research assistance.

References

Agarwal, A., Hosanagar, K., & Smith, M. D. (2011). Location, location, location: An analysis of profitability of position in online advertising markets. *Journal of Marketing Research, 48*(6), 1057–1073. https://doi.org/10.1509/jmr.08.0468

Alhabash, S., McAlister, A., Lou, C., & Hagerstrom, A. (2015). From clicks to behaviors: The mediating effect of intentions to like, share, and comment on the relationship between message evaluations and offline behavioral intentions. *Journal of Interactive Advertising, 15*(2), 82–96. https://doi.org/10.1080/15252019.2015.1071677

An, S., Kerr, G., & Jin, H. S., (2019). Recognizing native ads as advertising: Attitudinal and behavioral consequences. *Journal of Consumer Affairs, 53*(4), 1421–1442. https://doi.org/10.1111/joca.12235

Angulo-Ruiz, F., Donthu, N., Prior, D., & Rialp, J. (2014). The financial contribution of customer-oriented marketing capability. *Journal of the Academy of Marketing Science, 42*, 380–399. https://doi.org/10.1007/s11747-013-0353-6

Angulo-Ruiz, F., Donthu, N., Prior, D., & Rialp-Criado, J. (2022). Funding marketing resources and capabilities during a recession: An empirical examination of top corporate advertisers. *European Journal of Marketing*, 56(8), 2138–2171. https://doi.org/10.1108/EJM-06-2020-0423

Baek, T. H., & Morimoto, M. (2012). Stay away from me. *Journal of Advertising, 41*(1), 59–76. https://doi.org/10.2753/JOA0091-3367410105

Baron, S., Brouwer, C., & Garbayo, A. (2014). A model for delivering branding value through high-impact digital advertising. *Journal of Advertising Research, 54*(3), 286–291. https://doi.org/10.2501/JAR-54-3-286-291

Bart, Y., Stephen, A. T., & Sarvary, M. (2014). Which products are best suited to mobile advertising? A field study of mobile display advertising effects on consumer attitudes and intentions. *Journal of Marketing Research, 51*(3), 270–285. https://doi.org/10.1509/jmr.13.0503

Boerman, S. C. (2020). The effects of the standardized Instagram disclosure for micro-and meso-influencers. *Computers in Human Behavior, 103*, 199–207. https://doi.org/10.1016/j.chb.2019.09.015

Boerman, S. C., & Van Reijmersdal, E. A. (2020). Disclosing influencer marketing on YouTube to children: The moderating role of para-social relationship. *Frontiers in Psychology, 10*, 3042. https://doi.org/10.3389/fpsyg.2019.03042

Boninsegni, M. F., Roy, A., Bakpayev, M., Kumar, S., Peronard, J. P., & Reimer, T. (2022). Opportunities of and threats to consumer well-being in the age of Fourth Industrial Revolution (IR 4.0) technologies. *Digital Policy, Regulation and Governance, 24*(1), 93–105. https://doi.org/10.1108/DPRG-06-2021-0080

Breves, P., Amrehn, J., Heidenreich, A., Liebers, N., & Schramm, H. (2021). Blind trust? The importance and interplay of parasocial relationships and advertising disclosures in explaining influencers' persuasive effects on their followers. *International Journal of Advertising, 40*(7), 1209–1229. https://doi.org/10.1080/02650487.2021.1881237

Chakraborty, D., Polisetty, A., & Rana, N. P. (2024). Consumers' continuance intention towards metaverse-based virtual stores: A multi-study perspective. *Technological Forecasting and Social Change, 203*, 123405. https://doi.org/10.1016/j.techfore.2024.123405

Cho, S., Huh, J., & Faber, R. (2014). The influence of sender trust and advertiser trust on multistage effects of viral advertising. *Journal of Advertising, 43*(1), 100–114. https://doi.org/10.1080/00913367.2013.811707

Choi, K. (2020). Divisional advertising efficiency in the consumer car purchase funnel: A network DEA approach. *Journal of the Operational Research Society, 71*(9), 1411–1425. https://doi.org/10.1080/01605682.2019.1609886

Chun, K. Y., Song, J. H., Hollenbeck, C., & Lee, J. H. (2014). Are contextual advertisements effective? The moderating role of complexity in banner advertising. *International Journal of Advertising, 33*(2), 351–371. https://doi.org/10.2501/IJA-33-2-351-371

Chung, Y. H., Fare, R., & Grosskopf, S. (1997). Productivity and undesirable outputs: A directional distance function approach. *Journal of Environmental Management, 51*, 229–240. https://doi.org/10.1006/jema.1997.0146

Clark, T., Key, T. M., Hodis, M., & Rajaratnam, D. (2014). The intellectual ecology of mainstream marketing research: An inquiry into the place of marketing in the family of business disciplines. *Journal of the Academy of Marketing Science, 42*, 223–241. https://doi.org/10.1007/s11747-013-0362-5

Danaher, P. J., & Dagger, T. S. (2013). Comparing the relative effectiveness of advertising channels: A case study of a multimedia blitz campaign. *Journal of Marketing Research, 50*(4), 517–534. https://doi.org/10.1509/jmr.12.0241

Danaher, P. J., Smith, M. S., Ranasinghe, K., & Danaher, T. S. (2015). Where, when, and how long: Factors that influence the redemption of mobile phone coupons. *Journal of Marketing Research, 52*(2), 710–725. https://doi.org/10.1509/jmr.13.0341

De Jans, S., Van De Sompel, D., De Veirman, M., & Hudders, L. (2020). # Sponsored! How the recognition of sponsoring on Instagram posts affects adolescents' brand evaluations through source evaluations. *Computers in Human Behavior, 109*, 106342. https://doi.org/10.1016/j.chb.2020.106342

De Keyzer, F., Dens, N., & De Pelsmacker, P. (2015). Is this for me? How consumers respond to personalized advertising on social network sites. *Journal of Interactive Advertising, 15*(2), 124–134. https://doi.org/10.1080/15252019.2015.1082450

Deighton, J., & Kornfeld, L. (2009). Interactivity's unanticipated consequences for marketers and marketing. *Journal of Interactive Marketing, 23*, 4–10. https://doi.org/10.1016/j.intmar.2008.10.001

Dinner, I. M., Van Heerde, H. J., & Neslin, S. A. (2014). Driving online and offline sales: The cross-channel effects of traditional, online display, and paid search advertising. *Journal of Marketing Research, 51*(5), 527–545. https://doi.org/10.1509/jmr.11.0466

Diwanji, V. S., Cortese, J., & Lee, J. (2024). Is consumer generated branding the way forward for digital advertising: Examining the effects of message source, presentation format and involvement on consumer decisions on X (Formerly Twitter). *Journal of Current Issues & Research in Advertising, 46*(1), 90–112. https://doi.org/10.1080/10641734.2024.2334957

Duff, B., & Faber, R. (2011). Missing the mark. *Journal of Advertising, 40*(2), 51–62. https://doi.org/10.2753/JOA0091-3367400204

Fournier, S., & Avery, J. (2011). The uninvited brand. *Business Horizons, 54*, 193–207. https://doi.org/10.1016/j.bushor.2011.01.001

Gehman, J., Glaser, V. L., Eisenhardt, K. M., Gioia, D., Langley, A., & Corley, K. G. (2018). Finding theory–method fit: A comparison of three qualitative approaches to theory building. *Journal of Management Inquiry, 27*(3), 284–300. https://doi.org/10.1177/1056492617706029

Ghose, A., Li, B., & Liu, S. (2019). Mobile targeting using customer trajectory patterns. *Management Science, 65*(11), 5027–5049. https://doi.org/10.1287/mnsc.2018.3188

Gioia, D. A., Corley, K. G., Hamilton, A. L. (2013). Seeking qualitative rigor in inductive research notes on the Gioia methodology. *Organizational Research Methods*, *16*, 15–31. https://doi.org/10.1177/1094428112452151

Goldstein, D. G., Suri, S., Mcafee, R. P., Ekstrand-Abueg, M., & Diaz, F. (2014). The economic and cognitive costs of annoying display advertisements. *Journal of Marketing Research, 51*(6), 742–752. https://doi.org/10.1509/jmr.13.0439

Gomes, M. A., Marques, S., & Dias, Á. (2022). The impact of digital influencers' characteristics on purchase intention of fashion products. *Journal of Global Fashion Marketing*, *13*(3), 187–204. https://doi.org/10.1080/20932685.2022.2039263

Goodrich, K., Schiller, S., & Galletta, D. (2015). Consumer reactions to intrusiveness of online-video advertisements. *Journal of Advertising Research*, *55*(1), 37–50. https://doi.org/10.2501/JAR-55-1-037-050

Guo, Z., Yang, H., & Yang, W. (2025). A new social media programme for brands? A study of the relationship between virtual influencers and brand followers. *Journal of Retailing and Consumer Services*, *84*, 104241. https://doi.org/10.1016/j.jretconser.2025.104241

Han, X., Wang, L., & Fan, W. (2022). Cost-effective social media influencer marketing. *INFORMS Journal on Computing*, *35*(1), 138–157. https://doi.org/10.1287/ijoc.2022.1246

Hennig-Thurau, T., Wiertz, C., & Feldhaus, F. (2015). Does Twitter matter? The impact of microblogging word of mouth on consumers' adoption of new movies. *Journal of the Academy of Marketing Science, 43*, 375–394. https://doi.org/10.1007/s11747-014-0388-3

Hoban, P. R., & Bucklin, R. E. (2015). Effects of internet display advertising in the purchase funnel: Model-based insights from a randomized field experiment. *Journal of Marketing Research, 52*(3), 375–393. https://doi.org/10.1509/jmr.13.0277

Hu, H., & Ma, F. (2023). Human-like bots are not humans: The weakness of sensory language for virtual streamers in livestream commerce. *Journal of Retailing and Consumer Services*, *75*(11), 103541. https://doi.org/10.1016/j.jretconser.2023.103541

Hudders, L., De Pauw, P., Cauberghe, V., Panic, K., Zarouali, B., & Rozendaal, E. (2017). Shedding new light on how advertising literacy can affect children's processing of embedded advertising formats: A future research agenda. *Journal of Advertising*, *46*(2), 333–349. https://doi.org/10.1080/00913367.2016.1269303

Jenkins, H., Ford, S., & Green, J. (2013). *Spreadable media: Creating value and meaning in a networked culture*. New York: New York University Press.

Jerath, K., Ma, L., & Park, Y. H. (2014). Consumer click behavior at a search engine: The role of keyword popularity. *Journal of Marketing Research, 51*(4), 480–486. https://doi.org/10.1509/jmr.13.0099

Jing, Z., Xu, X., Gu, C., Zhang, Y., & Shu, Q. (2024). A security-enhanced advertising platform based on blockchain and edge computing in generative AI. *Applied Artificial Intelligence*, *38*(1). https://doi.org/10.1080/08839514.2024.2340395

Kareklas, I., Muehling, D., & Weber, T. J. (2015). Reexamining health messages in the digital age: A fresh look at source credibility effects. *Journal of Advertising*, *44*(2), 88–104. https://doi.org/10.1080/00913367.2015.1018461

Kay, S., Mulcahy, R., & Parkinson, J. (2020). When less is more: The impact of macro and micro social media influencers' disclosure. *Journal of Marketing Management*, *36*(3–4), 248–278. https://doi.org/10.1080/0267257X.2020.1718740

Kim, J. S. (2020). National culture and advertising sensitivity to business cycles: A reexamination. *Journal of International Marketing, 28*(4), 41–57. https://www.jstor.org/stable/26979585

Kim, D. Y., Lee, H. K., & Chung, K. (2023). Avatar-mediated experience in the metaverse: The impact of avatar realism on user-avatar relationship. *Journal of Retailing and Consumer Services, 73*, 103382. https://doi.org/10.1016/j.jretconser.2023.103382

Kumar, A., Bezawada, R., Rishika, R., Janakiraman, R., & Kannan, P. K. (2016). From social to sale: The effects of firm-generated content in social media on customer behavior. *Journal of Marketing, 80*(1), 7–25. https://doi.org/10.1509/jm.14.0249

Kwon, E. S., Kim, E., Sung, Y., & Yoo, C. Y. (2014). Brand followers: Consumer motivation and attitude towards brand communications on Twitter. *International Journal of Advertising, 33*(4), 657–680. https://doi.org/10.2501/IJA-33-4-657-680

Lawrence, B., Fournier, S., & Brunel, F. (2013). When companies don't make the ad: A multimethod inquiry into the differential effectiveness of consumer-generated advertising. *Journal of Advertising, 42*(4), 292–307. https://doi.org/10.1080/00913367.2013.795120

Levesque, N., Hachey, A., & Pergelova, A. (2023). No filter: Navigating well-being in troubled times as social media influencers. *Journal of Marketing Management, 39*(11–12), 1098–1131. https://doi.org/10.1080/0267257X.2023.2218858

Lewis, H. F., & Sexton, T. R. (2004). Network DEA: Efficiency analysis of organizations with complex internal structure. *Computers & Operations Research, 31*(9), 1365–1410. https://doi.org/10.1016/S0305-0548(03)00095-9

Li, H., & Kannan, P. (2014). Attributing conversions in a multichannel online marketing environment: An empirical model and a field experiment. *Journal of Marketing Research, 51*(1), 40–56. https://doi.org/10.1509/jmr.13.0050

Li, H., & Lo, H. Y. (2015). Do you recognize its brand? The effectiveness of online in-stream video advertisements. *Journal of Advertising, 44*(3), 208–218. https://doi.org/10.1080/00913367.2014.956376

Li, O., Pan, Z., Qiu, H., & Qian, H. (2024). How virtual reality can increase effectiveness of prosocial advertising. *Journal of Advertising Research, 64*(2), 229–244. https://doi.org/10.2501/JAR-2024-011

Liu, H., Jayawardhena, C., Shukla, P., Osburg, V. S., & Yoganathan, V. (2024). Electronic word of mouth 2.0 (eWOM 2.0) – The evolution of eWOM research in the new age. *Journal of Business Research, 176*, 114587. https://doi.org/10.1016/j.jbusres.2024.114587

Ma, J., & Du, B. (2018). Digital advertising and company value: Implications of reallocating advertising expenditures. *Journal of Advertising Research, 58*(3), 326–337. https://doi.org/10.2501/JAR-2018-002

Manchanda, P., Arora, N., & Sethi, V. (2022). Impact of beauty vlogger's credibility and popularity on eWOM sharing intention: The mediating role of parasocial interaction. *Journal of Promotion Management, 28*(3), 379–412. https://doi.org/10.1080/10496491.2021.1989542

Martínez-López, F. J., Anaya-Sánchez, R., Esteban-Millat, I., Torrez-Meruvia, H., D'Alessandro, S., & Miles, M. (2020). Influencer marketing: Brand control, commercial orientation, and post credibility. *Journal of Marketing Management, 36*(17–18), 1805–1831. https://doi.org/10.1080/0267257X.2020.1806906

Mayrhofer, M., Matthes, J., Einwiller, S., & Naderer, B. (2020). User generated content presenting brands on social media increases young adults' purchase intention.

International Journal of Advertising, 39(1), 166–186. https://doi.org/10.1080/02650487.2019.1596447.

Melnychuk, H.-A., Arasli, H., & Nevzat, R. (2024). How to engage and attract virtual influencers' followers: A new non-human approach in the age of influencer marketing. *Marketing Intelligence & Planning, 42*(3), 393–417. https://doi.org/10.1108/MIP-06-2023-0251

Musku, U., & Yadav, P. (2021). Supply path optimization in video advertising landscape. In: Singh, M., Tyagi, V., Gupta, P. K., Flusser, J., Ören, T., & Sonawane, V. R. (eds) *Advances in Computing and Data Sciences. ICACDS 2021. Communications in Computer and Information Science*, vol 1440, pp. 488–499. Cham: Springer. https://doi.org/10.1007/978-3-030-81462-5_44

Orazi, D., Bove, L., & Lei, J. (2016). Empowering social change through advertising co-creation: The roles of source disclosure, sympathy and personal involvement. *International Journal of Advertising, 35*(1), 149–166. https://doi.org/10.1080/02650487.2015.1096101

Pergelova, A., & Hachey, A. (2023): #Sponsored: Understanding the boundary conditions of resistance coping activation in influencer advertising. *Journal of Interactive Advertising, 23*(2), 128–148. https://doi.org/10.1080/15252019.2023.2196549

Pergelova, A., Prior, D., & Rialp, J. (2010). Assessing advertising efficiency. *Journal of Advertising, 39*(3), 39–54. https://doi.org/10.2753/JOA0091-3367390303

Rafdinal, W., Wibisono, N., & Setiawati, L. (2024). Customer-centric virtual reality applications adoption in the hospitality industry: Quality-value-based adoption model. *Journal of Hospitality and Tourism Insights, 7*(3), 1594–1614. https://doi.org/10.1108/JHTI-11-2023-0835

Reinikainen, H., Munnukka, J., Maity, D., & Luoma-aho, V. (2020) 'You really are a great big sister' – parasocial relationships, credibility, and the moderating role of audience comments in influencer marketing. *Journal of Marketing Management, 36*(3–4), 279–298. https://doi.org/10.1080/0267257X.2019.1708781

Rodgers, S., & Thorson, E. (2000). The interactive advertising model: How users perceive and process online ads. *Journal of Interactive Advertising, 1*(1), 42–61. https://doi.org/10.1080/15252019.2000.10722043

Rutz, O. J., Bucklin, R. E., & Sonnier, G. P. (2012). A latent instrumental variables approach to modeling keyword conversion in paid search advertising. *Journal of Marketing Research, 49*(3), 306–319. https://doi.org/10.1509/jmr.10.0354

Sexton, T. R., & Lewis, H. F. (2003). Two-stage DEA: An application to major league baseball. *Journal of Productivity Analysis, 19*(2–3), 227–249. https://doi.org/10.1023/A:1022861618317

Sharma, L., Kaushik, N., Maggon, M., & Sivathanu, B. (2025). Cognitive and cultural factors in metaverse acceptance: A TAM-based meta-analysis. *Acta Psychologica, 254*, 104855. https://doi.org/10.1016/j.actpsy.2025.104855

Sheth, J. N., & Sisodia, R. S. (2002). Marketing productivity: Issues and analysis. *Journal of Business Research, 55*(5), 349–362. https://doi.org/10.1016/S0148-2963(00)00164-8.

Shi, B., & Wang, H. (2023). An AI-enabled approach for improving advertising identification and promotion in social networks. *Technological Forecasting and Social Change, 188*, 122269. https://doi.org/10.1016/j.techfore.2022.122269

Srivastava, M., Abhishek, S., & Pandey, N. (2023). Electronic word-of-mouth (eWOM) and customer brand engagement (CBE): Do they really go hand-in-hand? *Electronic Commerce Research*, 1–69. https://doi.org/10.1007/s10660-023-09743-z.

Stewart, D., & Pavlou, P. (2002). From consumer response to active consumer: Measuring the effectiveness of interactive media. *Journal of the Academy of Marketing Science*, *30*(4), 376–396. https://doi.org/10.1177/009207002236912

Stylos, N., Jiang, Y., & Pergelova, A. (2024). Guest editorial: Marketing via smart technologies in hospitality and tourism. *Journal of Hospitality and Tourism Insights*, *7*(3), 1285–1293. https://doi.org/10.1108/JHTI-07-2024-969

Su, L. Y.-F., Chen, T., Ng, Y. M. M., Gong, Z., & Wang, Y.-C. (2024). Integrating human insights into text analysis: Semi-supervised topic modeling of emerging food-technology businesses' brand communication on social media. *Social Science Computer Review*, *42*(2), 416–437. https://doi.org/10.1177/08944393231184532

Turow, J., King, J., Hoofnagle, C. J., Bleakley, A., & Hennessy, M. (2009). *Americans reject tailored advertising and three activities that enable it.* Retrieved from https://repository.upenn.edu/cgi/viewcontent.cgi?article=1138&context=asc_papers

Wang, X., Zhang, Z., & Jiang, Q. (2024). The effectiveness of human vs. AI voice-over in short video advertisements: A cognitive load theory perspective. *Journal of Retailing and Consumer Services*, *81*, 104005. https://doi.org/10.1016/j.jretconser.2024.104005

Yadav, M., & Varadarajan, R. (2005). Interactivity in the electronic marketplace: An exposition of the concept and implications for research. *Journal of the Academy of Marketing Science*, *33*(4), 585–603. https://doi.org/10.1177/0092070305278487

Yang, J., Chu, S. C., & Cao, Y. (2024). Adopting AI advertising creative technology in China: A mixed method study through the Technology-Organization-Environment (TOE) framework, perceived value and ethical concerns. *Journal of Current Issues & Research in Advertising*, 1–24. https://doi.org/10.1080/10641734.2024.2403485

Yang, J., Zhang, J., & Zhang, Y. (2025). Engagement that sells: Influencer video advertising on TikTok. *Marketing Science*, *44*(2), 247–267. https://doi.org/10.1287/mksc.2021.0107

Yeh, L. T., & Chang, D. S. (2023). Measuring the lagged effects of advertising goodwill on dynamic promotional efficiency in the automobile industry. *Journal of the Operational Research Society*, *74*(10), 2094–2108. https://doi.org/10.1080/01605682.2022.2128910

Yoo, C. Y. (2014). Branding potentials of keyword search ads: The effects of ad rankings on brand recognition and evaluations. *Journal of Advertising*, *43*(1), 85–99. https://doi.org/10.1080/00913367.2013.845541

Yuan, S., & Lou, C. (2020). How social media influencers foster relationships with followers: The roles of source credibility and fairness in parasocial relationship and product interest. *Journal of Interactive Advertising*, *20*(2), 133–147. https://doi.org/10.1080/15252019.2020.1769514

Zaki, H. O., Fernandez, D., Dastane, O., Aman, A., & Sanusi, S. (2023). Virtual reality in digital marketing: Research agenda based on bibliometric reflection. *Marketing Intelligence & Planning*, *41*(4), 505–524. https://doi.org/10.1108/MIP-12-2022-0568

Zhang, Y., Zhu, J., Chen, H., & Jiang, Y. (2025). Enhancing trust and empathy in marketing: Strategic AI and human influencer selection for optimized content persuasion. *Journal of Consumer Behaviour*, *24*(2), 866–885. https://psycnet.apa.org/doi/10.1002/cb.2423

5 Hybrid Pathways to Persuasion

Integrating Online and Offline Advertising and Consumer Behavior

Patrick De Pelsmacker, Gudrun Roose and Cristian Buzeta

Introduction

For decades, mass offline advertising, via television, print, and outdoor media, dominated marketing communications strategies. However, the rise of digital technologies has fundamentally reshaped how individuals consume media and interact with brands. The proliferation of digital devices, particularly smartphones, and the widespread adoption of social media platforms have led consumers to increasingly turn to online channels for information search and purchase decisions. In response, advertisers have followed consumers into these digital spaces, leveraging online platforms to deliver more targeted, interactive, and measurable advertising experiences.

Despite these advancements, offline media and channels remain relevant. Consumers still engage with traditional formats such as TV, magazines, and physical retail environments. As a result, a challenge for contemporary advertisers lies in integrating online and offline advertising efforts to reflect the reality of consumers' hybrid media use and fluid behaviors across digital and physical contexts. As Wind et al. (2002) conceptualized, the "hybrid consumer" seamlessly navigates between online and offline media and environments. Such behavioral complexity underscores the need for cohesive, context-aware communication frameworks.

This chapter aims to contribute to a more holistic understanding of advertising effectiveness in a hybrid consumer landscape by mapping the key challenges of offline-online advertising integration, specifically in terms of strategic decision-making, generating effective online and offline consumer responses, and uncovering underlying mechanisms as identified in the literature. More specifically, this chapter provides an overview of academic articles that report the results of empirical studies related to the integration of offline and online advertising and consumer behavior published over the last ten years. In the next section, we first briefly explain how we selected the articles. The following sections discuss three theme categories: (1) cross-media studies, (2) location-based

DOI: 10.4324/9781003567523-7

advertising (LBA), and (3) integrating offline and online advertising across the stages of the consumer journey. Within these three themes, seven offline-online advertising integration challenges are discussed. Finally, we offer inspiration for further research.

Method

In order to develop our literature review, we first defined appropriate search terms to identify a broad scope of articles published over the last ten years using the Web of Science Core Collection (i.e., SCIE, SSCI, A&HCI, ESCI, CPCI, and BCI). Within the marketing communication and advertising context, these search terms were explored in titles, abstracts, and key terms focusing on offline-online integration (e.g., omnichannel advertising, cross-channel advertising). After removing duplicates, we obtained a sample of 587 unique documents. These articles were then screened using ASReview Lab (Van De Schoot et al., 2021). This open-source machine-learning tool applies active learning to (re-) sort articles so that the authors can assess the relevance of identified articles based on their titles and abstracts. Two authors annotated the papers using a relevant/irrelevant coding system. In order to be classified as relevant, the papers had to comply with the following criteria: (1) a clear advertising/brand communication context, (2) an explicit offline-online integration, and (3) a dependent variable directly tied to advertising effectiveness. Drawing on the SAFE principles (Boetje & Van De Schoot, 2024), when 50 consecutive occurrences were coded as irrelevant to the topic, this implied that the rest of the literature was also irrelevant, and the screening was stopped. The two combined lists of relevant records comprised 149 papers without duplicates. Their coding was then compared, and discrepancies were resolved through discussion. We excluded 91 articles using this last procedure, leading to 58 articles to be considered to be included in this chapter.

Thematic Categories

We organize our review into three overarching categories: (1) cross-media advertising studies, (2) LBA studies, and (3) studies investigating the offline-online advertising integration across the stages of the consumer journey. Within these three research streams, we identify seven key challenges in the field that were addressed through empirical research.

Cross-Media Advertising

Where companies used to select a combination of offline media, todays focus is on delivering a consistent and integrated customer experience across relevant advertising channels, allowing the consumer to interact seamlessly wherever they choose, both online and offline. The shift toward hybrid consumption and media use has made media selection more complicated than before. The following three challenges appear to be focal points in the literature: (1) selecting the right media, the right place, and the right time to reach and persuade consumers, (2) guaranteeing a synergetic effect of the cross-channel approach, and (3) finding concrete means to operationalize the advertising integration across media.

Selecting the Right Media, the Right Place, and the Right Time for Advertising

A first challenge of cross-media advertising is the selection of which media to use. Oz and Istanbulluoglu (2022) compared the short-term effects on sales of four media vehicles (i.e., online, print, outdoor, and TV) based on the advertising expenditures and sales data from 88 companies over 11 years. Overall, total advertising expenditure positively relates to sales in the same period. They find that TV and outdoor advertising positively affect contemporaneous sales, while print and online ads do not. Their results suggest that TV advertising consistently boosts sales across companies and markets, while the effect of the other three media vehicles largely depends on factors like market growth opportunities, industry, and firm size.

A second challenge is advertising at the right time in the right place. *Moment-based* advertising is the practice of synchronizing real-time online advertising (e.g., sponsored search) with relevant offline TV advertising closely tied to current moments or events in a retail or media environment. Using technology that detects live TV ads and triggers synchronized sponsored search advertising, advertisers can instantly adjust keyword and demographics targeting, bids, and messaging based on the detected TV ad. The goal of moment marketing for sponsored search advertising is to ensure that top-ranked search ads with the right messages reach the right consumers at contextually relevant moments.

Liu and Hill (2021) studied this challenge by using extensive TV ad spending data and granular search data, analyzing click-through rates (CTRs) as a performance metric for both sponsored and organic search. Results indicate that TV-moment-based search ads effectively boost CTRs for both the advertised brand and its competitors, showing a positive cross-media effect. Chae (2022) explored the role of context centrality in TV ads (i.e., the extent to which the external content is central to the ad's message) and its influence on viewers' online behavior related to the TV ad. When a TV ad tied to a major event is aired at the right moment, it can quickly go viral, especially since consumers often use multiple screens (e.g., checking phones while watching TV). Viewers immediately search for more information about a brand in a TV ad (online search behavior) or go to a social media site to talk about the ad with others or to see what others have said while watching it (social action). Using data from 1,223

TV ads aired during the Rio Olympics and NCAA events, the author found that TV ads with high context centrality led to less online search behavior but more online social actions, indicating that context-central ads encourage sharing over searching (Chae, 2022).

Creating Synergy

Media synergy occurs when multi-media campaigns create added value for the brand beyond the sum of individual executions (Lim et al., 2015). Cross-media synergy is explained by four mechanisms: (1) the multiple-source effect (different media enhance central information processing), (2) the differential attention hypothesis (cross-media repetition avoids wear-out), (3) the forward encoding hypothesis (early exposures leave memory traces for later ones), and (4) the repetition-variation theory (varied exposures in different media elicit stronger affective responses than repeated exposures in a single medium) (Lim et al., 2015). Several studies explore these synergy effects across online and offline media in advertising campaigns.

Digital media consumption has changed viewing habits, from serial to non-linear media use across devices like mobile TV, tablets, and smartphones (Lim et al., 2015). In their experiments comparing paired and single-media exposure, Lim et al. (2015) found that combining TV, mobile TV, and online video ads leads to higher perceived credibility, brand attitude, and purchase intention than repetitive ads in a single medium. Another type of creating potential synergy is having price promotions running in both offline and online media channels. In a field experiment across 59 grocery stores, Maier and Dost (2024) manipulated promotion channels and product types and assessed the added effects of print and online media above and beyond a sales promotion's base discount level effect on sales. They find that the effectiveness of these advertising channels depends on the beneficiary. Digital ads increase sales of the promoted product mainly via cross-brand switching, benefiting the manufacturer (but not the retailer). In contrast, traditional print ads raised category-wide sales over time, at the benefit of the retailer. A combined offline-online approach yielded the strongest sales gains, suggesting synergy in omnichannel promotion.

Operationalizing Offline-Online Advertising Integration

A third challenge is to find means to operationalize media integration. This is often done via *phygitals*. Phygital tools are technologies that integrate physical touchpoints (like stores, billboards, and packaging) with digital components (like apps, QR codes, sensors, or data systems) to enhance consumer interaction, engagement, or experience. Literature up to now has focused on quick response codes (QR codes), point-of-purchase (POP) communication, interactive screens, and augmented reality (AR) or mixed reality (MR) technologies as advertising tools that enable seamless transitions between physical touchpoints and digital content in real time.

QR codes are two-dimensional codes (scannable via smartphones) that connect offline ads to digital destinations (e.g., websites, apps, coupons), enabling pull-based engagement. QR codes facilitate consumer transitions from print to digital media, by empowering consumers to access additional information while allowing marketers to track engagement by scan source. Notably, the user initiates the QR-code-based consumer engagement process. Consequently, it is deemed less intrusive and more engaging. According to Trivedi et al. (2020), combining pull-based promotional QR codes with traditional push ads can effectively trigger action. Today, QR codes are often combined with call to actions (CTAs) and incentives with the aim to encourage viewers to scan the code and enter the digital environment.

Wei et al. (2021) examined how CTAs and incentive framing in outdoor ads, including QR codes, prompt product searching and further offline-to-online interactions and online communications. By means of a field experiment, they tested three factors: (1) CTA (e.g., positive "scan to win" vs. negative "scan or regret" framing), definiteness of incentives (definitive "clear" vs. indefinite "interact-to-know" rewards), and (3) incentive forms (discount vs. gift). Outdoor ads prompt a three-step process: scanning, clicking, and registration. Positive CTA increases engagement at all three steps of offline-to-online interaction. Indefinite interact-to-know incentives elicit a higher rate of QR code scanning and clicking than definite incentive forms, while definiteness has a non-significant effect on registration. Interestingly, discounts work better when incentives are indefinite, while gifts are more effective when the incentive is definite. Other moderating factors of QR code effectiveness are ad appeal and product involvement. Trivedi et al. (2020) show, for example, that QR codes steer purchase intention in a low-involved product category if used alongside an emotional appeal. Advertisements for high-involvement products benefit from QR codes that are combined with an informational appeal. Also, Ávila-Muñoz et al. (2024) reviewed strategies for enhancing and customizing QR codes without reducing functionality, offering design guidelines for effective integration.

While in most studies offline-online integration starts from offline touchpoints, Anagnostopoulos et al. (2018) reverse the flow. They propose a method for improving QR-based targeted outdoor ads using social media. Using geo-tagged Twitter/X data, they tracked user trajectories and performed user profiling to identify interests and recommend the most promising physical billboard locations for outdoor (QR) advertising. Their results show that even with a low budget in terms of the number of zones in which ads can be placed, for all categories, they were able to cover a consistently higher portion of the interested users (QR scanners) compared to simply placing ads at top crowded areas.

In addition to QR codes, *POP advertising* can also contribute to cross-media integration. Traditionally, static and digital in-store POP displays attempt to draw consumers' attention at the point of transaction. Nevertheless, location-based (LBA) POP ads now offer context-aware promotions. Gazley et al. (2015) used a scenario-based online survey to investigate the effects of customization, permission, and intrusiveness in LBA messages on attitudes and purchase intentions at the POP. Their findings show that higher customization, explicit user permission, and lower perceived intrusiveness lead to increasing positive attitudes toward the LBA and, ultimately, higher purchase intentions. Consumers preferred POP messages to at-home ones, and static displays were still favored over mobile messages. These results suggest that static displays still have a place as an effective POP advertising technique.

The digital and physical worlds are increasingly merging in retail settings. In fact, typical online functionalities are increasingly embedded in physical store environments via phygitals such as *interactive screens*. As consumers grow with the habituation to in-store screens and interactive content, in-store displays are evolving. Also, physical stores are increasingly dependent on impulse visits and the impulse purchases of passersby. Moes et al. (2022) examined the effect of interactive shop window screens on impulse urges. Using three field experiments in a clothing store, they found that highly (vs. less) interactive advertising screens in-store windows positively affect impulse visits and impulse-buying urges. According to the agency model of customization, interactivity enhances self-agency, which could increase positive attitudes toward displayed content.

Finally, also *AR* and *MR technologies* blur the boundaries between physical and digital environments, enabling immersive advertising experiences that connect offline and online consumer touchpoints. They allow consumers to experience digital content in physical spaces—such as AR product previews in retail environments—or engage with physical representations in fully virtual settings, like VR recreations of real-world stores or events. As such, MR can be a key enabler of offline-online integration, functioning as an immersive gateway between the two realms. MR distinguishes itself from earlier technologies such as QR codes, digital screens, or POP displays in that it does not merely serve as a bridge between offline and online (and is thus not purely cross-media) but rather integrates both domains within a single, unified medium. Cowan et al. (2024) posit that advertisers are still cautious about investing in AR or MR, pointing to concerns about return on investment, audience reach, and long-term financial implications. These strategic considerations underscore the importance of understanding when and how MR contributes to integrated advertising value.

Several empirical studies provide insights into consumer responses to MR-based advertising. Ham et al. (2023) show that in mixed-reality social media contexts, virtual influencers interacting with real products can enhance perceptions of anthropomorphism and authenticity, but too much blending of reality and virtuality may dilute these effects. Wu et al. (2025) apply construal level theory to demonstrate that the match between immersive media types (AR vs. VR) and advertising appeals (rational vs. emotional) affects consumer outcomes such as product attitudes and purchase intentions, moderated by product involvement. Focusing on brand experience, Lee and Cho (2023) introduce the concept of Virtual Brand Experience (VBE) and validate a five-dimensional scale capturing the social, intellectual, sensory, behavioral, and affective aspects of digital reality engagement. Their findings suggest that VBE can replicate the impact of direct offline experiences, reinforcing MR's integrative function across online and offline brand interactions. Pozharliev et al. (2022) use physiological measures to show that, compared to traditional formats, AR advertising leads to heightened arousal and willingness to pay, effects potentially explained by increased processing fluency. Similarly, Tsai et al. (2020) explore the role of interactivity and message design in AR ads, identifying instrumental AR interactions and telepresence as key drivers of ad effectiveness. Finally, Von der Au et al. (2023) emphasize the importance of the physical context in shaping the perceived plausibility and presence of AR content. Their findings reveal that contextual congruence enhances rational evaluations but can reduce the sensation of local presence, which in turn affects perceived tangibility and utilitarian value.

Taken together, the studies presented in this section underscore the increasing complexity and strategic potential of cross-media advertising in a digital-first environment. The effectiveness of combining online and offline channels hinges not only on media selection and timing but also on how campaigns are synchronized, contextualized, and personalized. Synergistic effects emerge when advertisers integrate content across platforms in ways that align with consumers' evolving media habits and engagement patterns. Moreover, the ability to trigger online responses through offline stimuli, such as QR codes, location-based technologies, interactive displays, and AR and VR technology, offers valuable opportunities to extend consumer journeys and track behaviors across touchpoints. Cross-media integration is not merely a tactical choice but a critical driver of advertising effectiveness and consumer interaction/response in omnichannel contexts.

Location-Based Advertising

LBA, or location-based mobile marketing, is marketer-controlled information specially tailored to the location where users access the advertising medium. Traditionally, this included billboards and posters directly linked to the user's location. However, the emergence of smartphones with GPS-tracking technology has revolutionized marketers' ability to deliver location-specific messages to consumers in real-time (Gazley et al., 2015). Advertisements containing geo-specific information are now sent to mobile devices via SMS, MMS, mobile websites, and apps to users near businesses running campaigns (Lin & Bautista, 2020). LBA targets consumers individually, in real-time, and based on precise geographic location. These three factors usually enhance advertising effectiveness by increasing advertising relevance, attention, brand recall, and positive attitude toward the brand. LBA has been widely studied within and beyond this review's timeframe, with many studies focusing on LBA campaigns aimed at driving in-store behavior, often through incentives (e.g., coupons) or some other form of sales promotion. Two challenging themes investigated in literature are (1) LBA consumer responses to different strategies and (2) optimizing LBA context dependency (moderating contextual factors).

Consumer Responses to Different Strategies

LBA uses two approaches to deliver messages to consumers' mobile devices, i.e., push and pull, depending on whether or not the consumer initiates the request for information about preferred product categories. *Mobile push* refers to mostly automated, firm-initiated notifications by branded apps that appear directly on consumers' phones. These apps are often integrated with the company's loyalty program, allowing marketers to observe consumers' exact real-time location and know their previous consumption behavior. *Mobile pull* requires consumers to initiate requests for ad content. The mobile pull is initiated by users' active content delivery requests, often through in-app content feeds (Bernritter et al., 2021; Molitor et al., 2025; Shieh et al., 2019). In addition, LBA effectiveness depends on collecting and examining data to target the right customers at the right time and place (Keshanian et al., 2023). Therefore, not surprisingly, much research has focused on exploring the role of proximity (distance from the store) and timing. As to the former, these studies compare in-store and out-store LBA. *In-store (or context-congruent) LBA* research mainly investigates the effects of mobile messages on consumers who are already in the store. *Out-store LBA* explores how location targeting (near the store, in competitors' stores, and other places (e.g., subway)) can encourage consumers to visit the focal store or brand advertised (Bernritter et al., 2021; Ketelaar et al., 2017). Timing relates to factors representing stages in the shopping journey that make consumers receptive to LBA messages (see "Offline and Online Advertising Integration across the Customer Journey" section). Both research streams also consider other location and/or message factors and explore mediating and moderating variables.

LBA enables marketers to deliver context-aware messages tied to consumers' real-world locations. While its potential for personalized engagement is widely acknowledged, the actual effectiveness of LBA depends on a range of factors—cognitive, emotional, technological, and contextual. We discuss recent research on LBA consumer responses in three themes: psychological engagement, trust and privacy, and contextual relevance. Special attention is given to studies that assess actual consumer behavior as a response to LBA, as the latter reflects the real integration that ultimately matters.

One body of research examines how LBA influences *psychological engagement and attitudinal responses* such as identification, perceived value, and ad acceptance. Thapa et al. (2024) focus on consumer-brand identification (CBI) as a key variable, and their study finds that personalized and location-congruent ads lead to stronger CBI, which in turn predicts consumer engagement. Notably, LBA only drives engagement when CBI is present, identifying it as a critical mediator. Lin and Bautista (2020) explore how ad features such as relevance, credibility, entertainment, and contextualization shape perceived value, which positively influences use intention. Among the predictors, credibility had the strongest effect, followed by entertainment. Lee (2018) contrasts LBA with social-local-mobile (SoLoMo) advertising, where messages are linked to users' real-time social media location. For example, Starbucks sends ads and coupons to Facebook users near a Starbucks store, and movie ads can be sent to users near a movie theater. Consumers perceive a higher level of brand interaction, entertainment, informativeness, perceived location awareness, and sociability in SoLoMo advertising than in traditional LBA. Interpersonal connectivity, intimacy, and sociability are key determinants of mobile phone users' participation in social media. This social dimension fosters actual word-of-mouth behavior, expanding the ad's reach through interpersonal networks and enhancing its behavioral impact.

Another major research stream emphasizes *privacy, control, and trust* as determinants of consumer behavior following LBA. Shieh et al. (2025) posit two fundamental issues regarding the LBA practices of companies and brands: privacy management and information service quality. *Privacy management* ensures that companies access and use consumers' personal information reasonably. *Information service quality* relates to whether service providers offer accurate, relevant, helpful, personalized, complete, and timely information with an easy-to-navigate interface in a responsive manner. Their research emphasizes the importance of implementing a filtering mechanism in LBA systems that allows consumers to autonomously select advertising categories based on their preferences, such that the messages are customized to match consumers' shopping needs (mobile pull). Two field experiments were conducted in a large shopping center. The results reveal that filtered (pull-based) vs. unfiltered (push-based) LBA leads to more favorable behavioral intentions through reduced psychological distance and enhanced trust.

Le et al. (2024) posit that *brand credibility and trustworthiness* are central to consumers' acceptance of LBA technology and their intention to engage with mobile promotions. Importantly, social influence and privacy concerns moderate the relationship between customers' LBA acceptance and engagement behaviors. Notably, high privacy concerns decrease the impact of mobile technology acceptance on mobile advertisement acceptance. LBA apps facilitate location sharing when users check in at suggested places, allowing significant social network individuals to engage and respond to these activities. Also, this social influence moderates the effect of LBA acceptance on engagement intentions: a high level of social influence lowers the effect of mobile technology acceptance on mobile advertisement acceptance. At the same time, it enhances the impact of mobile technology acceptance on engagement in promotions advertised through this technology (Le et al., 2024). Trust and privacy concerns also play a critical role in how consumers respond to different delivery modes of LBA. Shieh et al. (2019) found that push-based LBA tends to trigger stronger privacy concerns and a sense of lost control, making it less effective in generating click intentions. In contrast, pull-based LBA elicits higher click intentions, especially among those with high time consciousness. Their study, based on two field experiments with participants located within 3 km of a shopping mall, further shows that time-conscious consumers are more likely to engage with pull-based ads, while those with low time consciousness show no significant difference in response to either LBA approach.

A third group of studies explores how the instrumental value and contextual relevance of LBA contribute to consumer responses. Lin et al.'s (2016) study shows that privacy concerns have a stronger negative effect on perceived LBA value than perceived sacrifice, while perceived utility, utilizing contextual information, and trust positively predict *LBA value*. Perceived LBA value is positively associated with consumer responses to purchasing advertised brands, followed by searching for brand information and passing LBA to others. Shieh et al. (2025) provide an example of relevance and more specific behavioral customization through a mobile pull system that allowed users to choose the type of LBA they received. This personalization mechanism improved behavioral intention by supporting autonomy and relevance, both key psychological triggers of action. *Context relevance* also plays a central role. Hühn et al. (2017) investigated the effect of location-congruent mobile messages through a field experiment to determine in situ if location-congruent mobile ads on the participants' smartphones have a better effect on the user perception and evaluation of mobile ads than non-location-congruent ones. To that end, they developed a mobile application for students that featured campus news and information concerning class schedules. This application also included daily ads for the university restaurant, which were either location-(semi)congruent or location-incongruent. Immediately after viewing the ads, the app presented a short questionnaire to the participants for four weeks, thereby measuring the perceived intrusiveness, relevance, and value of these ads. The results show that the participants perceived location-(semi)congruent ads as significantly more valuable and relevant, whereas no significant results were found for perceived intrusiveness (Hühn, 2017).

A couple of studies go beyond studying attitudes and intentions and focus specifically on LBA behavioral effects. Bernritter et al. (2021) suggest that LBA efficacy depends on its potential to minimize consumer reactance, which can be achieved by effectively combining location targeting (in-store vs. out-store), behavioral targeting (based on consumers' product category involvement [PCI]), and the type of promotion offered (price vs. non-price promotion). The results of their virtual reality lab experiment show that, although in-store mobile ads are generally more effective in increasing sales than out-store mobile ads, this is only the case if consumers have low PCI with the advertised product category because this decreases their reactance. To attract consumers to stores by out-store LBA, they show that firms should offer price promotions to consumers with low PCI and non-price promotions to consumers with high PCI because these combinations of location targeting, behavioral targeting, and type of promotion elicit the least reactance and therefore result in a higher probability to buy (Bernritter et al., 2021).

Zhang et al. (2018) focus on daily customer visits as a behavior effect of LBA. More specifically, they point out that *location-based social networks* (LBSNs, like Foursquare) can help businesses not in prime locations become visible to nearby customers. After partnering with an LBSN, this channel was used in two ways. First, after users reveal their location to the LBSN, a business with a profile on the LBSN can thus be discovered by potential customers. It can use LBSNs to share promotions and gain visibility. Using a large longitudinal time-series data set of approximately 14 million venues in Foursquare, Zhang et al. (2018) examine the short- and long-term effects of promotions through the platform. Their main finding is that check-in-based promotions have minimal impact on daily customer visits. Chauhan et al. (2016) explore whether users' Twitter activity can be used to predict their following physical location. They found that Twitter-based models significantly improve prediction accuracy and may be used for more targeted LBA. Finally, Grewal et al. (2016) provide an overarching framework to synthesize findings in mobile advertising and a further research agenda.

Across all reviewed studies, one clear insight emerges: consumer responses to LBA are highly contingent on the ad's contextual fit, emotional tone, and perceived value. Whether measured through clicks, purchase intention, information search, or sharing, behavioral responses are stronger when consumers feel in control, trust the sender, and perceive the ad as useful and relevant. At the same time, privacy concerns and a lack of control remain significant barriers to behavioral engagement. Pull-based, filtered, and contextually embedded formats show the most promise in facilitating action, particularly when they lead to feelings of trust and transparency.

Optimizing Context Dependency (Moderating Contextual Factors)

An important stream of LBA research focuses on optimizing the effectiveness of ads by aligning them with contextual factors. This line of research explores how the situational context in which an LBA ad is delivered influences consumer responses. Three key approaches to investigating context dependency in LBA include: the (in)congruency between the ad and the user's current location, the physical distance between the user and the consumer who receives the location-based ad and the store, and the level of physical crowdedness in the user's environment at the moment of ad delivery.

Ketelaar et al. (2017) aim to disentangle the effects of location (in)congruency and the type of ad medium (mobile vs point-of-sales) on LBA effectiveness. Using a virtual reality lab experiment, they show that location-congruent ads increase choice for the target brand compared to location-incongruent ads, independent of medium type. However, mobile ads attract more attention in location-incongruent situations than point-of-sales display ads. Compared to point-of-sales advertising, the merits of mobile advertising thus seem to lie in the fact that consumers are more likely to pay attention to an advertisement received in a location-incongruent situation (Ketelaar et al., 2017). Also, Felka et al. (2022) show that, contrary to the prevailing assumption that location congruence yields the best LBA redemption rates, more distant locations such as commuting hubs perform at least as well as location-congruent LBA. They explain this by speculating that consumers in or near stores might be too busy and stressed to appreciate the receipt of LBA. LBAs' potential to evoke positive feelings in their recipients may determine consumers' redemption behavior more strongly than the cognitive component of ad perception.

In addition, the effect of distance needs to be disentangled from the effect of the advertising strategy (i.e., push vs. pull mobile). Unlike standardized push advertising, which typically delivers a single coupon with minimal interface design, pull-based LBA requires thoughtful structuring of information to support user decision-making. In addition, in mobile pull advertising, users engage more actively with a selection of offers. A central question in this context is how to present multiple location-based coupons in a way that maximizes relevance and usability. Molitor et al. (2020) investigated how distance influences coupon effectiveness through two interface design variables: the sorting mechanism (distance-based vs. random) and the inclusion of distance information. They conducted a large-scale field experiment, comprising nearly 400,000 observations across thousands of stores and promotions. Coupons sorted by distance are the most effective compared to randomly sorted coupons. Ranking effects were less negative if distance was not the primary sorting mechanism. However, distance seems more important for coupon choices than the display rank, indicating that distance-based transportation costs dominate ranking-based search costs when combined with random rankings.

Furthermore, also *physical crowdedness* as a contextual factor plays an important role. Physical crowdedness is the number of people per unit area. Andrews et al. (2016) examined the effects of contextual targeting with physical crowdedness on consumer responses to LBA. They used field data from a telecom provider that could gauge physical crowdedness in real-time regarding the number of active mobile users in subway trains. The telecom provider randomly sent targeted mobile ads to individual users, measured online purchase rates, and surveyed purchasers and non-purchasers. The results suggest that commuters in crowded subway trains are about twice as likely to purchase vis-à-vis non-crowded trains. The authors attribute this to mobile immersion, where crowding leads people to focus more on personal screens and become more susceptible to mobile ads (Andrews et al., 2016).

Taken together, the reviewed studies highlight the nuanced and context-sensitive nature of LBA. LBA's effectiveness is based on multiple interrelated factors, including location congruency, personalization, and delivery mode (push vs. pull). While LBA has shown a clear potential to enhance relevance, engagement, and in-store behavior, its success is contingent upon managing privacy concerns, minimizing perceived intrusiveness, and adapting message delivery to users' situational and psychological states. Notably, the reviewed literature demonstrates that even distant or unconventional locations can outperform proximity-based targeting under certain conditions, challenging assumptions of "spatial congruence" as a universal principle. Moreover, the interplay between interface design, consumer traits (e.g., time consciousness or product involvement), and contextual cues (e.g., crowdedness) reveals the strategic importance of tailoring LBA beyond geographic coordinates. LBA should be regarded as a flexible, data-driven practice that requires thoughtful integration of behavioral, spatial, and technological dimensions to optimize consumer and business outcomes.

Offline and Online Advertising Integration across the Customer Journey

One of the most critical factors for effective online-offline advertising integration is the alignment with the customer journey. Advertisers should identify strategic points where consumers switch media environments. The challenge is leveraging cross-media features as gateways that not only connect media environments but also seamlessly align with the customer journey. For example, QR codes and app-based features play a central role in connecting offline interactions with digital experiences, especially during the awareness and exploration phases. A second challenge is selecting and utilizing the right data sources essential to understand and support the journey. Clickstream data can capture online exploration behavior, while physical-movement trajectories and contextual factors, such as time of day or weather conditions, offer insight into offline patterns and situational relevance. The following two subsections examine how existing literature has investigated these tools and data sources in order to align them with the specific stages of the customer journey: (1) finding a gateway to media and cross-media features and (2) selecting data.

Finding a Gateway to Media and Cross-Media Features

QR codes are often considered a gateway from the physical world to the digital world. However, it is important to provide this touchpoint at the right moment in the customer journey. Trivedi et al. (2020) studied QR code effects in print advertising along five decision-making stages: closer ad examination intention, information search intention, positive attitude change, integration into a relevant brand set, and purchase intention. Based on survey data from 326,212 consumer evaluations of 792 print ads from 26 product categories, they found that 6.7% of ad evaluations were close to ad examination intention, 16.4% fell into information search intention, 5.9% selected positive attitude change, 9.6% represented integration into the relevant set, and 4.9% indicated purchase intention (Trivedi et al., 2020).

A gateway in the integration of online and offline advertising that can be embedded throughout the whole customer journey is the *shopping app***.** Shopping apps, mobile apps developed and branded by a specific retailer, offer a variety of online-to-offline and offline-to-online features for different touchpoints throughout the customer journey. These features can support the pre-purchase stage, e.g., product finding tools (filter) or chats with the staff, support the purchase stage, e.g., data preservation or shipment tracking, and enable channel switching, e.g., multi-channel technologies such as click and collect, check and reserve, product availability check, or QR code scanning. Sinemus et al. (2022) emphasize the role of shopping app features in enhancing the impact of advertising by supporting customer satisfaction and loyalty across different stages of the customer journey. They categorize app features into three groups: pre-purchase features, transaction features, and cross-channel features. *Cross-channel features* support switching between the online and physical store channels, e.g., consumers can scan products in the physical store to obtain information about the products online (QR code reader or consumers can return a product in the physical store with the electronic receipt within the app). Among these, pre-purchase and cross-channel features are particularly relevant for advertising, as they shape how consumers engage with promotional content and product information before making a purchase decision. For instance, cross-channel features, such as QR code scanning or accessing online product details while in-store, help bridge online advertisements with offline experiences, reinforcing ad message and facilitating informed choices. These features enable consumers to act on advertising prompts, whether they originate online or offline, by providing seamless access to additional product information, comparisons, and store availability.

Sinemus et al. (2022) test the effects of shopping app features on customer satisfaction and attitudinal loyalty and to what extent consumers have different channel preferences for the pre-purchase and the purchase stage. They studied three different retail sectors, i.e., electronics, apparel, and cosmetics, and find that app users are generally more satisfied and loyal to the retailer than non-users. Pre-purchase features, often linked to product advertising, have a significant effect on satisfaction in all three sectors studied. However, the perceived usefulness of these features is more relevant for consumers with offline pre-purchase channel preference than for consumers with online pre-purchase channel preference. Transaction features seem important for both consumer groups. Cross-channel features are essential for electronics. They have an effect on customer satisfaction with the app and on retailer satisfaction. Cross-channel features support the buying process in two stages of the customer journey. Consumers first search for information on the Internet. After getting enough information, they want to touch and see the product in the shop. In this case, multi-channel technologies simplify the buying process as the customers only need to pick up the product in the shop. In the second stage, consumers first want to go to a shop to touch and see the product. If customers need more information, they can use the QR code scanner or visual search to get more information. For the apparel and cosmetics sector, the importance of cross-channel features depends on consumers' channel preferences. Consumers' offline pre-purchase and purchase channel preferences strengthen the impact of cross-channel features on customer satisfaction. For consumers with strong online (and weak offline) channel preference, the effect of cross-channel features is small or even non-significant. In summary, shopping apps seem more interesting for consumers who prefer to shop in-store. In general, pre-purchase and cross-channel features are most strongly related to app and retailer satisfaction (Sinemus et al., 2022).

Finally, also *AR or MR* acts as a gateway for offline and online advertising integration throughout the customer journey. Unlike traditional cross-media strategies, which rely on sequential transitions across offline and online channels, AR enables simultaneous interaction with both realms within a single immersive environment. Rauschnabel et al. (2022) emphasize this integrative potential by proposing "Augmented Reality Marketing" as a distinct and potentially disruptive subdiscipline. Their customer journey model, structured around the BICK FOUR framework—branding, inspiring, convincing, and keeping—illustrates how AR (advertising) can be embedded holistically across the entire decision-making process. This approach encourages marketers to go beyond fragmented campaign tactics and instead align AR interventions with strategic goals throughout the journey. By collapsing the boundaries between physical and digital realities, AR creates media experiences that are not just cross-media, but trans-reality—shaping new forms of engagement, branding, and long-term customer relationships.

Selecting Data

A second challenge to effectively align advertising with the customer journey is to base decisions on relevant and timely data. Different types of data provide insight into consumer behavior across both online and offline contexts. This section discusses three key data sources: clickstream data, physical-movement trajectories, and contextual factors that help advertisers understand where consumers are in the journey and how best to target them across channels.

A first data source is *clickstream data*. Clickstream data refers to the sequence of clicks and interactions a user performs while navigating a website or app. It includes page visits, time spent per page, navigations paths, clicks on ads (click-through), etc. Goh et al. (2022) used clickstream panel data from an automobile ad campaign to promote an automobile show, to investigate the relevance of mobile advertising and the interrelationships between ad content, information search behavior, and advertising response. In addition, the authors also tested two components of online advertising, i.e., the campaign in terms of the stage in the customer journey (before and during the show) and the campaign's distance to the show's location (in the city or outside the city where the show took place). The dependent variable in their study was whether or not receivers of a mobile ad registered for a car test drive (i.e. actual behavior). The results show that mobile users in the city where the automobile show took place search more broadly and deeply before the show and tend to book a test drive more often than people from outside the city. The positive effects of search depth and breadth on test drive bookings were consistently larger during the focal campaign event compared to the period before the event. The effects of the advertisements were much larger during the show than before (Goh et al., 2015).

A particular subset of clickstream data is click-through data (tracking when a user clicks on an ad or link) and conversion data (completing a purchase or signing up), which is often the end of the clickstream. Ho et al. (2020) explored the differences in response depending on two stages in the purchase funnel, i.e. click-through and conversion. They argue that distance (i.e., the mileage from a consumer to a focal establishment) and local competition (i.e., the number of alternatives in the consumer vicinity) play a decisive role in consumers' responses to LBA. A data set of geofencing ad impressions was collected from a location-based marketing agency in the United States. Data consisted of all geofence campaigns the marketing agency runs in a given month. The results suggest that local competition (but not distance) matters in the click stage, while distance (but not local competition) influences the conversion propensity. They also found a significant interaction effect whereby a higher degree of local competition amplifies the negative impact of distance on the likelihood of conversions. In other words, a higher local competition makes the conversion rate more sensitive to distance.

A second data source is offline *physical-movement trajectory* data which refers to data that tracks a person's movements in the physical world, typically using GPS, Wi-Fi, Bluetooth, or mobile signal data. It shows where, when, and how individuals move through physical spaces such as stores or streets and can be used to infer patterns such as store visits, dwell time, or routes taken. This data helps advertisers understand offline behavior and target consumers online based on their real-world locations and movement patterns. In this respect, Ghose et al. (2019) propose a novel "trajectory-based" targeting strategy for mobile advertising that leverages detailed information on consumers' offline physical-movement trajectories, using fine-grained behavioral information from different mobility dimensions. They designed a field experiment in a large shopping mall that involved 83,370 unique user responses for 14 days and sent mobile coupons by SMS. They found that trajectory-based mobile targeting can, compared with other baselines, lead to higher coupon redemption, faster redemption behavior, and higher transaction amounts in the focal store. It can also facilitate higher revenues for the focal store and shopping mall. Moreover, the effect of trajectory-based targeting came from improvements in the efficiency of customers' current shopping processes and from its ability to nudge customers toward changing their future shopping patterns and, thereby, generate additional revenues. Importantly, they also find that trajectory-based ads are especially effective in attracting shoppers in a more focused later shopping stage. This strategy was less effective for those shoppers who were in the process of exploring across different product categories (awareness, exploration), than for shoppers in the later stages of the journey (engagement, consideration) (Ghose et al., 2019).

A third type of data relevant for aligning advertising with the customer journey is *contextual data* that captures situational factors that may influence consumer behavior. Yoon et al. (2022), for example, address when exactly a persuasive message should be sent by exploring contextual timing (meal and non-meal hours of the day) and weather factors (amount of sunshine). The central idea of a context-related strategy is to utilize contextual information to determine consumers' "point of need," so this information can be used to design mobile advertising in order to increase the revenue of restaurant campaigns on social media. In a field experiment with a newly launched restaurant partner, they developed product promotion and brand messages on Facebook and collected daily transaction data from restaurant diners and delivery app orders. Ads delivered at consumers' pre-decision stage (i.e., non-meal time, searching for information, evaluating alternatives) were more effective for the on-site service than those delivered at the decision stage (i.e., meal time; making a purchase decision) to increase consumer spending on the dining-in service. Furthermore, unpleasant weather conditions (i.e., less sunlight) increased the effectiveness of advertising on consumer spending on mobile app food delivery orders. The authors argue that ads delivered at the pre-decision stage should indeed have a stronger persuasion effect than that delivered at the decision stage for dining-in services because it allows more time for travel planning. In contrast, since ordering food delivery by mobile apps does not have the same level of time constraints as with dining-in, ads delivered at either the pre-decision stage or the decision stage do not lead to significantly different results. Ads delivered under unpleasant weather conditions tend to enhance travel constraints, thus functioning more effectively for mobile app food delivery orders. Ads delivered under pleasant weather conditions (e.g., more sunlight) generate more consumer spending on dining in, while ads delivered under unpleasant weather conditions (e.g., less sunlight) generate more consumer spending on app orders (Yoon et al., 2022).

In sum, integrating online and offline advertising throughout the customer journey is important for advertising effectiveness, and research investigating this challenge adopts a dual focus: identifying gateways that connect media environments and selecting data sources that reveal consumer behavior across contexts. Ads and app features that resonate with consumers at the right moment (during early stage exploration or later-stage decision-making) enhance satisfaction, loyalty, and behavioral response. The effectiveness of such integration is amplified when it accounts for individual contexts (e.g., mobility patterns, weather, local competition) and offers seamless transitions between digital and physical environments. These findings suggest that advertisers must go beyond static targeting to design responsive, adaptive communication strategies that reflect today's consumer journeys' non-linear, hybrid nature.

Conclusions and Further Research

Conclusions

Based on a systematic literature review, we provide an overview of empirical studies of the last ten years that focused upon the integration of online and offline advertising and consumer behavior. Three theme categories of studies are distinguished: cross-media studies, LBA, and integrating offline and online advertising across the stages of the consumer journey. Within these three themes, seven offline-online advertising integration challenges are discussed. These are selecting the right media, the right place, and the right time to reach and persuade unique consumers, guaranteeing a synergetic effect of the cross-channel approach, finding concrete means to operationalize the advertising integration across media, LBA consumer responses to different strategies, optimizing LBA context dependency (moderating contextual factors), finding gateways to media and cross-media features across the stages of the customer journey, and selecting data to explore persuasive effects across customer journey stages.

The studies underscore not only the increasing complexity but also the strategic potential of cross-media advertising in a digital-first environment. The effectiveness of combining online and offline media depends on media selection and timing, how campaigns are synchronized, contextualized, and personalized and align with consumers' evolving media habits and engagement patterns. Cross-media integration is not merely a tactical choice but a critical driver of advertising effectiveness and consumer interaction/response in omnichannel contexts. Location-based advertisements are highly contingent on the ad's contextual fit, emotional tone, and perceived value. Behavioral responses are stronger when consumers feel in control, trust the sender, and perceive the ad as useful and relevant. At the same time, privacy concerns and a lack of control remain significant barriers to behavioral engagement. Pull-based, filtered, and contextually embedded formats are important factors for triggering consumer behavior, particularly when supported by trust and transparency. Integrating online and offline advertising throughout the customer journey is important for advertising effectiveness. Ads and app features that resonate with consumers at the right moment enhance satisfaction, loyalty, and behavioral response. The effectiveness of such integration is amplified when it accounts for individual contexts and offers seamless transitions between digital and physical environments.

Further Research

Our literature review provides inspiration for future research in a number of domains: theory building, different contexts, and methods.

Theory Building

A number of approaches have been used as theoretical lenses: advertising synergy theories (e.g., Lim et al., 2015), contextual and moment marketing theories (e.g., Liu & Hill, 2021; Chae, 2022), congruency/relevance and personalization/customization frameworks (e.g., Thapa et al., 2024; Moes et al., 2022), privacy concerns and reactance theories (e.g., Shieh et al., 2019; Bernritter et al., 2021), consumer journey and timing theories (e.g., Yoon et al., 2022; Goh et al., 2022), behavioral targeting, and spatial frameworks (e.g., Ghose et al., 2019; Ketelaar et al., 2017). However, most of them are rooted in classical advertising- or marketing-related theories. It seems there is no formal theorization about the online-offline integration interplay. Maier and Dost (2024) and Anagnostopoulos et al. (2018) point at the need for more complete online-to-offline (and vice versa) cross-channel effect estimates and posit that a multi-channel retailer or sales platform is required to assess the full set of effects in an integrated study. Studies that explicitly make the distinction between stages in the customer journey and studies that investigate the synergy in online-offline cross-media campaigns are rare, especially in terms of measuring real (buying) behavior. Integrating online and offline touchpoints along the customer journey requires more than technological coordination; it demands strategic alignment with contextual cues, stage-specific behavior, and individual preferences. The effectiveness of cross-channel features and mobile advertising relies on their ability to support consumers in real-time, adapt to their location and mindset, and facilitate seamless transitions between digital and physical environments. Future research should take these gaps in theory building and testing into account.

Different Contexts

There are relatively novel or emerging contexts that warrant further investigation. For instance, a number of different media types and platforms (e.g., TV, print, online, outdoor advertising, mobile TV, digital video, social media platforms (e.g., Facebook, Twitter/X), QR codes, POP displays, shopping apps, location-based mobile advertising) have been studied in past research. However, future research could prioritize newer social media, such as TikTok, and digital out-of-home devices. Interesting studies related to urban mobility and physical crowdedness contexts (e.g., subways, commuting hubs) have been carried out but should be tested in more depth. There is an interesting potential for replication studies across countries/cultures, with different mobility practices, commuting infrastructure, and transportation modes (walking, driving, using public transport, stationary). A number of situational factors, such as time of day, weather conditions, consumer mobility patterns, and physical proximity to store, have also been explored. However, future studies could focus on other situational or individual factors, such as the social context (presence of others), emotional or mood states predicted by wearables, social setting (public vs. private), cognitive load, physical environment conditions (noise level, lighting, environmental comfort), economic context, and health or physical state. More work also needs to be done with respect to different product categories, in terms of their utilitarian or hedonistic nature, search or experience products, and levels of PCI or retail contexts. There is also a need for integrating in-store online and offline advertising (e.g. smart screens, QR advertising).

The Internet of Things (IoT) further amplifies the potential of advertising by generating rich behavioral data that allows for hyper-personalized advertising targeting and experiences. Data from IoT devices can indicate not only when the device is used but also how the device is used via load sensors, motion, temperature, and other types of sensors, or via indicating which settings are chosen. IoT devices can be supported by smartphone applications allowing for gathering additional data and communication with the user. IoT devices can create "smart environments" that, for example, dynamically adapt advertising content based on users' immediate context, preferences, and behavioral patterns. For instance, a smart refrigerator might display targeted food product advertisements based on a user's consumption history, or a connected car could provide location-specific promotional content during a commute. Published IoT research in advertising is very scarce. What type of content can be communicated without inducing feelings of awe or creepiness? Can IoT be used to generate more empathic advertising interactions? Do these new forms of interaction fit into the standard theories of advertising communication and attitude formation and change theories or should new theories be developed? What are optimal design principles for IoT advertising to seamlessly transit across smart home, mobile, and wearable platforms?

Voice-based advertising via smart speakers is a relatively novel and emerging topic that warrants further investigation. For instance, Alexa users are also hearing voice-based ads (Guerreiro et al., 2022). This calls for studying how and when consumers are willing to accept recommendations and voice-based ads via such AI-enabled devices, and which factors are important to maximize these persuasion attempts. Further studies of advertising in the metaverse are also needed (Kim, 2021; Lee & Cho, 2020; Marder et al., 2024).

Methods

Studies using real behavioral data are relatively scarce; most studies focus upon perceptions, attitudes, and intentions. Those that focus upon behavior often measure pre-purchase behavior (e.g. clicks, downloads) and not actual sales. The need for more real-life behavioral data is mentioned by, among others, Lim et al. (2015), Lin and Bautista (2020), Molitor et al. (2020), Liu and Hill (2021), Keshanian et al. (2023). Longitudinal studies, such as the effect of repetition of ads, relationship marketing, and exploring loyalty/repeat buying behavior, are extremely rare. The need for more of these studies is mentioned by, among others, Gazley et al. (2015), Livas and Skotis (2022), Sinemus et al. (2022), Thapa et al. (2024), Molitor et al. (2025).

Several studies about the topics in this paper were not published in advertising journals, but in marketing, management, computer science, or big data journals, such as Marketing Science (Andrews et al., 2016), Journal of Distribution Science (Chae, 2022), Management Science (Ghose et al., 2019), International Journal of Distributed Sensor Networks (Chauhan et al., 2016), Information Systems Research (Ho et al., 2020; Molitor et al., 2025), Journal of Computer Information Systems (Liu & Hill, 2021), and Data Mining and Knowledge Discovery (Anagnostopoulos et al., 2018). The papers in these journals use very different methodological approaches than the ones advertising academics are used to and the articles in advertising journals and are often interesting in that they measure real behavior. Advertising scholars may need to team up with academics of these disciplines and companies that have the data and the expertise to make sense of them.

More research attention should also be devoted to different analytical techniques, such as behavioral tracking (GPS, trajectory analysis, geo-tagged social media), statistical analysis of ad effectiveness (CTRs, conversion rates, purchase intentions), and multi-factor experiments manipulating ad appeals, incentive framing, personalization, and timing.

References

Anagnostopoulos, A., Petroni, F., & Sorella, M. (2018). Targeted interest-driven advertising in cities using Twitter. *Data Mining and Knowledge Discovery*, *32*(3), 737–763.

Andrews, M., Luo, X., Fang, Z., & Ghose, A. (2016). Mobile ad effectiveness: Hyper-contextual targeting with crowdedness. *Marketing Science*, *35*(2), 218–233.

Ávila-Muñoz, R., Bonales-Daimiel, G., & Suárez-Carballo, F. (2024). Strategies and guidelines for the aesthetic design of QR codes in advertising. *Doxa Comunicación*, *39*, 183–202.

Bernritter, S. F., Ketelaar, P. E., & Sotgiu, F. (2021). Behaviorally targeted location-based mobile marketing. *Journal of the Academy of Marketing Science*, *49*(4), 677–702.

Boetje, J., & Van De Schoot, R. (2024). The SAFE procedure: A practical stopping heuristic for active learning-based screening in systematic reviews and meta-analyses. *Systematic Reviews*, *13*(1), 81. https://doi.org/10.1186/s13643-024-02502-7

Chae, M. J. (2022). Context centrality in distributions of advertising messages and online consumer behavior. *Journal of Distribution Science*, *20*(8), 123–133.

Chauhan, A., Tejwani, R., & Toshniwal, D. (2016). Twitter can predict your next place of visit. *International Journal of Distributed Sensor Networks*, *12*(2), 9274715.

Cowan, K., Plangger, K., & Javornik, A. (2024). Insights for advertisers on immersive technologies: The future of ads using VR, AR, MR and the metaverse. *Journal of Advertising Research*, *64*(3), 249–254.

Felka, P., Mihale-Wilson, C., & Hinz, O. (2022). Understanding mediators in location-based mobile marketing and why commuting hubs are so effective—A mediation analysis of a randomized field experiment. *Journal of Media Economics*, *34*(1), 1–28.

Gazley, A., Hunt, A., & McLaren, L. (2015). The effects of location-based-services on consumer purchase intention at point of purchase. *European Journal of Marketing*, *49*(9/10), 1686–1708.

Ghose, A., Li, B., & Liu, S. (2019). Mobile targeting using customer trajectory patterns. *Management Science*, *65*(11), 5027–5049.

Goh, K. Y., Chu, J., & Wu, J. (2015). Mobile advertising: An empirical study of temporal and spatial differences in search behavior and advertising response. *Journal of Interactive Marketing*, *30*(1), 34–45.

Grewal, D., Bart, Y., Spann, M., & Zubcsek, P. P. (2016). Mobile advertising: A framework and research agenda. *Journal of Interactive Marketing*, *34*(1), 3–14.

Guerreiro, J., Loureiro, S. M. C., & Ribeiro, C. (2022). Advertising acceptance via smart speakers. *Spanish Journal of Marketing-ESIC*, *26*(3), 286–308.

Ham, J., Li, S., Shah, P., & Eastin, M. S. (2023). The "mixed" reality of virtual brand endorsers: Understanding the effect of brand engagement and social cues on technological perceptions and advertising effectiveness. *Journal of Interactive Advertising*, *23*(2), 98–113.

Ho, Y. J., Dewan, S., & Ho, Y. C. (2020). Distance and local competition in mobile geofencing. *Information Systems Research*, *31*(4), 1421–1442.

Hühn, A. E., Khan, V. J., Ketelaar, P., van't Riet, J., Konig, R., Rozendaal, E., ... & Markopoulos, P. (2017). Does location congruence matter? A field study on the effects of location-based advertising on perceived ad intrusiveness, relevance & value. *Computers in Human Behavior*, *73*, 659–668.

Keshanian, K., Ramasubbu, N., & Dutta, K. (2023). Mobile advertisement campaigns for boosting in-store visits: A design framework and case study. *Production and Operations Management*, *32*(8), 2438–2454.

Ketelaar, P. E., Bernritter, S. F., van't Riet, J., Hühn, A. E., Van Woudenberg, T. J., Müller, B. C., & Janssen, L. (2017). Disentangling location-based advertising: The effects of location congruency and medium type on consumers' ad attention and brand choice. *International Journal of Advertising*, *36*(2), 356–367.

Kim, J. (2021). Advertising in the metaverse: Research agenda. *Journal of interactive Advertising*, *21*(3), 141–144.

Lee, H., & Cho, C. H. (2020). Uses and gratifications of smart speakers: Modelling the effectiveness of smart speaker advertising. *International Journal of Advertising*, *39*(7), 1150–1171.

Lee, H., & Cho, C. H. (2023). Virtual brand experience in digital reality advertising: Conceptualization and measurement. *Journal of Consumer Behaviour*, *22*(2), 300–313.

Le, H. T. P. M., Yoo, W., & Park, J. (2024). The effects of brand trustworthiness and credibility on location-based advertising: Moderating effects of privacy concern and social influence. *International Journal of Advertising*, *43*(5), 798–823.

Lee, Y. C. (2018). Comparing factors affecting attitudes toward LBA and SoLoMo advertising. *Information Systems and E-Business Management*, *16*, 357–381.

Lim, J. S., Ri, S. Y., Egan, B. D., & Biocca, F. A. (2015). The cross-platform synergies of digital video advertising: Implications for cross-media campaigns in television, Internet and mobile TV. *Computers in Human Behavior*, *48*, 463–472.

Lin, T. T., Paragas, F., & Bautista, J. R. (2016). Determinants of mobile consumers' perceived value of location-based advertising and user responses. *International Journal of Mobile Communications*, *14*(2), 99–117.

Lin, T. T., & Bautista, J. R. (2020). Content-related factors influence perceived value of location-based mobile advertising. *Journal of Computer Information Systems, 60*(2), 184–193.

Liu, J., & Hill, S. (2021). Frontiers: Moment marketing: Measuring dynamics in cross-channel ad effectiveness. *Marketing Science*, *40*(1), 13–22.

Livas, C., & Skotis, A. (2022). Factors affecting the impact of text message advertising. *International Journal of Internet Marketing and Advertising*, *16*(3), 230–256.

Maier, E., & Dost, F. (2024). Decomposing cross-channel advertising support of retailer price promotions. *Journal of Retailing*, *100*(3), 362–381.

Marder, B., Yau, A., Yule, J., Osadchaya, E., Angell, R., Zhang, W. Z., … & Li, J. (2024). What Drives advertisers toward or away from immersive virtual spaces? The metaverse conundrum: Affordances and "disaffordances" through the eyes of advertisers. *Journal of Advertising Research*, *64*(3), 255–283.

Moes, A., Fransen, M., Fennis, B., Verhagen, T., & Van Vliet, H. (2022). In-store interactive advertising screens: The effect of interactivity on impulse buying explained by self-agency. *Journal of Research in Interactive Marketing*, *16*(3), 457–474.

Molitor, D., Spann, M., Ghose, A., & Reichhart, P. (2020). Effectiveness of location-based advertising and the impact of interface design. *Journal of Management Information Systems*, *37*(2), 431–456.

Molitor, D., Spann, M., Ghose, A., & Reichhart, P. (2025). Mobile push vs. pull targeting and geo-conquesting. *Information Systems Research*, *36*(1), 184–201.

Oz, S., & Istanbulluoglu, D. (2022). Advertising expenditures on media vehicles and sales. *Accounting Perspectives*, *21*(1), 31–60.

Pozharliev, R., De Angelis, M., & Rossi, D. (2022). The effect of augmented reality versus traditional advertising: A comparison between neurophysiological and self-reported measures. *Marketing Letters*, *33*(1), 113–128.

Rauschnabel, P. A., Babin, B. J., tom Dieck, M. C., Krey, N., & Jung, T. (2022). What is augmented reality marketing? Its definition, complexity, and future. *Journal of Business Research*, *142*, 1140–1150.

Shieh, C. H., Ling, I. L., Chen, Y. J., & Liu, Y. F. (2025). Effect of location-based advertising filtering mechanism in smart service. *Journal of Retailing and Consumer Services*, *82*, 104113.

Shieh, C. H., Xu, Y., & Ling, I. L. (2019). How location-based advertising elicits in-store purchase. *Journal of Services Marketing*, *33*(4), 380–395.

Sinemus, K., Zielke, S., & Dobbelstein, T. (2022). Shopping app features: Their impact on customer satisfaction and loyalty. *The International Review of Retail, Distribution and Consumer Research*, *32*(4), 423–449.

Thapa, S., Guzmán, F., & Paswan, A. (2024). We are just 10 feet away! How does location-based advertising affect consumer-brand engagement? *Journal of Business Research*, *172*, 114425.

Trivedi, R., Teichert, T., & Hardeck, D. (2020). Effectiveness of pull-based print advertising with QR codes: Role of consumer involvement and advertisement appeal. *European Journal of Marketing*, *54*(1), 145–167.

Tsai, W. H. S., Tian, S. C., Chuan, C. H., & Li, C. (2020). Inspection or play? A study of how augmented reality technology can be utilized in advertising. *Journal of Interactive Advertising*, *20*(3), 244–257.

Van De Schoot, R., De Bruin, J., Schram, R., Zahedi, P., De Boer, J., Weijdema, F., Kramer, B., Huijts, M., Hoogerwerf, M., Ferdinands, G., Harkema, A., Willemsen, J., Ma, Y., Fang, Q., Hindriks, S., Tummers, L., & Oberski, D. L. (2021). An open source machine learning framework for efficient and transparent systematic reviews. *Nature Machine Intelligence*, *3*(2), 125–133.

von der Au, S., Rauschnabel, P. A., Felix, R., & Hinsch, C. (2023). Context in augmented reality marketing: Does the place of use matter? *Psychology & Marketing*, *40*(11), 2447–2463.

Wei, Z., Dou, W., Jiang, Q., & Gu, C. (2021). Influence of incentive frames on offline-to-online interaction of outdoor advertising. *Journal of Retailing and Consumer Services*, *58*, 102282.

Wind, Y., Mahajan, V., & Günther, R. E. (2002). *Convergence Marketing: Strategies for Reaching the New Hybrid Consumer.* Financial Times Prentice Hall.

Wu, J. F., Zhang, Z., Wu, Y., & Tang, X. J. (2025). The effectiveness of immersive media in promoting consumer Products: Augmented vs. virtual reality. *Journal of Retailing and Consumer Services*, *86*, 104323.

Yoon, G., Li, C., & Choi, J. J. (2022). In search of time to bring the message on social media: Effects of temporal targeting and weather on digital consumers. *Frontiers in Psychology*, *13*, 1042714.

Zhang, K., Pelechrinis, K., & Lappas, T. (2018). Effects of promotions on location-based social media: Evidence from foursquare. *International Journal of Electronic Commerce*, *22*(1), 36–65.

6 Rethinking the Role of Reversal Theory in Digital Advertising

Jae Min Jung, Kyeong Sam Min and Drew Martin

Inevitably, companies increasingly use interactive or personalized online marketing tools to engage customers and remain relevant in the market place (Jai et al., 2021; Moes et al., 2023; Rau et al., 2006; Wang, 2021). These tools include artificial intelligence, chatbots, websites, banners, short-form videos, virtual reality, location-based messaging, mobile apps, and social media. As the prevalence of the internet and digital media ushers in an era of unprecedented, two-way communication between companies and consumers, the value of popular websites that provide interactive features has skyrocketed (Cheung et al., 2017; Jung et al., 2014; Lee & Cho, 2020). At the heart of interactive marketing is digital advertising. This chapter introduces a relatively under-researched theory called reversal theory (Apter, 2007, 2015, 2016) that offers promising utility in understanding consumer behavior in the era of social media and digital marketing.

While prior research demonstrates that interactive advertisements are effective (Kim & Forsythe, 2008; Köhler et al., 2011; Lucia-Palacios & Pérez-López, 2021; Van Berlo et al., 2021), relatively little attention has been devoted to identifying the conditions under which the interactivity may harm persuasion (Jung et al., 2011; Schlosser, 2003; Sreejesh et al., 2020; Yang & Shen, 2018). For instance, Schlosser (2003) found that interactivity is effective for casual internet browsers who do not have specific goals in mind, but that it is ineffective for searchers with specific goals. Jung et al. (2011) further advanced the notion of contingency to game advertising. Specifically, they found that for casual internet browsers, interactivity enhances persuasion regardless of the user's need for cognitive closure. For information searchers, interactivity's persuasive effect is contingent upon the searchers' need for cognitive closure. Under high need for cognitive closure, interactivity tends to harm persuasion for searchers (see Schlosser, 2003); however, under low need for cognitive closure, interactivity still facilitates persuasion, even for searchers. Thus, Jung et al. (2011) showed that consumer characteristics, such as the need for cognitive closure, can determine the effectiveness of interactivity. More recently, Sreejesh et al. (2020) tested whether media type can influence the effectiveness of interactive advertisements. They found that consumers were less likely to pay attention to,

DOI: 10.4324/9781003567523-8

recall, and recognize banner ads that were placed in the social media newsfeeds when the level of social media interactivity was high (e.g., Facebook), rather than low (e.g., LinkedIn). The authors demonstrated that interactivity's adverse effects were mitigated when the ads contained vivid elements (e.g., high resolution graphics) or anthropomorphic messages. However, all these studies assume that consumers remain static and they pursue only one goal.

According to reversal theory, individuals' metamotivational modes fluctuate between telic (i.e., serious-minded) and paratelic (i.e., playful-minded) states due to situation, frustration, and satiation (Apter, 2007). Taking this multi-static, non-rational view of consumers (Holbrook, 1994), Rodgers and Thorson's (2000) Interactive Advertising Model (IAM), as explained in Chapter 1, could encapsulate reversal theory's potential role in explaining consumers' online behaviors insofar as motivational states are concerned. However, to date, the advertising and marketing literatures are still slow in adopting reversal theory even though it allows researchers to capture a dynamic nature of a human behavior. This chapter introduces reversal theory, discusses the theory's relevance to online consumer behavior, reviews the interactive digital advertising literature from the reversal theory perspective, and suggests emerging areas for future research.

A Review of Reversal Theory and Implications for Online Consumer Behavior

What Is Reversal Theory?

In the mid-1970s, K.C.T. Smith and Michael Apter proposed reversal theory to explain the structure of mental life. Reversal theory relates to motivation, emotion, and personality (Apter, 1981, 2007). Apter further developed the theory in the 1980s, which has generated sustained interest in various fields of psychology and other disciplines, including marketing and advertising (e.g., Davis, 2009). Surprisingly, the theory remains relatively under-utilized by marketing scholars. Apter (1981) rejects the notion that people's motivational states remain static (homeostatic) and contends that their motivational states fluctuate between two opposite states instead. Thus, most individuals display bi-stability such as "serious-mindedness" and "playfulness." Sometimes, people are motivated to achieve goals by minimizing their felt arousal and engaging in a goal-directed way, which often involves planning for the future. Other times, their behaviors are directed by pleasurable feelings at the present state. Basically, everyone experiences the same universal set of states differently not only from each other but also from within a person at different moments. These universal common experiences are metamotivational states operationalized as four pairs of opposites: (1) telic and paratelic (means-ends dimension), (2) conformist and negativistic (rules dimension), (3) mastery and sympathy (transaction dimension), and (4) autic and alloic (relationship dimension) (Apter, 2015). Each pair of states has basic psychological value and a different range of emotions. The outcome is seeing the world from a particular perspective. Among them, the telic and paratelic states are most widely researched (Apter, 2013) and arguably most relevant for understanding consumer behavior in the digital world.

An Overview of Telic and Paratelic States

Telic and paratelic metamotivational states display interesting contrasting features. Telic states (from Greek *telos* meaning a "goal") refer to a serious-minded state in which individuals prefer a low level of arousals and seriously engage in a purposeful way to achieve a goal. They also plan carefully and rationally and do not pay attention to emotions. In contrast, paratelic states (*para* from Greek meaning "alongside") refer to a playful state. Individuals in a paratelic state engage in an activity seeking immediate enjoyment, spontaneously. They prefer a high arousal level and seek to maintain this state as long as possible. Accordingly, telic and paratelic states are polar opposite metamotivational states representing a means-ends domain (Apter, 1981).

Whereas the telic state focuses on important future goals and planning ahead, the paratelic state focuses only on the present. As a result, a telic state seeks achievement and progress, and a paratelic state prefers fun and immediate gratification. Further, telic and paratelic states include a range of emotions associated with the arousal level (see Figure 6.1).

Figure 6.1 shows that telic emotions vary from relaxation to anxiety as the arousal level changes from low to high. Heightened arousal induced by a demanding task causes individuals in a telic state to become anxious, but they become pleasantly relaxed once the task is completed. In contrast, paratelic emotions vary from boredom to excitement as the arousal level changes from low to high. When individuals in a paratelic state are highly involved and psychologically aroused with an activity, they become pleasantly excited. When the activity lacks enough stimulation, the person in a paratelic state gets bored. As a result, individuals experiencing the same level of arousal may have completely opposite emotions depending on the person's metamotivational state. For example, the same high arousal level can lead to anxiety or excitement, depending on the person's bi-stable state or mode in which the person interprets the motivational experience. This condition provides a unique perspective for reversal theory, which differs from optimal arousal theory (Hebb, 1955), which posits an inverted u-shaped curve with a medium level of arousal showing greater pleasantness than either low or high arousal levels (Apter, 2007).

Reversal theory employs a bi-stability concept; both high and low arousal levels are viewed as two opposite points that are optimal at a given time, and either arousal level can be effective under certain situations (Apter, 2007). Further, telic-paratelic states provide a different experiential structure. The paratelic state creates a "protective frame" (not in a telic state) that helps individuals feel immune from the consequences of failure. This feature helps explain why some people

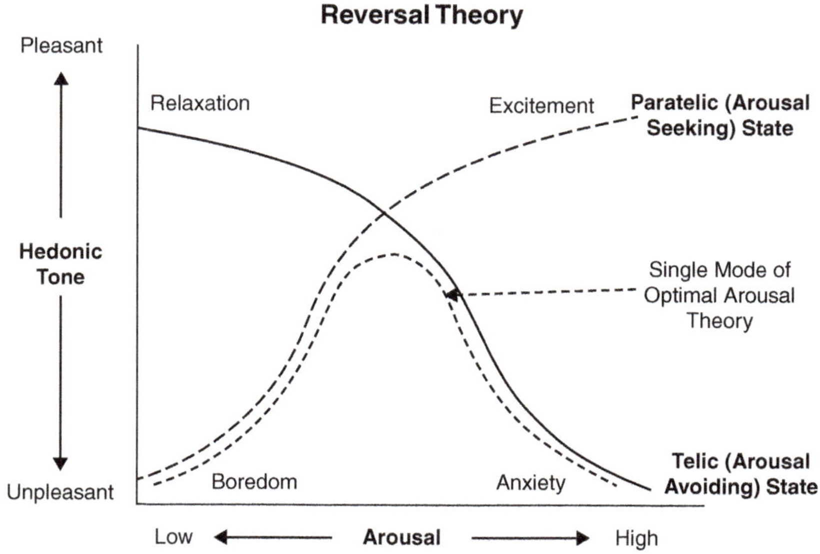

Figure 6.1 The Relationship between Arousal and Hedonic Tone according the Reversal Theory.

Source: Adapted from Apter (2007, p. 19).

Note: The solid line and dashed line presents bi-stable metamotivational state, a telic state and a paratelic state, respectively, according to the reversal theory. The dotted line is the inverted U-shape that represents the single mode of optimal arousal theory.

engage in dangerous sports such as parachuting and rock-climbing (Apter & Batler, 1997). While this behavior initially creates anxiety, overcoming the danger creates a protective frame and induces switching of the person's mental state from telic to paratelic mode. The outcome is excitement as intense as the initial anxiety.

Causes of Reversals in Telic-Paratelic States

According to Apter (2007), psychological conditions, including (1) contingency, (2) frustration, and (3) satiation, may cause reversals in metamotivational states. A reversal likely occurs when the strength of the conditions for change is greater than that of the conditions against change.

Contingency

Contingent conditions refer to situations that give rise to reversals. Specifically, faced with a threat or duty, individuals normally switch to a telic state, if not already in this mode. Removing a threat or absence of duty leads to a paratelic state (Apter, 2007). Additionally, other enduring conditions induce the metamotivational mode.

For example, different locations can prompt contingent reversals (Kerr & Tacon, 1999; Tacon & Kerr, 1999). A university library and a lecture hall were shown to foster a telic state, whereas a university sports center and a student union building triggered a paratelic state. Students in a lecture hall who were in a telic mode were switched to paratelic mode when they were given a surprise break in the middle of a lecture (Kerr & Tacon, 2000). Prior studies of competitive sports demonstrate reversals by recording the activities and interviewing the players (Bellew & Thatcher, 2002; Cox & Kerr, 1990; Males, 1999). Laboratory experiments also demonstrate metamotivational state reversals. When participants were presented with a financial reward, a telic state was induced, but when they were presented with comedy films, a paratelic state was induced (Svebak & Apter, 1987).

Reversals also likely occur due to contingency in the digital world. Filling out an online purchase order form presumably creates a telic state, as the consumer feels relaxed or anxious. Once the form is completed, the same person switches to a paratelic state, feeling either bored or excited. In addition to random events, online or offline retail or service establishments can produce rather enduring conditions that evoke either telic or paratelic modes.

Frustration

Frustration is the second condition for reversal to occur. When individuals become frustrated, they switch from a paratelic to a telic mode (Apter, 2007). For instance, a person who simply wants to have fun playing a game online may become increasingly frustrated if unable to improve the performance. Failing to achieve a higher score, the player becomes increasingly frustrated as the game continues. At a certain point, improving the score outweighs the fun of just playing the game. The game's excitement gives way to the anxiety of not achieving the goal. Frustration results in a reversal from arousal-seeking to arousal-avoidance and a concomitant reversal from paratelic to telic state.

Further, frustration can motivate individuals to switch from telic to paratelic mode. Suppose Bob wants to buy an air purifier to use at home for his family. As he searches for product information online, Bob discovers many brands and technologies with prices varying from less than $100 to over $1,000. Each manufacturer's website includes videos and testimonials claiming superior product technology. Information overload leads to simply too many evaluative criteria. "What should I look for? What would be the right size? Which technology is better for me? Is there any unknown harmful effect of the technology?" Yet, he has a limited time to make an informed decision. Bob becomes frustrated and gives up searching. He thinks to himself,

> Let me just try a product that is priced at or below the median price with an acceptable star rating at a popular ecommerce site. How bad could it be? Having any purifier would be better than not having anything at all.

Bob suddenly finds himself thinking about goal achievement for the family's welfare. At the start of the information search, Bob was in a serious mode, but his telic mode is now switched to a playful, paratelic mode as he visualizes goal achievement. The unachievable goal of buying the best air purifier loses centrality and is replaced by immediate gratification and excitement of anticipating positive responses from his family.

An empirical study demonstrates both types of reversals due to frustration (Barr et al., 1993). The stimulus was a jigsaw puzzle with over 300,000 incorrect ways and only one correct way of combining the pieces. Participants' metamotivational states were measured using telic/paratelic state scales before and after they attempted to assemble the puzzle. Surprisingly, six out of 30 participants (50% female) successfully solved the difficult puzzle. None of these puzzle masters showed reversals in their metamotivational state, probably due to the absence of frustration. Most participants (79.2%) who experienced frustration, however, experienced reversals. Whereas 41.7% reversed from a paratelic to a telic state, 37.5% reversed from a telic to a paratelic state. Further, the researchers confirm that participants' arousal-seeking tendency changed accordingly, reflecting their telic/paratelic state before and after the puzzle task.

Satiation

A third reason for reversal could be metamotivational satiation—an internal dynamic that leads naturally to reversal unless something else happens. Satiation is an underlying rhythm that moves forward and backward between telic and paratelic states (Apter, 2007). People gratuitously switch from one state to another for no apparent reason other than being "fed up" with current trivial daily activities such as gardening, interior decoration, and browsing on social media sites (Apter, 2007). Many consumers spend a significant portion of their time on computers to read newspapers, search for product information, visit blogs about personal interest topics, and check their news feeds on social media. During the course of these routine activities, satiation can kick in, and consumers may experience reversals in their metamotivational states. Lafreniere et al. (1988) confirm that indeed such satiation can explain reversals. Students from statistics classes were recruited to participate in a study of personality and attitudes about computers. Participants were asked to spend two hours on a computer. All participants were given a set of teaching programs on statistics and a varied set of video games. Results showed that 80.6% of participants changed either from a statistics program to video games or vice versa, suggesting reversals in metamotivational states. Subsequent questionnaires and interviews revealed that participants offered no reason for wanting to change the materials.

State Dominance and Individual Difference

Walters et al. (1982) found that some participants' preferences for arousal-seeking or avoidance remain unchanged considerably longer than others, typically toward one of the two polar ends. This behavior does not imply, however, that those traits are stable because metamotivational states did reverse in all participants despite the differences in duration that the one mode lasted (Apter, 2007). This form is the so-called state dominance. Individuals can be telic dominant or paratelic dominant. However, this condition does not mean that those individuals never experience the opposite state. State dominance differs from many personality traits, such as extraversion or introversion.

Murgatroyd et al. (1978) developed the Telic Dominance Scale (TDS). Their scale used 42 items to operationalize the state dominance of individuals in terms of telic dominance. Scale instructions asked participants to choose one of the two courses of action, telic- versus paratelic-related actions, based on which one they would most usually prefer or most closely apply to them. The TDS consisted of three subscales, namely *serious-mindedness* (14 items), *planning-orientation* (14 items), and *arousal-avoidance* (14 items). Although these three dimensions likely correlate, they represent three distinctive phenomena. In addition, Cook and Gerkovich (1993) developed the Paratelic Dominance Scale, which consists of 30 items. These items primarily employed temporal components (e.g., "I often take risks," "I usually take life seriously").

Svebak and Murgatroyd (1985) compared extremely telic-dominant individuals with extremely paratelic-dominant individuals in in-depth interviews. Paratelic-dominant individuals tended to engage in a greater variety of activities, act more flexibly and spontaneously, and appear less well-organized than telic-dominant individuals. In contrast, telic-dominant individuals executed their planned activities more carefully, spent more time carefully monitoring their activities and performance, and showed concerns about achieving their longer term goals. When describing their account of activities, the two groups were also quite different. Telic-dominant individuals were detailed and described events in a more systematic way, whereas paratelic-dominant individuals described events more generally. In addition, the two groups differed in their language use. Telic-dominant people used descriptive language, whereas the paratelic-dominant group favored evaluative language (Apter, 2007).

State Balance, State Dominance, and Change

According to reversal theory, personality is about patterns over a period of time rather than fixed traits. Thus, individuals are flexible and change in their metamotivational states. A consumer might spend more time in a paratelic state than in a telic state over a weekend. This same person might spend more time in a telic state than in a paratelic state on a weekday. Thus, the balance of time spent on one state rather than the other can change. This weekday versus weekend partitioning is referred to as a "state balance," and the state balance changes over time (Apter & Larsen, 1993). State balance differs from state dominance. State balance refers to the actual time spent in one state rather than the other, whereas state dominance refers to the individual's innate bias or tendency to be in one state rather than the other. State balance and dominance tend to associate strongly; however, they do not necessarily move in the same direction all the time (Apter, 2007). Girodo (1985) reports that generally paratelic-dominant individuals changed to telic-dominance after undergoing dramatically serious and potentially traumatic training (e.g., undercover police training). Further, some evidence suggests consumers' state dominance changes toward telic dominance over the span of their lives. Prior studies find strong, positive correlations between age and telic dominance; the older consumers are, the more they exhibit telic dominance (Murgatroyd, 1985; Tacon & Abner, 1993).

Summary

In sum, the telic state is goal-oriented, serious-minded, and arousal-avoiding, whereas the paratelic state is spontaneous, playful, and arousal-seeking (Apter, 1984). Reversal theory is primarily concerned with how consumers interpret experiences (e.g., arousal) rather than the specific content (Apter, 1981). Consumers' complex and inconsistent behaviors challenge traditional psychological theories. Acknowledging that consumers reverse between those psychological states depending on their particular motive felt at a particular time offers a compelling explanation for consumer behavior (Apter & Batler, 1997). Researchers have adopted reversal theory to explain individuals' complex and inconsistent behaviors in various contexts such as stress-moderating effects (Habe & Biasutti, 2024; Martin et al., 1987), design (Fokkinga & Desmet, 2014; Gielen & Van Leeuwen, 2014; Reiners et al., 2024), sports (Hick & Derksen, 2017; Sit & Lindner, 2006; Watkins et al., 2022), tourism (Nørfelt et al., 2023; Zhu & Xu, 2022), behavioral counseling (Blaydon et al., 2004; Hughes et al., 2023), management (Carter, 2005; Rosing et al., 2022), and digital advertising (Jung et al., 2014; Rodgers & Thorson, 2000; Seyedghorban et al., 2016).

Reversal Theory's Role in Interactive Digital Advertising

Interactivity in Digital Advertising and Reversal Theory

Online advertising or communication between firms and consumers can be characterized as interactive (Yadav & Varadarajan, 2005). A computer-mediated environment allows consumers to control online media and communicate back to the sender of the message at any time of the day. With digital technology advancing, new and innovative interactive technologies extend computer-mediated communication's capabilities to a whole new level. The online advertising literature includes several studies investigating how online interactivity affects persuasion (Jung et al., 2011; Schlosser, 2003). These studies manipulate goal types (e.g., information vs. entertainment) and observe the effectiveness of the interactivity in the ads from a rather homeostatic, traditional consumer behavior perspective. Traditional models such as the integrative attitude formation model (MacInnis & Jaworski, 1989) may be adequate in a static environment. However, some evidence suggests that internet users differ from traditional consumers. Internet consumers tend to be more active searching for information (Hoffman et al., 2000; Rosenkrans, 2009). Further, consumers appear to be multi-static and non-rational (Holbrook, 1994), especially when using technology (Mick & Fournier, 1998). Rodgers and Thorson (2000) integrate the psychological reversals into the consumer-controlled aspect "internet user mode" as part of their IAM.

According to the IAM, internet users' motives (e.g., research vs. entertainment) interact with their likely user mode, which, in turn, influences information processing (i.e., attention, memory, and attitude). The user's motives also interact directly with information processing because motives encourage the user to put more or less effort into carrying out any online activity. Based on motives such as researching, shopping, entertaining, communicating, or socializing, online users differentially attend to, comprehend, and form attitudes about interactive advertisements (Rodgers & Thorson, 2000). Further, an internet user's motives closely relate to user mode (e.g., serious vs. playful). An internet user searching for product information arguably is serious-minded. In contrast, a user seeking entertainment is playful. Because users' motives change more frequently while using the internet than traditional media, their mode likely changes frequently as well. Hence, the IAM incorporates reversal theory and classifies an internet user mode as "telic" (high goal-oriented, seriousness, and present-oriented) and "paratelic" (low goal-oriented, playfulness, and future-oriented) along the goal-directedness continuum. Further, building on multi-stability (Apter, 1984; Mick & Fournier, 1998), Davis (2009) reported the coexistence of two reversal states, such as telic and paratelic states, when consumers encounter multimedia messaging services.

Online Consumers' Mode and Advertising Interactivity

Li and Bukovac (1999) found that larger banner ads invited a higher click-through rate from playful versus serious mode online users, suggesting reversal theory's potential value in digital advertising. The Internet Advertising Model suggests that paratelic users respond more positively to interactive online advertising, whereas telic users respond more negatively to interactive online advertising because interactive features interfere with telic users' goal pursuit process. Since then, several studies have employed reversal theory to shed light on the relationship between online consumer mode and advertising interactivity. These studies focus on the persuasiveness of online interactive ads (e.g., Jung et al., 2014) and ad avoidance (e.g., Seyedghorban et al., 2016; Singaraju et al., 2022).

Persuasiveness of Online Interactive Ads

Drawing on the reversal theory and the IAM, Jung et al. (2014) conducted a field experiment to examine how online consumers' user mode influences their evaluation of advertisements that vary in their interactivity. The study used a 2 (advertising interactivity: high vs. low) x 2 (user mode: telic vs. paratelic) between-subjects design. Advertising interactivity was manipulated with a banner ad embedded on a cell phone section of a fictitious online retailer. The user mode was measured using a ten-item, seven-point semantic differential scale: five items for serious-mindedness and five items for playfulness. Before responding to the scale, participants read the instructions, "Please click on the number that best indicates how you were feeling in the last few minutes, just before you started this survey." The authors dichotomized the sample on each dimension based on the neutral point of four, identifying telic users (those who score high on serious-mindedness and low on playfulness) and paratelic users (those who score high on playfulness and low on serious-mindedness).

Results of Jung et al. (2014) showed an interactive effect between user mode and advertising interactivity, such that telic state online viewers formed a more favorable attitude toward the low interactivity ad, whereas paratelic state online viewers formed a more favorable attitude toward the high interactivity ad. Further, the study found that when exposed to the low (high) interactive ad, the telic (paratelic) state online viewers exhibited a more positive ad attitude than the paratelic (telic) state online viewers. Consistent with a mediation hypothesis, the study confirmed that the impact of user mode (telic vs. paratelic) on ad attitude was mediated through an arousal-seeking tendency. When exposed to a low interactivity ad, paratelic state consumers, compared with telic consumers, developed a less favorable attitude toward the ad because paratelic state consumers had a greater level of arousal-seeking tendency, which made them evaluate the ad with low interactivity less favorably. When exposed to a high interactivity ad, paratelic state consumers formed a more favorable attitude toward the ad than telic state consumers because the former had a greater level of arousal-seeking tendency, prompting them to more favorably evaluate the ad with high interactivity.

Online Ad Avoidance

Another fruitful way to investigate the persuasiveness of online ads explores why online ads are avoided. Thus, understanding factors influencing ad avoidance and the role of reversal theory complements the assessment of the persuasiveness of online ads and the role of reversal theory. Ad avoidance takes the form of cognitive (e.g., intentionally ignoring an ad), affective (e.g., disliking an ad), and behavioral (e.g., scrolling down a webpage to avoid banner ads) responses (Bang et al., 2018; Cho & Cheon, 2004). Cho and Cheon (2004) theorized perceived goal impediment, perceived ad clutter, and prior negative experience as the three main factors that increase consumers' avoidance of ads online.

Seyedghorban et al. (2016) extended the original Cho and Cheon (2004) model on internet ad avoidance by including user mode as a moderator. The authors confirmed Cho and Cheon's (2004) original findings. More interestingly, they found that the user mode moderated the relationship between perceived goal impediment and ad avoidance as well as the relationship between the prior negative experience and ad avoidance. Specifically, the positive impact of perceived goal impediment on ad avoidance was stronger among telic users, whereas the positive impact of prior negative experience on ad avoidance was stronger among paratelic users.

While Seyedghorban et al.'s research (2016) explored ad avoidance in the context of browsing the internet, excluding online gaming and social networking sites (SNSs), Singaraju et al. (2022) expanded the scope to include SNSs by investigating ad avoidance on mobile YouTube, a video-based SNS platform. Singaraju et al. (2022) found that the positive impact of privacy concern on ad avoidance was weaker for higher levels of entertainment and informativeness, whereas the positive impact of goal impediment on ad avoidance was weaker for higher levels of personalization. Drawing on reversal theory, the authors reasoned that personalized, entertaining, and informative ads can trigger reversals among the YouTube viewers who are goal-oriented, telic mode, thereby lowering the chances of ad avoidance and increasing attention to ads.

Conclusion

This chapter demonstrates that reversal theory provides a valuable framework relevant to online consumer behavior in general, and digital advertising in particular. While reversal theory is a well-established psychological theory, historical background, causes, state dominance, and state balance demonstrate ample opportunities for future work in consumer behavior and advertising. A review of the interactive advertising literature reveals that the reversal theory has been applied to digital advertising to some extent (i.e., Davis, 2009; Jung et al., 2014; Li & Bukovac, 1999; Rodgers & Thorson, 2000; Seyedghorban et al., 2016; Singaraju et al., 2022). Jung et al.'s (2014) research is one of the first empirical studies rooted in the reversal theory in marketing and contributes to the literature by incorporating the metamotivational state's role in the context of an interactive ad effectiveness. The research demonstrates that the users' metamotivational state and arousal-seeking tendency affect persuasiveness of digital advertising that varies in interactivity. Seyedghorban et al.'s (2016) research on ad avoidance demonstrates the usefulness of reversal theory on ad avoidance when users browse on the web. The positive impacts of goal impediment and prior negative experience on ad avoidance are reduced significantly when consumers are in a paratelic mode.

Findings from the extant research have significant implications for practitioners. Online consumers' metamotivational state changes from telic to paratelic or vice versa during the course of their digital experiences, and the user mode at the time of their exposure to an ad influences the persuasiveness of an interactive ad. This behavior suggests that digital advertising professionals should include both high and low interactivity advertisements (Jung et al., 2014). On the other hand, Seyedghorban et al.'s (2016) finding that user mode moderates the positive impact of goal impediment and prior negative experience on ad avoidance is welcome news to online advertisers. To minimize ad avoidance, advertisers are advised to find a way to put consumers in paratelic mode. One such contingency is when consumers are on SNSs such as Mobile YouTube (Singaraju et al., 2022). In this case, consumers are more likely to be in paratelic mode and more tolerant of advertisements. Further, advancements in digital technology potentially enable advertisers to identify the metamotivational state of online consumers. Enlightened digital advertisers can show either high or low interactive advertising that matches online consumers' modes to maximize ad effectiveness. For example, artificial intelligence-driven marketing campaigns are helping align messaging with consumers' metamotivational states (Graham, 2024).

Since Rodgers and Thorson (2000) first incorporated telic versus paratelic user modes as an essential part of the IAM, more and more studies have employed reversal theory in exploring the effectiveness of digital advertising. Because the rapidly growing use of new technology and innovation (e.g., artificial intelligence, chatbots, virtual reality, voice search optimization, short-form videos) in digital advertising will determine a firm's future performance, however, researchers need to pay more attention to the value of reversal theory as a plausible explanation for changeable bi-stability of human behavior when using the new digital media or technology. This chapter aims to encourage others to employ user mode in the advanced technologies. Further, this chapter only examines one dimension, the telic-paratelic dimension, but three more dimensions (conformity-negativity, autocentric-allocentric, mastery-sympathy) remain unexplored in this context. An essential first step is developing scales to measure these constructs. Moreover, more experiments are needed to show different types of metamotivational states that affect different types of advertisements beyond interactivity.

References

Apter, M. J. (1981). The possibility of a structural phenomenology: The case of reversal theory. *Journal of Phenomenological Psychology, 12*, 173–187.

Apter, M. J. (2007). *Reversal theory: The dynamics of motivation, emotion, and personality* (2nd ed.). Oxford: Oneworld.

Apter, M. J. (2013). Developing reversal theory: Some suggestions for future research. *Journal of Motivation, Emotion, and Personality, 1*(1), 1–8.

Apter, M. J. (2015). Exploring the concept of focus in reversal theory. *Journal of Motivation, Emotion, and Personality, 4*(4), 1–8.

Apter, M. J. (2016). Understanding reversal theory: Six critical questions. *Journal of Motivation, Emotion, and Personality, 5*(1), 1–7.

Apter, M. J., & Batler, R. (1997). Gratuitous risk: A study of parachuting. In S. Svebak & M. J. Apter (Eds.), *Stress and health: A reversal theory perspective* (pp. 119–129). Washington, DC: Taylor & Francis.

Apter, M. J., & Larsen, R. (1993). Sixty consecutive days: Telic and paratelic states in everyday life. In J. H. Kerr, S. Murgatroyd, & M. J. Apter (Eds.), *Advances in reversal theory* (pp. 107–122). Amsterdam: Swets & Zeitlinger.

Bang, H., Kim, J., & Choi, D. (2018). Exploring the effects of ad-task relevance and ad salience on ad avoidance: The moderating role of internet use motivation. *Computers in Human Behavior, 89*, 70–78.

Barr, S. A., McDermott, M. R., & Evans, P. (1993). Predicting persistence: A study of telic and paratelic frustration. In J. H. Kerr, S. Murgatroyd, & M. J. Apter (Eds.), *Advances in reversal theory* (pp. 123–136). Amsterdam: Swets & Zeitlinger.

Bellew, M., & Thatcher, J. (2002). Metamotivational state reversals in competitive sport. *Social Behavior and Personality, 30*(6), 613–624.

Blaydon, M. J., Lindner, K. J., & Kerr, J. H. (2004). Metamotivational characteristics of exercise dependence and eating disorders in highly active amateur sport participants. *Personality and Individual Differences, 36*, 1419–1432.

Carter, S. (2005) Reversal theory: Changing you and your organization for the better. *Training Journal, 2*, 20–22.

Cheung, M. Y., Hong, W., & Thong, J. Y. (2017). Effects of animation on attentional resources of online consumers. *Journal of the Association for Information Systems, 18*(8), 605–632.

Cho, C.-H., & Cheon, H. J. (2004). Why do people avoid advertising on the internet? *Journal of Advertising, 33*(4), 89–97.

Cook, M. R., & Gerkovich, M. M. (1993). The development of a Paratelic Dominance Scale. In J. H. Kerr, S. Murgatroyd, & M. J. Apter (Eds.), *Advances in reversal theory* (pp. 177–188). Amsterdam: Swets & Zeitlinger.

Cox, T., & Kerr, J. H. (1990). Self-reported mood in competitive squash. *Personality and Individual Differences, 11,* 199–203.

Davis, R. (2009). Do consumers experience a reversal state when encountering mobile commerce services? Proceedings from ANZMAC '09: *Australian and New Zealand Marketing Academy Annual Conference*. Melbourne: Australia and New Zealand.

Fokkinga, S., & Desmet, P. (2014). Reversal theory from a design perspective. *Journal of Motivation, Emotion, and Personality, 2*(2), 12–26.

Gielen, M. A., & Van Leeuwen, L. (2014). Found in translation: Bringing reversal theory to design for play. *Journal of Motivation, Emotion, and Personality, 2*(2), 27–40.

Girodo, M. (1985, May). Telic and paratelic modes in operational undercover and field narcotics agents. *Paper presented at the Second International Conference on Reversal Theory*, Toronto: York University.

Graham, M. (2024, November 15). Taco Bell and KFC's owner says AI-driven marketing is boosting purchases. *The Wall Street Journal*. https://www.wsj.com/articles/taco-bell-and-kfcs-owner-says-ai-driven-marketing-is-boosting-purchases-ab3a5f36?mod=author_content_page_4_pos_4

Habe, K., & Biasutti, M. (2024). Theoretical and practical challenges in dealing with music performance anxiety. In R. Timmers & S. Nikolić (Eds.), *Psychological perspectives on musical experiences and skills: Research in the Western Balkans and Western Europe* (pp. 323–349). Cambridge, UK: Open Book Publishers.

Hebb, D. O. (1955). Drives and the C.N.S. (Conceptual Nervous System). *Psychological Review, 62*, 243–254.

Hick, D. H., & Derksen, C. (2017). The problem of tragedy and the protective frame. *Emotion Review*, *9*(2), 140–145.

Hoffman, D. L., Novak, T. P., & Schlosser, A. E. (2000). *Consumer control in online environments*. Nashville, TN: Owen Graduate School of Management, Vanderbilt University.

Holbrook, M. B. (1994). The nature of customer value. In T. R. Roland, & L. O. Richard (Eds.), *Service quality: New directions in theory and practice* (pp. 21–71). Thousand Oaks: Sage Publications.

Hughes, D. C., Ortiz, A., Garcini, L., Serra, M., Kilpela, L., Patel, D., … & Cuevas, B. T. (2023). Feasibility of a pilot study using reversal theory states to test holistic interventions to maximize cancer survivors' quality of life. *Journal of Motivation, Emotion and Personality*, *8*, 6–20.

Jai, T. M., Fang, D., Bao, F. S., James III, R. N., Chen, T., & Cai, W. (2021). Seeing it is like touching it: Unraveling the effective product presentations on online apparel purchase decisions and brain activity (an fMRI study). *Journal of Interactive Marketing, 53*(1), 66–79.

Jung, J. M., Hui, H. C., Min, K. S., & Martin, D. (2014). Does telic/paratelic user mode matter on the effectiveness of interactive Internet advertising? A reversal theory perspective. *Journal of Business Research, 67*, 1303–1309.

Jung, J. M., Min, K. S., & Kellaris, J. J. (2011). The games people play: How the entertainment value of online ads helps or harms persuasion. *Psychology & Marketing, 28*(7), 661–681.

Kerr, J. H., & Tacon, P. (1999). Psychological responses to different types of locations and activities. *Journal of Environmental Psychology, 19,* 287–294.

Kerr, J. H., & Tacon, P. (2000). Environmental events and induction of metamotivational reversals. *Perceptual and Motor Skills, 91,* 337–338.

Kim, J., & Forsythe, S. (2008). Adoption of virtual try-on technology for online apparel shopping. *Journal of Interactive Marketing, 22*(2), 45–59.

Köhler, C. F., Rohm, A. J., De Ruyter, K., & Wetzels, M. (2011). Return on interactivity: The impact of online agents on newcomer adjustment. *Journal of Marketing, 75*(2), 93–108.

Lafreniere, K. D., Cowles, M. P., & Apter, M. J. (1988). The reversal phenomenon: Reflections on a laboratory study. In M. J. Apter, J. H. Kerr, & M. P. Cowles (Eds.), *Progress in reversal theory* (pp. 247–254). Amsterdam: Elsevier Science.

Lee, H., & Cho, C. H. (2020). Digital advertising: Present and future prospects. *International Journal of Advertising, 39*(3), 332–341.

Li, H., & Bukovac, J. L. (1999). Cognitive impact of banner ad characteristics: An experimental study. *Journalism and Mass Communication Quarterly, 76*(2), 341–353.

Lucia-Palacios, L., & Pérez-López, R. (2021). Effects of home voice assistants' autonomy on intrusiveness and usefulness: Direct, indirect, and moderating effects of interactivity. *Journal of Interactive Marketing, 56*(1), 41–54.

MacInnis, D. J., & Jaworski, B. J. (1989). Information processing from advertisements: Toward an integrative framework. *Journal of Marketing, 53*(4), 1–23.

Males, J. R. (1999). Individual experience in slalom canoeing. In J. H. Kerr (Ed.), *Experiencing sport: Reversal theory* (pp. 189–208). Chichester: Wiley Publications.

Martin, R. A., Kuiper, N. A., Olinger, L. J., & Dobbin, J. (1987). Is stress always bad? Telic versus paratelic dominance as a stress-moderating variable. *Journal of Personality and Social Psychology, 53*(5), 970–982.

Mick, D. G., & Fournier, S. (1998). Paradoxes of technology: Consumer cognizance, emotions, and coping strategies. *Journal of Consumer Research, 25*(2), 123–143.

Moes, A., Fransen, M. L., Verhagen, T., & Fennis, B. M. (2023). From direct marketing toward interactive marketing: The evolving interactive marketing tools. In C. L. Wang (Ed.), *The Palgrave handbook of interactive marketing* (pp. 43–63). London: Palgrave Macmillan.

Murgatroyd, S. (1985). The nature of telic dominance. In M. J. Apter, D. Fontana, & S. Murgatroyd (Eds.), *Reversal theory: Applications and developments* (pp. 20–41). Cardiff: University College Cardiff Press.

Murgatroyd, S., Rushton, C., Apter, M. J., & Ray, C. (1978). The development of the telic dominance scale. *Journal of Personality Assessment, 42*(5), 519–528.

Nørfelt, A., Kock, F., Karpen, I. O., & Josiassen, A. (2023). Pleasure through pain: An empirical examination of benign masochism in tourism. *Journal of Travel Research, 62*(2), 448–468.

Rau, P. L. P., Chen, J., & Chen, D. (2006). A study of presentations of mobile web banners for location-based information and entertainment information websites. *Behaviour & Information Technology, 25*(03), 253–261.

Reiners, S., Ostern, N., & Fischer, S. (2024). Decoding ambivalence: The potential of cue-based design for Customer Facing Technologies. *Electronic Commerce Research and Applications, 68*, 101444.

Rodgers, S., & Thorson, E. (2000). The interactive advertising model: How users perceive and process online adv. *Journal of Interactive Advertising, 1*(1), 42–61.

Rosenkrans, G. (2009). The creativeness and effectiveness of online interactive rich media advertising. *Journal of Interactive Advertising, 9*(2), 18–31.

Rosing, F., Boer, D., Buengeler, C., & Scheel, T. (2022). The effectiveness of absence of humour in leadership in firefighting frontline communication: A reversal theory perspective. *European Journal of Work and Organizational Psychology, 31*(2), 200–213.

Schlosser, A. E. (2003). Experiencing products in the virtual world: The role of goal and imagery in influencing attitudes versus purchase intentions. *Journal of Consumer Research, 30*, 184–198.

Seyedghorban, Z., Tahernejad, H., & Matanda, M. J. (2016). Reinquiry into advertising avoidance on the Internet: A conceptual replication and extension. *Journal of Advertising, 45*(1), 120–129.

Singaraju, S. P., Rose, J. L., Arango-Soler, L. A., D'Souza, C., Khaksar, S. M. S., & Brouwer, A. R. (2022). The dark age of advertising: An examination of perceptual factors affecting advertising avoidance in the context of mobile YouTube. *Journal of Electronic Commerce Research, 23*(1), 13–32.

Sit, C., & Lindner, K. J. (2006). Situational state balances and participation motivation in youth sport: A reversal theory perspective. *British Journal of Educational Psychology, 76*(2), 369–384.

Sreejesh, S., Paul, J., Strong, C., & Pius, J. (2020). Consumer response towards social media advertising: Effect of media interactivity, its conditions and the underlying mechanism. *International Journal of Information Management, 54*, 102155.

Svebak, S., & Apter, M. J. (1987). Laughter: An empirical test of some reversal theory hypotheses. *Scandinavian Journal of Psychology, 28,* 189–198.

Svebak, S., & Murgatroyd, S. (1985). Metamotivational dominance: A multimethod validation of reversal theory constructs. *Journal of Personality and Social Psychology, 48*(1), 107–116.

Tacon, P., & Abner, B. (1993). Normative and other data for the Telic Dominance and Negativism Dominance Scales. In J. H. Kerr, S. Murgatroyd, & M. J. Apter (Eds.), *Advances in reversal theory* (pp. 165–176). Amsterdam: Swets & Zeitlinger.

Tacon, P., & Kerr, J. H. (1999). Metamotivational states in sport locations and activities. In J. H. Kerr (Ed.), *Experiencing sport: Reversal theory* (pp. 175–187). Chichester: Wiley Publications.

Van Berlo, Z. M., Van Reijmersdal, E. A., & Eisend, M. (2021). The gamification of branded content: A meta-analysis of advergame effects. *Journal of Advertising, 50*(2), 179–196.

Walters, J., Apter, M. J., & Svebak, S. (1982). Colour preference, arousal and the theory of psychological reversals. *Motivation and Emotion, 6,* 193–215.

Wang, C. L. (2021). New frontiers and future directions in interactive marketing: Inaugural Editorial. *Journal of Research in Interactive Marketing, 15*(1), 1–9.

Watkins, L., Wilson, M., & Buscombe, R. (2022). Examining the diversity of ultra-running motivations and experiences: A reversal theory perspective. *Psychology of Sport and Exercise, 63*, 102271.

Yadav, M. S., & Varadarajan, R. (2005). Interactivity in the electronic marketplace: An exposition of the concept and implication for research. *Journal of the Academy of Marketing Science, 33*(4), 585–603.

Yang, F., & Shen, F. (2018). Effects of web interactivity: A meta-analysis. *Communication Research, 45*(5), 635–658.

Zhu, D., & Xu, H. (2022). Novice tourists' play experience in commercial outdoor adventure tourism: The perspective of reversal theory. *Journal of Outdoor Recreation and Tourism, 39*, 100529.

Part III

Experience

Interactivity, Immersion, and Engagement

7 Theoretical Landscapes in Influencer Advertising

A Framework-Based Review and Future Directions

Chen Lou, Zhuoman Li, Mingxi Sun, Diotima Chattoraj and Jiayue Sun

By looking into the research published between 2003 and 2025 (e.g., Ye et al., 2021), we have identified the top theories widely tested or applied in influencer advertising. We categorize the theories into five groups: influencer-centered, influencer content-centered, influencer–follower relationship-centered, platform/context-centered, and user/follower-centered. For instance, for theories associated with influencers, we recognized the top four theories, including source credibility, brand personality, human brand theory (HBT), and authenticity framework. For theories often applied in explicating how consumers or followers respond to influencer advertising, the following theories emerged: persuasion knowledge model (PKM), social learning theory (SLT), uses and gratifications (U&G), dual processing theories, social comparison theory (SCT), and computers are social actors (CASA) theory. We elaborate on each theory and review how they have been applied or tested in examining influencer advertisements below.

Influencers

Source Credibility

The concept of source credibility, originating from Hovland and Weiss (1951), posits that the persuasiveness of a message is largely determined by the perceived credibility of its source. Credibility is generally defined through two fundamental dimensions: expertise and trustworthiness. Expertise refers to the extent to which the source is perceived as competent or knowledgeable, while trustworthiness concerns the degree to which the source is viewed as honest, ethical, or unbiased. McGuire (1985) further proposed a third dimension of source credibility—attractiveness—describing a source's physical appeal or overall likeability. Recently, research on influencer advertising adopted a fourth dimension—source similarity or the perceived likeness of the source to the audience—to further extend the conceptualization of source credibility (Lou & Yuan, 2019; Munnukka, Uusitalo, & Toivonen, 2016).

DOI: 10.4324/9781003567523-10

Indeed, recent research reinforce source credibility's multifaceted impact: In commercial settings, trustworthiness, attractiveness, and similarity were found to positively predict followers' trust in influencers' sponsored posts, which in turn was positively correlated with consumers' brand awareness and purchase intentions (Lou & Yuan, 2019). In prosocial domains, influencer credibility has also been found to shape public health behavior. For instance, recent research has shown that influencers can enhance individuals' willingness to receive COVID-19 vaccines, with trust in vaccines mediating the link between influencer credibility and behavioral intentions (Alam et al., 2024). Overall, these findings highlight source credibility as a critical factor shaping consumer responses in both promotional and social marketing contexts and position it as an indispensable theoretical lens for understanding consumer engagement and decision-making in the context of influencer advertising.

Brand Personality

Brand personality, defined by Aaker (1997) as "the set of human characteristics associated with a brand" (p. 347), provides a foundational framework for understanding consumer–brand relationships through traits such as sincerity, excitement, competence, sophistication, and ruggedness (Escalas & Bettman, 2005). Carlson and Donavan (2013) argue for a more focused conceptualization, limiting brand personality to traits that are both applicable and relevant to brands, typically expressed as descriptive adjectives. This refined perspective highlights how specific traits of influencers affect consumer perceptions, trust, and loyalty, especially when aligned with consumer expectations and contextual relevance (Lee & Eastin, 2020; Misiak, Kowalczyk, & Guzik, 2025).

Initially applied in marketing and sport management to connect team traits with fan identification and engagement (Azoulay & Kapferer, 2003; Carlson, Donavan, & Cumiskey, 2009; Heere, 2010), brand personality theory has expanded to digital marketing, especially influencer advertising. Social media influencers (SMIs) operate as "human brands" who curate personas embodying brand personality traits, effectively analyzed within this framework (Khamis, Ang, & Welling, 2017). Empirical studies show that followers' perceptions of influencers' traits—such as sincerity, excitement, competence, and trustworthiness—enhance consumer attitudes and purchase intentions. For example, sincerity and excitement improve attitudes toward influencers (Lim et al., 2017), while competence and trustworthiness strengthen the link between influencer appeal and purchase intention, highlighting the importance of personality congruence (Jin, Muqaddam, & Ryu, 2019). Moreover, alignment between influencer's personality and brand identity enhances endorsement authenticity, psychological proximity, and consumer engagement (Djafarova & Rushworth,

2017). Personality transfer strengthens brand perception, as followers project influencer traits onto endorsed brands, consistent with Keller's (2009) associative brand transfer concept (Lou & Yuan, 2019). Furthermore, influencer personality traits foster parasocial bonds that increase message receptivity and deepen emotional brand connections (Schouten, Janssen, & Verspaget, 2020). Overall, these findings position brand personality theory as a robust framework explaining how influencers function as effective brand messengers in digital marketing.

Human Brand Theory

Thomson (2006) defines a human brand as "any well-known persona who is the subject of marketing communication efforts" (p. 104). HBT conceptualizes individuals as brands with distinct, consistent traits—such as name, image, and personality—that shape consumer perceptions and emotional responses (Kim & Kim, 2022; Thomson, 2006). These traits are deliberately managed to enhance appeal and differentiation, particularly in digital and influencer marketing contexts (Lee & Eastin, 2020; Khamis, Ang, & Welling, 2017). Human brands often embody qualities like sincerity, authenticity, and attractiveness, which increase credibility and emotional resonance (Ki, Park, & Kim., 2020; Lee & Eastin, 2020). HBT has been widely applied and empirically tested in influencer advertising, demonstrating how SMIs operate as human brands by strategically cultivating trust, authenticity, and expertise to foster strong consumer engagement and brand outcomes (Thomson, 2006; Kim & Kim, 2021; Lee & Eastin, 2020).

Research has shown that influencers are perceived as human brands when they fulfil followers' psychological needs and maintain sincerity, interactivity, and consistency (Ki, Park, & Kim, 2020; Malik, Thapa, & Paswan, 2023). These qualities increase identification, trust, and parasocial bonds, which in turn improve endorsement effectiveness and brand attitudes (Kim & Kim, 2021; Jin & Ryu, 2020; Janssen et al., 2022). Studies also find that traits like honesty, attractiveness, and approachability strengthen emotional resonance and parasocial engagement (Lee & Eastin, 2020), while perceived expertise enhances persuasion and purchase intent (Jin & Ryu, 2020). Positive influencer traits often transfer to endorsed products, especially when branding is consistent and authentic (Choi & Rifon, 2012; Lee & Watkins, 2016). Importantly, research highlights that smaller or micro-influencers may outperform larger ones in fostering trust and engagement due to their perceived relatability (De Veirman, Cauberghe, & Hudders, 2017). Overall, HBT has proven valuable in explaining how SMIs create and sustain influence through strategic self-branding, enabling effective advertising outcomes by fostering authenticity, emotional connection, and perceived expertise (Ki et al., 2020; Lee & Eastin, 2020; Malik et al., 2023; Jin & Ryu, 2020; Janssen et al., 2022).

Authenticity Framework

Authenticity is widely regarded as a significant component of advertising success, as it enhances brand trust (Grayson & Martinec, 2004), fosters emotional connections between consumers and brands, elicits consumer empathy (Stern, 1994), and helps overcome consumer skepticism toward advertisements (Becker et al., 2019; Darke & Ritchie, 2007).

Although there is no universally accepted definition, authenticity is often considered paradoxical, as labeling something as authentic—especially in advertising contexts—can actually undermine its perceived genuineness (Ebben & Bull, 2023; Schulze, 2017). Broadly, authenticity refers to what is perceived as genuine, real, and true (Beverland & Farrelly, 2010; Grayson & Martinec, 2004). From a psychological perspective, it has been defined as the unobstructed operation of one's true or core self in daily life (Kernis & Goldman, 2006). In advertising research, authenticity is often conceptualized as either indexical authenticity, grounded in factual evidence and direct connections to reality, or iconic authenticity, based on perceived resemblance or symbolic representation (Grayson & Martinec, 2004).

In the context of influencer advertising, authenticity refers to the perception that influencers present their genuine and unfiltered selves to their audiences, which profoundly shapes the complex relationships between brands, influencers, and consumers (Amini, 2025). Research in this domain has largely focused on followers' perceptions of SMI authenticity and its impact on advertising outcomes. Specifically, authenticity often functions as an independent variable or mediator, explaining how different types of influencers affect advertising effectiveness. Key outcomes examined include consumers' willingness to pay for endorsed products, attitudes toward the brand, and electronic word-of-mouth (eWOM), with studies consistently finding that authenticity positively predicts these outcomes (e.g., Boerman et al., 2017; Campbell & Evans, 2018; Evans et al., 2017; Kim & Wang, 2024; Weismueller et al., 2020). There is also an emerging research focus on virtual influencers (VIs). Generally, VIs are considered to lack of authenticity (Kádeková & Holienčinova, 2018; Sands et al., 2022). However, recent findings suggest VIs can match the effectiveness of human influencers (HIs), especially in non-commercial messaging where they even elicit higher perceptions of authenticity (Kim & Wang, 2024).

However, research on how influencers perceive their own authenticity remains limited (Balaban & Szambolics, 2022). Moreover, understanding how advertising disclosure practices, different influencer types (such as VIs), and message intent (profit vs. non-profit) influence authenticity perceptions represents a critical yet understudied area that is vital for comprehending their impact on consumer responses and marketing effectiveness (Kim, Park, Kim, 2023; Kim & Wang, 2024).

Influencer Content

Narrative Transportation Theory

Narrative transportation theory, first introduced by Green and Brock (2000), describes a psychological process in which individuals become mentally and emotionally immersed in a story, leading to reduced counterarguing and heightened empathy toward characters. Compared with the traditional dual-processing models that emphasize rational scrutiny, narrative processing engages both cognitive and affective systems. When consumers are prompted to imagine themselves using or experiencing the promoted product, mental simulation increases narrative transportation and improves persuasion (Escalas, 2004).

Influencer marketing, especially when embedded in storytelling formats on social media, provides fertile ground for narrative transportation. Influencer posts that combine text, visuals, and personal experiences often act as narrative episodes with identifiable characters and plotlines. This enables followers to become absorbed in the story world and connect emotionally with both the influencer and the associated brand (e.g., Feng, Chen, & Kong, 2020; Lim & Childs, 2020). The effectiveness of such narrative experiences can also be different in terms of the influencer type. For example, human or VI comparisons show that VIs may offer unique emotional benefits and novelty effects (Jain et al., 2024). Narrative transportation can be disrupted when persuasion cues, such as sponsorship disclosures, activate consumers' persuasion knowledge; yet, this negative effect may be relieved by social proof, such as likes and shares (Seo et al., 2018).

Overall, narrative transportation theory is a solid theoretical framework for understanding how influencer marketing works, especially in digital and visual contexts. Its effectiveness depends on various factors: narrative style, influencer identity, disclosure practices, and platform affordance, among others.

Advertising Value Theory

Advertising value theory (AVT), introduced by Ducoffe (1995), defines advertising value as consumers' subjective assessment of an ad's utility or worth, extending Zeithaml's (1988) concept of product value. Ducoffe (1995, 1996) contends that consumers evaluate ads by the time and attention they invest, with perceived informativeness, entertainment, and irritation shaping ads' overall value.

AVT has been applied in influencer marketing to explain how audiences evaluate influencer (sponsored) content, which, in turn, affects brand awareness, trust, or purchase intentions (e.g., Lou & Yuan, 2019; Lou & Kim, 2019). When influencers embed product information within emotionally engaging or visually appealing narratives—such as tutorials or lifestyle vlogs—perceived ad value increases (De Veirman, Cauberghe, & Hudders, 2017; Djafarova & Rushworth, 2017; Lou & Yuan, 2019). Informativeness, especially through detailed reviews or how-to content, enhances brand awareness and purchase intent (Lou & Yuan, 2019), while entertainment via humor, storytelling, or visuals boosts engagement and recall (Lim et al., 2017). In contrast, irritation from intrusive or inauthentic promotions reduces credibility and leads to disengagement, including unfollowing (Evans et al., 2017; Wojdynski & Evans, 2016), with long-term trust also being affected (Campbell & Grimm, 2019). These findings affirm AVT's adaptability in explaining consumer responses to influencer (sponsored) content.

Influencer–Follower Relation

PSR, PSI, and Trans-PSR

PSR, first introduced by Horton and Wohl (1956), refers to a one-sided engagement and emotional attachment that resembles, to some extent, real-life interpersonal connections, typically formed with media figures such as celebrities, TV personalities, or influencers. Similarly, parasocial interaction (PSI) involves individuals' one-sided situational reactions toward characters portrayed in mass media (Liebers & Schramm, 2023). Abidin (2015) challenged the classical PSR and PSI frameworks within the context of SMIs, demonstrating that influencer–follower relationships are fundamentally more interactive, reciprocal, and co-constructed than traditional conceptions of parasocial connections. In line with this, Lou (2022) proposes a trans-parasocial relationship (trans-PSR) that is (a)synchronously interactive, collectively reciprocal, and co-created, extending these traditional frameworks by emphasizing that contemporary interactions between influencers and followers transcend unilateral engagement, highlighting a dynamic, ongoing exchange that significantly blurs the lines between parasocial and genuine social interactions.

In advertising research, PSI and PSR are regarded as crucial factors for the persuasive success of influencer marketing (e.g., Beckert & Naderer, 2023; Bizjak Zabukovec & Faganel, 2024; Hudders, De Jans, & De Veirman, 2021). Studies indicate that PSI positively influences various persuasive outcomes of influencer marketing, such as brand trust, brand and product attitudes, purchase intentions, and eWOM intentions (Breves et al., 2021; Hwang & Zhang, 2018; Lou, 2022; Sokolova & Kefi, 2020; Sundermann & Munnukka, 2022). Typically, PSI and PSR are examined as moderators, influencing the strength of the relationship between persuasion knowledge activation and consumer responses. Strong PSI and PSR can mitigate the negative impact of recognizing manipulative advertising tactics, enhancing consumer resilience when they feel personally connected to the influencer (e.g., Boerman & Van Reijmersdal, 2020; Borchers, Hagelstein, & Beckert, 2022; Hwang & Zhang, 2018; Lou & Kim, 2019; Yuan &

Lou, 2020). However, some studies have found no moderating effect of PSR in specific contexts, such as the marketing of unhealthy products, suggesting that the role of PSR can vary based on contextual factors.

Social Media Platform and Context

Congruence Theory

Congruency theory, also known as congruity or consistency theory, was firstly introduced by Osgood and Tannenbaum (1955). It proposes that individuals look for cognitive consistency between their attitudes, beliefs, and the information they encounter. In influencer marketing, congruency theory explains how the perceived fit between an influencer and a brand or product affects consumer responses (De Veirman, Cauberghe, & Hudders, 2017; Ju & Lou, 2022). When the influencer's characteristics such as the expertise, lifestyle, or social status align with the brand's image or values, the endorsement is more likely to be perceived as authentic and persuasive (Breves et al., 2019; Schouten, Janssen, & Verspaget, 2020). This congruence facilitates symbolic meaning transfer from the influencer to the brand, enhancing brand equity and visibility. Importantly, the effectiveness of congruent endorsements varies by influencer type (e.g., Djafarova & Rushworth, 2017; Sokolova & Perez, 2021). Studies have found that macro-influencers, due to their wide reach, tend to be more effective for mainstream, high-popularity brands. In contrast, micro-influencers, who are perceived as more relatable and trustworthy, are better suited for niche or emerging brands (Djafarova & Rushworth, 2017; Sokolova & Perez, 2021).

Recent experiments show that influencer–brand congruence can significantly boost purchase intentions, particularly when the influencer's popularity aligns with the brand's perceived popularity (Ceylan & Hayran, 2025). Furthermore, PSRs may moderate the effect of congruency (Stein, Breves, & Anders, 2022). In particular, when consumers feel emotionally connected to an influencer, they may extend their trust to the endorsed brand, even in cases of moderate incongruence. Overall, congruency theory provides a useful lens for understanding how and why the fit between influencers and brands influences consumer perceptions and reactions.

Followers or Consumers

Persuasion Knowledge Model

The PKM, originally developed by Friestad and Wright (1994), is a seminal theoretical framework for understanding how individuals interpret and respond to persuasive communications. It posits that consumers develop "persuasion knowledge"—a sophisticated understanding of persuasive tactics and marketing communications that accumulates throughout their lifetime experiences with advertising. This concept is closely aligned with what scholars refer to as "advertising literacy" (Boerman et al., 2018). Within PKM, it can be classified into three core components: persuasion knowledge, agent knowledge, and topic knowledge (Friestad & Wright, 1995).

Later developments to the model conceptualize persuasion knowledge operate along two distinct dimensions: conceptual persuasion knowledge (CPK) and attitudinal persuasion knowledge (APK) (Rozendaal et al., 2011). CPK represents consumers' cognitive ability to recognize and identify commercial content and persuasive intent, encompassing advertising recognition (Boerman & Muller, 2022) and understanding of selling and persuasive intent (Borchers, Hagelstein, & Beckert, 2022; Evans et al., 2022; Lou, 2022; Van der Bend et al., 2023). Additionally, APK captures the affective and evaluative responses that consumers develop toward persuasive attempts, manifesting through critical attitudes such as skepticism, distrust, and moral evaluations of advertising practices (Boerman et al., 2018; Friestad & Wright, 1994).

PKM has been widely applied to examine how different types of sponsorship disclosures and varying levels of consumer involvement influence perception and processing of advertising content (Boerman & Muller, 2022; Giuffredi-Kahr, Petrova, & Malär, 2022; Voorveld, Meppelink, & Boerman, 2024; Yang, 2022). The framework has also proven particularly valuable for understanding how influencer characteristics, including influencer tier and perceived personality traits, affect the activation and subsequent effects of consumers' persuasion knowledge (e.g., Boerman et al., 2024; Lou, 2022). Additionally, PKM serves as an explanatory framework for understanding advertising effects mechanisms, with researchers utilizing key constructs such as advertisement recognition and advertisement resistance as mediating variables in influencer marketing effectiveness models (e.g., Yang, 2022).

Social Learning Theory

SLT explains how individuals acquire behaviors and attitudes by observing others—particularly when those behaviors appear rewarded—through four key processes: attention, retention, reproduction, and motivation (Bandura, 1977, 2009). In advertising context, SLT often explains how message content and the observer's traits and perceived rewards actively influence recall, attitudes, and purchase intentions (Fullagar & Barling, 1983).

SLT has been used to explain how followers, particularly younger users, learn by observing and imitating influencers' behaviors, attitudes, and consumption practices (De Jans, Cauberghe, & Hudders, 2017; De Jans et al., 2020; Gannon & Prothero, 2018; Shen & Ho, 2020). Several studies confirm SLT in influencer contexts: audiences (especially youth) tend to observe and imitate influencer behaviors and choices. For instance, influencer-led beauty communities can operate as informal learning spaces, enabling users to develop expertise through peer exchange and influencer demonstration (Gannon & Prothero, 2018). Research also indicates that children may model their identities and consumption practices after YouTubers (Martínez & Olsson, 2019). Moreover, exposure to influencer promotions has been linked to increased snack consumption among children, even when advertising disclosures are present (Coates et al., 2019a, 2019b).

These findings suggest that SLT effectively explains how influencers act as aspirational role models who shape consumer identity, behavior, and learning, particularly among youth, thereby driving emotional engagement and influencing consumption patterns.

Social Identity Theory

Social identity theory (SIT) was originally proposed by Tajfel and Turner (1979); it posits that individuals obtain part of their self-concept from the social groups they belong to, such as those defined by race, gender, lifestyle, or ideology. People tend to favor their in-group members (the group they identify with) while distancing themselves from out-group members. This in-group bias can influence individuals' cognitive processing, perception of message credibility, and/or behavioral responses (Hornsey, 2008).

In the context of influencer marketing, SIT has been applied to explore how identity alignment between consumers and influencers affects message effectiveness (e.g., Farivar & Wang, 2022). For example, identity alignment between influencers and followers enhances message credibility, authenticity, and persuasiveness, ultimately increasing purchase intentions (Farivar & Wang, 2022). It also shows that the effect of social identity surpasses that of interest fit and opinion leadership, highlighting the central role of identity congruence in influencer marketing. Similarly, out-group messages were found to provoke skepticism or rejection, further reinforcing the in-group/out-group dynamics predicted by SIT (Bee & Dalakas, 2015).

Additionally, certain factors can amply these identity effects. For example, storytelling by influencers amplifies the effect of social identity on purchase intention by fostering a deeper emotional connection between followers and influencers (Farivar & Wang, 2022). Similarly, cue consistency, which is defined as the alignment of an influencer's messaging and image across platforms, was found to strengthen followers' identification with the influencer, thereby boosting purchase and word-of-mouth intentions (Hsieh, 2023). These findings evidenced the importance of identity congruence as a key determinant of message credibility and persuasion in influencer marketing, as predicted by SIT.

Uses and Gratifications

The U&G theory, developed by Elihu Katz and Jay Blumler in the 1970s, focuses on understanding the motivations underlying individuals' media consumption choices. This theoretical framework fundamentally reconceptualizes media audiences as active agents who deliberately seek out specific media content to satisfy psychological and social needs, rather than positioning them as passive recipients of media messages. The theory has demonstrated remarkable adaptability, finding widespread application across both traditional media formats such as newspapers and radio, as well as contemporary digital technologies, including social media platforms, mobile applications, and immersive technologies like virtual and augmented reality (Alhabash & Ma, 2017).

A fundamental distinction within U&G theory centers on two primary modes of media engagement: "instrumental use," characterized by goal-directed consumption aimed at achieving specific outcomes, and "ritualized use," which encompasses habitual consumption patterns often driven by relaxation or entertainment seeking. This conceptual framework provides researchers with valuable analytical tools for understanding and predicting media usage patterns across diverse platforms and contexts (Flanagin & Metzger, 2001; Kim & Rubin, 1997).

Regarding the application of U&G theory in influencer advertising, a lot of prior research examined the motivational factors driving consumers to follow SMIs (e.g., Croes & Bartels, 2021; Lee et al., 2022; Morton, 2020), investigating how various gratifications influence audience engagement behaviors. Research has identified several instrumental uses—including hedonic value, information seeking, social connection, entertainment, and companionship—that serve as significant predictors of consumer behavior when following SMIs (Croes & Bartels, 2021; Lee et al., 2022; Morton, 2020). Extending this line of work, U&G applications have been extended to VI contexts, showing that users derive gratification such as novelty, information acquisition, entertainment, aesthetics, and social integration from interactions with AI-generated personas (Lou et al., 2023).

Dual Processing Theories (HSM/ELM)

Dual process theories, particularly the Elaboration Likelihood Model (ELM) developed by psychologist Richard Petty and John Cacioppo (1981, 1986) and the Heuristic-Systematic Model (HSM), serve as foundational frameworks for understanding individuals' information process in persuasive research, political communication, and advertising research (Petty & Cacioppo, 1981, 1986). These models explain how individuals process persuasive messages through distinct cognitive pathways based on their motivation, ability, and involvement levels (Petty, 1977; Petty & Cacioppo, 1981, 1986).

Specifically, both models posit that individuals process messages through dual routes: ELM's central and peripheral processing, and HSM's systematic and heuristic processing, respectively. The central/systematic route operates when consumers possess high motivation and ability, leading to effortful evaluation of message arguments (Bhattacherjee & Sanford, 2006). Conversely, the peripheral/heuristic route activates when consumers have limited processing capacity, resulting in reliance on superficial cues such as source attractiveness, celebrity endorsements, or visual aesthetics rather than argument quality (Tam & Ho, 2005).

In contemporary advertising research, these theories are frequently employed as foundational theoretical frameworks across three key areas. First, they explain how consumer involvement levels determine message processing strategies, with high-involvement situations prompting central processing and low-involvement contexts favoring peripheral cues (Petty, Cacioppo, & Schumann, 1983). Recent applications extend to VI research, where Park et al. (2024) applied the ELM framework to examine high- versus low-involvement products, finding that perceived attractiveness significantly influences consumer attitudes across both involvement levels, contrary to traditional ELM predictions. Second, they illuminate consumer responses to influencer endorsements, particularly in social media environments where peripheral cues significantly impact engagement intentions due to typically low-involvement contexts (Waltenrath Brenner, C., & Hinz, 2022). Third, they examine how different disclosure strategies influence cognitive processing routes, affecting advertising recognition and credibility perceptions. For instance, research has investigated how influencers' intimate self-disclosures affect followers' purchase intentions, testing direct effects as outcomes of heuristic processing and indirect effects via perceived altruistic motives through systematic processing (Zheng et al., 2024). Similarly, studies drawing upon ELM show that combined sponsorship disclosures (e.g., brand influence and compensation type) increase processing motivations, which in turn prompts central route processing and enhances influencer credibility, brand attitudes, and purchase intentions (Xie & Feng, 2023).

In a nutshell, these dual process models continue providing valuable theoretical foundations for understanding persuasive advertising mechanisms across diverse digital contexts.

Social Comparison Theory

SCT, introduced by Leon Festinger, asserts that individuals are intrinsically motivated to evaluate their own opinions, abilities, and self-worth by comparing themselves to others (Festinger, 1957). These comparisons help individuals determine the perceived desirability and attainability of certain traits or outcomes, thus shaping self-concept, aspirations, and behavior (Festinger, 1957). SCT distinguishes between upward comparisons, which can evoke feelings of inadequacy or inspire personal growth, and downward comparisons, which tend to enhance self-esteem (Choi, 2020).

Research shows that exposure to idealized influencer content often triggers upward social comparisons, particularly among adolescents and young women, resulting in either benign envy (aspiration) or malicious envy (resentment) depending on perceived similarity and attainability (Feijoo & Verdú, 2024; Van De Ven, Zeelenberg, & Pieters, 2009). Inauthentic or overly idealized portrayals by influencers can heighten stress, anxiety, and distrust (Lee et al., 2024; Mundel et al., 2024). Individual traits, including gender, self-esteem, and social comparison orientation, further shape such responses: men tend toward envy-driven consumption, while women seek emotional connection and authenticity (Choi, 2020; Jin & Ryu, 2020). Thus, SCT explains how influencer advertising shapes consumer behavior via social comparisons, with effects varying based on perceived authenticity and individual traits like gender and self-esteem, demonstrating that influencer content can both motivate and harm depending on context and audience vulnerability.

Computers Are Social Actors

The CASA theory, introduced by Reeves and Nass (1996), posits that individuals apply human social norms, such as politeness, reciprocity, and trust, to computers and other interactive media during interactions. CASA suggests that the presence of social cues (e.g., voice, facial expressions, interactivity) can trigger perceptions of social presence and foster human-like engagement with digital agents (Lee, 2004; Nowak & Biocca, 2003; Reeves & Nass, 1996). Originally developed to explain early human–computer interaction, CASA has been applied to examine VIs.

Empirical studies have shown that users develop PSRs with VIs that are similar in depth and form to that with HIs, in line with the CASA theory. For instance, users tend to apply the same relational scripts to virtual agents as they do to HIs (Looi, Kim (Anna), & Zihang, 2025). In addition, social cues are crucial in enabling virtual influencers to establish emotional connections through identity presentation and interaction (Looi & Kahlor, 2024). Moreover, perceived anthropomorphism (human-like qualities) in computer-generated influencers can enhance their social presence, making them perceived to be attractive and relatable. This increased social presence, in turn, positively influences consumer attitudes toward both the influencer and the endorsed brand, particularly among Generation Z consumers (Ahn, Cho, & Tsai, 2022). This connection underscores the importance of anthropomorphic traits in fostering engagement, as also evidenced by Stein, Breves, and Anders (2022), who found that users' PSIs with VIs can be as strong as those with HIs in immersive contexts, such as gaming.

In conclusion, the application of CASA theory in studying VIs evidenced how perceived human-like qualities in VIs enhance social presence and engagement.

Summary and Future Directions

While a wide range of advertising and communication theories have been applied or tested in influencer advertising, most current theory testing tends to focus primarily on influencer- or consumer-related topics. This is understandable, as influencer advertising fundamentally concerns advertising effects and consumer behavior. However, theories are less frequently applied to examine influencer relationships or platform/contextual factors. The only notable advancement in the theoretical landscape is the proposed trans-PSR framework, which addresses an updated influencer–follower relationship.

Looking ahead, several promising directions warrant further exploration. One is the rapidly evolving world of VIs, the AI powered personas begin to blur the line between human and machine, this trending raise questions about authenticity, consumer trust and emotional engagement. Another direction is the impact of emerging platforms and formats (from short-form video to virtual reality) on influencer effectiveness. The trans-PSR provides a useful theoretical tool for examining these phenomena. Finally, future research should also incorporate cross-cultural and global perspectives to better capture the diversity of influencer advertising practices and audience responses across contexts.

Acknowledgment

This work was supported by a Thematic Tier 1 grant (RT15/21) in the Wee Kim Wee School of Communication and Information, Nanyang Technological University, Singapore.

References

Aaker, J. L. (1997). Dimensions of brand personality. *Journal of Marketing Research, 34*(3), 347–356.

Abidin, C. (2015). Communicative intimacies: Influencers and perceived interconnectedness. *Ada: A Journal of Gender, New Media, & Technology 8*, 1–16.

Abidin, C. (2019). Yes Homo: Gay influencers, homonormativity, and queerbaiting on YouTube. *Continuum, 33*(5), 614–629.

Ahn, R., Cho, S., & Tsai, W. (2022). Demystifying Computer-Generated Imagery (CGI) influencers: The effect of perceived anthropomorphism and social presence on brand outcomes. *Journal of Interactive Advertising, 22*, 327–335.

Alam, F., Tao, M., Rastogi, R., Mendiratta, A., & Attri, R. (2024). Do social media influencers influence the vaccination drive? An application of source credibility theory and uses and gratification theory. *Technological Forecasting and Social Change, 198*, 122973.

Alhabash, S., & Ma, M. (2017). A tale of four platforms: Motivations and uses of Facebook, Twitter, Instagram, and Snapchat among college students?. *Social Media+ Society, 3*(1), 2056305117691544.

Amini, M. (2025). Authenticity in the realm of influencer marketing: A systematic review. *Journal of Promotional Communications, 11*(1), 1–22.

Azoulay, A., & Kapferer, J. N. (2003). Do brand personality scales really measure brand personality? *Journal of Brand Management, 11*, 143–155.

Balaban, D. C., & Szambolics, J. (2022). A proposed model of self-perceived authenticity of social media influencers. *Media and Communication, 10*(1), 235–246.

Bandura, A. (1977). *Social Learning Theory*. Englewood Cliffs, NJ: Prentice-Hall.

Bandura, A. (2009). Social cognitive theory of mass communication. In J. Bryant & D. Zillmann (Eds.), *Media Effects* (pp. 110–140). New Jersey, US: Routledge.

Becker, M., Wiegand, N., & Reinartz, W. J. (2019). Does it pay to be real? Understanding authenticity in TV advertising. *Journal of Marketing*, *83*(1), 24–50.

Beckert, J., & Naderer, B. (2023). Advertising to inspire-inspiring to persuade: How factors related to the source, message, and audience affect the persuasive effectiveness of influencer advertising. *International Journal of Advertising*, *42*(4), 641–661.

Bee, C., & Dalakas, V. (2015). Rivalries and sponsor affiliation: Examining the effects of social identity and argument strength on responses to sponsorship-related advertising messages. *Journal of Marketing Communications*, *21*, 408–424.

Beverland, M. B., & Farrelly, F. J. (2010). The quest for authenticity in consumption: Consumers' purposive choice of authentic cues to shape experienced outcomes. *Journal of Consumer Research*, *36*(5), 838–856.

Bizjak Zabukovec, B., & Faganel, A. (2024). The issue of scales for measuring parasocial interaction and parasocial relationship between followers and influencers on social media. *Sustainability*, *16*(17), Article 7782.

Bhattacherjee, A., & Sanford, C. (2006). Influence processes for information technology acceptance: An elaboration likelihood model. *MIS Quarterly*, *30*(4), 805–825.

Boerman, S. C., Willemsen, L. M., & Van Der Aa, E. P. (2017). "This post is sponsored" effects of sponsorship disclosure on persuasion knowledge and electronic word of mouth in the context of Facebook. *Journal of Interactive Marketing*, *38*(1), 82-92.

Boerman, S. C., Van Reijmersdal, E. A., Rozendaal, E., & Dima, A. L. (2018). Development of the persuasion knowledge scales of sponsored content (PKS-SC). *International Journal of Advertising*, *37*(5), 671–697.

Boerman, S. C., & Müller, C. M. (2022). Understanding which cues people use to identify influencer marketing on Instagram: An eye tracking study and experiment. *International Journal of Advertising*, *41*(1), 6–29.

Boerman, S. C., Van Reijmersdal, E. A., & Rozendaal, E. (2024). A closer investigation of dispositional persuasion knowledge of sponsored content: Exploring determinants and clusters. *Journal of Marketing Communications*, *30*(6), 660–680.

Boerman, S. C., & Van Reijmersdal, E. A. (2020). Disclosing influencer marketing on YouTube to children: The moderating role of para-social relationship. *Frontiers in Psychology*, *10*, 3042.

Borchers, N. S., Hagelstein, J., & Beckert, J. (2022). Are many too much? Examining the effects of multiple influencer endorsements from a persuasion knowledge model perspective. *International Journal of Advertising*, *41*(6), 974–996.

Breves, P. L., Liebers, N., Abt, M., & Kunze, A. (2019). The perceived fit between Instagram influencers and the endorsed brand: How influencer-brand fit affects source credibility and persuasive effectiveness. *Journal of Advertising Research*, *59*, 440–454.

Breves, P., Amrehn, J., Heidenreich, A., Liebers, N., & Schramm, H. (2021). Blind trust? The importance and interplay of parasocial relationships and advertising disclosures in explaining influencers' persuasive effects on their followers. *International Journal of Advertising*, *40*(7), 1209–1229.

Campbell, C., & Evans, N. J. (2018). The role of a companion banner and sponsorship transparency in recognizing and evaluating article-style native advertising. Journal of *Interactive Marketing*, *43*(1), 17–32.

Campbell, C. & Farrell, J. R. (2020). More than meets the eye: The functional components underlying influencer marketing. *Business Horizons*, *63*(4), 469–479.

Campbell, C., & Grimm, P. E. (2019). The challenges native advertising poses: Exploring potential federal trade commission responses and identifying research needs. *Journal of Public Policy & Marketing*, *38*(1), 110–123.

Carlson, B. D., & Donavan, D. T. (2013). Human brands in sport: Athlete brand personality and identification. *Journal of Sport Management*, *27*(3), 193–206.

Carlson, B. D., Donavan, D. T., & Cumiskey, K. J. (2009). Consumer-brand relationships in sport: brand personality and identification. *International Journal of Retail & Distribution Management*, *37*(4), 370–384.

Ceylan, M., & Hayran, C. (2025). Social media influencer marketing: The role of influencer type, brand popularity, and consumers' need for uniqueness. *International Journal of Advertising*, *44*(7), 1–28.

Choi, A. (2020). Social comparison in fashion blogging: "Creative self" as the new genre in fashion communication. *Journal of Fashion Marketing and Management: An International Journal*, *24*(4), 651–665.

Choi, S. M., & Rifon, N. J. (2012). It is a match: The impact of congruence between celebrity image and consumer ideal self on endorsement effectiveness. *Psychology & Marketing*, *29*(9), 639–650.

Coates, A. E., Hardman, C. A., Halford, J. C. G., Christiansen, P., & Boyland, E. J. (2019a). The effect of influencer marketing of food and a "protective" advertising disclosure on children's food intake. *Pediatric Obesity*, *14*(10), e12540.

Coates, A. E., Hardman, C. A., Halford, J. C., Christiansen, P., & Boyland, E. J. (2019b). Social media influencer marketing and children's food intake: A randomized trial. *Pediatrics*, *143*(4), 1–9.

Croes, E., & Bartels, J. (2021). Young adults' motivations for following social influencers and their relationship to identification and buying behavior. *Computers in Human Behavior*, *124*, 106910.

Darke, P. R., & Ritchie, R. J. (2007). The defensive consumer: Advertising deception, defensive processing, and distrust. *Journal of Marketing Research*, *44*(1), 114–127.

De Jans, S., Van De Sompel, D., De Veirman, M., & Hudders, L. (2020). # Sponsored! How the recognition of sponsoring on Instagram posts affects adolescents' brand evaluations through source evaluations. *Computers in Human Behavior*, *109*, 106342.

De Veirman, M., Cauberghe, V., & Hudders, L. (2017). Marketing through Instagram influencers: The impact of number of followers and product divergence on brand attitude. *International Journal of Advertising*, *36*(5), 798–828.

Djafarova, E., & Rushworth, C. (2017). Exploring the credibility of online celebrities' Instagram profiles in influencing the purchase decisions of young female users. *Computers in Human Behavior*, *68*, 1–7.

Ducoffe, R. H. (1995). How consumers assess the value of advertising. *Journal of Current Issues & Research in Advertising*, *17*(1), 1–18.

Ducoffe, R. H. (1996). Advertising value and advertising on the web. *Journal of Advertising Research*, *36*(5), 21–21.

Ebben, M., & Bull, E. (2023). Constructing authenticity: Social media influencers and the shaping of online identity. *Online Identity-An Essential Guide*, 37–53.

Escalas, J. E. (2004). Narrative processing: Building consumer connections to brands. *Journal of Consumer Psychology*, *14*(1–2), 168–180.

Escalas, J. E., & Bettman, J. R. (2005). Self-construal, reference groups, and brand meaning. *Journal of Consumer Research*, *32*(3), 378–389.

Evans, N. J., Balaban, D. C., Naderer, B., & Mucundorfeanu, M. (2022). How the impact of social media influencer disclosures changes over time: Discounting cues and exposure level can affect consumer attitudes and purchase intention. *Journal of Advertising Research, 62*(4), 353–366.

Evans, N. J., Phua, J., Lim, J., & Jun, H. (2017). Disclosing Instagram influencer advertising: The effects of disclosure language on advertising recognition, attitudes, and behavioral intent. *Journal of Interactive Advertising, 17*(2), 138–149.

Farivar, S., & Wang, F. (2022). Effective influencer marketing: A social identity perspective. *Journal of Retailing and Consumer Services, 67*, Article 103026.

Feijoo, B., & Vizcaíno-Verdú, A. (2024). To be fit, or not to be: How influencer-driven advertising reinforces idealized beauty standards in adolescents. *Journal of Marketing Communications, 32*(4), 1–16.

Feng, Y., Chen, H., & Kong, Q. (2020). An expert with whom I can identify: The role of narratives in influencer marketing. *International Journal of Advertising, 40*, 972–993.

Festinger, L. (1957). Social comparison theory. *Selective Exposure Theory, 16*(401), 16–18.

Flanagin, A. J., & Metzger, M. J. (2001). Internet use in the contemporary media environment. *Human Communication Research, 27*(1), 153–181.

Friestad, M., & Wright, P. (1994). The persuasion knowledge model: How people cope with persuasion attempts. *Journal of Consumer Research, 21*(1), 1–31.

Friestad, M., & Wright, P. (1995). Persuasion knowledge: Lay people's and researchers' beliefs about the psychology of advertising. *Journal of Consumer Research, 22*, 62–74.

Fullagar, C., & Barling, J. (1983). Social learning theory: A psychological approach to advertising effectiveness?. *South African Journal of Psychology, 13*(1), 18–22.

Gannon, V., & Prothero, A. (2018). Beauty bloggers and YouTubers as a community of practice. *Journal of Marketing Management, 34*(7–8), 592–619.

Giuffredi-Kähr, A., Petrova, A., & Malär, L. (2022). Sponsorship disclosure of influencers–a curse or a blessing?. *Journal of Interactive Marketing, 57*(1), 18–34.

Grayson, K., & Martinec, R. (2004). Consumer perceptions of iconicity and indexicality and their influence on assessments of authentic market offerings. *Journal of Consumer Research, 31*(2), 296–312.

Green, M. C., & Brock, T. C. (2000). The role of transportation in the persuasiveness of public narratives. *Journal of Personality and Social Psychology, 79*(5), 701–721.

Heere, B. (2010). A new approach to measure perceived brand personality associations among consumers. *Sport Marketing Quarterly, 19*(1), 17–24.

Hornsey, M. J. (2008). Social identity theory and self-categorization theory: A historical review. *Social and Personality Psychology Compass, 2*(1), 204–222.

Horton, D., & Richard Wohl, R. (1956). Mass communication and para-social interaction: Observations on intimacy at a distance. *Psychiatry, 19*(3), 215–229.

Hovland, C. I., & Weiss, W. (1951). The influence of source credibility on communication effectiveness. *Public Opinion Quarterly, 15*(4), 635–650.

Hsieh, J. (2023). The impact of influencers' multi-SNS use on followers' behavioral intentions: An integration of cue consistency theory and social identity theory. *Journal of Retailing and Consumer Services, 74,* 103397.

Hudders, L., De Jans, S., & De Veirman, M. (2021). The commercialization of social media stars: A literature review and conceptual framework on the strategic use of social media influencers. *Social Media Influencers in Strategic Communication, 40(3)*, 24–67.

Hwang, K., & Zhang, Q. (2018). Influence of parasocial relationship between digital celebrities and their followers on followers' purchase and electronic word-of-mouth intentions, and persuasion knowledge. *Computers in Human Behavior, 87*, 155–173.

Janssen, L., Schouten, A. P., & Croes, E. A. (2022). Influencer advertising on Instagram: product-influencer fit and number of followers affect advertising outcomes and influencer evaluations via credibility and identification. *International Journal of Advertising*, *41*(1), 101–127.

Jain, R., Schuster, L., Luck, E., & Jin, H. (2024). Influencer marketing, narrative transportation, and consumer well-being: An exploration of how virtual influencers impact followers' well-being. *International Journal of Consumer Studies*, *48*, e13105.

Jin, S. V., & Ryu, E. (2020). "I'll buy what she's# wearing": The roles of envy toward and parasocial interaction with influencers in Instagram celebrity-based brand endorsement and social commerce. *Journal of Retailing and Consumer Services*, *55*, 102121.

Jin, S. V., Muqaddam, A., & Ryu, E. (2019). Instafamous and social media influencer marketing. *Marketing Intelligence & Planning*, *37*(5), 567–579.

Ju, I., & Lou, C. (2022). Does influencer–follower relationship matter? Exploring how relationship norms and influencer–product congruence affect advertising effectiveness across product categories. *Journal of Interactive Advertising*, *22*(2), 157–177.

Kádeková, Z., & Holienčinová, M. (2018). Influencer marketing as a modern phenomenon creating a new frontier of virtual opportunities. *Communication Today*, *9*(2), 90–105.

Keller, K. L. (2009). Building strong brands in a modern marketing communications environment. *Journal of marketing communications*, *15*(2), 139.

Kernis, M. H., & Goldman, B. M. (2006). A multicomponent conceptualization of authenticity: Theory and research. *Advances in Experimental Social Psychology*, *38*, 283–357.

Khamis, S., Ang, L., & Welling, R. (2017). Self-branding, 'micro-celebrity' and the rise of social media influencers. *Celebrity Studies*, *8*(2), 191–208.

Ki, C. W. C., Cuevas, L. M., Chong, S. M., & Lim, H. (2020). Influencer marketing: Social media influencers as human brands attaching to followers and yielding positive marketing results by fulfilling needs. *Journal of Retailing and Consumer Services*, *55*, 102133.

Kim, D. Y., & Kim, H. Y. (2022). Social media influencers as human brands: An interactive marketing perspective. *Journal of Research in Interactive Marketing*, *17*(1), 94–109.

Kim, D. Y., Park, M., & Kim, H. Y. (2023). An influencer like me: Examining the impact of the social status of Influencers. *Journal of Marketing Communications*, *29*(7), 654–675.

Kim, J., & Rubin, A. M. (1997). The variable influence of audience activity on media effects. *Communication Research*, *24*(2), 107–135.

Kim, D., & Wang, Z. (2024). Social media influencer vs. virtual influencer: The mediating role of source credibility and authenticity in advertising effectiveness within AI influencer marketing. *Computers in Human Behavior: Artificial Humans*, *2*(2), 100100.

Lee, K. M. (2004). Presence, explicated. *Communication Theory*, *14*(1), 27–50.

Lee, J. A., & Eastin, M. S. (2020). I like what she's #endorsing: The impact of female social media influencers' perceived sincerity, consumer envy, and product type. *Journal of Interactive Advertising*, *20*(1), 76–91.

Lee, J. A., Cho, Y., Jung, Y., Kim, J., & Sung, Y. (2024). Social comparison on Instagram among millennial mothers: The relationships between envy and parental stress. *New Media & Society*, *27*(8), 14614448241243098.

Lee, J. A., Sudarshan, S., Sussman, K. L., Bright, L. F., & Eastin, M. S. (2022). Why are consumers following social media influencers on Instagram? Exploration of consumers' motives for following influencers and the role of materialism. *International Journal of Advertising*, *41*(1), 78–100.

Lee, J. E., & Watkins, B. (2016). YouTube vloggers' influence on consumer luxury brand perceptions and intentions. *Journal of Business Research*, *69*(12), 5753–5760.

Liebers, N., & Schramm, H. (2023). The history and scope of Parasocial research. *The Oxford Handbook of Parasocial Experiences*, pp. 13–32, New York, NY: Oxford University Press.
Lim, H., & Childs, M. (2020). Visual storytelling on Instagram: Branded photo narrative and the role of telepresence. *Journal of Research in Interactive Marketing, 14*, 33–50.
Lim, X. J., Radzol, A. M., Cheah, J., & Wong, M. W. (2017). The impact of social media influencers on purchase intention and the mediation effect of customer attitude. *Asian Journal of Business Research*, *7*(2), 19–36.
Looi, J., & Kahlor, L. A. (2024). Artificial intelligence in influencer marketing: A mixed-method comparison of human and virtual influencers on Instagram. *Journal of Interactive Advertising*, *24*(2), 107–126.
Looi, J., Kim, E. (Anna), & Zihang, E. (2025). Sponsorship disclosure in virtual influencer marketing: Assessing users' sentiment and engagement toward virtual influencer endorsements. *Journal of Advertising Research*, *65*(3), 1–23.
Lou, C. (2022). Social media influencers and followers: Theorization of a trans-parasocial relation and explication of its implications for influencer advertising. *Journal of Advertising*, *51*(1), 4–21.
Lou, C., Kiew, S. T. J., Chen, T., Lee, T. Y. M., Ong, J. E. C., & Phua, Z. (2023). Authentically fake? How consumers respond to the influence of virtual influencers. *Journal of Advertising*, *52*(4), 540–557.
Lou, C., & Kim, H. K. (2019). Fancying the new rich and famous? Explicating the roles of influencer content, credibility, and parental mediation in adolescents' parasocial relationship, materialism, and purchase intentions. *Frontiers in Psychology*, *10*, 2567.
Lou, C., & Yuan, S. (2019). Influencer marketing: How message value and credibility affect consumer trust of branded content on social media. *Journal of Interactive Advertising*, *19*(1), 58–73.
Lou, C., Zhou, X., & Xu, Q. (2024). Social media influencers helping the world? uncovering their advantages and tipping factors in cause-related marketing. *International Journal of Advertising*, *43*(8), 1315–1341.
Malik, A. Z., Thapa, S., & Paswan, A. K. (2023). Social media influencer (SMI) as a human brand–a need fulfillment perspective. *Journal of Product & Brand Management*, *32*(2), 173–190.
Martínez, C., & Olsson, T. (2019). Making sense of YouTubers: How Swedish children construct and negotiate the YouTuber Misslisibell as a girl celebrity. *Journal of Children and Media, 13*(1), 36–52.
McGuire, W. J. (1985). Attitudes and attitude change. In *Handbook of Social Psychology* (vol.2., pp. 233–346). G. Lindzey, & E. Aronson, eds., New York: Random House.
Misiak, M., Urbanek, A., Frackowiak, T., & Sorokowski, P. (2025). Who wants to be a YouTuber? Personality traits predict the desire to become a social media influencer. *Telematics and Informatics*, *98*, 102248.
Morton, F. (2020). Influencer marketing: An exploratory study on the motivations of young adults to follow social media influencers. *Journal of Digital & Social Media Marketing*, *8*(2), 156–165.
Mundel, J., Wan, A., & Yang, J. (2024). Processes underlying social comparison with influencers and subsequent impulsive buying: The roles of social anxiety and social media addiction. *Journal of Marketing Communications*, *30*(7), 834–851.
Munnukka, J., Uusitalo, O., & Toivonen, H. (2016). Credibility of a peer endorser and advertising effectiveness. *Journal of Consumer Marketing*, *33*(3), 182–192.

Nowak, K. L., & Biocca, F. (2003). The effect of the agency and anthropomorphism on users' sense of telepresence, copresence, and social presence in virtual environments. *Presence: Teleoperators and Virtual Environments, 12*(5), 481–494.

Osgood, C. E., & Tannenbaum, P. H. (1955). The principle of congruity in the prediction of attitude change. *Psychological Review, 62*(1), 42–55.

Park, S., Wei, X., & Lee, H. (2024). Revisiting the elaboration likelihood model in the context of a virtual influencer: A comparison between high-and low-involvement products. *Journal of Consumer Behaviour, 23*(4), 1638–1652.

Petty, R. E. (1977). *A cognitive response analysis of the temporal persistence of attitude changes induced by persuasive communications.* Unpublished doctoral dissertation. Ohio State University, Columbus.

Petty, R. E., & Cacioppo, J. T. (1981). *Attitudes and Persuasion: Classic and Contemporary Approaches*. Dubuque, IA: Wm. C. Brown.

Petty, R. E., Cacioppo, J. T. (1986). The elaboration likelihood model of persuasion. In Berkowitz, L. (Ed.), *Communication and Persuasion*, pp. 123–205. Springer Series in Social Psychology. New York: Springer.

Petty, R. E., Cacioppo, J. T., & Schumann, D. (1983). Central and peripheral routes to advertising effectiveness: The moderating role of involvement. *Journal of Consumer Research, 10*(2), 135–146.

Reeves, B., & Nass, C. I. (1996). *The Media Equation: How People Treat Computers, Television, and New Media Like Real People and Places*. Center for the Study of Language and Information. New York, NY: Cambridge University Press.

Rozendaal, E., Lapierre, M. A., Van Reijmersdal, E. A., & Buijzen, M. (2011). Reconsidering advertising literacy as a defense against advertising effects. *Media Psychology, 14*(4), 333–354.

Sands, S., Campbell, C. L., Plangger, K., & Ferraro, C. (2022). Unreal influence: Leveraging AI in influencer marketing. *European Journal of Marketing, 56*(6), 1721–1747.

Schouten, A. P., Janssen, L., & Verspaget, M. (2020). Celebrity vs. influencer endorsements in advertising: The role of identification, credibility, and product-endorser fit. *International Journal of Advertising, 39*(2), 258–281.

Schulze, D. (2017). *Authenticity in Contemporary Theatre and Performance: Make it Real*. London: Bloomsbury Publishing.

Seo, Y., Li, X., Choi, Y., & Yoon, S. (2018). Narrative transportation and paratextual features of social media in viral advertising. *Journal of Advertising, 47*, 83–95.

Shen, C. W., & Ho, J. T. (2020). Technology-enhanced learning in higher education: A bibliometric analysis with latent semantic approach. *Computers in Human Behavior, 104*, 106177.

Sokolova, K., & Perez, C. (2021). You follow fitness influencers on YouTube. But do you exercise? How parasocial relationships, and watching fitness influencers, relate to intentions to exercise. *Journal of Retailing and Consumer Services, 58*, 102276.

Sokolova, K., & Kefi, H. (2020). Instagram and YouTube bloggers promote it, why should I buy? How credibility and parasocial interaction influence purchase intentions. *Journal of Retailing and Consumer Services, 53*, 101742.

Stern, B. B. (1994). Classical and vignette television advertising dramas: Structural models, formal analysis, and consumer effects. *Journal of Consumer Research, 20*(4), 601–615.

Stein, J. P., Breves, P. L., & Anders, N. (2022). Parasocial interactions with real and virtual influencers: The role of perceived similarity and human-likeness. *New Media & Society, 26*(6), 3433–3453.

Sundermann, G., & Munnukka, J. (2022). Hope you're not totally commercial! Toward a better understanding of advertising recognition's impact on influencer marketing effectiveness. *Journal of Interactive Marketing*, *57*(2), 237–254.

Tajfel, H., Turner, J. C., Austin, W. G., & Worchel, S. (1979). An integrative theory of intergroup conflict. *Organizational Identity: A Reader*, *56*(65), 9780203505984–16.

Tam, K. Y., & Ho, S. Y. (2005). Web personalization as a persuasion strategy: An elaboration likelihood model perspective. *Information Systems Research*, *16*(3), 271–291.

Thomson, M. (2006). Human brands: Investigating antecedents to consumers' strong attachments to celebrities. *Journal of Marketing*, *70*(3), 104–119.

Van De Ven, N., Zeelenberg, M., & Pieters, R. (2009). Leveling up and down: The experiences of benign and malicious envy. *Emotion*, *9*(3), 419.

Van der Bend, D. L., Gijsman, N., Bucher, T., Shrewsbury, V. A., Van Trijp, H., & Van Kleef, E. (2023). Can I@ handle it? The effects of sponsorship disclosure in TikTok influencer marketing videos with different product integration levels on adolescents' persuasion knowledge and brand outcomes. *Computers in Human Behavior*, *144*, 107723.

Voorveld, H. A., Meppelink, C. S., & Boerman, S. C. (2024). Consumers' persuasion knowledge of algorithms in social media advertising: Identifying consumer groups based on awareness, appropriateness, and coping ability. *International Journal of Advertising*, *43*(6), 960–986.

Vrontis, D., Makrides, A., Christofi, M., & Thrassou, A. (2021). Social media influencer marketing: A systematic review, integrative framework and future research agenda. *International Journal of Consumer Studies*, *45*(4), 617–644.

Waltenrath, A., Brenner, C., & Hinz, O. (2022). Some interactions are more equal than others: The effect of influencer endorsements in social media brand posts on engagement and online store performance. *Journal of Interactive Marketing*, *57*(4), 541–560.

Weismueller, J., Harrigan, P., Wang, S., & Soutar, G. N. (2020). Influencer endorsements: How advertising disclosure and source credibility affect consumer purchase intention on social media. *Australasian Marketing Journal*, *28*(4), 160–170.

Wojdynski, B. W., & Evans, N. J. (2016). Going native: Effects of disclosure position and language on the recognition and evaluation of online native advertising. *Journal of Advertising*, *45*(2), 157–168.

Xie, Q., & Feng, Y. (2023). How to strategically disclose sponsored content on Instagram? The synergy effects of two types of sponsorship disclosures in influencer marketing. *International Journal of Advertising*, *42*(2), 317–343.

Yang, G. (2022). The effects of sponsorship disclosures, advertising knowledge, and message involvement in sponsored influencer posts. *International Journal of Advertising*, *41*(8), 1502–1520.

Ye, G., Hudders, L., De Jans, S., & De Veirman, M. (2021). The value of influencer marketing for business: A bibliometric analysis and managerial implications. *Journal of Advertising*, *50*(2), 160–178.

Yuan, S., & Lou, C. (2020). How social media influencers foster relationships with followers: The roles of source credibility and fairness in parasocial relationship and product interest. *Journal of Interactive Advertising*, *20*(2), 133–147.

Zeithaml, V. A. (1988). Consumer perceptions of price, quality, and value: A means-end model and synthesis of evidence. *Journal of Marketing*, *52*(3), 2–22.

Zheng, L., Huang, B., Qiu, H., & Bai, H. (2024). The role of social media followers' agency in influencer marketing: A study based on the heuristic-systematic model of information processing. *International Journal of Advertising*, *43*(3), 554–579.

8 What's in a Name? Exploring Consumer Perceptions of Social Media Personalities

Influencers, Content Creators, and Celebrities

Marijke De Veirman, Laurien Desimpelaere, Serena D'Hooge, Eveline Mollaert and Ilse Bruwiere

Introduction

> Influencers are walking billboards. I suppose they have become known for something on the internet, gained fame and then keep making posts to promote something. Content creators are people who create content on the internet, I believe for an intrinsic reason [...]. Celebrities are people who work 90% of the time, like actors or musicians who have turned their hobby into their job and become famous that way.
>
> (Male, 20 y.o.)

This quote, drawn from one of 34 exploratory in-depth interviews with Belgian youth (aged 16–24; see De Veirman, Bruwiere, & Mollaert, 2023) that served as the starting point for the present study, illustrates how young audiences attach distinct meanings to the label's influencer, content creator, and celebrity. Indeed, the rise of social media platforms as dominant marketing channels has introduced a spectrum of influential personas, most notably influencers, content creators, and celebrities. While previous studies have compared influencers to traditional celebrities (e.g., Schouten, Janssen, & Verspaget, 2019; Gräve & Bartsch, 2022), the specific role and perception of content creators remain relatively underexplored. Although the terms influencer and content creator are often used interchangeably, assumptions can be made, both in popular discourse and within industry practice, that content creator conveys a more professional and value-laden identity. The label content creator is frequently associated with creativity, originality, and production-oriented work, while influencer tends to evoke commercial intent and, at times, carries more negative connotations. Influencers are commonly perceived as being driven by monetized promotion, whereas content creators are assumed to be more authentic and intrinsically motivated.

DOI: 10.4324/9781003567523-11

Despite these prevalent assumptions, there is limited empirical research that examines how consumers perceive and differentiate between these social media personas, and how labels such as "celebrity," "influencer," or "content creator" shape audience perceptions (Jiménez-Castillo & Sánchez-Fernández, 2019; Haenlein et al., 2020). Moreover, few studies have investigated whether simple framing effects, such as the label one adopts ("influencer" vs. "content creator"), can influence how trustworthy, creative, or authentic a person is perceived to be.

The current chapter aims to identify the trait attributions associated with influencers, content creators, and celebrities. Hence, it provides important insights for marketers seeking to optimize their brand partnerships in an increasingly complex and perception-driven digital ecosystem.

Social Media Personas in Digital Advertising

Celebrity endorsement has long been a cornerstone of advertising strategy, grounded in the idea that celebrities transfer their symbolic meaning to the products they promote, which in turn transfers to the consumer (McCracken, 1989). Traditionally, this form of endorsement was mediated through television, print, and radio, relying on mass media to reach large, often undifferentiated audiences. With the advent of social media, the endorsement landscape has undergone a significant transformation. Social media have not only expanded the landscape for celebrity endorsement by offering a new platform for message dissemination, but they have also transformed the nature of endorsement itself by introducing new types of influential figures whose fame originates entirely within the digital sphere. Whereas traditional celebrities, such as actors, musicians, and athletes, have historically leveraged their visibility in mass media to support brand campaigns, social platforms now enable them to engage in brand promotion via their personal accounts. This allows for a more intimate and seemingly authentic mode of communication, where product endorsements are embedded into everyday content and personal narratives (Khamis, Ang, & Welling, 2017).

Moreover, social media have given rise to a new category of endorsers: influencers whose status and credibility are not inherited from mainstream media exposure but are instead cultivated through consistent engagement, niche expertise, and algorithmic visibility on platforms like Instagram, TikTok, and YouTube (Abidin, 2016; Marwick, 2015; Lou & Yuan, 2019; Campbell & Farell, 2020; Lou, 2021). Influencers are often described as popular online personalities, creating and sharing content through which they attract a large number of followers and have a significant impact on followers' purchase behavior (De Veirman, Cauberghe, & Hudders 2017; Lou et al., 2019; Lou, 2021). These platform-native figures blur the line between peer and promoter, and their perceived authenticity, accessibility, and relatability have made them especially appealing to younger audiences (Schouten, Janssen, & Verspaget, 2019).

At the same time, concerns have been raised about the growing commercialization of influencer content, particularly in cases where sponsored posts are perceived as overly frequent or not fully consistent with the influencer's typical tone and values (Abidin, 2016; Marwick, 2015). This shift in audience perception, often referred to as "influencer fatigue," has contributed to increasing consumer sensitivity around issues of authenticity and transparency in digital endorsements (Boerman, Willemsen, & Van Der Aa, 2017). In response to this evolving landscape, the term content creator has gained prominence, both within the industry and among social media personalities themselves.

Although the terms influencer and content creator are often used interchangeably, popular discourse increasingly suggests a preference for the latter among those who seek to emphasize the creative, technical, or narrative aspects of their work rather than mere persuasion or brand affiliation. Content creator is frequently framed as a more professional and craft-oriented identity, one that prioritizes content development and storytelling over commercial promotion (Influencer Marketing Hub, 2023; Kozinets, Gretzel, & Gambetti, 2023).

The following section delves deeper into the characteristics commonly associated with celebrities, influencers, and content creators, in order to map out the distinct trait profiles that shape how consumers evaluate these personas. Understanding these perceptions is essential, as they have been shown to significantly affect message credibility, brand attitudes, and consumer behavior (Ohanian, 1990; Erdogan, 1999; Eisend & Langner, 2010).

Characteristics Attributed to Social Media Personalities

A central theoretical lens for the current study is the Source Credibility Model (Ohanian, 1990), which identifies expertise, trustworthiness, and attractiveness as the three key dimensions that shape the persuasive power of a source. The first dimension, expertise, refers to the perception that an endorser possesses knowledge, skills, or competence in a particular domain (Ohanian, 1990). For traditional celebrities, perceptions of expertise are often grounded in their professional accomplishments outside of social media (Brooks, Drenten, & Piskorski, 2021). This includes success in domains such as acting, music, sports, or other performance-based or creative industries. Moreover, unlike influencers and content creators who often demonstrate expertise directly through their content (e.g., tutorials, product reviews, educational posts), celebrities are less likely to engage in such skill-demonstration behavior on social media platforms. On the other hand, influencers and content creators often emphasize these traits more explicitly, positioning themselves as skilled artists, educators, or storytellers. They often build their expertise through ongoing engagement and informational content within a niche (e.g., skincare, fitness, finance), which can lead audiences to view them as more experts. In addition, content creators are frequently associated with creative or technical mastery (such as videography, graphic design, or storytelling) which contributes to perceptions of professional quality and specialized talent (Jeffres, Atkin, & Neuendorf, 2024).

The second dimension of source credibility is trustworthiness, which captures the extent to which a source is seen as honest, authentic, and reliable. Influencers and content creators often build trust by sharing personal experiences, revealing behind-the-scenes moments, and maintaining a consistent tone and personality across content, eventually fostering a sense of parasocial intimacy (Abidin, 2016). This creates the perception that they are "people like us," which can boost feelings of reliability and sincerity (Djafarova & Rushworth, 2017). At the same time, the trustworthiness of influencers is increasingly under scrutiny due to the rise of undisclosed sponsorships and content that appears overly curated or commercially driven. Content creators are typically perceived as more intrinsically motivated, producing content out of passion, creativity, or expertise, rather than for promotional purposes alone (Somerfield, 2023). Celebrities, on the other hand, have historically been associated with a greater distance between endorser and audience, which can make their messages seem less personally invested or sincere (Winterich, Gangwar, & Grewal, 2018).

Finally, the physical appearance and overall attractiveness of a source significantly contribute to their perceived credibility and, in turn, to their persuasive impact (Kahle & Homer, 1985; Kamins, 1989; McCracken, 1989; Ohanian, 1990). Source attractiveness is shaped by several interrelated factors, including familiarity, likability, and similarity (McGuire, 1985). Familiarity refers to the degree to which an audience recognizes or feels acquainted with the source through repeated exposure. Likability involves the positive effect elicited by the source's appearance or behavior, while similarity refers to perceived shared characteristics or experiences between the source and the receiver (McGuire, 1985). Celebrities are often perceived as highly attractive, not only in terms of physical appearance but also because of their glamorous lifestyles, fame, and status. This contributes to their aspirational appeal, making them natural role models in the eyes of consumers. However, this idealization can also create psychological distance between the celebrity and the audience, reducing relatability (Schouten et al., 2019). Influencers and content creators often derive their attractiveness not only from appearance but also from relatability (Foster, 2022). The interactive nature of social media enables influencers to foster close relationships with their followers, positioning themselves more as approachable peers than distant celebrities. To strengthen this connection, influencers actively cultivate perceptions of similarity, familiarity, and likability, which are central to their perceived attractiveness and persuasive appeal (see Hudders, De Jans & De Veirman, 2020).

Beyond source credibility, authenticity has emerged as a central construct in evaluating social media personalities, particularly within the context of influencer marketing. Authenticity is commonly associated with being "true to self," "sincere," and "not overly commercial" (Audrezet, De Kerviler, & Moulard, 2018).

Among influencers, authenticity is not only central to their appeal but also frequently contested. As their content becomes more commercialized, they face growing pressure to maintain transparency and coherence between personal and sponsored messaging. While many influencers present themselves as relatable and accessible, their dependence on brand partnerships may lead to audience skepticism, especially if sponsorships appear inconsistent or insincere (Boerman et al., 2017). In contrast, content creators are typically perceived as more intrinsically motivated, with their authenticity often rooted in the perceived originality and passion behind their creative work. Their branding is often seen as an extension of their craft rather than a marketing strategy, which can enhance their credibility. Regarding celebrities, the study of Klostermann et al. (2023) found that most celebrities tend to share less private content than what would be considered optimal for fostering audience engagement. At the same time, prior studies have supported evidence that self-presentation can lead to stronger relationships with fans (Chung & Cho, 2017). As a result, their limited sharing of personal content may cause their social media presence to be perceived as strategic and distant, rather than genuinely authentic.

In addition, recent literature highlights the importance of attainability as a distinctive characteristic that differentiates influencers from traditional celebrities, offering a potential explanation for differences in persuasive power (Harff, Dekoninck, & Schmuck, 2025). Social media influencers are often seen as more attainable than traditional celebrities, precisely because of the informal, self-produced nature of their content and the proximity they maintain with their audiences (Jin, Muqaddam, & Ryu, 2019; Khamis, Ang, & Welling, 2017). For instance, Enke and Borchers (2019, p. 264) suggest that influencers foster a "sense of equality" with their followers, allowing audiences to perceive them as peers rather than distant icons.

Taken together, these theoretical perspectives provide a useful foundation for understanding the perceived differences between social media personas. However, there remains a lack of empirical clarity regarding how these characteristics are distributed across different types of social media personas. In particular, it is unknown whether consumers systematically attribute distinct trait profiles to celebrities, influencers, and content creators, or whether such distinctions are blurred in practice. To address this, we conducted a mixed-methods study to explore how audiences perceive and differentiate between these three persona types.

Methodology

The first study, conducted between November 2022 and January 2023, surveyed 5,287 Belgians aged 16–39 (Mage = 26.46 years, SDage = 6.76; 57.00% females, 42.10% males) in which they selected characteristics considered typical of each type of social media personality.

The second study, carried out between November 2023 and January 2024, included 4516 participants from the same age group (16–39 years old, Mage = 27.80 years, SDage = 6.87; 63.6% females, 35.6% males). This wave enabled inferential rather than merely descriptive analysis. For each type, respondents who follow an influencer (*N* = 1915), a content creator (*N* = 1977), and/or a celebrity (*N* = 2051) on social media needed to assign to what degree each characteristic fits the type of media personality on a five-point Likert scale. This resulted in a final subsample of 835 participants who follow all three types of social media personalities.

The surveys used in this study were part of a broader annual research initiative known as the SMI Barometer (Social Media & Influencer Marketing Barometer; www.smibarometer.be), which explores how young Belgians (aged 16–39) use social media and how they engage with brand communication via social platforms, influencers, and podcasts.

Table 8.1 Results of the Multiple Response Crosstab Analysis in Study 1

Characteristics	*Influencers* (*N* = 3726) *(%)*	*Content Creators* (N = 2281) *(%)*	*Celebrities* (N = 3177) *(%)*
1. Has many followers	**54.60**	38.50	**57.60**
2. Is credible, reliable	39.90	38.80	29.30
3. Is a role model, someone I look up to	37.00	23.70	**46.00**
4. Is attractive	25.40	22.20	27.50
5. Can teach me something	38.10	**46.90**	22.90
6. Advertises, is sponsored by brands	**40.30**	29.40	28.50
7. Reacts to comments and posts	16.90	26.50	10.20
8. Is creative	36.40	**56.20**	20.60
9. Posts fun, original content	**42.80**	**55.80**	23.10
10. Posts content of professional quality	28.00	37.30	27.00
11. Has a special talent, excels at something (specialization)	13.10	25.60	**34.20**
12. Shows how he/she really is (doesn't act, is not fake)	25.50	23.80	22.60
13. Shows an ideal image of what life could be like	18.90	11.00	20.40
14. Shares a similar life context, resembles me	9.50	10.20	5.40
None of the above	1.10	2.10	2.50

Results

In study 1, a multiple response frequency analysis was carried out (see Table 8.1). The top three characteristics associated with an influencer are having many followers (54.60%), posting fun, original content (42.80%), and advertising/being sponsored by brands (40.30%). For content creators, these are being creative (56.20%), posting fun/original content (55.80%), and the ability to teach their audience (46.90%). Celebrities' top three associated characteristics are having many followers (57.60%), being a role model, someone to look up to (46.00%), and having a special talent/excelling at something (34.20%). Note that "posting fun/original content" is included in the top three of both influencers and content creators but is more pronounced for the latter.

In study 2, a repeated measures ANOVA revealed a significant two-way interaction ($F(20.93, 17459.17) = 67.42$, $p < .001$, $\eta_p^2 = .075$, power = 1.00). All characteristics differed significantly between the different social media types (see Table 8.2). Content creators score highest with regard to creativity, reacting to comments and resembling followers. They are the least associated with having many followers. Celebrities are least associated with fun, original, creative, and high-quality content and being able to teach followers something. They resemble followers least and react least to comments but are also linked least to advertising.

Table 8.2 EM Means Results of the Repeated Measures ANOVA in Study 2 Presented in Order Following Effect Size

		Pairwise Comparisons: M(SD), p		
Characteristic	*Multivariate Test*	*Influencers versus Content Creators*	*Influencers versus Celebrities*	*Content Creators versus Celebrities*
Is creative	$F(2,833) = 133.56$, $p < .001$, $\eta_p^2 = .243$, power = 1.000	3.84(0.88) versus 4.04(0.85), $p < .001$	3.84(0.88) versus 3.37(1.03), $p < .001$	4.04(0.85) versus 3.37(1.03), $p < .001$
Posts fun, original content	$F(2,833) = 116.16$, $p < .001$, $\eta_p^2 = .218$, power = 1.000	3.96(0.84) versus 4.03(0.87), $p = .075$	3.96(0.84) versus 3.46(0.99), $p < .001$	4.03(0.87) versus 3.46(0.99), $p < .001$
Reacts to comments and posts	$F(2,833) = 99.72$, $p < .001$, $\eta_p^2 = .193$, power = 1.000	3.39(0.98) versus 3.56(0.93), $p < .001$	3.39 (0.98) versus 2.96(1.12), $p < .001$	3.56 (0.93) Versus 2.96(1.12), $p < .001$
Has many followers	$F(2,833) = 66.45$, $p < .001$, $\eta_p^2 = .138$, power = 1.000	3.91(0.96) versus 3.74(1.02), $p < .001$	3.91(0.96) versus 4.21(0.96), $p < .001$	3.74(1.02) versus 4.21(0.96), $p < .001$

(Continued)

Table 8.2 (Continued)

		Pairwise Comparisons: M(SD), p		
Characteristic	*Multivariate Test*	*Influencers versus Content Creators*	*Influencers versus Celebrities*	*Content Creators versus Celebrities*
Advertises, is sponsored by brands	$F(2,833) = 57.03$, $p < .001$, $\eta_p^2 = .120$, power = 1.000	3.97(0.97) versus 3.73(0.97), $p < .001$	3.97(0.97) versus 3.55(1.02), $p < .001$	3.73(0.97) versus 3.55(1.02), $p < .001$
Shares a similar life context, resembles me	$F(2,833) = 55.47$, $p < .001$, $\eta_p^2 = .118$, power = 1.000	2.78(1.15) versus 2.97(1.12), $p < .001$	2.78(1.15) versus 2.56(1.21), $p < .001$	2.97(1.12) versus 2.56(1.21), $p < .001$
Has a special talent, excels at something (specialization)	$F(2,833) = 53.52$, $p < .001$, $\eta_p^2 = .114$, power > .999	3.40(1.03) versus 3.65(0.94), $p < .001$	3.40(1.03) versus 3.83(0.96), $p < .001$	3.65(0.94) versus 3.83(0.96), $p < .001$
Can teach me something	$F(2,833) = 48.50$, $p < .001$, $\eta_p^2 = .104$, power > .999	3.75 (0.89) versus 3.72 (0.91), $p = 1.00$	3.75 (0.89) versus 3.38 (1.00), $p < .001$	3.72 (0.91) versus 3.38 (1.00), $p < .001$
Is a role model, someone I look up to	$F(2,833) = 39.66$, $p < .001$, $\eta_p^2 = .087$, power > .999	3.35(1.02) versus 3.35(0.99), $p = 1.00$	3.35(1.02) versus 3.65(0.96), $p < .001$	3.35(0.99) versus 3.65(0.96), $p < .001$
Is credible, reliable	$F(2,833) = 21.96$, $p < .001$, $\eta_p^2 = .050$, power > .999	3.35(1.01) versus 3.58(0.95), $p < .001$	3.35(1.01) versus 3.51(0.98), $p < .001$	3.58(0.95) versus 3.51(0.98), $p = .128$
Is attractive	$F(2,833) = 21.76$, $p < .001$, $\eta_p^2 = .050$, power > .999	3.50(0.94) versus 3.37(0.98), $p = .001$	3.50(0.94) versus 3.61(0.94), $p = .005$	3.37(0.98) versus 3.61(0.94), $p < .001$
Posts content of professional quality	$F(2,833) = 11.77$, $p < .001$, $\eta_p^2 = .027$, power = .994	3.85(0.92) versus 3.87(0.92), $p = 1.00$	3.85(0.92) versus 3.69(0.98), $p < .001$	3.87(0.92) versus 3.69(0.98), $p < .001$
Shows an ideal image of what life could be like	$F(2,833) = 8.81$, $p < .001$, $\eta_p^2 = .021$, power = .971	3.33(1.13) versus 3.27(1.05), $p = .485$	3.33(1.13) versus 3.43(1.07), $p = .024$	3.27(1.05), versus 3.43(1.07), $p < .001$
Shows how he/she really is (doesn't act, is not fake)	$F(2,833) = 3.62$, $p = .027$, $\eta_p^2 = .009$, power = .669	3.36(1.17) versus 3.41(1.04), $p = .616$	3.36(1.17) versus 3.30(1.10), $p = .486$	3.41(1.04) versus 3.30(1.10), $p = .022$

Celebrities are most assigned with having a special talent/being someone to look up to, being attractive, and showing an ideal image of what life can be like.

Influencers also fit better with a large following and are more attractive compared to content creators, while they are assigned more to posting fun, original, creative, and high-quality content, being able to teach followers something, resembling participants, and reacting to comments compared to celebrities. Influencers fit best with advertising, and being sponsored by brands, and are perceived as the least credible. In addition, we identified subtle statistically significant differences within gender and age groups. However, these differences did not exert a substantial influence on the main findings.

Conclusion and Implications

This research demonstrates that consumers attribute distinct characteristics to different types of social media personalities, namely influencers, content creators, and celebrities, who are frequently used as brand endorsers. Both studies reveal that these labels carry different sets of associations in the mind of consumers. While influencers are mainly associated with a large following and commercial motives, content creators are predominantly esteemed for their creativity and engaging videos. Conversely, celebrities are seen as talented individuals admired for their fame and professional success.

Our findings highlight that the way social media personalities frame their identity, whether as an influencer, content creator, or celebrity, can significantly impact how they are perceived in terms of key attributes such as credibility, trustworthiness, and authenticity. In this way, the study extends classical models such as the Source Credibility Model (Ohanian, 1990) by demonstrating that not only behavioral cues but also semantic framing (i.e., the labels individuals adopt) can shape audience judgments of credibility and influence.

This distinction also offers practical implications. By clarifying the specific traits attributed to each type of social media personality, brands can strategically leverage their potential. The study shows that consumers attribute systematically different characteristics to influencers, content creators, and celebrities, even when their roles as endorsers may overlap. This suggests that the label a social media personality adopts can function as a powerful framing device that shapes consumer expectations and responses, particularly regarding perceived expertise, trustworthiness, authenticity, and attainability.

Brands that are aware of these perceptual distinctions can align their partnership strategies more effectively with campaign objectives. For instance, if a brand seeks to emphasize the educational value of its products or services, partnering with content creators who are perceived as knowledgeable or insightful may be more beneficial. If the goal is to enhance brand visibility and reach a broader audience, collaborating with influencers known for their extensive follower base may be more advantageous. Celebrities, whose image remains tied to talent, aspirational appeal, and status, may be ideal for brand positioning efforts that rely on symbolic or prestige transfer.

Although the current study employed a robust mixed-method approach, including large sample sizes and a well-represented segment of the Belgian population aged 19–36, it is not without limitations. Below, we outline several key constraints and suggest directions for future research.

First, differential perceptions of social media personalities may vary across demographic and cultural contexts. The current findings are based on a Belgian sample, and it remains unclear whether similar associations would emerge in other countries, cultures, or age groups.

Second, while the current study compared three different endorser types, it did not account for variation within these categories. For example, recent studies showed that micro-influencers (smaller audience) may elicit different perceptions (e.g., in terms of trustworthiness) compared to macro-influencers (larger audience) (e.g., Cascio Rizzo et al., 2024). Further research should consider these subcategories to refine our understanding of how different social media personality labels are perceived. Moreover, new types of digital personas continue to emerge, such as virtual influencers (e.g., Lou et al., 2022), further complicating the landscape. As the world of digital endorsers continues to expand, emerging roles and dynamics call for more nuanced research into their differential perceptions and potential consequences.

Third, the current study only studied the perceptions of consumers toward the three endorser types, without assessing how these perceptions influence responses toward the endorsed brands. Although previous studies have shown that characteristics such as trustworthiness, expertise, and attractiveness impact brand attitudes and purchase intentions (e.g., Ohanian, 1990), including comparisons between celebrities and influencers (e.g., Schouten, Janssen, & Verspaget, 2019), the distinction with content creators and its consequences for consumer behavior requires further investigation.

Finally, while the study provides evidence for associative differences in how people interpret labels such as "influencers" and "content creators," it does not experimentally isolate the framing effect of the name itself. To establish causality, future research could manipulate only the label of an otherwise identical and unfamiliar endorser to examine whether naming alone evokes differential trait attributions. In the current study, consumers' perceptions were likely shaped by prior experiences and cultural associations with each type. Whether such framing effects persist for newly encountered endorsers remains an open question.

Despite these limitations, the current study demonstrates how consumers perceive different types of social media personalities and highlights the persuasive power of identity framing in digital advertising. By clarifying the characteristics associated with labels such as "influencers," "content creators," and "celebrities," this research contributes to a more nuanced understanding of digital endorsement practices and their consequences. It also opens promising avenues for future research into the increasingly complex interplay between digital identity and consumer responses, within the rapidly evolving landscape of digital advertising.

References

Abidin, C. (2016). "Aren't these just young, rich women doing vain things online?": Influencer selfies as subversive frivolity. *Social Media+ Society*, *2*(2), 1–17.

Audrezet, A., De Kerviler, G., & Moulard, J. G. (2018). Authenticity under threat: When social media influencers need to go beyond self-presentation. *Journal of Business Research, 117*, 557–569.

Boerman, S. C., Willemsen, L. M., & Van Der Aa, E. P. (2017). 'This post is sponsored': Effects of sponsorship disclosure on persuasion knowledge and electronic word of mouth in the context of Facebook. *Journal of Interactive Marketing, 38*, 82–92.

Brooks, G., Drenten, J., & Piskorski, M. J. (2021). Influencer celebrification: How social media influencers acquire celebrity capital. *Journal of Advertising*, *50*(5), 528–547.

Campbell, C., & Farrell, J. R. (2020). More than meets the eye: The functional components underlying influencer marketing. *Business Horizons, 63*(4), 469–479. https://doi.org/10.1016/j.bushor.2020.03.003

Cascio Rizzo, G. L., Ordenes, V., Pozharliev, F., De Angelis, R., M., & Costabile, M. (2024). How High-Arousal Language shapes Micro-versus Macro-Influencers' impact. *Journal of Marketing*, *88*(4), 107–128.

Chung, S., & Cho, H. (2017). Fostering parasocial relationships with celebrities on social media: Implications for celebrity endorsement. *Psychology & Marketing*, *34*(4), 481–495.

De Veirman, M., Bruwiere, I., & Mollaert, E. (2023). SMI Barometer 2023. Insights into how Belgians experience branding through social media and influencer marketing. *Arteveldehogeschool.*

De Veirman, M., Cauberghe, V., & Hudders, L. (2017). Marketing through Instagram influencers: The impact of number of followers and product divergence on brand attitude. *International Journal of Advertising*, *36*(5), 798–828.

Djafarova, E., & Rushworth, C. (2017). Exploring the credibility of online celebrities' Instagram profiles in influencing the purchase decisions of young female users. *Computers in Human Behavior*, *68*, 1–7.

Eisend, M., & Langner, T. (2010). Immediate and delayed advertising effects of celebrity endorsers' attractiveness and expertise. *International Journal of Advertising*, *29*(4), 527–546.

Enke, N., & Borchers, N. S. (2019). Social media influencers in strategic communication: A conceptual framework for strategic social media influencer communication. *International Journal of Strategic Communication*, *13*(4), 261–277.

Erdogan, B. Z. (1999). Celebrity endorsement: A literature review. *Journal of Marketing Management*, *15*(4), 291–314.

Foster, J. (2022). "It's all about the look": Making sense of appearance, attractiveness, and authenticity online. *Social Media+ Society*, *8*(4), 1–11.

Gräve, J., & Bartsch, F. (2022). #Instafame: Exploring the endorsement effectiveness of influencers compared to celebrities. *International Journal of Advertising, 41*(4), 591–622.

Harff, D., Dekoninck, H. & Schmuck, D. (2025). Idols Within Reach: Measuring Perceptions of Media Role Models' Attainability. Journalism & Mass Communication Quarterly. 10.1177/10776990251336388.

Haenlein, M., Anadol, E., Farnsworth, T., Hugo, H., Hunichen, J., & Welte, D. (2020). Navigating the new era of influencer marketing: How to be successful on Instagram, TikTok, & Co. *California Management Review*, *63*(1), 5–25.

Hudders, L., De Jans, S., & De Veirman, M. (2020). The commercialization of social media stars: A literature review and conceptual framework on the strategic use of social media influencers. *International Journal of Advertising, 40*(3), 327–375.

Influencer Marketing Hub. (2023). *20 Creator Economy Statistics That Will Blow You Away in 2023*. Retrieved from https://influencermarketinghub.com/creator-economy-stats/

Jeffres, L., Atkin, D., & Neuendorf, K. (2024). Content creators as social influencers: Predicting online video posting behaviors. *Online Media and Global Communication, 3*(4), 631–658.

Jiménez-Castillo, D., & Sánchez-Fernández, R. (2019). The role of digital influencers in brand recommendation: Examining their impact on engagement, expected value and purchase intention. *International Journal of Information Management, 49*(6), 366–376.

Jin, S.V., Muqaddam, A., & Ryu, E. (2019). Instafamous and social media influencer marketing. *Marketing Intelligence & Planning, 37*(5), 567–579.

Kahle, L. R., & Homer, P. M. (1985). Physical attractiveness of the celebrity endorser: A social adaptation perspective. *Journal of Consumer Research, 11*(4), 954–961.

Kamins, M. A. (1989). Celebrity and noncelebrity advertising in a two-sided context. *Journal of Advertising Research, 29*(3), 34–42.

Khamis, S., Ang, L., & Welling, R. (2017). Self-branding, 'micro-celebrity' and the rise of Social Media Influencers. *Celebrity Studies, 8*(2), 191–208.

Klostermann, J., Meißner, M., Max, A., & Decker, R. (2023). Presentation of celebrities' private life through visual social media. *Journal of Business Research, 156*, 113524.

Kozinets, R. V., Gretzel, U., & Gambetti, R. C. (2023). *Influencers and Creators: Business, Culture and Practice*. Sage Publications Ltd.

Lou, C. (2021). Social media influencers and followers: Theorization of a trans-parasocial relation and explication of its implications for influencer advertising. *Journal of Advertising, 51*(1), 4–21.

Lou, C., Kiew, S., Chen, T.,Lee, T., Ong, J. & Phua, Z. (2022). Authentically Fake? How Consumers Respond to the Influence of Virtual Influencers. Journal of Advertising. 10.1080/00913367.2022.2149641.

Lou, C., & Yuan, S. (2019). Influencer marketing: How message value and credibility affect consumer trust of branded content on social media. *Journal of Interactive Advertising, 19*(1), 58–73.

Marwick, A. (2015). You may know me from YouTube: (Micro)-celebrity in social media. In P. D. Marshall & S. Redmond (Eds.), *A Companion to Celebrity* (pp. 333–350). John Wiley & Sons Inc.

McCracken, G. (1989). Who is the celebrity endorser? Cultural foundations of the endorsement process. *Journal of Consumer Research, 16*(3), 310–321. https://doi.org/10.1086/209217

McGuire, W. J. (1985). Attitudes and attitude change. In G. Lindzey & E. Aronson (Eds.), *Handbook of Social Psychology* (3rd ed., Vol. 2, pp. 233–346). Random House.

Ohanian, R. (1990). Construction and validation of a scale to measure celebrity endorsers' perceived expertise, trustworthiness, and attractiveness. *Journal of Advertising, 19*(3), 39–52.

Schouten, A. P., Janssen, L., & Verspaget, M. (2019). Celebrity vs. influencer endorsements in advertising: The role of identification, credibility, and product-endorser fit. *International Journal of Advertising, 39*(2), 258–281.

Somerfield, K. (2023). *Sharing the love: Motivation and reward in brand-related user-generated content creation for social media*. Doctoral dissertation, University of Northampton.

Winterich, K. P., Gangwar, M., & Grewal, R. (2018). When celebrities count: Power distance beliefs and celebrity endorsements. *Journal of Marketing, 82*(3), 70–86.

9 Digital Advertising Clutter in an Age of Mobile Media and Artificial Intelligence

Louisa Ha and Man Luo

What is clutter? Is all advertising clutter? These are the basic questions that we need to ask before embarking on research on advertising clutter. Clutter has been defined as "a large amount of non-editorial content in an editorial medium" (Ha & McCann, 2008, p. 570). It is more about density rather than quantity of such non-editorial content. If the non-editorial content refers to advertisements, then it is advertising clutter. Clutter is described as a "difficult media environment" (Webb, 1979, p. 225). The key to this definition of advertising clutter is that the advertising is placed in a *third-party* editorial media vehicle, such as magazines or television programs (Ha, 2008). Some important characteristics of clutter are that clutter is unwanted, undesirable, excessive, and interferes with the consumption of editorial content.

Relevance of the ads to the individual is one major factor of whether the advertising is considered desirable (Kim & Sundar, 2010). The entertainment value of the ad also affects the consumer's receptiveness of the ads (Ducoffe, 1995; Ko, Cho, & Roberts, 2005). In addition, the goal of the user in the media consumption process moderates clutter perception (Ha & McCann, 2008; Heinz, Hug, Nugaeva, & Opwis, 2013; Seyedghorban, Tahernejad, & Matanda, 2015). Hence, perceived clutter levels vary by individuals (Ha, 1996). When advertising has a high level of ad-context congruity (Zanjani, Diamond, & Chan, 2011) or high compatibility with editorial content (Ha, 1996) and being seen as relevant (Kim & Sundar, 2010), then advertising is not clutter but is considered desirable and useful content to the audience.

Evolution of the Research on Clutter

Research on advertising clutter can be dated back to the late 1970s and had focused primarily on TV advertising clutter from Webb (1979) to Mord and Gilson (1985), Brown and Rothchild (1993), Pieters and Bijmolt (1997), and Zhao (1997) to more recent researchers, such as Hammer, Riebe, and Kennedy (2009). The captivity of television as a mass medium and the high stakes TV advertising poses to the TV and advertising industry are the main reasons for such focus

DOI: 10.4324/9781003567523-12

on TV advertising clutter. However, Ha (1996) demonstrates that the effect of clutter is not limited to TV but can affect any media outlets, including self-paced media such as magazines.

The online and digital media context presents new challenges because the passive and captive environment of traditional offline media is replaced by the active and self-paced environments in digital media. The competition for users' attention online is fierce, as users can easily move to another web page at the click of a mouse or the touch of a finger in mobile media. Theoretically, users are less subject to advertising control in digital media with the abundance of choices at their fingertips. Yet, online advertising formats range from complete control by advertisers, such as pre-roll video ads, that show the TV commercial before the display of an online video users want to watch and pop-up ads that block the whole screen for several seconds before the user can move to anything else, to ads as non-intrusive as a sponsored link on a Google search page and banners along the edges or bottom of a web page.

Burns and Lutz's (2006) experiment compared different consumer responses to six online advertising formats: banners, floating ads, large rectangles, interstitials, skyscrapers, and pop-ups. Their experiment showed that pop-up ads and floating ads scored highest on the annoyance factor, while interstitial ads scored highest on the entertainment factor. Banner ads scored highest on the information factor and received the highest overall positive attitude from consumers and performed the best on all behavioral measures, such as click-through percentage, percent visit later, and click-through frequency. Cho and Cheon (2004) developed a model of online advertising avoidance prompted by perceived goal impediment, perceived ad clutter, and prior negative experience using a student sample. Perceived ad clutter was found to be the most important predictor of advertising avoidance. This result was replicated in a later study of a general consumer sample in Iran (Seyedghorban, Tahernejad, & Matanda, 2015).

Causes of Advertising Clutter

One fundamental issue challenging advertisers is that some consumers have an overall negative attitude toward advertising in general due to its profit-making persuasion motive and its negative effect on society. Advertising is seen by some to lower the quality of content and sacrifice the independent nature of the news media. The use of ad-blocker software on computers and subscriptions to ad-free premium program packages are examples of overt manifestations of those online users who do not like to see any ads at all. A Backlinko (2024) blog reports that an estimated 912 million internet users use ad blocking across desktop and mobile, and almost one-third of internet users (31.5%) worldwide and American internet user (32.2%) use ad blocking tools at least sometimes. The trade association for digital advertising, the Interactive Advertising Bureau, views ad-blockers as a threat to the digital advertising industry, especially condemning those who replace the blocked ads with their own programmatic ads (Tribbey, 2016).

Three Dimensions of Clutter as Advertising Environment

Unlike the extreme of complete hatred toward advertising and total ad avoidance, complaints about advertising clutter are more commonly caused by the ways advertisements are presented to the audience in an editorial media unit, be it as an issue of a magazine, a TV program, a newspaper, or a web page. Ha (1996) proposed three dimensions of advertising clutter, or essentially three ways that advertisements can constitute clutter to the audience: quantity, competitiveness, and intrusiveness. Quantity is the large number of ads or proportion of ads (degree of commercialization) in the space of an editorial media unit, or the so-called list length effect, and commercial load (Bellman et al., 2012). Competitiveness is the degree of similarity of the product categories in the ads in an editorial media unit, causing confusion and perceived duplication among the audiences. Intrusiveness is the degree the ads interfere with the audience's consumption of editorial content. So, a commercial inserted in between two programs would be considered less intrusive than the one inserted in an unexpected commercial break that interrupts the flow of a program. Although Ha's (1996) study showed that both the quantity and intrusiveness dimensions had the most negative impact on advertising effectiveness in terms of recall, recognition, and attitude toward the ad, the competitiveness dimensions of clutter could still be a concern when researchers examine ads that are of similar product categories in a more captive medium such as television and not in a self-paced medium such as magazines. The many similar product/service sponsored links in a Google search are a common example of highly competitive digital ad clutter as consumers can be confused by the highly similar product listings.

Effects of Clutter

Approaches to Clutter Effects

Despite the interest of advertisers and researchers in the effects of clutter, the results are inconclusive due to several reasons. First is due to the difference in the captivity of media, which is the degree to which the user can control the pace of flow of content of the medium. Captive media, such as TV and radio, usually result in higher ad recall than self-paced media, such as print and online. For example, Hammer, Riebe, and Kennedy (2009) found that there is no difference in the recall of ads and ad avoidance in radio and TV with more or fewer ads. Creative execution is a better predictor of recall than clutter. Second is the difference in user task orientations. If users have a clear task, their tolerance of clutter is lower. If they are in a leisure/surfing mode, they are less resistant toward clutter. Third is the difference between laboratory and field research settings. The lab environment that controls many variables and forces ad/editorial exposure to participants could result in higher recall and recognition than the many distractions the audience would be faced with in field settings.

Ha and McCann (2008) proposed an integrated model of advertising clutter to provide a comprehensive model of understanding perception formation and its effects in both the digital and traditional media environments. Their model includes (1) the structural approach, (2) the information processing approach, and (3) the goal impediment (functional) approach in examining the effect of advertising clutter. The difference between online and offline advertising clutter is mainly in the increase in advertiser control of advertising display time/customization, and variety in ad formats for user control (see Figure 9.1).

The structural approach is about the physical attributes of ads. In this case, it is advertising clutter, which is controllable by advertisers and the media firm. These attributes include the duration of ads, number of ads, location and visibility of ads, ad-context/editorial congruity, and the execution (production quality) of the ads. These factors can affect the perception of clutter level among the audiences.

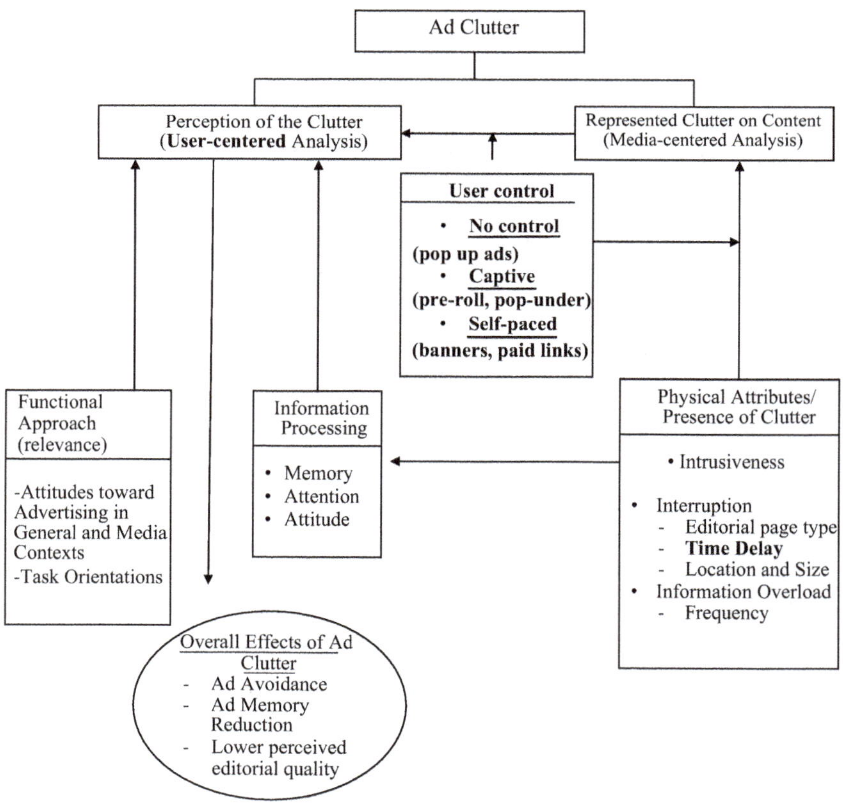

Figure 9.1 A Conceptual Framework of Advertising Clutter in Online Media (Bold faces indicate differences from offline media).

Although physical attributes as a media-centered analysis can influence perception of clutter, there are other information processing factors affecting perception of clutter such as overall attitudes toward advertising (e.g., Muehling, 1987), persuasion knowledge or the awareness of a persuasive intent in advertising (e.g., Campbell & Kirmani, 2000). Capability of processing advertising messages among the audiences (perceived message overload) can also affect the perceived advertising clutter level. Reactance theory and overload theory are the common theories used to explain the negative effects of clutter. Reactance theory argues that audiences resist external control over them and react negatively toward efforts to persuade them (Brehm & Brehm, 1981; Edwards, Li, & Lee, 2002), while overload theory explains the inability of audiences to process large amounts of messages in a cluttered situation (Malhotra, Jain, & Lagakos, 1982). In addition, users select advertising that is perceived as relevant or interesting for them to process based on selective attention theory to save their attention resources (Smith & Buchholz, 1991).

Finally, the consumer's involvement in the advertised product will affect their processing of the advertising based on the Elaboration Likelihood Model proposed by Petty, Cacioppo, and Schumann (1983). Consumers highly involved in the advertised product will use a central processing route and pay attention to the information contained in the advertising. Consumers not involved in the advertised product will use peripheral cues such as advertising execution elements to process the ads. When advertising clutter consists largely of products that consumers are not involved in, then the entertainment value of the ads becomes a critical factor for them to process and remember the ads. Hence, researchers on advertising clutter should also take into consideration the information processing approach in examining effects of advertising clutter on the processing of advertising messages.

There is also the functional approach that can be applied to the study of clutter by examining how clutter affects the editorial content consumption process and the goal or user task in media content consumption. Similar to the user mode in Rodgers and Thorson's (2000) Interactive Advertising Model, Ha and McCann's (2008) integrated model proposed that user task orientations affected perceived clutter levels. Informational searches and task-oriented consumers will have a higher perceived level of ad clutter than entertainment, exploration, and shopping-oriented consumers. Subsequent empirical research by Zanjani, Diamond, and Chan (2011) confirmed that information seekers were more likely to be affected by ad clutter than surfers. Their experiment shows that advertising clutter has little effect on surfers who have no particular purpose in consuming the e-magazine. But those who have the task of seeking information found the ad clutter intrusive and avoided the ads. Their recognition and recall of ads were lower when the ad-context congruity increased. Nonetheless, Seyedghorban, Tahernejad, and Matanda (2016) found that paratelic users (surfers) were more likely to perceive higher advertising clutter than telic users (task performers) because they were more likely to have prior negative experiences with online advertising, e.g., they had clicked on ads that were not useful to them.

Segev, Wang, and Fernandes's (2014) study of advertising on blogs found that importance of ad-context congruency is contingent upon consumers' issue involvement. Ad-context congruency is especially important to those who feel the issue in the editorial content is very relevant to them. But to those who are less involved with the issue, ads that are incongruent with context are better perceived.

Types of Clutter Effects

There are three types of clutter effects on audiences: cognitive, affective, and behavioral. Cognitive effects refer to the impact of advertising clutter in the processing of the advertisements especially in terms of how advertising is be remembered and understood by consumers. Affective effects are about the impacts of clutter on the consumers' attitudes and emotional reactions toward the advertising. Behavioral effects are actions taken by the consumer because of perceived advertising clutter such as avoiding or resisting the persuasive message of the advertising.

Cognitive Effects of Advertising Clutter

The most common measures of the effects of clutter are its negative cognitive effects on memory of advertisements. For memory of ads, unaided and aided recall, and recognition of ads with choices are common measures. Lee and Cho's (2010) experiment found that there is an interactive effect between frequency of the ads and online advertising clutter. In a highly cluttered web page, frequency of the target ad facilitated memory, but not recognition, of the banner ad. Bellman et al.'s (2012) experiment found that beyond three minutes of commercials within the primetime shows online, there was a marked decline in ad recall and recognition. The negative cognitive effect is related to the quantity of advertising, but not the intrusiveness of advertising. Such contradictory result of the effect of intrusiveness on memory of ads between online videos (Bellman et al., 2012) and print (Ha, 1996) probably is caused by the different measure of intrusiveness: "perceived" intrusiveness of magazines ads (Ha, 1996) and the researcher's own manipulation of number of commercial breaks in the videos on the consumption assuming everyone has the same perceived level of intrusiveness (Bellman et al., 2012).

Affective Effects of Advertising Clutter

Affective effects of clutter include attitude toward the advertisement (A_{ad}) in the medium/media vehicle, attitude toward advertising in general, attitude toward the brand (A_{br}), perceived editorial quality, and enjoyment of media content.

It is a well-known fact that consumers have different expectations and attitudes toward advertising in different media. For example, the Millward Brown Global AdReactions Report of 6,000 mobile media users worldwide (Statista, 2016) results showed that consumers have much more favorable attitudes toward TV (51%), radio (50%), and magazine ads than online media such as online video ads (28%), mobile ads (23%), and e-mail ads (18%). Elliot and Speck (1998) found different receptiveness toward advertising clutter for different media. The attitude transfer process can explain how negative attitudes toward advertising that appears in media may affect attitude toward the ad (A_{ad}) and attitude toward a specific brand (A_{br}).

It is also important to understand that ad clutter as a measurement of commercialization can also affect perceived editorial quality of the media vehicle. For example, too many ads in a magazine will adversely affect the audience's perception of the quality of the magazine and lower the value of the advertisement to the advertiser (Ha & Litman, 1997). Kim and Sundar's (2010) experiment also found that subjects who saw relevant ad clutter evaluated the website that displayed the ads significantly more positively than the website that had irrelevant ad clutter. So, it is not just amount but also *relevancy* that determines the affective effect of clutter. Hence, advertising clutter does not only threaten effectiveness of advertising but also the editorial media that carry the advertising as well.

Clutter can also affect the enjoyment of editorial content. Disengagement and adaptation are two psycho-physiological responses to the video programs resulting from ad clutter (Bellman et al., 2012). Disengagement is a decline in autonomic arousal after watching commercials in a video. Adaptation is the disruption and welcome break of the hedonic experience of media content through commercials that led to increasing enjoyment.

Behavioral Effects of Advertising Clutter

Behavioral effects of advertising clutter include advertising avoidance and reactance, such as not clicking through the ads. One commonly studied behavioral effect of ad clutter is advertising avoidance. Many advertising avoidance studies, including Cho and Cheon's (2004) model, include perceived advertising clutter as a factor causing advertising avoidance. Almost all advertising avoidance studies included one or more clutter dimension in their studies to explain why people avoid advertising (Rejón-Guardia & Martínez-López, 2014; Seyedghorban, Tahernejad, & Matanda, 2016).

Another behavioral effect is advertising reactance, that is, the resistance to be persuaded by the advertisement after exposure to the ads. When consumers feel overwhelmed by advertisements and cannot avoid them for whatever reasons (such as loud noise, blocked screen), they will resist the advertising and purposely reject the advertising messages they are exposed to. They can ignore or refuse to follow the suggestions and actions recommended by the advertisers, such as clicking through the link/ad. Schumann, von Wangenheim, and Groene (2014) found lower click-through rates (CTRs) among consumers who reported higher ad clutter in their experiment of receptiveness toward digital advertising.

Attention to Advertising in Multiple Web Pages

How do online users process ads in a cluttered environment? Goodrich's (2011) study used a dual attitude model to explain users' processing of ads in a cluttered environment by comparing mere exposure versus conscious processing of online advertising shown in a sequence of eight web pages with some containing banner ads. Her experiment found interaction effects of ad types and ad locations. Visual ads on the right side of a web page and text ads on the left side of the page resulted in higher attention. However, high attention was negatively correlated with brand attitude. The tested product, an electric shaver, did not have a contextual fit with the web pages. The Goodrich (2011) study showed that attention to the ad due to structural factors such as advertising types and location may not result in liking of the brand. Breaking through the clutter is not just about generating attention to the ad but also creating a positive brand attitude.

In the following section, clutter-related issues in several major digital advertising formats are examined.

Digital Advertising Clutter in Different Ad Formats

Search Advertising and Competitiveness of Ads

Search advertising revenue in the U.S. reached $132 billion in 2024, which is 40% of the total revenue of all digital advertising types (Statista, 2024). Despite this, relatively little research has been published about search ads (Ha, 2008). Even when it was studied, it was mainly for relevance (ad-contextual congruity), rather than competitiveness in relation to ad clutter. Dou, Linn, and Yang's (2001) study examined the online ad industry's use of smart banners by typing in 345 keywords for 115 product categories in 11 search engines. They found that many smart banners did not find relevant results. Kim and Sundar's (2010) experiment using a small student sample ($N = 13$) found that advertising clutter could be reduced by increasing the relevance of ads to the website context without reducing the number of ads. Haans, Raassens, and Van Hout (2013) found that evidence type used in the text affected the CTR of the sponsored links (search ads) in low-involvement products. Expert and statistical evidence were considered the most credible and attractive to the searchers. An interaction effect was found in Yoo's (2011) experiment between positivity of advertising message frame and presence of keywords in the search results in facilitating the sponsored link click-through.

One main assumption in search advertising is that when consumers type in a keyword or a phrase into a search engine, such as Google, they are interested in the product/service and, subsequently, are in a shopping mode. But if the consumer tries to research specific information on a topic rather than shopping, then these so-called smart ads become an impediment to completing that goal because shopping is not a goal at that time. The consumer must browse through all the paid listings to find relevant listing to their search. This extra effort will not lead to more use of the ads but may add to the consumers' resentment toward the advertisers (and search engines) that serve the ads.

Even with the smart ads or personalized ads, there is another issue of trust in the advertisers. Those advertisers to whom the consumers are unfamiliar but who used personalized ads will create a backlash effect because they are seen as violating privacy and stealing personal data from the consumer, i.e., they will be considered less trustworthy and manipulative by consumers (Bleier & Eisenbeiss, 2015). There are also ethical and legal concerns about targeted online behavioral advertising (Nill & Aalberts, 2014). Hence, adding the relevance of the ads is not as effective as it seems. Schumann, von Wangenheim, and Groene's (2014) experiment showed that normative reciprocity, i.e., reminding consumers that receiving targeted advertising as a return for getting free services, was more effective in gaining consumer acceptance than emphasizing the utility value of the targeted advertising to the consumers. The CTR of the targeted ads was higher even in higher perceived clutter level when the reciprocity argument was presented.

Banner Blindness Effects

Banner blindness refers to the overlooking of banner ads on a web page. Several studies about consumers' attention to banner ads (Benway, 1998) have found a banner blindness effect if the banners are placed in an F shape on a screen (i.e., too high or on the edges) or for users who are to perform a goal-directed search for information (Pagendarm & Schaumburg, 2001). Banner ads on Facebook attracted much lower attention levels than the friends' recommendations of the user (Barreto, 2013). Consumers easily overlook these banner ads. However, these banner blindness studies did not vary the number of banners (quantity) or whether the banners pop-up or animate on the users' screen (intrusiveness) to examine if banner blindness still occurred. Frequency of banner ads has been shown to positively relate to recall in clutter situations (Zanjani, Diamond, & Chan, 2011). Prior studies have shown that pop-up ads (Cho & Cheon, 2004; Edwards, Li, & Lee, 2002) caught the consumers' attention despite the negative effect of stimulating their intention to avoid the ads. Animated ads can arouse consumers and draw attention to the ads (Sundar & Kalyanaraman, 2004; Yoo, Kim, & Stout, 2004). Hence, the manner of how banners are presented to consumers is critical for them to be viewed as clutter.

Pre-Roll Ads vs. Mid-Roll Commercials in Online Videos and TV Shows

Despite the increasing use of in-stream video advertising in online videos, not many published studies examine video advertising from a clutter perspective. One major concern of clutter in online in-stream video ads is the position of the ads that can affect the intrusiveness of the ads. There are three types of positions: pre-roll (before the video is shown), mid-roll (inserted in the middle of the video content like TV commercial breaks), and post-roll ads (shown after the video is over or between episodes). Krishnan and Sitaraman's (2013) study of Akamai's video delivery network with 65 million unique viewers watching 362 million videos and 257 million ad video of 33 video providers found that mid-roll ads were 18.1% more likely to complete when placed as a mid-roll than as a pre-roll. Bellman et al.'s (2012) study comparing different levels of mid-roll advertising clutter in TV shows online revealed that that the optimal level of online video advertising was three minutes per hour with six different ads and was similar to research on traditional TV advertising clutter. They also found a primacy order effect in that only the first ad being shown had a greater advantage in getting attention and was better remembered than other ads.

Li and Lo's (2015) experiment showed that mid-roll ads led to better brand name recognition than pre-roll and post-roll ads and the interaction effect of ad-position and ad-context congruity. They explained that the mid-roll ads performed better due to attention spillover from the video when editorial content for ads was congruent with the content, such as watches shown in fashion programs. But when the ad was unrelated to the video content, the audiences simply ignored the ads with no benefit of brand recognition even if they were put as mid-roll ads. They found that incongruent ads with content worked best in post-roll ads. However, it should be noted that all these studies about online video ads only measured their effects on memory and brand recognition, rather than attitude toward the ad or brand. We believe that the latter are more important measures of advertising effectiveness if we consider the main purpose of advertising is persuasion.

With these lab-based experimental findings supporting the effectiveness of mid-roll ads, it is interesting that YouTube, the largest online video provider, still employs pre-roll full ads and TrueView ads, which allow users to skip ads after five seconds. It is because pre-roll ads can capture the most viewers and must be viewed for consumers to watch the video (and can even include those consumers who did not finish the video). Hence, the provision of choice may reduce consumers' resistance toward the ads. Even if there is only one commercial, which is typical in a YouTube video, consumers may view it as unwanted or an obstacle to the use of the video content, which puts it squarely in the realm of an ad clutter effect study.

Measures of Digital Editorial Unit and Digital Advertising Clutter

A critical need for researchers of digital advertising clutter is to determine the editorial unit. An editorial unit should be the primary content that the users consume in an editorial medium such as a blog, the non-sponsored social media feed on a user's screen, a non-advertising web page shown to the user on the display device rather than the entire website or all social media feeds which consists of multiple screens. Hence, the editorial unit will vary by the type of display device in which the digital advertising is placed. Nonetheless, the first screen visible to the user without scrolling down probably is the most conservative and standardized measure of editorial unit. It is because scrolling down a page will become another page of content on the screen and that requires extra effort by users of the content. It is hard to estimate how many users scroll down the screen to view the entire page.

Other deep-link destination pages of a website are a further step for a user to explore the site, and more research is needed to estimate the likelihood of users to scroll further down a website. In a digital video setting, the duration of the video should be an editorial unit. A smartphone screen is much smaller than a tablet or a computer screen, so the likelihood of perceived clutter level is higher in a smartphone screen than its bigger screen counterparts when advertising is displayed as a proportion of space. It is important that advertisers prepare different versions of ads for different versions of the page. Many web pages now have a computer version and a mobile version. Advertisers should also prepare their ads accordingly for the mobile version and computer version to minimize the perceived advertising clutter.

If we still use the conceptualization of three dimensions of clutter as the advertising environment presented to the audiences, then we need to develop measures of the digital advertising clutter corresponding to the three dimensions regarding different advertising formats. For example, the clutter level from a quantity dimension would be the proportion of the screen or number of advertisement/sponsored links or both, depending on the ad format of interest. If sponsored links and small buttons/banners are used for comparison, then the number of ads will be a better measure. But if prominence or size is the key issue of concern, then the proportion of screen devoted to digital banner ads/sponsored links should be a measure of digital ad quantity. If the digital ad is in the form of in-stream video, the proportion of the duration of the commercial over the actual video can be used to measure the quantity of ads in addition to commercial load.

As for the competitiveness dimension, the degree of similar product categories being shown on a screen should be a measure of competitiveness. Hence, in a Google search page, the proportion of sponsored links from the same product/service categories among all the sponsored links will be the competitiveness measure. In fact, judging from this perspective, even the sponsored links occupy little physical space of a page, because of their high similarity in product categories; its competitiveness clutter level is likely quite high. Yet, because of the high ad-context congruity in the search algorithm and display of the sponsored links, the perceived competitiveness may be viewed as favorable instead of confusing. But whether users may be confused or more willing to try different sponsors in more sponsored links in different search settings will require more research.

For the intrusive dimension, whether the user is forced to view the ad on a screen or per video/podcast will be the main measure. The most intrusive one is the total blocking of the use of editorial content until the ad is fully displayed, such as pop-up ads and non-skippable video ads on online videos. The moderately intrusive one will be the TrueView type of skippable ads (after five seconds of compulsory display, the users can opt out of the ad) and the mid-roll ads. The non-intrusive one will be banner ads or sponsored links on the side of the screen that users can easily ignore and where no editorial content is blocked from the users. As new digital formats emerge with either higher or lower levels of intrusiveness, researchers should continue to monitor advertising formats and measure the perceived intrusiveness of digital ads to consumers (Table 9.1).

Table 9.1 Measurement of Clutter Dimension in Different Platforms

	Quantity	*Competitiveness*	*Intrusiveness*
TV	Number of commercials and breaks between programs	Number of commercials of the same/similar product category in the same break	Number of commercial breaks within a program
Print	Number of advertisements or proportion of advertising space to editorial space	Number of advertisements of the same/similar product category in the newspaper/magazine	Number of advertisements that are inserted within an article
Computer	Total number of online video ads Total number of banner ads	Number or proportion of similar product ads or search results listing on the same screen	Online video ad: number of pre-roll and mid-roll ads, number of pop-up ads
Mobile phone/ devices	Social media: number and size of non-pop-up sponsored ads/ feeds Phone apps: number of brand apps on one phone screen Web browser: number of banner ads showing on a phone screen within a period of time (such as five minutes)	Social media: number or proportion of similar products listing on the same feed Phone apps: number of brand apps from the same category on one phone screen Web browser: number of banner ads of the same product category showing on a phone screen within a period of time (such as five minutes)—number or proportion of similar product ads or search results listing	Social media/Web browser: number and size of pop-up ads/ sponsored content blocking part of the screen, number and size of alerts of video and sponsored ads Online video ads: number of pre-roll and mid-roll ads, number of pop-up ads

Mobile Advertising and New Levels of Ad-Context Congruity

Now, mobile media represents a large portion of online access. Ceci (2025) reported that 62.5% of global internet users used their mobile devices to access the internet. Hence, digital ads are much more likely to be displayed on mobile media, which have smaller screens. The Global Positioning System and other access of mobile users' data allow even more possibility of customization for advertisers. These so-called location-based advertising and targeting created more opportunities for ad-context congruity. It raises ad-context congruity to a much high level by the sheer ability to put the ad near the actual purchase time and location. Indeed, Bauer and Strauss's (2016) review of location-based advertising studies on mobile devices identified at least 12 types of contextual information from mobile phones that can aid advertisers: (1) users' location, (2) the time the ad can be delivered when users use the device, (3) users' profiles, (4) users' interests, (5) users' preferences, (6) users' behaviors, (7) user' demographics, (8) weather at the user's location, (9) characteristics of the surrounding environment, (10) type of mobile device the user is using, (11) users' needs (related to search), and (12) users' activities. Despite all these possibilities, an important concern is how much the advertiser should take advantage of such contextual information without being seen as violating the privacy of the individual user. Weather is public information while user demographic information is not. Some types of relevancies may be more welcomed than others. For example, location may be a welcome customization. When someone searches a restaurant, a local restaurant ad display would be more relevant than a restaurant at a far distance from the user unless the user specifies the location of the restaurant. Or when someone is in a shopping mall, ads and sales discount offers from stores in the shopping mall would be highly relevant.

Okazaki, Molina, and Hirose (2012) argue that the perceived ubiquity of mobile ads to the consumers led to the avoidance of mobile ads. Yet, how many of the customized mobile ads they would like to receive and how these ads should be displayed (pointers on maps, text messages, banners, buttons, or videos) should be further studied. In addition to traditional measures of clutter's impact on advertising effectiveness such as memory of the ad, other screen-specific attention metrics measures on users' focus on the ad such as scroll depth (tracking how deep the users scroll down the page) and time-in-view (tracking how long an advertisement is displayed on the screen) can be used as the outcome measure for mobile ad and other digital ad clutter.

Future of Digital Advertising Clutter Research

Differences between Pull and Push Advertising

A final factor to be considered in clutter research is whether the advertising is requested by the consumer (on-demand) or given to the consumer. Ads may not be perceived as clutter when consumers are the ones who request the information/ads (pull), such as a product search on Amazon.com for shopping. But when ads are presented without consumers' requesting it (push), they are more easily perceived as clutter (Brettel & Spilker-Attig, 2010; Grusell, 2007). Consumers are much more likely to find the ads helpful when they choose to receive the ads (pull), and they resent misleading ads that do not deliver what they were promised (Truong & Simmons, 2010). It is easy to push digital targeted ads to consumers using computer programming, but consumers' reactance can be much higher if the ads interrupt the consumption of other digital content.

Digital ads, while they are relatively easy to be customized to the consumer based on their location, use time, and other contextual information available in mobile devices, so are they also more likely to be seen as clutter impeding the consumption of editorial content if the customization is seen as illegitimate (e.g., advertisers should not know the user's information, such as an advertiser with no prior relationship with the user). In other words, customization is a double-edged sword that advertisers need to be aware of. A hierarchy will need to be developed by researchers to determine an acceptable level of relevance and customization and how much consumers trust and view the utility value of such information.

Research questions that would guide this inquiry include: How many ads (quantity) and how many ads from companies from the same category (competitiveness) interrupt the flow of editorial content (intrusiveness)? And, in different usage situations (pull vs. push), what effect does customization have on consumer responses (e.g., avoidance, anger, resentment, and ad blocking)?

One important question in digital advertising is the blurring boundaries between ads and editorial content. The increasing call for "native advertising," such as product brand placement and sponsored content, to combat avoidance of clearly identified advertisements (Verhellen, Dens, & De Pelsmacker, 2013) may push the concept of clutter to another level. Should we include native ads in the measurement of clutter level? If yes, then we need to first determine what is pure editorial content and what is sponsored content. All sponsored content should be considered clutter, including product placement, but it is part of the editorial content. Hence, it may be better to put advertising clutter in perspective by limiting it to third-party editorial media, such as a mobile app or a web page (either regular or mobile version) not owned by the advertiser and exclude subtle brand placements.

Although this chapter has proposed measurement of digital editorial units and clutter levels, it would also be helpful for researchers to examine the degree of discrepancy between the physical attributes of advertising clutter and perceived levels of clutter by varying each functional and individual information processing factor to see which factor(s) affect the perceived clutter level most. It should be noted that creativity in advertising would facilitate the acceptance of ads as entertainment instead of clutter.

Artificial Intelligence and Advertising Clutter

Artificial intelligence (AI) is a new kind of creative resource. It is constantly changing the way humans innovate because it can inspire not only creative thinking methods but also enhance the human ability to create and provide new ideas. In addition, AI often breaks the limits of traditional thinking and encourages people to explore unconventional ideas, further promoting human creativity (Pagani & Wind, 2024). For example, more and more AI software (such as ChatGPT, Midjourney, and Make-A-Video) can generate images, videos, texts based on customers' instructions, and these AI-generated contents can be used for advertising creation.

Another advantage of AI-generated advertising content (e.g., ChatGPT) is that it can reduce costs and quickly complete an advertisement campaign in just five minutes by entering only a few keywords, including multiple versions of advertisement copy. This cannot be completed by human copywriters. Such use of AI-generated advertisement is not just a short-term fad: 82% of digital advertisers recognize that AI will play a central role in their advertising efforts within five years (Jatoi, 2025). AI can also generate a large amount of content in a short time, and there is no doubt that this new way of content creation greatly improves creative efficiency. The increased supply of these AI-generation advertisements is going to increase advertising clutter by the sheer quantity.

One worry about the use of generative AI is that it could lead to a reduction in content diversity, even resulting in content homogenization as shown in Anderson, Shah, and Kreminski (2024) study. This is because the AI-generated content is based on the same popularly used images and texts available online; they are likely to be similar. If creators rely on AI tools, it could result in a lot of homogeneous content appearing on the audiences' screens. More importantly, this phenomenon of homogenization not only affects the creativity but also exacerbates the spread of racial/ethnicity and gender groups stereotypes. Researcher has found that ChatGPT tends to portray different racial/ethnicity groups (such as African, Asian, and Hispanic America) and gender groups (such as women) in a more uniform way, lacking diversity, which further intensifies racial and gender homogenization (Lee, Montgomery, & Lai, 2024). Hence, generative AI can add more of the same advertising content, causing higher perceived advertising clutter.

However, AI can also analyze large amounts of data to understand audience preferences and then create personalized advertisements that match their interests and resonate with them through AI-based algorithm (Gujar & Panyam, 2024). Besides, Gu et al.'s (2024) study found that AI-generated advertisements that are lively, realistic, and creative make the audience feel more authentic and therefore are more likely to be liked and accepted. If AI-generated advertisements seem dogmatic, lack vitality, and feel too synthetic, consumers are less likely to accept those ads. Furthermore, it is difficult for humans to distinguish between human-created images and AI-generated images. A quantitative study involving 50 participants to analyze human versus AI-generated image found that only 38.7% of them could accurately recognize the difference, and they only relied on some flaws of AI-generated images as clues to recognize the difference. Therefore, as the number and sophistication of AI-generated advertisements increase, it will become even harder for the public to recognize these contents (Lu et al., 2023). Hence, AI is creating a paradox for advertising clutter in the future: it may worsen the clutter with more homogeneous ads and larger quantity of ads. It may also contribute to a better advertising environment with less perceived clutter if the ads are of better quality and are relevant to the individuals.

References

Anderson, B. R., Shah, J. H., & Kreminski, M. (2024) Homogenization effects of large language models on human creative ideation. In *Proceedings of the 16th Conference on Creativity & Cognition* (pp. 413–425). Chicago, Illinois: ACM.

Backlinko (September 2, 2024). Ad blocker usage and demographic characteristics. https://backlinko.com/ad-blockers-users#adblock-top-picks

Barreto, M. A. (2013). Do users look at banner ads on Facebook? *Journal of Research in Interactive Marketing*, *7*(2), 119–139. https://doi.org/10.1108/JRIM-Mar-2012-0013

Bauer, C., & Strauss, C. (2016). Location-based advertising on mobile devices. *Management Review Quarterly*, *66*(3), 159–194. https://doi.org/10.1007/s11301-015-0118-z

Benway, J. P. (1998). Banner blindness: The irony of attention grabbing on the World Wide Web. In *Proceedings of the Human Factors and Ergonomics Society Annual Meeting*, *42*(5), 463–467. https://doi.org/10.1177/154193129804200504

Bellman, S., Treleaven-Hassard, S., Robinson, J. A., Rask, A., & Varan, D. (2012). Getting the balance right: Commercial loading in online video programs. *Journal of Advertising*, *41*(2), 5–24. https://doi.org/10.2753/JOA0091-3367410201

Bleier, A., & Eisenbeiss, M. (2015). The importance of trust for personalized online advertising. *Journal of Retailing*, *91*(3), 390–409. https://doi.org/10.1016/j.jretai.2015.04.001

Brehm, S. S., & Brehm, J. W. (1981) *Psychological reactance: A theory of freedom and control.* New York: Academic Press.

Brettel, M., & Spilker-Attig, A. (2010). Online advertising effectiveness: A cross-cultural comparison. *Journal of Research in Interactive Marketing*, *4*(3), 176–196. https://doi.org/10.1108/17505931011070569

Brown, T. J., & Rothschild, M. L. (1993). Reassessing the impact of television advertising clutter. *Journal of Consumer Research, 20*(1), 138–146. https://doi.org/10.1086/209339

Burns, K. S., & Lutz, R. J. (2006). The function of format: Consumer responses to six on-line advertising formats. *Journal of Advertising*, *35*(1), 53–63. https://doi.org/10.2753/JOA0091-3367350104

Campbell, M. C., & Kirmani, A. (2000). Consumers' use of persuasion knowledge: The effects of accessibility and cognitive capacity on perceptions of an influence agent. *Journal of Consumer Research*, *27*(1), 69–83. https://doi.org/10.1086/209339

Ceci, L. (February 5, 2025). Mobile internet usage worldwide – statistics and facts. Statista. https://www.statista.com/topics/779/mobile-internet/#topicOverview

Cho, C., & Cheon, H. J. (2004). Why do people avoid advertising on the internet? *Journal of Advertising, 33*(4), 89–97. https://doi.org/10.1080/00913367.2004.10639175

Dou, W., Linn, R., & Yang, S. (2001). How smart are 'smart banners'? *Journal of Advertising Research, 41*(4), 31–43. https://doi.org/10.2501/jar-41-4-31-43

Ducoffe, R. H. (1995). How consumers assess the value of advertising. *Journal of Current Issues & Research in Advertising, 17*(1), 1–18. https://doi.org/10.1080/10641734.1995.10505022

Edwards, S. M., Li, H., & Lee, J. H. (2002). Forced exposure and psychological reactance: Antecedents and consequences of the perceived intrusiveness of pop-up ads. *Journal of Advertising, 31*(3), 83–96. https://doi.org/10.1080/00913367.2002.10673678

Elliot, M. T., & Speck, P. S. (1998). Consumer perceptions of advertising clutter and its impact across various media. *Journal of Advertising Research, 38*(1), 29–41.

Goodrich, K. (2011). Anarchy of effects? Exploring attention to online advertising and multiple outcomes. *Psychology & Marketing 28*(4), 417–440. https://doi.org/10.1002/mar.20371

Grusell, M. (2007). Advertising? Yes please, but only when it's my choice. *Journal of Media Business Studies, 4*(3), 87–101. https://doi.org/10.1080/16522354.2007.11073457

Gu, C., Jia, S., Lai, J., Chen, R., & Chang, X. (2024). Exploring consumer acceptance of AI-Generated advertisements: From the perspectives of perceived eeriness and perceived intelligence. *Journal of Theoretical and Applied Electronic Commerce Research, 19*(3), 2218–2238. https://doi.org/10.3390/jtaer19030108

Gujar, P., & Panyam, S. (2024). Generative AI in digital advertising campaigns. *International Journal of Computer Trends and Technology, 72*(5), 51–55. https://doi.org/10.14445/22312803/IJCTT-V72I5P106

Ha, L. (1996). Advertising clutter in consumer magazines: Dimensions and effects. *Journal of Advertising Research, 36*(4), 76–85. https://doi.org/10.1080/00218499.1996.12466507

Ha, L., & Litman, B. (1997). Does advertising clutter have diminishing returns? *Journal of Advertising, 26*(1), 31–42. https://doi.org/10.1080/00913367.1997.10673516

Ha, L., & McCann, K. (2008). An integrated model of advertising clutter in offline and online media environment. *International Journal of Advertising, 27*(4), 569–592. https://www.tandfonline.com/doi/abs/10.2501/S0265048708080153

Ha, L. (2008). Online advertising research in advertising journals: A review. *Journal of Current Issues and Research in Advertising, 30*(1), 33–50. https://doi.org/10.1080/10641734.2008.10505236

Haans, H., Raassens, N., & Van Hout, R. (2013). Search engine advertisements: The impact of advertising statements on clickthrough and conversion rates. *Marketing Letters, 24*(2), 151–163. https://doi.org/10.1007/s11002-013-9226-5

Hammer, P., Riebe, E., & Kennedy, R. (2009). How clutter affects advertising effectiveness. *Journal of Advertising Research, 49*(2), 159–163. https://doi.org/10.2501/S0021849909090217

Heinz, S., Hug, M., Nugaeva, C., & Opwis, K. (2013, April). Online ad banners: The effects of goal orientation and content congruence on memory. In *CHI'13 Extended Abstracts on Human Factors in Computing Systems* (pp. 1875–1880). Paris, France: ACM.

Jatoi, U. S. (2025). AI ad creation services that replace manual copywriting. *Pearl Lemon.* https://pearllemon.com/rise-of-ai-generated-ads/#elementor-toc__heading-anchor-9

Kim, N. Y., & Sundar, S. S. (2010). Relevance to the rescue: Can "smart ads" reduce negative response to online ad clutter? *Journalism & Mass Communication Quarterly, 87*(2), 346–362. https://doi.org/10.1177/107769901008700208

Ko, H., Cho, C. H., & Roberts, M. S. (2005). Internet uses and gratifications: A structural equation model of interactive advertising. *Journal of Advertising*, *34*(2), 57–70. https://doi.org/10.1080/00913367.2005.10639191

Krishnan, S. S., & Sitaraman, R. K. (2013, October). Understanding the effectiveness of video ads: A measurement study. In *Proceedings of the 2013 Conference on Internet Measurement Conference* (pp. 149–162). Barcelona, Spain: ACM.

Lee, M. H. J., Montgomery, J. M., & Lai, C. K. (2024). Large language models portray socially subordinate groups as more homogeneous, consistent with a bias observed in humans | *proceedings of the 2024 ACM Conference on Fairness, accountability, and transparency*. ACM DL Digital Library. https://dl.acm.org/doi/10.1145/3630106.3658975

Lee, S. Y., & Cho, Y. S. (2010). Do web users care about banner ads anymore? The effects of frequency and clutter in web advertising. *Journal of Promotion Management, 16*(3), 288–302. https://doi.org/10.1080/10496490903582594

Li, H., & Lo, H. Y. (2015). Do you recognize its brand? The effectiveness of online in-stream video advertisements. *Journal of Advertising*, *44*(3), 208–218. https://doi.org/10.1080/00913367.2014.956376

Lu, Z., Huang, D., Bai, L., Qu, J., Wu, C., Liu, X., & Ouyang, W. (2023). Seeing is not always believing: Benchmarking human and model perception of AI-generated images. *Advances in Neural Information Processing Systems*, *36*, 25435–25447.

Malhotra, N. K., Jain, A. K., & Lagakos, S. W. (1982). The information overload controversy: An alternative viewpoint. *Journal of Marketing*, *46*(2), 27–37. https://doi.org/10.1177/002224298204600204

Mord, M. S., & Gilson, E. (1985). Shorter units: Risk-responsibility-reward. *Journal of Advertising Research*, *25*(4), 9–19. https://doi.org/10.1080/00218499.1985.12467898

Muehling, D. D. (1987). An investigation of factors underlying attitude-toward-the-advertising in general. *Journal of Advertising, 16*(1), 32–40. https://doi.org/10.1080/00913367.1987.10673058

Nill, A., & Aalberts, R. J. (2014). Legal and ethical challenges of online behavioral targeting in advertising. *Journal of Current Issues & Research in Advertising*, *35*(2), 126–146. https://doi.org/10.1080/10641734.2014.899529

Okazaki, S., Molina, F. J., & Hirose, M. (2012). Mobile advertising avoidance: Exploring the role of ubiquity. *Electronic Markets*, *22*(3), 169–183. https://doi.org/10.1007/s12525-012-0087-1

Pagani, M., & Wind, Y. (2024). Unlocking marketing creativity using artificial intelligence. *Journal of Interactive Marketing*, *60*(1), 1–24. https://doi.org/10.1177/10949968241265855

Pagendarm, M., & Schaumburg, H. (2001). Why are users banner-blind? The impact of navigation style on the perception of web banners. *Journal of Digital Information, 2*(1). https://journals.tdl.org/jodi/index.php/jodi/article/view/36/38

Petty, R., Cacioppo, J. T., & Schumann, D. (1983). Central and peripheral routes to advertising effectiveness: The moderating role of involvement. *Journal of Consumer Research, 10*(3), 135–146. https://doi.org/10.1086/208954

Pieters, R. G. M., & Bijmolt, T. H. A. (1997). Consumer memory for television advertising: A field study of duration, serial position, and competition effects. *Journal of Consumer Research*, *23*, 362–372. https://doi.org/10.1086/209489

Rejón-Guardia, F., & Martínez-López, F. J. (2014). Online advertising intrusiveness and consumers' avoidance behaviors. In *Handbook of strategic e-business management* (pp. 565–586). Springer Berlin Heidelberg.

Rodgers, S., & Thorson, E. (2000). The interactive advertising model: How users perceive and process online ads. *Journal of Interactive Advertising*, *1*(1), 41–60. https://doi.org/10.1080/15252019.2000.10722043

Schumann, J. H., von Wangenheim, F., & Groene, N. (2014). Targeted online advertising: Using reciprocity appeals to increase acceptance among users of free web services. *Journal of Marketing*, *78*(1), 59–75. https://doi.org/10.1509/jm.11.0316

Segev, S., Wang, W., & Fernandes, J. (2014). The effects of ad–context congruency on responses to advertising in blogs: Exploring the role of issue involvement. *International Journal of Advertising*, *33*(1), 17–36. https://doi.org/10.2501/IJA-33-1-017-036

Seyedghorban, Z., Tahernejad, H., & Matanda, M. J. (2016). Reinquiry into advertising avoidance on the internet: A conceptual replication and extension. *Journal of Advertising*, *45*(1), 120–129. https://doi.org/10.1080/00913367.2015.1085819

Smith, R. E., & Buchholz, L. M. (1991). Multiple resource theory and consumer processing of broadcast advertisements: An involvement perspective. *Journal of Advertising*, *20*(3), 1–8. https://doi.org/10.1080/00913367.1991.10673343

Statista (2016). Millward Brown AdReaction 2012 – global report. Retrieved from https://www.statista.com/statistics/247891/mobile-users-attitudes-towards-different-advertising-formats-worldwide/

Statista (2024). Search advertising in the United States - statistics & facts https://www.statista.com/topics/4312/search-advertising/

Sundar, S. S., & Kalyanaraman, S. (2004). Arousal, memory, and impression-formation effects of animation speed in Web advertising. *Journal of Advertising*, *33*(1), 7–17. https://doi.org/10.1080/00913367.2004.10639152

Tribbey, C. (February 1, 2016). Ad-blocking remains high hurdle for digital video. *Multichannel News*, p. 15.

Truong, Y., & Simmons, G. (2010). Perceived intrusiveness in digital advertising: Strategic marketing implications. *Journal of Strategic Marketing*, *18*(3), 239–256. https://doi.org/10.1080/09652540903511308

Verhellen, Y., Dens, N., & De Pelsmacker, P. (2013). Consumer responses to brands placed in YouTube movies: The effect of prominence and endorser expertise. *Journal of Electronic Commerce Research*, *14*(4), 287–303.

Webb, P. H. (1979). Consumer initial processing in a difficult media environment. *Journal of Consumer Research*, *6*, 225–236. https://doi.org/10.1086/208764

Yoo, C. Y. (2011). Interplay of message framing, keyword insertion and levels of product involvement in clickthrough of keyword search ads. *International Journal of Advertising*, *30*(3), 399–424. https://doi.org/10.2501/IJA-30-3-399-424

Yoo, C. Y., Kim, K., & Stout, P. A. (2004). Assessing the effects of animation in online banner advertising: Hierarchy of effects model. *Journal of Interactive Advertising*, *4*(2), 49–60. https://jiad.org/vol4/no2/yoo/index.htm

Zanjani, S. H. A., Diamond, W. D., & Chan, K. (2011). Does ad-context congruity help surfers and information seekers remember ads in cluttered e-magazines? *Journal of Advertising 40*(4), 67–84. https://doi.org/10.2753/JOA0091-3367400405

Zhao, X. (1997). Clutter and serial order redefined and retested. *Journal of Advertising Research*, *37*(5), 57–74. https://doi.org/10.1080/00218499.1997.12466696

10 Immersion in Games Exemplifies Why Digital Media Create Complex Responses to Ads

Mike Schmierbach

Digital advertising involves many platforms where traditional theories of advertising do not apply and thus require employment of theories and concepts borrowed from other literatures. Advertising in video games is an excellent example. Video games are popular sites for branded content, and their role in advertising is a growing phenomenon. Because games provide a platform wherein individuals can interact directly with virtual representations of the product as well as view branded messages in a more immersive virtual environment, it is not surprising that research consistently demonstrates the effectiveness of linking brand messages with games. Additionally, broader research into interactive advertising and virtual environments offers opportunities to apply lessons from game-advertising scholarship. But future research in this area will require thinking more carefully about how features of the game-player experience shape responses to the brand message, and this means a more nuanced understanding is required of the games themselves.

As an illustration, we can consider how in-game branded content can both benefit and suffer from immersive game characteristics. To do so successfully, it is important to (1) clearly explicate concepts borrowed from other research domains; (2) carefully define specific features of game platforms; (3) evaluate how brand message characteristics may function differently with different platform features; and (4) use appropriate analytical strategies based upon a coherent theoretical model.

Presence, Flow, and Transportation

Immersion in games involves many attributes, including spatial presence, narrative transportation, and flow. Spatial presence is broadly understood as the sense of physically being in the game space, and research shows that it results from factors such as head-mounted displays and motion controls (Caroux, 2023). Narrative transportation describes how much people become involved in the story and is sometimes described as narrative presence. In addition to being linked to persuasive outcomes in other media, transportation in games can help generate

DOI: 10.4324/9781003567523-13

empathy and emotional responses that align with character behavior (Mahood & Hanus, 2017). Finally, flow is understood as a highly immersive state that occurs when the challenge represented by a task is appropriately matched to the skill of the player. A long-standing argument suggests that flow directly correlates with video game enjoyment (Sherry, 2004). Scholars have further explored how these factors might relate to one another as well as enjoyment (e.g., Jin, 2011; Weible & Wissmath, 2011)—conflicting results and measurement mean no clear causal model has been established.

Early research identified presence as an important mediator linking in-game advertising exposure and persuasive outcomes (e.g., Nelson et al., 2006). But subsequent research has not always supported this finding. For example, a study that attempted to manipulate presence through using VR instead of a flat screen did not find effects on brand recall or main effects on purchase intention (Wang & Yao, 2020). Furthermore, Chen and Yao (2022) found a negative association between presence and recall of virtual marketing content. Instead, they found that transportation predicted positive attitudes toward the marketed content, and while presence amplified this effect, it actually interfered with the ability of transportation to generate recall.

Another study by Yang and Kang (2021) also found that transportation increased "love" of the marketed brand. (It is worth noting that these studies tested interactive marketing and not actual games.) However, some studies fail to support a positive role for transportation. Huang and Waddell (2020) found that transportation diminished the effectiveness of brand choice on recall but did not have a clear direct effect on brand attitudes, for example. More broadly, the inconsistent results point to a potential discrepancy between research on games and research on in-game advertising. While advertisers can turn to the former to learn how to better achieve involvement in the place and story, if those elements are not directly linked to the goals of the advertiser, they might not result in benefits for the brand.

In addition to affecting attention and recall, immersion might matter if it relates to positive experiences. For example, Sherrick (2023) found mixed evidence related to the use of narrative and persuasion in a health message. Although narrative helped increase flow in a non-branded condition, it failed to do so when a brand was present. Furthermore, flow was only weakly and inconsistently tied to persuasive outcomes. Although positive emotional states such as flow might be expected to result in affective transfer and thus positive attitudes toward ads, this has not always proven to be the case (e.g., Dardis et al., 2019; Vyvey et al., 2018).

Vyvey and coauthors (2018) argue that the limited capacity of individuals to attend to messages may help account for why immersion in games doesn't necessarily make in-game advertising more effective. A person losing track of their surroundings due to flow may be so focused on the game that advertising elements go unnoticed or unprocessed. Another consideration is the inconsistency in the meaning and measurement of immersion (Sherrick, 2021). A lack of results for a measure of presence might be because the authors accidentally generated or tested flow or transportation instead. Clarity on this point is a vital step, but it is not enough.

The Impact of Differing Game Characteristics

Games are not a uniform medium, and differences in their technology and content likely moderate the influence of in-game advertisements. The reasons for this relate to and help expand our understanding of immersion. For example, Roettl and Terlutter (2018) found that individuals using a head-mounted VR had less recall of branded content than those in a more typical 2D environment, even though the former should be more immersive. Difficulty of the game can also be a predictor of recall and brand attitude, with players showing lower levels of each when playing a more difficult game (Dardis et al., 2015). At least one possible explanation is that even though a difficult game generates more focus and immersion, the combination of negative associations with the brand and increased cognitive demands due to the challenge can lead to the negative outcomes.

The Nature of the Branded Content in the Games

The finding from Dardis et al. (2015) was limited to the focal brand in the game, with other messages largely ignored. This points to the third important consideration: the nature of the branded content. Both focus and congruency play a role in whether more immersive experiences increase persuasive outcomes. Lee and Faber (2007) provided relatively early data on the application of the limited capacity model to the effectiveness of game advertising, showing that "focal" brands requiring less attention were more readily remembered. But centrality can be more than physical location. Ingendahl et al. (2023) manipulated whether branded content was directly linked to a game story and found that this form of centrality was important in determining the effectiveness of the ad. Critically, though, this was beneficial to the advertiser only if the story experience was positive, suggesting that transportation and game content are interacting. That's an important point—making an ad easier to notice or more connected with an immersive experience probably benefits recall, but the interaction with other aspects of the game experience—such as positive emotions, frustration from difficulty, or even motion sickness in a VR setup—determines whether the advertiser should want to be remembered.

Another meaningful aspect of the branded content is congruency, or the alignment between the brand and the context in which it appears. Congruent ads seem less likely to reduce immersion, but they may also be less memorable. An optimal ad not only won't anger players but also shouldn't go unnoticed

(Lewis & Porter, 2010), and meeting this criterion is challenging. There are also differences in how congruency between brands and games is defined. For example, congruency in the context of a racing game may involve car-related products, but in real-life auto sports, many advertisers are common brand names. Is Budweiser "congruent" when placed on a stock car? Similarly, billboards in a city-based action game could depict a range of brands while still being perceived as congruent. One might reasonably assume that an incongruent ad would disrupt narrative transportation. By extension, this could explain the poor performance of incongruent ads. Meanwhile, when players can actually interact with a branded product, spatial presence may be more important, with the performance of the product affecting the evaluation of the brand.

Conflicting and Non-Linear Influences

A broader picture emerges that suggests immersion as an umbrella label is a poor way to predict how well a game experience will translate into an effective branded message. We want players to be involved in the game, including the story and the physical space. Distracted players are less likely to notice ads. However, highly focused players might only notice ads that are directly involved in their task. So, we want ads that get the attention of players and make them actively process the message—however, these risks are inhibiting the kind of focused experience that makes a game pleasurable and potentially has a halo effect on branded content present within the game. A single measure of immersion cannot capture this nuance.

Another point is to consider whether the effects of immersion might be non-linear. Feelings of spatial immersion might help people recognize branded elements when the environment is immersive enough to keep the full attention of the player, but when it becomes so overwhelmingly vivid that players must consume all their focus on game elements, the impact of the game on the brand may become negative. Similarly, individuals who are having fun and starting to experience flow might be in a good position to favorably process an ad, but a true flow state often results in a loss of time and sense of self, factors that may not lead to recall for intrusive branded content (or favorable impressions if the content disrupts the enjoyable state).

Developing a More Coherent Model

As we have seen, the literature on what about impact embedding advertising in digital games has many contradictory results. A first suggestion is that the central concepts of presence, flow, and transportation need clear and consistent definitions. Their relationship to "immersion" must be clearly articulated. A second suggestion is that research must clearly distinguish the role of different kinds of games; and it must differentially predict the role of immersion as it varies in those different games. Third, immersion may not have linear effects, and statistical approaches should account for this.

A final suggestion involves better integrating the advertising literature with research on games and other immersive experiences. On this point, some caution is needed. Factors such as presence, transportation, and flow are consistent positive outcomes from the standpoint of gaming researchers. Even those considering pro-social outcomes want gamers to be immersed and happy. But as the examples of advertising research presented above show, these factors do not have the same consistent benefits for branding and persuasion purposes. Advertising scholars can learn from gaming research how to increase immersion, but more direct research is needed to determine how much and what kind of immersion actual benefits brands.

References

Caroux, L. (2023). Presence in video games: A systematic review and meta-analysis of the effects of game design choices. *Applied Ergonomics*, *107*, 103936. https://doi.org/10.1016/j.apergo.2022.103936

Chen, C., & Yao, M. Z. (2022). Strategic use of immersive media and narrative message in virtual marketing: Understanding the roles of telepresence and transportation. *Psychology & Marketing*, *39*(3), 524–542. https://doi.org/10.1002/mar.21630

Dardis, F. E., Schmierbach, M., Ahern, L., Fraustino, J., Bellur, S., Brooks, S., & Johnson, J. (2015). Effects of in-game virtual direct experience (Vde) on reactions to real-world brands. *Journal of Promotion Management*, *21*(3), 313–334. https://doi.org/10.1080/10496491.2015.1021503

Dardis, F., Schmierbach, M., Sherrick, B., & Luckman, B. (2019). How game difficulty and ad framing influence memory of in-game advertisements. *Journal of Consumer Marketing*, *36*(1), 1–11. https://doi.org/10.1108/JCM-07-2016-1878

Huang, Y., & Waddell, T. F. (2020). The impact of ad customization and content transportation on the effectiveness of online video advertising. *Journal of Current Issues & Research in Advertising*, *41*(3), 284–300. https://doi.org/10.1080/10641734.2019.1626304

Ingendahl, M., Vogel, T., Maedche, A., & Wänke, M. (2023). Brand placements in video games: How local in-game experiences influence brand attitudes. *Psychology & Marketing*, *40*(2), 274–287. https://doi.org/10.1002/mar.21770

Jin, S.-A. A. (2011). "I feel present. Therefore, I experience flow:" A structural equation modeling approach to flow and presence in video games. *Journal of Broadcasting & Electronic Media*, *55*(1), 114–136. https://doi.org/10.1080/08838151.2011.546248

Lee, M., & Faber, R. J. (2007). Effects of product placement in on-line games on brand memory: A perspective of the limited-capacity model of attention. *Journal of Advertising*, *36*(4), 75–90. https://doi.org/10.2753/JOA0091-3367360406

Lewis, B., & Porter, L. (2010). In-game advertising effects: Examining player perceptions of advertising schema congruity in a massively multiplayer online role-playing game. *Journal of Interactive Advertising*, *10*(2), 46–60. https://doi.org/10.1080/15252019.2010.10722169

Mahood, C., & Hanus, M. (2017). Role-playing video games and emotion: How transportation into the narrative mediates the relationship between immoral actions and feelings of guilt. *Psychology of Popular Media Culture*, *6*(1), 61–73. https://doi.org/10.1037/ppm0000084

Nelson, M. R., Yaros, R. A., & Keum, H. (2006). Examining the influence of telepresence on spectator and player processing of real and fictitious brands in a computer game. *Journal of Advertising*, *35*(4), 87–99. https://doi.org/10.2753/JOA0091-3367350406

Roettl, J., & Terlutter, R. (2018). The same video game in 2D, 3D or virtual reality – How does technology impact game evaluation and brand placements? *Plos One*, *13*(7), e0200724. https://doi.org/10.1371/journal.pone.0200724

Sherrick, B. (2021). Empirically comparing flow, narrative engagement, and enjoyment as responses to a computer game. *Atlantic Journal of Communication*, *29*(4), 230–245. https://doi.org/10.1080/15456870.2020.1755289

Sherrick, B. (2023). The impact of casual gameplay on health attitudes and behaviors: Examining persuasion in a branded game about nutrition through narrative, gameplay, and flow. *Atlantic Journal of Communication*, *31*(5), 404–419. https://doi.org/10.1080/15456870.2022.2123485

Sherry, J. L. (2004). Flow and media enjoyment. *Communication Theory*, *14*(4), 328–347. https://doi.org/10.1111/j.1468-2885.2004.tb00318.x

Vyvey, T., Castellar, E. N., & Van Looy, J. (2018). Loaded with fun? The impact of enjoyment and cognitive load on brand retention in digital games. *Journal of Interactive Advertising*, *18*(1), 72–82. https://doi.org/10.1080/15252019.2018.1446370

Wang, Y. (Mia), & Yao, M. Z. (2020). Did you notice the ads? Examining the influence of telepresence and user control on the effectiveness of embedded billboard ads in a VR racing game. *Journal of Interactive Advertising*, *20*(3), 258–272. https://doi.org/10.1080/15252019.2020.1846642

Weibel, D., & Wissmath, B. (2011). Immersion in computer games: The role of spatial presence and flow. *International Journal of Computer Games Technology*, *2011*, 1–14. https://doi.org/10.1155/2011/282345

Yang, K. C. C., & Kang, Y. (2021). Predicting the relationships between narrative transportation, consumer brand experience, love and loyalty in video storytelling advertising. *Journal of Creative Communications*, *16*(1), 7–26. https://doi.org/10.1177/0973258620984262

11 Advertising in Video Games

An Overview and Future Research Considerations

Anthony M. Limperos and Will R. Silberman

Video Games and Advertising: A Promising Trend

Though video games aren't typically thought of as a traditional venue for advertising, total spending on in-game advertising and branding has increased dramatically in recent years, solidifying that this form of advertising remains a promising trend. Though no comprehensive history of advertising in video games exists, this form of advertising was first seen in games like *Kool-Aid Man* and *Avoid the Noid* for the Atari 2600 and the personal computer (PC) in late 1970s and early 1980s. These games are often cited as early examples of what is now commonly referred to as in-game advertising (Skalski et al., 2010). Gaming advertisements have evolved to meet the staggeringly large, dynamic, and broad audience of gamers of 2025; analysts estimate that 78% of U.S. households have played at least one gaming device (i.e., PC, mobile, and/or console) in the past 12 months (Entertainment Software Association, 2024).

Even though in-game advertising was once considered a niche market, analysts estimate that nine to ten billion USD was spent globally in 2024 on these types of ads (Tibaldi & Vaughan, 2024). The returns generated from the spending were even higher, with game franchises like Fortnite reporting revenue of three to four billion USD annually, with most of it coming from in-game purchases (Iqbal, 2025). Though once uncertain, it is now clear that video game advertising is very effective at getting gamers to continue to purchase a variety of digital assets (e.g., playable characters and special items) in the gaming world and as a complementary piece in larger marketing/branding campaigns that exist outside of the gaming world. Therefore, the purpose of this exposition is to explain and give examples of in-game advertising, present a brief synopsis of the research in this area, and then to discuss what researchers and practitioners should consider when thinking about the future of this form of advertising and its effectiveness.

Common Contexts of Gaming Advertisements (Micro, Mezzo, and Macro)

While there are many different forms of game-related advertising, gaming advertisements can be slotted into three contextual categories: micro (e.g., in-game

DOI: 10.4324/9781003567523-14

advertisements), mezzo (e.g., ecosystem/platform advertisements), and macro (e.g., branded partnerships and collaborations).

At the microlevel, in-game advertisements are perhaps the ads most players can think of and see. These ads reside in the software and appear during gameplay. Freemium mobile games contain advertisements, such as an ad that plays when the player "loses" and gets an opportunity for an extra life in exchange for watching an ad. These advertisements tend to be used by developers to monetize their free games (Williams, 2019).

At the mezzo level, gaming advertisements emerge on gaming home screens/dashboards. For instance, when a player turns on their PlayStation 5 or opens the Steam application on their computer, they may see an advertisement for the newest game or microtransactions for trending games. These advertisements tend to be curated by publishers for the purposes of keeping players in a specific ecosystem, such as encouraging Game Pass subscribers to play another XBOX game on Game Pass instead of playing a game on a Nintendo Switch. While some publishers may be flip-flopping on injecting ads on startup (Yin-Poole, 2024), players are frustrated with the pervasiveness of these ads which may ultimately undermine their effectiveness (Robertson, 2024).

Finally, the macrolevel of gaming advertisements encompasses gaming-specific ads that make their way across ecosystems or merge with "the real world." These types of advertisements can emerge in the form of collaborations with other brands. In 2021, Riot Games collaborated with Louis Vuitton to create a set of in-game cosmetics alongside high-fashion physical products (i.e., watches, clothing; Oloman, 2021). Epic Games' *Fortnite* has led the way in cross-platform partnerships, including paid cosmetics that let players look like Ariana Grande, Snoop Dogg, LeBron James, and Mr. Beast (Pinera, 2025). These ads tend to be quite extensive but dominate headlines in the fast-paced 24/7 news cycle, bringing in current, former, and new players to boost a game's audience.

Video Game Advertising Research: A Picture of Mixed Effectiveness

While video game advertising has been around for quite some time, research on the subject first began to appear in communication and related marketing journals about 25 years ago. Early studies in this area illustrated that simply playing a game with embedded brand messaging is enough to impact simple recall of that brand, but not for all players (Nelson, 2002; Yang et al., 2006). Not surprisingly, this finding was replicated across many studies and scholarship eventually moved toward gaining a more comprehensive understanding of the conditions and processes under which brand messaging and advertising in games can be effective.

To date, researchers have focused on understanding how individual differences (Sparks & Chung, 2016), game genres (Lull et al., 2018), technological features (Dardis et al., 2012), gamified advertising formats (Ghosh & Dwivedi,

2022), and game difficulty (Dardis et al., 2019) can influence how advertising messages are recalled and how this might lead to consumer action. Perhaps unsurprisingly, both the early and more current research in this area paint a rather complex picture of how individuals process ads in games and whether they are ultimately effective.

As is the case with most research focused on understanding the cognitive processing of media and persuasive messages, there is no all-encompassing theory or set of studies that can definitively explain both the value and effectiveness of forms of video game advertising. Many of the studies referenced above are experimental in nature. Even though some of these studies have done a nice job of linking individual differences and characteristics of games to recall and cognition, relatively few studies have been able to explain how advertisements in games translate into purchase intentions or actual purchase of products or services. This is not to say that the theoretically driven laboratory studies are deficient in any way. In fact, without these studies, practitioners would merely be taking a shot in the proverbial dark in terms of message design for branded games, partnerships, and in-game advertising efforts. Research needs to continue to focus on the entire process. The research illustrates at a very baseline level that video game advertising can be effective. However, as video games continue to evolve, the way that players interact and respond to games will also change. Future research will need to account for this.

Future Considerations for Video Game Advertising

Van Berlo et al. (2023) provide an overview and synthesis of 20 years of video game advertising research, highlighting key theories that have been applied while advancing a framework that outlines key variables of interest often found in studies that focus on understanding the reception and effectiveness of video game ads. For anyone hoping to conduct research on the effectiveness of video game advertising, this article provides a great road map of the literature, complete with future research suggestions. Van Berlo et al. (2023) explain that a combination of game characteristics (e.g., genre, technological format/features), player characteristics (e.g., cognition and motivation), and ad characteristics (e.g., brand placement and message framing) are catalysts for psychological responses and behavior responses to different types of video game ads. Of the independent variables mentioned, technological variations are perhaps the most interesting because technologies in gaming continue to evolve. For example, things like augmented reality, virtual reality (VR), and other interactive simulations can allow for potentially greater interactivity and immersion with brands and products in video games. Some research has been done in this area, but we believe that future research should focus on isolating and explaining how variations in "game technologies" and specific technological affordances may contribute to or detract from the effects of video game advertising. While individual differences, context, and types of games certainly matter, playing a console game on a 100-inch TV is fundamentally different than playing a mobile game on a smartphone. Additionally, a game advertisement with interactive elements is different than an advertisement that does not contain these elements. Therefore, understanding how technological and structural advances influence the effectiveness of in-game advertising will likely remain an important question for years to come.

Although video games have reached critical mass and are very popular with a wide audience, tracking the return on in-game advertising expenditures remains challenging. The more that researchers can do to bridge the gap between what is theoretically and what is practically relevant, the more promising the future will be for practitioners concerned with understanding the effectiveness of in-game advertising. On a final note, although it will continue to be important to conduct research related to the traditional game advertising, the future of advertising involving AI and VR elements present a novel and vibrant area for future research consideration, especially since the traditional means of reaching consumers are impacted by an increasingly crowded gaming market.

References

Dardis, F. E., Schmierbach, M. G., & Limperos, A. M. (2012). The impact of game customization and control mechanism on videogame advertising effects. *Journal of Interactive Advertising, 12,* 1–12. https://doi.org/10.1080/15252019.2012.10722192

Dardis, F., Schmierbach, M., Sherrick, B., & Luckman, B. (2019). How game difficulty and ad framing influence memory of in-game advertisements. *Journal of Consumer Marketing, 36*(1), 1–11. https://doi.org/10.1108/JCM-07-2016-1878

Entertainment Software Association. (2024). *2024 Essential facts about the U.S. video game industry.* https://www.theesa.com/resources/essential-facts-about-the-us-video-game-industry/2024-data/

Ghosh, T., S, S., & Dwivedi, Y. K. (2022). Brands in a game or a game for brands? Comparing the persuasive effectiveness of in-game advertising and advergames. *Psychology & Marketing, 39*(12), 2328–2348. https://doi.org/10.1002/mar.21752

Iqbal, M. (2025, January 22). Fornite Usage and Revenue Statistics (2025). *Business of Apps.* https://www.businessofapps.com/data/fortnite-statistics/

Lull, R. B., Gibson, B., Cruz, C., & Bushman, B. J. (2018). Killing characters in video games kills memory for in-game ads. *Psychology of Popular Media Culture, 7,* 87–97. https://doi.org/10.1037/ppm0000108

Nelson, M. R. (2002). Recall of brand placements in computer/video games. *Journal of Advertising Research, 42,* 80–92. https://doi.org/10.2501/jar-42-2-80-92

Oloman, J. (2021, July 12). Gaming is entering its fashion-forward phase. *Washington Post.* https://www.washingtonpost.com/video-games/2021/07/12/video-game-fashion-esports-streetwear/

Pinera, A. (2025, January 13). Fornite: 13 best celebrity skins. *The Gamer.* https://www.thegamer.com/fortnite-best-celebrity-skins/

Robertson, J. (2024, June 13). Xbox users are sick of being shown full-screen ads. *The Gamer*. https://www.thegamer.com/xbox-users-are-tired-sick-of-being-full-screen-ads/

Skalski, P., Campanella-Bracken, C., & Buncher, M. (2010) Advertising: It's in the game. In M. S. Eastin, T. Daugherty, & N. M., Burns (Eds.), *Handbook of research on digital media and advertising: User generated content consumption* (pp. 437–455). Hershey, PA: Information Science Reference.

Sparks, J. V., & Chung, S. (2016). The effects of psychobiological motivational traits on memory of in-game advertising messages. *Psychology of Marketing, 33*, 60–68. https://doi.org/10.1002/mar.20840

Tibaldi, B., & Vaughan, M. (2024, March 26). IAB study reveals games advertising among top three investment growth areas alongside digital video. *Interactive Advertising Bureau*. https://www.iab.com/news/new-iab-study-reveals-games-advertising-among-top-three-investment-growth-areas/

Van Berlo, Z. M., Van Reijmersdal, E. A., & Waiguny, M. K. (2023). Twenty years of research on gamified advertising: A systematic overview of theories and variables. *International Journal of Advertising, 42*(1), 171–180. https://doi.org/10.1080/02650487.2022.2143098

Williams, R. (2019, December 19). *Study: 94% of free mobile games have in-game ads as developers fortify strategies*. https://www.marketingdive.com/news/study-94-of-free-mobile-games-have-in-game-ads-as-developers-fortify-stra/569500/

Yang, M., Roskos-Ewoldsen, D. R., Dinu, L., & Arpan, L. M. (2006). The effectiveness of "in-game" advertising: Comparing college students' explicit and implicit memory for brands. *Journal of Advertising, 35*, 143–152. https://doi.org/10.2753/JOA0091-3367350410

Yin-Poole, W. (2024, October 1). PS5 homescreen now replaces unique video game art with annoying ads you can't turn off. *IGN*. https://www.ign.com/articles/ps5-homescreen-now-replaces-unique-video-game-art-with-annoying-ads-you-cant-turn-off

12 Using Digital Media to Improve Public Health Communication for Both Physical and Emotional Health

Kathrynn Pounders, Marla Royne Stafford, Marian Levy and Amy Rebecca Jones

Consumers increasingly encounter a wide range of health issues. Four of the ten leading causes of death in the United States (heart disease, cancer, diabetes, and stroke) are due to chronic diseases, with heart disease, cancer, diabetes, and stroke accounting for nearly half of all deaths (CDC, 2025). In addition to being the leading causes of death and disability in the United States, these chronic diseases are also key drivers of the nation's $4.5 trillion spent in annual healthcare costs (CDC, 2025). Chronic diseases are the leading cause of illness, disability, and death in America, with most being caused by controllable actions like smoking, poor nutrition, physical inactivity, and excessive alcohol use (CDC, 2025). "Six in 10 Americans have at least one chronic disease, and 4 in 10 have two or more chronic diseases" (CDC, 2025). Additionally, the world was recently faced with an unprecedented pandemic, COVID-19, which is associated with both significant physical and emotional health issues.

Emotional health is also a significant priority today, with more awareness of mental health diseases moving to the forefront of society (Prince et al., 2007). For example, many adults in the United States suffer from mental illnesses with estimates stating that more than one in five adults live with mental illness (NIMH, 2024) like depression or mood disorders. Mental illnesses are not only common in the United States but also around the world (NIMH, 2024). In addition, suicide rates increased by 37% during the early 2000s, declined briefly, and then returned to peak levels in 2022 (CDC, 2025). The United States also continues to face an opioid addiction crisis that has persisted since the 1990s and is characterized by widespread misuse of prescription and illicit opioids, as well as overdose deaths. In addition, many consumers suffer from other forms of addiction, including online gambling addiction, which has become increasingly prevalent as gambling has been legalized in many U.S. states (Wisconsin Policy Forum, 2025). In addition, with the upbeat of consumption of social media platforms, issues such as bullying (Kee, Al-Anesi, & Al-Anesi, 2022) and eating disorders are on the rise worldwide (Pastore et al., 2023). As our society is increasingly plagued by a plethora of health issues, effective health communication appears more important than ever.

DOI: 10.4324/9781003567523-15

The rapidly changing nature of the healthcare environment demands that consumers become more engaged and take an active role in their own healthcare needs and are increasingly doing so using digital media (Tolentino, Costa & Jiang, 2023). However, to accomplish this, they need deeper knowledge of evident and underlying health issues, and research indicates that many consumers are unaware of various risks and health issues. For example, unhealthy lifestyles related to eating, exercise, and controversial behaviors are often attributed to a lack of knowledge about the importance of these behaviors and how to more easily integrate them into busy lifestyles with many people highlighting poor family eating education received during their childhood as the basis (Beltran-Carillo et al., 2022) or watching family members engage in controversial behaviors such as gambling.

The need for increased health information among consumers to help promote healthy lifestyles in our nation is apparent. In fact, Royne and Levy (2011) commented that "public health professionals have recently called for public health to utilize the same successful practices that marketers use to influence their customers." However, despite the success of implementing sound persuasion strategies in the corporate world, such approaches have not been utilized as effectively in public health. Clearly, it is time for the public health sector to engage in effective marketing techniques by using contemporary media and creative messages to reach those in need of important information to help improve individual lives and well-being. This type of marketing can have a huge impact on the healthcare system by bridging the relationship between patients and critical services offered by healthcare entities that disseminate important health information (Kay, 2007; Rahman et al., 2022). As such, it is important for health messages to be more effective in message and media strategies, as well as in reaching the target audience. With the phenomenal growth of digital marketing tools, the use of digital media is paramount in communicating health messages to consumers. Accordingly, the purpose of this chapter is to discuss how digital media can be used to effectively deliver health communications in a world of changing healthcare, increased chronic disease, and growing access to controversial activities.

First, we provide an overview of the health issues that are permeating our society. This is followed by an overview of the social-ecological model of health promotion, a discussion of digital and social media usage, and health issues and behaviors, positive and negative aspects. We conclude with a discussion of relevant theories and message strategies that may be effective in health messaging.

Physical Health Issues Related to Lifestyle

Our nation currently faces a public health crisis that has critical, personal, societal, and economic implications. Many chronic diseases share risk factors related to three modifiable lifestyle behaviors: tobacco use, unhealthy diet, and physical inactivity. Obesity is a significant and underlying factor in these conditions and has been fueled by substantial increases in food intake and sedentary behavior over the past few decades. Currently, 41.9% of U.S. adults are obese (CDC, 2025), and the direct and indirect cost of adult obesity is estimated at $173 billion, representing a significant portion of U.S. healthcare expenditures (Cawley & Meyerhoefer, 2012). Projections from the World Obesity Foundation indicate that obesity prevalence is predicted to reach 18% in men and surpass 21% in women, prompting governments to commit to prioritizing investment in addressing obesity. These rapidly increasing high BMI rates are estimated to cost health services globally $990 billion per year (World Obesity, 2025). The volume of overweight individuals has contributed to over 589 million adults recorded as having diabetes worldwide (International Diabetes Federation, 2025). Many Americans do not exercise on a regular basis and often fail to adhere to a healthy diet. Only 28% of Americans are adhering to physical activity guidelines distributed by the Centers for Disease Control and Prevention (Porterfield, 2024), and about one-fifth of Americans describe their diets as not too or not at all healthy (Kikuchi et al., 2025). Further, nearly 19.3% of U.S. children and adolescents are obese (CDC, 2025). This is a significant cause for concern because obesity in childhood often continues into adulthood (Ogden et al., 2012), and childhood obesity is associated with several negative health consequences (Freedman et al., 2007; Han et al., 2010; Sutherland, 2008; Puhl & Latner, 2007).

Mental Health Issues

The United States is facing a mental health crisis that has intensified in recent years, marked by rising rates of depression, anxiety, substance use, and suicide across all age groups. According to the National Alliance on Mental Illness (2023), one in five U.S. adults experience mental illness each year, and suicide is the second leading cause of death among individuals aged 10–34. The COVID-19 pandemic exacerbated existing vulnerabilities, particularly among adolescents and young adults, with the U.S. Surgeon General declaring a youth mental health crisis in 2021 (Office of the Surgeon General, 2021). Contributing factors include social isolation, academic pressure, economic instability, and most notably, excessive social media usage.

Social media platforms foster unrealistic appearance ideals and facilitate constant social comparison, which can lead to heightened symptoms of anxiety, depression, and body dissatisfaction—particularly among girls and young women (Fioravanti et al., 2024; De Valle et al., 2021). These appearance-related concerns are linked to an alarming increase in eating disorders and body dysmorphic disorders (BDDs). BDD—a preoccupation with perceived flaws in appearance—is increasingly recognized among adolescents and young adults, often triggered or exacerbated by exposure to idealized and filtered images on platforms like Instagram and TikTok (e.g., Hawes, Zimmer-Gembeck, & Campbell, 2020).

Research has shown that appearance-based comparisons on social media are directly associated with disordered eating behaviors and reduced body satisfaction (Lewallen & Behm-Morawitz, 2016). The normalization of "thinspiration" or "fitspiration" content online continues to fuel unhealthy beauty ideals and promote self-objectification, contributing to the broader decline in mental health and well-being.

At the same time, substance misuse remains a significant public health concern, particularly as it intersects with untreated mental health issues. The opioid epidemic continues to devastate communities across the country. In 2023, more than 112,000 people in the United States died from drug overdoses, most of them involving synthetic opioids such as fentanyl (CDC, 2025). Many individuals struggling with mood disorders, such as depression or PTSD, also experience co-occurring substance use disorders, further compounding both the mental and physical consequences of illness (Substance Abuse and Mental Health Services Administration [SAMHSA], 2025). Co-occurring disorders are common. Approximately half of individuals who experience a substance use disorder will also experience a mental illness during their lifetime, and vice versa (National Institute on Drug Abuse [NIDA], 2022). The growing prevalence of poly-substance use, combined with gaps in access to mental health services, makes comprehensive intervention more difficult. Addressing this crisis requires multifaceted solutions that span social policy, mental healthcare, education, and media literacy.

Addictions are not limited to substances. For example, gambling addiction has become a significant issue, with the CDC long recognizing that gambling disorder is a public health problem (e.g., Livingstone & Rintoul, 2020). Moreover, with the 2018 Supreme Court decision that allowed states to allow sports gambling, gambling addiction has grown significantly among young male adults, a market that utilizes social media regularly. At the same time, problem gambling is well-linked to anxiety and depression (Moore & Grubbs, 2021).

Social-Ecological Model for Health Promotion

The social-ecological model for health promotion is based on the understanding that behavior change is a function not only of educational activities but also advocacy, organizational change, policy development, economic support, environmental change, and multimethod strategies (McLeroy et al., 1988; Stokols, 1996). Specifically, individuals interact within multiple levels of influence; they exist within social networks, which in turn exist within surrounding environments. Thus, individual, social, and environmental factors affect health behaviors.

This ecological perspective focuses attention on both individual *and* social environmental factors as targets for health promotion interventions. It highlights the importance of approaching public health problems at multiple levels and advocates the simultaneous, concurrent change across five more complex levels of influence: individual, interpersonal, organizational, community, and public policy. The model assumes that appropriate changes in the social environment will produce changes in individuals, and that mutual and interdependent support of individuals within the population is essential for implementing environmental changes. These levels of influence play an important role in both physical and mental health issues.

The first level of influence comprises individual factors. This includes specific personal characteristics that influence behaviors, such as knowledge, attitudes, beliefs, and preferences. The second level includes interpersonal factors and involves interpersonal processes and primary relationships with family, friends, and peers that provide social identity, support, and role definition. For example, parents help shape youth attitudes and behaviors by modeling food and gambling behaviors. The next level, organizational factors, includes rules, policies, environmental, and informal structures within an institution or system, such as schools, worksites, neighborhoods, or casinos, where social relationships occur. Community factors refer to the social networks, norms, standards, and practices that exist formally or informally in relationships among organizations, such as church groups. Finally, public policy factors include local, state, and federal policies and laws that regulate or support desired behaviors.

In sum, this social-ecological perspective of effective health communication stresses the interaction and integration of factors both within and across all five levels (McLeroy et al., 1988) and recognizes that behavior is influenced by the complex and interwoven relationships that exist between an individual and his/her environment. Therefore, this theory acknowledges that while consumers are responsible for their lifestyle choices, consumer behavior is also largely influenced by social and environmental influences related to community norms, regulations, and policies. As such, health messages from health practitioners should start at the individual level of the social-ecological model and capitalize on digital tools and appropriate messages to reach the social networks at a greater level.

Digital Media Usage

The growth and acceptance of digital media, along with the increased need for public health information, suggest that the use of the newest techniques may be highly appropriate for health communication in today's society. About 96% of adults in the United States say they utilize some form of digital media (Pew Research Center, 2025). At the same time, vulnerable populations and ethnic groups, who at one time were less likely to use technology, are now regular users of digital media. For example, the **Anderson (2015)** notes, "blacks and whites are on more equal footing when it comes to ...mobile platforms." About 86.6% of Asian/Pacific Islanders, 83% of African Americans, 82.4% of Hispanics, 75.7% of Native American or Alaskan Native, and 74.2% of Whites have a smartphone

(Nielsen, 2025). Accordingly, it appears that digital media may prove effective in reaching the public, including minority and vulnerable populations.

A wide range of digital tools can be used to effectively disseminate public health information on a range of physical and emotional topics. Big data and targeting software make it easier to specialize and target health messages to consumers based on their demographic, psychographic, and behavioral data. This new vast information resource offers precise information, allowing today's public health professionals to have very specific knowledge about their intended market. This includes information ranging from target audience demographics, behavioral data, and psychographic information in the form of product and brand likes and dislikes, activities and interests, as well as the use of social media and other digital tools. It is widely established that consumers rely on information they find online and use the Internet to connect with other consumers about issues related to health. In fact, about 58% of Whites, 67% of African Americans, and 73% of Hispanics have used their phone throughout the year to seek information about a health condition (Pew Research Center, 2015).

Social media usage is at an all-time high and allows for targeted communication based on big data and other interest-sought information. Current popular social media include Facebook, Instagram, WhatsApp, TikTok, Snapchat, Telegram, WeChat, X (formally known as Twitter), Pinterest, GooglePlus, YouTube, and many more with new platforms emerging regularly. With more than 3 billion monthly active users and over 2 billion daily active users worldwide, approximately 37% of the world's population (Facebook, 2025), Facebook is larger than most countries and the largest social media platform globally. That is a significant percentage of the population considering several large countries have blocked and banned Facebook.

Instagram is a resource where pictures and short clips can be shared by users. Members can connect to certain groups whose members might share recipes, exercises, and health tips. In January 2025, there were over 2 billion active users on Instagram worldwide. Meta tools show that Instagram ads reached 1.74 billion users in January 2025 (DataReportal, 2025a, 2025b).

Twitter rebranded as X in 2023, reportedly resulting in a loss of approximately 32 million users. Nevertheless, as of January 2025, X remained one of the world's most popular social media platforms, with approximately 611 million monthly active users (Search Logistics, 2025). X, known for people sharing various messages, provides opportunities for sharing short bursts of important information. Although physicians have successfully used X for health education, it can be used by anybody to share any type of health-related tip. For example, a nutritionist or nurse can share a simple tweet about increasing the intake of vegetables; such information may be retweeted by one individual, and then either the original tweet or the retweet is liked by others. This chain or link of information has the opportunity to be endless and create mass dissemination across a range of healthcare topics that could potentially change someone's health knowledge.

Even former First Lady Michelle Obama used Twitter to promote healthy meals, tweeting previously that "healthy food is delicious too," showing the power of social media.

Pinterest is a highly specialized digital media tool, where a simple subject search may lead to numerous options to click on links for another site or groups of sites. This allows people to customize their settings and only view things that are of interest to them. In January of 2025, Pinterest had at least 340 million users worldwide (DataReportal, 2025a, 2025b), trailing another social media powerhouse, YouTube, which had approximately 2.70 billion monthly active users as of mid-2025 (Global Media Insight, 2025). YouTube is a popular digital tool where myriad videos are posted. Organizations and individuals can even create their own YouTube channel. Health organizations such as physicians' offices, cancer and addiction support groups, and gyms can post videos on YouTube to convey information or demonstrate healthy behaviors. Users can post, share, like, or comment on videos.

TikTok is the leading social platform for short-form mobile videos (TikTok, 2025). Within this mobile app and online platform, users can watch, share, and even create short-form videos. TikTok has become a popular social platform due to the creativity that is inspired by the videos, resulting in over 1.59 billion users worldwide as of January 2025 (DataReportal, 2025a, 2025b). Due to its popularity, many healthcare professionals are active on TikTok and help play a pertinent role in sharing accurate information and connecting with patients. These healthcare professionals have realized the power of the app and have used TikTok to engage with the diverse young audience participating on the platform.

Digital Media and Health: The Advantages

Digital media continue to evolve, and a wide range of digital tools are available to reach the public and provide informative messages that can encourage healthy lifestyles. Digital tools represent an intersection between interpersonal communication and mass media. This is noteworthy because interpersonal communication is related to health behavior change (Seo & Matsaganis, 2013). Thus, using digital media platforms to communicate health information has the potential to result in improved health outcomes. Because digital media interpersonal communication channels ultimately lead to mass communications channels as part of the shared social network, digital tools seem particularly appropriate for the social-ecological model, which is grounded in individual, environmental, and social levels.

Some consumers seek to connect with other patients to learn about conditions or gain support, while others seek information about physicians and healthcare facilities. According to the Journal of Medical Internet Research (2021), participants in a study indicated that they had a desire to take preventative health actions after reading and engaging in patient blogs. The term "cyberchondriacs" has arisen due to the questionable online health information that can misinform patients, leading to many physicians engaging in blogging themselves to provide patients with the correct health information (Chang et al., 2021). The Internet also provides resources for chronic disease self-management through the provision of specialized health information, social support, and psychosocial benefits (cf., Dobransky & Hargittai, 2012; Househ, Borycki, & Kushniruk, 2014) via online communities. Such communities have grown in general, and in particular, online health communities have exploded. Online health communities can productively decrease patients' visits to hospitals, increase the possibility of timely diagnosis, and help ensure the safety and well-being of the patients (Zhang et al., 2023). Fox (2010) reports that about one in four consumers engages regularly with an online health community. These communities provide emotional support and shared knowledge to consumers by engaging with similar individuals online (Frost & Massagli, 2008). This is consistent with Seo and Matsaganis (2013), who find that interpersonal channels are more successful in changing both attitudes and behaviors. Moreover, existing work shows the power of mass media in reaching and informing large audiences (Wakefield, Loken, & Hornik, 2010). That is, online health communities are essentially an intersection of mass media and interpersonal communication (Walther et al., 2010), offering a digital alternative for activating health behavior change (Webb et al., 2010) through online interaction.

Online tools are not limited to online communities, and consumers use the internet for a wide range of health activities. Wang and Terlizzi (2023) reported that '58.5% of U.S. adults used the Internet to look for health or medical information, 41.5% used it to communicate with a doctor or doctor's office, and 46.1% used it to look up medical test results." Thus, it is important for healthcare providers to utilize online tools to provide consumers with updated information and to enhance services. For instance, a healthcare provider (physician's office, pharmacy) could use various outlets to communicate information about flu shots and/or tips on how to reduce illness risk. Patient portals have become standard for medical groups and have proved effective in providing a wealth of healthcare information to patients. A healthcare provider can also use digital platforms to host virtual patient visits, introduce new doctors, update the community on relevant health issues, and provide wellness tips to patients. These digital platforms may include individual, corporate, or organizational websites; external website communication sources; text messages; digital billboards; or social media. Text messages and phone app scans can be used to remind consumers about needed medications or health-related behaviors (e.g., walking). Social media are a particularly popular and effective means for health communication because they not only allow public health advocates to disseminate public health information, but they also enable users to share these posts with others in their networks.

Digital devices such as smartphones, smart watches, and tablets also link consumers to a variety of health-related apps. Such apps are increasing in popularity, with hundreds of millions of people using health apps and the health app industry generating billions of dollars in annual revenue (Business of Apps, 2025). Health apps exist to monitor calorie intake, calories burned, steps per day, blood glucose, pulse rate, and sleep patterns. These apps, often free or available for a minimal charge, have a potentially huge impact on consumers and their physical health. Consumers can use these tools to monitor and track behaviors and outcomes that directly influence their health. In particular, the FitBit, a bracelet-like device tied to a mobile app, has helped thousands of people transition to a healthier lifestyle, and the company documents its success stories at the FitBit blog online.

Other digital apps are readily available to help individuals with emotional issues related to relaxation/sleep (e.g., Calm), anxiety (e.g., Mindshift), mood (Happify), substance abuse (Am Sober), and gambling addictions (GamBan). Many of these have success stories that have helped individuals in their emotional journey to wellness.

In addition to self-monitoring, many apps allow consumers the opportunity to share information with their social network and/or others who are using the same app. Interacting with others may serve as a source of motivation for some consumers. Social Comparison Theory (Festinger, 1954) states that self-evaluation, self-improvement, and self-enhancement are primary motivations for social comparisons. Making an upward comparison to a referent who is perceived to be better than oneself on a specific attribute may motivate a person to improve on the attribute. For example, if a consumer has the Nike app and realizes that most people in the network are more active than he is, he may be inspired to increase his level of physical activity. Social comparisons can be particularly motivating when consumers compare themselves to peers or friends (Lockwood & Kunda, 1997). Social Capital Theory has been explored by many researchers in a variety of contexts but overarchingly states that social relationships can lead to the creation and accumulation of human capital which is the value derived from the connections, networks, and relationships between people (Bisung & Elliott, 2014). It measures your strength of social connections but has been explored within the social media realm as well. Studies have shown that bridging social capital had an impact on the intent to participate in social movements, and those who engaged in social participation were higher among social media users who had higher social capital via a well-developed network (Hwang & Kim, 2015). This could drive populations to be more active in building and nurturing their social networks by sharing content that would motivate themselves and others through social comparisons. Health communication practitioners could implement campaigns that encourage consumers to utilize their apps to compete with their friends for physical activity, a healthy diet, or an emotional health challenge. Hence, health communication efforts can utilize these types of apps to learn more about consumers' health, communicate with consumers about health issues, and motivate consumers to engage in healthy behaviors.

In sum, public health officials should take note and incorporate these social media platforms to help promote healthy lifestyles and to keep up with this new technology shift that other powerful marketers are utilizing (Royne & Levy, 2011).

Digital Media and Health: The Disadvantages

As noted by the World Health Organization, the proliferation of social media use has contributed to infodemics, defined as "too much information, including false or misleading information, in digital and physical environments during a disease outbreak." Misinformation is false or inaccurate information deliberately intended to deceive and represents a significant threat to public health. Infodemics containing rumors, stigma, and conspiracy theories were rampant during the COVID-19 pandemic and fueled misinformation among the public (Islam, 2020). False claims of coronavirus cures related to "eating garlic," "drinking bleach," "drinking alcohol," "drinking cow urine and cow dung," or "camel urine with lime" are not only misguided but also potentially harmful when scientific evidence is ignored. (Islam et al., 2020). Significant potential harm has been caused by the amplification of vaccine misinformation on social media, including its role in fostering vaccine hesitancy and perpetuating false medical treatments.

Thus, misinformation promulgated by social media is detrimental to public health during a pandemic. During the first six months of the COVID-19 vaccination campaign, the rapid spread of online misinformation was linked to vaccine hesitancy rates. Associations between vaccine outcomes and misinformation remain significant when accounting for political as well as demographic and socioeconomic factors. Pierri Ahmed et al. demonstrated that the use of social media sites Twitter and Facebook as sources of health information and influenza knowledge has a significant inverse association with influenza vaccine uptake. Tomeny, Vargo, and El-Toukhy (2017) coded 549,972 Twitter tweets between 2009 and 2015 and found 50% of the tweet volume contained anti-vaccine beliefs. In a randomized control study, exposure to misinformation on Twitter regarding side effects of the COVID-19 vaccine led to reduced intent to vaccinate. (Loomba et al., 2021). Wilson and Wiysonge (2020) evaluated social media globally and noted the presence of foreign disinformation campaigns, which are used to promote anti-vaccination content trans-nationally. Gunasekeran et al. (2022) highlight the potential of social media to support public health preparedness, crisis communication, and disaster response. For example, infoveillance (i.e. information surveillance) can be used to detect events, trace outbreaks, identify critical needs, and support crisis communication.

Misinformation has also affected the uptake of the polio vaccine in Pakistan. In 2019, a fake video falsely claimed adverse side effects of the polio vaccine. Disinformation quickly spread across social media platforms, including Facebook, Twitter, WhatsApp, and YouTube, and produced civil unrest, leading to a mob attack. Consequently, Pakistan's polio eradication campaign suffered a great setback (Ittefaq et al., 2024). More recently, vaccine hesitancy promulgated by social media has also led to the resurgence of measles in the United States (Mathis et al., 2025). According to the Centers for Disease Control and Prevention, 23 outbreaks of measles have been reported in the first six months of 2025 (CDC.gov).

However, social media can be a useful tool to combat misinformation. As Tomeny, Vargo, and El-Toukhy (2017) suggest, monitoring social media sites can be used to detect false claims and inaccurate information, identify shifts in public opinion, and provide public health and medical providers with targeted strategies and media campaigns to counter anti-vaccine beliefs in real-time online. On a global basis, the World Health Organization is combating infodemics through a new information platform called WHO Information Network for Epidemics (EPI-WIN), using amplifiers to distribute tailored information to specific target groups (Zarocostas, 2020).

Message Strategies and Theories for Digital Media and Health

Effective communication will only result if an effective message strategy is in place. Message framing for the various media should start at the individual level of the socio-ecological model and capitalize on digital tools to reach and integrate the social network.

In the advertising literature, most message types fall within a simple two-level categorization model: rational and emotional messages. Rational messages focus more on functional benefits, facts, and statistics to communicate the information. This approach appeals to the consumer's logic. In contrast, emotional messages appeal to a person's feelings with the goal of eliciting an emotional response such as humor, happiness, fear, or guilt. The belief is that emotional appeals provide a connection at a visceral level. Both rational and emotional appeals can be effective. Considerable research has focused on the situations that might prove one appeal to be more effective than the other. While a review of this body of literature is outside the scope of this chapter, we do provide an overview of rational and emotional appeals in health messages that may prove effective in digital media. This distinction is important for two reasons.

First, in digital media, and social media in particular, engagement is extremely important, and the message content directly affects consumer engagement. Second, consumers respond to emotional appeals and rational appeals differently, and the various types of appeals within these two broad categories will generate different responses. Moreover, reactions to digital media will be digital in nature by virtue of their characteristics. For example, people will share information online more quickly and more readily than they would in traditional media.

Recognizing the different emotional reactions among consumers, Facebook recently expanded its traditional "Like" button to include an additional five animated emoji reactions: Love, Haha, Wow, Sad, and Angry. This allows individuals to specifically express their emotional response to the posted message when a simple thumbs-up is just not enough.

Finally, different types of digital media may be more relevant for emotional versus rational messages. For instance, certain rational messages might be best communicated via Twitter, because it is a verbally based platform. However, effective emotional messages may require visual elements and, hence, may be more suited to Facebook and YouTube than Twitter.

Rational Appeals

Health messages typically utilize common message elements. For example, most health communication advertisements convey risk, advocate a healthy action or unhealthy inaction, and appeal to the self or one's family. It is important to understand how combining these elements influences the efficacy of health communication. Accordingly, this section will focus on these various message elements and identify when they are most efficacious. Because health messages typically illustrate the undesired consequences of contracting an illness or disease while advocating a behavior to promote a healthier outcome, a substantial body of research has examined the role of regulatory focus in health message effectiveness.

Regulatory Focus Theory suggests people are motivated to minimize the discrepancy between actual and desired end states (Higgins, 1997, 1998). Specifically, people seek pleasure and avoid pain (Higgins, 1997, 1998). To achieve this goal, Regulatory Focus Theory suggests two types of self-regulation systems: promotion-focused and prevention-focused. A promotion-focused regulation system is associated with emphasizing aspirations and achievements and focuses on the presence and absence of positive outcomes. Additionally, a promotion-focused regulation system uses an approach strategy of goal attainment. A prevention-focused regulation system is associated with emphasizing safety and protection and focuses on the presence of negative outcomes. A prevention-focused regulation system is associated with an avoidance strategy of goal attainment.

A large stream of research in persuasion has focused on regulatory fit, which refers to the notion that although a goal may be pursued with either a promotion or prevention focus, some goals are more compatible with a specific self-regulatory strategy, resulting in a higher level of "fit" (Higgins, 2002a, 2002b). For example, approach goals that strive toward a desirable end state tend to be more compatible with a promotion focus, whereas avoidance goals that seek to deter an undesirable end state tend to be more compatible with a prevention focus (Cesario, Grant, & Higgins, 2004; Higgins, 2002a, 2002b). The fit occurs because striving for a gain involves more eagerness than guarding against a non-gain and guarding against a loss involves more vigilance than striving for a non-loss (Idson, Liberman, & Higgins, 2000).

Although regulatory focus was initially conceptualized as a relatively stable chronic trait (Higgins, 1997, 1998, 2000), it can be situationally induced (Higgins, 1997, 1998; Lee & Aaker, 2004). For example, messages can emphasize the positive outcomes of targeted behaviors (e.g., "regular exercise can promote a healthy heart!") and encourage audiences to pursue gains. In contrast, messages can focus on negative outcomes resulting from noncompliance with targeted behaviors and focus on the prevention of those outcomes (e.g., "regular exercise can prevent heart disease!"). Thus, much work on regulatory focus has concentrated on understanding the effectiveness of promotion-focused and prevention-focused messages.

A large stream of prior research has focused on the effects of regulatory fit in persuasion. That is, when the regulatory focus of a message is consistent with individuals' dispositional tendency or primed goal direction, the persuasive effects are increased. Promotion-focused messages are more persuasive among those with promotion goals while the opposite holds true for those with prevention goals (e.g., Cesario, Grant, & Higgins, 2004). Such regulatory fit has been shown to result in positive persuasion outcomes. Kim (2006) examined how message framing influenced the effectiveness of antismoking messages. Results showed that when regulatory goals were congruent with the antismoking message frame, participants perceived lower benefits related to smoking and indicated they were less likely to smoke in the future.

Lee and Aaker (2004) found that regulatory focus moderates message framing on persuasion. Their work demonstrated gain frames are more persuasive when the message is promotion-focused, whereas loss frames are more persuasive when the message is prevention-focused. Additionally, this work showed increased eagerness toward positive outcomes and increased vigilance against negative outcomes when there was a match between the message frame and the regulatory focus of the message. This was attributed to fluency and "feeling" right when processing the message. This has implications for health communications in terms of pairing message frames with the appropriate type of message.

Self-efficacy and response-efficacy have long been central components of health communication strategy. Self-efficacy refers to the ease of the advocated behavior, and response-efficacy refers to the effectiveness of the advocated behavior (Roger, 1983). Keller (2006) identified a match effect between regulatory focus and the type of efficacy (self-efficacy or response-efficacy) conveyed in communication about health behaviors. Findings from two studies demonstrate greater regulatory-efficacy fit and higher intention to perform the advocated healthy behaviors when self-efficacy features are paired with a promotion focus and when response-efficacy features are paired with a prevention focus.

A substantial number of health messages convey the risk of a health hazard. Prior work has examined the effectiveness of various temporal frames in regard to conveying risk. Much of the work is rooted in Construal Level Theory, which proposes that people use higher level construals to represent information about future distant events and lower level construals to represent near future events

(Liberman & Trope, 1998; Trope & Liberman, 2003). Higher level construals are conceptualized as abstract and schematic, whereas lower level construals are conceptualized as concrete and contextualized (Trope & Liberman, 2003). Chandran and Menon (2004) found that conveying risk in a proximal frame (i.e., every day) is more effective than conveying risk in a distal frame (i.e., every year) because the risk of health issues is construed as more proximal or perceived to be closer.

However, recent work has identified that self-construal influences the impact of temporal frame in health advertising. Self-construal is described as an assembly of thoughts, feelings, and behaviors concerning the self as distinct from others (Singelis, 1994). Research in self-construal focuses on the distinction between an independent and interdependent construal of the self (Markus & Kitayama, 1991). People with an accessible, independent self tend to place a high value on independence and are associated with promotion goals. On the other hand, people with an accessible interdependent self-view tend to place importance on relationships with others and belonging. They tend to think and behave under the consideration of "we" rather than "I," and group interests often override individual concerns (Kitayama, Markus, & Matsumoto, 1995).

While self-view has been considered a chronic trait dependent on culture, several studies have revealed that one's accessible self-view can be situationally manipulated (e.g., Aaker & Lee, 2001). In the marketplace, health advertisements often emphasize consequences for the self (i.e., independent self-construal) or one's close others, such as family and friends (i.e., an interdependent self-construal). Thus, self-construal can be operationalized as a type of message framing health communication advertising (Pounders, Bouchacourt, & Kemp, 2024). In academic research, self-construal is oftentimes primed using both copy and imagery in the ad (e.g., Aaker & Lee, 2001; Pounders, Bouchacourt, & Kemp, 2024).

Pounders, Lee, and Mackert (2015) found temporal frame interacts with self-construal in the contexts of heart disease and skin cancer prevention. Specifically, a proximal frame is more effective when paired with an interdependent self, whereas a distal frame is more effective when paired with an independent self. They suggest this is the result of consistent cognitive processing. People with an interdependent self-view construe information concretely and specifically, while people with an independent self-view construe information more schematically and abstractly (Spassova & Lee, 2013). Further, they find that the mediating process differs for those with an interdependent versus independent self-view. For those with an interdependent self-view, message concreteness mediates the relationship between temporal frame and message persuasiveness, and message persuasiveness then mediates the impact of message concreteness on intention to engage in healthy behaviors. However, for those with an independent self-view, only message persuasiveness plays a mediating role in understanding the impact of temporal frame on intention to engage in healthy behaviors. This finding is consistent with the different ways that interdependent versus independent people construe information.

Additionally, a substantial body of work has focused on the relationship between self-construal and regulatory focus. For example, Aaker and Lee (2001) found that people with an accessible interdependent self-view are more persuaded by prevention-focused information consistent with an avoidance goal, whereas people with an accessible independent self-view are more persuaded by promotion-focused information consistent with an approach goal. When there is a match between self-view and regulatory focus of the message, people demonstrate greater message recall. Lee, Keller, and Sternthal (2010) extended this work by establishing that promotion-focused people are more likely to construe information at abstract, high levels, whereas prevention-focused people are more likely to construe information at concrete, low levels. A fit between one's regulatory focus and the construal level of the information resulted in enhanced attitude due to processing fluency. Specifically, a PSA that features what one has to gain by engaging in a healthy behavior should also focus on the self, whereas a PSA that features what one has to lose by not engaging in a healthy behavior should focus on one's family. This serves as yet another example of match effects between message elements in persuasion.

Emotional Appeals

The use of emotional appeals in health messages is not a new concept. Health communication research has long investigated discrete emotions such as fear and humor. Multiple theoretical frameworks exist in health and fear appeals. These include the Health Belief Model, Theory of Reasoned Action, Protection Motivation Theory, and Extended Parallel Process Model. In the advertising arena, Protection Motivation Theory has been widely used to understand consumer response to fear appeals in the context of conveying risk of health hazards (Rogers, 1975). Fear is defined as a negative emotional response to a perceived threat (Rogers, 1983). The general premise of Protection Motivation Theory is that a threat message includes four components: probability of the threat, magnitude of the threat, effectiveness of the recommended response (response-efficacy), and one's ability to perform a recommended response (self-efficacy) (Rogers, 1983). The first two components refer to the threat appraisal, whereas the latter two components refer to the coping appraisal. High levels of all four components result in the greatest amount of change in behavior (Rogers, 1983). However, work in fear appeals has demonstrated divergent findings. Generally, research has found that fear appeals can work until a certain point, beyond which it creates anxiety and is ineffective (Keller & Block, 1996; Keller, 1999).

Berger and Milkman (2012) demonstrated that high-arousal negative emotions, such as anxiety and anger, can also increase the likelihood that content will be shared online, illustrating this effect through the success of an anxiety-inducing campaign. Powerful fear appeals also have the potential to generate the needed arousal to activate engagement and create online activity. Hence, advertisers must develop the appropriate ad campaign and generate the desired emotions they seek to effectively communicate health information with the intended target audience.

Recently, researchers have shifted focus to guilt and shame appeals. Guilt and shame are negative self-conscious emotions because the internal attribution is the self (Tangney & Dearing, 2002). Although much of the existing literature refers to guilt and shame interchangeably, guilt and shame are two different emotions with unique cognitive appraisals and coping mechanisms (Tracy, Robins, & Tangney, 2007; Tangney & Dearing, 2002). Guilt is a negative emotion that occurs when individuals appraise information about their behavior that violates some social or moral standard (Izard, 1997; Tangeny & Dearing, 2002). Shame is a negative emotion that arises when an individual appraises negative information about the global self. Therefore, guilt is associated with the notion "I did something bad," while shame is associated with the notion "I am a bad person" (Tangney & Dearing, 2002; Tracy, Robins, & Tangney, 2007). Guilt and shame also differ in coping mechanisms. Guilt is associated with adaptive or approach coping, whereas shame is associated with maladaptive or avoidance coping (Tracy, Robins, & Tangney, 2007).

Recent work in the arena of consumer behavior and marketing has examined the impact of guilt and shame in the context of motivating healthy behaviors (Agrawal & Duhachek, 2010; Boudewyns, Turner, & Paquin, 2013; Duhachek, Agrawal, & Han, 2012). Agrawal and Duhachek (2010) investigated how the two emotional states influence the effectiveness of messages that highlight the socially undesirable consequences of binge drinking. They find that compatible appeals, or appeals which are the same elicited by the manipulated message frame, are less effective. This is due to defensive processing; specifically, consumers discount the negative consequences because they are motivated to reduce the negative emotion (Agrawal & Duhachek, 2010). Additionally, Duhachek, Agrawal, and Han (2012) found that guilt appeals are more effective when paired with gain frames, and shame appeals are more effective when paired with loss frames. This finding is attributed to coping mechanisms. Specifically, gain frames elicit the use of problem-solving coping strategies, which are accompanied with feelings of guilt. In addition, loss frames elicit the use of emotion-focused coping strategies, which are accompanied with feelings of shame (Duhachek, Agrawal, & Han, 2012). More recently, Pounders, Royne, and Lee (2019) investigated guilt and shame appeals alongside temporal frame, revealing that a guilt appeal is more effective when matched with a proximal temporal frame and a shame appeal is more effective when matched with a distal temporal frame. Additionally, Pounders, Lee and Royne (2018) examined guilt and shame appeals in conjunction with regulatory focus message frames and found a guilt appeal is more effective when matched with a promotion message frame, while a shame appeal is more effective when matched with a prevention message frame, and that self-efficacy mediated the match between a guilt appeal and a promotion message frame.

Health communication research has also examined positive emotions, such as humor. The use of humor in advertising has a long history, yet there is still not a universal agreement about the definition. Speck (1987) offered a broad perspective of humor arguing that humor is multi-dimensional, a concept consistent with the idea that humor has many types. Specifically, Speck notes that humor is "a family of related phenomena made up a several distinct humor species" (p. 61). There are also questions about the underlying mechanism that drives humor and its success in the advertising arena, with several different theories proposed to explain how it works. However, the success of humor in the commercial marketplace has led to a call for health communications that offers more than basic information and education. Rather, edutainment, or the integration of educational messages with entertaining approaches, including humor, has been advanced (e.g., Lister et al., 2014). Lister et al. (2014) propose the Laugh Model as one method to reach the public with an entertaining and somewhat humorous approach. Specifically, they found that implementation of their model in the Utah Partnership for Healthy Weight campaign produced successful results and, as such, argue for moving toward this model to improve health communications in society.

Interestingly, recent research has examined the interplay between shame and humor. Yoon (2015) found that the individual factor, fear of negative evaluation, moderates the interplay between shame and humor. Those with low fear of negative evaluation favored humor ads when the level of shame was low and preferred no-humor ads when shame induction was high. However, for those with high fear of evaluation, the results demonstrate humor is important when shame induction is high.

When utilizing digital media, emotional appeals are often more effective when portrayed in platforms that utilize pictures and/or videos such as Instagram and YouTube. This may be particularly true for positive emotions, such as humor, as suggested by Lister et al. (2015), who also indicate that emotional content may be more likely to be shared on social media.

In sum, the work discussed in this section lends insight into how to create effective health messages to be delivered using digital media. The match effect between various message elements enhances processing of the message, or fluency, and results in positive outcomes. Thus, health marketers may consider using message elements that "match," particularly when using digital platforms that may not be able to convey as much information as more traditional outlets (i.e., print). Providing information that "matches" may be particularly important when using digital media because consumers are likely multitasking and less likely to pay attention or have a smaller screen to view the information.

Conclusions

With the considerable influence of advertising, it is imperative that the best practices of research and technology be considered to confront adverse influences on health by effectively communicating important health information to consumers. With continuing advances in technology, digital advertising represents an opportunity to promote healthy lifestyles by augmenting current actions of public health.

Numerous digital tools exist that offer enormous resources to health practitioners. Social media, apps, and wearables both offer vast information about consumers to healthcare providers and also serve as a tool for healthcare providers to communicate with consumers. In addition, big data and other information provided on social media offer a unique lens by which healthcare providers can better understand and target consumers. As important as it is to utilize digital tools in the arena of health communication, it is also necessary to utilize a sound message strategy when creating health messages for those tools. A wide body of research has been conducted to identify a match between various message elements that results in more effective persuasion. Health communicators should be aware of this work and strive to convey information in an effective manner, particularly when utilizing digital media, because of the need to actively engage consumers with the posted content.

A final consideration is the need to tailor digital tools and messaging to the target audience for each physical or mental issue. Considering the numerous lifestyle factors that contribute to pervasive chronic diseases, messages related to food intake, physical activity, tobacco and cannabis, and addictive behaviors will likely make the most impact on improving health outcomes and containing healthcare costs. Moreover, further specialized content should be developed to support positive physical and emotional health behaviors in vulnerable populations: underserved minorities, limited English speaking, low-income, children, and the elderly, all of whom are at increased health risk. Perhaps most important is the need for collaboration between marketing and public health professionals. Marketing experts are needed to help shape the format and develop the content of digital advertising to realize the true potential of digital advertising to improve public health for overall community well-being.

References

Aaker, J.L., & Lee, A.Y. (2001). 'I' seek pleasures and 'we' avoid pains: The role of self- regulatory goals in information processing and persuasion. *Journal of Consumer Research*, *28*(1), 33–49.

Agrawal, N., & Duhachek, A. (2010). Emotional compatibility and the effectiveness of antidrinking messages: A defensive processing perspective on shame and guilt. *Journal of Marketing Research*, *47*(2), 263–273.

Ahmed, N., Quinn, S.C., Hancock, G.R., Freimuth, V.S., & Jamison, A. (2018). Social media use and influenza vaccine uptake among white and African American adults. *Vaccine*, *36*(49), 7556–7561.

Beltrán-Carrillo, V. J., Megías, Á., González-Cutre, D., & Jiménez-Loaisa, A. (2022). Elements behind sedentary lifestyles and unhealthy eating habits in individuals with severe obesity. *International Journal of Qualitative Studies on Health and Well-being*, *17*(1), 2056967. https://doi.org/10.1080/17482631.2022.2056967

Berger, J., & Milkman, K. L. (2012). What makes online content viral? *Journal of Marketing Research*, *49*(2), 192–205. https://doi.org/10.1509/jmr.10.0353

Bisung, E., & Elliott, S. (2014). Toward a social capital based framework for understanding the water-health nexus. *Social Science & Medicine*, *108*, 194–200.

Boudewyns, V., Turner, M.M., & Paquin, R.S. (2013). Shame-free guilt appeals: Testing the emotional and cognitive effects of shame and guilt appeals. *Psychology and Marketing*, *30*(9), 811–825.

Business of Apps. (2025). *Health app revenue and usage statistics.* https://www.businessofapps.com/data/health-app-market/

Cawley, J., & Meyerhoefer, C. (2012). The medical care costs of obesity: An instrumental variables approach. *Journal of Health Economics*, *31*(1), 219–230.

CDC.gov Measles Cases and Outbreaks. https://www.cdc.gov/measles/data- research/index.html accessed 6/21/25.

Centers for Disease Control and Prevention. (2025a). About chronic diseases. Retrieved from https://www.cdc.gov/chronic-disease/about/index.html.

Centers for Disease Control and Prevention. (2025b). Death and mortality. NCHS Fast-Stats web site. Retrieved from https://www.cdc.gov/nchs/fastats/deaths.htm.

Cesario, J., Grant, H., & Higgins, E.T. (2004). Regulatory fit and persuasion: Transfer from 'feeling right'. *Journal of Personality and Psychology*, *86*(3), 388–404.

Chandran, S., & Menon, G. (2004). When a day means more than a year: Effects of temporal framing on judgments of health risk. *Journal of Consumer Research*, *31*(2), 375–389.

Chang, I.C., Cheng, K.C., Hsu, H.M., & Yen, D.C. (2021). Factors influencing physicians' continuous blogging: A survey. *Healthcare (Basel)*, *9*(8), 958. https://doi.org/10.3390/healthcare9080958. PMID: 34442095; PMCID: PMC8394209.

DataReportal. (2025a). Global social media statistics. Retrieved from https://datareportal.com/social-media-users.

DataReportal. (2025b). Instagram users, stats, data & trends for 2025. Retrieved from https://datareportal.com/essential-instagram-stats.

De Valle, M.K., Gallego-García, M., Williamson, P., & Wade, T.D. (2021). Social media, body image, and the question of causation: Meta-analyses of experimental and longitudinal evidence. *Body Image*, *39*, 276–292.

Dobransky, K., & Hargittai, E. (2012). Inquiring minds acquiring wellness: Uses of online and offline sources of health information. *Health Communication*, *27*(4), 331–343.

Duhachek, A., Agrawal, N., & Han, D. (2012). Guilt versus shame: Coping, fluency, and framing in the effectiveness of responsible drinking message. *Journal of Marketing Research*, *49*(60), 928–941.

Festinger, L. (1954). A theory of social comparison processes. *Human Relations*, *7*(2), 117–140.

Fioravanti, G., Cassioli, E., Rossi, E., Lucherini Angeletti, L., Casale, S., Ricca, V., & Castellini, G. (2024). The relationship between problematic Instagram use and eating disorders psychopathology: An explanatory structural equation model. *Social Psychiatry and Psychiatric Epidemiology*, *59*(9), 1617–1627.

Fox, S. (2010). Patients and online communities. *Pew Research Center*. Retrieved from https://www.pewinternet.org.

Freedman, D.S., Mei, Z., Srinivasan, S.R., Berenson, G.S., & Dietz, W.H. (2007). Cardiovascular risk factors and excess adiposity among overweight children and adolescents: The Bogalusa heart study. *Journal of Pediatrics, 150*(1), 12–17.

Frost, J.H., & Massagli, M.P. (2008). Social uses of personal health information within PatientsLikeMe, an online patient community: What can happen when patients have access to one another's data. *Journal of Medical Research, 10*, e15.

Global Media Insight. (2025). *YouTube users statistics 2025 (users by country + demographics).* https://www.globalmediainsight.com/blog/youtube-users-statistics/

Gunasekeran, D. V., Tseng, R. M. W. W., Tham, Y.-C., & Wong, T. Y. (2022). The impact and applications of social media platforms for public health responses before and during the COVID-19 pandemic: Systematic review. *Journal of Medical Internet Research, 24*, e33680. https://doi.org/10.2196/33680

Han, J. C., Lawlor, D. A., & Kimm, S. Y. S. (2010). Childhood obesity. *The Lancet, 375*(9727), 1737–1748.

Hawes, T., Zimmer-Gembeck, M.J., & Campbell, S.M. (2020). Unique associations of social media use and online appearance preoccupation with depression, anxiety, and appearance rejection sensitivity. *Body Image, 33*, 66–76.

Higgins, T.E. (1997). Beyond pleasure and pain. *American Psychologist, 52*(December), 1280–1300.

Higgins, T.E. (1998). Promotion and prevention: Regulatory focus as motivational principle. *Advances in Experimental Social Psychology, 30*, 1–46.

Higgins, T.E. (2002). How self- regulation creates distinct values: The case of promotion and prevention decision making. *Journal of Consumer Psychology, 12*(3), 177–191.

Higgins, T.E. (2002). Making a good decision: Value from fit. *American Psychology, 55*(11), 1217.

Househ, M., Borycki, E., & Kushniruk, A. (2014). Empowering patients through social media: The benefits and challenges. *Healthier Informatics Journal, 20*(1), 50–58.

Hwang, H., & Kim, K. O. (2015). Social media as a tool for social movements: The effect of social media use and social capital on intention to participate in social movements. *International Journal of Consumer Studies, 39*(5), 478–488.

Idson, L.C., Liberman, N., & Higgins, T.E. (2000). Distinguishing gains from nonlosses and losses from nongains: A regulatory focus perspective on hedonic intensity. *Journal of Experimental Social Psychology, 36*(3), 252–274.

International Diabetes Federation. (2025). *IDF Diabetes Atlas*. Retrieved from https://diabetesatlas.org/.

Islam, M. S., Sarkar, T., Khan, S. H., Mostofa Kamal, A.-H., Hasan, S. M. M., Kabir, A., Yeasmin, D., Islam, M. A., Amin Chowdhury, K. I., Anwar, K. S., Chughtai, A. A., & Seale, H. (2020). COVID-19-related infodemic and its impact on public health: A global social media analysis. *The American Journal of Tropical Medicine and Hygiene, 103*(4), 1621–1629. https://doi.org/10.4269/ajtmh.20-0812

Islam, M.S., Sarkar T., Khan, S.H., Mostofa Kamal, A.H., Hasan, S.M.M., Kabir, A., Yeasmin, D., Islam, M.A., Amin Chowdhury, K.I., Anwar, K.S., Chughtai, A.A., & Seale, H. (2020). COVID-19-related infodemic and its impact on public health: A global social media analysis. *American Journal of Tropical Medicine and Hygiene, 103*(4), 1621–1629.

Ittefaq, M., Kamboh, S.A., Zelaya, C., & Arif, R. (2024). Polio vaccine misinformation on social media: Challenges, efforts, and recommendations. *Journal of Science Communication, 23*(01), Y01.

Izard, C.E. (1997). Emotions and facial expressions: A perspective from differential emotions theory. *The Psychology of Facial Expression, 2*, 57–77.

Kay, M.J. (2007). Healthcare marketing: What is salient? *International Journal of Pharmaceutical and Healthcare Marketing, 1*(3), 247–263.

Kee, D.M.H., Al-Anesi, M.A.L., & Al-Anesi, S.A.L. (2022). Cyberbullying on social media under the influence of COVID-19. *Global Business and Organizational Excellence, 41*(6), 11–22.

Keller, P. A. (2006). Regulatory focus and efficacy of health messages. *Journal of Consumer Research, 33*(1), 109–114. https://doi.org/10.1086/504141

Keller, P.A. (1999). Converting the unconverted: The effect of inclination and opportunity to discount health-related fear appeals. *Journal of Applied Psychology, 84*(3), 403.

Keller, P.A., & Block, L.B. (1996). Increasing the persuasiveness of fear appeals: The effect of arousal and elaboration. *Journal of Consumer Research, 22*(4), 448–459.

Kikuchi, E., Pula, I., Tyson, A., & Yam, E. (2025, May 7). Americans on Healthy Food and eating. *Americans on Healthy Food and Eating*. Retrieved from https://www.pewresearch.org/science/2025/05/07/americans-on-healthy-food-and-eating/.

Kim, Y.J. (2006). The role of regulatory focus in message framing in antismoking advertisements for adolescents. *Journal of Advertising, 35*(1), 143–151.

Kitayama, S., Markus, H.R., & Matsumoto, H. (1995). Culture, self, and emotion: A cultural perspective on 'self-conscious' emotions. (439–464). In: June Price Tangney & Kurt W. Fischer (Eds.), *Self-conscious emotions: The psychology of shame, guilt, embarrassment, and pride.* New York: Guilford Press.

Lee, A.Y., & Aaker, J.L. (2004). Bringing the frame into focus: The influence of regulatory fit on processing fluency and persuasion. *Journal of Personality and Social Psychology, 86*(2),205–218.

Lee, A.Y., Keller, P.A., & Sternthal, B. (2010). Value from regulatory construal fit: The persuasive impact of fit between consumer goals and message concreteness. *Journal of Consumer Research, 36*(5), 735–747.

Lewallen, J., & Behm-Morawitz, E. (2016). *Pinterest or Thinterest? Social comparison and body image on social media*. Social Media + Society.

Liberman, N., & Trope, Y. (1998). The role of feasibility and desirability consideration in near and distant future decisions: A test of temporal construal theory. *Journal of Personality and Social Psychology, 75*(1), 5–18.

Lister, C., Royne, M., Payne, H. E., Cannon, B., Hanson, C., & Barnes, M. (2015). The Laugh Model: Reframing and rebranding public health through social media. *American Journal of Public Health, 105*(11), 2245–2251. https://doi.org/10.2105/AJPH.2015.302669

Lister, C., Royne, M.B., Payne, H., Cannon, B., Hanson, C., & Barnes, M. (2015). The laugh model: Reframing and rebranding public health through social media. *American Journal of Public Health, 105*(11), 2245–2251.

Livingstone, C., & Rintoul, A. (2020). Moving on from responsible gambling: A new discourse is needed to prevent and minimise harm from gambling. *Public Health, 184,* 107–112.

Lockwood, P., & Kunda, Z. (1997). Superstars and me: Predicting the impact of role models on the self. *Journal of Personality and Social Psychology, 73*(1), 91.

Loomba, S., De Figueiredo, A., Piatek, S.J., De Graaf, K., & Larson, H.J. (2021). Measuring the impact ofCOVID-19 vaccine misinformation on vaccination intent in the UK and USA. *Nature Human Behaviour*, *5*, 337–348.

Markus, H.R., & Kitayama, S. (1991). Culture and self: Implications for cognition, emotion, and motivation. *Psychological Review*, *98*(April), 224–253.

Mathis, A.D., Raines, K., & Filardo, T.D., et al. (2025). Measles Update — United States, January 1–April 17, 2025. *MMWR Morbidity and Mortality Weekly Report* 74, 232–238.

McLeroy, K.R., Bibeau, D., Steckler, A., & Glantz, K. (1988). An ecological perspective on health promotion programs. *Health Education & Behavior*, *5*(4), 351–377.

Moore, L.H.III., & Grubbs, J.B. (2021). Gambling Disorder and comorbid PTSD: A systematic review of empirical research. *Addictive Behaviors, 114,* Article 106713. https://doi.org/10.1016/j.addbeh.2020.106713.

National Alliance on Mental Illness (2023). SAMSHSA Releases 2022 National Survey on Drug Use and Health Report. Retrieved from https://www.nami.org/about-mental-illuness/research/research-news/2023-2/.

National Institute of Mental Health. (2024). Mental Illness. Retrieved from https://www.nimh.nih.gov/health/statistics/mental-illness.

National Institute on Drug Abuse. (2022). *Common comorbidities with substance use disorders research report.* National Institutes of Health. https://nida.nih.gov/publications/research-reports/common-comorbidities-substance-use-disorders

Nielsen. (2025). Smartphone Owners Are as Diverse as Their Devices. Retrieved from https://www.nielsen.com/insights/2015/smartphone-owners-are-as-diverse-as-their-devices/#:~:text=Asian%2FPacific%20Islanders%20(86.6%25),%25%20of%20non%2DHispanic%20whites.

Office of the Surgeon General. (2021). *Protecting youth mental health: The U.S. Surgeon General's advisory.*

Ogden, C.L., Carroll, M.D., Kit, B.K., & Flegal, K.M. (2012). Prevalence of obesity and trends in body mass index among US children and adolescents, 1999–2010. *JAMA*, *307*(5), 483–490.

Pastore, M., Indrio, F., Bali, D., Vural, M., Giardino, I., & Pettoello-Mantovani, M. (2023). Alarming increase of eating disorders in children and adolescents. *The Journal of Pediatrics*, *263,* 1–4.

Pew Research Center. (2025). Internet, Broadband Fact Sheet. Retrieved from https://pewresearch.org.

Pierri, F., Perry, B.L., DeVerna, M.R., Yang, K.C., Flammini, A., Menczer, F., & Bryden, J. (2022). Online misinformation is linked to early COVID-19 vaccination hesitancy and refusal. *Scientific Reports*, *12*(1), 5966. https://doi.org/10.1038/s41598-022-10070-w. PMID: 35474313; PMCID: PMC9043199.

Porterfield, C. (2024, February 20). *Just 28% of Americans are exercising enough, CDC says- and it's even lower in some regions.* Forbes: https://www.forbes.com/sites/carlieporterfield/2023/01/26/just-28-of-americans-are-exercising-enough-cdc-says-and-its-even-lower-in-some-regions/.

Pounders, K. R., Lee, S., & Royne Stafford, M. B. (2018). The effectiveness of guilt and shame ad appeals in social marketing: The role of regulatory focus. *Journal of Current Issues & Research in Advertising, 39*(4), 386–403. https://doi.org/10.1080/10641734.2017.1372322

Pounders, K. R., Royne Stafford, M. B., & Lee, S. (2019). The influence of temporal frame on guilt and shame appeals. *Journal of Current Issues & Research in Advertising, 40*(3), 245–257. https://doi.org/10.1080/10641734.2018.1503115

Pounders, K., Kemp, D., & Bouchacourt, L. (2024). We're all in this together! Self-construal pride and guilt appeals in health advertising. *Journal of Current Issues & Research in Advertising, 45*(1), 71–87.

Pounders, K.R., & Mackert, M.S. (2015). Matching temporal frame, self-view, and message frame valence: Improving persuasiveness in health communications. *Journal of Advertising, 44*(4), 388–402.

Prince, M., Patel, V., Saxena, S., Maj, M., Maselko, J., Phillips, M. R., & Rahman, A. (2007). No health without mental health. *The Lancet, 370*(9590), 859–877.

Puhl, R.M., & Latner, J.D. (2007). Stigma, obesity, and the health of the nation's children. *Psychology Bulletin, 133*(4), 557–580.

Rahman, A.N., Nuryakin, & Pribadi, F. (2022). Effective marketing strategies in health services: Systematic literature review. *Expert Journal of Marketing, 10*(2), 73–84.

Rogers, R.W. (1983). Cognitive and physiological processes in fear appeals and attitude change: A revised theory of protection motivation. (153–176). In: Cacciopo, J. T., & Petty, R., (Eds.) *Social psychophysiology: A sourcebook.* New York: Guildord Press.

Royne, M.B., & Levy, M. (2011). Marketing for public health: We need an app for that. *Journal of Consumer Affairs, 45*(1), 1–6.

Search Logistics. (2025). *Twitter (X) user statistics 2025: What happened after "X"?*https://www.searchlogistics.com/learn/statistics/twitter-user-statistics/

Seo, M., & Matsaganis, M.D. (2013). How interpersonal communication mediates the relationship of multichannel communication connections to health-enhancing and health- threatening behaviors. *Journal of Health Communication, 18*, 1002–1020.

Singelis, T.M. (1994). The measurement of independent and interdependent self-construals. *Personality and Social Psychology Bulletin, 20*(October), 580–591.

Spassova, G., & Lee, A.Y. (2013). Looking into the future: A match between self-view and temporal distance. *Journal of Consumer Research, 40*(1), 159–171.

Speck, P.S. (1987). On humor in advertising. *Unpublished Doctoral Dissertation; Texas Tech University.*

Stokols, D. (1996). Translating social ecological theory into guidelines for community health promotion. *American Journal of Health Promotion, 10*, 282–298.

Substance Abuse and Mental Health Services Administration. (2025). *Key substance use and mental health indicators in the United States: Results from the 2023 National Survey on Drug Use and Health* (HHS Publication No. PEP25-07-022, NSDUH Series H-61). U.S. Department of Health and Human Services. https://www.samhsa.gov/data/report/2023-nsduh-annual-national-report

Sutherland, E.R. (2008). Obesity and asthma. *Immunology Allergy Clinic of North America, 28*(3), 589–602.

Tangney, J.P., & Dearing, R.L. (2002). *Shame and guilt.* New York: Guildford Press.

Taylor, K.A., & Humphrey, W.F. Jr. (2021). Impact of medical blog reading and information presentation on readers' preventative health intentions: Mixed methods, multi-study investigation. *Journal of Medical Internet Research, 23*(12), e23210. https://doi.org/10.2196/23210. PMID: 34941543; PMCID: PMC873491s3.

TikTok. (2025). About TikTok. Retrieved from https://www.tiktok.com/about.

Tolentino, D.A., Costa, D.K., & Jiang, Y. (2023). Determinants of American adults' use of digital health and willingness to share health data to providers, family, and social media: A cross-sectional study. *Computers, Informatics, Nursing : CIN*, *41*(11), 892–902.

Tomeny, T.S., Vargo, C.J., & El-Toukhy, S. (2017). Geographic and demographic correlates of autism-related anti-vaccine beliefs on Twitter, 2009–15. *Social Science & Medicine*, *191*, 168–175. https://doi.org/10.1016/j.socscimed.2017.08.041. Epub 2017 Sep 4. PMID: 28926775; PMCID: PMC5623105.

Tracy, J.L., Robins, R.W., & Tangney, J.P. (2007). *The self-conscious emotions: Theory and research.* New York: Guilford Press.

Trope, Y., & Liberman, N. (2003). Temporal construal. *Psychological Review*, *110*(3), 403–421.

Wakefield, M.A., Loken, B., & Hornik, R.C. (2010). Use of mass media campaigns to change health behavior. *The Lancet*, *376*, 1261–1271.

Walther, J.B., Carr, C.T., Choi, S.S.W., DeAndrea, D.C., Kim, J., Tong, S.T., & Van Der Heide, B. (2010). Interaction of interpersonal, peer, and media influence sources online. *A Networked Self: Identity, Community, and Culture on Social Network Sites*, *17*, 17–38.

Wang, X., & Terlizzi, E. P. (2023). *Health information technology use among adults: United States, July–December 2022*(NCHS Data Brief No. 482). National Center for Health Statistics, Centers for Disease Control and Prevention. https://www.cdc.gov/nchs/products/databriefs/db482.htm

Webb, T., Joseph, J., Yardley, L., & Michie, S. (2010). Using the internet to promote health behavior change: A systematic review and meta-analysis of the impact of theoretical basis, use of behavior change techniques, and mode of delivery on efficacy. *Journal of Medical Internet Research*, *12*(1), e4.

Wilson, S.L., & Wiysonge, C. (2020). Social media and vaccine hesitancy. *BMJ Glob Health*, *5*(10), e004206. https://doi.org/10.1136/bmjgh-2020–004206. Epub 2020 Oct 23. PMID: 33097547;PMCID: PMC7590343.

Wisconsin Policy Forum. (February 2025). As states approve sports betting, Wisconsin does so on limited scale. Retrieved from https://wispolicyforum.org/research/as-states-approve-sports-betting-wisconsin-does-so-on-limited-scale/.

World Health Organization https://www.who.int/health-topics/infodemic#tab=tab_1 accessed 6/17/2025

World Obesity Federation. (2025). *World Obesity Atlas 2025.*

Yoon, H.J. (2015). Humor effects in shame-inducing health issue advertising: The moderating effects of fear of negative evaluation. *Journal of Advertising*, *44*(2), 126–139.

Zarocostas, J. (2020). How to fight an infodemic. *The Lancet*, *395*(10225), 676.

Zhang, Q., Zhang, R., & Lu, X. et al. (2023). What drives the adoption of online health communities? An empirical study from patient-centric perspective. *BMC Health Services Research, 23*, 524. https://doi.org/10.1186/s12913-023-09469-6.

Part IV

Data

Computational, AI, and Programmatic Systems

13 Past, Present, and Future of Computational Advertising and Research Directions

Joanna Strycharz, Claire M. Segijn and Jisu Huh

Introduction

Computational advertising has become a cornerstone of the digital media landscape, transforming how advertising messages are created and delivered, and their effects are evaluated. It represents a fundamental shift from traditional mass advertising to data-driven, algorithmic persuasion (Zarouali et al., 2022). As defined by Huh and Malthouse (2020, p. 1), computational advertising is "a broad, data-driven advertising approach relying on or facilitated by enhanced computing capabilities, mathematical models/algorithms, and the technology infrastructure to create and deliver messages and monitor/surveil an individual's behaviors." Building on this, Pearson (2024) expands its scope to also include the anticipation of societal trends and media planning that adapt to evolving dynamics in the economy, society, and environment.

With the development of communication technologies and infrastructures, the volume, velocity, and variety of data available and processed for computational advertising have significantly increased (Yun et al., 2020). Today, various types of data, such as advertising investments, media activities, and granular consumer behavior, are systematically collected and analyzed to optimize the match between the advertising message and the receiver (Araujo et al., 2020; Yun et al., 2020). Advertisers can apply various strategies to process such consumer data and personalize ads. One common approach is content-based filtering, which relies on explicit data (i.e., explicit or overtly collected data that consumers are aware of being collected), including searches or clicks, to deliver personalized recommendations (e.g., searching for flights to Tokyo results in ads promoting discounted airfare for flights to Tokyo). A second method is collaborative filtering, which utilizes data from similar consumers to make recommendations (First, 2018). For instance, if consumers with certain characteristics booked flights to a specific destination, this destination might get recommended to others with similar interests. Beyond these, advertisers may also employ probabilistic data usage, where multiple data points, often across platforms, are combined to infer consumer interests (i.e., implicit or covertly collected data). For example, for

DOI: 10.4324/9781003567523-17

consumers who have researched flights to Tokyo on an airline's website and searched for popular tourist spots in Tokyo on social media platforms, it can be inferred that they might be interested in hotels in Tokyo and thus shown ads promoting a discount on stays in Tokyo.

This chapter presents an overview of the evolution of computational advertising, reviews emerging research on the topic and the theoretical frameworks explaining computational advertising effects and influencing factors, and proposes future research directions. It begins by providing a historical perspective on how computational advertising has evolved from early direct marketing to artificial intelligence (AI)-driven advertising, setting the stage for a discussion on the present state of research in the field. Next, it traces the theory development, highlighting key models applied in computational advertising research. This chapter concludes by outlining future research directions, emphasizing both the need for continued theoretical innovation and the methodological advancements required to keep pace with the fast-evolving computational advertising landscape.

Historical Development of Computational Advertising

Although generally associated with online media, data-driven advertising has a much longer history than online digital media. Already in the 19th century, strategies used in direct marketing established the foundation for modern computational advertising practices (Malthouse et al., 2024). First-party data (i.e., data owned by companies from their own customers; Zarouali et al., 2022) gathered in customer databases were later enriched with second-party data (first-party data from another company; Malthouse et al., 2018) and third-party data (data purchased from data brokers, such as data management platforms; Zarouali et al., 2022). Later, the rise of the internet led to major changes and rapid developments in computational advertising by establishing a digital environment in which consumer behaviors could be continuously tracked and processed. At first, it enabled so-called contextual advertising, i.e., targeting consumers based on their interests inferred from the content of the webpage on which ads are to be displayed (Goldfarb & Tucker, 2011). Soon after, ad agencies began offering to help their clients identify websites that their target audience would likely visit, marking the beginning of demographic targeting in digital advertising (Hesterberg, 2021).

A significant innovation in the computational advertising evolution was the emergence of online behavioral advertising (OBA), which relies on online behavioral data (e.g., browsing history, searches, likes) to tailor ads to individual users (Boerman et al., 2017). OBA utilizes tracking technologies (e.g., cookies) to build user profiles across websites, enabling higher personalization (Smit et al., 2014). This marked a shift from broad segment-based targeting to individualized behavioral profiling, reinforcing the data-driven nature of computational advertising. A major milestone that accelerated this shift was the launch of

DoubleClick, which not only improved tracking consumer interactions with ads but also popularized third-party cookies (Oberoi, 2013). Another important step was the rise of programmatic advertising (i.e., computational systems for automated ad inventory transactions) in the early 2000s. In 2000, Google launched AdWords, and by 2002, it allowed advertisers to bid on keywords for ads displayed in Google's search results (Google, 2000). Over time, keyword bidding evolved into more dynamic models: so-called real-time bidding emerged around 2004, enabling real-time banner ad transactions on websites (Jones, 2021). In real-time bidding, ad inventories are bought and sold in automated auctions that occur in milliseconds, allowing advertisers to target specific users as they load a webpage (Strycharz et al., 2019).

The next major change involved targeting consumers across devices. This strategy focuses on reaching the same consumer across multiple devices. Cross-device targeting gained popularity with the rise of smartphones, and Google's Enhanced Campaigns, among others, led the way in the early 2010s. Later, more advanced solutions, such as Google's Customer Match and Facebook Pixel, allowed advertisers to link consumer identity across multiple devices and apps. An extension of this approach is synced advertising, which coordinates advertising content across devices in real-time (Segijn, 2019).

Computational advertising has evolved further with the integration of machine learning, which enables more dynamic, data-driven decisions about when, where, and to whom ads are delivered. In fact, the term *computational advertising* was first introduced by Microsoft in 2013 in an article that introduced the use of machine learning to optimize large-scale ad placement systems, enabling the design of algorithms that predict and evaluate the impact of small changes in ad-ranking models on user engagements and revenues (Bottou et al., 2013).

More recently, the advancement of AI presents new disruptions and opportunities in computational advertising message creation and placement. Generative AI (genAI) tools enable fully AI-generated visuals, copy, and video ads (so-called synthetic advertising, Campbell et al., 2022). Synthetic advertising is actively embraced by big tech platforms. For example, Meta's genAI tool for Facebook and Instagram will allow brands to upload product images and budget, and then it will automatically generate complete ads, including tailored images, videos, text, and audience targeting (Bobrowsky & Coffee, 2025). Such tools can also be used to create AI-influencers, synthetic personas that simulate human-like behaviors and appearance to engage audiences, promote brands, and influence consumer decisions on social media platforms (Thomas & Fowler, 2021). Additionally, AI enables hyper-personalization of synthetic advertising content that is created to match the individual consumer's exact interest and intention inferred from their past online behaviors (Kapoor & Kumar, 2025). Furthermore, AI has revolutionized media planning, where it is used to analyze large volumes of consumer, market, and performance data to optimize computational advertising campaigns (Lee, 2025).

Computational Advertising Research and Theory Development

As technological developments continue to reshape the computational advertising landscape, researchers have sought to understand the complex mechanisms, processes, and contextual factors that shape its development and impact. A wide range of theories and conceptual models have emerged to explain how computational advertising messages are created, measured, processed, and received by consumers. This section synthesizes key theoretical perspectives in computational advertising research in five interconnected subsections.

Computational Advertising Ecosystem

To understand computational advertising as more than a set of technological tools or campaign strategies, researchers have examined the unique ecosystem in which it operates. The computational advertising ecosystem is shaped by complex interdependencies and tensions among platforms, advertisers, algorithms, consumers, regulatory entities, and surrounding macro environments. It highlights how computational advertising is embedded within broader digital and socio-technical systems and conceptualizes computational advertising's dynamics and persuasive potential.

The concepts of the digital ecosystem and the computational advertising ecosystem provide foundational perspectives for understanding the broader environment in which computational advertising operates. Araujo et al. (2020) describe the digital ecosystem as a dynamic network of interdependent actors, such as large technology platforms, hardware and data brokerage companies, publishers, advertisers, and users, whose interactions are shaped by digital infrastructures and algorithmic systems. Importantly, this ecosystem enables a fundamental shift in advertising: advertising no longer constitutes one-way messages but has transformed into omnichannel, multi-actor interactions throughout the consumer journey.

Extending this perspective, Helberger et al. (2020) define the computational advertising ecosystem more specifically as the socio-technical system through which advertising is algorithmically produced, distributed, and optimized. This ecosystem includes not only technological elements, such as data infrastructures and machine learning algorithms, but also normative and institutional components, such as regulation, platform policies, and user expectations. It reflects a shift from advertiser-controlled one-way communication to platform-mediated, algorithmic persuasion, where targeting and content delivery are continuously optimized through data-driven feedback loops. Within this evolving system, consumers increasingly take on active roles as data providers, content creators, and distributors. This multifaceted role not only enhances their influence within the system but also raises concerns about transparency, autonomy, and control, particularly as many of these processes operate on inferred data with limited consumer awareness or oversight. Understanding computational advertising within such ecosystems highlights the increasing power of intermediaries, such as large technology platforms, and the evolving dynamics of consumer participation and platform accountability in computational advertising.

As such dynamics become more complex, regulatory frameworks have evolved to address the emerging risks associated with computational advertising. Privacy regulations, such as the General Data Protection Regulation and ePrivacy Directive in the European Union (EU) as well as the California Consumer Privacy Act in the United States, have fundamentally reshaped how personal data are collected and used in computational advertising (Li et al., 2019). They have introduced strict requirements for user consent for data collection, transparency about how data are collected and processed, and data minimization (i.e., the requirement to only collect data that are adequate, relevant, and limited to what is necessary for the purposes for which they are processed). They also grant consumers rights to know, delete, and opt out of the collection and processing of their personal data. Regarding the use of AI, the EU's Digital Services Act imposes transparency obligations on digital platforms regarding computational advertising driven by algorithms and restricts personalization based on sensitive data (Duivenvoorde & Goanta, 2023).

While regulatory frameworks aim to provide a level playing field in computational advertising, understanding how persuasion in computational advertising operates requires a comprehensive theoretical lens. Two complementary process models offer valuable theoretical insights into persuasion in computational advertising. The Algorithmic Persuasion Model proposed by Zarouali et al. (2022) conceptualizes how platforms and advertisers leverage algorithmic systems to influence consumer attitudes and behaviors. It highlights the role of data-driven personalization and the influence of platform affordances in driving consumer responses, often without consumers' full awareness. It also highlights that computational advertising may have both intended persuasive effects and unintended effects, such as selective exposure to content and polarization in the long term. Overall, this model shows how algorithmic persuasion differs from traditional advertising by being continuous, adaptive, and embedded in everyday digital interactions, making it more pervasive and potentially more powerful.

Complementing this perspective, the Personalization Process Model (Vesanen & Raulas, 2006) and its extension the Dataveillance in Interactive Advertising Model (Strycharz et al., 2025) offer an overview of how individual-level data are collected, analyzed, and transformed into personalized ads. They map the process from data collection that occurs when consumers interact with content online, through data processing when data are transformed into customer profiles to message customization, drawing attention to the multistep process of advertising personalization. These models bring into focus the operational logic behind computational advertising, revealing how personalization is not a single act but a sequence of technical and strategic decisions, many of which remain invisible to consumers. Together, these models illuminate the role of data and algorithms in persuasion, clarifying how computational advertising systems leverage consumer data to optimize influence and shape consumer experiences in dynamic and personalized ways.

Creation of Computational Advertising Messages

The creation of computational advertising messages involves the automated generation of ads based on data inputs, user profiling, and algorithmic decision-making. One of the key models explaining this process is the Automated Brand-Generated Content Model (Van Noort et al., 2020). This model introduces "automated brand-generated content as the transformation of brand and consumer data into a message that is created and delivered with some level of automation" (p. 412) and outlines how brands increasingly rely on AI systems to autonomously produce advertising messages. Historically, brand-generated content was the product of a creative process led by advertising professionals working on behalf of brands (Goh et al., 2013). However, due to recent advances in AI, brand-generated content today is increasingly computer-generated based on consumer data, with minimal or no human involvement. Such advertising relies on various AI techniques, such as deepfakes and generative adversarial networks, to automatically create content that depicts an unreal, but convincing, artificial version of reality (Campbell et al., 2022).

Importantly, Van Noort et al. (2020) emphasize that automated brand-generated content must be evaluated not only in terms of its effectiveness and scalability but also in terms of authenticity, brand fit, and consumer trust. As algorithmic systems are increasingly able to independently create persuasive messages, the boundaries between human and machine authorship blur, raising new questions about creative control, brand consistency, and ethics of AI generation of content. While automation enhances scalability and efficiency, empirical studies show that consumer responses vary depending on content type and context. Arango et al. (2024), for example, showed that consumer awareness of synthetic content can reduce emotional engagement. Emerging research findings underscore the need to assess not only the effectiveness and fit of AI-generated content but also its authenticity and emotional impact.

Beyond synthetic content, consumers can also play an active role in the creation of computational advertising messages. Liu-Thompkins and colleagues (2020) proposed the conceptual framework for user-brand relationships in advertising. The framework identifies three distinct consumer roles in computational advertising, each defined by the type of engagement and data the engagement generates. Content creators contribute original or derivative brand-related material (e.g., reviews), providing rich, expressive data. Metavoicers interact with existing content by liking, commenting, or rating, offering evaluative signals. Propagators share content across their networks, generating data uniquely tied to social connections and diffusion dynamics. Together, these roles illustrate how consumers shape and amplify computational advertising content, while producing diverse and rich data.

Media Planning and Placement of Computational Advertising Messages

Relative to research on computational advertising content, investigation of the media planning and message placement aspect of computational advertising has been more limited. However, emerging research suggests a fruitful research avenue. Huang and Rust (2021) offer a three-stage framework detailing how various types of AI, namely mechanical, thinking, and feeling, can enhance computational advertising media planning. At the marketing research stage, mechanical AI systematically collects and structures large-scale consumer data, thinking AI interprets market trends through data analyses, and feeling AI enriches insights by understanding consumer emotions and motivations. At the marketing strategy stage, mechanical AI identifies distinct consumer segments, thinking AI recommends optimal targeting strategies, and feeling AI fine-tunes positioning to emotionally resonate with specific consumer segments. Finally, during the marketing action stage, mechanical AI ensures standardization of marketing communications across channels, thinking AI enables personalized ads tailored to individual profiles, and feeling AI increases relational engagement, ensuring stronger emotional connections with consumers.

With the emergence of digital ecosystems (see the "Introduction" section), the traditional exposure-driven media planning framework has shifted toward more interaction-driven planning, emphasizing consumer engagement rather than mere reach. This approach involves more dynamic media planning approaches to foster deeper, ongoing relationships between brands and consumers and interactions as a source of richer consumer data (Araujo et al., 2020). Additional considerations for computational advertising media planning and placements include brand safety and misinformation prevention, which have become crucial as human involvement in choosing where ads are placed is reduced. Zarouali et al. (2025) demonstrate that when ads appear alongside disinformation content, consumer trust and brand attitudes decrease, particularly when there is thematic congruence between the advertised brand and the disinformation content. Such unintended brand-unsafe ad placing can not only damage the brand's image but also amplify the perceived credibility of the disinformation itself, making the advertised brand appear as if it validates misleading information. More research is warranted in this area.

Perceptions and Receptivity of Computational Advertising

Consumers' as well as advertising professionals' perceptions of computational advertising constitute a critical factor in understanding computational advertising effects, and a key theoretical construct in connection to such perceptions is the affordances offered by platforms. In this context, affordances can be understood as relational opportunities for action that a platform's algorithms and features both enable and constrain for users (Nagy & Neff, 2015). These affordances are not just based on the design and actual functionalities of platforms but also strongly shaped by users' perceptions of design cues. For example, social media platforms offer advertisers the possibility to personalize and optimize their campaigns, but in practice, it is the interplay between actual system capabilities and the advertiser's expectations (advertisers' expectations about the campaign and the target group) that shape choices in computational advertising.

From the consumer's perspective, privacy plays a central role in shaping their perceptions of computational advertising. More specifically, the privacy paradox refers to the tension between the perceived benefits and costs of computational advertising. On the one hand, computational advertising can improve relevance and consumer experience by matching content to individual preferences. On the other hand, computational advertising can feel intrusive, leading to privacy concerns, discomfort, or resistance when consumers perceive that their personal data are being overused or misused, which may result in a feeling of resignation (De Groot, 2022). Hence, computational advertising is seen as both beneficial for consumers and one that comes with privacy costs. From the perspective of Communication Privacy Management theory, consumers manage privacy by forming personal boundaries around their data and developing rules for disclosure, similar to interpersonal contexts. When these boundaries are violated, such as through intrusive data collection or opaque personalization practices, privacy turbulence occurs, which prevents consumers from sharing information with advertisers (Metzger, 2007).

Another critical perceptual factor related to computational advertising is consumer trust. Trust plays a pivotal role in shaping consumer attitudes and behaviors, especially in situations involving uncertainty and risk (e.g., Roy et al., 2017). Thus, trust acts as a key facilitator of sustainable interactions, particularly in online environments where data-sharing is involved. Prior research has demonstrated that trust enhances various communication outcomes (McKnight et al., 2002; Roy et al., 2017; Shin et al., 2025). In advertising research, studies suggest that consumers' trust in websites or digital media platforms significantly influences their responses to data-driven personalized advertising, even mitigating negative reactions to personal data collection when ads appear on more trustworthy websites or platforms (Aguirre et al., 2015; Shin et al., 2025). This is supported by the trust transfer theory (Stewart, 2003), which suggests that trust in a platform can extend to associated advertising practices, increasing consumer receptivity to computational advertising.

To explore how the different perceptions jointly affect consumers' receptivity of computational advertising, researchers have applied the Technology Acceptance Model among others. The model helps explain how consumers' perceptions of the usefulness of technology (e.g., relevance of personalized content) and its ease of use influence their attitudes toward it and willingness to engage with it (Davis, 1989). Applying the model to computational advertising, Le et al. (2024) extend it by proposing brand credibility and brand trustworthiness as significant antecedents of computational advertising acceptance.

Additionally, Shin et al. (2025) propose the Privacy and Trust Equilibrium (PATE) model of Personalization Acceptance, which integrates the positive (i.e., trust) and negative (i.e., privacy concern) perceptual factors influencing consumers' receptivity of computational advertising. The PATE model sheds light on the complex and competing roles of privacy and trust factors in consumers' acceptance of computational advertising practices and explains how the push-pull equilibrium of privacy concern and trust perceptions is influenced by different types of data collection practices.

Consumer Processing and Responses to Computational Advertising

Rapidly growing research examines how consumers process computational advertising messages and resulting effects, as well as influencing factors. The unique characteristics of computational advertising have prompted researchers to revisit and expand upon traditional advertising effect theories and look into theoretical frameworks from adjacent fields (e.g., human-AI interaction) in order to better understand the distinct ways in which consumers process and respond to computational advertising.

A distinct mechanism of computational advertising effects is the degree to which the ad matches the target consumer's profile. To examine such computational advertising effects, researchers have applied perceived relevance theory. Research has suggested that personalized advertising is only effective if it is perceived as relevant by the consumer, whether it is content relevance (e.g., De Keyzer et al., 2015) or relevance of the targeted personality traits (e.g., Zarouali et al., 2024).

Another central theoretical framework for explaining computational advertising effects in connection to its personalization characteristics is impression management and identification theories. The concept of the algorithmic mirror refers to how algorithmic systems, such as computational advertising, reflect and amplify our past behaviors, preferences, and biases back to us (so-called feedback loop). Computational advertising selectively mirrors what the algorithm has "learned" from our past interactions, shaping what we see and reinforcing certain identities or views. As a result, consumers may experience a distorted version of themselves or their environment, curated through computational advertising (French, 2018).

Consumer identity is particularly important when psychographic data on consumers are used in computational advertising. More specifically, while relevance is central to ads personalized based on one's past behavior, ads personalized based on one's psychographic profile are related to one's self-image. They are evaluated by consumers based on the social desirability of the traits they target. For example, when a consumer realizes an ad targets them based on socially undesirable traits, they will not want to be seen this way and will consequently become more negative about the ad as they try to preserve their positive image (Zhang et al., 2024).

To further examine and explain consumers' negative responses to computational advertising, the Persuasion Knowledge Model (PKM) (Friestad & Wright, 1999) provides useful theoretical framework. This model explains how consumers cope with persuasive attempts depending on their knowledge of persuasive tactics, topics, and agents. In the context of computational advertising, studies applying PKM have examined how computational advertising can lead to higher resistance to ads (e.g., Morimoto, 2021). Building on this model, Strycharz and Segijn (2022) developed the Dataveillance in Advertising Effects Landscape framework. This framework explains how an observable instance of surveillance (e.g., data-driven personalized ad) affects perceived surveillance, which subsequently affects advertising outcomes (e.g., brand attitude, resistance) and surveillance outcomes (e.g., privacy concerns). Testing this model, Sifaoui and Segijn (2024) found that when the advertised brand matches the consumer's previous online search for that brand, this increased perceived surveillance and generated less positive attitudes and higher advertising avoidance.

Another traditional theory applied to examining computational advertising effects is the signaling theory (Spence, 1974). It explains how advertisers can use cues such as personalization as signals to convey their characteristics, relevance, or value to consumers. Computational advertising can be perceived as a positive signal indicating the advertiser values consumers because computational advertising addresses them individually (Pfiffelmann & Pfeuffer, 2022).

Going beyond traditional advertising and communication theories, researchers have increasingly drawn on theoretical frameworks from the field of human-AI interaction. For example, the Human-AI Interaction Theory of Interactive Media Effects (HAII-TIME) model (Sundar, 2020) applies the dual-process model of the TIME (Sundar et al., 2015) to human-AI interaction, proposing that consumers' processing of any algorithmic system happens via two simultaneous routes: the cue route, where consumers form judgments based on visible system attributes, and the action route, shaped by consumers' direct interactions with the system and perceived agency in this interaction. Recent research shows that personalized ads with anthropomorphic transparency cues heighten algorithmic awareness, leading consumers to simultaneously perceive the ad as both transparent and surveilling, resulting in resistance to the ad (Lee et al., 2024). These findings suggest that the anthropomorphizing of algorithmic systems like computational advertising can encourage deeper information processing through the action route but may also increase advertising resistance.

Furthermore, the data-driven characteristic of computational advertising makes privacy-related mechanisms central to its effectiveness. The privacy paradox, described above, is central to consumer perceptions of computational advertising, and the perceived benefits and costs directly influence advertising effectiveness: according to the privacy calculus theory (Dinev & Hart, 2006), consumers evaluate computational advertising by weighing the perceived benefits against the potential costs. When the perceived costs outweigh the benefits, ad effectiveness generally declines (e.g., Jung & Heu, 2022; Segijn & Voorveld, 2021). Information boundary theory further explains this by suggesting that when consumers feel their informational boundaries are crossed, the positive link between the benefit of perceived relevance and attitude weakens (De Groot, 2022). Similarly, psychological ownership theory, when applied to computational advertising, suggests that the use of data in computational advertising can undermine consumers' sense of ownership over their personal data, leading to more negative attitudes toward the ad and reduced behavioral intentions (Kim & Jeong, 2023).

Factors Influencing Computational Advertising Effects

Some theories focus on the boundary conditions of computational advertising, helping to explain when and for whom it succeeds or backfires, or moderating factors influencing computational advertising effects. First, trust is a crucial factor that can significantly affect computational advertising effects and effectiveness. When consumers trust the advertiser, computational advertising, especially those with high relevance and narrow focus, can increase perceived usefulness and click-through intentions. However, for less trusted advertisers, relevance can lead to increased reactance and skepticism, reducing ad effectiveness (Bleier & Eisenbeiss, 2015). Research also shows that consumers' general trust in online environments strengthens the positive effects of computational advertising on user engagement, while low trust diminishes these effects and may lower the perceived value of personalization (Kang et al., 2016).

Perceived autonomy, linked to the psychological reactance theory, is another boundary condition. More specifically, perceived privacy intrusiveness in personalized advertising can be seen as a threat to consumers' autonomy, triggering psychological reactance. This reactance manifests primarily in cognitive resistance, particularly in the form of skepticism toward the advertiser's motives, resulting in reduced engagement with the ad (Alhellay et al., 2025).

Related to perceived autonomy, another potential factor that impacts how consumers respond to computational advertising is consumer control, which is defined as "the extent to which individuals can start, stop, or maintain what personal data firms collect, process, or share (exchange) with the purpose of generating personalized communication" (Segijn et al., 2021, p. 123). One can distinguish between actual control (i.e., the amount of control offered to consumers) and perceived control (i.e., the amount of control consumers think they have), although actual and perceived control are related (Hu & Wise, 2024).

According to the Transparency-Awareness-Control framework (Segijn et al., 2021), control is a product of consumer awareness (i.e., the degree to which consumers are cognizant about data usage for personalization), the ability to control, and the desire to control (i.e., motivation). Consumers can become more aware of computational advertising practices through disclosures by companies (i.e., transparency).

Future Directions of Computational Advertising Research

Research on computational advertising is rapidly emerging, and the growing consumer data and advancement of AI technologies will fuel increasing research in this field. Looking ahead, further theoretical development is needed to understand how emerging technologies like genAI will shape consumer behavior and advertising practice. At the same time, methodological innovation and interdisciplinary collaboration will be crucial to advancing the field and keeping up with the developments in the industry. These developments also bring conceptual, ethical, and normative challenges that must be addressed to ensure rigorous and responsible computational advertising research.

The growing dependence on data-driven processes in computational advertising calls for changes in how advertising research is conducted, requiring new tools and methods to keep pace with evolving technologies. Given the methodological challenges in conducting computational research, multidisciplinary collaborations across advertising, computer science, statistics, and decision science fields will be imperative. For meaningful and fruitful multidisciplinary collaborations contributing to advertising theory building, a strong theoretical framework and rigorous concept explication that makes theoretically sound matching between a concept and valid proxy measure indicators will be crucial. New frameworks developed for computational advertising and adaptations of existing theories to the computational context introduced in this chapter provide examples of the necessary theoretical and conceptual developments. They can also serve as the starting point for clear communication among members of the multidisciplinary project team and will allow us to bridge the differences across disciplines in understanding and using theoretical concepts and terms.

Building on the need for strong theoretical foundations and interdisciplinary collaboration, it is equally important to address the measurement challenges that arise in computational advertising research. For each concept-indicator mapping, thorough measurement validity tests should be conducted for face, content, criterion-related, and construct validity. New technologies and complex social networks introduce novel types of data that present both opportunities and challenges for measurement in computational advertising research. For example, datasets containing network edges (i.e., links or connections between network actors such as likes, follows, or shares), which are very common in social media research, may appear similar across platforms but can represent fundamentally different user behaviors or relationships. Befriending someone or liking something on Facebook, liking or commenting on videos on YouTube, might represent different concepts and should not be assumed to have the same meaning to consumers (Wagner et al., 2021). Interpreting these signals accurately requires careful conceptual mapping and measurement validation, as assuming equivalence across contexts risks misleading conclusions. As such, advancing computational advertising research and theory development will depend not only on new or better data but also on the thoughtful operationalization of digital interactions as valid indicators of psychological and behavioral constructs.

New types of digital data offer fresh possibilities for expanding the scope of computational advertising research. While the studies described in this chapter often focus on readily observable outcomes, such as clicks or purchases, more abstract psychological constructs, such as attention and emotions, may now be inferred from emerging forms of digital trace data and biometric measures. Advances in web analytics, user interaction data, and psychophysiological tools open the door to capturing consumer responses that were previously difficult to measure. Data collection tools like data donation platforms and browser tracking plug-ins enable consumers to voluntarily share their individual-level data across platforms with researchers in a privacy-conscious manner (e.g., Angus et al., 2024; Zhou et al., 2024), providing insights into real-time ad exposure, targeting, and engagement that were previously difficult to access. As discussed by Hofacker et al. (2016), such behavioral data can be used to infer underlying states, such as satisfaction, emotional engagement, or even moment-to-moment attitude shifts, allowing researchers to examine a broader set of theoretical concepts with greater ecological validity. At the same time, biometric and psychophysiological methods, such as EEG, eye-tracking, and facial coding, offer innovative insights by directly measuring cognitive and emotional processes that are not observable through self-reports (Read et al., 2024). These tools can help researchers examine what drives consumers' attention, memory, and affective responses to advertising in a more ecologically valid manner. By combining digital traces with biometric signals, researchers can both deduce and directly observe psychological responses to ads, substantially enhancing theoretical development in computational advertising.

Furthermore, expanding the source of digital data beyond website browsing and social networking data would open new possibilities for computational advertising research. For example, virtual reality and online games are especially interesting environments where human psychology and behaviors can be observed in a virtual environment that mimics the real-world social atmosphere. All these new data sources offer researchers access to unstructured data in multiple modalities. Hence, researchers must explore how such data can be analyzed to reveal new insights into consumer behavior and advertising phenomena in real-world environments. Advances in computational content analysis and machine learning enable the large-scale analysis of unstructured data, allowing to uncover sentiment, themes, visual strategies, and emotional cues among others. Research provides overviews of how different automated object detection methods can analyze video, audio, images, and text in advertising (Barari & Eisend, 2024; Segijn et al., 2024). These methods offer powerful tools for analyzing multimodal advertising data, allowing researchers to better understand how consumers perceive and respond to real-world ad stimuli. Moreover, affective computing offers new possibilities for computational advertising research by enabling multimodal emotion recognition to account for emotional cues in content creation, anticipate the emotional impact of media placement, and assess both the immediate and long-term emotional effects of computational advertising campaigns (Wen et al., 2024). Extensive discussions of various computational research methods and tools applied to growing computational advertising research are offered in the *Journal of Advertising*'s Computational Advertising Research Methodology Themed Issue published in 2024.

With the profound shift in digital advertising focus to computational advertising and the availability of rich data capturing consumer activities and interactions with ads, computational advertising research has huge potential for revealing new insights and building theories explaining and predicting consumers' behaviors related to advertising. The availability of large-scale behavioral data and the tools to analyze them open new opportunities for understanding and predicting how consumers engage with advertising in the changing environment. This shift calls for new theoretical models, methodological innovations, and critical reflection on the ethical and societal implications of data use in advertising. By combining conceptual clarity with careful measurement and leveraging new data sources and computational tools, the field can advance in a way that keeps pace with technological developments as well as ensures that research on computational advertising research remains theoretically meaningful, methodologically sound, and socially impactful.

References

Aguirre, E., Mahr, D., Grewal, D., De Ruyter, K., & Wetzels, M. (2015). Unraveling the personalization paradox: The effect of information collection and trust-building strategies on online advertisement effectiveness. *Journal of Retailing, 91*(1), 34–49. https://doi.org/10.1016/j.jretai.2014.09.005

Alhelaly, Y., Dhillon, G., & Oliveira, T. (2025). The Impact of Privacy Intrusiveness on Individuals' Responses and Engagement Toward Personalization in Online Interactive Advertising. *Journal of Interactive Advertising, 25*(1), 38–60. https://doi.org/10.1080/15252019.2024.2440318

Araujo, T., Copulsky, J. R., Hayes, J. L., Kim, S. J., & Srivastava, J. (2020). From purchasing exposure to fostering engagement: Brand–consumer experiences in the emerging computational advertising landscape. *Journal of Advertising, 49*(4), 428–445. https://doi.org/10.1080/00913367.2020.1795756

Angus, D., Hayden, L., Obeid, A. K., Tan, X. Y., Carah, N., Burgess, J., ... & Bagnara, J. (2024). Computational methods for improving the observability of platform-based advertising. *Journal of Advertising*, *53*(5), 661–680. https://doi.org/10.1080/00913367.2024.2394156

Arango, L., Singaraju, S. P., & Niininen, O. (2023). Consumer responses to AI-generated charitable giving ads. *Journal of Advertising*, *52*(4), 486–503. https://doi.org/10.1080/00913367.2023.2183285

Barari, M., & Eisend, M. (2024). Computational content analysis in advertising research. *Journal of Advertising*, *53*(5), 681-699. https://doi.org/10.1080/00913367.2024.2407642

Bleier, A., & Eisenbeiss, M. (2015). The importance of trust for personalized online advertising. *Journal of Retailing*, *91*(3), 390–409. https://doi.org/10.1016/j.jretai.2015.04.001

Boerman, S. C., Kruikemeier, S., & Zuiderveen Borgesius, F. J. (2017). Online behavioral advertising: A literature review and research agenda. *Journal of Advertising*, *46*(3), 363–376. https://doi.org/10.1080/00913367.2017.1339368

Bobrowsky, M., & Coffee, P. (2025). Meta aims to fully automate ad creation using AI. *The Wall Street Journal*. https://www.wsj.com/tech/ai/meta-aims-to-fully-automate-ad-creation-using-ai-7d82e249/

Bottou, L., Peters, J., Quiñonero-Candela, J., Charles, D. X., Chickering, D. M., Portugaly, E.,… Snelson, E. (2013). Counterfactual reasoning and learning systems: The example of computational advertising. *Journal of Machine Learning Research, 14*(1), 3207–3260.

Campbell, C., Plangger, K., Sands, S., & Kietzmann, J. (2022). Preparing for an era of deepfakes and AI-generated ads: A framework for understanding responses to manipulated advertising. *Journal of Advertising, 51*(1), 22–38. https://doi.org/10.1080/00913367.2021.1909515

Campbell, C., Plangger, K., Sands, S., & Kietzmann, J. (2022). Preparing for an era of deepfakes and AI-generated ads: A framework for understanding responses to manipulated advertising. *Journal of Advertising, 51*(1), 22–38. https://doi.org/10.1080/00913367.2021.1909515

Davis, F. D. (1989). Perceived usefulness, perceived ease of use, and user acceptance of information technology. *MIS Quarterly, 13*(3), 319–340. https://doi.org/10.2307/249008

De Groot, J. I. M. (2022). The personalization paradox in Facebook advertising: The mediating effect of relevance on the personalization–brand attitude relationship and the moderating effect of intrusiveness. *Journal of Interactive Advertising, 22*(1), 57–74. https://doi.org/10.1080/15252019.2022.2032492

De Keyzer, F., Dens, N., & De Pelsmacker, P. (2015). Is this for me? How consumers respond to personalized advertising on social network sites. *Journal of Interactive Advertising, 15*(2), 124–134. https://doi.org/10.1080/15252019.2015.1082450

Dinev, T., & Hart, P. (2006). An extended privacy calculus model for e-commerce transactions. *Information Systems Research, 17*(1), 61–80. https://doi.org/10.1287/isre.1060.0080

Duivenvoorde, B., & Goanta, C. (2023). The regulation of digital advertising under the DSA: A critical assessment. *Computer Law & Security Review, 51*, 105870. https://doi.org/10.1016/j.clsr.2023.105870

French, M. R. (2018). *Algorithmic mirrors: An examination of how personalized recommendations can shape self-perceptions and reinforce gender stereotypes* (Publication No. 28115243) [Doctoral dissertation, Stanford University]. ProQuest Dissertations and Theses Global.

Friestad, M., & Wright, P. (1999). Everyday persuasion knowledge. *Psychology & Marketing, 16*(2), 185–194. https://doi.org/10.1002/(SICI)1520-6793(199903)16:2<185::AID-MAR7>3.0.CO;2-N

Goh, K. Y., Heng, C. S., & Lin, Z. (2013). Social media brand community and consumer behavior: Quantifying the relative impact of user- and marketer-generated content. *Information Systems Research, 24*(1), 88–107. https://doi.org/10.1287/isre.1120.0469

Google. (2000, October 23). *Google launches self-service advertising program*. Google Blog. https://googlepress.blogspot.com/2000/10/google-launches-self-service.html

Goldfarb, A., & Tucker, C. (2011). Online display advertising: Targeting and obtrusiveness. *Marketing Science, 30*(3), 389–404. https://doi.org/10.1287/mksc.1100.0583

Helberger, N., Huh, J., Milne, G., Strycharz, J., & Sundaram, H. (2020). Macro and exogenous factors in computational advertising: Key issues and new research directions. *Journal of Advertising, 49*(4), 377–393. https://doi.org/10.1080/00913367.2020.1811179

Hesterberg, K. (2021). *A brief history of online advertising*. HubSpot. https://blog.hubspot.com/marketing/history-of-online-advertising

Hofacker, C. F., Malthouse, E. C., & Sultan, F. (2016). Big data and consumer behavior: Imminent opportunities. *Journal of consumer marketing, 33*(2), 89–97. https://doi.org/10.1108/JCM-04-2015-1399

Hu, X., & Wise, K. (2024). Disentangling control and personalization: exploring the effects of ad choice and ad personalization in digital advertising effectiveness. *Journal of Interactive Advertising, 24*(3), 265–288. https://doi.org/10.1080/15252019.2024.2375970

Hesterberg, K. (2021). A brief history of online advertising. HubSpot. https://blog.hubspot.com/marketing/history-of-online-advertising

Hofacker, C. F., Malthouse, E. C., & Sultan, F. (2016). Big data and consumer behavior: Imminent opportunities. *Journal of consumer marketing, 33*(2), 89–97. https://doi.org/10.1108/JCM-04-2015-1399

Hu, X., & Wise, K. (2024). Disentangling control and personalization: exploring the effects of ad choice and ad personalization in digital advertising effectiveness. *Journal of Interactive Advertising, 24*(3), 265–288. https://doi.org/10.1080/15252019.2024.2375970

Huang, M. H., & Rust, R. T. (2021). A strategic framework for artificial intelligence in marketing. *Journal of the Academy of Marketing Science, 49*(1), 30–50. https://doi.org/10.1007/s11747-020-00749-9

Huh, J., & Malthouse, E. C. (2020). Advancing computational advertising: Conceptualization of the field and future directions. *Journal of Advertising, 49*(4), 367–376. https://doi.org/10.1080/00913367.2020.1795759

Jung, A. R., & Heo, J. (2022). The effects of mobile phone use motives on the intention to use location-based advertising: The mediating role of media affinity and perceived trust and risk. *International Journal of Advertising, 41*(5), 930–947. https://doi.org/10.1080/02650487.2021.1974204

Jones, H. (2021, October 18). Real-time bidding: The ad industry has crossed a very dangerous line. *Forbes*. https://www.forbes.com/sites/hessiejones/2021/10/18/real-time-bidding-the-ad-industry-has-crossed-a-very-dangerous-line/

Kang, M., & Gong, T. (2016). The role of personalization, engagement, and trust in online communities. *Information Technology & People, 29*(3), 580-596. https://doi.org/10.1108/ITP-01-2015-0023

Kapoor, A., & Kumar, M. (2025). Frontiers: Generative AI and personalized video advertisements. *Marketing Science, 44*(4), 733–747. https://doi.org/10.1287/mksc.2023.0494

Kim, J., & Jeong, H. J. (2023). 'It's my virtual space': the effect of personalized advertising within social media. *International Journal of Advertising*, 42(8), 1267-1294. https://doi.org/10.1080/02650487.2023.2274243

Le, H. T. P. M., Yoo, W., & Park, J. (2024). The effects of brand trustworthiness and credibility on location-based advertising: Moderating effects of privacy concern and social influence. *International Journal of Advertising, 43*(5), 798–823. https://doi.org/10.1080/02650487.2023.2251287

Lee, E. (2025, February). How AI will transform media buying & planning. *Think with Google*. https://www.thinkwithgoogle.com/marketing-strategies/data-and-measurement/ai-media-buying-transformation/

Lee, S., Moon, W. K., & Song, Y. G. (2025). Is It transparent or surveillant? The effects of personalized advertising and privacy policy on advertising effectiveness. *Journal of Interactive Advertising, 25*(1), 1–21. https://doi.org/10.1080/15252019.2024.2417422

Lee, S., Moon, W. K., & Song, Y. G. (2025). Is it transparent or surveillant? The effects of personalized advertising and privacy policy on advertising effectiveness. *Journal of Interactive Advertising, 25*(1), 1–21. https://doi.org/10.1080/15252019.2024.2417422

Li, H., Yu, L., & He, W. (2019). The impact of GDPR on global technology development. *Journal of Global Information Technology Management, 22*(1), 1–6. https://doi.org/10.1080/1097198X.2019.1569186

Liu-Thompkins, Y., Maslowska, E., Ren, Y., & Kim, H. (2020). Creating, metavoicing, and propagating: A road map for understanding user roles in computational advertising. *Journal of Advertising, 49*(4), 394–410. https://doi.org/10.1080/00913367.2020.1795758

Malthouse, E. C., Maslowska, E., & Franks, J. U. (2018). Understanding programmatic TV advertising. *International Journal of Advertising, 37*(5), 769–784. https://doi.org/10.1080/02650487.2018.1461733

Malthouse, E. C., Maslowska, E., Strycharz, J., Block, M., & Araujo, T. (2024). Data quality measures for computational research: Ensuring informed decisions with emerging data sources. *Journal of Advertising*, *53*(5), 644–660. https://doi.org/10.1080/00913367.2024.2403609

McKnight, D.H., Choudhury, V. & Kacmar, C. (2002). Developing and validating trust measures for e-commerce: An integrative typology. *Information Systems Research, 13*(3), 334–359. https://doi.org/10.1287/isre.13.3.334.81

Metzger, M. J. (2007). Communication privacy management in electronic commerce. *Journal of Computer-Mediated Communication, 12*(2), 335–361. https://doi.org/10.1111/j.1083-6101.2007.00328.x

Morimoto, M. (2021). Privacy concerns about personalized advertising across multiple social media platforms in Japan: The relationship with information control and persuasion knowledge. *International Journal of Advertising, 40*(3), 431–451. https://doi.org/10.1080/02650487.2020.1796322

Nagy, P., & Neff, G. (2015). Imagined affordance: Reconstructing a keyword for communication theory. *Social Media+ Society*, *1*(2), 2056305115603385. https://doi.org/10.1177/2056305115603385

Oberoi, A. (2013, July 3). *The history of online advertising*. AdPushup. https://www.adpushup.com/blog/the-history-of-online-advertising/

Pearson, S. (2024). Computational advertising for meaningful brands, the public purpose, and a sustainable ecology: A call for research into a systems approach and modeling applications of LLMs in marketing and advertising. *Journal of Current Issues & Research in Advertising, 45*(3), 357–367. https://doi.org/10.1080/10641734.2024.2382208

Pfiffelmann, J., & Pfeuffer, A. (2022). Understanding personalized recruitment ads' effectiveness: The role of personalization type and message involvement. *Journal of Interactive Advertising, 22*(3), 311–326. https://doi.org/10.1080/15252019.2022.2132124

Read, G. L., Holiday, S., Hayes, J. L., & Britt, B. C. (2024). Biometric tools in a computational advertising context: An overview of use and application. *Journal of Advertising, 53*(5), 754–770. https://doi.org/10.1080/00913367.2024.2399657

Roy, A., Huh, J., Pfeuffer, A., & Srivastava, J. (2017). Development of trust scores in social media (TSM) algorithm and application to advertising practice and research. *Journal of Advertising, 46*(2), 269–282. https://doi.org/10.1080/00913367.2017.1297272

Segijn, C. M. (2019). A new mobile data driven message strategy called synced advertising: Conceptualization, implications, and future directions. *Annals of the International Communication Association, 43*(1), 58–77. https://doi.org/10.1080/23808985.2019.1576020

Segijn, C. M., Menheer, P., Lee, G., Kim, E., Olsen, D., & Hofelich Mohr, A. (2024). Automated object detection in mobile eye-tracking research: Comparing manual coding with tag detection, shape detection, matching, and machine learning. *Communication Methods and Measures*, 1–21. https://doi.org/10.1080/19312458.2024.2443396

Segijn, C. M., & Voorveld, H. A. (2021). A first step in unraveling synced advertising effectiveness. *International Journal of Advertising, 40*(1), 124–143. https://doi.org/10.1080/02650487.2020.1778279

Shin, S., Kim, E., & Huh, J. (2025). Young adults' acceptance of data-driven personalized advertising: Privacy and Trust Equilibrium (PATE) model. *Young Consumers, 26*(2), 189–206. https://doi.org/10.1108/YC-06-2024-2105

Sifaoui, A., & Segijn, C. M. (2024). Surveillance in the advertising landscape: Application of the DEAL framework to investigate online behavioral advertising, surveillance, and users' responses on Instagram. *Journal of Current Issues & Research in Advertising*, 1–15. https://doi.org/10.1080/10641734.2024.2419602

Smit, E. G., Van Noort, G., & Voorveld, H. A. (2014). Understanding online behavioural advertising: User knowledge, privacy concerns and online coping behaviour in Europe. *Computers in Human Behavior*, *32*, 15–22.

Spence, M. (1974). Competitive and optimal responses to signals: An analysis of efficiency and distribution. *Journal of Economic Theory*, *7*(3), 296–332. https://doi.org/10.1016/0022-0531(74)90098-2

Stewart, K. J. (2003). Trust transfer on the World Wide Web. *Organization Science, 14*(1), 5–17. https://doi.org/10.1287/orsc.14.1.5.12810

Strycharz, J., & Segijn, C. M. (2022). The future of dataveillance in advertising theory and practice. *Journal of Advertising*, *51*(5), 574–591. https://doi.org/10.1080/00913367.2022.2109781

Strycharz, J., Van Noort, G., Helberger, N., & Smit, E. (2019). Contrasting perspectives–practitioner's viewpoint on personalised marketing communication. *European Journal of Marketing, 53*(4), 635–660. https://doi.org/10.1108/EJM-11-2017-0896

Strycharz, J., Zhang, D., & Segijn, C. M. (2025). Dataveillance in interactive advertising: Transforming consumer-advertiser interactions and its unintended consequences. *Journal of Interactive Advertising*, 1–13. https://doi.org/10.1080/15252019.2025.2547850

Sundar, S. S., Jia, H., Waddell, T. F., & Huang, Y. (2015). Toward a theory of interactive media effects (TIME) four models for explaining how interface features affect user psychology. *The Handbook of the Psychology of Communication Technology*, 47–86. https://doi.org/10.1002/9781118426456.ch3

Sundar, S. S. (2020). Rise of machine agency: A framework for studying the psychology of human–AI interaction (HAII). *Journal of Computer-Mediated Communication, 25*(1), 74–88. https://doi.org/10.1093/jcmc/zmz026

Thomas, V. L., & Fowler, K. (2021). Close encounters of the AI kind: Use of AI influencers as brand endorsers. *Journal of Advertising, 50*(1), 11–25. https://doi.org/10.1080/00913367.2020.1810595

Van Noort, G., Himelboim, I., Martin, J., & Collinger, T. (2020). Introducing a model of automated brand-generated content in an era of computational advertising. *Journal of Advertising, 49*(4), 411–427. https://doi.org/10.1080/00913367.2020.1795954

Vesanen, J., & Raulas, M. (2006). Building bridges for personalization: A process model for marketing. *Journal of Interactive Marketing, 20*(1), 5–20. https://doi.org/10.1002/dir.20052

Wagner, C., Strohmaier, M., Olteanu, A., Kıcıman, E., Contractor, N., & Eliassi-Rad, T. (2021). Measuring algorithmically infused societies. *Nature*, *595*(7866), 197–204. https://doi.org/10.1038/s41586-021-03666-1

Wen, T. J., Chuan, C. H., Anghelcev, G., Sar, S., Yun, J. T., & Xu, Y. (2024). Infusing affective computing models into advertising research on emotions. *Journal of Advertising, 53*(5), 710–731. https://doi.org/10.1080/00913367.2024.2409254

Yun, J. T., Segijn, C. M., Pearson, S., Malthouse, E. C., Konstan, J. A., & Shankar, V. (2020). Challenges and future directions of computational advertising measurement systems. *Journal of Advertising, 49*(4), 446–458. https://doi.org/10.1080/00913367.2020.1795757

Zarouali, B. (2025). The contextual interplay between advertising and online disinformation: How brands suffer from and amplify deceptive content. *Communications, 50*(1), 149–172. https://doi.org/10.1515/commun-2022-0110

Zarouali, B., Boerman, S. C., Voorveld, H. A., & Van Noort, G. (2022). The algorithmic persuasion framework in online communication: Conceptualization and a future research agenda. *Internet Research, 32*(4), 1076–1096. https://doi.org/10.1108/INTR-01-2021-0049

Zarouali, B., Dobber, T., & Schreuder, J. (2024). Personality and susceptibility to political microtargeting: A comparison between a machine-learning and self-report approach. *Computers in Human Behavior*, *151*, 108024.

Zhang, W., Tsou, T. H., Rodgers, S., & Willett, J. F. (2024). Comparing personalization strategies in social network advertising: The role of impression motivation in persuasion outcomes. *Journal of Interactive Advertising, 24*(3), 247–264. https://doi.org/10.1080/15252019.2024.2337057

Zhou, A., Metaxa, D., Kim, Y. M., & Jaidka, K. (2024). User-centric behavioral tracking: Lessons from three case studies with do-it-yourself computational pipelines. *Journal of Advertising*, *53*(5), 791–809. https://doi.org/10.1080/00913367.2024.2403613

14 Personalization in the Age of Artificial Intelligence-Powered Digital Advertising

Weilu Zhang

Introduction

Artificial intelligence (AI) is a transformative technology often described as a cornerstone of the *Fourth Industrial Revolution* (Chen & Zhou, 2018), offering unprecedented opportunities for digital advertising practice and theory (Huh et al., 2023). In advertising, AI refers to brand communication powered by machine learning functions capable of performing persuasive tasks based on human, machine, or hybrid input (Rodgers, 2021). Among AI's most significant contributions to digital advertising is its ability to enable personalization (Baek, 2023; Zanker et al., 2019) that brings marketers closer to the long-sought goal of delivering the right message to the right person at the right time (Tam & Ho, 2006). Scholars suggest we have entered an era of intelligent advertising (Li, 2019), where AI-powered personalization serves as a defining benchmark. Kotler and colleagues (2021) describe this shift as the advent of *Marketing 5.0*, characterized by widespread AI-driven marketing automation, and forecast the emergence of *Marketing 6.0*, which emphasizes immersive, omnichannel metamarketing (Kotler et al., 2023).

Personalization, broadly defined, refers to tailoring advertising content to match individual preferences or characteristics (Huh & Malthouse, 2020). It is distinguished by its use of consumer-specific information to construct persuasive messages (Bang et al., 2019). As technology has advanced, personalization has evolved from rule-based targeting (e.g., loyalty card or browsing history-based recommendations) to more complex AI-powered approaches that support multichannel synchronization and dynamic delivery across the consumer journey (Brinson et al., 2019; Van Noort et al., 2020; Malthouse & Copulsky, 2023).

Advertising research on personalization spans over two decades, dating back to Web 1.0 (e.g., Pavlou & Stewart, 2000), and highlights both its potential and its pitfalls (Girondaa & Korgaonkar, 2018). On the benefit side, personalization increases perceived relevance, activates self-referential processing, and enhances persuasive outcomes (Ahn & Bailenson, 2011; Brinson & Eastin, 2016). On the downside, it raises concerns over privacy and data ethics, particularly regarding

DOI: 10.4324/9781003567523-18

the collection and misuse of personal data (Baek & Morimoto, 2012; White et al., 2008). While this body of research has laid a strong foundation, the growing influence of AI necessitates an updated examination of personalization, its forms, mechanisms, and implications.

This chapter offers an updated overview of personalization in AI-powered advertising. It begins by defining personalization through a two-dimensional framework, consumer profiling, and message tailoring, and distinguishing it from related concepts such as targeting and customization. A technological overview then traces the evolution of personalization in tandem with AI advancements. Building on this foundation, this chapter introduces a typology of four personalization categories based on the level of AI involvement across the two dimensions. It proceeds to synthesize recent literature highlighting key theories and concepts relevant to AI-driven personalization and consumer response. This chapter concludes by outlining theory-driven directions for future research that reflect the increasing complexity of personalization in digital advertising.

A Two-Dimensional Framework of Personalization: Consumer Profiling and Message Tailoring

The foundational idea of personalization is to individualize advertising messages and their delivery to specific recipients while retaining the efficiency and scalability of mass message production (Brinson et al., 2019; Hu & Wise, 2024). As such, personalization typically requires a certain degree of automation and technological integration. Table 14.1 summarizes 20 definitions of personalization from advertising research over the past two decades to provide a broader understanding of the concept.

While the definitions vary slightly in wording and emphasis, two core dimensions consistently emerge across the literature: (1) the detailed profiling of the target audience and (2) the tailoring of advertising messages. Zanker et al.'s (2019) study has made a similar distinction. These dimensions commonly inform both the theoretical frameworks and empirical approaches used in advertising research on personalization. For instance, Li (2016) defined personalization as the delivery of "individualized information" based on an audience's "unique preference," while De Schaepdrijver et al. (2022) described it as offering tailored "content and service" based on knowledge of individuals' "preferences and behaviors" (see full list in Table 14.1). As the cornerstone of personalization, consumer data enables both individualized profiling and broader segment-level analysis to predict consumer preferences (Li, 2019). These insights inform message selection and design, effectively linking the two core dimensions of personalization.

Consumer profiling involves collecting and analyzing consumer data to identify specific individuals or audience segments (Bang et al., 2019). This process includes tracking both manifest data, such as name, photo, and location (Yoon et al., 2023), and latent characteristics, including needs, wants, beliefs, and

Table 14.1 Definitions of Personalization

Author(s) Year	*Definition*
Baek and Morimoto (2012)	Personalized advertising is defined as "a form of customized promotional messages that are delivered to each individual consumer through paid media based on personal information (such as consumers' names, past buying history, demographics, psychographics, locations, and lifestyle interests)." (p. 59)
Dijkstra and Ballast (2012)	"Personalizing refers to including pieces of information in a generic persuasive message that signal the reader that the message is addressed to him or her individually." (p. 60)
Li (2016)	Personalization was conceptualized as to deliver individualized information to the audience based on their unique preference.
Maslowska et al. (2016)	Personalization is defined as the "communication strategy that involves incorporating elements in a message that refer to each individual recipient and are based on the recipient's personal characteristics, such as name, gender, residence, occupation, and past behaviors." (p. 74)
Ahn et al. (2017)	Personalization is a computer-tailored persuasive strategy that "reflects personal information collected over time, such as prior purchasing or browsing behaviors, in a message." (p. 111)
Bang et al. (2019)	Personalized advertising refers to "advertising that incorporates information about each individual consumer based on personally identifying information (e.g. name, photo, email address, birthday, etc.), social identity-related information (e.g. gender, ethnicity, occupation, and etc.) or past shopping-related behaviour (e.g. purchase history or brand preference) (Dijkstra & Ballast, 2012; Wolin & Korgaonkar, 2005)." (p. 1)
Bartsch and Kloß (2019)	Personalization is a "specialized flow of communication that sends different recipients distinct messages tailored to their individual preferences or characteristics" (p. 347, cf. White et al., 2008, 40)
Brinson et al. (2019)	"Personalized advertising involves tailoring a message and/or delivery channel to each consumer while retaining principles of mass message production (Dolnicar & Jordaan, 2007)." (p. 56)
Dodoo and Wen (2019)	Personalized advertising was defined as the advertising strategy that "singly targets consumers by incorporating their unique preferences to design compatible messages based on these preferences." (p. 118–119)
Lee and Cho (2019)	Personalized advertising is defined as "advertising that is created for an individual consumer using information about the individual." (p. 101).
Huh and Malthouse (2020)	Personalization: tailoring of advertising content to each unique recipient based on individual preferences and or personal characteristics (Baek & Morimoto, 2012; Kim & Huh, 2017).
Morimoto (2021)	Personalization is an advertising strategy that "matches a promotional message to individual consumers based on their preferences." (p. 432)
De Groot (2022)	"Ad personalization can be defined as delivering ads that contain individualized information based on the unique preferences of the receiver (Li 2016)." (p. 60)

(*Continued*)

Table 14.1 (Continued)

Author(s) Year	*Definition*
De Schaepdrijver et al. (2022)	Personalization is defined as "the ability to provide content and service that are tailored to individuals based on knowledge about their preference and behaviors" (p. 134)
Youn et al. (2024)	Ad personalization is the extent to which advertisers utilize individualized personal details in an ad, ranging from totally generic (no personalization) to moderate personalization (e.g., geographic personalization) to extreme personalization (e.g., names or other personal details).
Zhang et al. (2023)	Personalized advertising refers to "the marketing practice that delivers tailored ads to individuals based on any type of personal information" (p. 394)
Zhang et al. (2024)	Personalization involves tailoring messages by incorporating personally identifiable elements to target individual consumers (De Keyzer et al., 2022; Pfiffelmann & Pfeuffer, 2022).
Hu and Wise (2024)	Personalization refers to the provision of personally relevant content, products, and services based on individual users' unique characteristics and needs (Xiao & Benbasat, 2007).
Alhelaly et al. (2025)	Personalization refers to tailoring advertisements to match individual characteristics, interests, preferences, and behaviors, thereby enhancing user experience by providing relevant and timely content (Bol et al., 2018) (p. 1).
Ahn and Haley (2025)	Personalized advertising sends advertising messages that increase message relevance and delivery timing (Bol et al., 2018) based on individuals' demographic information, preferences, and behavioral patterns (Hoy & Milne, 2010) (p. 3).
Sun et al. (2025)	Personalization of advertising, defined as tailoring ads to an individual's characteristics, interests, or tastes (De Keyzer et al., 2015) (p. 3).

personality traits (Bang et al., 2019; Dodoo & Wen, 2019). The information is systematically entered into consumer databases to generate insights, define target audiences, and inform personalization strategies.

Message tailoring draws on these consumer insights, along with advertiser input, strategic goals, and proprietary datasets, to create customized advertising content delivered in real time across one or multiple channels. Depending on the type and richness of the data, this process may include selecting the appropriate product or service (e.g., interactive recommendations; Kim et al., 2022), identifying effective messaging strategies (e.g., appeals; Zhang et al., 2024), incorporating personal characteristics into the message (e.g., personalized address; Dijkstra & Ballast, 2012), and optimizing delivery channels (e.g., synchronized advertising; Boerman & Segijn, 2022).

Importantly, these two dimensions are not separate but form a dynamic, interconnected process in which each influences and is shaped by the other (Araujo et al., 2020). For example, the contents and channels consumers frequently use can shape message format and content, while consumers' engagement with the content and conversions feed back into audience identification and future strategy refinement (Araujo et al., 2020; Malthouse & Copulsky, 2023). While some scholars have suggested adding *evaluation* as a distinct third stage in the personalization process (e.g., Zanker et al., 2019), this chapter treats evaluation as an integrated function. In AI-driven personalization, feedback mechanisms are inherently embedded within both profiling and message tailoring through machine learning, making evaluation a continuous and adaptive component of the system rather than a standalone phase. Based on this analysis, this chapter defines personalization as below:

> Personalization is an advertising strategy that employs automated or semi-automated systems to tailor persuasive messages at scale, based on detailed consumer profiles generated through large-scale data collection.

Targeting, Customization, and Personalization

Two related concepts, targeting and customization, are often used interchangeably with personalization due to their shared reliance on personal data and their common goal of delivering relevant content to individuals or consumer segments (e.g., Yoon et al., 2023). However, these terms can be meaningfully distinguished by the two core dimensions of personalization: targeting emphasizes consumer profiling, while customization centers on message tailoring. In this framework, both targeting and customization are considered subtypes of personalization, each highlighting a different facet of the broader personalization strategy.

Targeting primarily focuses on ad delivery without necessarily tailoring the message content to individual recipients (Huh & Malthouse, 2020). For instance, retargeting or online behavioral targeting delivers ads based on users' past online behavior (Boerman et al., 2017; Morimoto, 2021), while ethnic affinity targeting uses AI to classify consumers by ethnic affiliation to deliver culturally relevant messages (Zhang & Rodgers, 2023). In such approaches, advertisements may be pre-designed for specific audience segments and often contain generic product or service imagery. The content-matching process can be subtle and occur without consumers being fully aware of how their personal data has been used (Boerman et al., 2017). Still, consumer profiling can be highly sophisticated, incorporating multiple predictive characteristics aligned with marketing objectives (Malthouse & Copulsky, 2023).

Customization, by contrast, refers to content generation that allows consumers to modify aspects of the ad experience to enhance personal relevance (Eastin et al., 2019). It is typically a user-initiated process, where individuals input personal data to be combined with brand or product information (Morimoto, 2021). For example, Stitch Fix invites users to complete a style profile that informs product recommendations (Kim et al., 2022), while virtual advertising platforms may allow consumers to create avatars that appear in the ad as a form of self-endorsement (Ahn & Bailenson, 2011). In these cases, audience profiling is less crucial because data is provided directly by the consumer. Yet, the resulting message can be highly individualized, incorporating specific details to create a unique experience.

A Brief Overview of Personalization Development as Technology Evolves

Although AI-powered personalization marks a major leap in advertising, the core concept of personalization predates the AI era (Vesanen, 2007; Zanker et al., 2019). For decades, personalization has evolved alongside technological advancements. These developments have enabled more sophisticated approaches to both consumer profiling and message generation, the two core dimensions of personalization discussed earlier.

Technological advancements have dramatically increased the volume, variety, and integration of consumer data for profiling. In the pre-digital era, profiling relied on internal records and transactional data, occasionally supplemented by third-party lists (Vesanen, 2007; Peppers & Rogers, 1998). The rise of personal computers and the internet introduced cookies and web tracking, enabling more accurate targeting based on browsing and purchase history (Boerman et al., 2017). Social media further expanded personalization by capturing user-generated content, social connections, real-time interactions, and psychological traits such as personality, ideology, and preferences (Morimoto, 2021; Orazi & Nyilasy, 2019). Smartphones and wearable devices that allow location tracking add context-rich, real-time data (Hong et al., 2024; Le et al., 2024). The CRM platforms, like those from Salesforce and IBM, can integrate online and offline data using machine learning and predictive analytics, enabling more detailed, holistic consumer profiling (Kimla, 2024).

Technological advancements have enabled more dynamic and nuanced message tailoring using diverse consumer data. Early efforts, such as direct mail, used basic segmentation based on frequency or spending, with unchanged message content (Rao & Steckel, 1995). Later, surface-level personalization, like inserting names, gender, or zip codes, was common but did not alter the message's core (Dijkstra & Ballast, 2012; Tam & Ho, 2006; Maslowska et al., 2016). Digital platforms introduced interactive personalization, including behavioral targeting and synchronized advertising, allowing real-time adaptation to user behavior and media use (Lee & Cho, 2019; Segijn & Voorveld, 2021). Today, advertisers are able to adjust all aspects of advertising messages, including images, appeals, sources, and communication styles, based on individual preferences.

AI for Personalization

Building on decades of data-driven innovation, AI-powered personalization marks a new era in advertising. Unlike earlier rule-based or segmented approaches, AI enables real-time, predictive personalization at scale by continuously learning from large, diverse datasets. Campbell et al. (2022b) identify three key AI types in advertising: analytic AI (analyzing complex data), interpretive AI (supporting decision-making), and creative AI (generating content). Personalization now integrates all three, enhancing both audience profiling and message tailoring.

In profiling, AI analyzes large volumes of consumer data, ranging from demographic and psychographic traits to behavioral patterns and multimedia inputs, collected across diverse advertising channels (Van Noort et al., 2020). This data fuels the delivery of personalized advertising solutions (Malthouse & Copulsky, 2023). Analytic AI plays a central role by identifying individual preferences and behavioral patterns using machine learning, deep learning, and other techniques like supervised, unsupervised, and reinforcement learning (Rodgers, 2021; Malthouse & Copulsky, 2023). Tools such as natural language processing, computer vision, and neural networks process this data to uncover insights and generate predictive outputs (Helberger et al., 2020), which inform interpretive AI in shaping tailored strategies (Campbell et al., 2022b).

In message tailoring, interpretive AI determines effective content and optimal delivery channels. Creative or generative AI then assembles the ad, integrating consumer insights with brand assets and persuasive elements such as emotional appeals and visual formats (Chen et al., 2019). Machine learning enhances computational creativity by optimizing content based on audience preferences and campaign performance (Kallevig et al., 2022). Technologies like deepfakes support synthetic advertising by generating realistic, personalized content (Campbell et al., 2022a; Kietzmann et al., 2021), which is then distributed through the chosen channels (Segijn & Voorveld, 2021; Wu et al., 2022). For example, visual AI enables the use of consumer images or avatars to boost identification and relevance (Ahn et al., 2017; Eastin et al., 2019; Haikel-Elsabeh, 2023), while chat-based AI fosters interactive, real-time customization.

Technology-Based Typology of Personalization

Personalization is an umbrella concept encompassing a wide range of advertising practices. To clarify its scope and guide model development, prior research has proposed various frameworks to categorize personalization. For instance, Li (2016) distinguishes between actual and perceived personalization based on marketers' manipulations and consumers' subjective evaluations. Bang et al. (2019) classify personalization by targeting scale, differentiating between group-level and individual-level approaches. Zhang et al. (2024) focus on the type of consumer information used, distinguishing behavioral from psychological personalization. Building on this body of work, this chapter introduces a typology of four personalization types based on AI involvement across two core dimensions: audience profiling and message tailoring (see Figure 14.1). Each category represents distinct practices and raises unique research questions.

The first category, *Rule-Based Personalization*, appears in the lower left quadrant of Figure 14.1, where AI involvement is low in both audience profiling

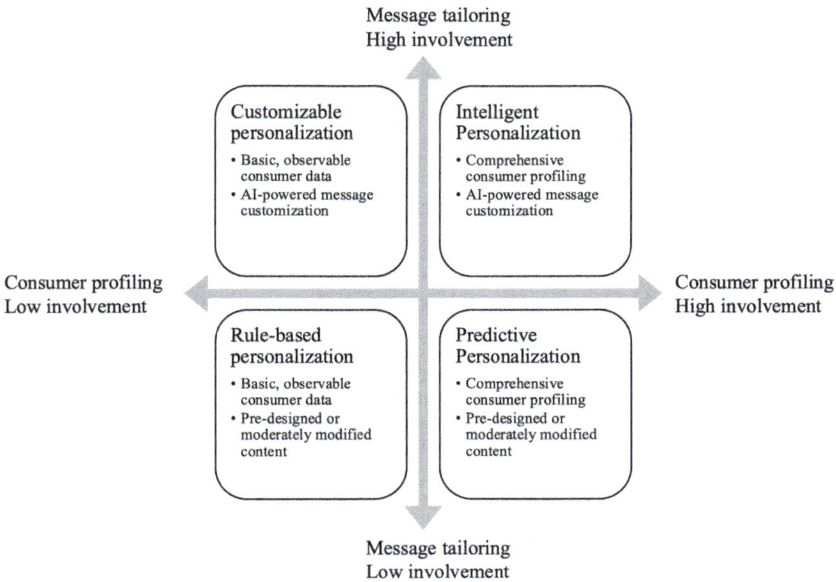

Figure 14.1 Technology-Based Typology for Personalization in Digital Advertising.

and message tailoring. This approach employs traditional content-matching strategies rooted in direct marketing. Consumer profiling relies on basic, observable data—such as past clicks, demographics, or location—collected via cookies or trackers to trigger predefined responses. Message tailoring typically involves delivering static, pre-designed content to users who meet simple rule-based criteria, sometimes incorporating personal details like the recipient's name or photo (e.g., Maslowska et al., 2016). Common examples include retargeting ads and personalized email campaigns.

The second category, *Predictive Personalization*, is located in the lower right quadrant, where AI involvement is high in audience profiling but low in message tailoring. Like rule-based personalization, it often uses pre-designed messages, but it enhances targeting through AI-driven profiling. These systems infer latent attributes—such as personality traits, contextual factors, and evolving preferences—from behavioral data with high precision (Huh & Malthouse, 2020). AI selects and delivers the most relevant message type for each user and continuously refines audience models using feedback from prior interactions (Malthouse & Copulsky, 2023). Personalization on platforms like Meta and TikTok exemplifies this approach, focusing on content-audience matching at scale.

The third category, *Customizable Personalization*, occupies the upper-left quadrant, where AI involvement is high in message tailoring but low in audience profiling. Aligned with the concept of customization, this type involves consumer-initiated data input, such as names, images, or preferences, used to generate tailored content through AI tools. Rather than profiling audiences, the AI customizes message content directly based on user-provided information. Applications include virtual fitting rooms, branded augmented reality (AR) lenses, and interactive metaverse product experiences.

The fourth category, *Intelligent Personalization*, is in the upper-right quadrant, where AI plays a central role in both audience profiling and message tailoring. This type combines the strengths of predictive and customizable personalization. AI systems analyze large-scale, multimodal consumer data to segment audiences and use generative tools, such as large language models, visual synthesis engines, and chatbots, to dynamically assemble personalized content in real time (Deng et al., 2019). Messages vary in tone, appeal, format, and interactivity across channels, creating a seamless and adaptive communication experience. Examples include real-time product recommendations, conversational agents, and dynamic creative optimization, representing a fully AI-integrated approach to advertising.

Theoretical Foundations and Research of Personalization

Theory-driven advertising research on personalization typically addresses both its challenges (e.g., intrusiveness, ad avoidance) and its benefits (e.g., enhanced attention, recall, relevance, usefulness, and social value), providing insights that help advertisers refine and optimize individualized marketing strategies (Bang et al., 2019; Brinson et al., 2019; Zhang et al., 2024). In this section, I will review recent research on AI-driven personalization through the lens of the two key dimensions, with particular attention to how the challenges and benefits of personalization tend to be emphasized within each dimension.

Privacy and Ethical Concerns from Consumer Profiling

As AI-driven personalization shifts toward the right two quadrants of Figure 14.1, its enhanced ability to access and analyze vast, cross-channel data allows for the creation of more detailed and predictive consumer profiles. A growing body of research, particularly those focusing on predictive personalization, has examined the implications of such extensive audience profiling, particularly in relation to privacy.

Several theoretical frameworks have been applied to explain how consumers evaluate the trade-offs between personalization benefits and privacy risks. The Persuasion Knowledge Model (Friestad & Wright, 1994) suggests that consumers who recognize personalization as a persuasion tactic become more skeptical, scrutinize the ad more closely, and adjust their responses based on perceived appropriateness and intent (Zhang & Rodgers, 2023). Privacy Calculus Theory (Girondaa & Korgaonkar, 2018) posits that consumers weigh the benefits of personalized content against perceived privacy risks and make decisions accordingly (Kim et al., 2023). Communication Privacy Management Theory (Petronio, 2010) highlights how individuals establish, coordinate, and adjust the boundaries of personal information disclosure, particularly when privacy expectations are breached (Xie & Karan, 2019). Together, these frameworks offer valuable insight into how consumers navigate personalization in the context of data privacy.

Privacy concerns, defined as "concerns about [the] possible loss of privacy as a result of information disclosure to a specific external agent" (Xu et al., 2012, p. 2), remain a central predictor of advertising effectiveness. For example, Segijn et al. (2021) found that privacy concerns reduced attention and memory for personalized ads, although this effect was moderated by ad synchronicity across devices. Morimoto (2021) linked higher privacy concerns to increased ad avoidance and perceived intrusiveness on social media. Similarly, Zhang et al. (2023) found that privacy concerns moderated consumer responses to online behavioral targeting.

Recent work has begun exploring strategies to mitigate these negative effects, including enhancing consumer control (Bright et al., 2022; Kim et al., 2019; Morimoto, 2021) and improving data security through blockchain technology (Yun & Strycharz, 2023). These approaches reflect a broader shift toward recognizing consumers as active participants in the personalization process, particularly in their willingness to share personal data for more relevant recommendations (De Schaepdrijver et al., 2022). Rather than assuming consumer passivity, recent research highlights the importance of consumer autonomy (Coffin, 2022) in shaping attitudes toward privacy, persuasion, and technology adoption.

As AI becomes more embedded in audience profiling, ethical and regulatory issues have come to the fore. For example, Zhang and Rodgers (2023) raise concerns about the discriminatory implications of AI-powered ethnic affinity targeting, while Desimpelaere et al. (2024) show how personalization referencing children's hobbies can heighten ad persuasiveness and product desire, raising ethical questions about exploitation and vulnerability.

Content Relevance Enhanced by Message Tailoring

On the message-tailoring side, research has focused on identifying content features that enhance effectiveness and the mechanisms behind them. A central explanation is the self-referencing effect: individuals tend to better process and recall information that relates to themselves (Ahn et al., 2017). Self-relevant messages activate the self-schema (i.e., complex cognitive structures shaped by personal experience), which facilitates deeper encoding and comprehension (Greenwald & Banaji, 1989; Markus, 1977). Much of the personalization literature has thus examined how specific message elements enhance perceived relevance.

Relevancy refers to the degree to which consumers see ad content as aligned with their personal needs and values (De Groot, 2022). Research consistently shows that greater perceived relevance improves attention, elaboration, and persuasion while reducing perceived intrusiveness (Bartsch & Kloß, 2019; Maslowska et al., 2016; Morimoto, 2017). Relevant messages are also more useful, increasing their effectiveness and consumer satisfaction (Kim et al., 2022; Yoon et al., 2023). AI enhances message tailoring by enabling more granular targeting based on nuanced consumer traits, allowing advertisers to increase relevance and reduce risks.

An emerging focus in AI-driven personalization is self-endorsing—a strategy that visually depicts consumers or their avatars using the product (Ahn & Bailenson, 2011; Ahn et al., 2017). This overt form of personalization increases perceived relevance by enabling consumers to visualize themselves with the product. Advances in AI have made integrating self-images or avatars into ads more realistic and immersive, enhancing persuasion potential (Hamilton et al., 2021). Recent studies have shown that self-endorsing via virtual mirrors or AR tools improves engagement, satisfaction, and purchase intentions (Lin et al., 2024; Hamilton et al., 2021).

Future Theoretical Directions and Research Opportunities

As AI continues to advance personalization toward more intelligent and adaptive forms, scholarly inquiry into personalization design is expanding accordingly. Thorson and Rodgers (2019) organized advertising research into six key components: audience, message, source, channel, device, and organization under a certain context. Most personalization research to date has centered on two of these, audience and message, through the lenses of consumer profiling and message tailoring. However, as AI-driven personalization becomes more sophisticated and as foundational work in traditional settings matures, new opportunities are emerging to explore less-studied facets within these elements. Furthermore, the increasingly integrated nature of personalization, situated at the intersection of multiple components, presents promising directions for future research.

Extending the Research on Message and Audience

As AI enables increasingly granular use of consumer data in persuasive communication, privacy concerns remain central to understanding consumer responses. On one hand, greater digital literacy may enhance consumers' ability to detect inappropriate data collection, thereby amplifying privacy concerns in shaping persuasive outcomes. On the other hand, the ubiquity and convenience of data collection may lead consumers to deprioritize privacy, contributing to the well-documented privacy paradox (Brinson & Eastin, 2016). Future research should continue to examine this paradox, particularly in the context of AI-powered personalization.

The broader integration of consumer data also invites more active consumer participation and greater user control. Active participation involves consumers voluntarily engaging with personalization processes, sharing data, customizing content, interacting across platforms, initiating product-related conversations, and co-creating branded experiences, often supported by AI tools. Research should investigate factors influencing technology adoption, co-creation, and data-sharing behavior. Perceived control, for example, has been shown to mitigate privacy concerns (Brinson et al., 2024; Feng & Xie, 2019), underscoring the importance of user empowerment.

A growing body of research addresses ethical concerns surrounding algorithmic fairness and transparency. As AI becomes more embedded in advertising, issues of trust, data ethics, and consumer autonomy gain prominence (Boerman & Segijn, 2022; Xie & Karan, 2019; Zhang & Rodgers, 2023). Future studies should examine how control over data, ease of use, algorithmic transparency, and digital literacy contribute to ethical personalization and reduce privacy risks.

In message tailoring, intelligent personalization allows for highly individualized content based on detailed user data (Campbell et al., 2022a). Yet, empirical research on AI-generated content in this context remains limited. Generative technologies not only enable benefits such as greater realism, creativity, and accessibility but also introduce challenges, including perceptions of falsity, algorithm aversion, and ethical concerns about misinformation and deception (Campbell et al., 2022a; Kietzmann et al., 2021). Future research should explore the conditions under which AI-generated messages are effective and trustworthy. As generative AI accelerates the spread of persuasive content, addressing its ethical implications is essential to maintaining consumer trust and safeguarding brand integrity.

Integrate Other Advertising Elements into Personalization Research

Future research should broaden personalization scholarship by examining how it intersects with other advertising components, particularly source, device, and channel. One promising direction is exploring how backstage personalization (e.g., data profiling) interacts with front-end AI sources, such as virtual agents or influencers, and how this interplay shapes user engagement and perception (Kim et al., 2022). While recent studies have examined AI personas like virtual influencers, they are typically analyzed in one-to-many contexts (Byun & Ahn, 2023); their potential for delivering individualized, one-to-one personalization remains underexplored.

Another critical AI source is the chatbot, which enables real-time, two-way communication and personalized recommendations. Research by Lou et al. (2022) conceptualizes contingency, also known as message interactivity, as the extent to which system responses meaningfully relate to user input (see also Rafaeli, 1988; Sundar et al., 2016). Higher contingency, supported by memory and user data, can increase message accuracy and persuasiveness, as exemplified by AI chatbots like ChatGPT. For instance, Lim and Zhang (2022) found that perceived contingency enhances consumer intention to adopt AI personalization platforms. Chat-based AI, such as ChatGPT, thus presents an opportunity to study personalized interactions at scale.

Personalization also deserves further examination within multichannel and omnichannel environments. A central concept in this area is synchronization—the ability to track media behavior, gather contextual data, and deliver consistent, coordinated messages across platforms (Segijn, 2019; Segijn & Voorveld, 2021). AI-enabled synced advertising represents a sophisticated form of personalization that adapts both audience profiles and message content across devices and formats. Though promising, this practice raises privacy concerns: Segijn et al. (2021) found that greater privacy concern reduced attention to synced ads, while Boerman and Segijn (2022) reported that many Dutch consumers viewed such advertising as inappropriate.

Future studies could investigate how personalization variables, such as personality traits, motivations, message congruency, and perceived relevance, moderate the effectiveness of synced advertising. Additionally, research should move beyond conventional platforms like smartphones and TVs to examine newer interfaces, including voice assistants, wearables, virtual reality, and public displays. Understanding how personalization varies across channels and how synchronization across formats (e.g., voice-to-screen or screen-to-AR) affects engagement will be essential. Identifying message and channel combinations that boost receptiveness without triggering privacy concerns remains a key direction for future inquiry.

Conclusion

As AI transforms digital advertising, personalization has advanced from static, rule-based methods to intelligent systems that tailor messages and delivery at the individual level. This chapter introduced a two-dimensional framework—audience profiling and message tailoring—and categorized personalization into four types based on AI involvement, offering a structured lens for analysis. By integrating relevant advertising theories and emerging concepts such as contingency, self-endorsing, and synchronization, this chapter highlights how AI-driven personalization is becoming more dynamic, interactive, and cross-platform. As this evolution raises new questions around consumer experience, brand perception, and ethics, continued research is essential to ensure that personalization remains both effective and aligned with consumer autonomy and social responsibility.

References

Ahn, S. J., & Bailenson, J. N. (2011). Self-endorsing versus other-endorsing in virtual environments. *Journal of Advertising*, 40(2), 93–106.

Ahn, S. J. G., Phua, J., & Shan, Y. (2017). Self-endorsing in digital advertisements: Using virtual selves to persuade physical selves. *Computers in Human Behavior*, *71*, 110–121.

Ahn, H. Y., & Haley, E. (2025). Are My Photos Worth a Thousand Ads? Gen Z Consumers' Perspectives on Personalized Myselfie Advertising and Its Implication for AI Algorithms. *Journal of Current Issues & Research in Advertising*, *46*(4), 473–502.

Araujo, T., Helberger, N., Kruikemeier, S., & De Vreese, C. H. (2020). In AI we trust? Perceptions about automated decision-making by artificial intelligence. *AI & Society*, *35*(3), 611–623.

Alhelaly, Y., Dhillon, G., & Oliveira, T. (2025). The Impact of Privacy Intrusiveness on Individuals' Responses and Engagement Toward Personalization in Online Interactive Advertising. *Journal of Interactive Advertising*, *25*(1), 38–60.

Baek, T. H. (2023). Digital advertising in the age of generative AI. *Journal of Current Issues & Research in Advertising*, 44(3), 249–251.

Baek, T. H., & Morimoto, M. (2012). Stay away from me. *Journal of Advertising*, 41(1), 59–76.

Bang, H., Choi, D., Wojdynski, B. W., & Lee, Y. I. (2019). How the level of personalization affects the effectiveness of personalized ad messages: The moderating role of narcissism. *International Journal of Advertising*, 38(8), 1116–1138.

Bartsch, A., & Kloß, A. (2019). Personalized charity advertising. Can personalized prosocial messages promote empathy, attitude change, and helping intentions toward stigmatized social groups? *International Journal of Advertising*, 38(3), 345–363.

Bol, N., T. Dienlin, S. Kruikemeier, M. Sax, S. C. Boerman, J. Strycharz, N. Helberger, and C. H. De Vreese. 2018. "Understanding the Effects of Personalization as a Privacy Calculus: Analyzing Self-Disclosure across Health, News, and Commerce Contexts." *Journal of Computer-Mediated Communication 23* (6): 370–388. https://doi.org/10.1093/jcmc/zmy020.

Boerman, S. C., Kruikemeier, S., & Zuiderveen Borgesius, F. J. (2017). Online behavioral advertising: A literature review and research agenda. *Journal of Advertising*, 46(3), 363–376.

Boerman, S. C., & Segijn, C. M. (2022). Awareness and perceived appropriateness of synced advertising in Dutch adults. *Journal of Interactive Advertising*, 22(2), 187–194.

Bright, L. F., Logan, K., & Lim, H. S. (2022). Social media fatigue and privacy: An exploration of antecedents to consumers' concerns regarding the security of their personal information on social media platforms. *Journal of Interactive Advertising*, 22(2), 125–140.

Brinson, N. H., & Eastin, M. S. (2016). Juxtaposing the persuasion knowledge model and privacy paradox: An experimental look at advertising personalization, public policy and public understanding. *Cyberpsychology: Journal of Psychosocial Research on Cyberspace*, 10(1), 43(1), 58–77.

Brinson, N. H., Eastin, M. S., & Bright, L. F. (2019). Advertising in a quantified world: A proposed model of consumer trust, attitude toward personalized advertising and outcome expectancies. *Journal of Current Issues & Research in Advertising*, 40(1), 54–72.

Brinson, N. H., Holiday, S., & George, J. L. (2024). Response to advertising delivered by voice assistants: the mediating role of persuasion knowledge, perceived control, social presence, and privacy concerns. *Journal of Interactive Advertising*, *24*(4), 344–367.

Byun, K. J., & Ahn, S. J. (2023). A systematic review of virtual influencers: Similarities and differences between human and virtual influencers in interactive advertising. *Journal of Interactive Advertising*, 23(4), 293–306.

Campbell, C., Plangger, K., Sands, S., & Kietzmann, J. (2022a). Preparing for an era of deepfakes and AI-generated ads: A framework for understanding responses to manipulated advertising. *Journal of Advertising*, 51(1), 22–38.

Campbell, C., Plangger, K., Sands, S., Kietzmann, J., & Bates, K. (2022b). How deepfakes and artificial intelligence could reshape the advertising industry: The coming reality of AI fakes and their potential impact on consumer behavior. *Journal of Advertising Research*, 62(3), 241–251.

Chen, H., & Zhou, L. (2018). The myth of big data: Chinese advertising practitioners' perspective. *International Journal of Advertising,* 37(4), 633–649.

Chen, G., Xie, P., Dong, J., & Wang, T. (2019). Understanding programmatic creative: The role of AI. *Journal of Advertising*, 48(4), 347–355.

Coffin, J. (2022). Asking questions of AI advertising: A maieutic approach. *Journal of Advertising*, 51(5), 608–623.

De Groot, J. I. M. (2022). The personalization paradox in Facebook advertising: The mediating effect of relevance on the personalization–brand attitude relationship and the moderating effect of intrusiveness. *Journal of Interactive Advertising*, 22(1), 57–74.

De Keyzer, F., N. Dens, and P. De Pelsmacker. 2015. "Is This for Me? How Consumers Respond to Personalized Advertising on Social Network Sites." *Journal of Interactive Advertising 15* (2): 124–134. https://doi.org/10.1080/152 52019.2015.1082450.

De Keyzer, F., N. Dens, and P. De Pelsmacker. 2022. "How and When Personalized Advertising Leads to Brand Attitude, Click, and WOM Intention." *Journal of Advertising 51* (1): 39–56. https://doi.org/10.1080/00913367.2021.1888339.

Deng, S., Tan, C. W., Wang, W., & Pan, Y. (2019). Smart generation system of personalized advertising copy and its application to advertising practice and research. *Journal of Advertising*, 48(4), 356–365.

Desimpelaere, L., Hudders, L., & Van De Sompel, D. (2024). Children's hobbies as persuasive strategies: The role of literacy training in children's responses to personalized ads. *Journal of Advertising*, 53(1), 70–85.

Dijkstra, A., & Ballast, K. (2012). Personalization and perceived personal relevance in computer-tailored persuasion in smoking cessation. *British Journal of Health Psychology*, 17(1), 60–73.

Dodoo, N. A., & Wen, J. (2019). A path to mitigating SNS ad avoidance: Tailoring messages to individual personality traits. *Journal of Interactive Advertising*, 19(2), 116–132.

Dolnicar, S., & Yolanda, J. (2007). A Market-Oriented Approach to Responsibly Managing Information Privacy Concerns in Direct Marketing. *Journal of Advertising, 36* (2), 123–149.

Eastin, M. S., Netto, J. J., Xu, F., Lee, J. A., & Mabry-Flynn, A. (2019). Customizing the win: Demonstrating a positive way to consumer brand attitude. *Journal of Interactive Advertising*, 19(3), 236–245.

Feng, Y., & Xie, Q. (2019). Privacy concerns, perceived intrusiveness, and privacy controls: An analysis of virtual try-on apps. *Journal of Interactive Advertising*, 19(1), 43–57.

Friestad, M., & Wright, P. (1994). The persuasion knowledge model: How people cope with persuasion attempts. *Journal of Consumer Research*, 21(1), 1–31.

Gironda, J. T., & Korgaonkar, P. K. (2018). iSpy? Tailored versus invasive ads and consumers' perceptions of personalized advertising. *Electronic Commerce Research and Applications*, 29, 64–77.

Greenwald, A. G., & Banaji, M. R. (1989). The self as a memory system: Powerful, but ordinary. *Journal of Personality and Social Psychology*, 57(1), 41.

Haikel-Elsabeh, M. (2023). Virtual influencers versus real influencers advertising in the metaverse, understanding the perceptions, and interactions with users. *Journal of Current Issues & Research in Advertising*, 44(3), 252–273.

Hamilton, K. A., Lee, S. Y., Chung, U. C., Liu, W., & Duff, B. R. (2021). Putting the "Me" in endorsement: Understanding and conceptualizing dimensions of self-endorsement using intelligent personal assistants. *New Media & Society*, 23(6), 1506–1526.

Helberger, N., Araujo, T., & De Vreese, C. H. (2020). Who is the fairest of them all? Public attitudes and expectations regarding automated decision-making. *Computer Law & Security Review*, 39, 105456.

Hong, J., Im, I., & Park, S. (2024). It's all about timing: Captive targeting through mobile ads. *Journal of Advertising*, *53*(2), 242–261.

Hoy, M., and G. Milne. 2010. "Gender Differences in Privacy-Related Measures for Young Adult Facebook Users. *Journal of Interactive Advertising*, *10*(2), 28–45. https://doi.org/10.1080/15252019.2010.10722168.

Hu, X., & Wise, K. (2024). Disentangling control and personalization: Exploring the effects of Ad choice and Ad personalization in digital advertising effectiveness. *Journal of Interactive Advertising*, 24(3), 265–288.

Huh, J., & Malthouse, E. C. (2020). Advancing computational advertising: Conceptualization of the field and future directions. *Journal of Advertising*, 49(4), 367–376.

Huh, J., Nelson, M. R., & Russell, C. A. (2023). ChatGPT, AI advertising, and advertising research and education. *Journal of Advertising*, 52(4), 477–482.

Kallevig, A., Zuem, W., Willis, M., Ranfagni, S., & Rovai, S. (2022). Managing creativity in the age of data-driven marketing communication: A model for agencies to improve their distribution and valuation of creativity. *Journal of Advertising Research*, 62(4), 301–320.

Kietzmann, J., Mills, A. J., & Plangger, K. (2021). Deepfakes: Perspectives on the future "reality" of advertising and branding. *International Journal of Advertising*, 40(3), 473–485.

Kim, H., and J. Huh. (2017). Perceived relevance and privacy concern regarding online behavioral advertising (OBA) and their role in consumer responses. *Journal of Current Issues & Research in Advertising 38* (1):92–105. doi:10. 1080/10641734.2016.1233157

Kim, J., Kang, S., & Bae, J. (2022). The effects of customer consumption goals on artificial intelligence driven recommendation agents: Evidence from Stitch Fix. *International Journal of Advertising*, 41(6), 997–1016.

Kim, W., Ryoo, Y., Lee, S., & Lee, J. A. (2023). Chatbot advertising as a double-edged sword: The roles of regulatory focus and privacy concerns. *Journal of Advertising*, 52(4), 504–522.

Kim, H. Y., Song, J. H., & Lee, J. H. (2019). When are personalized promotions effective? The role of consumer control. *International Journal of Advertising*, 38(4), 628–647.

Kimla, N. (2024). *How AI can maximize your CRM: The future of customer relationship management.* Retrieved from https://www.forbes.com/councils/forbesbusinesscouncil/2024/07/11/how-ai-can-maximize-your-crm-the-future-of-customer-relationship-management/

Kotler, P., Kartajaya, H., & Setiawan, I. (2021). *Marketing 5.0: Technology for Humanity*. John Willey & Sons.

Kotler, P., Kartajaya, H., & Setiawan, I. (2023). *Marketing 6.0: The Future is Immersive*. Wiley.

Le, H. T. P. M., Yoo, W., & Park, J. (2024). The effects of brand trustworthiness and credibility on location-based advertising: moderating effects of privacy concern and social influence. *International Journal of Advertising*, 43(5), 798–823.

Lee, H., & Cho, C. H. (2019). An empirical investigation on the antecedents of consumers' cognitions of and attitudes towards digital signage advertising. *International Journal of Advertising*, 38(1), 97–115.

Li, C. (2016). When does web-based personalization really work? The distinction between actual personalization and perceived personalization. *Computers in Human Behavior*, 54, 25–33.

Li, H. (2019). Special section introduction: Artificial intelligence and advertising.*Journal of Advertising*, 48(4), 333–337.

Lim, J. S., & Zhang, J. (2022). Adoption of AI-driven personalization in digital news platforms: An integrative model of technology acceptance and perceived contingency. *Technology in Society*, 69, 101965.

Lin, H-F., Yeo, B., & Lu, T-Y. (2024). How virtual mirrors in advertising influence attitudes about beauty products: Consumer viewing perspectives, beautification, and endorsement in AR advertising. *Journal of Advertising Research*, 64(3), 372–392.

Lou, C., Kang, H., & Tse, C. H. (2022). Bots vs. humans: How schema congruity, contingency-based interactivity, and sympathy influence consumer perceptions and patronage intentions. *International Journal of Advertising*, 41(4), 655–684.

Malthouse, E., & Copulsky, J. (2023). Artificial intelligence ecosystems for marketing communications. *International Journal of Advertising*, 42(1), 128–140.

Maslowska, E., Smit, E. G., & Van den Putte, B. (2016). It is all in the name: A study of consumers' responses to personalized communication. *Journal of Interactive Advertising*, 16(1), 74–85.

Markus, H. (1977). Self-schemata and processing information about the self. *Journal of Personality and Social Psychology*, 35(2), 63.

Morimoto, M. (2017). Personalization, perceived intrusiveness, irritation, and avoidance in digital advertising. In S. Rodgers & E. Thorson (Eds.), *Digital Advertising* (pp. 110–123). Routledge.

Morimoto, M. (2021). Privacy concerns about personalized advertising across multiple social media platforms in Japan: The relationship with information control and persuasion knowledge. *International Journal of Advertising*, 40(3), 431–451.

Orazi, D. C., & Nyilasy, G. (2019). Straight to the heart of your target audience: Personalized advertising systems based on wearable technology and heart-rate variability. *Journal of Advertising Research*, 59(2), 137–141.

Pavlou, P. A., & Stewart, D. W. (2000). Measuring the effects and effectiveness of interactive advertising: A research agenda. *Journal of Interactive Advertising*, 1(1), 61–77.

Peppers, D., & Rogers, M. (1998). Better business–one customer at a time. *The Journal for Quality and Participation*, 21(2), 30.

Petronio, S. (2010). Communication privacy management theory: What do we know about family privacy regulation? *Journal of Family Theory & Review*, 2(3), 175–196.

Pfiffelmann, J., & Pfeuffer A. (2022). Understanding Personalized Recruitment Ads' Effectiveness: The Role of Personalization Type and Message Involvement. *Journal of Interactive Advertising 22* (3), 311–326. https://doi.org/10.1080/15252019.2022.2132124.

Rafaeli, S. (1988). From new media to communication. Sage annual review of communication research. *Advancing Communication Science*, 16(1), 110–134.

Rao, V. R., & Steckel, J. H. (1995). Selecting, evaluating, and updating prospects in direct mail marketing. *Journal of Direct Marketing*, 9(2), 20–31.

Rodgers, S. (2021). Themed issue introduction: Promises and perils of artificial intelligence and advertising. *Journal of Advertising*, 50(1), 1–10.

Segijn, C. M., & Voorveld, H. A. (2021). A first step in unraveling synced advertising effectiveness. *International Journal of Advertising*, 40(1), 124–143.

Segijn, C. M., Voorveld, H. A., & Vakeel, K. A. (2021). The role of ad sequence and privacy concerns in personalized advertising: An eye-tracking study into synced advertising effects. *Journal of Advertising*, 50(3), 320–329.

Segijn, C. M. (2019). A new mobile data driven message strategy called synced advertising: Conceptualization, implications, and future directions. *Annals of the International Communication Association*, *43*(1), 58–77.

Schaepdrijver, L. D., Baecke, P., & Tackx, K. (2022). What makes consumers willing to share their data in addressable TV advertising? The influence of personal and situational factors on consumer willingness to disclose information. *Journal of Advertising Research*, 62(2), 131–147.

Sun, H., Xie, P., & Sun, Y. (2025). The inverted U-shaped effect of personalization on consumer attitudes in AI-generated ads: Striking the right balance between utility and threat. *Journal of Advertising Research*, *65*(2), 237–258.

Sundar, S. S., Bellur, S., Oh, J., Jia, H., & Kim, H. S. (2016). Theoretical importance of contingency in human-computer interaction: Effects of message interactivity on user engagement. *Communication Research*, 43(5), 595–625.

Tam, K. Y., & Ho, S. Y. (2006). Understanding the impact of web personalization on user information processing and decision outcomes. *MIS quarterly*, *30*(4), 865–890.

Thorson, E., & Rodgers, S. (2019). Advertising theory in the digital age. In S. Rodgers & E. Thorson (Eds.), *Advertising Theory* (pp. 3–17). Routledge.

Van Noort, G., Himelboim, I., Martin, J., & Collinger, T. (2020). Introducing a model of automated brand-generated content in an era of computational advertising. *Journal of Advertising*, 49(4), 411–427.

Vesanen, J. (2007). What is personalization? A conceptual framework. *European Journal of Marketing*, 41(5/6), 409–418.

Wolin, L., and P. Korgaonkar. 2005. Web advertising: Gender differences in beliefs, attitudes, and behavior. *Journal of Interactive Advertising*, *6*, 125–136.

White, T. B., Zahay, D. L., Thorbjørnsen, H., & Shavitt, S. (2008). Getting too personal: Reactance to highly personalized email solicitations. *Marketing Letters*, 19, 39–50.

Wu, L., Dodoo, N. A., Wen, T. J., & Ke, L. (2022). Understanding Twitter conversations about artificial intelligence in advertising based on natural language processing. *International Journal of Advertising*, 41(4), 685–702.

Xiao, Bo, and Izak Benbasat. 2007. "E-Commerce Product Recommendation Agents: Use, Characteristics, and Impact." *MIS Quarterly 31* (1): 137–209. https://doi.org/10.2307/25148784.

Xie, W., & Karan, K. (2019). Consumers' privacy concern and privacy protection on social network sites in the era of big data: Empirical evidence from college students. *Journal of Interactive Advertising*, 19(3), 187–201.

Xu, H., Gupta, S., Rosson, M. B., & Carroll, J. M. (2012). Measuring mobile users' concerns for information priv- acy. In *Proceedings of the 33rd International Conference on Information Systems* (ICIS) Paper 10, Orlando, FL.

Yoon, H. J., Huang, Y., & Kim, T. (2023). The role of relevancy in native advertising on social media. *International Journal of Advertising*, 42(6), 972–999.

Youn, K., Pittman, M., & Haley, E. (2024). Using the FCB grid to understand privacy concerns in social media advertising. *International Journal of Advertising*, 43(3), 405–433.

Yun, J. T., & Strycharz, J. (2023). Building the future of digital advertising one block at a time: How blockchain technology can change advertising practice and research. *Journal of Current Issues & Research in Advertising*, 44(1), 24–37.

Zanker, M., Rook, L., & Jannach, D. (2019). Measuring the impact of online personalisation: Past, present and future. *International Journal of Human-Computer Studies*, 131, 160–168.

Zhang, W., & Rodgers, S. (2023). Linking ethnicity targeting with artificial intelligence and data collection: Perceptions and behavioral responses of black consumers. *Journal of Current Issues & Research in Advertising*, 44(3), 373–391.

Zhang, W., Tsou, T. H., Rodgers, S., & Willett, J. F. (2024). Comparing personalization strategies in social network advertising: The role of impression motivation in persuasion outcomes. *Journal of Interactive Advertising*, 24(3), 247–264.

Zhang, D., Voorveld, H., & Boerman, S. C. (2023). Privacy concerns matter, knowledge does not: Investigating effects of online behavioral advertising among Chinese and Dutch adults. *Journal of Current Issues & Research in Advertising*, 44(3), 392–410.

15 Defining Ads in Metaverse

Concept Explication of Augmented and Virtual Reality Advertising

Ting-Hao Tsou

Introduction

Imagine this: Skyler Parker, an ordinary white-collar worker who stepped into the workforce, has finally saved enough for that long-dreamed-of down payment on buying the very first home. Although the house is still under construction, the advertiser hands Skyler a virtual reality (VR) headset to experience a life-sized simulation of the future home promoted by every customizable detail: the angle and size of bedroom windows, ceiling height, wall colors, and more, tailored to daily routines and habits. Months later, standing in the constructed but still empty house becomes a unique experience when simply lifting a phone with an augmented reality (AR) filter from Ashley Furniture to arrange the sofa and desk at where showing light supported focus, and to match the wardrobe with clothing needs and storage preferences, through recommendations all tailored to Skyler's living patterns.

AR and VR create tremendous opportunities for various advertising formats to engage consumers in immersive ways, blending physical worlds with virtual content or creating totally virtual environments, such as virtual product try-ons and placements, gamified ads, and immersive storytelling within the metaverse. The global metaverse market was valued at approximately $105.4 billion in 2024 (RaveSpace, 2025), and AR advertising (ARA) and VR advertising (VRA) are forecasted to grow to about $24.2 billion by 2033 (Market.us, 2024), reflecting a dominant force with rapid adoption among 3.7 billion users by 2029 (International Data Corporation, 2023). Although AR and VR have been defined in various fields (e.g., computer science, healthcare, education, and marketing), including advertising (e.g., Kim & Kim, 2014; Yaoyuneyong et al., 2016; Tsai et al., 2020; De Ruyter et al., 2020), they are still expanding their applications in advertising, and no study has systematically applied formal concept explication procedures to define ARA and VRA as the distinct constructs. Hence, corresponding definitions for ARA and VRA that reflect their various practical applications and that are developed through systematic, scientific, and justifiable procedures are urgently needed (Bergkvist & Eisend, 2023).

DOI: 10.4324/9781003567523-19

A concept explication on ARA and VRA can enhance theoretical clarity, improve measurement validity, and guide future empirical research and practical applications in the metaverse advertising domain (MacKenzie, 2003; Bergkvist & Eisend, 2023). Without such explication, conceptual ambiguity may persist, leading to inconsistent operationalizations, weak theoretical advancement, and difficulties in accumulating and comparing empirical findings (Bergkvist & Eisend, 2023), as well as in evaluating the practical effectiveness and informing policy and regulatory frameworks surrounding ARA and VRA (Spotts et al., 2014; Taylor, 2021).

For developing a clear definition and for adapting to a wide range of metaverse applications in advertising, this chapter (1) follows the recommended procedures for concept explication (e.g., Chaffee, 1991; McLeod et al., 2005) to define ARA and VRA and (2) uses the popular application of AR and VR in narrative advertising (Tsou & Rodgers, 2024) as an example, illustrating how metaverse advertising can be conceptually defined and adapted to various practical applications to ensure theoretical consistency and operational clarity when it is used in a specific format of advertising.

Literature Review on Definitions

Early conceptualizations of AR and VR can be traced back to the field of computer science. The original definition of AR is the system that has the following three characteristics: (1) combines real and virtual, (2) interactive in real time, and (3) registered in 3D (Azuma, 1997). On the other hand, VR is the system that (1) displays computer-generated images in real time, (2) changes according to the user's movements and inputs, and (3) provides visual, auditory, and haptic feedback (Sutherland, 1965). From these origins, the key distinction between AR and VR lies in their relationship to the physical world: AR enhances reality by overlaying virtual elements, while VR fully replaces it with a simulated environment (De Ruyter et al., 2020; Sands et al., 2024). Although this distinction reflects differences in physical integration, both AR and VR are fundamentally defined by their technological foundations that facilitate the immersion of environment (Errmann, 2025).

This technological emphasis has shaped how AR and VR are subsequently defined, leading scholars to refine their focus on AR's and VR's technological aspects. For example, one definition of AR, derived from Azuma et al. (1997), defines AR as "a system that combines real and computer-generated information in a real environment, interactively and in real time, and aligns virtual objects with physical ones" (Höllerer & Feiner, 2004, p. 222). Similarly, VR has been defined as one in which the user is immersed in a responsive, computer-generated environment (Slater & Wilbur, 1997). While these definitions closely mirror the originals, the phrase "computer-generated" encompasses a wide range of message genres, enabling AR and VR to be applied across diverse contexts beyond computer science and thus broadening their conceptual development in other fields.

In communication-related fields beyond advertising, AR and VR definitions still not only emphasize technological functions but also incorporate communication elements such as messages and receivers that reflect the specific communication purposes AR and VR serve. For example, in education, AR is defined as "a wide spectrum of technologies that project computer-generated materials, such as text, images, and video, onto users' perceptions of the real world" (Yuen et al., 2011, p. 120). In communication, VR is defined as "a communication medium that enables users to experience computer-generated environments through multisensory interaction, shaping how messages are delivered and how users cognitively and emotionally respond" (Steuer, 1992). Subsequent definitions would emphasize the objects of which messages are presented and receivers' responses, adapting the technological functions to specific communication contexts. In marketing, for example, AR has been defined as "a computer-simulated interactive technology that overlays a projected 3-D visualization of products on the user's view of the real world," and VR has been defined as a computer-generated immersive environment that enables users to interact with virtual products and experiences, blending sensory input to influence perceptions and behaviors in marketing contexts (Yim & Park, 2019, p. 582). These definitions recast computer-generated objects as "products" within marketing communication.

To analyze the foci of technology-related concepts' definitions in communication contexts, Kiousis's (2002) table cells (see Figure 15.1) offer a useful structure for analyzing previous AR and VR definitions in advertising. In this figure, definitions can be categorized along two dimensions: object emphasized, which refers to the primary elements scholars focus on, including technology, communication, and perceiver; and intellectual perspective originated, the fields/contexts in which these concepts are defined and used, divided into communication or non-communication fields/contexts. This figure helps to: (1) identify what is emphasized or de-emphasized from AR's and VR's technological origins and (2) highlight what has been added or omitted regarding the communication aspect, thereby advancing the process of defining AR and VR in advertising. Definitions that originate from computer science typically fall in the top-right quadrant, where technology is emphasized within non-communication fields/contexts. Unsurprisingly, early definitions in advertising often emphasized technological functions. For example, AR was described as a concept of supplementing the real world with the virtual world" (Kim & Kim, 2014, p. 386), while VR was defined as a computer-generated, immersive environment that replaces the user's perception of reality through interactive three-dimensional simulations (Li et al., 2002).

These definitions fall within the top-left quadrant of Figure 15.1, where technology remains the primary focus but is applied within communication contexts. Over time, definitions began to place greater emphasis on communication-related

Focus of Previous AR and VR Definitions

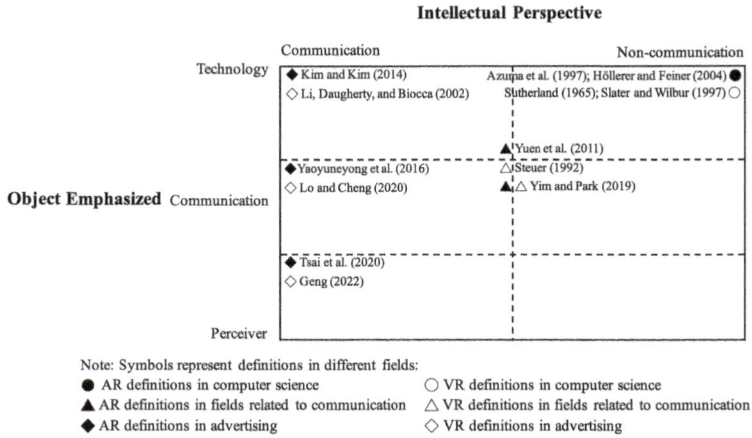

Figure 15.1 Focus of Previous AR and VR Definitions.

elements. For example, Yaoyuneyong et al. (2016) defined AR as "technology in which virtual information is superimposed over users' perceptions of the real world" (p. 16), highlighting the receiver's perceptions in advertising. Lo and Cheng (2020) described VR as "a computer-generated environment that allows a user to interact with various stimuli and experience scenery, objects, and sound effects in a virtual medium, giving the user the sense of actually 'being there'" (p. 539), reflecting attention to message features. Lee and Cho (2019) further incorporated more communication components—receiver, message, and medium—to define AR as "a technology that places augmented 3D images into print ads, which are viewed using an app on consumers' mobile phones or on tablet computers in real time" (p. 22).

Compared with the definitions situated in the top-left area, these definitions are at where the aspects of communication and perceiver are emphasized more within the advertising field. More recent definitions in advertising have more closely integrated technological features with core communication elements tailored to advertising contexts. For example, AR is defined as "an advanced form of image interactivity technology that can not only simulate direct product experience but also deliver multisensory (e.g., visual, motion, interactivity), enjoyable brand experience in consumers' own physical environments" (Tsai et al., 2020, p. 245). These evolving definitions reflect a shift toward the bottom-left area, where technological functions are more intricately connected with communicative elements.

These definitions are useful in illustrating the intent to adapt concepts from other fields to advertising and specific research contexts. However, they: (1)

often rely on referring to prior studies without being developed through a systematic and rigorous concept explication process; (2) may lack clear specification of characteristics relevant to communication or advertising, resulting in blurred boundaries with definitions from other fields; and (3) do not change accordingly when applied to specific advertising types or formats—such as narrative, comparative, or prosocial advertising—within the digital and interactive advertising landscape.

Hence, a concept explication of the proposed ARA and VRA concepts is essential. This process should focus on how ARA and VRA function within key elements of the Interactive Advertising Model—such as message structure, user control, interactivity level, and outcome processing paths (Rodgers & Thorson, 2000)—to develop domain-specific definitions that align with construct clarity principles for advertising research (Bergkvist & Eisend, 2023).

Examining Operational Properties

Following McLeod et al. (2005) steps for concept explication, examining a concept's operational properties in prior studies helps illustrate how it may manifest empirically and, in turn, supports conceptualization. Accordingly, this chapter examines the operational properties of AR and VR in existing research to inform the conceptualization of ARA and VRA. Previous advertising studies have shown that the *contextualization* of advertising content is core of the practical applications of AR (De Ruyter et al., 2020) and VR (Gonçalves et al., 2022) in advertising. In ARA, contextualization refers to the ability to tailor content in real time based on consumers' physical environments, linking advertising content to their immediate surroundings to influence their experiences and responses to the advertised objects (Zhao & Balague, 2015).

In VRA, contextualization means the ability to tailor content based on consumers' behaviors and environments within a simulated virtual world that replaces their physical reality (e.g., Wedel et al., 2020; Nam et al., 2025), integrating advertising content into a fully virtual setting, rather than projecting onto consumers' physical surroundings, to shape their experiences and responses to the advertised objects (Sands et al., 2024). Contextualization is proposed as a critical antecedent to AR and VR evaluations, as it represents a core practical design feature in AR (e.g., Hilken et al., 2017; Zhu & Owen, 2008) and VR (e.g., Tain, 2020; Nam et al., 2025), serving as the key factor in their effectiveness (Wedel et al., 2020; Sands et al., 2024).

According to McLeod et al. (2005), analyzing a concept's operational properties, particularly its antecedents identified in prior research, can support the conceptualization process. Therefore, examining how contextualization functions as an operational property of AR and VR in detail in existing studies can aid in defining ARA and VRA. Research has identified three dimensions of contextualization—context mapping, content matching, and consumer experience—as the key operational properties for ARA (De Ruyter et al., 2020) and VRA (Wu et al., 2018).

In ARA, context mapping is the ability to locate physical objects within consumers' environments and compute their perspectives toward those objects (De Ruyter et al., 2020). In studies operationalizing AR (e.g., Sung et al., 2022; Tsai et al., 2020; Yaoyuneyong et al., 2016), participants used mobile devices (e.g., smartphones or tablets) to aim the camera and scan their physical surroundings. This process allows context mapping to visualize and simulate participants' real-world perceptions from their point of view, building a spatial map for placing virtual content in accurate, meaningful positions, thereby enabling subsequent AR experiences (Silva et al., 2003).

In VRA, context mapping refers to the ability to translate consumers' actions into changes within a mediated virtual environment in a natural and predictable manner that mirrors real-life movement (Steuer, 1992; Wu et al., 2018). In studies operationalizing VR (e.g., Lee & Cho, 2023; Nam et al., 2025; Wu et al., 2018), VR systems simulate real-world human movements and objects to enable participants to interact naturally within fully virtual environments. By enabling intuitive control and embodiment through realistic motion correspondence between participants' physical actions and their virtual representations, context mapping enhances the VR experience (Tussyadiah et al., 2018). Thus, context mapping emphasizes that the conceptualization of ARA and VRA must be grounded in consumers' physical environments and movements, which serve as the foundation for placing or generating virtual advertising content, respectively.

Content matching refers to the real-time adaptation of advertising messages to consumers' physical surroundings (De Ruyter et al., 2020), serving as another key operational property of ARA. Once AR maps the environment and simulates consumers' perceptions, it overlays virtual advertising content onto their real-world settings (Yaoyuneyong et al., 2016). This allows participants to see virtual content embedded within their physical environments through creative executions that deliver information fitted to their need and responds to their actions in real time (De Ruyter et al., 2020).

In VRA, content matching means aligning advertising messages with the simulation of consumer behaviors and virtual environment, ensuring that advertising content integrates seamlessly into the computer-generated surroundings to maintain coherence and realism (Lee & Cho, 2023; Wu et al., 2018). Unlike AR, which anchors content in the physical world, VR studies show that advertising content is dynamically tailored to participants' actions, preferences, or roles within the virtual space (Nam et al., 2025; Wedel et al., 2020). Thus, content matching in AR practices informs the definition of ARA, where advertising content is delivered in real time based on consumers' physical surroundings, actions, and needs. In contrast, content matching in VR applications informs the definition of VRA, where advertising relies on internal contextual cues, such as users' actions, gazes, and virtual locations, to deliver messages within a fully virtual environment.

Consumer experience in AR refers to the unique experience of contextualization resulting from real-time context mapping and content matching of physical surroundings (De Ruyter et al., 2020), which is often described as spatial presence in empirical AR research. When consumers perceive and freely interact with virtual advertising content tailored to their physical environments, needs, and actions, they experience a sense of non-mediation—the illusion that the mediated experience is not mediated at all (Lombard & Ditton, 1997). This means that ARA enables consumers to experience virtual advertising content as "being here" within their physical surroundings (Wedel et al., 2020), without consciously recognizing the role of media technology in creating the experience captured in prior studies (e.g., Smink et al., 2020; Sung et al., 2022; Wirth et al., 2007).

Consumer experience in VR refers to the sense of presence within a virtual environment created by VR technology (Steuer, 1992), which is commonly referred to telepresence as the outcome observed in prior VR operationalizations. Whether consumers perceive the environment as a simulation of a real-world scene or as a fully computer-generated or animated virtual world, they experience what Steuer (1992) describes as "a mediated perception of an environment." This suggests that VRA enables consumers to feel as if they are "being there" with the advertising content in the virtual environment as if it were real (Reeves, 1991), which is an experience measured in previous studies (e.g., Kim et al., 2021). The creation and observation of participants' AR and VR experiences in prior studies support the conceptualization of ARA and VRA by emphasizing the need for definitions to highlight consumers' unique contextual experiences, either perceiving advertising content as "being here" in their physical surroundings or "being there" in a virtual environment.

Developing Conceptual Definition

To address conceptual limitations in prior literature such as the overemphasis on technology and the lack of advertising-specific characteristics, this chapter proposes two tentative, yet systematically explicated, domain-specific definitions of ARA and VRA to enhance clarity within the metaverse advertising field. These definitions build upon existing AR and VR conceptualizations (e.g., Kim & Kim, 2014; Yaoyuneyong et al., 2016; Tsai et al., 2020; De Ruyter et al., 2020) and follow systematic concept explication procedures and recommendations (Chaffee, 1991; McLeod et al., 2005; Bergkvist & Eisend, 2023) to refine and tailor them for advertising-specific applications. Specifically, ARA is defined as:

> an advertising that superimposes virtual message content over consumers' real-time, physical environments to enable consumer spatial presence experiences for promoting a product or brand.

In parallel, VRA is defined as:

> an advertising that simulates real-life behaviors and settings and creates virtual message content and environments to enable consumer telepresence experiences for promoting a product or brand.

The proposed definitions align with the key elements of the Interactive Advertising Model (Rodgers & Thorson, 2000), including the composition and integration of ARA and VRA content (message structure), consumers' real-time or real-life interaction with the overlaid or simulated content (i.e., user control), the immediacy and responsiveness of the interactions (i.e., interactivity level), and the subsequent spatial or telepresence experiences (i.e., outcome processing paths). They can further serve as a foundation for advancing empirical research and guiding practical implementation in metaverse advertising practices.

Defining Operationally

Following the proposed conceptual definitions, the next step is to define the concepts operationally by identifying practices that serve as empirical indicators, which are observable elements implemented in real-world settings (Chaffee, 1991; McLeod et al., 2005). Accordingly, this chapter examines how context mapping, content matching, and consumer experience are addressed and manifested in actual advertising practices to develop the operational definitions of ARA and VRA.

In real-world ARA practices, context mapping is achieved through four key techniques: (1) applies computer vision and machine learning to recognize and interpret physical objects, helping advertisers understand consumers' real-world environments (Restrepo-Rodriguez et al., 2019); (2) gaze tracking that uses consumers' cameras to record and simulate their eye movement patterns in real surroundings, offering insights into their perspectives on physical surroundings (Van der Meulen et al., 2017); (3) real-time analytics that collects and analyzes consumer behaviors toward nearby physical objects, revealing their significance and motivational relevance (Binetti et al., 2019); and (4) affordance recognition that estimates the relevance and purpose of physical objects to consumers, generating contextually appropriate advertising messages (De Ruyter et al., 2020). AR can then guide consumers by recommending suitable locations for placing virtual advertising content or by connecting it to their real-world practices (Stevens, 2019). Thus, classifying physical objects, tracking eye movements, analyzing consumer behaviors, and estimating the relevance and purpose of physical objects serve as key indicators for operationalizing context mapping in ARA.

Based on previous studies (e.g., Steuer, 1992), context mapping in real-world VRA practices is primarily driven by, first, vividness that is the delivery of content with high sensory richness and representational clarity. This involves presenting advertising content with enhanced detail and realism to stimulate consumers' senses. Vividness is a stimulus-driven ability of VR technology, relying on its technical capacity to convey information seamlessly and shape consumers' sensory experiences (Rafaeli, 1985).

Two major technical characteristics of VR context mapping contribute to achieving vividness: (1) sensory breadth, which is the ability of VR technology to present advertising content across the senses such as visual, auditory, haptic, channels (Gibson, 1966); and (2) sensory depth, which denotes the resolution and richness of information delivered within each perceptual channel. Hence, the number of sensory channels (quantity) and the richness of information transmitted through them (quality) in a virtual environment represent real-world practices for operationalizing vividness as a key indicator of context mapping in VRA. Second, VRA's context mapping in real-world practice is also achieved through interactivity, which allows consumers to modify the form or content of advertising messages or virtual environments in real time (Steuer, 1992). This also reflects VR systems' stimulus-driven capacity for interactivity, shaped by their technological structure that enables dynamic exchanges between consumers and virtual content (Rafaeli, 1988).

There are three key structural elements of VR context mapping that enable interactivity: (1) speed that means the real-time interaction or response of the virtual content with or toward users' actions; (2) rang that refers to the variety and scope of content attributes users can manipulate; and (3) mapping that is the correspondence between users' real-world actions and virtual-world behaviors. To sum up, the extent of consumer control over advertising content and virtual objects, the number of action possibilities available at any moment, and the system's ability to naturally predict and reflect those actions in the virtual environment represent real-world practices for operationalizing interactivity as another key indicator of VRA's context mapping.

Content matching can be operationalized through three ARA tactics identified by advertising scholars: (1) embedding virtual objects that make virtual advertising content as well integrated into consumers' environments as possible (Hilken et al., 2017); (2) creative executions such as using 3D models, video, or virtual "try-on" overlays that are applied to enhance the connection between virtual advertising content and consumers' real surroundings (Hilken et al., 2017); and (3) fitting information to task that provides details matching consumers' real-time surroundings, actions, or needs when they are viewing the ARA content (Baek et al., 2018). Therefore, the extent to which ARA embeds virtual advertising content, employs creative executions, and tailors information to consumers' surroundings, actions, or needs serves as the indicators for operationalizing content matching in ARA.

VRA's content matching can be operationalized through three real-world practices documented in the literature (e.g., Marache-Francisco & Brangier,

2013): (1) real object simulation that designs virtual versions of real advertising elements (e.g., product 3D models, consumer avatars) integrated naturally into the virtual environment (e.g., game-like settings); (2) creative executions that use multisensory stimuli (e.g., visual, auditory, haptic) to help consumers interact with and experience advertising content in creative ways in the virtual environments; and (3) hyper-personalization that leverages behavioral data from VRA combined with other data related to consumption behaviors to generate tailored messages to influence consumer responses toward the advertised objects. Hence, the extent to which advertising content is designed into virtualized environments, presented through sensory stimuli, and personalized using consumers' behavioral data and personal information in VR to generate advertising messages serves as the indicators for operationalizing content matching in VRA.

In terms of consumer experience, spatial presence is the goal of conducting ARA since it allows consumers to perceive virtual advertising content as part of their real surroundings, thereby enhancing advertising content's personal relevance (Hilken et al., 2017). Hence, the extent to which ARA makes consumers feel advertising content is contextually realistic, personalized, and relevant to them serves as the key indicators for operationalizing consumer experience in real-world ARA observations. On the other hand, VRA practices aim to evoke the experience of telepresence, allowing consumers to perceive themselves as present in the virtual environment and interact with virtually realistic, sensory-rich, and responsive advertising content as part of the virtual settings, ultimately making the experience more immersive and personal. Therefore, the extent to which VRA makes consumers perceive advertising content as virtually realistic, engaging, and personalized serves as the key indicator of consumer experience in real-world VRA practices.

Application Example: Augmented and Virtual Narrative Advertising

One key advantage of AR and VR is their flexibility to integrate with various advertising formats such as gamified, social media, and narrative advertising (Scholz & Smith, 2016; Tsou & Rodgers, 2024). As AR and VR technologies evolve, there is a growing need for updated definitions that clearly delineate and guide their various applications in advertising (Bergkvist & Eisend, 2023). However, existing studies have not defined or demonstrated how to conceptualize specific types of advertising that fundamentally change when incorporating AR or VR, making it challenging to design and evaluate their effects with precision.

This chapter uses the popular integration of AR or VR technology with narrative messages, i.e., augmented narrative advertising (ANA) or virtual narrative advertising (VNA), as an example to illustrate how AR and VR transform specific formats of advertising and make them distinct. ANA and VNA are the concepts emerging from the integration of AR or VR functions with story structures (Nam, 2015), encompassing both AR or VR and narrative as core components. To enable precise identification, design, and evaluation of ANA and VNA in the advertising field, this chapter again follows the established concept explication procedures (Chaffee, 1991; McLeod et al., 2005), focusing specifically on narrative, to combine with the earlier explication of AR and VR to develop a clear, domain-specific definition of ANA and VNA.

Literature review on definitions of narrative. Compared to AR and VR, narrative has a longer history as a communication technique and has been widely applied across various contexts such as health, politics, science, and education where scholars have proposed definitions. For instance, Kreuter et al. (2007) defined narrative as "a representation of connected events and characters that has an identifiable structure, is bounded in space and time, and contains implicit or explicit messages about the topic being addressed" (p. 222), a definition that captures a broad range of story types within the health communication domain. A meta-analysis of narrative research in communication contexts defined narrative as "any cohesive and coherent story with an identifiable beginning, middle, and end that provides information about scene, characters, and conflict; raises unanswered questions or unresolved conflict; and provides resolution" (Hinyard & Kreuter, 2007, p. 778).

These definitions consistently highlight the core features of narrative (i.e., story elements, identifiable structure, and the topic being addressed), even when adapted for different purposes and contexts. Many scholars have also defined narrative specifically within advertising contexts. These definitions emphasize the communication perspective while adapting narrative's message features to fit advertising goals. For example, Escalas (2003) conceptualized narrative as a type of advertising that tells a story by depicting "one or more episodes consisting of actors engaged in actions to achieve goals" in a "sequence initiated by some events and actions result[ing] in outcome(s)" (p. 273).

Building on this, Chang (2013) defined narrative advertising as content that "depicts product consumption and its consequences or employs plots associated with what people desire, such as romance, achievement, adventure, or hopes" (p. 55). The most recent definition of narrative advertising describes it as "a type of advertisement that conveys the message of interest to the consumer about the brand and product through a plot by using narrative elements such as narrative characters, temporality, and spatiality" (Şahin & Yilmaz, 2022, p. 13). This definition adapts the earlier notion of the "topic being addressed" to fit the advertising context by framing it as "promoting products or brands to consumers." Based on the review of studies conceptualizing AR, VR, and narrative, defining ANA and VNA requires addressing three key points: (1) identifying the essential technological functions of AR and VR and the core message features of narrative used in advertising; (2) emphasizing the communication perspective and advertising elements; and (3) linking AR's and VR's technological functions to narrative structures in ways that are adaptable to advertising contexts.

Examining operational properties of narrative. Narrative has been operationalized across diverse contexts such as politics, education, health, law, and advertising

(Ryan, 2007); depending on the study's purpose and context, three core properties consistently emerge (i.e., story elements, identifiable structure, and topic being addressed), serving as a foundation for conceptualizing ANA and VNA. Story elements refer to the events, characters, settings, and supporting objects used jointly to tell a story (Branigan, 2013). In operationalizations of narrative, one or more scenes typically depict characters engaging in goal-directed actions initiated by specific events and culminating in particular outcomes (e.g., Escalas, 1998). Hence, prior operationalizations of narrative typically include specific story elements and depict their interrelationships to effectively convey a story (e.g., Escalas, 2003, 2004, 2007; Chang, 2009, 2013).

This informs the conceptualization of ANA and VNA by highlighting the overlaid content in AR or the simulation of VR content that serves as narrative elements, which are meaningfully connected to each other and to consumers' physical or virtual environments. Identifiable structures refer to the organized frameworks through which these story elements are arranged into coherent plots that drive story progression (Polkinghorne, 1995). In previous studies (e.g., Escalas, 2003, 2004, 2007; Chang, 2009, 2013; Lien & Chen, 2013), two key structural features of narrative have been identified: chronology and causality. Chronology refers to organizing story plots as a sequence of events unfolding over time (Polkinghorne, 1991). Causality means structuring events based on inferred cause-and-effect relationships (Escalas, 1998). For defining ANA and VNA, this means that the overlaid or simulated story content is structured according to the chronology and causality of the story plot. The topic being addressed refers to the central idea conveyed explicitly or implicitly by the story, intended to shape viewers' responses to the causes and potential solutions to a problem (Kreuter et al., 2007). In advertising studies, the topics conveyed through narratives typically center on the advertised objects such as products or brands by presenting plots related to consumers' needs or problems that can be addressed through consuming products or brands (Chang, 2012, 2013). This informs the conceptualization of ANA and VNA by highlighting that the topic expressed through virtual augmentation or simulation is focused on promoting a product or brand.

Developing conceptual definitions of ANA and VNA. Based on the literature review of prior definitions of AR, VR, and narrative, which identifies their essential elements, and the examination of their operational properties, which informs the conceptualization of ANA and VNA, this chapter proposes conceptual definitions for ANA and VNA. The definition of ANA requires that AR's technological functions enable story elements and structure to: (1) be superimposed onto consumers' physical environments; (2) be presented in response to consumers' real-time surroundings and actions; and (3) provide consumers with contextually realistic and relevant story experiences. Accordingly, the conceptual definition of ANA proposed in this chapter is:

"a story that superimposes virtual story content over consumers' real-time, physical environments to enable consumer spatial experiences of the story for promoting a product or brand."

Meanwhile, the definition of VNA requires that VR's technological functions enable story elements and structure to: (1) simulate consumers' real-life behaviors and environments; (2) be created in response to consumers' real-time movements and actions within the virtual world; and (3) provide consumers with virtually realistic and responsive story experiences. Accordingly, the conceptual definition of VNA proposed in this chapter is:

"a story that simulates real-life behaviors and settings and creates virtual story content and environments to enable consumer telepresence experiences of the story for promoting a product or brand."

The proposed definitions underscore the importance of examining how AR and VR technologies interact with specific advertising messages, such as narratives, thereby advancing both theoretical understanding and practical applications of metaverse technologies in advertising.

Defining ANA and VNA operationally. In advertising, narratives are operationalized through four key elements: (1) events, which meaningfully transform the world from one state to another to serve as the foundation for story plots (Polkinghorne, 1991); (2) settings, which define the temporal and spatial context of where and when events unfold (Murray, 2003); (3) characters, who perform actions that convey personality, attitudes, and interpersonal dynamics within the narrative (Young et al., 2013); and (4) supporting objects, including audiovisual media or props, which assist in telling the story (Phillips & McQuarrie, 2010). Hence, the presence of story events, settings, characters, and/or supporting objects overlaid or simulated serves as an indicator for the operationalization of story elements in ANA and VNA. Moreover, in storytelling practices, stories are commonly structured in three main ways based on the features of chronology and causality: (1) chronological order, which arranges and presents the causal relationships among story events from the earliest to the latest points of occurrence; (2) backward order, which proceeds from the latest to the earliest events, allowing viewers to encounter consequences before uncovering their causes; and (3) non-chronological order, which presents story events out of sequence, such as through flashbacks, embedded narratives, or flashforwards, to support specific understandings of causal relationships (Ushiro et al., 2011).

Therefore, the augmentation or simulation of story events based on their chronological sequence and causal relationships serves as indicators for operationalizing the structure of ANA and VNA. In narrative advertising practices, the topic being addressed typically involves conveying information about the advertised product or brand. This includes the origin and development of the product or brand, the experience of consuming or interacting with it, and the outcomes associated with its use (Solja, Liljander, & Söderlund, 2018). Therefore, the key indicator for operationalizing the "topic being addressed" in ANA and VNA is the promotion of the product or brand through augmentation or simulation.

In conclusion, this chapter provides a comprehensive framework for defining and operationalizing ARA and VRA through a formal, systematic concept explication process tailored to advertising research and further to specific formats of advertising. The proposed definitions enhance theoretical clarity and support empirical testing within the context of metaverse advertising. Looking ahead, future research can build upon these definitions to explore how evolving metaverse technologies can be integrated with diverse advertising message strategies. Continuous and specified conceptualization and further research will be essential in unlocking the full potential of metaverse technologies in interactive advertising.

References

Azuma, R. T. (1997). A survey of augmented reality. *Presence: Teleoperators & Virtual Environments, 6*(4), 355–385. https://doi.org/10.1162/pres.1997.6.4.355

Baek, T. H., Yoo, C. Y., & Yoon, S. (2018). Augment yourself through virtual mirror: The impact of self-viewing and narcissism on consumer responses. *International Journal of Advertising, 37*(3), 421–439. https://doi.org/10.1080/02650487.2016.1244887

Bergkvist, L., & Eisend, M. (2023). Changes in definitions and operationalizations in advertising research—Justified or not? *Journal of Advertising, 52*(3), 468–476. https://doi.org/10.1080/00913367.2022.2077268

Binetti, N., Cheng, T., Mareschal, I., Brumby, D., Julier, S., & Bianchi-Berthouze, N. (2019). Assumptions about the positioning of virtual stimuli affect gaze direction estimates during Augmented Reality based interactions. *Scientific Reports, 9*(1), 2566. https://www.nature.com/articles/s41598-019-39311-1

Branigan, E. (2013). *Narrative comprehension and film*. Routledge.

Chaffee, S. H. (1991). *Communication concepts: Explication*. Sage.

Chang, C. (2009). "Being hooked" by editorial content: The implications for processing narrative advertising. *Journal of Advertising, 38*(1), 21–34. https://doi.org/10.2753/JOA0091-3367380102

Chang, C. (2012). How people tell an ad story: Western vs. Asian styles. *Asian Journal of Communication, 22*(3), 235–252. https://doi.org/10.1080/01292986.2012.662516

Chang, C. (2013). Imagery fluency and narrative advertising effects. *Journal of Advertising, 42*(1), 54–68. https://doi.org/10.1080/00913367.2012.749087

De Ruyter, K., Heller, J., Hilken, T., Chylinski, M., Keeling, D. I., & Mahr, D. (2020). Seeing with the customer's eye: Exploring the challenges and opportunities of AR advertising. *Journal of Advertising, 49*(2), 109–124. https://doi.org/10.1080/00913367.2020.1740123

Errmann, A. (2025). Mindful immersion: Curating awe-inducing experiences to increase brand salience. *Journal of Advertising, 54*(2), 251–265. https://doi.org/10.1080/00913367.2024.2325144

Escalas, J. E. (2003). Advertising narratives: What are they and how do they work? In B. B. Stern (Ed.), *Representing Consumers* (pp. 283–305). Routledge. https://www.taylorfrancis.com/chapters/edit/10.4324/9780203380260-19/advertising-narratives-jennifer-edson-escalas

Escalas, J. E. (2004). Narrative processing: Building consumer connections to brands. *Journal of Consumer Psychology, 14*(1–2), 168–180. https://doi.org/10.1207/s15327663jcp1401&2_19

Escalas, J. E. (2007). Self-referencing and persuasion: Narrative transportation versus analytical elaboration. *Journal of Consumer Research, 33*(4), 421–429. https://doi.org/10.1086/510216

Gibson, J. J. (1966). *The senses considered as perceptual systems*. Houghton Mifflin.

Gonçalves, G., Meirinhos, G., Filipe, V., Melo, M., & Bessa, M. (2022). Virtual reality e-commerce: Contextualization and gender impact on user memory and user perception of functionalities and size of products. *IEEE Access*, *10*, 92491–92504. https://doi.org/10.1109/ACCESS.2022.3198957

Hilken, T., De Ruyter, K., Chylinski, M., Mahr, D., & Keeling, D. I. (2017). Augmenting the eye of the beholder: Exploring the strategic potential of augmented reality to enhance online service experiences. *Journal of the Academy of Marketing Science*, *45*(6), 884–905. https://doi.org/10.1007/s11747-017-0541-x

Hinyard, L. J., & Kreuter, M. W. (2007). Using narrative communication as a tool for health behavior change: A conceptual, theoretical, and empirical overview. *Health Education & Behavior*, *34*(5), 777–792. https://doi.org/10.1177/1090198106291963

Höllerer, T., & Feiner, S. (2004). Mobile augmented reality. In H. A. Karimi & A. Hammad (Eds.), *Telegeoinformatics: Location-based Computing and Services* (pp. 221–260). Taylor & Francis.

International Data Corporation (IDC). (2023). Worldwide spending on augmented and virtual reality forecast to reach $13.8 billion in 2023, according to a new IDC spending guide. https://www.idc.com/getdoc.jsp?containerId=prUS50932423

Kim, J. H., Kim, M., Park, M., & Yoo, J. (2021). How interactivity and vividness influence consumer virtual reality shopping experience: The mediating role of telepresence. *Journal of Research in Interactive Marketing*, *15*(3), 502–525. https://doi.org/10.1108/JRIM-07-2020-0148

Kim, Y. G., & Kim, W. J. (2014). Implementation of augmented reality system for smartphone advertisements. *International Journal of Multimedia and Ubiquitous Engineering*, *9*(2), 385–392. https://doi.org/10.14257/ijmue.2014.9.2.39

Kiousis, S. (2002). Interactivity: a concept explication. *New Media & Society*, *4*(3), 355–383.

Kreuter, M. W., Green, M. C., Cappella, J. N., Slater, M. D., Wise, M. E., Storey, D., … & Woolley, S. (2007). Narrative communication in cancer prevention and control: A framework to guide research and application. *Annals of Behavioral Medicine*, *33*(3), 221–235. https://doi.org/10.1007/BF02879904

Lee, H., & Cho, C.-H. (2019). Is augmented reality advertising a cure-all? An empirical investigation of the impact of innovation resistance on augmented reality advertising effectiveness. *International Journal of Contents*, *15*(3), 21–31.

Lee, H., & Cho, C. H. (2023). Virtual brand experience in digital reality advertising: Conceptualization and measurement. *Journal of Consumer Behaviour*, *22*(2), 300–313. https://doi.org/10.1002/cb.2126

Li, H., Daugherty, T., & Biocca, F. (2002). Impact of 3-D advertising on product knowledge, brand attitude, and purchase intention: The mediating role of presence. *Journal of Advertising*, *31*(3), 43–57.

Lien, N. H., & Chen, Y. L. (2013). Narrative ads: The effect of argument strength and story format. *Journal of Business Research*, *66*(4), 516–522. https://doi.org/10.1016/j.jbusres.2011.12.016

Lo, W. H., & Cheng, K. L. B. (2020). Does virtual reality attract visitors? The mediating effect of presence on consumer response in virtual reality tourism advertising. *Information Technology & Tourism*, *22*(4), 537–562.

Lombard, M., & Ditton, T. (1997). At the heart of it all: The concept of presence. *Journal of Computer-Mediated Communication*, *3*(2), JCMC321. https://doi.org/10.1111/j.1083-6101.1997.tb00072.x

MacKenzie, S. B. (2003). The dangers of poor construct conceptualization. *Journal of the Academy of Marketing Science, 31*(3), 323–326. https://doi.org/10.1177/0092070303031003011

Marache-Francisco, C., & Brangier, E. (2013). Process of gamification: Between graphical design and persuasive design. In *Proceedings of the 2013 DUXU/HCII*, 126–131. https://eric.brangier.free.fr/Pdf/centric_2013_6_40_30073%20(1)%20Marache+Brangier.pdf

Market.us. (2024). *AR and VR in marketing market to be worth USD 24.2 billion by 2033*. Scoop. https://www.market.us/report/ar-and-vr-in-marketing-market/

McLeod, J. M., Pan, Z., Dunwoody, S., & Becker, L. (2005). Concept explication and theory construction. In S. Dunwoody (Ed.), *The evolution of key mass communication concepts: Honoring Jack M. McLeod* (pp. 13–76). Lawrence Erlbaum Associates.

Murray, M. (2003). Narrative psychology and narrative analysis. In P. M. Camic, J. E. Rhodes, & L. Yardley (Eds.), *Qualitative research in psychology: Expanding perspectives in methodology and design* (pp. 95–112). American Psychological Association.

Nam, H. W., Lee, S. J., Kim, J. J., Lee, J. Y., & Cho, M. (2025). Development and training operation analysis results of virtual reality/augmented reality training simulator for radiation emergency medicine. *Nuclear Engineering and Technology*, 103477. https://doi.org/10.1016/j.net.2025.103477

Nam, Y. (2015). Designing interactive narratives for mobile augmented reality. *Cluster Computing, 18*(1), 309–320. https://doi.org/10.1007/s10586-014-0354-3

Phillips, B. J., & McQuarrie, E. F. (2010). Narrative and persuasion in fashion advertising. *Journal of Consumer Research, 37*(3), 368–392. https://doi.org/10.1086/653087

Polkinghorne, D. E. (1991). Narrative and self-concept. *Journal of Narrative and Life History, 1*(2–3), 135–153. https://doi.org/10.1075/jnlh.1.2-3.04nar

Polkinghorne, D. E. (1995). Narrative configuration in qualitative analysis. *International Journal of Qualitative Studies in Education, 8*(1), 5–23. https://doi.org/10.1080/0951839950080103

Rafaeli, S. (1985). If the computer is a medium, what is the message: Explicating interactivity. In *Proceedings of International Communication Association annual convention,* Dallas, TX.

Rafaeli, S. (1988). From new media to communication. *Sage Annual Review of Communication Research: Advancing Communication Science, 16*(1), 110–134.

RaveSpace. (2025). *The metaverse in 2025: A comprehensive analysis of its technology, economy, and society*. https://www.grandviewresearch.com/industry-analysis/metaverse-market-report

Reeves, B. (1991). Being there: Television as symbolic versus natural experience. *Unpublished manuscript, Institute for Communication Research, Stanford University.*

Restrepo Rodriguez, A. O., Casas Mateus, D. E., Gaona Garcia, P. A., Gomez Acosta, A., & Montenegro Marin, C. E. (2019). Segmentation methods for image classification using a convolutional neural network on AR-Sandbox. In J. MacIntyre, I. Maglogiannis, L. Iliadis, & E. Pimenidis (Eds.), *Proceedings of 2019 Artificial Intelligence Applications and Innovations: 15th IFIP WG 12.5 International Conference* (pp. 391–398). Springer International Publishing. https://doi.org/10.1007/978-3-030-19823-7_33

Rodgers, S., & Thorson, E. (2000). The interactive advertising model: How users perceive and process online ads. *Journal of Interactive Advertising, 1*(1), 41–60. https://doi.org/10.1080/15252019.2000.10722043

Ryan, M. L. (2007). Toward a definition of narrative. In D. Herman (Ed.), *The Cambridge Companion to Narrative*, (pp. 22–35). Cambridge University Press.

Şahin, S., & Yılmaz, R. (2022). Grandiose Mirrors of the Self: The Narcissistic Narrative in Ads. In *Narrative Theory and Therapy in the Post-Truth Era* (pp. 11–25). IGI Global. https://doi.org/10.4018/978-1-7998-9251-9.ch002

Sands, S., Ferraro, C., Demsar, V., Cohen, J., & Gvirtz, A. (2024). Immersive advertising—A review and research agenda: Potential effects of and considerations for AR, VR, and MR advertisements. *Journal of Advertising Research, 64*(3), 284–300. https://doi.org/10.2501/JAR-2024-018

Scholz, J., & Smith, A. N. (2016). Augmented reality: Designing immersive experiences that maximize consumer engagement. *Business Horizons, 59*(2), 149–161. https://doi.org/10.1016/j.bushor.2015.10.003

Silva, R., Oliveira, J. C., & Giraldi, G. A. (2003). Introduction to augmented reality. *National Laboratory for Scientific Computation, 11*, 1–11. https://lncc.br/~jauvane/papers/RelatorioTecnicoLNCC-2503.pdf

Slater, M., & Wilbur, S. (1997). A framework for immersive virtual environments (FIVE): Speculations on the role of presence in virtual environments. *Presence: Teleoperators and virtual environments, 6*(6), 603–616.

Smink, A. R., Van Reijmersdal, E. A., Van Noort, G., & Neijens, P. C. (2020). Shopping in augmented reality: The effects of spatial presence, personalization and intrusiveness on app and brand responses. *Journal of Business Research, 118*, 474–485. https://doi.org/10.1016/j.jbusres.2020.07.018

Solja, E., Liljander, V., & Söderlund, M. (2018). Short brand stories on packaging: An examination of consumer responses. *Psychology & Marketing, 35*(4), 294–306. https://doi.org/10.1002/mar.21087

Spotts, H. E., Weinberger, M. G., & Parsons, A. L. (2014). Assessing the effectiveness of advertising regulation: A policy analysis approach. *Journal of Public Policy & Marketing, 33*(1), 132–147.

Steuer, J. (1992). Defining virtual reality: Dimensions determining telepresence. *Journal of Communication, 42*(4), 73–93. https://doi.org/10.1111/j.1460-2466.1992.tb00812.x

Stevens, B. (2019). IKEA's AR App Now Lets You Visualise Entire Rooms and Introduces Visual Search. https://www.chargedretail.co.uk/2019/09/26/ikeas-ar-app-now-lets-you-visualise-entire-rooms-and-introduces-visual-search/

Sung, E., Han, D. I. D., & Choi, Y. K. (2022). Augmented reality advertising via a mobile app. *Psychology & Marketing, 39*(3), 543–558. https://doi.org/10.1002/mar.21632

Sutherland, I. E. (1965). The ultimate display. In *Proceedings of the IFIP Congress, 2*, 506–508.

Tain, J. (2020). The role of contextualization in immersive media: Frameworks for evaluating AR and VR experiences. *Journal of Interactive Media Research, 42*(3), 215–234.

Taylor, C. R. (2021). How should we regulate advertising in the evolving digital age?. *International Journal of Advertising, 40*(6), 849–853.

Tsai, W. H. S., Tian, S. C., Chuan, C. H., & Li, C. (2020). Inspection or play? A study of how augmented reality technology can be utilized in advertising. *Journal of Interactive Advertising, 20*(3), 244–257. https://doi.org/10.1080/15252019.2020.1738292

Tsou, T. H., & Rodgers, S. (2024). Augmented narrative advertising: Consumer responses to AR story filters and product placement primes. *Journal of Interactive Advertising, 24*(4), 303–323. https://doi.org/10.1080/15252019.2024.2383761

Tussyadiah, I. P., Wang, D., Jung, T. H., & Tom Dieck, M. C. (2018). Virtual reality, presence, and attitude change: Empirical evidence from tourism. *Tourism management, 66*, 140–154. https://doi.org/10.1016/j.tourman.2017.12.003

Ushiro, Y., Kai, A., Shimizu, H., Hoshino, Y., Nahatame, S., Hasegawa, Y., …& Nakagawa, C. (2011). Effects of flashback on Japanese EFL readers' narrative comprehension. *Arele: Annual Review of English Language Education in Japan, 22*, 111–126. https://doi.org/10.20581/arele.22.0_111

Van der Meulen, H., Kun, A. L., & Shaer, O. (2017, October). What are we missing? Adding eye-tracking to the hololens to improve gaze estimation accuracy. In *Proceedings of the 2017 ACM International Conference on Interactive Surfaces and Spaces* (pp. 396–400). Brighton, UK: ACM.

Wedel, M., Bigné, E., & Zhang, J. (2020). Virtual and augmented reality: Advancing research in consumer marketing. *International Journal of Research in Marketing, 37*(3), 443–465. https://doi.org/10.1016/j.ijresmar.2020.04.004

Wirth, W., Hartmann, T., Böcking, S., Vorderer, P., Klimmt, C., Schramm, H., …& Jäncke, P. (2007). A process model of the formation of spatial presence experiences. *Media Psychology, 9*(3), 493–525. https://doi.org/10.1080/15213260701283079

Wu, D. Y., & Lin, J. H. T. (2018). Ways of seeing matter: the impact of a naturally mapped perceptual system on the persuasive effects of immersive virtual reality advertising. *Communication Research Reports, 35*(5), 434–444.

Yaoyuneyong, G., Foster, J., Johnson, E., & Johnson, D. (2016). Augmented reality marketing: Consumer preferences and attitudes toward hypermedia print ads. *Journal of Interactive Advertising, 16*(1), 16–30. https://doi.org/10.1080/15252019.2015.1125316

Yim, M. Y. C., & Park, S. Y. (2019). "I am not satisfied with my body, so I like augmented reality (AR)": Consumer responses to AR-based product presentations. *Journal of Business Research, 100*, 581–589.

Young, R. M., Ware, S. G., Cassell, B. A., & Robertson, J. (2013). Plans and planning in narrative generation: A review of plan-based approaches to the generation of story, discourse and interactivity in narratives. *Sprache und Datenverarbeitung: Special Issue on Formal and Computational Models of Narrative, 37*(1–2), 41–64. https://www.justusrobertson.com/papers/Young%20Ware%20Cassell%20and%20Robertson%202013%20-%20Plans%20and%20Planning%20in%20Narrative%20Generation.pdf

Yuen, S. C. Y., Yaoyuneyong, G., & Johnson, E. (2011). Augmented reality: An overview and five directions for AR in education. *Journal of Educational Technology Development and Exchange (JETDE), 4*(1), 119–140.

Zhao, Z., & Balagué, C. (2015). Designing branded mobile apps: Fundamentals and recommendations. *Business Horizons, 58*(3), 305–315. https://doi.org/10.1016/j.bushor.2015.01.004

Zhu, W., & Owen, C. B. (2008). Design of the promopad: An automated augmented-reality shopping assistant. *Journal of Organizational and End User Computing, 20*(3), 41–56. https://doi.org/10.4018/joeuc.2008070103

16 The Advertising Experience and the Power of (Tele)Presence

Matthew Lombard and Jennifer Snyder-Duch

Introduction

> At the heart of the [flagship London] store sits a technological marvel — a custom-engineered 360-degree projection dome that serves as an immersive basecamp. This installation, only the second of its kind worldwide, transforms a The North Face tent into an extraordinary digital canvas. Five synchronized Optoma projectors utilizing advanced Vioso projection technology create an immersive experience through AI-generated content that flows through day-to-night transitions and seasonal changes. The 30-minute visual journey, enhanced by nature soundscapes and custom scenting, transports visitors from the city streets to remote wilderness locations. … The innovative approach has shown remarkable results in customer engagement, with the immersive elements significantly increasing dwell time and repeat visits. The combination of cutting-edge technology and thoughtful design has created a space that resonates with both outdoor enthusiasts and urban explorers, proving that experiential retail can successfully bridge the gap between product showcase and brand storytelling.
>
> –Mood Media (n/d)

> Using consumer data from various sources (e.g., browsing patterns, the user's demographics data, public Facebook Likes or Instagram posts) in combination with predictive algorithms, [companies] could first generate detailed profiles of their consumers' psychological traits. These profiles could then be automatically funneled to generative AI models designed to automatically create persuasive communication ("write an ad for toothpaste X that is shown to an extraverted, 33 years old man, who is likely to pay up to $6 for the product"). In addition to personalized textual content, such algorithms could also produce visual content (still or video) or auditory stimuli. The combined marketing message could subsequently be displayed to the consumer in real-time and adjusted dynamically based on the consumer's interaction with the content.
>
> – Matz et al. (2024)

DOI: 10.4324/9781003567523-20

> The ongoing progress of building the metaverse is creating abundant creative opportunities for advertisers in the near future. It's likely that advertising storytelling will shift toward a more immersive, personalized and memorable first-person experience, allowing for interactive engagement with brands and products and positive outcomes. Essentially, advertising will be both entertaining and effective. - Paula Celestino, SPRK Media Group Inc.
>
> – Forbes Council Expert Panel (2023, May 5)

Advertising in the traditional media environment was defined as "a form of controlled communication that attempts to persuade consumers, through use of a variety of strategies and appeals, to buy or use a particular product or service" (Defleur & Dennis, 1996, p. 564) and, relatedly, "paid nonpersonal communication from an identified sponsor using mass media to persuade or influence an audience" (Wells et al., 1998, p. 13). As the examples above suggest, we have entered a new age in which advertising is much more interactive and personalized to consumers. In addition, advances in technology have prompted users to engage much differently in their media environment, and this has presented advertisers with substantial challenges and strategic opportunities in developing the relationship between consumers and brands.

In this chapter, we describe key characteristics of advertising today and explain how the concept of telepresence, or presence, in which media users overlook or misperceive the role of technology in their experience, offers a valuable framework for the study and practice of advertising today and in the future.

The Changing Nature of Advertising

In 2001, we argued that advertisers had an opportunity to take advantage of emerging technologies to provide a new advertising experience:

> The internet and other interactive technologies make it possible to create ads that are not only more targeted, but more personal, in which advertising is an experience in which the consumer participates and is engaged. Thus, the model of advertising as communication that is nonpersonal and controlled exclusively by the sponsor seems to be evolving into one in which advertising is personal and interactive. Interactive advertising gives consumers more control by giving them a range of choices in their experience with product information. And it produces a sense that the communication is more personal than traditional media ads because it creates or simulates a one-on-one interaction.
>
> (Lombard & Snyder-Duch, 2001, p. 56)

Over the past quarter century, advertising has certainly evolved in the ways that we predicted. The goal of consumer advertising—to persuade individuals to purchase a product or service—remains the same. However, technological advances have drastically changed the nature of ads and media consumers' advertising experiences. Based on academic and industry literature, three characteristics strongly distinguish digital advertising from advertising in traditional media such as newspapers, magazines, radio, and television: interactivity, personalization, and engagement.

Interactivity

Interactivity emerged as a defining attribute of "new media" in the early years of the digital age (Kim & McMillan, 2008). It can be defined simply as "a characteristic of a medium in which the user can influence the form and/or content of the mediated presentation or experience" (Lombard & Snyder-Duch, 2001, p. 57). As Bezjian-Avery et al. (1998) explain,

> Whereas in traditional advertising, the presentation is linear and the consumer is passively exposed to product information, for interactive advertising, the consumer instead actively traverses the information. The pieces of information the consumer sees depends on where the consumer wants to go.
>
> (p. 24)

Media can vary in degree from not interactive to highly interactive based on several variables. While a banner ad is interactive in that it allows a user to click through for more information, advertising experiences like those described in the opening of this chapter allow users to enter a real-time, realistic experience where they feel as if they are using the product (see Table 16.1 for a description and examples of variables that affect degree of interactivity).

Research and commentary about interactive advertising are ultimately about the amount and nature of control given to the consumer in the digital environment. The literature makes it clear that digital media allow for a level of interactivity that has changed the relationship between the advertiser and the consumer (Jenkins et al., 2013; Rodgers & Thorson, 2017; Turow & Draper, 2014), with research suggesting that interactive ads promote more positive attitudes toward products and brands (Sundar & Kim, 2005) and contribute to ad effectiveness (Arroyo-Cañada & Gil-Lafuente, 2012). In many cases, interactivity enables the interested consumer to choose to learn more about the product, make a purchase decision, and order the product all in real time. On the other hand, ads that disrupt a consumer's media use, as traditional television and radio ads did, remove choice and are often judged as annoying and may cause negative attitudes toward a brand (Bright, 2011; Edwards et al., 2002; Smith, 2012; Tanyel et al., 2013).

The increasingly diverse contexts, forms, and degrees of interactivity in advertising messages—including on social media and in immersive in-store and

Table 16.1 Variables that Influence the Degree of Interactivity of a Mediated Experience

Variable	*Examples*
The number of inputs from the user that the medium accepts and to which it responds.	*A basic website accepts cursor movement and selection via keyboard/mouse while virtual reality may accept and respond to body and head movement via tracking sensors; selections via button-presses on controllers/joystick; and even audio/voice input, text via virtual keyboard, hand and finger movement, haptic pressure, eye movement, facial expression, or physiological inputs such as heart rate, muscle tension and skin conductance.*
The number and type of characteristics of the mediated presentation or experience that can be modified by the user.	*A viewer of streaming video (e.g., on YouTube) can modify image size and resolution, amount and language of text on the screen, volume and pace. A video game player can modify these, along with their avatar's appearance, content (e.g., the course of the game play, which parts of the game-world are explored), and duration.*
The range or amount of change possible in each characteristic.	*Users of basic videogames can select among a small set of generic virtual representations (avatars) and environments while users of virtual worlds such as Roblox can select and modify many elements of their avatar and environment.*
The speed at which the medium responds to user inputs (asynchronous vs. synchronous, long vs. short lag).	*Responses to an email message may take hours or days (asynchronous) while responses in a chatroom are immediate (synchronous). Responses to actions on a platform, operating system, or other software while using an older, slower computer can be noticeably slower than the responses to the same actions while using a modern, faster computer.*
The degree of correspondence between the type of user input and the type of medium response (natural mapping).	*Using a combination of keystrokes or moving a joystick to cause a player to kick a soccer ball in a basic video game represents unnatural mapping, while making a kicking movement with one's leg and foot to cause the same action in a virtual reality environment represents natural mapping.*

virtual environments—highlight the central role of interactivity in the contemporary consumer advertising experience.

Personalization

Personalization can be described broadly as the "tailoring of message content and delivery based on data collection or covert observation of users, to increase the personal relevance of the message" (Bang & Wojdynski, 2016, p. 868). Personalization has long been central to consumer advertising strategy. Advertisers want consumers to feel that ads are meant specifically for them. For over 50 years, advertisers have used psychographic research, in addition to basic demographic segmentation, to create personal advertising appeals through their media placement and through storytelling that addresses consumers' specific needs, values, and beliefs and depicts how products fit into their lives (Wells et al., 1998). Digital technology has provided the marketing and advertising industries with sophisticated new methods to assess consumers' demographic traits, media habits, and lifestyles and use the information to personalize messages. "As a consumer travels in the virtual, or digital world, everywhere he or she goes, and everything he or she does, leaves a trail of bits of information because almost all actions and activities are recorded" (Dickey & Lewis, 2011, p. 25).

The strong trend, then, has been toward more and more personal advertising. Today we find companies investing in sophisticated and expensive tracking (particularly on websites and social media platforms and increasingly in virtual reality [VR] environments), algorithms, and creative techniques such as "real-time bidding," which allows online advertisers to adapt content—including price, product details, and product variations—at the moment when users interact with the ad (Minsker, 2013; Viktoratos & Tsadiras, 2021).

The last decade has seen a significant increase in research on personalization in advertising, particularly as artificial intelligence (AI) has enabled many industries to streamline user experiences while collecting vast amounts of behavioral data and improved the capabilities and efficiency of research about and targeting of consumers (Kumar et al., 2024; Metz, 2025). Recent research on personalization focuses heavily on the balance between the appeal of tailored content and the intrusiveness some consumers experience as a result of the methods used to collect their data. Dominant findings suggest that too much personalization without transparency causes feelings of intrusiveness and lack of trust, but too little personalization risks irrelevance and lack of consumer attention or interest.

While personalized advertising often causes discomfort and privacy concerns, some research shows that this response can be reduced when consumers understand how their data is collected and used. In 2009, Turow et al. surveyed American adults and found that a majority were not in favor of personalized advertising, and the percentage of those who reported that they did not want personalized ads was even higher when they were made aware of the techniques used by marketers and advertisers to gather personal data. A recent study by Alhelaly et al. (2025) found that privacy intrusiveness had a direct negative effect on both emotional and behavioral responses to personalized ads even when personalization improved content relevance for consumers. Over-personalization (with lack of transparency) is even referred to by some as the "creepiness factor" (Alhelaly et al., 2025; Schomer, 2021). The creepiness factor plays a role in current perceptions of technology, as reflected in public discourse—such as suspicions that digital assistants like Apple's Siri and Amazon's Alexa are always listening, and the common belief that real-life conversations lead to targeted product recommendations on our devices. However, some of the current research finds that clear privacy policies and ability to understand, opt-in, or manage personalization settings can reduce the feeling of intrusion caused by ads (Alhelaly et al., 2025; Lee et al., 2024).

Other studies indicate that personalization is effective, but its impact is mediated by other variables, including the user's personal disposition, in particular the need for cognition (Tam & Ho, 2005); congruence between media content and ad content (Simola et al., 2013); the clarity and strength of product attributes in the ad (Howard & Kerin, 2004); consumer trust in the retailer (Bleier & Eisenbeiss, 2015); and the cognitive demand of the user's primary task when encountering the ad (Bang & Wojdynski, 2016). Lee et al. (2024) found that context and user expectations matter—what feels helpful in one context (e.g., shopping recommendations) may feel intrusive in another (e.g., health-related ads).

Engagement

Even as individual ads have become more interactive and personalized, advertisers realize that changes in the media environment at large provide new challenges and opportunities that require more than merely competing for the attention of consumers. In the advertising industry, *engagement,* a measure that goes beyond the traditional measure of advertising *reach* or *impressions,* has come to describe consumers' interactions with brands through social media, pop-up attractions, and a variety of other emerging channels. As Gangadharbatla (2012) explains:

> [Engagement] roughly translates to some evidence that the individual, i.e., the audience member, an advertiser is trying to reach is responding in some way to the message, e.g., by clicking the Like button or by commenting on the advertisers' wall on Facebook or by writing a review or by retweeting (RT) or downloading an app.
>
> (p. 409)

Posting responses to advertiser-funded real or virtual social media influencers, visiting and exploring advertisers' websites or spaces in virtual worlds, signing up for purchase discounts and email newsletters, and many other behaviors are further examples of this kind of "two-way conversation between the brand and its fans" (Schoenfeld, 2012, para. 8). Researchers continue to examine approaches to measuring these types of engagement in order to determine ROI. Advertisers can certainly count clicks, shares, and downloads, but recent research attempts to understand what causes those behaviors and what they indicate. The research suggests that engagement is characterized by multiple types of responses—cognitive, emotional, and behavioral (Brandow, 2016; Liu-Thompkins, 2018; Wang, 2006)—and seeks to understand the complex relationships among them. For example, Alhelaly et al. (2025) found that,

> ...irritation resulting from perceived privacy intrusiveness does not significantly influence engagement with personalized ads, whereas skepticism substantially reduces engagement. This finding suggests that different

> negative emotional responses to advertising technologies impact consumer behavior in varied ways. The lack of a significant relationship between irritation and engagement may indicate that although irritation is a common emotional reaction to intrusive ads, it is not strong enough to deter users from interacting with personalized content.
>
> (p. 51)

Jenkins et al. (2013) conceptualized engagement within a transmedia environment. They explain that an "appointment model" no longer characterizes consumer media use, where content is offered at particular times as it was in the traditional media environment. Rather, the user experience can be described as "engagement," where media users are "a collective of active agents whose labor may generate alternative forms of market value" (Jenkins et al., 2013, p. 116). This approach acknowledges that audiences interact with content across multiple channels. "Such models value the spread of media texts as these engaged audiences are more likely to recommend, discuss, research, pass along, and even generate new material in response" (Jenkins et al., 2013, p. 116). This means that advertisers must work differently to understand and shape the relationship between consumers and products or brands.

What is needed—in both academic research and industry practice—is a framework to better understand and take advantage of the interactivity, personalization, and engagement of modern (and future) digital advertising. The concept and phenomena of (tele)presence provide such a framework.

The Role of Presence in Advertising

The term presence (short for telepresence) emerged in technology studies as early as 1980 (Minsky, 1980) as VR and teleoperation (operation of technology at a distance) emerged and, to some extent, in the public sphere in the mid-2000s as companies, including Cisco, launched high-end teleconferencing equipment designed to replicate the in-person meeting experience (Cisco, 2006). Among academics the idea of mediated experiences that mimic non-mediated ones extends back many more decades, to at least Horton and Wohl's (1956) work on parasocial interaction and relationships with radio and television personalities. The term is often used imprecisely to refer to one or more different related phenomena, but in 2000 a panel of scholars associated with what would become the International Society for Presence Research developed a detailed definition and explication, which begins this way:

> Presence (a shortened version of the term "telepresence") is a psychological state or subjective perception in which even though part or all of an individual's current experience is generated by and/or filtered through human-made technology, part or all of the individual's perception fails to accurately

> acknowledge the role of the technology in the experience. Except in the most extreme cases, the individual can indicate correctly that s/he is using the technology, but at *some level* and to *some degree*, her/his perceptions overlook that knowledge and objects, events, entities, and environments are perceived as if the technology was not involved in the experience.
>
> (ISPR, 2000)

Since then, many authors have developed variations of this definition, describing different subsets of types or dimensions of presence (see Lombard & Jones, 2015 for a detailed review). Lombard and Sun's (2016) project, which explored how presence is experienced in everyday contexts, presented ten of these different but overlapping types of presence (see Table 16.2).

Table 16.2 Types of Presence

Presence Type	*First-Person Descriptor*	*Spatial vs Social Emphasis*
Spatial presence	I felt like I was in the *space or environment* created by the technology.	Spatial
Transportation	I felt like I *went* somewhere else, people or things *came* to me, or we went somewhere else *together.*	Spatial and social
Perceptual realism	The people, things and events I experienced through the technology *looked, sounded, and/or felt* as they would in the real world.	Spatial and social
Social realism	The people, things and events I experienced through the technology *could (or did) occur* in the real world.	Spatial and social
Engagement	I felt *mentally immersed*; I was focused on or absorbed in the experience.	Spatial and social
Social presence	I felt I was actually *with the people* who were available via technology.	Social
Actor within medium	Even though I *couldn't interact with them, I felt I was actually with the people* or characters who were available via the technology.	Social
Medium as social actor	The technology itself *seemed to have a personality* (including computers, phones, robots, and mannequins).	Social
Self-presence	I felt connected to the *avatar or other representation of me* in the world created by the technology.	Social
Inverse presence	Even though *I wasn't using technology, I felt like I was* (for example, I felt like I was in a movie when I was really walking in the street).	Spatial and social

Adapted from Lombard and Sun 2016.

Note: These types of presence are identified in the literature as distinct but they are not mutually exclusive—most presence experiences involve more than one and sometimes many of them.

Despite these disparate forms of presence, most scholars (see ISPR, 2000) seem to agree that the primary and most inclusive forms are spatial (a sense of being in the media-created physical environment) and social (a sense of being in the media-created social environment). A third form of presence particularly relevant in the context of advertising is presence as engagement: "'Engagement,' 'involvement,' and 'psychological immersion' occur when part or all of a person's perception is directed toward objects, events, and/or people created by the technology, and away from objects, events, and/or people in the physical world" (ISPR, 2000). This form of presence is measured in presence questionnaire items that ask media users to rate how much they felt "involved" and "enjoyed" their experience and how intense it was (Lessiter et al., 2001, p. 293), and how much they felt "mentally immersed," had their "senses engaged" and a "sensation of reality," how "relaxing or exciting" it was, and how "engaging [the story] was" (TPI; Lombard et al., 2011, pp. 293–294). This type of engagement is distinct from the behavioral-based and more specific accounts of engagement from the advertising industry and literature as discussed above, but it is clearly related, since presence as engagement is likely to be associated with user responses to advertising messages within and across media (see Mollen & Wilson, 2010 for a detailed explication of how interactivity, telepresence, and engagement have been defined and measured in different contexts and may be related).

A common view among scholars has been that presence, especially spatial presence, requires sophisticated and expensive technology that as nearly-as-possible reproduces our non-mediated experience. Much of the early scholarly work on the topic focused on nascent VR and teleoperation systems that were most often only available in laboratories and specialized industry settings (note the original subtitle of the MIT Press journal founded in 1992, *Presence: Teleoperators and Virtual Environments*). But researchers observed that even a good novel can produce sensations of spatial and social presence, which they identified as "the book problem" (Biocca, 2003; Schubert & Crusius, 2002). And as far back as the 1950s, Horton and Wohl (1956) wrote about radio and television audience members experiencing a "simulacrum" of social interaction with presenters and entertainers. Today, some of the most compelling social presence experiences come from text and images in social media, including ephemeral, low-production-value live streaming video (e.g., by influencers on YouTube and TikTok). The Covid-19 pandemic accelerated the adoption of relatively low-quality videoconferencing technologies for use in work, learning, and play (e.g., see Volmar et al., 2023), but they provide a strong sense of social presence. A logical explanation for the seeming contradiction is the fact that we do not respond directly to our sensory inputs but to our mental recreations of those inputs. Regardless of the sophistication of the technology, any mediated experience, including an advertising experience, that evokes strong spatial and social presence features vivid and compelling places, people, and/or events that create a sense of psychological, and even physiological, connection for the user. But any technology that allows advertising to become more interactive, personal, and engaging, for example, by giving them the experience of shopping in an interesting (virtual) store environment; examining and trying out a product they care about; having a conversation with a human or artificially intelligent chatbot in the role of salesperson or influencer; being the main character in an event or story related to the product, service, or brand; and, as described in any of the scenarios at the beginning of this chapter, is likely to evoke stronger presence.

Research on Advertising and Presence

From telling vivid stories by firelight and in novels, to painting and sculpture, photography, the electronic media of the 20th century, and today's rapidly evolving immersive, social, and hyper-realistic digital media, humans have always sought to make mediated experiences seem more direct and non-mediated. Reeves and Nass (1996) are among those who argue that our responses to these technologies are based in evolution; others point to aspects of our embodied experience (Haans & IJsselsteijn, 2012). In any case, it is clear that presence is both an important motivator and goal in human experience, and that presence experiences lead to a series of responses many of which are valuable to advertisers.

Even though the definitions and measures of presence and the impacts of presence experiences examined have varied across studies, the results of disparate research point to an important mediating role of presence in advertising effects. When ad messages and experiences are designed to evoke presence, those presence responses lead to a variety of cognitive, affective, and behavioral effects desired by advertisers, including enjoyment, positive attitude toward the ad and product, product knowledge, and purchase intention. This is the case with manipulations of different types of presence in different contexts. Researchers have examined media contexts, including online advertising (Choi et al., 2001; Debbabi et al., 2010; Fortin & Dholakia, 2005; Hopkins et al., 2004; Klein, 2003; Li et al., 2002; Yang, 2006); indoor (Yim et al., 2012) and outdoor (De Boer et al., 2010) 3D displays; noninteractive (Russell & Stern, 2006) and interactive (Cauberghe et al., 2011) television; video games (Nelson et al., 2006); virtual worlds (Grigorovici, 2003; Jin, 2009; Tikkanen et al., 2009); virtual and augmented reality (Jayawardena et al., 2023); and chatbots (Sun et al., 2024; Tsai et al., 2021). A consistent pattern in the results is that presence plays a key role in the positive effects of interactivity, anthropomorphic agents, modality (audio vs. text), the use of 3D displays, and other attributes of new and emerging media.

Presence-Evoking Marketing and Advertising Experiences

As presence-evoking technologies become more effective, practical, and widespread (at least in developed nations), they will present important opportunities for advertisers. The exact nature of these opportunities, especially in the far term, is difficult to predict, but we can look to examples (including the ones at the beginning of this chapter) of how advertisers are utilizing emerging presence technologies now and consider research findings and technology forecasts to predict how they may be utilized in the future. These technologies can be distinguished by their emphasis on evoking spatial and social presence as well as presence as engagement.

Spatial Presence

Home and Public Virtual, Mixed, and Augmented Reality

VR, from 360-degree navigable videos to fully interactive motion-tracked head-mounted displays at home or in public spaces (stores, hotels, bars, amusement centers, pop-up attractions, etc.), can be used to transport users to travel destinations and allow them to interact with and customize products (e.g., cars, appliances, home decor, make-up, and fashion) (e.g., Johnson, 2015a; Li, 2016; Robertson, 2015). Longer form virtual experiences centered on a product or brand (e.g., Johnson, 2015b) can be used to engage, entertain, and persuade. Full immersion headsets are being supplemented and may be supplanted, by headsets and less obtrusive eyeglasses that enable users to perceive a variety of seamless combinations of non-mediated and mediated (mixed and augmented) realities (Abrash, 2021; Werner Bandeira, 2023), creating more opportunities to evoke compelling advertising experiences.

Holographic Product Displays and Demonstrations

Although practical hologram technology has developed slowly, recent advances are likely to find their way into more interactive signage and in-store displays, and these can be personalized based on information provided actively or passively via sensors (as in the film *Minority Report*) (see Genuth, 2013).

Virtual Shopping Environments

Already used to simulate and test different store and product designs and configurations (InContext Solutions, 2024; Wang et al., 2021), virtual and augmented reality can provide users with a more familiar and intuitive digital version of the brick-and-mortar shopping experience. The shopping cart icon used by most retail websites can be made more literal, as the separate web pages for lists of products and product details and reviews can be made to match the physical space of a retail store (e.g., Buss, 2012).

Product Placement

Widely used in film and television, and more recently in video games, this technique in which a product or brand appears as a major or minor part of the story or environment is being extended to other presence-evoking experiences, including VR (Takahashi, 2014) and virtual worlds (Samad et al., 2023). The specific products/brands displayed are likely to be personalized based on information provided actively or passively by users, and even the prominence of the appearance might be adjusted based on such knowledge.

Social Presence

Customer Service via Real or Virtual Agents

The evolution of video conferencing services such as Zoom and FaceTime and the ubiquity of mobile media continue to make it easier and less expensive to communicate with customers and potential customers from home, brick-and-mortar stores, or anywhere else in ways that create an illusion of non-mediated face-to-face interaction. Given the power of these interactions, especially for high-involvement products and services, advertisers and businesses will likely make available and initiate more of them. Some banks are experimenting with ATMs that incorporate telepresence equipment that connects users to remote human tellers (Ginovsky, 2013), and the logic can be extended to other financial services, luxury purchases, and many others. The "person" at the other end of the conversation need not be human. In 2001, Amtrak began using an artificially intelligent voice-based agent named Julie to take rail reservations over the telephone (Nuance Communications, 2016). With the ascendance of Large Language Models and other forms of generative AI, many members of the public interact regularly with chatbots that sound remarkably like humans (Schreibelmayr & Mara, 2022) and increasingly look human as well (Abel & Larsen, 2024; Kolbe et al., 2006). Text-based chatbot assistants on websites are primitive versions of the digitally embodied, intelligent agents that will likely soon be available to advertisers.

Robots and Androids as Product/Brand/Retail Representatives

Service robots like Lowe's OSHbot (Rodriguez, 2014) and Giant's Marty (Moran, 2024) are already helping customers find and buy the right products, while other robots guide airport visitors (Blackman, 2012), serve hotel guests (Lewis-Kraus, 2016; see also Biba, 2025), and greet and serve food to customers at restaurants (Cha, 2020). Robots and androids evoke more than delight and interest; presence scholars have established that people tend to respond to them in many of the ways they respond to humans and animals (Reeves & Nass, 1996; Lombard & Xu, 2021). Robots and androids can therefore be used to advise and persuade customers and prospective customers in a variety of settings.

Engagement

Engaging Form: Virtual/Mixed Reality and Theme Parks

In the increasingly competitive "attention economy" (Nelson-Field, 2020; Newport, 2019), it is difficult to get and keep consumers' full and undivided attention, but technologies that shut out distractions are more likely to evoke presence as engagement. VR headsets that replace the sights and sounds from the non-mediated world encourage users to become mentally immersed in messages, including advertising messages. Mixed and augmented reality, in which virtual objects seem to interact with real ones in interesting ways and users can interact with either, should also produce a high level of engagement presence. Although mobile technologies are still a potential distraction, Disney, Universal, and many other theme parks, sections of parks devoted to franchises, including "Harry Potter" and "Star Trek," and many individual theme park rides all create a cohesive, immersive world for attendees to fully engage with and represent a logical context for sponsored messages (see Olson, 2004). Of course, the technologies must work properly and not draw attention to their operation to fully engage users.

Engaging Content: Supplementary and Transmedia

Media products are increasingly deemed successful not just because they reach a large audience, but because the audience members they do reach are devoted and passionate about the products (Arvidsson & Bonini, 2015; Jenkins et al., 2013; Napoli, 2011). Indicators of this passion include posting on and interacting with fan communities via social media, in real-time or otherwise; attending online and in-person conventions; and producing fan fiction based on content characters and storylines. Media producers and advertisers can encourage and take advantage of this type of passion first by developing compelling storylines, characters, and dialogue for their media products and then by providing additional opportunities for audiences to interact with the media content. In addition to behind-the-scenes and outtake videos, other "extra" online content, and fan convention appearances, producers are increasingly creating content-related, experience-based promotions across media platforms from websites to video games to VR (e.g., Knowles, 2016; Lazzaro, 2016). These techniques within and across media should increase audience mental immersion (engagement), loyalty, and receptiveness to (appropriately designed and placed) advertising messages.

Parasocial Interaction and Authenticity

As noted above, an effective presence experience need not rely on expensive technology and high production values. Low-fi, raw, imperfect but intimate first-person videos, as from news/weather/sports presenters, actors, musicians, program creators/writers, gamers, and influencers, can be extremely engaging because they evoke a sense of authenticity and personal connection. These represent key opportunities to enhance engagement presence and, if used wisely, promote products and services.

Presence in the More Distant Future

We can imagine spatial, social, and engagement presence reaching their full potential in the context of advertising in the more distant future. Here is one possible scenario:

You return home and enter your ironically named "Reality Room," an otherwise empty space containing the well-hidden holography generator technology that can create or recreate vivid, interactive representations of any combination of places, objects, people, and events. You ask your home's AI-powered virtual assistant (which has a human name, voice, and appearance you selected) to put you in the living room of your favorite dramedy series with your favorite fictional character from your collection of stories. The father of the series' family, who you've always liked and respected, appears on the couch next to you. Both the physical environment and the character are utterly realistic, and you begin to relax as you and he carry on a warm conversation. The topic eventually turns to the latest models of transport vehicle; the character describes the model he thinks you should consider purchasing. He makes a compelling argument, and though you realize he's likely been biased by his programming and an algorithm developed to collect data about you and influence your behavior, it is hard to resist him given your fondness for him and his (fictional) family. Together, you visit a virtual showroom where you take a test ride, feeling every aspect of being inside the vehicle as it speeds down familiar sun-drenched streets, as onlookers smile in admiration. On returning to the living room, you thank your companion and say goodbye. Your virtual assistant reappears and asks you if you enjoyed your experience and where you would like to go next, and as the room becomes a vivid, restful nature scene, you sit by the mountain stream, listen to the birds happily chirping back and forth with each other, and decide that you will buy the vehicle your "friend" introduced you to.

Ethical Considerations

It is important to acknowledge that the incredible possibilities created by emerging technologies also produce a number of ethical considerations. First, our environment is increasingly cluttered with persuasive media messages, including consumer advertisements. For both practical and ethical reasons, advertisers and media owners must act responsibly in avoiding interruptive ads (Manluccia, 2015). Second, beyond the inconvenience and invasiveness of clutter, the interactivity of new media allows advertisers access to a great deal of our personal information. A condition to using media content today, it seems, is giving up our rights to privacy. Although many consumers find the entertainment, education, and sense of community offered by digital media to be valuable, research suggests they do not unconditionally accept invasions of privacy for the sake of personalized advertising (Alhelaly et al., 2025; Lee et al., 2024; Turow et al., 2009), as the industry often argues. At the same time, media users often find it difficult to know the extent to which they are being monitored (Stole, 2014). Transparency should be the guiding principle, not only as a matter of ethics but also because it increases trust and thereby encourages attention and engagement. Rather than merely revealing the monitoring behind personalization, users should be given the ability to establish the scope and parameters of the personalization. Finally, the power of presence to blur the line between reality and fiction can be easily abused, with potential serious effects on individuals and even cultures (see Lombard, 2010; Olson, 2004; Veljković et al., 2024). Again, transparency is critical; users need to be reminded before and after high presence experiences about the nature of the illusions.

Conclusion

Presence is not a new phenomenon, but emerging technologies have brought it to the forefront of media experiences as they allow a range of possibilities for media users to enter more and more interesting, realistic, personalized, and interactive environments. Much of the industry and academic research on advertising does not adequately examine the complexity of users' perceptual experience with media and how this might impact advertiser-consumer interactions. Presence adds a layer of understanding by addressing the ways that people are spatially and socially immersed in all types of mediated experiences. Further, presence may help explain the appeal of interactive and personalized ads, as research indicates that people desire a sense of connection with the people and places they encounter in media.

Of course, the causes and consequences of presence experiences depend on the form and content of the media presentation, the attributes and motivations of the viewer or user, the type of product or service (or idea) being promoted, and likely, many other factors (see Lombard & Ditton, 1997). Researchers are just beginning to catalog, much less fully understand, the role of each of these factors (see Cummings & Bailenson, 2015; Oh et al., 2018). At the same time, the technologies that evoke presence continue to evolve: advertisers have moved from a relatively few, distinct options (print ads featuring combinations of text and image, radio ads featuring voice and music, and network and local television ads featuring all of these) to a complex, fragmented, digital media environment with a vast array of options, including everything from social media apps to AI chatbots and robots to immersive virtual worlds. In many cases, the presence-evoking technologies and the experiences they create are novel, and their ability to maintain their power to delight and persuade is unknown. But the evidence suggests (Reeves & Nass, 1996)—and we strongly believe—that because presence itself is a basic motivation, each time we adjust to a technology, a new "better" one will take its place—likely more capable of evoking presence. And advertisers, and all content producers, will need to adjust.

References

Abel, E., & Larsen, A. D. (2024, July). Exploring perceptions & reactions to digital humans. In *2024 16th IIAI International Congress on Advanced Applied Informatics (IIAI-AAI)* (pp. 632–637). IEEE. https://doi.org/10.1109/IIAI-AAI63651.2024.00119

Abrash, M. (2021). Creating the future: Augmented reality, the next human–machine interface. In *2021 IEEE International Electron Devices Meeting (IEDM)* (pp. 1–11). IEEE. https://doi.org/10.1109/IEDM19574.2021.9720526

Alhelaly, Y., Dhillon, G., & Oliveira, T. (2025). The impact of privacy intrusiveness on individuals' responses and engagement toward personalization in online interactive advertising. *Journal of Interactive Advertising, 25*(1), 38–60. https://doi.org/10.1080/15252019.2024.2440318

Arroyo-Cañada, F. J., & Gil-Lafuente, J. (2012). Considerations of interactive digital television as advertising media. *Journal of Promotion Management, 18*(3), 306–318. https://doi.org/10.1080/10496491.2012.696456

Arvidsson, A., & Bonini, T. (2015). Valuing audience passions: From Smythe to Tarde. *European Journal of Cultural Studies, 18*(2), 158–173. https://doi.org/10.1177/1367549414563297

Bang, H., & Wojdynski, B. W. (2016). Tracking users' visual attention and responses to personalized advertising based on task cognitive demand. *Computers in Human Behavior, 55*, 867–876. https://doi.org/10.1016/j.chb.2015.10.025

Bezjian-Avery, A., Calder, B., & Iacobucci, D. (1998). New media interactive advertising vs. traditional advertising. *Journal of Advertising Research, 38*(4), 23–32.

Biba, J. (2025, March 10). Top 27 Humanoid Robots in Use Right Now. *Built In.* https://builtin.com/robotics/humanoid-robots

Biocca, F. (2003, May). Can we resolve the book, the physical reality, and the dream state problems? From the two-pole to a three-pole model of shifts in presence. In *EU Future and Emerging Technologies, Presence Initiative Meeting*, Aalborg, Denmark. https://www.semanticscholar.org/paper/Can-we-resolve-the-book-%2C-the-physical-reality-%2C-to-Biocca/5bcd9bd256295823ba515f3ebec9eacd4f79208d

Blackman, S. (2012, August 21). Rise of the holograms: The next generation of airport employees. *Airport Technology.* https://www.airport-technology.com/features/featureholograms-next-generation-airport-employees/

Bleier, A., & Eisenbeiss, M. (2015). The importance of trust for personalized online advertising. *Journal of Retailing, 91*(3), 390–409. https://doi.org/10.1016/j.jretai.2015.04.001

Brandow, M. (2016, March 14). Engagement matters. Emotion sells. Data fuels [Web log post]. *Mediapost.* https://www.mediapost.com/publications/article/271175/engagement-matters-emotion-sells-data-fuels.html

Bright, L. F. (2011). Media evolution and web 2.0 technologies. In M. S. Eastin, T. D. Daugherty, & N. M. Burns (Eds.), *Handbook of research on digital media and advertising: User generated content consumption* (pp. 32–51). IGI-Global. Hershey, PA: Information Science Reference.

Buss, D. (2012, May 10). Peapod expands virtual grocery shopping to Chicago. *Brand Channel*. https://brandchannel.com/2012/05/10/peapod-expands-virtual-grocery-shopping-to-chicago/

Cauberghe, V., Geuens, M., & De Pelsmacker, P. (2011). Context effects of TV programme-induced interactivity and telepresence on advertising responses. *International Journal of Advertising*, *30*(4), 641–663. https://doi.org/10.2501/IJA-30-4-641-663

Cha, S. S. (2020). Customers' intention to use robot-serviced restaurants in Korea: Relationship of coolness and MCI factors. *International Journal of Contemporary Hospitality Management*, *32*(9), 2947–2968. https://doi.org/10.1108/IJCHM-01-2020-0046

Choi, Y. K., Miracle, G. E., & Biocca, F. (2001). The effects of anthropomorphic agents on advertising effectiveness and the mediating role of presence. *Journal of Interactive Advertising*, *2*(1), 19–32. https://doi.org/10.1080/15252019.2001.10722055

Cisco. (2006, October 23). Cisco announces the Cisco telepresence meeting solution – a breakthrough "in-person" experience for real-time, remote, business communication and collaboration [Press release]. https://www.cisco.com/cisco/web/UK/news/archive/2006/102306.html

Cummings, J. J., & Bailenson, J. N. (2015). How immersive is enough? A meta-analysis of the effect of immersive technology on user presence. *Media Psychology*, *19*(2), 272–309. https://doi.org/10.1080/15213269.2015.1015740

De Boer, C. N., Verleur, R., Heuvelman, A., & Heynderickx, I. (2010). Added value of an autostereoscopic multiview 3-D display for advertising in a public environment. *Displays*, *31*(1), 1–8. https://doi.org/10.1016/j.displa.2009.09.001

Debbabi, S., Daassi, M., & Baile, S. (2010). Effect of online 3D advertising on consumer responses: the mediating role of telepresence. *Journal of Marketing Management*, *26*(9–10), 967–992. https://doi.org/10.1080/02672570903498819

DeFleur, M. L., & Dennis, E. E. (1996). *Understanding mass communication*. Boston: Houghton Mifflin Company.

Dickey, I., & Lewis, W. (2011). An overview of digital media and advertising. In M. S. Eastin, T. D. Daugherty, & N. M. Burns (Eds.), *Handbook of research on digital media and advertising: User generated content consumption* (pp. 1–31). IGI-Global. Hershey, PA: Information Science Reference.

Edwards, S. M., Li, H., & Lee, J. H. (2002). Forced exposure and psychological reactance: Antecedents and consequences of the perceived intrusiveness of pop-up ads. *Journal of Advertising*, *31*(3), 83–95. https://doi.org/10.1080/00913367.2002.10673678

Forbes Council Expert Panel. (2023, May 5). 16 Innovative Ways Virtual Reality Could Revolutionize Advertising. *Forbes*. https://www.forbes.com/councils/forbesagencycouncil/2023/05/05/16-innovative-ways-virtual-reality-could-revolutionize-advertising/

Fortin, D. R., & Dholakia, R. R. (2005). Interactivity and vividness effects on social presence and involvement with a web-based advertisement. *Journal of Business Research*, *58*(3), 387–396. https://doi.org/10.1016/S0148-2963(03)00106-1

Gangadharbatla, H. (2012). Social media and advertising theory. In S. Rodgers & E. Thorson (Eds.), *Advertising theory* (pp. 402–416). New York, NY: Routledge.

Genuth, I. (2013, April 11). Nike launched a holographic 3D advertising campaign. *The Future of Things*. https://thefutureofthings.com/5069-nike-launched-a-holographic-3d-advertising-campaign/

Ginovsky, J. (2013, August 27). Banks need to rethink telepresence approach: Use it to improve customer engagement, not reinvent teller experience. *Banking Exchange.* https://www.bankingexchange.com/news-feed/item/3898-banks-need-to-rethink-telepresence-approach

Grigorovici, D. (2003). Persuasive effects of presence in immersive virtual environments. In G. Riva, F. Davide, & W. A. Ijsselsteijn (Eds.), *Being there: Concepts, effects and measurement of user presence in synthetic environments.* pp. 192–205, Amsterdam: IOS Press. https://www.neurovr.org/emerging/book4/4_13GRIGOR.PDF

Haans, A., & IJsselsteijn, W. A. (2012). Embodiment and telepresence: Toward a comprehensive theoretical framework. *Interacting with Computers, 24*(4), 211–218. https://doi.org/10.1016/j.intcom.2012.04.010

Hopkins, C. D., Raymond, M. A., & Mitra, A. (2004). Consumer responses to perceived telepresence in the online advertising environment: The moderating role of involvement. *Marketing Theory, 4*(1), 137–162. https://doi.org/10.1177/1470593104044090

Horton, D., & Wohl, R. (1956). Mass communication and para-social interaction: Observations on intimacy at a distance. *Psychiatry, 19*(3), 215–229. https://doi.org/10.1080/00332747.1956.11023049

Howard, D. J., & Kerin, R. A. (2004). The effects of personalized product recommendations on advertisement response rates: The "Try This. It Works!" technique. *Journal of Consumer Psychology, 14*(3), 271–279. https://doi.org/10.1207/s15327663jcp1403_8

InContext Solutions. (2024, November 25). *7 surprising ways virtual store testing might challenge everything we know about grocery profitability.* https://incontextsolutions.com/blog/7-ways-virtual-store-testing-grocery-profitability/

International Society for Presence Research. (2000). *The concept of presence: Explication statement.* https://ispr.info/about-presence-2/about-presence/

Jayawardena, N. S., Thaichon, P., Quach, S., Razzaq, A., & Behl, A. (2023). The persuasion effects of virtual reality (VR) and augmented reality (AR) video advertisements: A conceptual review. *Journal of Business Research, 160*, 113739. https://doi.org/10.1016/j.jbusres.2023.113739

Jenkins, H., Ford, S., & Green, J. (2013). *Spreadable media: Creating value and meaning in a networked culture.* New York: New York University Press.

Jin, S. A. (2009). Modality effects in second life: The mediating role of social presence and the moderating role of product involvement. *Cyberpsychology & Behavior, 12*(6), 717–721. https://doi.org/10.1089/cpb.2008.0273

Johnson, L. (2015a, April 9). Is virtual reality the next big form of in-bar entertainment? Jim Beam and Dos Equis have been quick to embrace the trend. *AdWeek.* https://www.adweek.com/news/technology/virtual-reality-next-big-form-bar-entertainment-163963

Johnson, L. (2015b, May 1). Drones are filming seriously jaw-dropping virtual reality video for brands: Patrón goes inside the agave field. *AdWeek.* https://www.adweek.com/news/technology/drones-are-filming-seriously-jaw-dropping-virtual-reality-video-brands-164433

Kim, J., & McMillan, S. J. (2008). Evaluation of internet advertising research. *Journal of Advertising, 37*(1), 99–112. https://doi.org/10.2753/JOA0091-3367370108

Klein, L. R. (2003). Creating virtual product experiences: The role of telepresence. *Journal of Interactive Marketing, 17*(1), 41–55. https://doi.org/10.1002/dir.10046

Knowles, K. (2016, April 27). Step into a spy's shoes: Top TV series launches first virtual reality spin-off. *The Memo.* https://www.thememo.com/2016/04/27/vr-le-bureau-des-legendes-virtual-reality-le-bureau-des-legendes-360-video/

Kolbe, L., Salomann, H., & Brenner, W. (2006). Self-services in customer relationships: Balancing high-tech and high-touch today and tomorrow. *e-Service Journal, 4*(2), 65–84. https://doi.org/10.2979/esj.2006.4.2.65

Kumar, A., Pandey, M., & Shreyaskar, P. K. P. (2024). Three decades of digital advertising: What the bibliometrics say and how AI came into play. *Vision*. Advance online publication. https://doi.org/10.1177/09722629241278149

Lazzaro, S. (2016, March 28). 7 movies you can experience in virtual reality. *Observer*. https://observer.com/2016/03/7-movies-you-can-experience-in-virtual-reality/

Lee, S., Moon, W.-K., & Song, Y. G. (2024). Is it transparent or surveillant? The effects of personalized advertising and privacy policy on advertising effectiveness. *Journal of Interactive Advertising*. Advance online publication. https://doi.org/10.1080/15252019.2024.2417422

Lessiter, J., Freeman, J., Keogh, E., & Davidoff, J. (2001). A cross-media presence questionnaire: The ITC-Sense of Presence Inventory. *Presence*, *10*(3), 282–297. https://doi.org/10.1162/105474601300343612

Lewis-Kraus, G. (2016, March 2). Check in with the velociraptor at the world's first robot hotel. *Wired*. https://www.wired.com/2016/03/robot-henn-na-hotel-japan/

Li, H., Daugherty, T., & Biocca, F. (2002). Impact of 3-D advertising on product knowledge, brand attitude, and purchase intention: The mediating role of presence. *Journal of Advertising*, *31*(3), 43–57. https://doi.org/10.1080/00913367.2002.10673675

Li, S. (2016, April 10). How retail stores are using virtual reality to make shopping more fun. *Los Angeles Times*. https://www.latimes.com/business/la-fi-retail-vr-20160410-story.html

Liu-Thompkins, Y. (2018). A decade of online advertising research: What we learned and what we need to know. *Journal of Advertising, 48*(1), 1–13. https://doi.org/10.1080/00913367.2018.1556138

Lombard, M. (2010). The promise and peril of telepresence. In Bracken, C.C., & Skalski, P. (Eds.). *Immersed in Media: Telepresence in Everyday Life* (pp. 215-246). New York, NY: Routledge.

Lombard, M., & Ditton, T. B. (1997). At the heart of it all: The concept of presence. *Journal of Computer-Mediated Communication, 3*(2), n.p. https://doi.org/10.1111/j.1083-6101.1997.tb00072.x

Lombard, M., & Jones, M. T. (2015). Defining presence. In M. Lombard, F. Biocca, W. A. Ijsselsteijn, J. Freeman, & R. Schaevitz (Eds.), *Immersed in media: Telepresence theory, measurement and technology* (pp. 13–34). London: Springer.

Lombard, M., & Snyder-Duch, J. (2001). Interactive advertising and presence: A framework. *Journal of Interactive Advertising*, *1*(2), 56–65. https://doi.org/10.1080/15252019.2001.10722051

Lombard, M., & Sun, W. (2016). *Outside the lab: A direct, mixed-method approach to examining telepresence experiences in everyday life.* Unpublished manuscript.

Lombard, M., Weinstein, L., & Ditton, T. (2011, October). *Measuring telepresence: The validity of the Temple Presence Inventory (TPI) in a gaming context.* Proceedings of the 2011 annual conference of the International Society for Presence Research (ISPR), Edinburgh, Scotland. Available: https://matthewlombard.com/ISPR/Proceedings/2011/Lombard_etal.pdf

Lombard, M., & Xu, K. (2021). Social responses to media technologies in the 21st century: The media are social actors paradigm. *Human-Machine Communication, 2*, 29–55. https://doi.org/10.30658/hmc.2.2

Manluccia, N. (2015, October 30). How to avoid the potential horrors of virtual reality marketing: Don't let virtual reality ads become virtual prisons for consumers. *Advertising Age*. https://adage.com/article/digitalnext/avoid-horrors-virtual-reality-marketing/301135/

Matz, S. C., Teeny, J. D., Vaid, S. S., Peters, H., Harari, G. M., & Cerf, M. (2024). The potential of generative AI for personalized persuasion at scale. *Scientific Reports, 14*, 4692. https://doi.org/10.1038/s41598-024-53755-0

Metz, C. (2025, May 21). By putting AI into everything, Google wants to make it invisible. *MIT Technology Review*. https://www.technologyreview.com/2025/05/21/1117251/by-putting-ai-into-everything-google-wants-to-make-it-invisible/

Minsker, M. (2013). Digital advertising gets personal. *CRM Magazine*, *17*(10), 22–26. https://www.destinationcrm.com/Articles/Editorial/Magazine-Features/Digital-Advertising-Gets-Personal-92024.aspx

Minsky, M. (1980). Telepresence. *OMNI magazine*. https://web.media.mit.edu/~minsky/papers/Telepresence.html

Mollen, A., & Wilson, H. (2010). Engagement, telepresence and interactivity in online consumer experience: Reconciling scholastic and managerial perspectives. *Journal of Business Research*, *63*(9/10), 919–925. https://doi.org/10.1016/j.jbusres.2009.05.014

Mood Media (n/d). The North Face Case Study. https://us.moodmedia.com/case-study/the-north-face/

Moran, C. D. (2024, January 22). How Stop & Shop promoted in-store robot Marty to brand ambassador. *Grocery Dive*. https://www.grocerydive.com/news/stop-and-shop-humanizing-marty-robot-grocery-technology/704512/

Napoli, P. M. (2011). *Audience evolution: New technologies and the transformation of media audiences*. New York: Columbia University Press.

Nelson, M. R., Yaros, R. A., & Keum, H. (2006). Examining the influence of telepresence on spectator and player processing of real and fictitious brands in a computer game. *Journal of Advertising, 35*(4), 87–99. https://doi.org/10.2753/JOA0091-3367350406

Nelson-Field, K. (2020). *The Attention Economy and How Media Works: Simple Truths for Marketers*. Singapore: Springer Nature.

Newport, C. (2019). *Digital minimalism: Choosing a focused life in a noisy world.* New York, NY: Portfolio/Penguin.

Nuance Communications. (2016). Amtrak's Julie gets callers on board. https://www.nuance.com/content/dam/nuance/en_au/collateral/enterprise/case-study/cs-amtrak-en-us.pdf

Oh, C. S., Bailenson, J. N., & Welch, G. F. (2018). A systematic review of social presence: Definition, antecedents, and implications. *Frontiers in Robotics and AI, 5*, 114. https://doi.org/10.3389/frobt.2018.00114

Olson, S. R. (2004). The extensions of synergy: Product placement through theming and environmental simulacra. *Journal of Promotion Management, 10*(1–2), 65–87. https://doi.org/10.1300/J057v10n01_06

Reeves, B., & Nass, C. (1996). *The media equation: How people treat computers, televisions, and new media as real people and places*. Cambridge: Cambridge University Press.

Robertson, A. (2015, September 10). What virtual reality postcards can tell us about the future of travel. *The Verge*. https://www.theverge.com/2015/9/10/9289073/marriott-virtual-reality-postcard-samsung-gear-vr

Rodriguez, A. (2014, October 28). Meet Lowe's newest sales associate – OSHbot, the robot. *Advertising Age.* https://adage.com/article/cmo-strategy/meet-lowe-s-newest-sales-associate-oshbot-robot/295591/

Russell, C. A., & Stern, B. B. (2006). Consumers, characters, and products - a balance model of sitcom product placement effects. *Journal of Advertising, 35*(1), 7–21. https://doi.org/10.2753/JOA0091-3367350101

Samad, A., Izani, M., Razak, A., & Mustaffa, F. (2023, May). Understanding advertising in virtual worlds and best practices for metaverse advertising. In *2023 Zooming Innovation in Consumer Technologies Conference (ZINC)* (pp. 45–50). IEEE, Novi Sad, Serbia. https://doi.org/10.1109/ZINC58345.2023.10174214

Schoenfeld, A. (2012, February 1). 5 Ways to Report on Engagement [Web log post]. https://simplymeasured.com/blog/5-ways-to-report-on-engagement/

Schomer, A. (2021, July 23). Most consumers are creeped out by ads that follow them across devices. *EMARKETER.* https://www.emarketer.com/content/most-consumers-creeped-out-by-ads-that-follow-them-across-devices

Schreibelmayr, S., & Mara, M. (2022). Robot voices in daily life: Vocal human-likeness and application context as determinants of user acceptance. *Frontiers in Psychology, 13*, 787499. https://doi.org/10.3389/fpsyg.2022.787499

Schubert, T., & Crusius, J. (2002). Five theses on the book problem: Presence in books, film and VR. *PRESENCE 2002-Proceedings of the fifth international workshop on Presence*. Porto, Portugal: Universidad Fernando Pessoa. https://www.igroup.org/projects/porto2002/SchubertCrusiusSlidesPorto2000.pdfigroup.org

Simola, J., Kivikangas, M., Kuisma, J., & Krause, C. M. (2013). Attention and memory for newspaper advertisements: Effects of ad-editorial congruency and location. *Applied Cognitive Psychology, 27*(4), 429–442. https://doi.org/10.1002/acp.2918

Smith, K. T. (2012). Longitudinal study of digital marketing strategies targeting millennials. *The Journal of Consumer Marketing, 29*(2), 86–92. https://doi.org/10.1108/07363761211206339

Stole, I. L. (2014). Persistent pursuit of personal information: A historical perspective on digital advertising strategies. *Critical Studies in Media Communication, 31*(2), 129–133. https://doi.org/10.1080/15295036.2014.921319

Sun, Y., Chen, J., & Sundar, S. S. (2024). Chatbot ads with a human touch: A test of anthropomorphism, interactivity, and narrativity. *Journal of Business Research, 172*, 114403. https://doi.org/10.1016/j.jbusres.2023.114403

Sundar, S. S., & Kim, J. (2005). Interactivity and persuasion: Influencing attitudes with information and involvement, *Journal of Interactive Advertising, 5*(2), 5–18. https://doi.org/10.1080/15252019.2005.10722097

Takahashi, D. (2014, December 8). MediaSpike creates cool in-game native ads for virtual reality. *VentureBeat.* https://venturebeat.com/2014/12/08/mediaspike-creates-cool-in-game-native-ads-for-virtual-reality/

Tam, K. Y., & Ho, S. Y. (2005). Web personalization as a persuasion strategy: An Elaboration Likelihood Model perspective. *Information Systems Research, 16*(3), 271–291. https://doi.org/10.1287/isre.1050.0058

Tanyel, F., Stuart, E. W., & Griffin, J. (2013). Have "Millennials" embraced digital advertising as they have embraced digital media? *Journal of Promotion Management, 19*(5), 652–673. https://doi.org/10.1080/10496491.2013.829161

Thorson, E., & Rodgers, S. (2017). Network advertising model (NAM). In S. Rodgers & E. Thorson (Eds.), *Digital advertising: Theory and research* (3rd ed., pp. 19–30). New York, NY: Routledge.

Tikkanen, H., Hietanen, J., Henttonen, T., & Rokka, J. (2009). Exploring virtual worlds: Success factors in virtual world marketing. *Management Decision, 47*(8), 1357–1381. https://doi.org/10.1108/00251740910984596

Tsai, W. H. S., Liu, Y., & Chuan, C. H. (2021). How chatbots' social presence communication enhances consumer engagement: The mediating role of parasocial interaction and dialogue. *Journal of Research in Interactive Marketing, 15*(3), 460–482. https://doi.org/10.1108/JRIM-12-2019-0200

Turow, J., & Draper, N. (2014). Industry conceptions of audience in the digital space. *Cultural Studies*, *28*(4), 643–656. https://doi.org/10.1080/09502386.2014.888929

Turow, J., King, J., Hoofnagle, C. J., Bleakley, A., & Hennessy, M. (2009, September 29). *Americans reject tailored advertising and three activities that enable it.* SSRN. https://doi.org/10.2139/ssrn.1478214

Veljković, S. Z., Ćurčić, M. T., & Gavrilović, I. P. (2024). Dark sides of deepfake technology. *Vojnotehnički glasnik/Military Technical Courier, 72*(3), 1441–1463. https://www.aseestant.ceon.rs/index.php/vtg/article/view/49630

Viktoratos, I., & Tsadiras, A. (2021). Personalized advertising computational techniques: A systematic literature review, findings, and a design framework. *Information*, *12*(11), 480. https://doi.org/10.3390/info12110480

Volmar, A., Kindervater, C., Randerath, S., & Mniestri, A. (2023). Mainstreaming Zoom: Covid-19, social distancing, and the rise of video-mediated remote cooperation. In C. Eisenmann, K. Englert, C. Schubert, & E. Voss (Eds.), *Varieties of cooperation* (Medien der Kooperation – Media of Cooperation). Wiesbaden, Germany: Springer VS. https://doi.org/10.1007/978-3-658-39037-2_6

Wang, A. (2006). Advertising engagement: A driver of message involvement on message effects. *Journal of Advertising Research*, *46*(4), 355–368. https://doi.org/10.2501/S0021849906060429

Wang, Q. J., Escobar, F. B., Da Mota, P. A., & Velasco, C. (2021). Getting started with virtual reality for sensory and consumer science: Current practices and future perspectives. *Food Research International, 145*, 110410. https://doi.org/10.1016/j.foodres.2021.110410

Wells, W., Burnett, J., & Moriarity, S. (1998). *Advertising principles & practices* (4th Ed.). Upper Saddle River, NJ: Prentice Hall.

Werner Bandeira, L. (2023). On the mainstream use of AR glasses: Why it matters, what are its ethical risks, and what to do about it (Master's thesis, University of Twente). https://essay.utwente.nl/95095/1/WernerBandeira_MA_BMS_pdf.pdf

Yang, K. C. (2006). The influence of humanlike navigation interface on users' responses to internet advertising. *Telematics and Informatics*, *23*(1), 38–55. https://doi.org/10.1016/j.tele.2005.03.001

Yim, M. Y. C., Cicchirillo, V. J., & Drumwright, M. E. (2012). The impact of stereoscopic three-dimensional (3-D) advertising. *Journal of Advertising*, *41*(2), 113–128. https://doi.org/10.2753/JOA0091-3367410208

17 Exploring the Roles and Impacts of Artificial Intelligence in Advertising

Chang-Dae Ham, WooJin Kim, and Seo-Jeong Heo

Introduction

Artificial intelligence (AI) has become one of the most transformative forces in contemporary advertising, reshaping how advertising is created and how it persuades. Advances in machine learning, natural language processing, and generative AI extend beyond current industry practices, creating both opportunities and challenges for scholarly inquiry. As advertisers increasingly deploy AI for conversational agents, creative development, hyper-personalization, and consumer engagement, researchers need to address the theoretical, methodological, and ethical implications of these AI-induced changes.

Recent scholarship reflects this transformation, with growing attention to AI's conceptualization, functions, and practical applications in advertising (Huang & Wang, 2023; Ford et al., 2023). To contribute to the emerging discourse, this chapter systematically reviews current research on AI in advertising. Using topical keywords (e.g., AI advertising, AI-generated advertising, AI marketing), we identified relevant works from Web of Science and Google Scholar, focusing on publications from 2019 to 2025. Among thousands of findings, our review includes 129 sources, including journal articles, book chapters, conference papers, and web-based materials.

To structure the analysis, we propose the ACET framework—an adaptation of the classic SMCR communication model—which recasts advertising into four components: agents, contents, engines, and targets. This framework provides a systematic lens for understanding AI's evolving roles and impacts in both advertising practice and scholarship.

ACET Framework—Agents, Contents, Engines, and Targets

Communication models provide simplified yet systematic representations of complex processes, helping to analyze the roles and interactions of different elements. Among these, Berlo's SMCR model conceptualizes communication as a linear sequence of Source, Message, Channel, and Receiver (Berlo, 1960). While

DOI: 10.4324/9781003567523-21

useful for its clarity, this framework has limitations for AI-powered advertising, as it assumes linearity and does not account for the dynamic, interactive nature of AI communication.

To address this, we adapt the SMCR model into the ACET framework by reconfiguring its components: *Source* to *Agents, Message* to *Contents, Channel* to *Engines,* and *Receiver* to *Targets. Agents* represent AI-powered communicators such as chatbots or virtual influencers (VIs) that simulate human marketers (Friestad & Wright, 1994; Ham & Nelson, 2019; Lee & Ham, 2023). *Contents* reflect the diverse persuasive materials generated by AI—including text, visuals, and interactive formats—that aim to shape consumer perceptions and behaviors. *Engines* denote the back-end technologies in the media, platform, and system that power AI persuasion, enabling behavioral analysis, predictive forecasting, and personalized targeting. Finally, *Targets* are consumers who, in interaction with agents, engage in a persuasion game that is dynamic and reciprocal rather than linear (Friestad & Wright, 1994; Ham & Nelson, 2019). The ACET framework positions AI advertising as an interactive ecosystem in which agents, contents, engines, and targets continuously influence one another. We propose ACET as a conceptual tool to analyze recent literature on AI-powered advertising, identifying key research topics and theoretical applications within each component to guide future inquiry (see Figure 17.1).

Evolutionary Landscape of AI-Powered Advertising: Topic Overview

Our analysis categorizes several related topics using the ACET framework, illustrating how these topics have been explored in the context of AI-powered

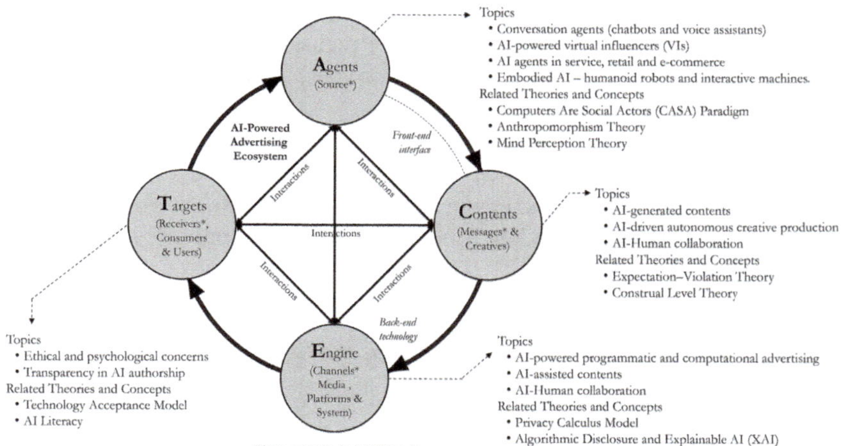

Figure 17.1 ACET (Agents, Contents, Engine, Targets) Framework.

advertising. In this first section, we highlight widely examined areas that have attracted scholarly attention and offer insights for advancing research on AI-driven advertising.

Topics in AI-Powered Persuasion Agents (Sources)

AI agents can be understood as autonomous systems that interpret and respond to consumer inquiries, functioning as mediating front-end interfaces in advertising. Enabled by machine learning and natural language processing, they personalize message delivery, generate creative content, and facilitate consumer interaction.

Conversational agents such as chatbots and voice assistants simulate dialogue, conversation, and interactions to guide consumer decisions. Research shows that anthropomorphic cues in AI agent can enhance persuasiveness in hedonic contexts (Youn & Cho, 2023) but may also trigger discomfort when perceived as overly human-like, a phenomenon described as the "uncanny valley of mind" (Kim et al., 2024). Perceptions of moral agency also matter: chatbots seen as morally responsible are held accountable during crises (Ahn et al., 2024). AI voice-overs increase cognitive load compared to human narration, though subtitles can mitigate this effect (Wang et al., 2024). Collectively, interface design and identity cues shape trust, engagement, and moral judgment.

Second, AI-powered VIs are algorithmically managed personas that blend curated aesthetics with brand storytelling. VIs with warm visual cues increase emotional trust (Chan et al., 2023), while transparency about VI identity strengthens perceptions of agency (Wang & Qiu, 2024). Diversity in race, body type, and ability enhances authenticity and engagement (Ferraro et al., 2024). Yet, responses to synthetic ads hinge on authenticity perceptions, with risks of perceived manipulation (Campbell et al., 2023). Effects often vary by product type, appeal, and consumer involvement.

A third area of research considers AI agents specialized in service, retail, and e-commerce. Service robots foster satisfaction through warmth and parasocial bonding (Ku, 2024), while AI service quality drives engagement, particularly for consumers inclined toward AI interaction (Prentice et al., 2020). Disclosure of AI use can reduce trust in services, especially when applied to intangible attributes, though effects are lessened when AI is confined to tangible elements (Grigsby et al., 2025).

A fourth research stream explores embodied AI agents such as humanoid robots and interactive machines. Robots' moderate anthropomorphism tends to build comfort and trust, whereas excessive human-likeness can cause discomfort, particularly in failure scenarios (Letheren et al., 2021; Mulcahy et al., 2024). Gesture-based interactivity enhances self-presence and engagement on large digital displays (Jung et al., 2022). Specialist consumers, however, distrust low-intelligence robots, revealing ideological biases in acceptance (Guido et al.,

2024). Social bonding with robots has also been shown to increase satisfaction and engagement (Ku, 2024), emphasizing the need for careful alignment of form, realism, and identity.

Topics in AI-Generated Contents (Messages and Creatives)

Generative and predictive AI are reshaping advertising by autonomously creating visuals, text, audio, and narratives tailored to consumers and brand contexts. Beyond serving as production tools, these systems increasingly act as ollaborative partners with human creators in ideation, design, and message optimization.

A growing body of research shows that AI-generated content can rival or even surpass human-created material. Hartmann et al. (2025) demonstrate that AI images outperform human designs in both aesthetics and effectiveness, while Wen and Laporte (2025) find that large language models produce narratives that evoke stronger emotional responses and purchase intentions. AI voices tuned to specific traits influence perceptions of product congruency (Efthymiou et al., 2024), and deep-learning models aligning music with ad timing enhance engagement (Fong et al., 2025). Similarly, Guo and Jiang (2025) report that

AI-generated personalized ad copy boosts engagement in field experiments, while Shumanov et al. (2022) show that tailoring appeals to predicted personality traits increases effectiveness, particularly for neurotic and extraverted consumers. Yet consumer responses remain nuanced. Hardcastle et al. (2025) find that while personalized contents can improve experiences, it also raises concerns about control and empowerment. Other studies caution that AI-authored content may reduce perceived authenticity: Brüns and Meißner (2024) note diminished trust in AI-created social media posts, while Kirk and Givi (2025) show that emotionally charged AI ads can elicit backlash. Wu et al. (2024) further demonstrate that transparency about AI authorship affects trust in context-dependent ways.

Research also highlights AI's impact on creative labor. Pagani and Wind (2025) outline a framework for agile, augmented, and unconventional creativity, while Akmeraner-Kökat and Pellandini-Simányi (2025) show how device-led creativity restructures agency in advertising work. Studies on human–AI collaboration confirm both potential and pitfalls: co-created ads can elevate expectations but risk greater disappointment when outcomes fall short (Ryoo et al., 2025a). Zhang et al. (2025) find that AI agents are more effective with rational appeals, while humans remain stronger communicators of emotional messages.

Finally, methodological contributions are emerging. Zamudio et al. (2024) propose the Rapid Artificial Intelligence Stimuli for Experiments method for producing AI-generated stimuli, and Van Berlo et al. (2024) introduce the Mapping, Assembling, Demonstrating, and Executing framework for ensuring ethical and valid use of generative AI in experiments.

Topics in AI-Driven Engines (Channels, Media, Platforms, or Systems)

The early stage of AI in advertising emerged with programmatic and computational systems that automated ad placement and delivery. This transition shifted advertising from static media planning to dynamic, data-driven architectures capable of adapting in real time to user feedback. Chen et al. (2019) introduced the concept of programmatic creative, illustrating how AI integrates media delivery with personalized content.

Biometric and affective-computing research further advanced this trajectory. Marques et al. (2025) show that electrodermal activity and facial expression analysis can predict ad preferences, while Alipour et al. (2024) demonstrate that convolutional neural networks classify engagement based on facial cues, with happiness indicating interest, and disgust or fear signaling disinterest. Yet scholars caution against uncritical adoption. Díaz Ruiz (2024) argues that programmatic infrastructures, though efficient, may diffuse accountability and inadvertently spread disinformation. Similarly, Beauvisage et al. (2024) find that despite sophisticated algorithmic tools, practitioners often revert to demographic segmentation, highlighting a persistent gap between technological potential and applied practice.

Topics in Persuasion Targets (Receivers, Consumers, or Users)

Advertising targets include consumers, users, and receivers of AI-generated contents, with research increasingly focused on ethical, regulatory, and normative concerns as AI assumes more autonomous and social roles. Paget (2024) critiques fragmented regulation of synthetic political ads and calls for national disclosure mandates, while Rodgers and Nguyen (2022) propose ethics-by-design frameworks grounded in deontological and utilitarian logics.

Consumer responses highlight significant ethical and psychological tensions. Kirk and Givi (2025) find that AI-authored, emotionally charged ads reduce perceptions of authenticity, evoke moral disgust, and reduce consumer trust. Gu et al. (2024) show that eeriness in AI-generated ads undermines acceptance unless offset by intelligence or vividness cues. In CSR contexts, AI involvement can reduce brand engagement by diminishing perceived sincerity (Aljarah et al., 2024), while in charity advertising, personalization may backfire by threatening autonomy unless framed as servant-style or choice-based (Lv & Huang, 2024). Transparency about AI authorship is also critical. Wu et al. (2024) demonstrate that disclosure generally decreases trust and effectiveness, though effects vary by task type, suggesting the importance of context-contingent strategies.

In sum, these findings demonstrate a shift in persuasion dynamics: effectiveness now depends not only on how content is designed but also on how AI agents appear, behave, and are perceived as moral and social actors. These advances also underscore AI's dual role as both a transformative production tool and a collaborative partner, while highlighting the importance of authenticity, disclosure, and ethical practice in shaping consumer acceptance. Advertising is thus no longer simply algorithmically mediated—it is co-produced through machine presence, affective resonance, and public accountability.

Applications of Theories in AI-Powered Advertising: Theory and Concept Overview

Our analysis revealed that several theories and concepts have been widely applied to address research questions in the context of AI-powered advertising. In this second section, we highlight theories and concepts that provide scholars with effective frameworks for examining AI-related advertising phenomena in the four areas of ACET framework.

Theories and Concepts in Agents

COMPUTERS ARE SOCIAL ACTORS (CASA) PARADIGM

The Computers Are Social Actors (CASA) paradigm posits that humans naturally and automatically apply social rules, norms, and expectations to computers, AI systems, and other interactive technologies (Reeves & Nass, 1996). According to CASA, individuals respond to these non-human entities as if they were social actors, even while fully aware that the entity is a machine. This response is triggered by minimal social cues—such as language use, tone of voice, conversational turn-taking, emotional expressiveness, or perceived responsiveness—that activate mindless social processing (Ham et al., 2024). In the context of AI advertising, CASA provides a foundational explanation for why consumers interact with AI-driven brand agents—such as chatbots, VIs, recommendation systems, and intelligent voice assistants—as if they were human representatives of the brand. When AI systems are designed with social features, they activate consumers' social cognition, making interactions feel more natural, trustworthy, and emotionally engaging. This social engagement enhances advertising outcomes such as brand liking, persuasion, brand loyalty, and purchase intention (Nkegbe & Abor, 2023). Understanding CASA is crucial for advertisers, as it underscores that even minimal anthropomorphic cues can meaningfully shape consumer perceptions and behaviors. Importantly, the effectiveness of AI agents in advertising is not solely determined by technological sophistication but also by the psychological and social dynamics they evoke (Xu et al., 2024).

ANTHROPOMORPHISM THEORY (THREE-FACTOR THEORY)

The Three-Factor Theory of Anthropomorphism explains why people attribute human qualities to non-human agents, identifying three motivations: elicited agent knowledge, sociality, and effectance (Epley et al., 2007). This framework is highly relevant to AI advertising as it clarifies the psychological mechanisms that lead consumers to perceive AI agents as human-like. Anthropomorphism enhances trust, relatability, and emotional engagement, making VIs, chatbots, recommendation systems, and voice assistants more approachable and socially present (Kim et al., 2023; Sun et al., 2024). In this context, elicited agent knowledge enables consumers to apply familiar human schemas to AI interactions, sociality motivation fulfills needs for connection and companionship with AI agents, and effectance motivation reduces uncertainty by increasing predictability and control in AI. Together, these processes provide advertisers with a foundational framework for designing AI agents that resonate with consumers cognitively, emotionally, and socially, ultimately strengthening persuasion and brand relationships.

MIND PERCEPTION THEORY

Mind perception theory posits that individuals attribute minds not only to humans but also to non-human agents, perceiving them along two independent dimensions: experience—the capacity to feel and sense emotional or biological states—and agency—the capacity to act intentionally, plan, and exercise self-control (Lee & Kim, 2025). This process serves as a pre-attribution mechanism for evaluating accountability, consciousness, and the ability to recognize others' emotions and needs (Wang & Qiu, 2024). In AI advertising contexts, some studies characterize VIs as mindless entities lacking both intention and emotional capacity, which affords brands greater flexibility in deploying them as persuasion agents (Willemsen et al., 2025). Other research, however, suggests that AI agents are not always perceived as mindless, particularly regarding agency. Consumers often view AI systems as capable of intentional, rational functions such as planning, efficiency, and execution—thereby enhancing perceptions of agency (Lee & Kim, 2024; Wang & Qiu, 2024). Overall, while experience is typically perceived as limited, perceptions of agency are more context-dependent, shaped by factors such as product domain, transparency cues, and the framing of AI capabilities.

Theories and Concepts in Contents

EXPECTATION–VIOLATION THEORY

Expectation–Violation Theory (EVT) posits that individuals evaluate interactions based on whether outcomes align with or deviate from prior expectations. Positive violations enhance satisfaction, while negative violations diminish trust and evaluations (Burgoon, 1992; Burgoon & Le Poire, 1993). In AI advertising, EVT offers a useful framework for understanding consumer responses when algorithmic performance either exceeds or falls short of anticipated standards.

In algorithmic creativity, expectations are grounded in human benchmarks for artistic and aesthetic quality. Research on AI-generated music shows that when outputs surpass expectations for creativity and enjoyment, they are perceived as positive violations, but when they fail to meet human standards, evaluations drop sharply, underscoring the importance of expectation gaps in persuasion outcomes (Hong et al., 2020). In collaborative advertising, expectations center on the added value of AI–human partnerships. Consumers often assume that collaboration will generate superior creativity and synergy; however, when these high expectations are unmet, the violation results in disappointment, skepticism, and reduced trust in both the AI system and the sponsoring brand (Ryoo et al., 2025b). In service communication, expectations are defined by both informational accuracy and relational cues. Users interacting with chatbots anticipate not only reliable information but also responsiveness and empathy. When these expectations are violated, consumers experience negative outcomes, lowering satisfaction with the chatbot and eroding trust in the AI system and the firm behind it (Rheu et al., 2024).

CONSTRUAL LEVEL THEORY

Construal Level Theory (CLT) posits that individuals interpret events, objects, or actions at varying levels of abstraction depending on their perceived psychological distance (Trope & Liberman, 2010). High-level construals are abstract, schematic, and decontextualized, emphasizing central and goal-relevant features. In contrast, low-level construals are concrete, contextualized, and detail-oriented, highlighting incidental or subordinate aspects (Trope et al., 2007; Liberman & Trope, 2008). Psychological distance—encompassing temporal, spatial, social, and hypothetical dimensions—is the key determinant of construal level. Events perceived as temporally or socially distant are processed at higher, more abstract levels, whereas events perceived as proximal are represented through lower, more concrete construals (Liberman & Trope, 1998). In the context of AI advertising, CLT helps explain why AI VIs tend to align more effectively with utilitarian messages, while human influencers are often better suited to hedonic appeals. This distinction arises because humans are typically associated with high-level construal, whereas AI systems are often perceived as better equipped to deliver concrete, utilitarian information (Kim & Duhachek, 2020; Lee & Ham, 2023).

Theories and Concepts in Engines

PRIVACY CALCULUS MODEL

The Privacy Calculus Model explains how individuals weigh the benefits and risks of disclosing personal information (Cloarec et al., 2024). Consumers are more willing to share data when perceived benefits—such as personalization, convenience, or rewards—outweigh perceived risks, including privacy invasion or data misuse (Kim et al., 2023). In AI-driven advertising, this framework is particularly relevant due to evolving personalization engines in the media, platforms, and systems. Personalized recommendation systems, chatbots, and VIs depend on extensive data collection and analysis, placing consumers in situations where they must implicitly evaluate whether the value of personalization justifies potential risks. Benefits often include greater relevance, efficiency, and enhanced user experiences, such as predictive product recommendations or interactive customer service (Wu & Wen, 2021). However, risks remain significant. Concerns include data privacy violations, loss of control, opaque data practices, and fears of algorithmic manipulation (Menard & Bott, 2025; Diakopoulos, 2016). Because consumers often lack clarity about how AI systems collect and use their data, uncertainty and distrust may arise (Dwivedi et al., 2023). As AI engines grow more sophisticated in inferring sensitive information, ethical questions around autonomy and consent intensify. When risks are judged to outweigh benefits, consumers are more likely to resist or disengage from AI-generated advertising.

ALGORITHMIC DISCLOSURE, TRANSPARENCY, AWARENESS, AND EXPLAINABLE AI (XAI)

The rise of AI in advertising has heightened concerns over consumer trust, ethical data use, and the legitimacy of algorithmically generated content. Scholars and practitioners often address these issues through four related but distinct concepts: algorithmic disclosure, algorithmic transparency, algorithmic awareness, and explainable AI (XAI) (Kim et al., 2024).

Algorithmic disclosure refers to informing consumers that content or recommendations are generated by algorithms rather than humans, such as labeling an ad as "AI-generated." Disclosure makes the non-human source visible and shapes consumer trust, skepticism, and processing strategies (Diakopoulos, 2016). Algorithmic transparency goes further by clarifying how algorithms function—their logic, inputs, and criteria. In advertising, this might mean explaining why a specific ad is shown based on browsing or demographic data. Transparency fosters perceptions of fairness, accountability, and informed consent (Diakopoulos & Koliska, 2017).

Algorithmic awareness reflects consumers' recognition that algorithms shape their media environment. Awareness does not require technical expertise but rather a general consciousness that algorithms influence what is seen and recommended. In AI advertising, greater awareness can lead consumers to critically evaluate content and question credibility (Shin et al., 2022).

XAI focuses on making AI systems interpretable by providing human-understandable rationales for outputs. By "opening the black box," XAI seeks to improve transparency, accountability, and trust, especially in contexts where opaque decision-making could raise ethical or legal concerns (Ali et al., 2023; IBM, 2025).

While interrelated, these concepts are not interchangeable: disclosure reveals the presence of algorithms; transparency reveals their mechanisms; awareness reflects consumer recognition; and XAI provides interpretable justifications. Disclosure and transparency are system-level practices, awareness is consumer-level, and XAI operates as both a transparency tool and a trust-building mechanism (see Table 17.1).

INTERACTIVITY

Interactivity is broadly defined as the extent to which users can influence or modify media content in real time (Johnson et al., 2006). In digital communication, it reflects the degree to which participants can exchange roles and affect one another, highlighting engagement, responsiveness, and reciprocal influence (Rafaeli & Sudweeks, 1997).

Table 17.1 Concept Comparisons in Algorithmic Disclosure, Transparency, Awareness, and Explainable AI (XAI)

Concept	*Definition*	*Focus*	*Actor Responsible*	*Application in AI Advertising*
Algorithmic disclosure	Informing users that content or a decision is generated by an AI or algorithm.	*Revealing the presence* of AI.	Platform/ Advertiser	Labeling ads as "AI-generated"; disclosing chatbot or AI involvement in brand interactions.
Algorithmic transparency	Making the operations, logic, and data use of the AI system understandable to users.	*Revealing the mechanism* behind AI outputs.	Platform/ Advertiser	Providing information about how ads are targeted or how recommendations are generated.
Algorithmic awareness	Consumers' subjective recognition that algorithms shape the content they see.	*Consumer's cognitive recognition* of algorithmic influence.	Consumer	Influences consumer processing of AI-generated ads; heightens critical evaluation.
Explainable AI (XAI)	Designing AI systems to offer human-understandable justifications for decisions.	*Providing interpretable explanations* for AI outputs.	Platform/ Advertiser (via AI system design)	Chatbots or recommendation engines explaining why a product or service was suggested.

In AI-driven advertising, interactivity plays a central role. Technologies such as chatbots, personalized platforms, and VIs create two-way exchanges that adapt dynamically to consumer input. For instance, a chatbot promoting skincare may ask about a user's skin type and tailor recommendations, enhancing relevance and engagement (Kim et al., 2023). High interactivity benefits persuasion in several ways. It increases consumers' sense of agency and personalization, fostering deeper cognitive processing, emotional involvement, and brand attachment (Yang et al., 2025). It can also reduce trust concerns by making AI agents appear more credible and responsive. At the same time, interactivity shapes privacy perceptions: while personalized exchanges may reassure users by offering control, they can also heighten concerns if data use appears opaque.

Theories and Concepts in Targets

TECHNOLOGY ACCEPTANCE MODEL

The Technology Acceptance Model (TAM; Davis, 1989) explains how individuals adopt new technologies, emphasizing two core beliefs: perceived usefulness and perceived ease of use. These perceptions shape attitudes toward the technology and, ultimately, intention to use it. Applied to AI-driven advertising, TAM helps explain how consumers evaluate and respond to AI systems such as recommendation engines, chatbots, and virtual agents. When AI ads are seen as useful, for example, by improving personalization, timeliness, or decision-making, consumers are more likely to engage (Cho, 2024). Ease of use is equally critical; intuitive, responsive, and non-intrusive systems encourage adoption, while opaque or difficult-to-navigate systems foster confusion, distrust, or rejection. Extensions of TAM, including the Unified Theory of Acceptance and Use of Technology, highlight additional factors such as trust, social influence, and perceived risk. These are particularly salient in AI advertising, where concerns about data privacy and algorithmic transparency can undermine both perceived usefulness and ease of use, ultimately shaping consumer acceptance or resistance (Wang et al., 2023).

AI LITERACY

Traditionally, literacy referred simply to the ability to read and write (McBride, 2015). In the digital age, however, the concept has broadened to include digital literacy, reflecting the skills needed to participate equitably in a knowledge-based society (Bawden, 2008). Extending this further, recent scholarship identifies four dimensions of AI literacy: (1) understanding AI concepts and techniques, (2) using and applying AI in practice, (3) evaluating and creating AI systems, and (4) considering ethical issues such as fairness, accountability, and transparency (Carolus et al., 2023; Ng et al., 2021a; Wang et al., 2023). First, understanding AI refers to knowledge of fundamental AI techniques and concepts across products and services, along with building perceived abilities, confidence, and readiness to engage with AI (Kandlhofer et al., 2016; Ng et al., 2021a). Second, using and applying AI emphasizes equipping individuals to apply AI concepts in real-world contexts. Third, evaluating and creating AI involves higher order thinking skills such as critical evaluation, prediction, and innovation regarding AI applications (Ng et al., 2021a). Finally, AI ethics highlights human-centered concerns related to fairness, accountability, transparency, and safety in AI development and deployment (Kajiwara et al., 2024). Scholars have proposed and developed scales to measure AI literacy. Carolus et al. (2023) introduced the Meta AI Literacy Scale, which assesses AI literacy across four key dimensions: AI literacy, AI creation, AI self-efficacy, and AI self-competency, using 34 items. Wang et al. (2023) developed a scale to evaluate users' competence in interacting with AI, consisting of four dimensions: Awareness, Use, Evaluation, and Ethics, with a total of 31 items. To develop a scale, Ng et al. (2021b) conducted an exploratory review of 30 studies conceptualizing AI literacy proposing four broad components essential for fostering AI literacy: knowing and understanding, using and applying, evaluating and creating, and addressing ethical considerations.

In advertising, AI literacy holds important implications for both consumers and practitioners. As AI increasingly shapes ad targeting, content generation, and consumer engagement, those with higher literacy are better able to recognize algorithmic persuasion, question data-driven practices, and resist potential manipulation (Kim et al., 2024). For advertisers, awareness of varying AI literacy levels among audiences is essential for designing effective and ethical campaigns. Transparency in AI use, responsible data practices, and attention to consumer concerns can foster trust and credibility, while reducing risks of backlash against manipulative strategies.

Conclusion

While a wide range of established theories and concepts provide valuable insights to interpret how AI advertising works in topics of each ACET framework, the rapid advancement and integration of AI technologies into persuasive communication settings necessitate a more comprehensive and adaptive theoretical approach. Traditional frameworks were largely developed in contexts where humans were the sole agents of persuasion or where technology functioned as a passive medium. In contrast, AI functions as an active, autonomous, and dynamic participant in the communication process, often blurring the boundaries between human and machine, transparency and opacity, and control and delegation.

One key theoretical implication is the need for integration and adaptation. Rather than relying on a single framework, scholars must consider the interplay between multiple concepts and theories to fully understand consumer responses to AI advertising. For example, combining the three-factor theory of anthropomorphism with the mind perception framework allows researchers to assess not only *why* consumers anthropomorphize AI agents but also *how* they perceive their mental capacities in terms of agency and experience—an essential determinant of emotional connection and moral judgment. Additionally, frameworks like AI literacy and algorithmic transparency/disclosure demand refinement or expansion of existing models such as the persuasion knowledge model (Friestad & Wright, 1994; Lee & Ham, 2023). As AI becomes the "persuader," the very nature of persuasion changes: it is not always clear to consumers whether the message has a human or algorithmic origin. This ambiguity complicates the activation of persuasion knowledge, highlighting the need for models that account for hybrid source processing and algorithmic intention attribution.

In summary, the integration of AI into advertising environments challenges the sufficiency of traditional psychological and communication theories. Future theoretical development should aim to synthesize social cognition, motivational frameworks, algorithmic awareness, and ethical reasoning into more nuanced models that reflect the hybrid, semi-autonomous, and data-intensive nature of AI advertising. Only through such an interdisciplinary and integrative approach can researchers adequately capture the evolving dynamics of consumer–AI interactions in persuasive contexts.

Future Research

As AI becomes increasingly embedded in advertising, future research can address the complex interplay between technology, persuasion, and consumer psychology. A central question is how persuasion itself changes when contents originate from AI algorithms rather than humans. Another direction involves the relationship between AI literacy and algorithmic transparency. As consumers better understand AI systems, they may respond with greater skepticism or, conversely, greater trust. Examining how disclosure, targeting explanations, and system explainability shape trust and resistance is critical. AI-driven personalization also warrants closer study. While personalization enhances relevance and convenience, it can simultaneously trigger concerns about manipulation, surveillance, or loss of autonomy. Research should explore when personalization fosters empowerment versus disengagement, depending on framing and disclosure. Individual and cultural differences further moderate responses. Traits such as privacy sensitivity or sociality motivation, as well as cultural values surrounding technology and authority, may shape how AI advertising is interpreted across markets. Finally, the ethical dimensions of AI advertising demand sustained attention. As AI is used for microtargeting, prediction, and automation, research should investigate where consumers perceive the boundary between assistance and manipulation. Insights on fairness, transparency, and ethics can guide theory, industry practice, and policy aimed at safeguarding consumer trust.

References

Ahn, J., Kim, J., & Sung, Y. (2024). The role of perceived freewill in crises of human–AI interaction: The mediating role of ethical responsibility of AI. *International Journal of Advertising, 43*(5), 847–873.

Akmeraner-Kökat, Y., & Pellandini-Simányi, L. (2025). Creativity re-distributed: How digitalisation changes creative advertising practice. *Journal of Marketing Management,* Advance online publication.

Ali, S., Abuhmed, T., El-Sappagh, S., Muhammad, K., Alonso-Moral, J. M., Confalonieri, R., … & Herrera, F. (2023). Explainable Artificial Intelligence (XAI): What we know and what is left to attain Trustworthy Artificial Intelligence. *Information Fusion, 99,* 101805.

Aljarah, A., Ibrahim, B., & Lopez, M. (2024). In AI, we do not trust! The nexus between awareness of falsity in AI-generated CSR ads and online brand engagement. *Internet Research, 35*(3), 1406–1426.

Alipour, P., Gallegos, E. E., & Sridhar, S. (2024). AI-driven marketing personalization: Deploying convolutional neural networks to decode consumer behavior. *International Journal of Human–Computer Interaction, 41*(2), 123–140.

Bawden, D. (2008). Origins and concepts of digital literacy. *Digital Literacies: Concepts, Policies and Practices, 30*(2008), 17–32.

Beauvisage, T., Beuscart, J. S., & Mellet, K. (2024). How online advertising targets consumers: The uses of categories and algorithmic tools by audience planners. *New Media & Society, 26*(10), 6098–6119.

Berlo, D. K. (1960). *The process of communication; An introduction to theory and practice*. New York: Holt, Rinehart and Winston.

Brüns, J. D., & Meißner, M. (2024). Do you create your content yourself? Using generative artificial intelligence for social media content creation diminishes perceived brand authenticity. *Journal of Retailing and Consumer Services*, 79, 103–790.

Burgoon, J. K. (1992). Applying a comparative approach to nonverbal expectancy violations theory. In J. Blumler, K. E. Rosengren, & J. M. McLeod (Eds.), *Comparatively speaking: Communication and culture across space and time*, 53–69. Beverly Hills, CA: Sage.

Burgoon, J. K., & Le Poire, B. A. (1993). Effects of communication expectancies, actual communication, and expectancy disconfirmation on evaluations of communicators and their communication behavior. *Human Communication Research, 20*, 75–107.

Campbell, C., Sands, S., & Mavrommatis, A. (2023). Diversity representation in advertising. *Journal of the Academy of Marketing Science,* Advance online publication.

Carolus, A., Augustin, Y., Markus, A., & Wienrich, C. (2023). Digital interaction literacy model: Conceptualizing competencies for literate interactions with voice-based AI systems. *Computers and Education: Artificial Intelligence, 4,* 100114.

Carolus, A., Koch, M. J., Straka, S., Latoschik, M. E., & Wienrich, C. (2023). MAILS - Meta AI literacy scale: Development and testing of an AI literacy questionnaire based on well-founded competency models and psychological change- and meta-competencies. *Computers and Education: Artificial Intelligence, 1,* 100114.

Chan, K. W., Septianto, F., & Kamal, R. S. (2023). Color effects on AI influencers' product recommendations. *European Journal of Marketing, 57*(9), 2290–2315.

Chen, G., Xie, P. H., & Wang, T. F. (2019). Understanding programmatic creative: The role of AI. *Journal of Advertising, 48*(4), 347–355.

Cho, Y. C. (2024). Application of AI in marketing strategy: Insights from Millennials and generation Z. *The Journals of Economics, Marketing & Management, 12*(1), 29–38.

Cloarec, J., Meyer-Waarden, L., & Munzel, A. (2024). Transformative privacy calculus: Conceptualizing the personalization-privacy paradox on social media. *Psychology & Marketing, 41*(7), 1574–1596.

Davis, F. D. (1989). Perceived usefulness, perceived ease of use, and user acceptance of information technology. *MIS Quarterly, 13*(3), 319–340.

Diakopoulos, N. (2016). Accountability in algorithmic decision making. *Communications of the ACM, 59*(2), 56–62.

Diakopoulos, N., & Koliska, M. (2017). Algorithmic transparency in the news media. *Digital Journalism, 5*(7), 809–828.

Díaz Ruiz, C. A. (2024). Disinformation and fake news as externalities of digital advertising: A close reading of sociotechnical imaginaries in programmatic advertising. *Journal of Marketing Management, 40*(1–2), 52–75.

Dwivedi, Y. K., Kshetri, N., Hughes, L., Slade, E. L., Jeyaraj, A., Kar, A. K., ... & Wright, R. (2023). Opinion Paper: "So what if ChatGPT wrote it?" Multidisciplinary perspectives on opportunities, challenges and implications of generative conversational AI for research, practice and policy. *International Journal of Information Management, 71*, 102642.

Efthymiou, F., Hildebrand, C., & Hampton, W. H. (2024). The power of AI-generated voices: How digital vocal tract length shapes product congruency and ad performance. *Journal of Interactive Marketing, 59*(2), 117–134.

Epley, N., Waytz, A., & Cacioppo, J. T. (2007). On seeing human: A three-factor theory of anthropomorphism. *Psychological Review, 114*(4), 864.

Ferraro, C., Sands, S., & Campbell, C. (2024). Diversity in the digital age: How consumers respond to diverse virtual influencers. *International Journal of Advertising, 43*(8), 1342–1365.

Friestad, M., & Wright, P. (1994). The persuasion knowledge model: How people cope with persuasion attempts. *Journal of Consumer Research, 21*(1), 1–31.

Ford, J., Jain, V., Wadhwani, K., & Gupta, D. (2023). AI advertising: An overview and guidelines, *Journal of Business Research, 166*, 114–124.

Fong, H., Kumar, V., & Sudhir, K. (2025). A theory-based explainable deep learning architecture for music emotion. *Marketing Science, 44*(1), 110–128.

Grigsby, J. L., Michelsen, M., & Zamudio, C. (2025). Service ads in the era of generative AI: Disclosures, trust, and intangibility. *Journal of Retailing and Consumer Services, 84,* 104519.

Gu, C. Y., Jia, S. Y., & Chang, X. S. Y. (2024). Exploring consumer acceptance of AI-generated advertisements: From the perspectives of perceived eeriness and perceived intelligence. *Journal of Theoretical and Applied Electronic Commerce Research, 19*(3), 2218–2238.

Guido, J. C. F. L., Kim, J. W., & Tuzovic, S. (2024). Retail robots as sales assistants: How speciesism moderates the effect of robot intelligence on customer perceptions and behaviour. *Journal of Service Theory and Practice, 34*(1), 127–154.

Guo, B., & Jiang, Z. B. (2025). Influence of personalised advertising copy on consumer engagement: A field experiment approach. *Electronic Commerce Research, 25*(2), 1281–1310.

Lee, G., & Kim, H. Y. (2025). Algorithm fashion designer? Ascribed mind and perceived design expertise of AI versus human. *Psychology & Marketing, 42*(1), 255–273.

Ham, C. D., & Nelson, M. R. (2019). The reflexive persuasion game: The Persuasion knowledge model (1994–2017). In S. Rodgers & E. Thorson (Eds.), *Advertising theory*, 124–140. New York, NY: Routledge.

Ham, J., Li, S., Looi, J., & Eastin, M. S. (2024). Virtual humans as social actors: Investigating user perceptions of virtual humans' emotional expression on social media. *Computers in Human Behavior, 155,* 108161.

Hardcastle, K., Vorster, L., & Brown, D. M., (2025). Understanding customer responses to AI-driven personalized journeys: Impacts on the customer experience. *Journal of Advertising, 54*(2), 176–195.

Hartmann, J., Exner, Y., & Domdey, S. (2025). The power of generative marketing: Can generative AI create superhuman visual marketing content? *International Journal of Research in Marketing, 42*(1), 13–31.

Huang, G. & Wang, S. (2023). Is artificial intelligence more persuasive than humans? A meta-analysis, *Journal of Communication, 73*(6), 552–562.

Hong, J. W., Peng, Q., & Williams, D. (2020). Are you ready for artificial Mozart and Skrillex? An experiment testing expectancy violation theory and AI music. *New Media & Society, 23*(7), 1920–1935.

IBM. (2025, February 13). What is explainable AI (XAI)? https://www.ibm.com/think/topics/explainable-ai

Johnson, G. J., Bruner II, G. C., & Kumar, A. (2006). Interactivity and its facets revisited: Theory and empirical test. *Journal of Advertising, 35*(4), 35–52.

Jung, S., Lee, D., & Kum-Biocca, H. (2022). The role of self-presence in interactive large digital displays. *International Journal of Human-Computer Interaction, 38*(16), 1576–1588.

Kajiwara, Y., & Kawabata, K. (2024). AI literacy for ethical use of chatbot: Will students accept AI ethics? *Computers and Education: Artificial Intelligence, 6,* 100251.

Kandlhofer, M., Steinbauer, G., Hirschmugl-Gaisch, S., & Huber, P. (2016, October). Artificial intelligence and computer science in education: From kindergarten to university. In *2016 IEEE Frontiers in Education Conference (FIE)* (pp. 1–9). IEEE.

Kim, T., & Duhachek, A. (2020). Artificial intelligence and persuasion: A construal-level account. *Psychological Science, 31*(4), 363–380.

Kim, W., Ryoo, Y., & Choi, Y. K. (2024). That uncanny valley of mind: When anthropomorphic AI agents disrupt personalized advertising. *International Journal of Advertising,* Advance online publication.

Kim, W., Ryoo, Y., Lee, S., & Lee, J. A. (2023). Chatbot advertising as a double-edged sword: The roles of regulatory focus and privacy concerns. *Journal of Advertising, 52*(4), 504–522.

Kirk, C. P., & Givi, J. (2025). The AI-authorship effect: Understanding authenticity, moral disgust, and consumer responses to AI-generated marketing communications. *Journal of Business Research, 186,* 113562.

Ku, E. C. S. (2024). Digital marketing innovation and industrial marketing: Evidence from restaurants' service robots. *Asia Pacific Journal of Marketing and Logistics, 36*(11), 3099–3117.

Lee, D., & Ham, C.-D. (2023) AI versus human: Rethinking the role of agent knowledge in consumers' coping mechanism with influencer marketing. *Journal of Interactive Advertising, 23*(3), 241–258.

Lee, G., & Kim, H.- Y. (2024). Algorithm fashion designer? Ascribed mind and perceived design expertise of AI versus human. *Psychology & Marketing, 41*(1), 255–273.

Letheren, K., Jetten, J., & Donovan, J. (2021). Robots should be seen and not heard… sometimes: Anthropomorphism and AI service robot interactions. *Psychology & Marketing, 38*(12), 2393–2406.

Liberman, N., & Trope, Y. (1998). The role of feasibility and desirability considerations in near and distant future decisions: A test of temporal construal theory. *Journal of Personality and Social Psychology, 75*(1), 5–18.
Liberman, N., & Trope, Y. (2008). The psychology of transcending the here and now. *Science, 322*(5905), 1201–1205.
Lv, L. X., & Huang, M. X. (2024). Can personalized recommendations in charity advertising boost donation? The role of perceived autonomy. *Journal of Advertising, 53*(1), 36–53.
Marques, J. A. L., Neto, A. C., & Bigné, E. (2025). Predicting consumer ad preferences: Leveraging a machine learning approach for EDA and FEA neurophysiological metrics. *Psychology & Marketing, 42*(1), 175–192.
McBride, C. (2015). Children's literacy development: A cross-cultural perspective on learning to read and write. 3rd edition, New York, Routledge.
Menard, P., & Bott, G. J. (2025). Artificial intelligence misuse and concern for information privacy: New construct validation and future directions. *Information Systems Journal, 35*(1), 322–367.
Mulcahy, R. F., Riedel, A., & Letheren, K. (2024). Avoiding excessive AI service agent anthropomorphism: Examining its role in delivering bad news. *Journal of Service Theory and Practice, 34*(1), 98–126.
Ng, D. T. K., Leung, J. K. L., Chu, K. W. S., & Qiao, M. S. (2021a). AI literacy: Definition, teaching, evaluation and ethical issues. *Proceedings of the Association for Information Science and Technology, 58*(1), 504–509.
Ng, D. T. K., Leung, J. K. L., Chu, K. W. S., & Qiao, M. S. (2021b). Conceptualizing AI literacy: An exploratory review. *Computers and Education: Artificial Intelligence, 2*(1), 100041.
Nkegbe, F., & Abor, Y. (2023). The role of social media in enhancing customer engagement and brand loyalty. *Journal of Policy Options, 6*(3), 26–34.
Pagani, M., & Wind, Y. (2025). Unlocking marketing creativity using artificial intelligence. *Journal of Interactive Marketing, 60*(1), 1–24.
Paget, A. (2024). (Synthetic) stump speech: Crafting generative AI disclosure regulations for political ads. *Fordham Law Review, 93*(1), 321–358.
Prentice, C., Weaven, S., & Wong, I. A. (2020). Linking AI quality performance and customer engagement: The moderating effect of AI preference. *International Journal of Hospitality Management, 90,* 102610.
Rafaeli, S., & Sudweeks, F. (1997). Networked interactivity. *Journal of Computer-Mediated Communication, 2*(4), JCMC243.
Reeves, B., & Nass, C. (1996). *The media equation: How people treat computers, television, and new media like real people.* Cambridge, 10(10), 19–36.
Rheu, M., Dai, Y., Meng, J., & Peng, W. (2024). When a chatbot disappoints you: Expectancy violation in human-chatbot interaction in a social support context. *Communication Research, 51*(7), 782–814.
Rodgers, W., & Nguyen, T. (2022). Advertising benefits from ethical artificial intelligence: Algorithmic purchase decision pathways. *Journal of Business Ethics, 178*(4), 1043–1061.
Ryoo, Y., Bakpayev, M., & Yoon, S. (2025a). High hopes, hard falls: Consumer expectations and reactions to AI–human collaboration in advertising. *International Journal of Advertising,* Advance online publication.
Ryoo, Y., Halfacre, V., & Yoon, H. J. (2025b). AI chatbot interventions in combatting marijuana-impaired driving: The role of gender, linguistic style, and hypocrisy induction. *International Journal of Advertising,* Advance online publication.

Shin, D., Kee, K. F., & Shin, E. Y. (2022). Algorithm awareness: Why user awareness is critical for personal privacy in the adoption of algorithmic platforms? *International Journal of Information Management, 65,* 102494.

Shumanov, M., Cooper, H., & Ewing, M. (2022). Using AI-predicted personality to enhance advertising effectiveness. *European Journal of Marketing, 56*(6), 1590–1609.

Sun, Y., Chen, J., & Sundar, S. S. (2024). Chatbot ads with a human touch: A test of anthropomorphism, interactivity, and narrativity. *Journal of Business Research, 172,* 114403.

Trope, Y., & Liberman, N. (2010). Construal-level theory of psychological distance. *Psychological Review, 117*(2), 440–463.

Trope, Y., Liberman, N., & Wakslak, C. J. (2007). Construal levels and psychological distance: Effects on representation, prediction, evaluation, and behavior. *Journal of Consumer Psychology, 17,* 83–95.

Van Berlo, Z. M. C., Campbell, C., & Voorveld, H. A, M. (2024). The MADE framework: Best practices for creating effective experimental stimuli using generative AI. *Journal of Advertising, 53*(5), 732–753.

Wang, B., Rau, P. L. P., & Yuan, T. (2023). Measuring user competence in using artificial intelligence: Validity and reliability of artificial intelligence literacy scale. *Behaviour & Information Technology, 42*(9), 1324–1337.

Wang, X. M., Zhang, Z., & Jiang, Q. Y. (2024). The effectiveness of human vs. AI voice-over in short video advertisements: A cognitive load theory perspective. *Journal of Retailing and Consumer Services, 81,* 104451.

Wang, X. Y., & Qiu, X. Y. (2024). The positive effect of artificial intelligence technology transparency on digital endorsers: Based on the theory of mind perception. *Journal of Retailing and Consumer Services, 78,* 103349.

Wen, Y. T., & Laporte, S. (2025). Experiential narratives in marketing: A comparison of generative AI and human content. *Journal of Public Policy & Marketing,* Advance online publication.

Willemsen, L. M., Withuis, I., Brom, M., & Boerman, S. C. (2025). How does persuasion knowledge differ between humanlike virtual influencers and human influencers? *International Journal of Advertising, 44*(1), 109–130.

Wu, L., & Jing Wen, T. (2021). Understanding AI advertising from the consumer perspective: What factors determine consumer appreciation of AI-created advertisements? *Journal of Advertising Research, 61*(2), 133–146.

Wu, L., Dodoo, N. A., & Wen, T. J. (2024). Disclosing AI's involvement in advertising to consumers: A task-dependent perspective. *Journal of Advertising, 54*(1), 20–38.

Xu, Y., Dai, H., & Yan, W. (2024). Identity disclosure and anthropomorphism in voice chatbot design: A field experiment. *Management Science, 72*(1), 223–241.

Yang, S., Guo, Y., Chen, Y., Li, Y., Zhou, S., & Jiang, H. (2025). Understanding service performance of frontline employees from employee–AI interaction perspective. *Journal of Service Management, 36*(3), 448–475.

Youn, K., & Cho, M. H. (2023). Business types matter: New insights into the effects of anthropomorphic cues in AI chatbots. *Journal of Services Marketing, 37*(8), 1032–1045.

Zamudio, C., Grigsby, J. L., & Michelsen, M. (2024). RAISE: A new method to develop experimental stimuli for advertising research with image generative artificial intelligence. *Journal of Advertising,* Advance online publication, *55*(2), 264–279

Zhang, Y. Y., Zhu, J. J., & Jiang, Y. S. (2025). Enhancing trust and empathy in marketing: Strategic AI and human influencer selection for optimized content persuasion. *Journal of Consumer Behaviour, 24*(2), 866–885.

Part V

Ethics and Responsibility in Digital Systems

18 Targeted Digital Advertising and Privacy

Heather Shoenberger

In the early days of internet advertising, practitioners predicted consumers would desire more personalized advertising as the capabilities of curating and creating messages emerged (McMillan, 2004). Fast-forward to 2025 and it appears that prediction has rung true, and new methods of personalization and hyperson-alization are becoming possible with evolving technologies (Blackwell, 2024). Research shows that relevant messages tailored to consumer interests are more helpful and interesting to consumers than randomly placed advertising messages (Shoenberger, Sableman, & Thorson, 2013).

Targeted digital advertising has grown rapidly and become increasingly sophisticated. The internet allows the collection, aggregation, and synthesis of clickstream data, purchase behavior, etc. to deliver advertisements tailored to previous online behavior (Barnes, 2002). Search engines, social media, and other types of digital content rank messages displayed to consumers based on algo-rithms or rules (Sullivan, 2002). Tailoring allows for potentially more relevant search results and accompanying advertisements based on consumer behavior in the digital context (e.g., past searches and clickstream activity) (FTC, 2007). For example, consider the newly released Pokemon Go application. The app is based on geo-location technology, which has attracted millions of users within days of its initial launch. The app is able to capture email addresses, webpages viewed before entering the app, geographic location, IP address, Google pro-file information (if a person signed into the app using a Google account), and more (Bernstein, 2016). All of the information captured by this popular app could be used to design and serve digital advertising specifically tailored to a consumer based on his/her behavior in the digital context. However, as tailored messaging in the digital context grows, so too does the concern that consumer privacy expectations may not be met.

The editors of this book note in Chapter 2 that in the realm of digital adver-tising, there is a network of message movements across platforms. The issue of targeted digital advertising and privacy touches upon message curation, manipulation, and creation of messages as information about consumers' online behavior is stored, analyzed, and used to create personalized search results and

DOI: 10.4324/9781003567523-23

serve targeted advertisements. There are clear benefits for advertisers and consumers, in that personalized messages based on past consumer behavior are the advertising that consumers see. Advertisers are able to offer more relevant content, and, subsequently, consumers receive more relevant messages.

As digital advertisers work to interpret and apply seemingly infinite amounts of data, curating the important pieces of information, and manipulating the information to provide messages to consumers, the issue of how to address consumer privacy concerns persists. What is meaning and value of privacy in relation to the benefits of digital advertising? Do consumers receive adequate notification and/or options for controlling their data? Where should the line be drawn between consumer-reported anxiety over data privacy and unfocused, rather nonchalant behavior regarding data protection?

In considering the above questions, this chapter will begin with a short discussion of privacy and digital advertising. In doing so, the current regulation of privacy in the digital advertising context will be discussed, and the literature on consumer concerns versus their actual behaviors online will be highlighted. This chapter concludes with some suggestions for future research to address the complex issue of privacy concerns as they relate to digital advertising.

Information and Privacy

People constantly negotiate a balance between privacy and the need to be stimulated by other human beings. Violation of expected privacy boundaries may harm the human psyche and cause emotional or even physical ailments to arise (Westin, 1967). Privacy is important to the emotional and cognitive functioning of people because it allows them to pursue self-actualization (Calo, 2015).

Privacy is easy to understand when considered analogous to a physical door that provides privacy for people in their homes. It becomes more complicated as it relates to how and when data about a person is used. It may not be as easy to grasp or protect privacy in a context that is not understood through physical boundaries. Companies involved in digital advertising have to grapple with defining an appropriate line between offering relevant messages based on profiles curated online and failing to respect the privacy expectations of the consumer. Privacy, in the digital advertising context, involves how the data collected about consumers is employed to deliver tailored advertisements. The tension is generated by what consumers *expect* advertisers to do with their personal information and what advertisers actually *do* the personal details that consumers provide online.

In the economic context, consumer advocates worry that unfettered data collection by companies for advertising purposes will be harmful to the consumer, incorrect digital profiles may be created, and using personal profiles may be used to discriminate against people and cause other harms (Podesta et al., 2014). The other side of the issue includes fear that stifling of data collection will result in stunted innovation and an inefficient marketplace (Calo, 2015).

Control over the information created by consumers in the digital context is controversial with some scholars advocating for the information to remain under the control of the consumer and others advocating for more control to be held by those who may curate and use the data for market purposes (Calo, 2015). Targeted digital advertising will be the focus of this chapter because the very existence of targeted digital advertising depends, in large part, on the data provided by consumers. While digital advertising could be any advertisement placed on digital media such as mobile devices, or the internet, targeted digital advertising uses consumer data to serve ads to consumers based on their behavior online.

Respect for information privacy can be useful to the growth and maintenance of markets because it has the capacity to increase trust between consumers and companies. Trust on the part of consumers is necessary for digital commerce to prove satisfactory to consumers and grow (Pavlou, 2003). Trust is especially important in this context as consumers have little bargaining power when it comes to digital transactions of personal data (Beldad, De Jong, & Steehouder, 2010). The Federal Trade Commission (FTC) enforces companies' privacy policies to mollify consumer trust issues and allow privacy to bolster an efficient marketplace (Calo, 2015). Privacy allows transactions online to take place based on relevant information (e.g., the price of a product) instead of based on entire profiles (e.g., information about the seller or buyer's spiritual practices) (Calo, 2015).

Some companies may keep consumer data collected via use of their website or application proprietary but may use the data in ways that violates consumer expectations of privacy. For example, Facebook holds consumer data proprietary within its own network to offer pieces of content such as news stories and friend photos to people based on their interests (Sutton, 2016). The idea of a consumer within Facebook's walls being served only stories interesting to them based on prior behavior is defended as a good business decision though some critics have noted the content may be biased toward Facebook leaders' sensibilities, especially in the news story realm (Sutton, 2016). Facebook also ran into trouble when its "People You May Know" feature was connected to geo-location data about people, although the company later denied it used geo-location data to suggest new friends (Burlacu, 2016). The feature, when based on geo-location and other information, may expose physical locations a consumer meant to keep private (Nicks, 2016). For example, one story included a consumer who received a friend suggestion based on an anonymous meeting he attended (Nicks, 2016). In both instances of companies housing vast amounts of consumer data, there is a concern over hacking. What if a hacker was able to expose nearly every aspect of someone's private life, including medical visits or anonymous meetings, with one successful attempt to access Facebook's data? Of course, once again, consumer control as a mechanism of privacy protection is paramount. In this and most digital advertising settings, the onus is on the consumer to opt out of geo-location tracking via their mobile settings and other privacy settings within each respective application or device.

The integrity of consumer data privacy remains an important topic upon which regulators and scholars routinely discuss and debate as more information is collected about consumer behavior via better analytics and emerging technologies. The discussion involves balancing consumer privacy expectations against the interests of the market. A right to privacy was not explicitly included in the U.S. law; thus, regulators and privacy advocates are forced to search for ways to carve out such a right or institute safeguards to hold companies accountable for data use and distribution and provide notice to consumers about how their data may be used.

Regulating Privacy in the Digital Advertising Context

The first mention of a right to privacy was spurred by technological advancement and a concern that the government may be able to conduct surveillance on citizens in ways that would chill behavior and information sharing (Solove, 2006). Warren and Brandeis (1890) noted that what was once whispered behind closed doors would one day be screamed from the rooftops. This sentiment of privacy, actions taken with no obvious onlooker, is relevant to the discussion of privacy in the context of digital advertising today.

Currently, the legal definition for privacy exists in the consumers' ability to show that they had an expectation of privacy in the matter at hand (Solove, 2006). If a consumer cannot show a reasonable expectation of privacy, there are few protections available under privacy law. Thus, the definition of privacy in the context of digital advertising is important.

Under the umbrella of digital advertising, privacy has often been synonymous with control (Solove, 2006; Brandimarte, Acquisti, & Lowestein, 2013). Thus, ensuring meaningful control over data in the digital context is the crux of the privacy debate in the digital advertising context. Privacy operationalized as control requires the consumer to awareness of how online sites use consumer data (Milne, Labrecque, & Cromer, 2009). In order for consumers to exert meaningful control over their data, they must digest each site, application, or device's privacy policy, if available, and to decide whether to agree with the terms and conditions. The U.S. legal system holds consumers to "click-thru" contracts in the same way as contracts physically signed despite the differences in the motivation to read the digital contracts, the asymmetry of the bargaining relationships, etc. (Moringiello, 2014), and privacy law expects consumers to proactively protect their interests (Moringiello, 2014; Schlosser, White, & Lloyd, 2006; Shield, 2014).

The FTC, in its regulatory role, works to ensure consumer control over data. The FTC began its foray into privacy protection in the 1990s when it started enforcing companies' existing privacy policies in the interest of preventing unfair or deceptive acts that affect commerce (Calo, 2015). The theory behind the enforcement was to encourage trust among consumers that privacy policies presented by companies could be relied on (Solove & Hartzog, 2014).

The FTC encourages notice and choice, often in the form of a link or icon directing the consumer to a stated privacy policy, in an effort to allow control over data collection and use (Federal Trade Commission, 2007). In addition to icons and links, privacy information may pop up just before a consumer downloads an application or navigates through a site. The looming issue for privacy advocates and regulators is how to approach the issue of consumers' control over data/privacy in a meaningful way. Consumers' paradoxical behavior makes privacy protection via notice and choice challenging.

Recent privacy laws like the EU's General Data Protection Regulation (GDPR) and a patchwork of state laws such as California Consumer Privacy Act and the Virginia Consumer Data Protection Act have introduced regulations on how advertisers can collect and use personal data, requiring some form of user consent or allowing consumers to opt out of targeted advertising (California Attorney General, 2024; Virginia Office of the Attorney General, 2023; GDPR, 2018). These regulations, enacted in 2018, 2020, and 2023, respectively, curtail tracking and behavioral targeting, forcing advertisers to pivot ad strategy or abide by the stricter rules (Wang, Jiang, & Yang, 2024). Early evidence suggests stricter laws (e.g., GDPR) reduce third-party trackers and diminish the effectiveness of targeted ads, resulting in lower advertising revenue especially for publishers (Wang, Jiang, & Yang, 2024). On the consumer side, individuals now have greater transparency and control—such as rights to know, delete, or not have their data sold or used for targeted ads—empowering them to opt out of personalized advertising (California Attorney General, 2024; Virginia Office of the Attorney General, 2023; GDPR, 2018). However, the laws have been criticized as leaving consumers with "take it or leave it" choices which negates the control bequeathed by them (Borgesius et al., 2017). These regulations also do not contemplate data collection and usage via newer technologies such as generative artificial intelligence (AI).

The Privacy Paradox: The Curious Case of Consumer Privacy Concern vs. Apathy

Digital advertising has become increasingly data-driven, leveraging personal information to tailor content to individual consumers. In recent years, advertisers have embraced new technologies—including AI and augmented reality (AR)—to enhance targeting and consumer engagement. These innovations not only promise more immersive and personalized ad experiences but also amplify privacy concerns. Recent scholarship acknowledges a surge of novel advertising formats, such as AR ads, AI-powered messaging, and "deepfake" endorsements, that have entered the marketing toolkit (Boerman & Smit, 2023; Campbell et al., 2022).

Each of these technologies gathers or utilizes consumer data in new ways. For example, AR campaigns often access cameras and sensors to overlay digital content on the user's real environment. Research on AR face filter apps finds that they can collect highly sensitive personal information—including biometric data like facial images and emotional expressions—raising heightened privacy issues (Cowan, Javornik, & Jiang, 2021). In fact, users consider biometric identifiers (e.g., facial data) especially private, more so than typical data collected by older digital ad techniques (Cowan, Javornik, & Jiang, 2021). AI has been a double-edged sword in digital advertising. On one hand, AI algorithms allow advertisers to analyze big data and micro-target consumers with unprecedented precision; on the other, this intensive data processing heightens the stakes for consumer privacy. Scholars note that the discussion of privacy in advertising now extends beyond traditional web tracking to new AI-driven tools. For instance, generative AI gives rise to significant privacy concerns due to the use and large amounts of personal and biometric data used for training, "including face and body biometrics for image generation and voice biometrics for speech generation" (Xiang, 2024, p. 288). Regardless of many calls for alarm in relation to data privacy or lack thereof in the training and use of generative AI, the new generative AI conversational chatbot, ChatGPT, reached 100 million users just two months after it was launched publicly (Reed, 2023). Some recent studies have begun examining how disclosing AI involvement in ads affects consumer perceptions. Wu, Dodoo, and Wen (2025) demonstrate that when companies are transparent about AI's role in creating or delivering ads, it can significantly influence consumer trust and engagement with those ads. The advertising industry has yet to reach consensus on best practices for AI transparency, but researchers emphasize that proactively informing consumers about data-driven techniques is crucial for maintaining trust (Wu, Dodoo, & Wen, 2025). Overall, the advent of AI and AR in marketing is transforming the privacy landscape—advertisers can now collect more intimate forms of data and reach consumers in novel settings, making robust data protection measures and ethical guidelines more important than ever.

Advertisers must strike a balance of the benefits of innovative, data-rich advertising against the potential of alienating consumers when privacy concerns are triggered. New advertising platforms (from AR try-on apps to in-game ads and AI chatbots) will need to address these privacy challenges to sustain consumer goodwill. As one review concludes, ongoing technological advances in computational advertising mean that consumer privacy will remain a critical issue in the foreseeable future (Boerman & Smit, 2023). Additionally, transparency about how data is collected and used in the AR context may increase perceived privacy protection (Sun et al., 2025).

Increasingly, regulators and platforms are imposing constraints—for example, stricter data consent requirements and limits on third-party tracking—in response to public privacy demands. Digital advertisers operating in this new era must adopt privacy-centric design and transparent data practices to reconcile personalized marketing with consumer data protection expectations. Consumers exhibit a spectrum of attitudes toward data-driven advertising, ranging from concern to apathy. A growing body of research confirms that privacy concerns are widespread and can significantly shape consumer responses to online ads. Many consumers are worried about the collection and use of their personal data by advertisers (Boerman & Smit, 2023; Strycharz & Segin, 2022). Studies in the last few years report consistent findings: individuals often feel uneasy knowing that their browsing behaviors, location, or demographic details inform the ads they see (Boerman & Smit, 2023). These privacy concerns are not merely abstract fears; they have tangible effects on how consumers behave. When people feel their privacy is invaded by personalized or targeted ads, they tend to react negatively perceiving such ads as intrusive and avoiding them whenever possible (Boerman & Smit, 2023). For instance, personalized banners or social media ads that appear "too knowing" about a user can trigger a sense of violation, prompting the user to ignore the ad or even install ad blockers (Boerman & Smit, 2023). In this way, heightened concern can undermine advertising effectiveness, reducing clicks, conversions, and overall consumer engagement.

At the same time, not all consumers respond to digital advertising with high alert. A notable segment displays apparent apathy or resignation toward data collection—a stance sometimes described as privacy fatigue or cynicism. These consumers have become desensitized to ubiquitous tracking and may feel powerless to control their personal information in the digital marketplace. Recent work refers to this phenomenon as privacy cynicism, where individuals believe they cannot meaningfully protect their data and therefore stop trying (Van Ooijen, Segin, & Opree, 2024). Symptoms of privacy fatigue include a sense of helplessness and mistrust toward companies and platforms, yet paradoxically a willingness to accept personalized services as inevitable. This leads to what researchers call the "privacy paradox": the disconnect between people's stated privacy concerns and their actual behaviors online (LaRose & Rifon, 2007; Yap, Beverland, & Bove, 2009; Norberg, Horne, & Horne, 2007). Even consumers who claim to value privacy highly often continue to hand over data for personalized services, discounts, or simply the convenience of using social media—effectively tolerating privacy invasions in exchange for perceived benefits. The privacy paradox is well-documented in advertising research (see LaRose & Rifon, 2007; Yap, Beverland, & Bove, 2009; Norberg, Horne, & Horne, 2007; Boerman & Smit, 2023). It suggests that many users, overwhelmed by the volume of data requests or the complexity of privacy settings, end up acquiescing to targeting practices that they find uncomfortable in principle. In other words, apathy can temper resistance: when fighting to protect one's data feels futile, concern might give way to inaction. While privacy concern discourages users from accepting personalized ads, a countervailing force—privacy fatigue—can set in when those concerns reach a standoff with other factors such as becoming fatigued, also, with social media platforms (Bright, Logan, & Lim, 2022) and avoiding advertisements (Alavi, Iyer, & Bright, 2024). In scenarios where users felt torn between disliking surveillance and enjoying tailored content, privacy fatigue tipped the balance by reducing their resistance, ultimately increasing acceptance of targeted ads (Shin, Kim, & Huh 2025). Such findings underscore that apparent apathy often masks an internal coping strategy: when consumers feel they cannot win on privacy, they rationalize or ignore the issue to resolve the dissonance (Shin, Kim, & Huh 2025).

Trust is a critical moderating factor in how consumers reconcile these feelings of concern or resignation. Trust in a company can significantly alleviate privacy worries and improve receptivity to ads (Jung & Heo, 2022). Trust can stem from various sources—a brand's reputation, strong data security measures, transparent privacy policies, or regulatory compliance—but its presence often serves as a buffer against privacy alarms. Importantly, trust and privacy concerns are not static; they interact dynamically. When companies take steps to be transparent and give users more control (such as clear privacy notices or easy opt-out tools), they can increase trust and reduce consumer cynicism (Boerman & Smit, 2023). Indeed, studies suggest that user empowerment (e.g., letting individuals customize how their data is used for ads) lowers feelings of vulnerability and can turn a reluctant consumer into a more willing participant in data-driven marketing (Boerman & Smit, 2023).

Contemporary consumers are not monolithic in their privacy attitudes—they range from the highly concerned to the seemingly apathetic, with trust acting as a deciding factor in their acceptance of digital advertising. Advertisers and researchers classify consumers into segments based on privacy preferences and trust levels (Boerman & Smit, 2023), recognizing that one-size-fits-all approaches to privacy may fail. Understanding these nuances is essential for digital advertisers aiming to navigate the fine line between personalization and privacy intrusion. If the pendulum swings too far—for instance, hyper-targeting without regard for transparency—concerned consumers will respond with avoidance and backlash. Conversely, if advertisers earn consumer trust and address privacy anxieties through clear communication and fair practices, even skeptical audiences may remain open to tailored advertising (Boerman & Smit, 2023; Sun et al., 2025). As data protection norms continue to evolve (with new laws and consumer expectations emerging globally), the relationship between digital advertising and consumer privacy will remain a focal point for advertising.

Conclusion

The concerns of data curation and manipulation by advertisers and companies who provide ad space to advertisers based on intricate consumer profiles (e.g. Facebook) to provide tailored advertising to consumers are problematic, first of all, because of the consumer privacy paradox. That is, consumers seem to desire (even ask for) greater privacy and greater control over their privacy online but frequently (and sometimes freely) give out personal information to brands and applications that request it. As we have seen in this chapter, there is much public concern over who controls the almost infinite amount of data generated in the communication digital network. At the same time, there is clear evidence that when people are in the network, they often divulge information without checking on how it will be used. Researchers and others have also pointed out how important it is in the digital marketplace to maintain consumer trust in the information and transactions they are presented with (Richards & Hartzog, 2015; Boerman & Smit, 2023).

This issue is further complicated when considering that search engines like Google, and social media sites, like Facebook, are becoming more and more adept at collecting, storing, and analyzing data. Although the algorithms these companies use are proprietary, it is clear that they are built on massive and detailed knowledge of what people are doing when they are in the digital communication network (see Chapter 2), and probably a lot of what they are doing outside their digital participation. Add to these the new and even more intrusive types of data being collected with huge potential for advertisers via AR and AI.

With respect to findings of consumer behavior in the privacy arena, future research must seek to find a way to understand what types of information being collected may harm consumers and with what effects. Additionally, based on consumer reliance on cues and their need for convenience in the digital context, more research is needed to discover how and when privacy policies/icons are processed and used by consumers.

Advertisers and regulators may seek to create uniform policies related to the type of information collected, perhaps to give consumers a visual cue of what the language of the policy contains without having to click through and digest a policy. Consumer privacy in the digital universe continues to be an important topic, and many new questions continue to arise as technologies fueled by consumer data evolve.

References

Alavi, S., Iyer, P., & Bright, L. F. (2024). Advertisement avoidance and algorithmic media: The role of social media fatigue, algorithmic literacy and privacy concerns. *Journal of Digital & Social Media Marketing*, *12*(3), 276–292.

Barnes, S. J. (2002). Wireless digital advertising: Nature and implications. *International Journal of Advertising*, *21*(3), 399–420.

Beldad, A., De Jong, M., & Steehouder, M. (2010). How shall I trust the faceless and the intangible? A literature review on the antecedents of online trust. *Computers in Human Behavior*, *26*(5), 857–869.

Bernstein, J. (2016). You should probably check your Pokemon Go privacy settings. *BuzzFeed*. Retrieved from https://www.buzzfeed.com/

Blackwell, V. (2024). Digital advertising trends 2025: AI Ad targeting - where privacy and personalization coexist. *G2.com*. Retrievable from: https://research.g2.com/insights/digital-advertising-trends-2025

Boerman, S. C., & Smit, E. G. (2023). Advertising and privacy: An overview of past research and a research agenda. *International Journal of Advertising*, *42*(1), 60–68.

Borgesius, Z., Kruikemeier, F., Boerman, S., & Helberger, N. (2017). Tracking walls, take-it-or-leave-it choices, the GDPR, and the ePrivacy regulation. *European Data Protection Law Review*, *3*, 353.

Brandimarte, L., Acquisti, A., & Loewenstein, G. (2013). Misplaced confidences privacy and the control paradox. *Social Psychological and Personality Science*, *4*(3), 340–347.

Bright, L. F., Logan, K., & Lim, H. S. (2022). Social media fatigue and privacy: An exploration of antecedents to consumers' concerns regarding the security of their personal information on social media platforms. *Journal of Interactive Advertising*, *22*(2), 125–140.

Burlacu, A. (2016). Facebook allegedly tracks phones' location to serve friend suggestions: How to turn this off. *TechTimes.com*. Retrieved from: https://www.techtimes.com/articles/167397/20160629/facebook-allegedly-tracks-phones-location-to-serve-friend-suggestions-how-to-turn-this-off.htm

California Attorney General (2024). *California Consumer Privacy Act (CCPA) regulations*. Retrievable from: https://oag.ca.gov/privacy/ccpa

Calo, R. (2015). Privacy and markets: A love story. *Notre Dame Law Review*, *91*, 649. Retrievable from https://heinonline.org/HOL/LandingPage?handle=hein.journals/tndl91&div=19&id =&page=

Campbell, C., Plangger, K., Sands, S., Kietzmann, J., & Bates, K. (2022). How deepfakes and artificial intelligence could reshape the advertising industry: The coming reality of AI fakes and their potential impact on consumer behavior. *Journal of Advertising Research*, *62*(3), 241–251.

Cowan, K., Javornik, A., & Jiang, P. (2021). Privacy concerns when using augmented reality face filters? explaining why and when use avoidance occurs. *Psychology Marketing*, *38*, 1799–1813. https://doi.org/10.1002/mar.21576

Federal Trade Commission (2007). FTC staff proposes online behavioral advertisingprivacy principles. Retrieved from https://www.ftc.gov/news-events/press-releases/2007/12/ftc-staff-proposes-online-behavioral-advertising-privacy

GDPR (2018). EU's general data protection regulation. Retrievable from: https://gdpr-info.eu/

Jung, A. R., & Heo, J. (2022). The effects of mobile phone use motives on the intention to use location-based advertising: The mediating role of media affinity and perceived trust and risk. *International Journal of Advertising, 41*(5), 930–947.

LaRose, R., & Rifon, N. J. (2007). Promoting i-safety: Effects of privacy warnings and privacy seals on risk assessment and online privacy behavior. *Journal of Consumer Affairs*, *41*(1), 127–149.

McMillan, S. J. (2004). Internet advertising: One face or many. *Internet Advertising: Theory and Research*, *2*(5), 1–30.

Milne, G. R., Labrecque, L. I., & Cromer, C. (2009). Toward an understanding of the online consumer's risky behavior and protection practices. *Journal of Consumer Affairs*, *43*(3), 449–473.

Moringiello, J. M. (2014). Notice, assent, and form in a 140 character world. *Southwestern Law Review*, *44*, 275.

Nicks, D. (2016). Facebook might be using your location to suggest friends: Here's how to make sure it doesn't. *Money.com.* Retrieved from https://time.com/money/4386138/facebook-friend-suggestions-privacy-concerns/

Norberg, P. A., Horne, D. R., & Horne, D. A. (2007). The privacy paradox: Personal information disclosure intentions versus behaviors. *Journal of Consumer Affairs*, *41*(1), 100–126.

Pavlou, P. A. (2003). Consumer acceptance of electronic commerce: Integrating trust and risk with the technology acceptance model. *International Journal of Electronic Commerce*, *7*(3), 101–134.

Podesta, J., Pritzker, P., Moniz, E., Holdren, J., & Zients, J. (2014). Big data seizing opportunities, preserving values. *Executive Office of the President.* Retrieved from https://www.whitehouse.gov/sites/default/files/docs/big_data_privacy_report_may_1_2014.pdf

Reed, B. (2023). ChatGPT reaches 100 million users two months after launch. *Guardian.com*. Retrieved from: https://www.theguardian.com/technology/2023/feb/02/chatgpt-100-million-users-open-ai-fastest-growing-app

Richards, N. M., & Hartzog, W. (2015). Taking trust seriously in privacy law. Available at SSRN. Retrieved from https://ssrn.com/abstract=2655719

Schlosser, A. E., White, T. B., & Lloyd, S. M. (2006). Converting web site visitors into buyers: How web site investment increases consumer trusting beliefs and online purchase intentions. *Journal of Marketing*, *70*(2), 133–148.

Shield Jr., J. J. (2014). Apple, Inc. v. Superior Court: Caveat emptor: The future of online credit card transactions. *DePaul Business & Commercial Law Journal*, *13*, 529.

Shin, W., Kim, E., & Huh, J. (2025). Young adults' acceptance of data-driven personalized advertising: Privacy and Trust Equilibrium (PATE) model. *Young Consumers*, *26*(2), 189–206.

Shoenberger, H., Sableman, M. & Thorson, E. (2013). Ads made for me?: Consumer attitudes roward relevant online behavioral advertising. Paper presented at American Academy of Advertising conference. Albuquerque, NM.

Solove, D. J. (2006). A taxonomy of privacy. *University of Pennsylvania Law Review*, *154*(3), 477–564.

Solove, D. J., & Hartzog, W. (2014). The FTC and the new common law of privacy. *Columbia Law Review*, *114*, 583–676.

Strycharz, J., & Segijn, C. M. (2022). The future of dataveillance in advertising theory and practice. *Journal of Advertising*, *51*(5), 574–591.

Sullivan, D. (2002). How search engines work. *SEARCH ENGINE WATCH*. Retrieved from https://www.searchenginewatch.com/webmasters/work.html

Sun, Y., Freeman, J., Shoenberger, H., & Shen, F. (2025). To tell or not to tell: Investigating the persuasive appeal of information transparency for AR-powered E-commerce sites. *International Journal of Human–Computer Interaction*, *41*(24), 15323–15337.

Sutton, K. (2016). With news feed values, Facebook pushes back against bias claims. *Politico.com*. Retrieved from: https://www.politico.com/media/story/2016/06/with-news-feed-values-facebook-pushes-back-against-bias-claims-004634

Van Ooijen, I., Segijn, C. M., & Opree, S. J. (2024). Privacy cynicism and its role in privacy decision-making. *Communication Research*, *51*(2), 146–177.

Virginia Office of the Attorney General. (2023). *Virginia Consumer Data Protection Act (VCDPA). Retrievable from:* https://law.lis.virginia.gov/vacodefull/title59.1/chapter53/

Warren, S. D., & Brandeis, L. D. (1890). The right to privacy. *Harvard Law Review*, 193–220.

Wang, P., Jiang, L., & Yang, J. (2024). The early impact of GDPR compliance on display advertising: The case of an ad publisher. *Journal of Marketing Research*, *61*(1), 70–91.

Westin, A. F. (1967) Privacy and freedom. *Washington and Lee Law Review*, *25*(1), 166.

Wu, L., Dodoo, N. A., & Wen, T. J. (2025). Disclosing AI's involvement in advertising to consumers: A task-dependent perspective. *Journal of Advertising*, *54*(1), 20–38.

Xiang, A. (2024). Fairness & privacy in an age of generative AI. *Science and Technology Law Review*, *25*(2), 12765.

Yap, J. E., Beverland, M. B., & Bove, L. L. (2009). A conceptual framework of the causes and consequences of the privacy paradox. The Australian and New Zealand Marketing Academy Conference.

19 The Role of Culture in Electronic Word-of-Mouth Communication

Shu-Chuan Chu and Hyejin Kim

Introduction

The number of global Internet users reached more than 5.56 billion in 2025 (Petrosyan, 2025). Meanwhile, digital advertising spending worldwide is forecasted to reach $870.85 billion by 2027 (Statista Research Department, 2024). Today, the Internet allows ordinary people to easily create and disseminate content about brands and services, namely user-generated content (UGC) (Smith, Fischer, & Chen, 2012). The global UGC market, currently valued at $5.36 billion, is projected to grow to $32.6 billion by 2030 (Grand View Research, 2025). As the market expands, advertisers increasingly leverage UGC to strengthen audience connections, recognizing its influence. For example, on Instagram, UGC drives nearly four times more engagement rates than advertising (Businesswire, 2024). As UGC continues to expand and shape digital engagement, electronic word-of-mouth (eWOM) has gained increasing prominence among researchers and professionals (Babić Rosario, De Valck, & Sotgiu, 2020; Baker, Donthu, & Kumar, 2016).

Primarily through the Internet, eWOM has been categorized as consumer-consumer interactions (Yadav & Pavlou, 2014) that play an important role in influencing consumer decision-making (Goodrich & De Mooij, 2014; Li, Chen, & Chen, 2023). Studies have found eWOM to be more trustworthy than corporate-driven information (Lee & Youn, 2009), and in recent years, companies are increasing their marketing budgets to generate and shape eWOM communication through influencers (e.g., Cheung et al., 2025; Rialti et al., 2024).

The growing significance of eWOM has driven substantial advancements in academic research, both theoretically and methodologically. Studies have explored its antecedents and consequences in various marketing contexts (e.g., Baker et al., 2016) and have increasingly adopted computer-assisted data collection and analysis approaches, including programming languages and machine learning models, to process large-scale eWOM data across various formats (e.g., text, image, video) (e.g., Oc et al., 2023). However, there remains a limited understanding of cross-cultural differences in eWOM effectiveness and its applicability in international contexts (Chan & Yang, 2021).

DOI: 10.4324/9781003567523-24

A few initial studies have examined the role of culture in eWOM. Park and Jun (2003) demonstrated differences in Internet usage and perceived risks of Internet shopping between Korean and American consumers. Dobele et al. (2007) argued that culture is a determining factor in influencing recipients' emotional responses to viral marketing campaigns and subsequent forwarding behavior. Given the influence of nationalities in the acceptance of viral marketing campaigns, cultural values and backgrounds need to be taken into account in this context (Dobele et al., 2007). It is likely that incongruities also exist in how people with various nationalities differ in terms of their engagement in eWOM. An interesting question arises: Do different cultural values (such as individualism vs. collectivism) have varying effects on eWOM? It would be theoretically interesting to examine cross-cultural differences in the context of eWOM, as culture has been identified as a key managerial consideration in online consumer behavior (Richard & Habibi, 2016).

The global nature of eWOM indicates that an understanding of how cultural values moderate the effects of eWOM on consumer product evaluation is needed. Therefore, the goal of this chapter is twofold: (1) to review the current literature on the role of cultural values in eWOM, and (2) to provide directions for future academic research on eWOM and to offer managerial implications for online marketing communications. Through improved understanding of the effects of global cultural differences on eWOM, this chapter contributes to research on digital advertising by identifying an underinvestigated yet important research topic. It is hoped that this chapter could generate increased research interest in eWOM across cultures and help international advertisers develop their eWOM strategy to better target Internet users in different countries, thereby building long-term consumer-brand relationships.

Electronic Word-of-Mouth and Culture

In Hennig-Thurau et al.'s (2004) seminal study, eWOM is defined as "any positive or negative statement made by potential, actual, or former customers about a product or company, which is made available to a multitude of people and institutions via the Internet" (p. 39). eWOM has been found to have an impact on purchase intention (Li, Chen, & Chen, 2023), sales (Rosario et al., 2016), attitude toward brands (Rialti et al., 2024), and brand activism (Chu, Kim, & Kim, 2023). What differentiates eWOM from offline WOM is that eWOM could lead to higher retransmission intentions than offline WOM conversations due to the easy accessibility of finding new people to generate online conversations on a global scale (Christodoulides, Michaelidou, & Argyriou, 2012; Dang & Raska, 2022). As a result, eWOM is considered to be more influential than offline WOM and has been recognized as an important marketing technique in online global branding (Chu & Choi, 2011).

Despite the importance of eWOM in online consumer decision-making, research on whether eWOM has the same effect in a cross-cultural setting is largely unexplored in the digital advertising literature (Christodoulides et al., 2012). According to Hofstede's (2001) definition, culture is "the collective programming of the mind, which distinguishes the members of one group from another" (p. 9). Culture has been found to influence consumer behavior and aspects of traditional WOM, such as WOM referral in relational service exchange (Schumann et al., 2010), the relationship between self-relevance and WOM (Chung & Darke, 2006), and the effects of consumers' cultural values on WOM transmission patterns (Lam, Lee, & Mizerski, 2009). Cultural values have also been found to influence the nature of online communication, but there is relatively little empirical research on the impact of culture on the eWOM process (Chan & Yang, 2021). Because Internet users from different cultures may use different channels and methods to create and disseminate messages, eWOM is expected to relate to international contexts and cultural values.

Prior research has shown the cultural influences on the creation and reception of eWOM on digital platforms designed for consumer opinion exchange. Regarding the creation of eWOM, one study found that culture-based motives (e.g., egocentrism, relationism) shape consumers' motivations for writing online reviews (Kaur & Singh, 2021). Another study found that consumers in individualistic cultures were more likely to write negative reviews when they perceived a discrepancy between a service's description and its actual performance, compared to those in collectivistic cultures (Kusawat & Teerakapibal, 2021). Cultural factors also influence the reception of eWOM. Leonhardt and colleagues (2020) found that online reviews exert a stronger impact on consumer decision-making in collectivistic cultures than in individualistic cultures. More specifically, in collectivist cultures, the consistency of social opinions, such as shared content and ratings, plays a greater role in shaping perceived eWOM credibility than in individualistic cultures (Luo et al., 2014). These findings are in line with the general assumption that Internet users from collectivistic cultures are more likely to be receptive to information transmitted in the form of eWOM due to their greater emphasis on reference groups and group norms (see Hofstede, 2001, for detailed discussion on the individualism/collectivism dimension).

With the introduction of social networking applications, social media has gained tremendous popularity, and research on eWOM in social media has received significant attention (Goodrich & De Mooij, 2014). Chu and Choi (2011) examined social relationship variables between the U.S. and China and found that culture plays a role in determining consumers' engagement in eWOM on social media in the two countries. Goodrich and De Mooij (2014) found that individuals from a collectivistic culture tend to rely more on social media than people from an individualistic culture, suggesting that social media has become an alternative to offline WOM. Additionally, recent studies have examined the role of influencers in eWOM behaviors and conceptualized influencer marketing as a form of eWOM communication (AlRabiah et al., 2022; Cheung et al., 2025; Valmohammadi et al., 2024). For example, Bingol et al. (2023) defined brand influencers as one of the social media factors and examined the impact of culture on social media between the U.S. and Turkey. Their study found that compared to American Facebook users, Turkish consumers are more sensitive to social media factors, including brand influencers, brand-generated content, consumer-generated content, and brand engagement on Facebook's global brand pages. Such findings provide evidence that the effects of eWOM on online behaviors vary by culture and open a door for future research.

Directions for Future Research

Digital and social media as well as a new emerging virtual world such as Metaverse have enabled consumers to share their brand experiences that help others (e.g., followers and friends) make more informed purchase decisions. Through the examination of the moderating role of culture on the effect of eWOM on product evaluations, the following suggestions for future research are proposed. First, while social media and social media influencers provide potential for eWOM, limited empirical studies have investigated how and why consumers use social media for a mediated form of WOM across cultures. Continued research could examine eWOM in a social media context through a cultural lens. Second, future academic research could look into the latest advancements in studying digital advertising and consider using computational methodologies to process a large-scale eWOM data. For example, Oc et al. (2023) used artificial intelligence and machine learning to collect and analyze eWOM marketing of luxury products to better refine content creation and increase consumer engagement. Third, additional studies could adopt an integrated communication model to study eWOM by incorporating cultural factors of the sources and receivers, message valence (i.e., positive or negative), communication channel characteristics, as well as individual factors (e.g., the level of self-concept and personality traits). The complex nature of culture's influence on eWOM and consumer decision-making requires continuous attention from researchers and practitioners. From a practical perspective, the cultural differences observed in eWOM will provide meaningful insights that help global advertisers adopt different strategies to better target diverse consumers across cultures.

References

AlRabiah, S., Marder, B., Marshall, D., & Angell, R. (2022). Too much information: An examination of the effects of social self-disclosure embedded within influencer eWOM campaigns. *Journal of Business Research*, *152*, 93–105.

Babić Rosario, A., De Valck, K., & Sotgiu, F. (2020). Conceptualizing the electronic word-of-mouth process: What we know and need to know about eWOM creation, exposure, and evaluation. *Journal of the Academy of Marketing Science*, *48*(3), 422–448.

Baker, A. M., Naveen, D., & Kumar, V. (2016). Investigating how word-of-mouth conversations about brands influence purchase and retransmission intentions. *Journal of Marketing Research*, *53*(2), 225–239.

Bingol, T., Samii, L., Dhakar, T., & Karakaya, F. (2023). Cross cultural analysis of Facebook on global purchase. *Journal of Marketing Development & Competitiveness, 17*(2), 39–51.

Businesswire. (2024). Emplifi reveals user-generated content helps drive 63% YoY revenue growth across B2C industries. Retrieved from https://www.businesswire.com/news/home/20241114389731/en/Emplifi-Reveals-User-Generated-Content-Helps-Drive-63-YoY-Revenue-Growth-Across-B2C-Industries#:~:text=One%20of%20the%20more%20interesting,rates%20compared%20to%20Instagram%20ads

Chan, H., & Yang, M. X. (2021). Culture and electronic word of mouth: A synthesis of findings and an agenda for research. *Journal of Global Marketing, 34*(3), 165–169.

Cheung, M. L., Leung, W. K. S., Chang, M. K., Shi, S., & Tse, S. Y. (2025). Harvesting sustainability: How social capital fosters cohesive relationships between green social media influencers and consumers to drive electronic word-of-mouth behaviours. *Psychology & Marketing, 42*(2), 444–469.

Christodoulides, G., Michaelidou, N., & Argyriou, E. (2012). Cross-national differences in e-WOM influence. *European Journal of Marketing, 46*(11/12), 1,689–1,707.

Chu, S., & Choi, S. M. (2011). Electronic word-of-mouth (eWOM) in social networking sites: A cross-cultural study of the U.S. and China. *Journal of Global Marketing, 24*(3), 263–281.

Chu, S., Kim, H., & Kim, Y. (2023). When brands get real: The role of authenticity and electronic word-of-mouth in shaping consumer response to brands taking a stand. *International Journal of Advertising, 42*(6), 1037–1064.

Chung, C. M., & Darke, P. R. (2006). The consumer as advocate: Self-relevance, culture, and word-of-mouth. *Marketing Letters, 17*, 269–279.

Dang, A., & Raska, D. (2022). National cultures and their impact on electronic word of mouth: A systematic review. *International Marketing Review, 39*(5), 1182–1225.

Dobele, A., Lindgreen, A., Beverland, M., Vanhammed, J., & Van Wijk, R. (2007). Why pass on viral messages? Because they connect emotionally. *Business Horizons, 50*(4), 291–304.

Goodrich, K., & De Mooij, M. (2014). How 'social' are social media? A cross-cultural comparison of online and offline purchase decision influences. *Journal of Marketing Communications, 20*(1–2), 103–116.

Grand View Research. (2025). User generated content platform market size, share & trends analysis report by product type (blogs, websites), by end-user (enterprises, individual), by region, and segment forecasts, 2023–2030. Retrieved from https://www.grandviewresearch.com/industry-analysis/user-generated-content-platform-market-report

Hennig-Thurau, T., Gwinner, K. P., Walsh, G., & Gremler, D. D. (2004). Electronic word-of-mouth via consumer-opinion platforms: What motivates consumers to articulate themselves on the Internet? *Journal of Interactive Marketing, 18*(1), 38–52.

Hofstede, G. (2001). *Culture's consequences: Comparing values, behaviors, institutions, and organizations across nations* (2nd ed.). Thousand Oaks, CA: Sage Publications.

Kaur, K., & Singh, T. (2021). What motivates consumers to write online reviews? Qualitative research in the Indian cultural context. *Journal of Global Marketing, 34*(3), 170–188.

Kemp, S. (2023). Digital 2023: Global overview report. Retrieved from https://datareportal.com/reports/digital-2023-global-overview-report

Kusawat, P., & Teerakapibal, S. (2021). The roles of culture in online user reviews: An empirical investigation. *Journal of Global Marketing, 34*(3), 189–204.

Lam, D., Lee, A., & Mizerski, R. (2009). The effects of cultural values in word-of-mouth communication. *Journal of International Marketing, 17*(3), 55–70.

Lee, M., & Youn, S. (2009). Electronic word of mouth: How eWOM platforms influence product judgment. *International Journal of Advertising*, *28*(3), 473–499.

Leonhardt, J. M., Pezzuti, T., & Namkoong, J-E. (2020). We're not so different: Collectivism increases perceived homophily, trust, and seeking user-generated product information. *Journal of Business Research*, *112*, 160–169.

Li, S., Chen, J., & Chen, Y. (2023). The effect of repeat purchase information in electronic word-of-mouth (eWOM) on purchase intention. *Journal of Consumer Behaviour*, *22*(6), 1493–1508.

Luo, C., Wu, J., Shi, Y., & Xu, Y. (2014). The effects of individualism–collectivism cultural orientation on eWOM information. *International Journal of Information Management*, *34*(4), 446–456.

Oc, Y., Plangger, K., Sands, S., Campbell, C. L., & Pitt, L. (2023). Luxury is what you say: Analyzing electronic word-of-mouth marketing of luxury products using artificial intelligence and machine learning. *Psychology & Marketing*, *40*(9), 1704–1719.

Park, C., & Jun, J. (2003). A cross-cultural comparison of Internet buying behaviour: Effects of Internet usage, perceived risks, and innovativeness. *International Marketing Review*, *20*(5), 534–553.

Petrosyan, A. (2025). Number of internet and social media users worldwide as of February 2025. Retrieved from https://www.statista.com/statistics/617136/digital-population-worldwide/

Rialti, R., Zollo, L., Kim, K., & Yoon, S. (2024). Mega-influencers and brand dynamics: Shaping attitudes toward leading and challenger brands through electronic word of mouth. *Psychology & Marketing*, *41*(12), 3041–3059.

Richard, M.-O., & Habibi, M. R. (2016). Advanced modeling of online consumer behavior: The moderating roles of hedonism and culture. *Journal of Business Research*, *69*(3), 1103–1119.

Rosario, A. B., Sotgiu, F., De Valck, K., & Bijmolt, T. H. A. (2016). The effect of electronic word of mouth on sales: A meta-analytic review of platform, product, and metric factors. *Journal of Marketing Research*, *53*(3), 297–299.

Schumann, J. H., v. Wangenheim, F., Stringfellow, A., Yang, Z., Blazevic, V., Praxmarer, S., Shainesh, G., Komor, M., Shannon, R. M., & Jiménez, F. R. (2010). Cross-cultural differences in the effect of received word-of-mouth referral in relational service exchange. *Journal of International Marketing*, *18*(3), 62–80.

Smith, A. N., Fischer, E., & Chen, Y. (2012). How does brand-related user-generated content differ across YouTube, Facebook, and Twitter? *Journal of Interactive Marketing*, *26*(2), 102–113.

Statista Research Department. (2024). Digital advertising spending worldwide from 2021 to 2027. Retrieved from https://www.statista.com/statistics/237974/online-advertising-spending-worldwide/#:~:text=Digital%20advertising%20spending%20worldwide%20%E2%80%93%20which,billion%20U.S.%20dollars%20by%202026

Valmohammadi, C., Asayesh, F., Mehdikhani, R., & Taraz, R. (2024). Influencer marketing, eWOM, e-brand experience, and retail e-brand loyalty: Moderating influence of e-brand love. *Journal of Relationship Marketing*, October, 1–27.

Yadav, M. S., & Pavlou, P. A. (2014). Marketing in computer-mediated environments: Research synthesis and new directions. *Journal of Marketing*, *78*(1), 20–40.

20 Algorithmic Absorption

Affective Alignment and Perceived Intrusiveness in ELM Persuasion Routes on Social Media

Attila Pohlmann, Bingxin Leng and Qimei Chen

The act of Liking online content is a routine task in the day-to-day interactions with family, friends, colleagues, and companies that advertise online. But are your Likes still yours? The emblematic thumbs-up button and other heart-shaped mechanisms across social media platforms woo us to signal positive affect toward online content. Whereas platforms once offered explicit reaction buttons (e.g., Love, Haha, Sad), they now infer engagement passively: through scroll hesitation, dwell time, and even biometric input (Epstein et al., 2022; Lamba & Shah, 2019). Meanwhile, the algorithm continuously models users' affective states in context, drawing on content and behavioral pattern analyses as social media landscapes are traversed (Gebhardt et al., 2024; Luangrath et al., 2022; Rocklin et al., 2023; Y. Wang et al., 2022).

Moreover, computational advertising and AI are opening new avenues: targeting customers dynamically based on their temporary affect rather than relying on static segmentation criteria (Lu et al., 2022; Malthouse & Copulsky, 2022; Yun et al., 2020), eliciting engagement (Schivinski, 2021), influencing emotions (Coldwell, 2021), and delivering personalized persuasive communications (Huh & Malthouse, 2020; Matz et al., 2024; Rodgers, 2021). Critically, affect has always played a central role in advertising research (Burke & Edell, 1989; Edell & Burke, 1987; Morris et al., 2002), and Petty and Cacioppo's (1986) dual-process approach of the Elaboration Likelihood Model (ELM) continues to contribute to explaining attitude change and persuasion phenomena (El Hedhli & Zourrig, 2023).

Today, passive social media engagement is dominated by inferred affect rather than explicit user reactions. If algorithms decide which cues to present based on inferred user affect, how can we reconcile this predictive affective steering with classic linear response hierarchy models? And does the central route to persuasion of the ELM still come into play when social media content is awash with peripheral cues, thereby taxing users' cognitive resources (Pittman & Haley, 2023)? These questions underscore a fundamental tension: classic persuasion process models, developed for an era of explicit user engagement, struggle to

DOI: 10.4324/9781003567523-25

capture the algorithmic mediation of emotion. To understand why, we must first examine these models in the context of the technological advances and human adaptations that have reshaped the digital experience.

The Technological Evolution of Persuasion

Whether thoughts or feelings are the better predictor of consumer intention is a highly debated topic in advertising and marketing research. Cognitive theories propose that viewers' attitude formation toward the object of an ad is mediated by their cognitive elaboration of the arguments that are presented in the persuasive communication (e.g., Greenwald & Leavitt, 1984; Tsal, 1985). The introduction of emotional response as a mediator for attitude formation (e.g., Batra & Ray, 1986) and as a predictor of behavioral outcomes (e.g., Smith et al., 1994) indicates that focusing exclusively on cognitive processes impedes our understanding of consumer behavior in its entirety (Allen et al., 1992).

Originally, the driving force behind the development of models such as the ELM was to understand the role of people's state of mind, to explain why they are persuaded by the same message in different ways. Marketers then used these insights to target broad groups based on assumed states of motivation with tailored messages. The subsequent advent of digital tracking and big data analytics allowed advertisers to construct psychographic profiles at the individual level to deliver micro-targeted messages (e.g., Kosinski et al., 2013).

Considering that most internet users try to avoid and ignore online ads (Cho & Cheon, 2004; Drèze & Hussherr, 2003; L. Kelly et al., 2021), merely processing them at pre-attentive levels (Epstein et al., 2022; Rocklin et al., 2023; Schweizer, 2001; Yoo, 2007), it is unlikely that users of social media will pause to carefully consider the persuasive appeals of an ad that they encounter in their social media stream. It is more likely that they are basing their attitudes on peripheral cues rather than establishing a lasting, centrally formed attitude that is bonded to the object of the persuasive message (Hwang, 2020; Lwin et al., 2020; Xu & Zhang, 2018; Zheng et al., 2022).

Toward an Affective Alignment Elaboration Likelihood Model for Social Media

In programmatic advertising, algorithms now optimize and automate the matching of tailored messages to inferred user states and characteristics. Building on this shift, Pohlmann and Chen (2017) proposed the *Interactive Response Model for Social Media* (Figure 20.1, center), which integrates the iterative approach of social media advertising algorithms into the ELM. The advertising display algorithm gauges incidental user affect based on the explicit reaction set (e.g., Wow, Sad, Angry) and purposefully sequences the content stream to prime positive affective states before introducing the attitude object paired with the persuasive communication. Eliciting positive affect before introducing the attitude object aims at increasing the likelihood of the desired reaction to the ad, such as higher purchase intent or stronger brand support (Pohlmann & Chen, 2017). Concurrently, social media users have adjusted to the changes in the social media landscape. For instance, while early platforms such as Facebook encouraged social connection and community building, newer platforms such as Instagram and TikTok (Douyin) are sought out primarily for escapism and entertainment, where the majority of users are passive content consumers (Yang & Ha, 2021).

This state of passive, entertainment-oriented consumption is actively cultivated by platforms, creating a user experience defined by an illusion of autonomous choice. Users perceive themselves as freely navigating their own digital experience through the simple act of scrolling, yet they are in fact following an algorithmically envisioned path. It is within this context that we propose the *Affective Alignment Elaboration Likelihood Model for Social Media* (AA-ELM), we argue that platforms persuade not so much through facts and arguments, but by curating the user's emotional experience. We posit that algorithms achieve persuasion by first inferring a user's mood from digital behavioral residue—such as dwell time, scroll velocity, temporal patterns, and analyzed audio-visual content (Epstein et al., 2022; Lamba & Shah, 2019)—and then aligning the feed's emotional resonance, i.e., the *vibe*, by adjusting content rhythm and tone, images, sounds, or textual cues (Brown et al., 2024). This process creates a state of ambient affective alignment that is continuously reinforced, thereby fundamentally altering the dynamic of deliberate user engagement as persuasion shifts away from conscious, critical evaluation and instead operates through subconscious, emotional alignment.

Figure 20.1 shows the progressive evolution of the peripheral route of the ELM (Petty & Cacioppo, 1986) and the *Interactive Response Model for Social Media* (Pohlmann & Chen, 2017), which illustrates the iterative ability of algorithms to evaluate and influence user affect. We now propose the AA-ELM, which draws from literature on persuasion and attitude change in digital environments (Figure 20.1, right side).

Since algorithms simply infer users' emotional states rather than relying on explicit user signals, each individual stream of content is uniquely algorithmically tuned, based on preferences, time, location, and cultural surroundings. As a result, each stream is composed of purposefully patterned content—termed *vibes* in Brown et al. (2024)—that serves to modulate, i.e. *tune*, user moods and propensities (Goldenfein & McGuigan, 2022; Lupinacci, 2024). When it comes to persuasive communications, the entire tapestry of contextual content that is served up by the algorithm needs to be considered to evaluate the persuasive effectiveness of sponsored messages. In essence, the classical conceptualization of the persuasive message as an isolated piece of content, which is perceived

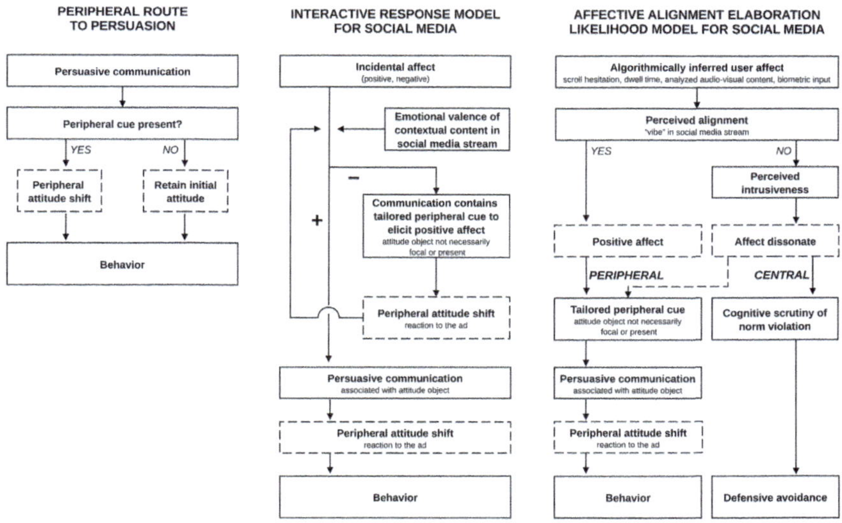

Figure 20.1 Persuasion Process Models in Digital Environments.

by social media users as such, does not encompass the contemporary holistic approach of algorithmic advertisement flow sequences (Beauvisage et al., 2024; Brown et al., 2024; Williams, 1974).

During these digital experiences, users encounter a critical branching point: in the case of perceived alignment, the cues embedded in the ad and the contextual structure of its delivery are aligned with the user's affective state and result in acceptance through affective fit (Brown et al., 2024; Williams, 1974). The algorithm may strategically seed the stream with user-generated content that contains additional pre-identified cues with the intent to influence user affect along the peripheral route (e.g., stories, reels, suggestion grids). In this preparatory stage, the attitudinal object of the ad may remain absent or non-focal. Once the affective groundwork is laid, the persuasive communication is deployed, now positioned to optimally elicit attitude shifts and trigger target behaviors with minimal cognitive resistance.

In more practical terms, the mechanisms for achieving affective alignment represent an evolution of the data-driven personalization pioneered by content-delivery platforms like Spotify (Jokinen, 2025; Ng, 2024) and Netflix (Gomez-Uribe & Hunt, 2016; Hallinan & Striphas, 2016). Where those platforms perfected the algorithmic matching of content based on tastes and behaviors, social media algorithms now guide the affective experience itself. Brown et al. (2024) illustrate this shift through their collection of over 5,000 sponsored advertisement screenshots from Australian youth, documenting how algorithmic systems construct commercially actionable *vibes*. For example, "the femme 'summer botanicals' vibe" (Figure 1 in Brown et al., 2024) captures the essence of an idealized vibe where high-end leisure and aesthetic pleasure are the main currencies. The visuals feature warm lighting and natural colors to evoke sophisticated relaxation and social indulgence. The assemblage suggests that a well-lived life is defined by experiences such as attending exclusive brunches and enjoying beautifully crafted cocktails. Consumption is framed as a social reward and an act of self-care, positioning stylish products and desirable destinations as the essential ingredients for achieving a consistently elegant, coveted lifestyle. Another example, "the masc 'long may we play' vibe" (Figure 2 in Brown et al., 2024), makes consumption, whether it is grabbing a snack or placing a bet, feel like a natural, essential part of being a sports fan. High-stakes gambling is promoted alongside official game action, familiar food brands, and celebration drinks. The configuration of ads normalizes the idea that to truly engage with the game, one must be invested in it financially: sports teams provide the passion; betting apps provide the action; and consumer brands provide the fuel and social rewards.

These assembled *vibes* demonstrate the operationalization of affect—where users' cultural practices are parsed into behavioral datasets. As such, *vibescapes*—algorithmically constructed scaffolds of affective tones, themes, images, sounds, or textual cues—constitute an evolving architectural feature of social media, dynamically transforming what is perceived as subjective experience into a fabricated real-time opportunity for ad targeting systems. From the algorithm's perspective, social media users are constructed as collections of behavioral and affective patterns. These patterns are dynamically modulated and organized into real-time, commercially optimizable matrices for programmed content delivery and commercial exploitation (Brown et al., 2024; Goldenfein & McGuigan, 2022).

Jumping ahead to the behavioral stage in the conceptual model, such algorithmically engineered *vibescapes* enable impulsive consumption, where emotionally primed desires (e.g., "The foodie 'feasting with the eyes' vibe") are paired with an immediate matched purchase option via embedded checkout (e.g., Uber Eats, DoorDash, Grubhub). Such frictionless consumption collapses the traditional temporal gap between attitude formation and behavior (He et al., 2016; Shen & Chen, 2007). When a gourmet burger, the ingredients for a spicy margarita, or an iced oat-milk latte can arrive in 20 minutes via one-tap ordering, the long-term attitude persistence of central route processing becomes functionally obsolete.

However, if the algorithm fails to achieve affective alignment—resulting in an ad perceived as intrusive or manipulative (Aguirre et al., 2015; De Groot, 2022)—it undermines the user's sense of psychological safety. This perceived norm violation, arising from excessive personalization (creepiness), goal disruption, or contextual inappropriateness (Aguirre et al., 2015), typically triggers central route processing, as users deliberately scrutinize the ad (Burgess et al., 2024; Masur & Trepte, 2021; Pittman & Haley, 2023; Z. Wang & Duff, 2016). Such cognitive evaluation presumably leads to a persistent negative and avoidant attitude toward the advertiser. Yet, algorithmic systems can even mitigate this resistance through adaptive learning: each skip, block, or session termination serves as training data to refine affective alignment (Riedel et al., 2024). By leveraging peripheral cues from user-generated content or strategically sequencing mood-recovery content, platforms can steer users back toward positive engagement—hinting at the resilient, self-correcting nature of algorithmic persuasion systems (Pohlmann & Chen, 2017).

The process articulated in the AA-ELM represents a fundamental inversion of the traditional advertising paradigm: the model no longer primarily seeks to match a pre-made ad to a static consumer profile. Instead, it continuously preps and tunes the user's entire informational context—the rhythmic flow of content and other ads—to cultivate a specific mood, propensity, or vulnerability, making the user receptive to a range of promotional stimuli. The consumer is dynamically engineered into a state of readiness, where the final ad serves less as a targeted message and more as the logical, activation-oriented culmination of a meticulously curated vibe.

Safeguarding Volition in an Age of Algorithmic Persuasion and Defensive Processing

The AA-ELM reveals a contradiction at the heart of contemporary digital advertising: platforms interpret continued, passive engagement—the mere act of scrolling—as a valid form of consent. This is not so much a conscious agreement but rather the product of pre-cognitive engineering enabled by privacy-undermining design strategies (D. Kelly & Burkell, 2025)—particularly those relying on differential visual salience (e.g., brightly colored "accept all" button) to exploit automatic attentional processes (Krüger & Scharlau, 2022). Platforms no longer merely respond to user preferences; they anticipate and sculpt affective states through algorithmic mood modulation (Brown et al., 2024; Lupinacci, 2024).

Consequently, our proposed AA-ELM model suggests that in stimuli-saturated social media environments, central route processing survives primarily as a defensive mechanism—activated when affective alignment fails and perceived intrusiveness triggers cognitive scrutiny of a perceived norm violation (Aguirre et al., 2015; De Groot, 2022; Masur & Trepte, 2021; Riedel et al., 2024). In this case, users engage deliberative thinking not to evaluate arguments, but to evaluate the evaluator—questioning the algorithm's intent when *vibes* dissonate with what feels right in the moment, most likely resulting in defensive avoidance (Çelik et al., 2023; D. Kelly & Burkell, 2025; L. Kelly et al., 2021; Morimoto, 2017). Given this blurred line between persuasion and manipulation, there is a growing imperative for research projects such as the Ad Observatory to track harmful industries advertising on social media (Angus, 2024; Carah et al., 2024), as well as legal instruments such as the US Algorithmic Accountability Act and the EU Artificial Intelligence Act to safeguard the volitional integrity and free will of users (Habib Lantyer, 2025; Mökander et al., 2022; Sahi, 2024).

This is the central paradox of modern (passive) engagement: the Like button remains, but the act of liking has been hollowed out. When emotions are algorithmically curated, persuasion becomes ambient—a harmonic resonance in the orchestrated *vibescape*, where ads are no longer solo performances but synchronized notes in a pre-composed emotional score. This leaves us all—users and researchers alike—to re-evaluate what "engagement" truly means and to confront an unsettling question: when our digital environments are designed to preempt our choices, what does it mean to genuinely "like" something?

References

Aguirre, E., Mahr, D., Grewal, D., De Ruyter, K., & Wetzels, M. (2015). Unraveling the personalization paradox: The effect of information collection and trust-building strategies on online advertisement effectiveness. *Journal of Retailing*, *91*(1), 34–49. https://doi.org/10.1016/j.jretai.2014.09.005

Allen, C. T., Machleit, K. A., & Kleine, S. S. (1992). A comparison of attitudes and emotions as predictors of behavior at diverse levels of behavioral experience. *Journal of Consumer Research*, *18*(4), 493–504. https://doi.org/10.1086/209276

Angus, D. (2024). *Alcohol Advertising Sequences* [Dataset]. Tableau Public. https://bit.ly/ipr-13-2

Batra, R., & Ray, M. L. (1986). Affective responses mediating acceptance of advertising. *Journal of Consumer Research*, *13*(2), 234–249.

Beauvisage, T., Beuscart, J.-S., Coavoux, S., & Mellet, K. (2024). How online advertising targets consumers: The uses of categories and algorithmic tools by audience planners. *New Media & Society*, *26*(10), 6098–6119. https://doi.org/10.1177/14614448221146174

Brown, M.-G., Carah, N., Robards, B., Dobson, A., Rangiah, L., & De Lazzari, C. (2024). No targets, just vibes: Tuned advertising and the algorithmic flow of social media. *Social Media+ Society*, *10*(1), 20563051241234691.

Burgess, J., Carah, N., Angus, D., Obeid, A., & Andrejevic, M. (2024). Why Am I Seeing This Ad? The affordances and limits of automated user-level explanation in Meta's advertising system. *New Media & Society*, *26*(9), 5130–5149. https://doi.org/10.1177/14614448241251796

Burke, M. C., & Edell, J. A. (1989). The impact of feelings on ad-based affect and cognition. *Journal of Marketing Research*, *26*(1), 69–83. https://doi.org/10.2307/3172670

Carah, N., Hayden, L., Brown, M. G., Angus, D., Brownbill, A., Hawker, K., Tan, X. Y., Dobson, A., & Robards, B. (2024). Observing "tuned" advertising on digital platforms. *Internet Policy Review*, *13*(2), 1–26. https://doi.org/10.14763/2024.2.1779

Çelik, F., Çam, M. S., & Koseoglu, M. A. (2023). Ad avoidance in the digital context: A systematic literature review and research agenda. *International Journal of Consumer Studies*, *47*(6), 2071–2105. https://doi.org/10.1111/ijcs.12882

Cho, C.-H., & Cheon, H. J. (2004). Why do people avoid advertising on the internet? *Journal of Advertising*, *33*(4), 89–97. https://doi.org/10.1080/00913367.2004.10639175

Coldwell, W. (2021, December 21). What happens when an AI knows how you feel? *Wired*. https://www.wired.com/story/artificial-emotional-intelligence/

De Groot, J. I. M. (2022). The personalization paradox in Facebook advertising: The mediating effect of relevance on the personalization–brand attitude relationship and the moderating effect of intrusiveness. *Journal of Interactive Advertising*, *22*(1), 57–74. https://doi.org/10.1080/15252019.2022.2032492

Drèze, X., & Hussherr, F.-X. (2003). Internet advertising: Is anybody watching? *Journal of Interactive Marketing*, *17*(4), 8–23. https://doi.org/10.1002/dir.10063

Edell, J. A., & Burke, M. C. (1987). The power of feelings in understanding advertising effects. *Journal of Consumer Research*, *14*(3), 421–433. JSTOR.

El Hedhli, K., & Zourrig, H. (2023). Dual routes or a one-way to persuasion? The elaboration likelihood model versus the unimodel. *Journal of Marketing Communications*, *29*(5), 433–454. https://doi.org/10.1080/13527266.2022.2034033

Epstein, Z., Lin, H., Pennycook, G., & Rand, D. (2022). *Quantifying attention via dwell time and engagement in a social media browsing environment* (No. arXiv:2209.10464). arXiv. https://doi.org/10.48550/arXiv.2209.10464

Gebhardt, C., Brombach, A., Luong, T., Hilliges, O., & Holz, C. (2024). Detecting users' emotional states during passive social media use. *Proceedings of the ACM on Interactive Mobile Wearable and Ubiquitous Technologies*, *8*(2), 77:1–77:30. https://doi.org/10.1145/3659606

Goldenfein, J., & McGuigan, L. (2022). Managed sovereigns: How inconsistent accounts of the human rationalize platform advertising. *Journal of Law and Political Economy*, *3*, 425.

Gomez-Uribe, C. A., & Hunt, N. (2016). The Netflix recommender system: Algorithms, business value, and innovation. *ACM Transactions on Management Information Systems*, *6*(4), 13:1–13:19. https://doi.org/10.1145/2843948

Greenwald, A. G., & Leavitt, C. (1984). Audience involvement in advertising: Four levels. *Journal of Consumer Research*, *11*(1), 581–592.

Habib Lantyer, V. (2025). *When AI Molds Thoughts and Desires: Pre-Cognitive Expropriation and Legal Challenges* (SSRN Scholarly Paper No. 5277665). Social Science Research Network. https://doi.org/10.2139/ssrn.5277665

Hallinan, B., & Striphas, T. (2016). Recommended for you: The Netflix Prize and the production of algorithmic culture. *New Media & Society*, *18*(1), 117–137. https://doi.org/10.1177/1461444814538646

He, Y., Chen, Q., & Alden, D. L. (2016). Time will tell: Managing post-purchase changes in brand attitude. *Journal of the Academy of Marketing Science*, *44*, 791–805.

Huh, J., & Malthouse, E. C. (2020). Advancing computational advertising: Conceptualization of the field and future directions. *Journal of Advertising*, *49*(4), 367–376. https://doi.org/10.1080/00913367.2020.1795759

Hwang, T. (2020). *Subprime Attention Crisis: Advertising and the Time Bomb at the Heart of the Internet*. Farrar, Straus and Giroux.

Jokinen, J. (2025). *Spotify and the algorithmic control of desire*. https://lutpub.lut.fi/handle/10024/169597

Kelly, D., & Burkell, J. (2025). Resisting online manipulation: How teens perceive and respond to privacy dark patterns on social media. *Internet Research*, 1–18. https://doi.org/10.1108/INTR-04-2024-0539

Kelly, L., Kerr, G., Drennan, J., & Fazal-E-Hasan, S. M. (2021). Feel, think, avoid: Tes ting a new model of advertising avoidance. *Journal of Marketing Communications*, *27*(4), 343–364. https://doi.org/10.1080/13527266.2019.1666902

Kosinski, M., Stillwell, D., & Graepel, T. (2013). Private traits and attributes are predictable from digital records of human behavior. *Proceedings of the National Academy of*

Sciences of the United States of America, 110(15), 5802–5805. https://doi.org/10.1073/pnas.1218772110

Krüger, A., & Scharlau, I. (2022). The time course of salience: Not entirely caused by salience. *Psychological Research, 86*(1), 234–251. https://doi.org/10.1007/s00426-020-01470-6

Lamba, H., & Shah, N. (2019). Modeling dwell time engagement on visual multimedia. *Proceedings of the 25th ACM SIGKDD International Conference on Knowledge Discovery & Data Mining*, 1104–1113. https://doi.org/10.1145/3292500.3330973

Luangrath, A. W., Peck, J., Hedgcock, W., & Xu, Y. (2022). Observing product touch: The vicarious haptic effect in digital marketing and virtual reality. *Journal of Marketing Research, 59*(2), 306–326. https://doi.org/10.1177/00222437211059540

Lupinacci, L. (2024). Phenomenal algorhythms: The sensorial orchestration of "real-time" in the social media manifold. *New Media & Society, 26*(7), 4078–4098. https://doi.org/10.1177/14614448221109952

Lu, X., Das, D., Huh, J., & Srivastava, J. (2022). Influence of consumers' temporary affect on ad engagement: A computational research approach. *Journal of Advertising, 51*(3), 352–368. https://doi.org/10.1080/00913367.2021.1977202

Lwin, M. O., Lu, J., Sheldenkar, A., Schulz, P. J., Shin, W., Gupta, R., & Yang, Y. (2020). Global sentiments surrounding the COVID-19 pandemic on Twitter: Analysis of Twitter trends. *JMIR Public Health and Surveillance, 6*(2), e19447. https://doi.org/10.2196/19447

Malthouse, E., & Copulsky, J. (2022). Artificial intelligence ecosystems for marketing communications. *International Journal of Advertising*. https://doi.org/10.1080/02650487.2022.2122249

Masur, P. K., & Trepte, S. (2021). Transformative or not? How privacy violation experiences influence online privacy concerns and online information disclosure. *Human Communication Research, 47*(1), 49–74. https://doi.org/10.1093/hcr/hqaa012

Matz, S. C., Teeny, J. D., Vaid, S. S., Peters, H., Harari, G. M., & Cerf, M. (2024). The potential of generative AI for personalized persuasion at scale. *Scientific Reports, 14*(1), 4692. https://doi.org/10.1038/s41598-024-53755-0

Mökander, J., Juneja, P., Watson, D. S., & Floridi, L. (2022). The US Algorithmic Accountability Act of 2022 vs. The EU Artificial Intelligence Act: What can they learn from each other? *Minds and Machines, 32*(4), 751–758. https://doi.org/10.1007/s11023-022-09612-y

Morimoto, M. (2017). Personalization, perceived intrusiveness, irritation, and avoidance in digital advertising. In Shelly R., & Esther, T. (Eds.), *Digital Advertising* (3rd ed.). Routledge.

Morris, J. D., Woo, C., Geason, J. A., & Kim, J. (2002). The power of affect: Predicting intention. *Journal of Advertising Research, 42*(3), 7–17. https://doi.org/10.2501/jar-42-3-7-17

Ng, T. (2024). *How to break free of Spotify's algorithm*. MIT Technology Review. https://www.technologyreview.com/2024/08/16/1096276/spotify-algorithms-music-discovery-ux/

Petty, R. E., & Cacioppo, J. T. (1986). The elaboration likelihood model of persuasion. In R. E. Petty & J. T. Cacioppo (Eds.), *Communication and Persuasion: Central and Peripheral Routes to Attitude Change* (pp. 1–24). Springer. https://doi.org/10.1007/978-1-4612-4964-1_1

Pittman, M., & Haley, E. (2023). Cognitive load and social media advertising. *Journal of Interactive Advertising, 23*(1), 33–54. https://doi.org/10.1080/15252019.2022.2144780

Pohlmann, A., & Chen, Q. (2017). Easy loving: Understanding affect in social media. In S. Rodgers & E. Thorson (Eds.), *Digital Advertising: Theory and Research* (pp. 439–445). Taylor & Francis.

Riedel, A. S., Weeks, C. S., & Beatson, A. T. (2024). Dealing with intrusive ads: A study of which functionalities help consumers feel agency. *International Journal of Advertising*, *43*(2), 361–387. https://doi.org/10.1080/02650487.2023.2197778

Rocklin, M. L., Garròn Torres, A. A., Reeves, B., Robinson, T. N., & Ram, N. (2023). The affective dynamics of everyday digital life: Opening computational possibility. *Affective Science*, *4*(3), 529–540. https://doi.org/10.1007/s42761-023-00202-4

Rodgers, S. (2021). Themed issue introduction: Promises and perils of artificial intelligence and advertising. *Journal of Advertising*, *50*(1), 1–10. https://doi.org/10.1080/00913367.2020.1868233

Sahi, E. (2024). *The impact of targeted advertising on consumers behaviour and ethical concerns*. https://lutpub.lut.fi/handle/10024/167900

Schivinski, B. (2021). Eliciting brand-related social media engagement: A conditional inference tree framework. *Journal of Business Research*, *130*, 594–602. https://doi.org/10.1016/j.jbusres.2019.08.045

Schweizer, K. (2001). Preattentive processing and cognitive ability. *Intelligence*, *29*(2), 169–186. https://doi.org/10.1016/S0160-2896(00)00049-0

Shen, F., & Chen, Q. (2007). Contextual priming and applicability: Implications for ad attitude and brand evaluations. *Journal of Advertising*, *36*(1), 69–80.

Smith, S. M., Haugtvedt, C. P., & Petty, R. E. (1994). Attitudes and recycling: Does the measurement of affect enhance behavioral prediction? *Psychology & Marketing*, *11*(4), 359–374. https://doi.org/10.1002/mar.4220110405

Tsal, Y. (1985). On the relationship between cognitive and affective processes: A critique of Zajonc and Markus. *Journal of Consumer Research*, *12*(3), 358–362. JSTOR.

Wang, Y., Song, W., Tao, W., Liotta, A., Yang, D., Li, X., Gao, S., Sun, Y., Ge, W., Zhang, W., & Zhang, W. (2022). A systematic review on affective computing: Emotion models, databases, and recent advances. *Information Fusion*, *83–84*, 19–52. https://doi.org/10.1016/j.inffus.2022.03.009

Wang, Z., & Duff, B. R. L. (2016). All loads are not equal: Distinct influences of perceptual load and cognitive load on peripheral ad processing. *Media Psychology*, *19*(4), 589–613. https://doi.org/10.1080/15213269.2015.1108204

Williams, R. (1974). *Television: Technology and Cultural Form* (3rd ed.). Routledge. https://doi.org/10.4324/9780203426647

Xu, W. (Wayne), & Zhang, C. (2018). Sentiment, richness, authority, and relevance model of information sharing during social Crises—The case of #MH370 tweets. *Computers in Human Behavior*, *89*, 199–206. https://doi.org/10.1016/j.chb.2018.07.041

Yang, Y., & Ha, L. (2021). Why people use TikTok (Douyin) and how their purchase intentions are affected by social media influencers in China: A uses and gratifications and parasocial relationship perspective. *Journal of Interactive Advertising*, *21*(3), 297–305. https://doi.org/10.1080/15252019.2021.1995544

Yoo, C. Y. (2007). *Preattentive Processing of Web Advertising*. Cambria Press.

Yun, J. T., Segijn, C. M., Pearson, S., Malthouse, E. C., Konstan, J. A., & Shankar, V. (2020). Challenges and future directions of computational advertising measurement systems. *Journal of Advertising*, *49*(4), 446–458. https://doi.org/10.1080/00913367.2020.1795757

Zheng, H., Goh, D. H., Lee, E. W. J., Lee, C. S., & Theng, Y. (2022). Understanding the effects of message cues on COVID-19 information sharing on Twitter. *Journal of the Association for Information Science and Technology*, *73*(6), 847–862. https://doi.org/10.1002/asi.24587

Part VI

The Evolution and Future of Digital Advertising

21 Social Media Advertising

Juan Mundel, Syed Ali Hussain and Saleem Alhabash

Inspired by Grimace, McDonald's anthropomorphic mascot, the brand launched a limited-edition Grimace Shake. The purple, berry-flavored milkshake quickly became the centerpiece of a viral TikTok trend, where users humorously depicted adverse effects after consuming the shake. These videos amassed billions of views, significantly boosting McDonald's online presence and engagement (Brito, 2023; Murray, 2023) and financial results, with sales increasing 12% globally (CBS News, 2023). The popularity of the Grimace Shake is an excellent example of how social media work, how it facilitates brand and product evolution, and most importantly, how it continues to alter the rules of advertising, marketing, and public relations, mainly by dissolving the boundaries between advertising, marketing, and public relations (Bernhard & Russmann, 2024; Scott, 2015).

While traditional advertising models generally applied a linear progression from ideation, strategic thinking, execution, to evaluation; social media advertising is an amalgamation of iterative processes intertwined to galvanize advertisers' strategic input, public relations efforts, offline strategies (including point-of-purchase), mobile tactics, and most importantly, use of approaches that build on the organic nature of social media content. Social media amplifies the importance of the human factor, as the highest salience is placed on understanding how consumers respond, react, and generate online content that fits (or modifies) an existing advertising strategy. The Grimace Shake phenomenon highlights the power of user-generated content (UGC) and the influence of social media trends on consumer behavior. Leveraging the power of organic content, McDonald's successfully connected with a younger audience, turning a simple product launch into a cultural moment that resonated widely (Murray, 2023). This does not mean that paid social media advertising is obsolete. Yet it is essential to acknowledge the significant changes within the environment that are transforming the nature of paid brand-related communication. This is especially notable as we examine the growing popularity of new advertising and public relations avenues related to influencer and creator marketing and advertising. More importantly, understanding the boundaries of advertising strategy

DOI: 10.4324/9781003567523-27

and effectiveness cannot take place without examining how consumers are using such platforms, specifically in relation to heightened information overload and the interplay of consumer behavior on these platforms vis-à-vis the plight for noticeability and optimization about algorithmic inclusion and salience.

Although the challenges are increasing, the projection for continued growth remains intact. Social media ad spending is rapidly increasing, reaching a value of $234.14 billion in 2024 and expected to grow by nearly 50% by the end of the decade, surpassing $345 billion by 2029 (Statista, 2024). However, social media advertisers face two major questions. First, how can advertisers create authentic, unique, personalized, targeted, and viral experiences that capture consumers' attention, engagement, and, hopefully, purchase behavior? Second, how can advertisers quantify the return on investment (ROI) from social media advertising? Or, a more pertinent question is, how *should* advertisers think about and continually reassess ROI from social media advertising, given its evolving nuances, intricacies, and complexities? Responses to these questions are detailed in the sections below.

Social Media and Advertising: Concepts

Compared to traditional media, which typically relies on one-way, top-down communication, social media allows consumers to view and access information and share, engage with, and create multimodal content. This shift transforms audiences from passive receivers into active participants, distributing content across private, semi-private, and public spheres through networks of friends, followers, and communities (Alhabash et al., 2017; Scharlach & Hallinan, 2023). We define social media advertising as any piece of digital content—whether paid, sponsored, or organically distributed—designed with a persuasive intent and/or distributed via a social media platform that enables users to view, save, share, comment, remix, and co-create. This includes static posts, dynamic formats such as short-form videos, live streams, influencer collaborations, and algorithmically targeted ads, among others.

Social media advertising can be classified into paid, owned, and earned media (Li, Larimo, & Leonidou, 2023). Platforms like TikTok, YouTube, and Instagram provide advertisers with many options to pay social media platforms for targeted reach, reaching consumers through display ads, promoted content, and various apps and plug-ins. Alternatively, advertisers may use strategic tactics leveraging organic presence, where the sender directly shares content with their followers online. Lastly, earned social media involves instances where users engage with content via eWOM (electronic word of mouth) or UGC related to the brand or service. In this process, advertisers invest in developing consumers as brand or service ambassadors and social media influencers who create content and generate online engagement, helping to spread the message across their social networks (De Veirman, Hudders, & Nelson, 2019; Jin & Muqaddam, 2019).

As social media evolves, "promoted" (or "sponsored") and "shared" roles are added to the social media categories previously discussed above (i.e., paid, owned, and earned media; Solis and Jess, n.d.). Promoted social media activities focus on paid influencer and creator content. At the same time, the sharing function emphasizes the use of brand-owned and brand-related content in a curatorial manner, allowing consumers to share, discuss, and comment on it (see Figure 21.1).

McDonald's Grimace, introduced earlier in this chapter, serves as a compelling example of user-generated brand mentions that extend beyond visibility to illustrate the increasingly converged nature of social media advertising. The viral Grimace Shake trend on platforms like TikTok and Instagram not only generated widespread user engagement but also blurred the lines between organic fandom, participatory culture, and brand strategy. The campaign's cultural impact was evident during Halloween, when fans dressed in Grimace costumes

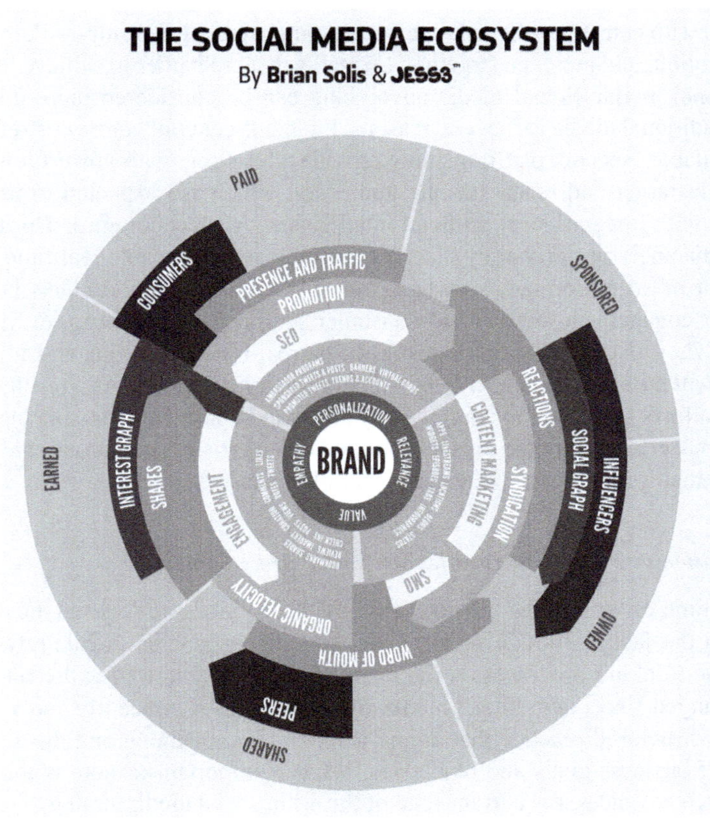

Figure 21.1 Social Media Brandsphere.

Source: Reproduced with permission from Solis and JESS3 (n.d.).

and shared themed content across social media platforms. McDonald's actively embraced this wave of UGC, engaging with and amplifying posts to sustain momentum and reinforce brand affinity. This illustrates that, though at the strategic level, the different functions and tactical uses of social media might be clear, when executed, tracked, and leveraged, the lines between the varying functions of paid, owned, earned, promoted (sponsored), and shared media are increasingly blurring.

Digital advertising has become the largest part of global ad spending, making up 73% of worldwide investment (Kemp, 2025). These figures only include activities where advertisers pay social media platforms for any form of advertising, excluding organic efforts. This provides two important insights. First, social media advertising is now a key element of contemporary brand strategies. Second, the continued investment by advertisers in these platforms suggests they are becoming more effective—an area that needs ongoing study. Chu, Deng, and Mundel (2024) pointed out that social media not only helps service businesses interact with consumers in real time but also improves relationship-building, personalization, and message targeting—benefits that are harder to achieve through traditional media. Social media advertising can be considered more effective than traditional media for several reasons. First, it is generally more cost-efficient and scalable. Second, platforms now provide advertisers with powerful tools to precisely target and reach specific audiences, which are expected to improve further with integration of artificial intelligence (AI) technologies. Third, digital media analytics, driven by machine learning and AI, enable real-time measurement of ad performance, tracking not just impressions and clicks but also broader engagement metrics and consumer sentiment (Chu, Deng, & Mundel, 2024). They also offer unique capabilities for real-time retargeting and adjusting ad content based on consumer behavior and performance data. As a result, social media allows marketers to continuously adapt and optimize their campaigns.

Despite clear advantages of social media for advertising, numerous challenges remain that we highlight in the remainder of this chapter.

Re-Envisioning Persuasion Theories in a Social Media Context

At the time of writing the previous edition of this book, we focused the discussion on the fact that much social media advertising practice, while relying on strategic thinking processes, is the result of considerable trial-and-error. A lot has changed since then. Social media advertising has significantly evolved into a more structured practice that aligns with strategic planning and the achievement of business goals and objectives. What is important to note is that even with such advances, the current state of the art in social media strategy—though largely informed by multi-sourced data, deep understanding of consumers, and real-time effectiveness tracking—still involves a degree of flexibility and coincidence. The nature of social media—how accessible, inexpensive (in most cases, free), and easy to use they are—has shifted industry standards in terms of strategic ad production processes. The era of pretesting, evaluating, and systematic consumer research has been replaced with systematic processes that reflect the "always-on" nature of social media and its users. The new era involves *research as we go*. And in the age of AI, it is *research as we go*—at scale! The key in this era of digital innovation and disruption is continuous evolution, adaptability, and iterative processes. This mode of executing social media advertising strategy, which lacks time boundaries, is further complicated by multi-source and multi-channel strategy inputs, making it difficult at times to discern linearity and pinpoint the sources of effectiveness in achieving goals and objectives. That said, existing persuasion theories can still be applied to design and measure social media advertising. The next section outlines how three theoretical frameworks—commonly employed in advertising and persuasion research—can be applied to analyze the phenomenon of social media advertising and its effects.

Dual Process Models of Persuasion

Among the multiple information processing models, the elaboration likelihood model (ELM, Petty & Cacioppo, 1981, 1986) and the heuristic-systematic model (HSM, Chaiken, 1980, 1987; Chaiken, Liberman, & Eagly, 1989) have been widely used in advertising research. The premise of ELM and HSM is that processing persuasive messages often occurs in two distinct ways: activating either the central route (systematic) or the peripheral route (heuristic) processing. Central route or systematic processing involves increased effort and critical thinking about a message's persuasive arguments, whereas the peripheral route (heuristic) processing is less cognitively demanding and more superficial, as humans rely on heuristic cues and shortcuts to evaluate the message and ultimately accept or reject arguments. Source factors (e.g., model attractiveness, expertise, trustworthiness), message factors (e.g., advertising appeal, argument quality), and receiver factors (e.g., involvement) are believed to influence the processing method, which is guided by an individual's motivation and ability to process information.

ELM/HSM envisioned the persuasive process as linear, similar to other communication models (e.g., Lasswell, 1971; Shannon & Weaver, 1949): a communicator develops a message, disseminates it through a channel to a receiver who is affected by that message with some instances of feedback. The uniqueness of social media persuasion lies in two areas: (1) information overload, and (2) blurring persuasive lines.

The persuasion process is increasingly nonlinear, shaped by information overload, content abundance, and multitasking. Social media users often consume content across multiple devices and platforms simultaneously, with television viewing commonly accompanied by second-screen usage on mobile devices (Beuckels et al., 2021; Chang & Thorson, 2023). In such fragmented contexts, advertisers face the challenge of cutting through clutter to secure attention and drive engagement. Persuasive messages that stand out typically balance novelty, emotional appeal, and personal relevance—factors that activate motivational processing and determine what information is encoded and remembered (Lang, 2006, 2014; Lang & Bailey, 2015). Personalization is especially powerful in this regard. When users perceive that content aligns with their preferences or identities, they attribute greater authenticity and creativity to it, which in turn increases their willingness to like, share, and act on it (Chu et al., 2024). The Grimace Shake trend on TikTok illustrates these processes: what began as a quirky product release evolved into a viral, user-driven campaign by leveraging humor, novelty, and nostalgic brand associations. Such examples demonstrate how persuasion now frequently emerges from the interplay of emotionality, cultural resonance, and user participation, rather than solely from top-down campaigns.

Equally important, the boundaries between sender, message, channel, and receiver are eroding in today's media environment. In UGC and eWOM ecosystems, consumers act as both receivers and redistributors, simultaneously serving as endorsers. A single ad may circulate with multiple layers of influence: a brand produces it, a celebrity features in it, a fan reposts it, and another user reshapes it with commentary. In this scenario, source attribution becomes diffuse, and persuasion becomes a networked, multidirectional process. Each participant is both consumer and co-creator, curating content flows across platforms. This decentralization requires a rethinking of persuasion models as circular, iterative, and context-dependent, where influence emerges through dynamic interactions between individuals, platforms, and content (see Figure 21.2).

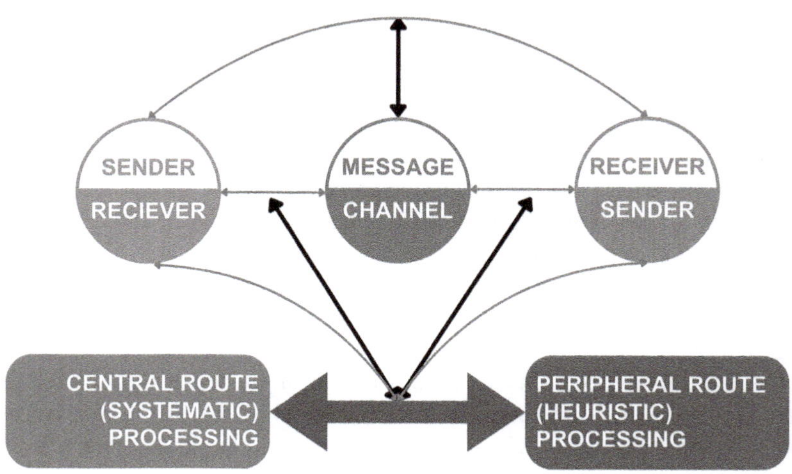

Figure 21.2 Integrating Social Media into Dual Process Models of Persuasion.

Behavior Change Models

Behavioral outcomes of persuasion in these environments can be understood through the theory of reasoned action (TRA) and the theory of planned behavior (TPB) (Ajzen, 1985). These frameworks link attitudes, subjective norms, and perceived behavioral control to behavioral intentions and actual behaviors. In social media contexts, online engagement intentions (OEIs)—liking, sharing, commenting, saving, or remixing content—are best understood as a form of behavioral intention. Research has shown that OEIs not only predict offline consumer behaviors but also serve as mediators between attitudes toward a message and subsequent purchase or behavior change (Alhabash & McAlister, 2014; Alhabash et al., 2015a, 2015b). Early experimental studies found that OEIs could explain nearly half of the variance in offline intentions, with "liking" emerging as the strongest predictor (Alhabash et al., 2015b). More recent work shows that ad characteristics such as authenticity, personalization, and even model age can shape OEIs, particularly among users with a high need for uniqueness (Alhabash et al., 2021; Chu et al., 2022). These findings reinforce that both psychological traits and contextual variables influence persuasion in digital spaces.

Based on this review, there is a need for a revised TPB model that explicitly incorporates OEIs as both outcomes of and mediators within the persuasion process (see Figure 21.3). In digital contexts, OEIs bridge online interactions with offline consumer behavior, reflecting the complex interrelationships among attitudes, subjective norms, and control. Importantly, they highlight how persuasion unfolds in stages, from initial online actions (e.g., liking, sharing) to more consequential outcomes (e.g., purchasing, behavioral change). While online engagement itself may be a strategic objective, the ultimate challenge remains

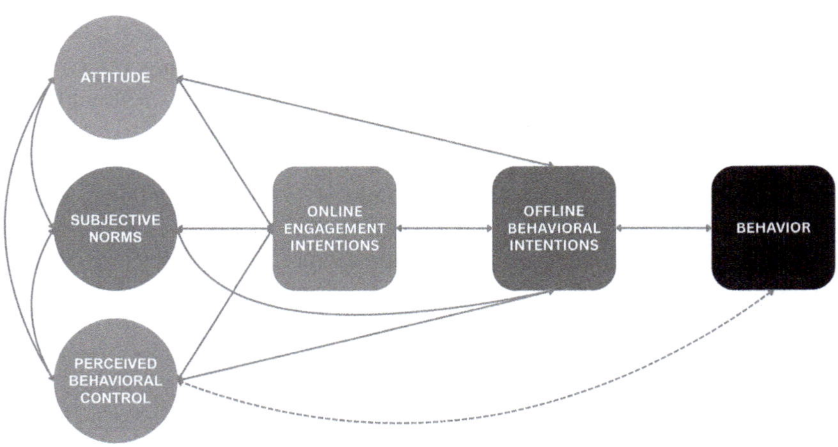

Figure 21.3 Integrating Social Media into Theory of Planned Behavior.

translating such engagement into durable offline behaviors—a task made not only more complex but also more dynamic, by today's nonlinear and networked persuasion environment.

Social Norms on Social Media

When making decisions, people often consider whether their behaviors are accepted within their social groups (Feng, Chen, & Ahn, 2021). Park and Smith (2007) identified five types of norms: subjective norms, personal descriptive norms, personal injunctive norms, societal descriptive norms, and societal injunctive norms. Subjective norms—key to the TPB—reflect perceptions of how others expect someone to behave and often represent descriptive or injunctive judgments. Descriptive norms refer to perceptions of how common a behavior is, while injunctive norms relate to perceptions of how accepted or approved the behavior is. These perceptions can occur at the individual level (close friends or key contacts) or at the societal level (broader groups, such as "Americans" or "college students").

On social media, these normative perceptions are often shaped by platform affordances. Descriptive cues appear through popularity metrics—views, shares, or trending hashtags—while injunctive cues emerge through evaluative behaviors such as likes, supportive comments, or positive reposts (Pittman & Abell, 2021). Thus, engagement metrics enable users to gauge both the prevalence and approval of content or influencers before interacting with them. Normative perceptions can also influence persuasion indirectly. For example, Chinn and Hasell (2024) demonstrated that perceived norms, as reflected in virality, mediated the impact of a national pro-vaccine campaign on vaccination intentions.

Tie strength also affects normative influence. While strong-tie platforms (e.g., Facebook, WeChat) strengthen existing relationships, weak-tie platforms (e.g., Twitter/X) promote broader information sharing (Haythornthwaite, 2002; Wellman, 1996). Research indicates that users on strong-tie platforms respond more favorably to specific and actionable appeals, whereas weak-tie users tend to engage more with abstract or generalized messages (Valenzuela et al., 2018; Lee & Kronrod, 2020; Yan et al., 2024). These dynamics demonstrate that both the type of norm and the characteristics of the social network influence persuasive outcomes.

Norms on social media are also reinforced through visibility and accountability. Because users' behaviors are publicly observable, the fear of reputational loss can drive conformity (Chu & Kim, 2011; Marwick & Boyd, 2011). Content creators often imagine diverse audiences and self-censor to avoid violating perceived norms. Networked sanctioning also plays a role: Marwick (2021) argues that norm violations may provoke collective harassment, further reinforcing conformity. Influencers hold a special position here, as they actively reinforce norms through reciprocal interactions with followers—liking or commenting on posts to foster visibility and a sense of belonging (Ouvrein et al., 2021). Such interactions increase the prominence of social norms around products and behaviors.

Ultimately, social norms on social media operate on multiple levels—individual and societal, descriptive and injunctive—and are amplified by the visibility and interactivity of digital platforms. Whether expressed through engagement metrics, peer behaviors, or influencer interactions, these norms influence how users interpret and respond to branded content. For advertisers and marketers, this means that successful campaigns must strategically activate and leverage the perceived norms embedded in users' networks to impact both online engagement and offline behavior.

Social Media Persuasion for Behavioral Change

The "million-dollar question" regarding social media advertising is: how can product- or brand-related behavioral outcomes (e.g., purchase and consumption) be attributed to social media ads? Additionally, how can online behaviors related to advertising messages lead to behavioral outcomes? As with previous models and studies of advertising effects, the most common indicator of behavioral change is behavioral intentions. According to TRA/TPB, behavioral intentions are considered the strongest predictors of actual behaviors. Therefore, the research reviewed in this section mainly examines the effects of social media advertising and persuasion on behavioral intentions and, in some cases, proxies of actual behaviors. This section is organized by theme of effects. Specifically, we categorize social media advertising into (1) incidental exposure effects, (2) engagement effects, (3) UGC effects, and (4) influencers.

Incidental Exposure

Incidental exposure is defined as situations when an individual encounters secondary information while focusing on a different primary task (Janiszewski, 1988). It is common to observe that advertisements usually receive only incidental attention from consumers because of the clutter surrounding them in society (Pham & Vanhuele, 1997). Although exposure to an ad might be brief and incidental, the widespread nature of advertising influences ad recognition, familiarity, and recall (Hawkins & Hoch, 1992; Holden & Vanhuele, 1999) and helps build brand familiarity (Fang, Singh, & Ahluwalia, 2007). Kelly, Kerr, and Drennan (2010) studied attitudes and message avoidance toward social media advertising and found that participants did not mind excessive clutter as long as using social media was free of charge.

While early research on digital advertising and incidental exposure focused on participants' attention to banners within search engines (Manchanda et al., 2006), the rise of social media platforms has prompted new investigations into whether online social media users registered the displayed ads. A 2013 study tracking participants' visual attention found that Facebook banners attract less notice compared to recommendations from friends (Barreto, 2013). However, this doesn't mean the ads went unnoticed. Instead, incidental exposure has been shown to increase the likelihood of being considered for a future purchase (Shapiro, 1999). In a study by Alhabash et al. (2016), participants were exposed to Facebook ads featuring either an alcoholic (beer) or non-alcoholic (water) brand. Not only did participants report greater behavioral intentions to consume alcohol after seeing beer ads compared to water ads, but they were also more likely to choose a gift card for a bar rather than a coffee shop at the end of the study. Alhabash et al.'s (2016) findings help us understand not only the significant—and often substantial—impact of ad exposure on social media, but also that once ads are noticed and processed, their potential for influence is also increased.

The effects of ad exposure and the potential to influence behavior are amplified in an era of AI-powered content dissemination and behavioral retargeting. Although incidental and initial exposure might not fit within the "magic bullet" framework, the opportunity for accessible and relatively inexpensive repeated exposure, based on data-driven decisions about who to retarget, offers insights into the value of ad exposure in today's digital or post-digital age. This is especially true in an environment where advertisers use multiple tactics across various channels, employing different appeals to target and retarget consumers. Ad exposure effects are therefore intensified by the proliferation and convenience of e-commerce and social commerce. For example, user X sees a paid social media ad for brand Y, and online behavioral data shows that user X watched a significant portion of the ad. The advertiser can then leverage other tactics to target user X, including omnichannel marketing, paid algorithmic placement of influencer content, and even prioritization of UGC content related to that brand. This multi-tactic strategy builds on repeated exposure of the same persuasive message, aiming to influence the user's responses and guide them through different stages of the purchase funnel.

Engagement Effects

Research on engagement effects also reveals strong links between intentions to like, share, and comment and the expression of intentions to perform message-induced behaviors either offline or online (e.g., buying a product from a store or online). Several studies by Alhabash and colleagues documented this strong effect among samples of college students (Alhabash et al., 2013, 2015a). Conceptually, these effects can be explained by understanding different stages of behavioral change. Behavior change models that emphasize the importance of readiness for change (e.g., Marcus, Selby, Niaura, & Rossi, 1992; Webb & Sheeran, 2006) clearly explain the relationship between online and offline behavioral intentions. Engaging with an online message involves and results from certain levels of cognitive and emotional mechanisms. Pressing the "like" button, sharing an ad, or commenting on someone else's brand-related post can indicate the individual's endorsement of the brand and behavior promoted in the advertisement. Therefore, readiness for behavior change may increase. Conversely, participating in viral behaviors with branded content reflects higher level information processing mechanisms and enhances memory storage of the ad content and related brand attributes.

User-Generated Content Effects

The link between creating persuasive content and whether consumers will buy or use a product or service has been documented in many studies. For example, Viken et al. (2016) showed that participants who reported posting about alcohol during a major celebration ended up drinking more alcohol than those who did not post about alcohol on Facebook. Based on Viken et al.'s (2016) findings, creating UGC appears to be strongly linked to offline behaviors. UGC can also indicate the source of persuasion. Comparing the effects of content marketing, sponsored marketing, and UGC on brand responses, Müller and Christandl (2019) found that sponsored content results in a more negative brand attitude than UGC and content marketing. Paek et al. (2011) argued that the effects of peer versus expert sources could be explained through the model similarity concept related to persuasive effects. Peer-generated messages seem more genuine and are perceived as less "ad-looking" compared to messages from experts or professional models. Additionally, UGC gains credibility and helps build parasocial relationships between creators and consumers (Lou & Yuan, 2019; Yuan & Lou, 2020).

Social media advertising suggests three distinct levels of outcomes: exposure, engagement, and UGC—all of which are believed to influence attitudes and offline behaviors. Lee (2015) offers a guide for measuring ROI from social media, based on identifying advertising goals, aggregating data, and measuring impact. However, these recommendations are limited to assigning monetary values to online activities based on hypothetical assumptions. Colicev and colleagues (2019) examined the relationship between brand-initiated content and UGC across the marketing funnel stages of awareness, consideration, purchase intent, and satisfaction. Their findings indicate that UGC content is more strongly linked to awareness and satisfaction, while company ads are more strongly associated with consideration and purchase intent. Valuing exposure to social media ads, online engagement, and UGC engagement requires further research that leverages big data, triangulates data from multiple sources, and employs various methodologies (e.g., combining server-level data with surveys and experiments). Additionally, to maximize the value of social media advertising budgets, it may be necessary to redefine which outcomes are attainable, measurable, and meaningful. In conclusion, is the immediate post-exposure sale the most crucial revenue from social media? Or is it the relationship and loyalty built through conversation, co-creation, and engagement?

Influencer Marketing

Social media influencers and content creators have become powerful agents of behavioral change because of their ability to build parasocial relationships—one-sided emotional bonds—through perceived credibility, authenticity, and interactive engagement with followers. These relationships are heavily influenced by the influencer's attractiveness, perceived similarity to the audience, and perceived fairness in communication, which includes being respectful and providing transparent, honest content (Yuan & Lou, 2020). When followers feel personally connected to influencers, they are more inclined to imitate their consumption behaviors, demonstrating that influencer marketing functions both as a persuasive and relational communication strategy.

The influence of influencers can be understood through theories like the Source Credibility Model and the ELM. According to the ELM, influencers can act as both central and peripheral cues depending on how involved the audience is with the content; their credibility, attractiveness, and authenticity can lead to attitude changes through either pathway (Petty & Cacioppo, 1986). Empirical research shows that when influencers are seen as trustworthy and knowledgeable, audiences are more likely to process branded messages thoroughly, resulting in increased persuasion and behavioral intention (Lou & Yuan, 2019; Jin et al., 2019).

However, the influence of social media influencers and content creators on behavioral change is not simple. Mundel, Yang, and Wan (2022) report negative effects of influencer marketing, including increased social comparison, anxiety, and even social media addiction. This happens as followers try to imitate the lifestyles shown by influencers, often leading to dissatisfaction when those goals are out of reach. Mimicking influencers can have unexpected impacts on well-being, especially among younger users who are more prone to social comparison and social norms. Therefore, while influencers effectively influence consumer behavior, ethical concerns are very important.

Impact of AI on Advertising

Social media advertising has drastically evolved over the last decade, with the most notable change being AI in content creation, delivery, and consumer engagement (Chu, Yim, & Mundel, 2024; Ford et al., 2023). For example, if the Grimace campaign were launched today, McDonald's could use AI to analyze consumer reactions on social platforms, customizing campaigns to increase engagement with this quirky purple icon among many other innovative strategies. In this section, we briefly discuss the AI-driven technologies used in social media advertising: (1) algorithmic targeting and AI-powered creative agencies, and (2) the creation of AI-synthesized content.

Using Algorithms for Audience Targeting and Personalization

AI algorithms are transforming social media advertising by shifting from broad demographics to highly personalized strategies (Teepapal, 2025). By analyzing extensive data on user behavior and preferences, these algorithms predict ideal ad audiences. Machine learning identifies detailed patterns, enabling advertisers to customize individual messages, which boosts engagement and efficiency (Marathe, 2024). The growth of the Internet and smartphones has expanded customer data, which AI leverages to improve engagement and services (Drydakis, 2022). AI also transforms advertising by creating compelling stories and competitive advantages (Kumar, shraf, & Nadeem, 2024). Additionally, AI allows for real-time campaign adjustments, optimizing bids, placements, and content for better results. These data-driven approaches enhance customer experiences, automate tasks, and increase ROI.

For example, in the case of Grimace, using AI, an agency might generate a dozen ads—videos of him spilling shakes or posters of their grin—while human creatives refine the humor and heart that define the character. In this way, the agencies can target specific audiences, such as Gen Z milkshake lovers or nostalgic Millennials, based on their online behavior. Additionally, machine learning could analyze data from social media posts about Grimace to craft personalized ads, such as promoting a Grimace-themed shake to users who frequently mention fast food.

AI-Based Creative Agencies

Creative agencies leverage AI to accelerate the creative process by generating ad copy, visuals, and campaign ideas. They use AI to analyze market trends, consumer preferences, and competitor tactics, producing optimized ad variations tailored to specific audiences and platforms. AI-powered tools generate high-quality content—such as copy, images, and videos—and identify the best channels and timing for delivery to maximize impact. This streamlines workflows, enabling human focus on strategic tasks.

Wang et al. (2024) examined the adoption of AI creative technology in China and identified several driving factors, including perceived usefulness, perceived control, corporate innovativeness, and competitive pressure. Vakratsas and Wang (2021) took a broader conceptual approach, introducing the Creative Advertising System, which frames creativity as a computational search process. Their model suggests AI can democratize creative work by using predefined rules to generate, assess, and refine ideas systematically—potentially reshaping the role of traditional creatives in agencies. Furthermore, Wang and Liu (2022) analyzed AI's role in programmatic advertising and found that while AI increases operational efficiency, it introduces challenges around transparency, such as sponsorship disclosure and clear brand attribution. Their study also shows a tendency toward product-centric, positively framed messaging in AI-generated advertisements. Holistically, Chu, Yim, and Mundel (2024) review the use of digital media in service businesses, including the growing role of AI and computational advertising. The authors outline how AI can analyze consumer data for personalized and targeted promotional campaigns for service industry clients. They suggest that creative agencies can leverage AI tools to enhance their service offerings.

Theoretically, we believe that the proliferation of highly accessible, user-friendly, and relatively inexpensive AI-powered technologies, including generative AI for advertising purposes, is likely to impact ad effectiveness in two conflicting ways. First, by reducing waste and streamlining ad strategy execution, AI can make advertising more personalized and targeted, providing a shortcut to effectiveness. In other words, AI-powered technologies can "zoom in" not only on who the consumers are but also on a wide range of relevant data points that could enhance effectiveness, refine targeting strategies, and inform post-behavior engagement with consumers. On the other hand, as observed in the early days of social media advertising, that same accessibility, marketing, targeting, and retargeting of consumers is now amplified, allowing advertisers to continue advertising to consumers without pause. However, this could lead to information overload, increasing ad avoidance and creating greater skepticism about persuasive intent.

Still, human oversight remains crucial to ensure brand consistency, emotional resonance, and ethical standards. For instance, AI might generate Grimace TikToks or Shake ads customized for fans, but human editors would make sure he keeps his goofy charm, avoiding issues like bias or an off-brand deepfake Grimace. The most successful agencies blend AI with human creativity, using AI's data analysis to understand customer behavior and customize offerings to meet audience expectations.

AI-Generated Content

AI-generated content creates personalized and engaging ads at scale across various formats. AI can accelerate content production, reducing costs and optimizing resources. Additionally, AI generates tailored ad variations and visuals using large datasets (Gozalo-Brizuela & Merchan, 2023). This enhances efficiency, personalization, and campaign performance while allowing humans to focus on creative tasks (Kshetri et al., 2024). However, it also raises security, privacy, and ethical concerns, including biased or inauthentic content, potential job displacement, and misuse such as deepfakes (Inie Falk, & Tanimoto, 2023). To address these issues, human oversight remains essential to ensure accuracy and brand consistency.

Generative AI boosts productivity by automating tasks like content creation and campaign optimization, providing personalized experiences. However, it also risks spreading biases or misinformation, highlighting the need for strong ethical guidelines. To fully realize its potential, future advertisers must carefully balance AI's advantages with ethical considerations, addressing issues like privacy, bias, and transparency through clear regulations.

Summary

The current chapter examined theoretical frameworks commonly used in advertising and persuasion research within social media advertising. It also reviewed recent studies addressing three key areas of social media advertising effects: exposure, engagement, and UGC. Previous studies have only partially answered the questions introduced at the start of this chapter. Advertising scholars and practitioners should continue to explore systematic ways to generate persuasive effects through evidence-based and strategically planned campaigns, aiming to convert investments of time, effort, and money into meaningful intentions and behaviors, both online and offline.

References

Ajzen, I. (1985). From intentions to actions: A theory of planned behavior. In J. Kuhl & J. Beckmann (Eds.), *Action control: From cognition to behavior* (pp. 11–39). Berlin and Heidelberg: Springer-Verlag.

Alhabash, S., & McAlister, A. R. (2014). Redefining virality in less broad strokes: Predicting viral behavioral intentions from motivations and uses of Facebook and Twitter. *New Media & Society, 17*(8), 1317–1339.

Alhabash, S., McAlister, A. R., Hagerstrom, A., Quilliam, E. T., Rifon, N. J., & Richards, J. I. (2013). Between likes and shares: Effects of emotional appeal and virality on the persuasiveness of anticyberbullying messages on Facebook. *Cyberpsychology, Behavior, and Social Networking, 16*(3), 175–182.

Alhabash, S., McAlister, A. R., Kim, W., Lou, C., Cunningham, C., Quilliam, E. T., & Richards, J. I. (2016). Saw it on Facebook, drank it at the bar! Effects of exposure to Facebook alcohol ads on alcohol-related behaviors. *Journal of Interactive Advertising, 16*(1), 44–58.

Alhabash, S., McAlister, A. R., Lou, C., & Hagerstrom, A. (2015). From clicks to behaviors: The mediating effect of intentions to like, share, and comment on the relationship between message evaluations and offline behavioral intentions. *Journal of Interactive Advertising, 15*(2), 82–96.

Alhabash, S., McAlister, A. R., Quilliam, E. T., Richards, J. I., & Lou, C. (2015). Alcohol's getting a bit more social: When alcohol marketing messages on Facebook increase young adults' intentions to imbibe. *Mass Communication and Society, 18*(3), 350–375.

Alhabash, S., Mundel, J., & Hussain, S. A. (2017). Social media advertising: Unraveling the mystery box. In Digital advertising (pp. 285–299). Routledge.

Alhabash, S., Mundel, J., Deng, T., McAlister, A., Quilliam, E. T., Richards, J. I., & Lynch, K. (2021). Social media alcohol advertising among underage minors: Effects of models' age. *International Journal of Advertising, 40*(4), 552–581.

Barreto, A. (2013). Do users look at banner ads on Facebook? *Journal of Research in Interactive Marketing, 7*(2), 119–139.

Bernhard, J., & Russmann, U. (2024). Blurring boundaries: A longitudinal analysis of skills required in journalism, PR, and marketing job ads. *Journalism & Mass Communication Quarterly*, *101*(3), 612–636.

Beuckels, E., Hudders, L., Cauberghe, V., Bombeke, K., Durnez, W., & Morton, J. (2021). To fit in or to stand out? An eye-tracking study investigating online banner effectiveness in a media multitasking context. *Journal of Advertising*, *50*(4), 461–478.

Brito, C. (2023). What are people doing with the Grimace shake? Here's the TikTok trend explained. *CBS News*. Retrieved from https://www.cbsnews.com/news/grimace-shake-mcdonalds-tiktok-meme

CBS News. (27 July 2023). Grimace shakes help send McDonald's sales surging. Retrieved from https://www.cbsnews.com/miami/news/grimace-shakes-help-send-mcdonalds-sales-surging

Chaiken, S. (1980). Heuristic versus systematic information processing and the use of source versus message cues in persuasion. *Journal of Personality and Social Psychology*, *39*(5), 752–756.

Chaiken, S. (1987). The heuristic model of persuasion. In M. P. Zanna, J. M. Olson, & C. P. Herman (Eds.), *Social influence: The Ontario Symposium* (pp. 3–39). Hillsdale, NJ: Erlbaum.

Chaiken, S., Liberman, A., & Eagly, A. H. (1989). Heuristic and systematic processing within and beyond the persuasion context. In J. S. Uleman & J. A. Bargh (Eds.), *Unintended thought* (pp. 212–252). New York: Guilford.

Chang, Y., & Thorson, E. (2023). Media multitasking, counterarguing, and brand attitude: Testing the mediation effects of advertising attention and cognitive load. *Computers in Human Behavior*, *139*. https://doi.org/10.1016/j.chb.2022.107544

Chinn, S., & Hasell, A. (2024). How different uses of social media inform perceptions of offline social norms and changes in vaccine intentions. *Health Communication*, *39*(6), 1198–1208. https://doi.org/10.1080/10410236.2023.2207284

Chu, S. C., & Kim, Y. (2011). Determinants of consumer engagement in electronic word-of-mouth (eWOM) in social networking sites. *International Journal of Advertising*, *30*(1), 47–75.

Chu, S. C., Deng, T., & Mundel, J. (2024). The impact of personalization on viral behavior intentions on TikTok: The role of perceived creativity, authenticity, and need for uniqueness. *Journal of Marketing Communications*, *30*(1), 1–20.

Chu, S. C., Yim, M. Y. C., & Mundel, J. (2024). Artificial intelligence, virtual and augmented reality, social media, online reviews, and influencers: A review of how service businesses use promotional devices and future research directions. *International Journal of Advertising*, 1–31. https://doi.org/10.1080/02650487.2024.2325835

Colicev, A., Kumar, A., & O'Connor, P. (2019). Modeling the relationship between firm and user generated content and the stages of the marketing funnel. *International Journal of Research in Marketing*, *36*(1), 100–116.

De Veirman, M., Hudders, L., & Nelson, M. R. (2019). What is influencer marketing and how does it target children? A review and direction for future research. *Frontiers in Psychology*, *10*, 498106.

Drydakis, N. (2022). Artificial Intelligence and reduced SMEs' business risks. A dynamic capabilities analysis during the COVID-19 pandemic. *Information Systems Frontiers*, *24*(4), 1223–1247.

Fang, X., Singh, S., & Ahluwalia, R. (2007). An examination of different explanations for the mere exposure effect. *Journal of Consumer Research, 34*(1), 97–103.
Feng, Y., Chen, H., & Ahn, H. (2021). How consumers react to woke advertising: Methodological triangulation based on social media data and self-report data. *Journal of Research in Interactive Marketing, 15*(4), 529–548.
Ford, J., Jain, V., Wadhwani, K., & Gupta, D. G. (2023). AI advertising: An overview and guidelines. *Journal of Business Research, 166*, 114124.
Gozalo-Brizuela, R., & Garrido-Merchán, E. C. (2023). A survey of generative AI applications. *arXiv preprint arXiv:2306.02781*.
Hawkins, S. A., & Hoch, S. J. (1992). Low-involvement learning: Memory without evaluation. *Journal of Consumer Research, 19*(2), 212–225.
Haythornthwaite, C. (2002). Strong, weak, and latent ties and the impact of new media. *The Information Society, 18*(5), 385–401.
Holden, S. J., & Vanhuele, M. (1999). Know the name, forget the exposure: Brand familiarity versus memory of exposure context. *Psychology and Marketing, 16*(6), 479–496.
Inie, N., Falk, J., & Tanimoto, S. (2023, April). Designing participatory AI: Creative professionals' worries and expectations about generative AI. In *Extended Abstracts of the 2023 CHI Conference on Human Factors in Computing Systems* (pp. 1–8). Association for Computing Machinery. https://doi.org/10.1145/3544549.3585714
Janiszewski, C. (1988). Preconscious processing effects: The independence of attitude formation and conscious thought. *Journal of Consumer Research, 15*(2), 199–209.
Jin, S. V., & Muqaddam, A. (2019). Product placement 2.0: Do brands need influencers, or do influencers need brands?. *Journal of Brand Management, 26*, 522–537.
Jin, S. V., Muqaddam, A., & Ryu, E. (2019). Instafamous and social media influencer marketing. *Marketing Intelligence & Planning, 37*(5), 567–579. https://doi.org/10.1108/MIP-09-2018-0375
Kelly, L., Kerr, G., & Drennan, J. (2010). Avoidance of advertising in social networking sites. The teenage perspective. *Journal of Interactive Advertising 10*(2), 16–27.
Kemp, S. (2025). Digital 2025: Global advertising trends. *Datareportal*. Retrieved from https://datareportal.com/reports/digital-2025-sub-section-global-advertising-trends
Kshetri, N., Dwivedi, Y. K., Davenport, T. H., & Panteli, N. (2024). Generative artificial intelligence in marketing: Applications, opportunities, challenges, and research agenda. *International Journal of Information Management, 75*, 102716.
Kumar, V., Ashraf, A. R., & Nadeem, W. (2024). AI-powered marketing: What, where, and how? *International Journal of Information Management, 77*, 102783.
Lang, A. (2006). Using the limited capacity model of motivated mediated message processing to design effective cancer communication messages. *Journal of Communication, 56*(S1), S57–S80.
Lang, A. (2014). Dynamic human-centered communication systems theory. *The Information Society, 30*(1), 60–70.
Lang, A., & Bailey, R. L. (2015). Understanding information selection and encoding from a dynamic, energy saving, evolved, embodied, embedded perspective. *Human Communication Research, 41*(1), 1–20.
Lasswell, H. D. (1971). *Propaganda technique in World War I.* Cambridge: MIT Press.
Lee, J. K., & Kronrod, A. (2020). The strength of weak-tie consensus language. *Journal of Marketing Research, 57*(2), 353–374. https://doi.org/10.1177/0022243720904957

Lee, K. (26 March 2015). *The delightfully short guide to social media ROI.* Retrieved from https://blog.bufferapp.com/guide-calculate-social-media-roi

Li, F., Larimo, J., & Leonidou, L. C. (2023). Social media in marketing research: Theoretical bases, methodological aspects, and thematic focus. *Psychology & Marketing*, *40*(1), 124–145.

Lou, C., & Yuan, S. (2019). Influencer marketing: How message value and credibility affect consumer trust of branded content on social media. *Journal of Interactive Advertising*, *19*(1), 58–73.

Manchanda, P., Dubé, J. P., Goh, K. Y., & Chintagunta, P. K. (2006). The effect of banner advertising on internet purchasing. *Journal of Marketing Research, 43*(1), 98–108

Marathe, S (2024). The Role of artificial intelligence in modern marketing: A review of current technologies, applications, and challenges. https://doi.org/10.58445/rars.1417

Marcus, B. H., Selby, V. C., Niaura, R. S., & Rossi, J. S. (1992). Self-efficacy and the stage of exercise behavior change. *Research Quarterly for Exercise and Sport, 63*(1), 60–66.

Marwick, A. E. (2021). Morally motivated networked harassment as normative reinforcement. *Social Media + Society*, *7*(2), 20563051211021378.

Marwick, A., & Boyd, D. (2011). To see and be seen: Celebrity practice on Twitter. *Convergence: The International Journal of Research into New Media Technologies, 17*(2), 139–158.

Müller, J., & Christandl, F. (2019). Content is king–But who is the king of kings? The effect of content marketing, sponsored content & user-generated content on brand responses. *Computers in Human Behavior*, *96*, 46–55.

Mundel, J., & Yang, J. (2022). Hispanics' response to ethnic targeting ads for unhealthy products: Examining the roles of endorser identification and endorser–product matchup. *Journal of Interactive Advertising*, *22*(1), 28–41.

Mundel, J., Yang, J., & Wan, A. (2022). Influencer marketing and consumer well-being: from source characteristics to social media anxiety and addiction. In J. H. Lipschultz, K. Freberg, & R. Luttrell (Eds.), *The Emerald handbook of computer-mediated communication and social media* (pp. 323–340). Bingley, UK: Emerald Publishing Limited.

Murray, C. (2023). McDonald's Credits 'Peak Absurdist Gen Z Humor' For Grimace Shake TikTok Trend. Forbes. Retrieved from https://www.forbes.com/sites/conormurray/2023/07/12/mcdonalds-credits-peak-absurdist-gen-z-humor-for-grimace-shake-tiktok-trend

Ouvrein, G., Pabian, S., Giles, D., Hudders, L., & De Backer, C. (2021). The web of influencers. A marketing-audience classification of (potential) social media influencers. *Journal of Marketing Management*, *37*(13–14), 1313–1342.

Paek, H.-J., Hove, T., Jeon, H. J., & Kim, M. (2011). Peer or expert? *International Journal of Advertising, 30*(1), 161–188.

Park, H. S., & Smith, S. W. (2007). Distinctiveness and influence of subjective norms, personal descriptive and injunctive norms, and societal descriptive and injunctive norms on behavioral intent: A case of two behaviors critical to organ donation. *Human Communication Research, 33*(2), 194–218. https://doi.org/10.1111/j.1468-2958.2007.00296.x

Petty, R. E., & Cacioppo, J. T. (1981). *Attitudes and persuasion: Classic and contemporary approaches*. Dubuque, IA: William C. Brown.

Petty, R. E., & Cacioppo, J. T. (1986). *Communication and persuasion: Central and peripheral routes to attitude change*. New York: Springer.

Pham, M. T., & Vanhuele, M. (1997). Analyzing the memory impact of advertising fragments. *Marketing Letters, 8*(4), 407–417.

Pittman, M., & Abell, A. (2021). More trust in fewer followers: Diverging effects of popularity metrics and green orientation social media influencers. *Journal of Interactive Marketing*, *56*(1), 70–82. https://doi.org/10.1016/j.intmar.2021.05.002

Scharlach, R., & Hallinan, B. (2023). The value affordances of social media engagement features. *Journal of Computer-Mediated Communication*, *28*(6), zmad040.

Scott, D. M. (2015). *The new rules of marketing and PR: How to use social media, online video, mobile applications, blogs, news releases, and viral marketing to reach buyers directly.* Hoboken, NJ: John Wiley & Sons.

Shannon, C. E., & Weaver, W. (1949). *The mathematical theory of communication.* Urbana: University of Illinois Press.

Shapiro, S. (1999). When an ad's influence is beyond our conscious control: Perceptual and conceptual fluency effects caused by incidental ad exposure. *Journal of Consumer Research*, *26*(1), 16–36.

Solis, B. & Jess3 (n.d.). Social media brandsphere. Retrieved from: https://jess3.com/projects/social-media-brandsphere/#gallery-4

Statista. (2024). Social media advertising spending worldwide from 2019 to 2029. Retrieved from https://www.statista.com/forecasts/1418549/social-media-ad-spend-worldwide

Teepapal, T. (2025). AI-driven personalization: Unraveling consumer perceptions in social media engagement. *Computers in Human Behavior*, *165*, 108549.

Vakratsas, D., & Wang, Z. (2021). Artificial intelligence in advertising creativity: Conceptualizations and applications. *International Journal of Advertising, 40*(7), 1034–1064.

Valenzuela, S., Correa, T., & Gil De Zúñiga, H. (2018). Ties, likes, and tweets: Using strong and weak ties to explain differences in protest participation across Facebook and Twitter use. *Political Communication*, *35*(1), 117–134.

Viken, G., Kim, W., Alhabash, S., & Smith, S. (2016). An analysis of celebratory drinking and related Facebook activity on college campuses. Poster presented to the 2016 *Kentucky Conference on Health Communication,* April 14–16, 2016, Lexington, KY.

Wang, L., & Liu, W. (2022). When AI meets programmatic advertising: Investigating disclosure, sentiment, and message appeal. *Journal of Marketing Communications, 29*(5), 564–584.

Wang, Y., Wang, X., Zhang, L., Liu, L., & Wang, K. (2024). Adoption of AI advertising creative technology in China: The role of ethics and firm characteristics. *International Journal of Advertising, 43*(1), 112–138.

Webb, T. L., & Sheeran, P. (2006). Does changing behavioral intentions engender behavior change? A meta-analysis of the experimental evidence. *Psychological Bulletin, 132*(2), 249–268.

Wellman, B. (1996). Are personal communities local? A Dumptarian reconsideration. *Social Networks*, *18*(4), 347–354.

Yan, J., Pan, J., Li, Z., & Chang, Y. (2024). Promoting eco-friendly advertising on social media: The fit between appeals and tie strength. *International Journal of Advertising, 43*(1), 202–230.

Yuan, S., & Lou, C. (2020). How social media influencers foster relationships with followers: The roles of source credibility and fairness in Parasocial relationship and product interest. *Journal of Interactive Advertising*, *20*(2), 133–147.

22 International Digital Advertising

Lessons from around the World

Charles R. Taylor, Eunjin (Anna) Kim and Heather Shoenberger

Introduction

Digital advertising media have come to dominate the global advertising landscape. Indeed, in 2025, digital advertising expenditures will account for three-quarters of the worldwide advertising market, which will be more than $1 trillion (Emarketer, 2025). The evolution of digital advertising and its various formats, including search engine ads, display ads, social media ads, native ads, video ads, and audio ads, has accelerated globally. Moreover, digital media have been profoundly affected by technological trends including the use of artificial intelligence (Ford et al., 2023), gamification (Van Berlo, Van Reijmersdal, and Waiguny, 2022), the advancement of the metaverse (Kim, 2021), and the growth of influencer marketing (Hudders and Lou, 2022). While researchers and managers have learned much about digital advertising in the past few decades, the dynamic nature of the technologies used and the growth of online access worldwide reflect the need for continued exploration of digital marketing internationally.

In this chapter, we will first briefly discuss some factors that have facilitated the rise of digital advertising across the globe and recent trends that have helped spur its growth. Next, we will discuss innovative research pertinent to international digital advertising from three perspectives. We then review recent literature on international digital advertising related to (1) consumer-centric factors, (2) executional factors related to ads, and (3) general philosophy/goals behind advertising in building the brand in the long term. Within these sections, we will evaluate whether the general principles related to digital advertising internationally, based on the Taylor (2009) framework (see Figure 22.1), still hold. We conclude each section by summarizing major findings and outlining future areas of international digital advertising research.

Factors Contributing to the Growth of Digital Advertising Worldwide

An early obstacle to the growth of digital advertising has been access to the internet and the speed of that access. As of 2025, there are 5.56 billion internet

DOI: 10.4324/9781003567523-28

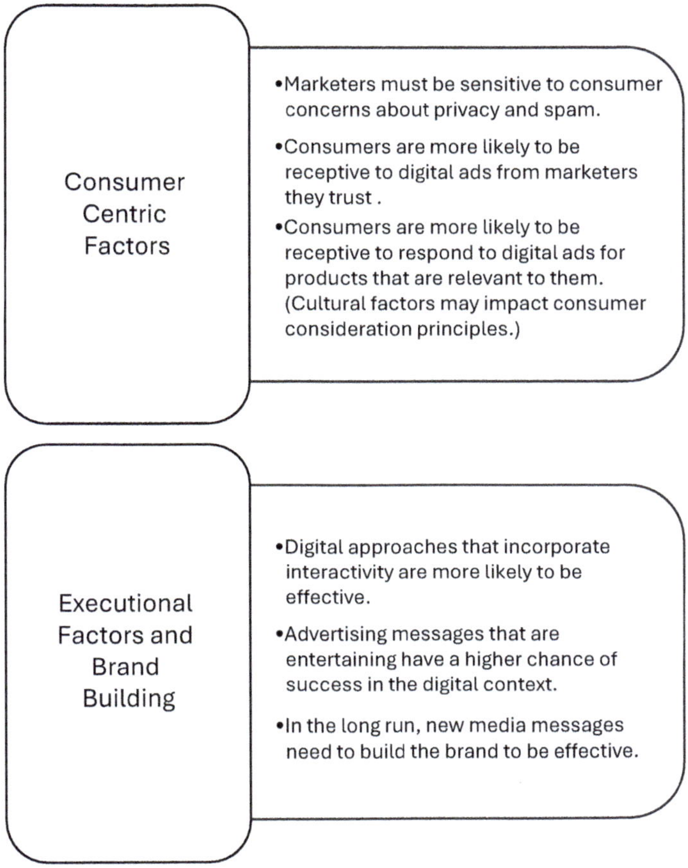

Figure 22.1 Principles of Digital Advertising (adapted from Taylor, 2009).

users globally, accounting for more than two-thirds (67.9%) of the world's population (Statista, 2025). Notably, there are also 5.24 billion social media users. It is also estimated that 78% of global internet users have broadband access, making access to all digital advertising formats, including video, more easily possible. When one considers that even in the United States, internet penetration was only 14%, the growth of internet access and speed over the past three decades has been dramatic (Pew Internet and American Life Project, 2014). While some disparities between the most economically developed countries and less developed countries persist (Gur and Kulesza, 2024), there is little doubt that internet access and use across the world have achieved impressive growth and that digital advertising formats can be effective in most of the world.

In addition to access to more viewers, it is also clear that the unique features of digital advertising have contributed to its global growth. The ability to personalize messages and more effectively target consumers is a clear advantage of the medium (Lee and Cho, 2020). In addition, the measurability of effectiveness has improved (Turnbull, 2022), and the medium is regarded as more cost-effective than it once was. In general, as will be discussed below, digital advertisers are aware that digital media often can foster engagement. Innovations such as the evolution of social media sites, the growth of the metaverse, the growth of influencer marketing, the use of artificial reality and virtual reality (VR), and the use of artificial intelligence to create ads have helped increase engagement even further.

The continued global expansion of digital advertising makes it more important than ever for firms to understand what principles apply across borders and what must be localized to fit the particular targeted culture. Understanding what is important to consumers of digital advertising is paramount. Some of the most important considerations related to these consumers are discussed in the following section. The analysis builds on Taylor's (2009) assertion that the primary principles of digital advertising are related to either consumer-related factors (i.e., "consumer-centric" factors) or executional factors. Additionally, we explore issues related to the unique ability of interactive advertising to contribute to brand-building.

Consumer-Centric Principles in International Digital Advertising

Taylor (2009) found that it is good practice in digital advertising to (1) understand and respond to consumer concerns about privacy; (2) build trust with the consumer; and (3) take care to deliver messages that are relevant to the customer. To create and execute successful digital advertising campaigns internationally, firms must understand consumers' preferences. As a relatively new medium, it is understandable that consumers may be concerned about issues related to their privacy and may vary in the level of trust they have in the firm's advertising to them. Additionally, given the importance of segmentation and targeting in marketing, it seems natural that the relevance of digital advertising content would largely impact the efficacy of an advertisement in the eye of the consumer. Research on consumers of digital advertising addresses these issues and has uncovered how consumer privacy, trust of the marketer, and relevance of advertisements impact advertising effectiveness. Also, a smaller stream of research has addressed how cultural differences between consumers may impact how they react to digital advertisements. Findings related to each of these issues will now be discussed in the following sections.

Consumer Privacy

As digital advertising expands globally, understanding consumer expectations about privacy becomes even more critical to campaign effectiveness. At the close of 2024, 58% of the world's population used the internet powered by mobile devices which has further brought consumers online, including developing nations. Mobile devices, often considered extensions of the self, foster an "always on" media experience where users expect a degree of control over their digital experiences (Hart, 2008). Digital advertising that fails to respect consumer privacy not only risks low engagement but also may generate negative sentiment toward the company.

An early study by Barwise and Strong (2002) surveyed 1,000 mobile phone users from the greater London area and found that explicit permission for SMS advertising messages was essential to favorable responses. The authors find that this type of service is especially effective for selling lower ticket items to younger consumers (Barwise and Strong, 2002). In a multi-method study of consumers in New Zealand on mobile SMS advertising, Carroll et al. (2007) also find that obtaining user trust and permission are necessities and remain the biggest challenge facing digital marketing. In the United States, Unni and Harmon (2007) investigated the important topic of location-based advertising (LBA) and how it impacts consumers' feelings of privacy. LBA describes "targeted advertising initiatives delivered to a mobile device from an identified sponsor that is specific to the location of the consumer" (Unni and Harmon, 2007, p. 28). They found that LBA-associated privacy concerns are high while perceived benefits and value of LBA are low (Unni and Harmon, 2007). LBA becomes more effective when the consumer grants permission to the marketer (Unni and Harmon, 2007). In France, Truong and Simmons (2010) found that consumers view a great deal of mobile advertising as intrusive. These consumers also expressed the desire for companies to ask permission before they begin sending advertisements to consumers' phones (Truong and Simmons, 2010). Another source of concern was a general mistrust of mobile operators and doubts that advertisers were adhering to government regulations related to consumer privacy (Truong and Simmons, 2010).

Building on this foundation, Tucker (2014) conducted a field experiment on Facebook and found that improved privacy controls—especially those that enhanced users' sense of control—led to a doubling in click-through rates on personalized ads. These results reinforce a key point: perceived autonomy over one's data significantly increases consumer responsiveness to targeted advertising.

In light of consumer desire for perceived autonomy over their data, a growing body of research suggests that transparency about how consumer data is collected can alleviate some privacy concerns (Baek and Morimoto, 2012; Martin, Borah, and Palmatier, 2017); however, advertisers must exercise caution, as disclosures that reveal practices consumers dislike can backfire (Aguirre et al., 2015; Bandara, Fernando, and Akter, 2020). Cross-cultural research posits that cultural context moderates the relationship between social media usage patterns and privacy concerns and suggests that cultural factors should be considered when combating privacy concerns (Zhong et al., 2024). And as far as online behavioral advertising, in general, Chinese consumers tend to have higher privacy concerns than Dutch consumers (Zhang, Voorveld, and Boerman, 2023). Certain types of data seem to implicate higher levels of privacy concern, such as location and biometric information (Boerman and Smit, 2023), and advertisers operating across borders should limit data collection to non-sensitive categories unless explicit permission is granted.

To protect consumer privacy in the digital space, recent global developments have changed regulations governing the ways advertisers, in some jurisdictions, collect and use personal information. The implementation of the European Union's General Data Protection Regulation in 2018 has shaped expectations for digital privacy not only in Europe but also globally, inspiring legislation such as Brazil's LGPD (2018) and India's Digital Personal Data Protection Act (2023). The United States does not have consumer data privacy regulation at a federal level but does have some state consumer privacy laws like the California Consumer Privacy Act (2018).

These global shifts underscore the need for advertisers to proactively obtain consumer consent, prioritize transparency about acceptable practices, and remain mindful of cultural differences in privacy expectations when designing international digital advertising strategies.

Trust

In addition to sensitivity to consumer privacy, early studies supported the notion that the marketer is important in the creation of effective digital advertising. Carroll et al. (2007) found that consumers in New Zealand prefer to have their mobile service provider screen advertisers to assure that advertising messages come from a trusted source when considering whether to respond to SMS messages. Okazaki, Katsukura, and Nishiyama (2007) studied mobile advertising campaigns in Japan and found that trust plays a pivotal role in both message recall and advertising toward the ad. In a cross-cultural study, Choi, Hwang, and McMillan (2008) found that both Koreans and Americans are more likely to express more positive attitudes and purchase intention for advertising that is trustworthy driving positive attitude and purchase intention for both Koreans and Americans (Choi, Hwang, and McMillan, 2008). Studies of social media advertising conducted in Australia and the United States also found that trust in a social media site affects whether consumers are receptive and responsive to advertising (Kelly, Kerr, and Drennan, 2010; Chu and Kim, 2011).

Research conducted in recent years continues to support the notion that trust in the advertiser is a key factor associated with the effectiveness of digital advertising. A U.S. study by Milne, Rohm, and Bahl (2009) found that consumers are more likely to view or be responsive to ads from a trusted website or a trusted firm. In a seminal study of influencer marketing, Lou and Yuan (2019) found that influencer trustworthiness was one key factor in trust in a branded post and that trustworthiness has a positive effect on awareness and purchase intention. Bleier and Eisenbeiss (2015) studied the impact of trust on banner ad effectiveness using a sample of German students. Their findings indicated that ads from trusted retailers were perceived as informative, whereas ads from less trusted retailers generated reactance and concerns about privacy.

In addition to influencer marketing, findings on the importance of trust in digital advertising have also been extended to new formats and technologies. Zhang, Anjum, and Wang studied Chinese consumers in the context of the metaverse and found that two types of trust (cognitive and affective) contributed to higher purchase intention after viewing ads. In separate studies using U.S. panel data, Li and Ma (2024) and Feng, Chen, and Xie (2024) both found that the use of humanlike (i.e., anthropomorphized) influencers has a positive impact on consumer perception of authenticity/trust, which then has a positive impact on ad effectiveness.

Relevance

As companies began to use large databases of merged consumer data and/or behavioral targeting, the ability to deliver more personalized messages to consumers became a significant capability of digital advertising (see e.g., Borenstein and Taylor, 2024). This approach is often beneficial, as early research on digital advertising found that consumers are more likely to respond to products and services that are relevant to them in a mixed methods study that included a survey of Italian and U.S. consumers and focus groups from six countries (Brazil, Germany, Italy, Singapore, United Kingdom, United States) found that relevance of the message was essential to the acceptance of MMS messages (Pagani, 2004). In a study of consumers in New Zealand, Carroll et al. (2007) found that relevancy of mobile advertising was important in gaining its acceptance. Merisavo et al. (2007) studied SMS advertising on a sample of over 4,000 Finnish mobile phone users and found that effective mobile advertising should provide utility and have relevance to the targeted consumer (Merisavo et al., 2007). In addition, Truong and Simmons (2010) found that French consumers are more likely to be accepting of digital advertisements they did not express permission to receive if that advertisement presents a relevant value proposition. In another early study in the context of social media communities, Zeng, Huang, and Dou (2009) found that Chinese social media users' perceptions of advertising on the sites depended on perceived relevance and perceived value of the advertising.

Recent studies affirm the special importance of message relevance to digital advertisers around the globe. In a study of subjects from the Netherlands and Poland, found that viewers were more responsive to personalized (hence, relevant) messages and that being transparent about the personalization aids effectiveness. Similarly, Zhu and Chang (2016) studied Taiwanese consumers and found that relevance was not only valued in its own right but could also offset consumer concerns about privacy. In an experimental study of Facebook users, Zhang et al. (2024) found that behavior personalization increased engagement. In a cross-cultural study of U.S. and Japanese consumers, Mueller, Kelleher, and Ibuki (2024) found that relevance is a key factor to the success of ads in both countries, as personalized messages outperformed those that were not personalized.

It is also clear that relevance is an important factor in the application of new technologies to advertising. As noted by Boerman and Smit (2023), artificial intelligence is used to help better target contexts that include influencer marketing, online games, the metaverse, and augmented reality (AR)/VR applications. Akhilkanov (2024) notes that AI's ability to identify patterns is now widely used in conjunction with data available on the web to efficiently predict the relevance of a message to a consumer.

Culture's Impact on Consumer Response

While privacy, trust, and relevance seem to be important when evaluating digital advertising in several national contexts, some research has also investigated how cultural differences may impact consumer response to ads. The Taylor (2009) framework does not specifically address the role culture plays in consumer response to digital advertising; however, whether cultural differences affect the six principles is an important consideration. For the most part, available literature supports each of the principles cross-culturally, though some studies find some nuances related to the principles.

Möller and Eisend (2010) studied the impact that national-level culture has on banner advertising effectiveness, analyzing survey data from 34 countries as well as click-through rates of over 2,000 users in 26 countries. The authors find that banner advertising effectiveness varies based on Hofstede's cultural dimensions of culture. Specifically, consumers who come from individualistic countries are less accepting of banner advertisements (Möller and Eisend, 2010). Notably, the authors' results do not suggest that any of the six principles are less relevant in one country vs. another; they do point out, however, that some digital advertising formats may be less effective in some countries compared to others.

While we conclude that relevance is an important factor that improves digital advertising effectiveness cross-culturally, the findings of Maslowska, Smit, and Van den Putte (2013) suggest that there may be differences in what is perceived as relevant by country. The study examined tailored advertising in the Netherlands, which has a long history with advertising, and Poland, which does not. Results showed that Polish consumers find the tailored advertising to be more relevant and, hence, "became more involved and were less skeptical towards the messages, which led them to have more positive attitudes" (Maslowska et al., 2013, p. 504).

Benmamoun, Singh, and Sobh (2019) conducted focus groups in Qatar and surveys in Qatar and the United Arab Emirates to examine whether cultural differences need to target Arab consumers differently. Results found that respondents were especially sensitive to privacy and security concerns and that e-marketers operating in the Middle East should follow strategies that engender trust with consumers, such as offering a favorable return policy, escrow services, strong warranties, or using third-party seals of approval. In finding that privacy and trust concerns are even more prominent in the Middle East due to cultural factors such as power distance, these findings support the privacy and trust principles. It was also noted that using localized approaches, including effective translation and being familiar with cultural norms, helps enhance the relevance of the message in these countries.

Liu et al. (2019) surveyed Australian and Chinese high school students on perceptions of the acceptance and value of mobile advertising. The authors found that in both countries, functional and credibility values are important to the acceptance of mobile advertising. This finding reinforces the importance of trust across cultures, and the authors suggested measures for building trust, including providing multiple contact formats and relevant links.

Strycharz and Segijn (2024) found somewhat higher levels of trust and less concern about privacy among Dutch and U.S. consumers. However, the authors attributed some of these differences to stricter regulation in the EU, and raw levels of concern about privacy were relatively high, while trust levels were lower, indicative of privacy and trust being important concerns in both nations.

Consumer-Centric Factors: Discussion

Existing literature from several international contexts supports the notion that the need to respect consumer privacy concerns is a cultural universal. In addition, studies from around the world find that consumers tend to react better to advertising from marketers they trust and are more responsive to relevant messages.

While extant evidence supports these first three principles holding cross-culturally, future research should focus on uncovering more nuances related to cultural differences and their impact. For example, consumers in different countries may have different attitudes toward specific issues related to privacy. In addition, there may be cross-cultural differences in what type of content is relevant or in the specific dimensions of trust that are most important. As digital advertising has grown in most parts of the world, research from diverse cultures is needed.

More research on how the principles of privacy, relevance, and trust apply to new digital formats and practices, including influencer marketing, AR/VR approaches, gamification, the metaverse, and the use of artificial intelligence, is also needed. Again, current research suggests that the principles still hold, but deeper insight into specifics of how the principle applies (e.g., what factors affecting privacy perceptions are affected by the use of artificial intelligence) is needed.

Executional Strategies and Brand-Building in International Digital Advertising

In addition to understanding how international consumers react to digital advertising, it is equally important to understand how specific features of the advertisement itself contribute to campaign success. Unlike traditional advertising formats, digital advertising offers a wider range of creative possibilities, from interactive functionalities and entertaining formats to immersive storytelling and personalized brand experiences. These executional strategies can influence key outcomes such as engagement, recall, and brand equity. However, what works in one market may not translate seamlessly to another. As advertisers seek to create effective campaigns across diverse cultural contexts, understanding which executional elements resonate globally and how they support long-term brand-building becomes essential. The following sections examine three such elements that have emerged as central to digital advertising success worldwide: interactivity, entertainment, and brand-building strategies.

Interactivity

Based on the advanced capabilities of the medium, digital advertisements are able to achieve levels of interactivity with the consumer that are generally not possible in traditional forms of advertising such as television or radio. Research has shown that across the globe, digital advertisements that promote interactivity engage consumers and improve the effectiveness of the advertisements. In a study that focused on website advertising, McMillan, Hwang, and Lee (2003) used a field study that included a sample of consumers who had recently used one of several hotel websites. The authors found that the perceived level of interactivity is the best predictor of consumer attitudes (McMillan, Hwang, and Lee, 2003). In an early study of SMS advertising, Dickinger et al. (2004) conducted a qualitative study on European mobile marketing experts from industry and academia to understand success factors for digital advertising. The authors found that interactivity is related to more effective SMS advertisements (Dickinger et al., 2004). In another example, for fashion brand consumers in Korea, Kim and Ko (2012) found that interactivity is an important variable for digital marketing and suggest that social media marketing is pivotal for companies attempting to build brand equity. The intrinsically interactive nature of social media platforms makes interaction with the content integral to advertising success (Borah, 2020). Interactive experiences foster stronger trust in both the brand and the advertising platform (De Vierman et al., 2017; Lou, Tan, and Chen, 2019).

Beyond typical digital advertising and social media, new immersive technologies such as AR, VR, and the Metaverse are further redefining interactivity, offering consumers immersive and highly personalized brand experiences that enhance effectiveness (Jayawardena et al., 2023; Wu, Lin, and Bowman, 2022).

Another emerging technology, generative AI, is in its infancy, and so too is research. As artificial intelligence continues to advance, it presents novel opportunities for brands to engage audiences in increasingly meaningful and personalized ways, thereby contributing to a growing convergence between advertising and interactive entertainment (Gujar, Paliwal, and Panyam, 2024). It seems that the interactive capabilities allowed for with conversational chatbots, a hallmark of the technology, may also see better advertising attitudes when interactivity is higher (Sun, Chen, & Sundar, 2024). Interactive and immersive advertisements increase user engagement by grabbing and sustaining attention (Gujar, Paliwal, and Panyam, 2024).

These findings emphasize that interactivity is a key principle of effective digital advertising worldwide. Its successful application requires incorporating interactive elements on websites and other digital spaces and suggests that interactivity cultivates trust and continued interaction with a brand's content.

Entertainment

Entertainment has emerged as a critical success factor in digital advertising, particularly in a landscape saturated with content and increasingly shaped by mobile and immersive formats. Globally, entertaining content has been consistently linked to increased engagement, more favorable brand attitudes, and stronger purchase intentions (e.g., Raney et al., 2003; Chen et al., 2009; Flecha-Ortiz et al., 2023). Whether through humor, narrative, audiovisual richness, or interactive formats, ads that delight and engage consumers have proven especially effective across cultures and platforms. As digital technologies evolve, understanding how entertainment functions across varying cultural contexts and media formats has become essential for building effective international campaigns.

Early research established entertainment's foundational role in shaping digital advertising outcomes. Raney et al. (2003) studied the role of entertainment on the websites of four automotive brands and found that the website that was high in entertainment value, especially sites featuring a mini-movie, generated the most positive evaluations, greatest revisit intentions, and highest levels of arousal and purchase intent. In a cross-national lab study, Chen et al. (2009) examined digital banner ads in Thailand and Taiwan and found that animated, entertaining ads and localized website content were preferred in both national samples.

Mobile advertising further demonstrates the value of entertaining content. Okazaki and Taylor (2008) found that Japanese teenagers were more responsive to SMS messages that were perceived as entertaining. Similarly, in France, Truong and Simmons (2010) reported that consumers not only preferred entertaining mobile ads but also often expected them. A cross-national comparison by Choi, Hwang, and McMillan (2008) showed that mobile ads with entertaining content improved ad attitudes and purchase intentions in both the U.S. and Korean contexts. Beyond static, message-based formats, gamified digital advertising, such as advergames, has shown strong entertainment effects. Yeu et al. (2013), in a Korean sample, demonstrated that banner ads embedded within advergames significantly increased both implicit and explicit recall. Building on this, Cheng et al. (2009) examined four types of digital advertising in Taiwan and found that MMS and internet-based (e-advertising) formats were perceived as more entertaining than SMS or email. This aligns with findings by Wang, Shih, and Peracchio (2013), who reported that banner ads combining verbal and visual cues were more easily processed and more engaging than those using only a single modality.

Social media has emerged as a dynamic platform for entertainment-driven brand-building. Ko and Kim (2010, 2012), in a study of Korean fashion brands, identified entertainment as a significant factor influencing engagement and campaign effectiveness across social media platforms. Recent work has explored entertainment in the context of emerging digital formats, particularly short-form video platforms such as TikTok, Instagram Reels, and YouTube Shorts. These platforms highlight the growing importance of entertainment, storytelling, and emotional immediacy in digital advertising. Bite-sized video content thrives on its ability to quickly evoke laughter, surprise, or relatability—elements shown to increase user attention and brand engagement (Youn, Shah, and Dodoo, 2024; Flecha-Ortiz et al., 2023). These environments are fertile ground for viral humor, aesthetic experimentation, and user-generated remixing, especially among Gen Z consumers across global markets.

Artificial intelligence further amplifies entertainment value in digital advertising by enabling hyper-personalized, adaptive content delivery. Brands such as Duolingo have embraced algorithmically tuned humor and meme culture on TikTok, producing short-form, culturally resonant content that consistently garners high engagement (The Drum, 2025; Smith, 2023). AI also powers interactive storytelling through brand chatbots, dynamic content generators, and synthetic influencers. Baek and Kim (2023) found that AI-generated content is more effective when it aligns with local norms of authenticity, humor, and interactivity, underscoring the need for culturally calibrated artificial intelligence-driven entertainment strategies.

Immersive technologies like AR and VR deepen entertainment by enhancing sensory and narrative engagement. AR and VR make brand experiences more vivid and emotionally engaging. For example, AR try-on tools like Sephora's Virtual Artist allow consumers to experiment with products in their environments, making the experience playful, visually rich, and functionally useful (Nascimento and Loureiro, 2024). VR storytelling campaigns such as Hyundai's metaverse experience illustrate how immersive narratives can transport users, evoking emotional connection, exploration, and surprise (Sung, Han and Choi, 2022).

These findings demonstrate that entertainment in digital advertising has evolved from static enjoyment to interactive, personalized, and immersive brand experiences. As platforms and technologies continue to advance, entertainment will remain a vital tool for driving engagement, sustaining consumer attention, and enhancing the overall effectiveness of digital advertising strategies. These findings reinforce that entertainment is a core driver of digital advertising effectiveness across media formats and global markets.

Brand-Building

Thus far, we have discussed what factors have led to the growth of digital advertising worldwide, important consumer-centric principles that lead to successful responses to ads, and findings related to what executional variables have proven effective in international digital advertising. This final section will suggest a general philosophical principle that should apply to all digital advertising and discuss research that supports and relates to this principle. This principle is that most digital advertising, no matter the national context, must build the brand in the long run to be effective.

In an early conceptual piece, Chiagouris and Wansley (2000) highlighted the Internet's unique capacity to strengthen the relationship between brands and consumers. They argued that digital media offered a powerful yet underutilized opportunity for deepening brand bonds, stating that "never have so many talked so little of what may be the Internet's most stunning capability—strengthening the bond with customers and prospects" (p. 35). Although digital technologies have advanced dramatically since then, the central idea endures: regardless of format or innovation, the ultimate goal of digital advertising is to build the brand.

Empirical research has reinforced this brand-building potential across a range of digital formats. In a cross-national survey of marketing managers of multinational companies operating in the United States, Europe, and Japan, Okazaki and Taylor (2008) found that the adoption of SMS advertising was driven in part by its perceived value for brand development. Managers across these markets believed that SMS could help generate excitement and prompt consumer action, outcomes that contribute meaningfully to long-term brand equity.

In an early study of banner advertising, Manchanda et al. (2006), using consumer data set of an online-only health and beauty retailer, demonstrated that exposure to banner ads increased purchase likelihood, particularly among existing customers. They also found that the effect size of banner advertising was comparable to that of traditional media (Manchanda et al., 2006), reinforcing digital advertising's potential for brand-building.

Dinner, Van Heerde, and Neslin (2014) extended this conversation by analyzing a high-end U.S. clothing retailer and showing that advertising influences purchases across both online and offline channels. Their findings indicate that online display and search ads can be more effective than traditional advertising, partly due to their cross-channel impact on in-store sales effects on the offline channel (Dinner, Van Heerde, & Neslin, 2014). Importantly, the authors argue that brands may be underestimating the return on investment of online advertising if they overlook these offline effects. This point echoes broader concerns raised by Cheong, De Gregorio, and Kim (2010) who reported that many managers feel challenged by the limited tools available to evaluate how digital campaigns contribute to brand growth.

Social media has become a powerful channel for building brand equity. Kim and Ko (2012), in a study of Korean fashion brands, found that social media marketing strategies incorporating entertainment, interaction, trendiness, customization, and word of mouth positively influence value equity, relationship equity, and brand equity—each of which contributes to purchase intention. Similarly, Bruhn, Schoenmueller, and Schafer (2012) found that social media communications have a stronger positive influence on brand image than traditional advertising. Their findings support the broader shift toward digital platforms as effective tools for brand-building. A growing body of empirical research has further supported this connection. In a study of Polish social media users, Schivinski and Dabrowski (2015) found that both firm- and user-generated content had a stronger effect on brand loyalty and perceived brand quality, underscoring the value of participatory brand ecosystems in digital platforms. Lou, Tan, and Chen (2019) showed that active brand pages build trust, emotional connection, and a sense of community, key drivers of loyalty. Moreover, Lou and Xie (2020) found that content that is entertaining and informative increases engagement, which in turn reinforces long-term loyalty and brand advocacy.

Beyond social media, immersive technologies like AR and VR have opened new pathways for brand-building. Nascimento and Loureiro (2024) found that AR-powered campaigns offering interactive, sensory-rich experiences enhanced perceived brand value and memorability. Similarly, Sung, Han, and Choi (2022) demonstrated that narrative and spatial immersion in AR ads deepens emotional and cognitive engagement with brands. However, researchers like Jayawardena et al. (2023) caution that poorly designed AR/VR experiences can backfire, reducing enjoyment and damaging brand perceptions. AI-driven personalization also plays a growing role. Kumar, Ashraf, and Nadeem (2024) indicate that AI-powered, tailored interactions, when transparently managed, strengthen brand trust and engagement, showing that personalization, while powerful, must be ethically implemented to sustain brand equity.

On the advertiser side, strong brand equity contributes to long-term ROI by boosting customer lifetime value, price premiums, and competitive insulation. Ford et al. (2023) highlight that integrating digital and traditional media (e.g., TV, print) amplifies brand familiarity and trust, reinforcing that digital does not replace but enhances holistic brand-building strategies. Co-creation and participatory branding, as observed by Jayawardena et al. (2023), deepen consumer loyalty by transforming customers into brand advocates. Cotter (2019) warns, however, that authenticity management remains crucial—overly polished influencer partnerships or algorithm-driven promotions can erode trust if perceived as inauthentic.

Executional Strategies and Brand-Building: Discussion

A growing body of cross-national research continues to highlight the importance of interactivity, entertainment, and brand-building strategies in effective digital advertising. While these executional variables have shown consistent value across global markets, research also suggests that their effectiveness is often moderated by cultural context. For example, Zorn et al. (2016) found that interactive television advertising was generally effective across cultures, but that entertaining messages were particularly influential in the United Kingdom due to a cultural preference for soft-sell approaches. Similarly, Wang and Sun (2010) reported that Romanian consumers responded more strongly to entertaining digital ads than U.S. consumers, in part because online media was still relatively new in Romania at the time. These findings illustrate that cultural norms, market maturity, and media familiarity can all shape the impact of executional elements.

As digital technologies evolve, the need to better understand how specific tactics perform in different cultural environments becomes more urgent. Prior research on consumer-centric principles (e.g., privacy, trust, relevance) has shown that certain digital formats are more effective in some cultures than others; for example, banner ads may be more accepted in collectivist cultures. A similar line of inquiry is needed for executional variables: how do cultural values influence responses to immersive storytelling, gamified ad formats, or AI-generated brand interactions?

Recent studies offer early insight into this question. For example, high-context cultures are more likely to appreciate subtle, symbolic cues in XR environments, while low-context cultures prefer direct and explicit narratives (Hall, 1976). Jung et al. (2016) also found that AR-based brand experiences were more enjoyable in collectivist societies when reinforced by social influence. Zorn et al. (2016) further revealed that gamified AR tools enhanced brand loyalty differently across markets—playfulness had more impact in Pakistan, while novelty and aesthetics mattered more in China. These studies underscore the importance of matching executional strategies to cultural communication preferences and motivational drivers.

Another area for future research involves the challenge of cross-platform brand coherence. As consumers engage with brands across a growing array of digital touchpoints, from social media and mobile apps to AR/VR environments, marketers must ensure that brand voice, values, and personality remain consistent and compelling. Future studies should explore whether consistency across platforms enhances brand trust and recall, or whether tailored messaging that aligns with each platform's culture and functionality drives deeper engagement. Although some evidence supports the benefits of integrated campaigns across digital and traditional media, the optimal strategies for maintaining brand identity in fragmented media ecosystems remain underexplored.

In sum, while interactivity, entertainment, and brand-building remain critical drivers of digital advertising effectiveness, their successful implementation requires attention to cultural variation, technological adaptation, and strategic integration across platforms.

Conclusion and Future Research

As digital advertising continues to expand globally, its strategic importance across industries and regions has become indisputable. With most of the world's population now online and a rapidly growing base of mobile and broadband users, digital advertising has become a central tool for brand engagement across cultures. This chapter revisited and extended Taylor (2009)'s foundational framework for digital advertising, confirming that the six core principles—privacy, trust, relevance, interactivity, entertainment, and brand-building—remain widely applicable across diverse markets. However, as digital platforms evolve and consumer expectations shift, these principles are not static; instead, they must be continuously reinterpreted through the lens of emerging technologies and cultural nuance.

Consumer-centric principles remain foundational. Research across contexts confirms that users are more receptive to digital ads when their privacy is respected, when the advertiser is trusted, and when the message is perceived as relevant. These insights are now complicated by rapid technological advancements. The emergence of AI, for instance, not only offers powerful tools for personalization and adaptive storytelling but also introduces fresh privacy and trust concerns. These developments highlight the importance of transparency, consent, and cultural sensitivity as universal design considerations for digital campaigns.

Executional strategies such as interactivity and entertainment have likewise gained traction as global drivers of digital advertising effectiveness. Immersive platforms like AR, VR, and the metaverse have amplified consumers' expectations for vivid, engaging brand experiences. At the same time, brand-building remains the long-term imperative. Whether through community-building on social media, gamified AR, or AI-powered chatbots, the ability to forge emotional, functional, and symbolic bonds with consumers is what ultimately distinguishes high-impact campaigns.

However, one-size-fits-all solutions are unlikely to succeed. Cultural values such as individualism vs. collectivism, uncertainty avoidance, and communication style can shape how consumers interpret brand messages, experience immersion, or assign trust in tech-driven environments. For example, while playful virtual influencers might resonate in East Asia, Western audiences may demand more "authentic" interactions. Similarly, consistent brand messaging across platforms might build familiarity in some markets, while others may respond better to localized, platform-specific storytelling.

In light of these cross-cultural differences, several key areas emerge as valuable directions for future research. First, as consumers interact with brands across multiple digital touchpoints, scholars should examine how consistency versus platform-specific adaptation influences brand equity across diverse media ecosystems. Second, more work is needed to understand how immersive advertising formats and AI-driven tools can be designed to reflect local values, humor norms, and narrative expectations, ensuring cultural fluency in global campaigns. Third, because much of the existing literature has focused on developed markets, future studies must prioritize underrepresented and emerging regions where digital access is accelerating, capturing a fuller picture of international consumer behavior. Finally, as advertising increasingly blends storytelling, real-time AI interaction, and immersive AR/VR experiences, researchers and practitioners alike need more sophisticated tools to assess campaign effectiveness both in terms of short-term engagement and long-term brand impact.

References

Aguirre, E., Mahr, D., Grewal, D., De Ruyter, K., & Wetzels, M. (2015). Unraveling the personalization paradox: The effect of information collection and trust-building strategies on online advertisement effectiveness. *Journal of Retailing*, *91*(1), 34–49.

Akhilkanov, A. (2024). AI and personalization in marketing. (Jan 5), https://www.forbes.com/councils/forbescommunicationscouncil/2024/01/05/ai-and-personalization-in-marketing/

Baek, Y. M., & Kim, E. (2023). Is ChatGPT scary good? How user motivations affect creepiness and trust in generative artificial intelligence. *Telematics and Informatics*, *83*, 102072. https://doi.org/10.1016/j.tele.2023.102072

Baek, T. H., & Morimoto, M. (2012). Stay away from me: Examining the determinants of consumer avoidance of personalized advertising. *Journal of Advertising, 41*(1), 59–76.

Bandara, R., Fernando, M., & Akter, S. (2020). Explicating the privacy paradox: A qualitative inquiry of online shopping consumers. *Journal of Retailing and Consumer Services*, *52*, 101947.

Barwise, P. & Strong, C. (2002) Permission-based mobile advertising. *Journal of Interactive Marketing*, 16(1), pp. 14–24.

Benmamoun, M., Singh, N., & Sobh, R. (2019). How advertisers can target Arab e-Consumers more effectively: A framework for localizing digital advertising and marketing content to Arab e-Consumers. *Journal of Advertising Research*, *59*(2), 171–184.

Bleier, A., & Eisenbeiss, M. (2015). The importance of trust for personalized online advertising. *Journal of Retailing, 91*(3), 390–409.

Boerman, S. C., & Smit, E. G. (2023). Advertising and privacy: An overview of past research and a research agenda. *International Journal of Advertising*, *42*(1), 60–68.

Borah, A., Banerjee, S., Lin, Y. T., Jain, A., & Eisingerich, A. B. (2020). Improvised marketing interventions in social media. *Journal of Marketing*, *84*(2), 69–91.

Borenstein, B. E., & Taylor, C. R. (2024). The effects of targeted digital advertising on consumer welfare. *Journal of Strategic Marketing*, *32*(3), 317–332.

Bruhn, M., Schoenmuller, V., & Schäfer, D. B. (2012). Are social media replacing traditional-media in terms of brand equity creation?. *Management Research Review*, *35*(9), 770–790.

CCPA (2018). California consumer privacy act. Retrieved from https://oag.ca.gov/privacy/ccpa

Carroll, A., Barnes, S. J., Scornavacca, E., & Fletcher, K. (2007). Consumer perceptions and attitudes towards SMS advertising: recent evidence from New Zealand. *International Journal of Advertising*, *26*(1), 79–98.

Chen, J. V., Ross, W. H., Yen, D. C., & Akhapon, L. (2009). The effect of types of banner ad, Web localization, and customer involvement on Internet users' attitudes. *CyberPsychology & Behavior*, *12*(1), 71–73.

Cheng, J. M. S., Blankson, C., Wang, E. S. T., & Chen, L. S. L. (2009). Consumer attitudes and interactive digital advertising. *International Journal of Advertising*, *28*(3), 501–525.

Cheong, Y., De Gregorio, F., & Kim, K. (2010). The power of reach and frequency in the age of digital advertising. *Journal of Advertising Research*, *50*(4), 403–415.

Chiagouris, L., & Wansley, R. (2000). Branding on the internet. *Marketing Management*, *9*(2), 34–38.

Choi, Y. K., Hwang, J. S. & McMillan, S. J. (2008) Gearing up for mobile advertising: A cross-cultural examination of key factors that drive mobile messages home to consumers. *Psychology & Marketing*, *25*(8), 756–768.

Chu, S. C., & Kim, Y. (2011). Determinants of consumer engagement in electronic word-of-mouth (eWOM) in social networking sites. *International Journal of Advertising*, *30*(1), 47–75.

Cotter, K. (2019). Playing the visibility game: How digital influencers and algorithms negotiate influence on Instagram. *New Media & Society*, *21*(4), 895–913.

De Vierman, M., Cauberghe, V., Hudders, L., & De Pelsmacker, P. (2017). Consumers motivations for lurking and posting in brand communities on social networking sites. In S. Rodgers & E. Thorson (Eds.) Digital advertising. (pp. 207–221). Routledge.

Dickinger, A., Haghirian, P., Murphy, J. & Scharl, A. (2004) An investigation and conceptual model of SMS marketing. *Proceedings of the 37th Hawaii International Conference on System Sciences*. IEEE.

Dinner, I. M., Van Heerde, H. J., & Neslin, S. A. (2014). Driving online and offline sales: The cross-channel effects of traditional, online display, and paid search advertising. *Journal of Marketing Research*, *51*(5), 527–545.

Emarketer (2025). Worldwide Ad Spending Forecast 2025, (Jan 28), https://www.emarketer.com/content/worldwide-ad-spending-forecast-2025

Feng, Y., Chen, H., & Xie, Q. (2024). AI influencers in advertising: the role of AI influencer-related attributes in shaping consumer attitudes, consumer trust, and perceived influencer–product fit. *Journal of Interactive Advertising*, *24*(1), 26–47.

Flecha-Ortiz, J. A., Feliberty-Lugo, V., Santos-Corrada, M., Lopez, E., & Dones, V. (2023). Hedonic and utilitarian gratifications to the use of TikTok by Generation Z and the parasocial relationships with influencers as a mediating force to purchase intention. *Journal of Interactive Advertising*, *23*(2), 114–127.

Ford, J., Jain, V., Wadhwani, K., & Gupta, D. G. (2023). AI advertising: An overview and guidelines. *Journal of Business Research*, *166*, 114124.

Gur, B. A., & Kulesza, J. (2024). Equitable access to satellite broadband services: Challenges and opportunities for developing countries. *Telecommunications Policy*, *48*(5), 102731.

GDPR (2018). General data protection regulation. Retrieved from https://www.google.com/search?q=gdpr&oq=gdpr+&gs_lcrp=EgZjaHJvbWUyBggAEEUYOTIKCAEQABi-xAxiABDIKCAIQABixAxiABDIHCAMQABiABDIHCAQQABiABDIKCAUQABi xAxiABDIHCAYQABiABDIHCAcQABiABDIHCAgQABiABDINCAkQABiDARix-AxiABNIBCDIyMDVqMGo3qAIAsAIA&sourceid=chrome&ie=UTF-8

Gujar, P., Paliwal, G., & Panyam, S. (2024, October). Generative AI and the Future of Interactive and Immersive Advertising. In *2024 IEEE Eighth Ecuador Technical Chapters Meeting (ETCM)* (pp. 1–6). IEEE.

Hall, E. T. (1976). *Beyond culture*. Anchor Books.

Hart, K. (2008). Advertising sent to cellphones opens new front in war on spam. *Washington Post*, 10 March, p. A1.

Hudders, L., & Lou, C. (2022). A new era of influencer marketing: Lessons from Recent Inquires and Thoughts on Future Directions. *International Journal of Advertising*, *41*(1), 1–5.

India Digital Personal Data Protection Act (2023). Retrieved from https://egazette.gov.in/WriteReadData/2023/248045.pdf

Jayawardena, C., Ahmad, A., Valeri, M., & Jaharadak, A. A. (2023). Technology acceptance antecedents in digital transformation in hospitality industry. *International Journal of Hospitality Management*, *108*, 103350.

Jung, J., Shim, S. W., Jin, H. S., & Khang, H. (2016). Factors affecting attitudes and behavioral intention towards social networking advertising: A case of Facebook users in South Korea. *International Journal of Advertising, 35*(2), 248–265.

Kelly, L., Kerr, G., & Drennan, J. (2010). Avoidance of advertising in social networking sites: The teenage perspective. *Journal of Interactive Advertising, 10*(2), 16–27.

Kim, A. J., & Ko, E. (2010). Impacts of luxury fashion brand's social media marketing On customer relationships and purchase intentions. *Journal of Global Fashion Marketing*, *1*(3), 164–171.

Kim, A. J., & Ko, E. (2012). Do social media marketing activities enhance consumer equity? An empirical study of luxury fashion brand. *Journal of Business Research*, *65*(10), 1480–1486.

Kim, J. (2021). Advertising in the metaverse: Research agenda. *Journal of Interactive Advertising*, *21*(3), 141–144.

Kim, K., & Baek, T. H. (2023). Virtually authentic? Examining the match-up hypothesis between human vs. virtual influencers and product types. *Journal of Product & Brand Management*. https://doi.org/10.1108/JPBM-03-2023-4418

Kumar, V., Ashraf, A. R., & Nadeem, W. (2024). AI-powered marketing: What, where, and how? *International Journal for Multidisciplinary Research,* 102783.

Lee, H., & Cho, C. H. (2020). Digital advertising: Present and future prospects. *International Journal of Advertising*, *39*(3), 332–341.

Li, J., & Ma, Y. (2024). Virtual influencers in advertisements: Examining the role of authenticity and identification. *Journal of Interactive Advertising*, *24*(1), 1–12.

Liu, F., Kanso, A., Zhang, Y., & Olaru, D. (2019). Culture, perceived value, and advertising acceptance: A cross-cultural study on mobile advertising. *Journal of Promotion Management*, *25*(7), 1028–1058.

Lou, C., & Yuan, S. (2019). Influencer marketing: How message value and credibility affect consumer trust of branded content on social media. *Journal of Interactive Advertising*, *19*(1), 58–73.

Lou, C., Tan, S. S., & Chen, X. (2019). Investigating consumer engagement with influencer- vs.brand-promoted ads: The roles of source and disclosure. *Journal of Interactive Advertising, 19*(3), 169–186. https://doi.org/10.1080/15252019.2019.1667928

Lou, C., & Xie, Q. (2020). Something social, something entertaining? How digital content marketing augments consumer experience and brand loyalty. *International Journal of Advertising, 40*(3), 376–402. https://doi.org/10.1080/02650487.2020.1788311

LGPD (2018). Lei Geral de Protecao de Dados. Retrieved from https://gdpr.eu/gdpr-vs-lgpd/

Manchanda, P., Dubé, J. P., Goh, K. Y., & Chintagunta, P. K. (2006). The effect of banner advertising on internet purchasing. *Journal of Marketing Research, 43*(1), 98–108.

Martin, K. D., Borah, A., & Palmatier, R. W. (2017). Data privacy: Effects on customer and firm performance. *Journal of Marketing, 81*(1), 36–58.

Maslowska, E., Smit, E. G., & Van den Putte, B. (2013). Assessing the cross-cultural applicability of tailored advertising: a comparative study between the Netherlands and Poland. *International Journal of Advertising, 32*(4), 487–511.

McMillan, S. J., Hwang, J.-S. & Lee, G. (2003) Effects of structural and perceptual factors on attitudes toward the website. *Journal of Advertising Research, 43*(4), 400–409.

Merisavo, M., Kajalo, S., Karjaluoto, H., Virtanen, V., Salmenkivi, S., Raulas, M., & Leppäniemi, M. (2007). An empirical study of the drivers of consumer acceptance of mobile advertising. *Journal of Interactive Advertising, 7*(2), 41–50.

Milne, G. R., Rohm, A., & Bahl, S. (2009). If it's legal, is it acceptable? *Journal of Advertising, 38*(4), 107–122.

Möller, J., & Eisend, M. (2010). A global investigation into the cultural and individual antecedents of banner advertising effectiveness. *Journal of International Marketing, 18*(2), 80–98.

Mueller, S., Kelleher, T., & Ibuki, Y. (2024). US and Japanese consumer attitudes toward tailored and targeted communication with human and chatbot Agents. *Journal of Interactive Advertising, 24*(1), 84–101.

Nascimento, J., & Loureiro, S. M. C. (2024). Boosting heritage recommendations through awe and augmented reality. *International Journal of Contemporary Hospitality Management, 36*(11), 3841–3864.

Okazaki, S., Katsukura, A. & Nishiyama, M. (2007) How mobile advertising works: The role of trust in improving attitudes and recall. *Journal of Advertising Research, 47*(2), 165–178.

Okazaki, S., & Taylor, C. R. (2008). What is SMS advertising and why do multinationals adopt it? Answers from an empirical study in European markets. *Journal of Business Research, 61*(1), 4–12.

Pagani, M. (2004). Determinants of adoption of third generation mobile multimedia services. *Journal of Interactive Marketing, 18*(3), 46–59.

Pew Internet & American Life Project (2014). *Internet Use Over time*, January, available at https://www.pewinternet.org/Shared-Content/Data-Sets/2000/April-2000-Survey- Data.aspx, https://www.pewinternet.org/data-trend/internet-use/internet-use-over-time/

Raney, A. A., Arpan, L. M., Pashupati, K., & Brill, D. A. (2003). At the movies, on the web: An investigation of the effects of entertaining and interactive web content on site and brand evaluations. *Journal of Interactive Marketing, 17*(4), 38–53.

Schivinski, B., & Dabrowski, D. (2015). The impact of brand communication on brand equity through Facebook. *Journal of Research in Interactive Marketing, 9*(1), 31–53.

Smith, L. (2023, November 7). Ryanair: How the airline became a TikTok favourite. *BBC News*. https://www.bbc.com/news/newsbeat-67333386

Statista (2025). Number of internet and social media users worldwide as of February 2025. https://www.statista.com/statistics/617136/digital-population-worldwide/#:~:text=As%20of%20February%202025%2C%205.56,population%2C%20were%20social%20media%20users

Strycharz, J., & Segijn, C. M. (2024). Ethical side-effect of dataveillance in advertising: Impact of data collection, trust, privacy concerns and regulatory differences on chilling effects. *Journal of Business Research, 173*, 114490.

Sun, Y., Chen, J., & Sundar, S. S. (2024). Chatbot ads with a human touch: A test of anthropomorphism, interactivity, and narrativity. *Journal of Business Research, 172*, 114403.

Sung, E., Han, S., & Choi, J. (2022). Augmented reality advertising and consumer escapism: The roles of narrative transportation and spatial immersion. *Journal of Business Research, 147*, 392–402.

Taylor, C. R. (2009). Editorial: The six principles of digital advertising. *International Journal of Advertising, 28*(3), 411–418.

The Drum. (2025, February 25). Duolingo's TikTok mastermind on its unhinged social strategy and killing its mascot. *The Drum*. https://www.thedrum.com/news/2025/02/25/duolingo-s-tiktok-mastermind-its-unhinged-social-strategy-and-killing-its-mascot

Truong, Y., & Simmons, G. (2010). Perceived intrusiveness in digital advertising: Strategic marketing implications. *Journal of Strategic Marketing, 18*(3), 239–256.

Tucker, C. E. (2014). Social networks, personalized advertising, and privacy controls. *Journal of Marketing Research, 51*(5), 546–562.

Turnbull, S. (2022). Digital advertising: Measurement, metrics and future research agenda. In Annmarie Hanlon, Tracy L. Tuten, & Sarah Turnbull (Eds.), *The SAGE handbook of digital marketing* Sage Publications Ltd., 465–478.

Unni, R., & Harmon, R. (2007). Perceived effectiveness of push vs. pull mobile location based advertising. *Journal of Interactive Advertising, 7*(2), 28–40.

Van Berlo, Z. M. C., Van Reijmersdal, E. A., & Waiguny, M. K. J. (2022). Twenty years of research on gamified advertising: A systematic overview of theories and variables. *International Journal of Advertising, 42*(1), 171–180.

Wang, K. Y., Shih, E., & Peracchio, L. A. (2013). How banner ads can be effective: Investigating the influences of exposure duration and banner ad complexity. *International Journal of Advertising, 32*(1), 121–141.

Wang, Y., & Sun, S. (2010). Examining the role of beliefs and attitudes in online advertising: A comparison between the USA and Romania. *International Marketing Review, 27*(1), 87–107.

Wu, D. Y., Lin, J. H. T., & Bowman, N. D. (2022). Watching VR advertising together: How 3D animated agents influence audience responses and enjoyment to VR advertising. *Computers in Human Behavior, 133*, 107255.

Yeu, M., Yoon, H. S., Taylor, C. R., & Lee, D. H. (2013). Are banner advertisements in Online Games Effective?. *Journal of Advertising, 42*(2–3), 241–250.

Youn, S., Shah, P., & Dodoo, N. A. (2024). Engaging with branded content on short-video sharing apps: How motivations affect attitude toward branded content, brand experience, and relationship quality. *Journal of Interactive Advertising, 24*(3), 215–237.

Zeng, F., Huang, L., & Dou, W. (2009). Social factors in user perceptions and responses to advertising in online social networking communities. *Journal of Interactive Advertising*, *10*(1), 1–13.

Zhang, D., Voorveld, H., & Boerman, S. C. (2023). Privacy concerns matter, knowledge does not: Investigating effects of online behavioral advertising among Chinese and Dutch adults. *Journal of Current Issues & Research in Advertising*, *44*(3), 392–410.

Zhang, L., Anjum, M. A., & Wang, Y. (2024). The impact of trust-building mechanisms on purchase intention towards metaverse shopping: The moderating role of age. *International Journal of Human–Computer Interaction*, *40*(12), 3185–3203.

Zhong, B., Sun, T., Zhou, Y., & Xie, L. (2024). Privacy matters: Reexamining internet privacy concern among social media users in a cross-cultural setting. *Atlantic Journal of Communication*, *32*(2), 180–197.

Zorn, S. F., Bellman, S., Robinson, J. A., & Varan, D. (2016). Cultural differences affect interactive television advertising. *Journal of Marketing Communications*, *22*(1), 3–17.

Zhu, Y. Q., & Chang, J. H. (2016). The key role of relevance in personalized advertisement: Examining its impact on perceptions of privacy invasion, self-awareness, and continuous use intentions. *Computers in Human Behavior*, *65*, 442–447.

Index

Note: **Bold** page numbers refer to tables and *italic* page numbers refer to figures.

For Product Safety Concerns and Information please contact our EU representative GPSR@taylorandfrancis.com Taylor & Francis Verlag GmbH, Kaufingerstraße 24, 80331 München, Germany

Batch number: 10725983

Printed by Printforce, the Netherlands